THE RESOURCE TEACHER

a guide to effective practices

second edition

J. Lee Wiederholt
Donald D. Hammill
Virginia L. Brown

Allyn and Bacon, Inc.
Boston London Sydney Toronto

Library of Congress Cataloging in Publication Data

Weiderholt, J. Lee.
    The resource teacher.

    Includes bibliographical references and index.
    1. Resource programs (education) I. Hammill,
Donald D., 1934-   . II. Brown, Virginia, 1931-
III. Title.
LB1028.8.W53 1983b 371.9   83-8784
ISBN 0-205-07978-4 (pbk.)

10 9 8 7 6 5   88 87 86

CONTENTS

PREFACE

The Resource Teacher: A Guide to Effective Practices was first published in 1978. We have been very pleased with its acceptance since that time. However, it was now time for an extensive revision of that 1978 manuscript. This revision was called for by several major points.

First, many of our colleagues have made excellent suggestions for expanding the original text. For example, they suggested additional attention to adolescents in need of resource support. They also suggested that we include information about study skills. Finally, they encouraged us to review and discuss the efficacy research on resource programs. All of these suggestions have been incorporated into this revision.

Second, we wished to include a significant body of research and literature, which reaffirms the positions overviewed in the first edition. We remain committed to the belief that many, probably most, of the problems that students encounter in learning are the direct effect of the environments in which they find themselves rather than of "defects" in their physical makeup. Consequently, we continue to advocate what is variously called an "ecological," "environmental," or "situational" approach to assessment and instruction. Therefore, we have placed a great deal of emphasis in this book on analyzing and modifying elements of the environment — the teachers, peers, parents, and curricula — to fit the specific needs of individual students. Of course, strategies are also delineated for analyzing and modifying the behavior of students who are referred for resource support.

We also continue to hold the belief that assessing and instructing of students with learning and behavior difficulties should be undertaken in their natural environments. Specifically, we regret the continued pervasive practice of testing and instructing these students outside the regular classroom. We recognize, of course, that on occasion this is both a necessary and desirable practice; however, it is not likely to be a particularly effective procedure in most instances. Since students usually are referred to resource programs because they are experiencing difficulty in their regular classrooms, it is there that we must ultimately help them to succeed. Sometimes success is accomplished by altering their behaviors. More often, however, the major changes required are in the instructional program, the teaching strategies, and/or the classroom climate.

We continue to believe that the duties of an effective resource teacher are demanding and require a high level of competence. After reading this book, a few readers may think that we expect too much of any one individual. Yet we maintain that all of the competencies discussed are necessary and can be acquired by most resource teachers through continued training, study, and practice.

We have attempted to prepare a book that is comprehensive in scope and contains specific overviews of recommended approaches, many of them quite recent. Readers will need to study both this book and the references cited throughout if they wish to become thoroughly acquainted with the recommended techniques.

Readers may be surprised that some of their favorite approaches to assessment and instruction are not included. Indeed, we have dropped many of the approaches discussed in the first edition. No doubt, we may have overlooked a few valuable procedures. We wish to assure the reader, however, that omissions are not always the result of our ignorance; some techniques are omitted by design because research indicates that they lack validity or promise. The approaches overviewed in this book represent what we believe to be the most professionally defensible practices available at the present time. We also strongly encourage resource teachers to evaluate our recommended procedures in light of their own experiences in working with students.

This is an advocacy book! By that, we mean that very little time is spent telling teachers what *not* to do. Instead, we recommend the resource program as a viable mechanism for serving most students with learning and behavior difficulties. In addition, we delineate three roles to be performed by resource teachers in the schools, and we suggest particular materials and methods for use in assessment and instruction. We hope that readers will find many effective practices in this book and that their use will result in programs that work for students.

J. Lee Wiederholt
Donald D. Hammill
Virginia L. Brown

I

THE RESOURCE CONCEPT

Part I of this text describes both the resource program and the role of the resource teacher in that program. Resource teachers, administrative personnel, parents, and teachers should understand what a resource teacher is, what a resource program is and is not, and also what services it offers before attempting to implement such a program in their schools. This information is presented in Chapters 1 and 2.

    The first chapter discusses the rationale behind the resource approach and the historical development of this service arrangement. It goes on to describe how the resource program relates to other school programs and the variety of resource models that can be set up. Chapter 1 concludes with a list of unique advantages associated with the resource program as well as a review of the efficacy research.

    The potential roles of resource teachers are described in the second chapter. Specifically, we believe that resource teachers should conduct the educational assessment of referred children; should instruct some childrer in a special room and/or in the regular classroom; and should consult with teachers, other school staff, and parents about the educational problems of referred children and about school curricular matters.

1

The Resource Program Concept

In the schools today, nearly 15 to 20 percent of the students cannot meet the curriculum's requirements. Many of the students come from backgrounds that do not prepare them to meet the demands of the educational system; as a result, they fall behind from the start, become discouraged early, and drop out as soon as possible. In addition, some students have physical, intellectual, psychological, and/or social problems that seriously impede their advancement in the curriculum. Other students fail for no apparent reason. Some of these students perform normally or even excel in some school subjects but are marginal or totally inadequate in the rest. Other students function below average in almost every area of school performance. Most students who have problems in their school work also develop some emotional and/or social problems because they cannot conform to the standards of behavior required by the schools.

To cope with the uniqueness, diversity, and range of the educational problems of these students, the schools over the years have implemented a wide variety of instructional service arrangements, including special classes and schools, evaluation centers, provisions for home-bound instruction, tutoring and remedial programs, vocational education, and alternative schools. Since the late 1960s, the resource program has been the most popular of these new arrangements. Before 1970, resource programs were used almost exclusively for providing remedial reading and speech therapy services; they now exist in one form or another in most of the nation's schools and offer many services to students and teachers alike. This chapter will acquaint readers with: (1) the basic rationale underlying the resource program; (2) the historical development of the interest in this approach; (3) the relationship between the resource program and other services in the school; (4) the different types of resource models that are available; (5) the potential benefits to be obtained by adopting a resource service system, and (6) the effectiveness of the resource model.

RATIONALE UNDERLYING THE RESOURCE PROGRAM

This book deals specifically with the practices involved in organizing and managing resource programs. But what is a resource program? What kinds of services does it provide? Who should receive these services? The answers to these important questions illustrate the rationale underlying this concept of the resource program.

Basically, a resource program is any school operation in which a person (usually the resource teacher) has the responsibility of providing supportive educationally related services to students and/or to their teachers. The resource teacher may provide the student with direct services in the form of analytic, remedial, developmental, or compensatory teaching and/or behavioral management. Such services may be conducted either in the regular classroom or in a room designated for that purpose, such as the resource room or center. The services offered to the regular or special teachers may include, but are not limited to, helping them either to adjust or to select curricula to meet the unique needs of some children and to manage the classroom behavior of disruptive students. In addition, the resource teacher also discusses with parents the problems evidenced by their students.

The resource program approach is flexible enough to include assessment, teaching, and consulting services that are specifically related to reading, arithmetic, handwriting, spelling, spoken language, and behavior. These services may be provided by one resource teacher or several, depending on the competencies of the resource teachers, the policies of the school, the preferences of the administrators, and the particular resource model that is used. The variety of models available are described later in this chapter.

The resource room is an important part of a complete resource program. A resource room is any setting in the school to which a student comes to receive specific instruction on a regularly scheduled basis, while receiving the major part of his/her education elsewhere (usually in a regular or special class program). Therefore, resource rooms are not part-time special education classes where, for example, handicapped students are integrated with regular students only for lunch, gym, or art. Neither are they study halls, discipline or detention centers, or crisis rooms. These arrangements have legitimate places in the schools, but they are not resource rooms according to our definition.

Unfortunately, many schools confine their resource program to the resource room. Only in this room does the resource teacher assess the students' instructional and skill needs, make his/her teaching plans, and carry out his/her remediation program. Little attention is given to assessing the factors in the school classroom, home, and/or curriculum that might be contributing to the students' failure or to the attitudes and expectations of the referring teacher.

In fact, the resource teacher is not expected or encouraged to deal with regular class teachers to any appreciable extent; and the communication that does take place between them usually is restricted to general discussions of students who attend the resource room, In short, the idea that the resource teacher is a support person for the whole school as well as for the few students enrolled in the resource room is not often recognized. To avoid this interpretation, the resource 'room' should be thought of more broadly as the resource 'program.'

Thus, the resource program concept encompasses more than merely "running resource rooms." The resource format is a promising means by which many services can be provided in a variety of school settings, to students, parents, and teachers. Even though a well-equipped resource room is an important component of a comprehensively planned resource program, it should not be the only place in the school where resource teachers perform their duties. Readers desiring more information on the principles underlying the resource program are referred to Reger's article "What is a resource room program" (1973) and to Hawisher and Calhoun's book *The Resource Room: An Educational Asset for Children with Special Needs* (1978).

HISTORICAL BACKGROUND OF THE RESOURCE CONCEPT

The resource concept is not a new idea. Dr. Robert Irwin operated resource programs for the visually handicapped as early as 1913, and similar arrangements for the hard-of-hearing were developed soon after (Frampton and Gall, 1955; Frampton and Rowell, 1940). During the 1950s and 1960s, many schools implemented resource programs specifically to help students assigned to the regular classrooms overcome difficulties in reading, math, and speech.

Until the 1970s, special education placements were almost the only service arrangements that school districts provided for the education of "handicapped" students who had moderate to severe problems in learning and behavior. Despite the history of resource programs in both elementary and special education, they did not become popular in the schools until serious questions arose about the educational and social consequences of the segregated special self-contained classes and schools. To a considerable degree, the many resource programs that are being established today are seen as supplements to (and even substitutes for) traditional special education placements.

Reasons for the disenchantment with special classes and schools have been well documented by such observers as Dunn (1968), Christopolos and Renz (1969), Cegelka and Tyler (1970), Ross, De Young, and Cohen (1971), Garrison and Hammill (1971), Iano (1972), and Hammill and Wiederholt (1972). These writers delineate many weaknesses associated with the unrestricted use of the special classes or of the special school setting. Their research strongly suggests that the benefits derived by most students taught in such special placements are virtually nonexistent, or at the very least, not readily apparent. These critics become particularly distressed when the children who are placed in these segregated classes come from poor and/or minority backgrounds.

Because of professional criticism of existing services and of parental pressure, a variety of resource models have been implemented widely in the schools. One goal of these resource programs is to provide enough support to "handicapped" students so that many of them can progress through the grades along side their nonhandicapped peers. Thus, these students are kept in mainstream education, rather than being isolated in order to receive the special instruction or help that they might require.

THE RELATIONSHIP OF THE RESOURCE PROGRAM TO OTHER SCHOOL SERVICES

The general relationships existing between the resource program and other instructional service arrangements that the schools provide is depicted (in simplified form) in Figure 1-1. This figure shows that the schools provide instruction for students in one of four settings: the regular classroom, a resource room of some type, a special class, or at home. From time to time, students (and teachers, too) need additional help that is obtained from one or more supplemental support persons, such as the school psychologist or guidance counselor.

The instructional activities in these teaching settings generally are the same; most teachers do some developmental, remedial, and compensatory education from time to time. The goals of instruction also are usually similar; all teachers want their students to read and write and to be able to take a useful place in society. In terms of teaching, the main differences relate directly to the degree of individualization, to the methods used to reach the goals, and to the intensity of instruction that may be required to deal effectively with a student and his or her problem.

For many known, suspected, or unknown reasons, some students cannot manage in a room with a teacher and twenty-five to forty other students. These students need a more sheltered instructional environment on a temporary or perhaps a more permanent basis.

The amount of shelter required usually determines whether the student is eventually placed in the resource program, a special class, or on homebound instruction. In most cases, the resource teacher can show regular teachers how to accommodate referred students in their classrooms; failing this, the students can be taught in the resource room. The special class and homebound alternatives are reserved for the few students who do not or cannot progress in the other settings. The principle governing all placements is that the student receive instruction in the least restrictive environment possible; that is, in the alternative closest to the regular classroom where the student can find success

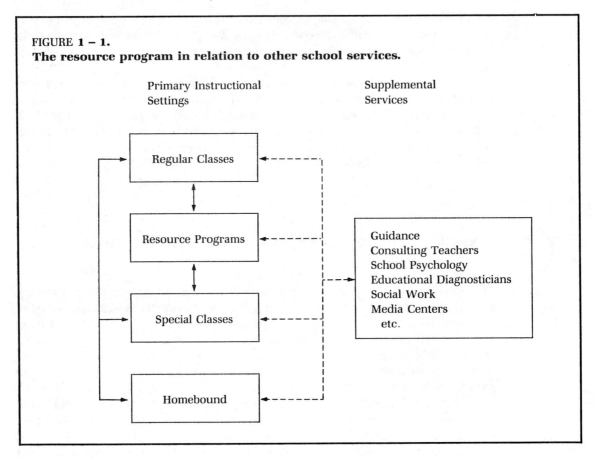

FIGURE **1 – 1.**
The resource program in relation to other school services.

TYPES OF RESOURCE MODELS

At least five different types of resource programs currently operate in the schools: the categorical, the cross-categorical, the noncategorical, the specific skill varieties, and the itinerant. Even though services such as diagnostic teaching classes, school psychology, counseling, and mental health agencies also are often set up as resource programs, we will focus our attention on the programs that relate most directly to classroom instruction.

The Categorical Resource Program

Like traditional self-contained special education classes, services provided in the categorical resource program are reserved for students who are officially diagnosed as handicapped, including the mentally retarded, learning disabled, emotionally disturbed, sensory impaired, speech disordered, and physically handicapped. In this model, one resource room enrolls only educable mentally retarded students; another serves only emotionally disturbed youngsters, and so forth.

The rationale for categorical programs, where personnel are trained specifically in a particular disability area, is that such teachers will have a better idea of the problems, related services, and recent advances associated with each handicap. Presumably, they will be able to suggest and/or provide appropriate educational evaluation and programming. The disadvantage of the categorical resource program is primarily one of continuing to group students by disability label.

Some school districts have replaced all of their classes for the educable retarded, emotionally disturbed, and learning disabled students with categorically based resource rooms. Others have found it more beneficial and expedient to maintain several self-contained classes for each type of disability in order to provide back-up support for their categorical resource programs. Under this arrangement, the mildly to moderately involved students are mainstreamed; they are assigned to regular classes and receive supplemental help from a resource teacher who is specially trained in a particular disability area of special education. The more severe students, who may require a total approach to management on either a temporary or a permanent basis, are placed in special classes.

Because the categorical resource program model conforms to existing legal definitions of handicapping conditions, to funding patterns, and to teacher certification requirements, it is particularly attractive to many educators, administrators, teachers, parents, and legislators. Of all the resource models, the categorical variety is perhaps the most popular at the present time. Detailed descriptions of categorical resource programs have been provided by Barksdale and Atkinson (1971), Tilley (1970), and Rodee (1971) for the educable mentally retarded; by Glavin et al. (1971) for the emotionally disturbed; and by Sabatino (1971) and Bersoff et al. (1972) for the learning disabled.

The Cross-Categorical Resource Program

As in the special class and the categorical resource program, enrollment in cross-categorical programs is reserved for students who have been classified as handicapped. In this model, however, the resource teacher serves students from two or more disability categories. For example, the teacher may work wth a group of educables during the first period of the day, a group of disturbed youngsters the second period, and a group of learning disabled students, disturbed students, and educable students the next period. This last grouping is the most popular because it allows the teacher to group the students according to instructional level rather than according to diagnostic label. Sometimes this model is called "interrelated" rather than "cross-categorical."

The rationale for the cross-categorical program involves both administrative expediency and instructional assumption. If the number of handicapped students of a particular category is too low to justify a teacher for each area, then programs are combined under one teacher who is usually certified in at least one of the categorical areas. The instructional assumption is a behavioral one: where specific instructional groupings are formed through identified common level or need, the categorical label of the student is irrelevant. The label is also irrelevant where the resource program is simply a tutorial study hall for the regular class program.

The major problems associated with cross-categorical resource programs are associated with their emphasis upon instructional level or need. Such programs often assume an invariant instructional sequence of curriculum — usually that of the regular program — through which all students must go. It further assumes that a retarded, a disturbed, a gifted, and a learning disabled student who at a point in time are all at a third-grade instructional level can and should be taught the same thing, in the same manner, at the same time, and with the same goals in mind. Furthermore, as teachers in a cross-categorical program get caught up in "same instructional needs," they, like those who teach in categorical programs, may lose sight of the uniqueness of each student and the need for programming that encompasses more than an academic instructional level or task.

When these programs were first introduced, they presented administrators with several important difficulties pertaining to securing financial support and in locating appropriately trained, certifiable personnel. These problems were caused by the fact that until the late 1970s, funding for special education programs was provided on a strictly categorical basis and teachers were certified only in those fundable categories of handicap.

At first, to get the programs started, programs were funded on a trial or experimental basis. Experienced teachers holding a certificate in any area of special education qualified to be a resource teacher in most school districts. Officials with the Bureau of Teacher Certification became legitimately concerned when they discovered that a resource teacher who was certified in learning disabilities was providing instruction to mentally retarded, physically handicapped, and/or emotionally disturbed students. Many parents also objected when they learned that the resource teacher had neither specific training nor experience in their child's handicap.

These problems have lessened considerably during recent years in no small part due to the rapid development of multicategorical, generic, or general special education teacher preparation programs in colleges and universities. No doubt, the primary purpose of these programs is to provide trained personnel for the cross-categorical resource model. In addition, funding criteria have been changed in some states to accommodate the cross-categorical resource model.

The Noncategorial Resource Program

The noncategorical resource program is designed to meet the educational needs of students with mild or moderate learning and/behavior problems, including both handicapped and nonhandicapped students. Students may be referred to this program from both regular and special education classes, and they may or may not be legally classified as handicapped.

A major strength of this arrangement is that disability labels are not considered in determining eligibility; students do not have to be diagnosed as handicapped in order to receive appropriate services. The noncategorical approach avoids the present-day administrative necessity of having to classify students as handicapped so that they can qualify for special services. This labeling is particularly objectionable to many educators, especially when the problems exist in mild to moderate degrees. Eligibility for placement is predicated strictly on the student's need for the services and on the availability of space for them in the program.

Administratively, the noncategorical arrangement is situated in the grey area between special education and regular education. Even though these programs usually are placed under the director of special services (special education), they just as reasonably could be placed under the director of elementary or secondary curriculum. Noncategorical services support about equally the efforts of regular education teachers to manage instructional and behavioral problems and the desire of special educators to mainstream handicapped students.

Educators have expressed a strong preference for this model. Gickling, Murphy, and Malloy (1979) surveyed regular and resource teachers and found that both groups favored the noncategorical model by wide margins. Although the model is preferred by educators, it has not been used widely in the schools, probably because of the many difficulties involved in its implementation. The administrative problems, for example, are considerable. If students no longer have to be diagnosed as handicapped in order to receive resource help, then what specific criteria, if any, should be used instead? How are teachers to be selected for these programs when suitable college courses of study and state teaching certificates do not exist? How will school administrators estimate the number of resource teaching units that will be needed when the population to be served is defined so loosely? Where will the funding come from to support such programs?

Even though many educators recognize the distinct advantages of and the needs for the noncategorical approach, we know of no state legislatures that have changed their laws so that these noncategorical programs can be openly financed. Where noncategorical programs do exist, local districts provide the necessary funds or else the programs are classified as experimental, which means that state monies can be expended in their behalf on a year-to-year basis.

The current popularity of both the categorical and cross-categorical approaches may represent a transition between the almost exclusive use of the categorical special class and the eventual acceptance of the noncategorical model — a bridge between special and regular education. However, the money required to support the noncategorical program should not come exclusively from allocations intended for use with handicapped students. At present, little financial support is available for truly handicapped school-aged students; to spend the meager funds that are available on nonhandicapped students would be ill advised and also would violate the intent of the law. Instead, new money (nonspecial education money) should be added to the current allocations to support at least part of the operation of noncategorical resource programs.

The noncategorical approach to resource programming must not be considered as a substitute for special (categorical) education. Many handicapped students, perhaps 5 percent of the school population, still require special classes and/or resource programs. Assigning these handicapped students to noncategorical resource programs and/or to regular classes would not help them. Most noncategorical teachers are not equipped to handle the specific instructional requirements of many young blind, deaf, disturbed, or language disordered children. The noncategorical resource program is a promising alternative for many of the handicapped but by no means is it intended to be the only alternative.

Readers who wish more information about the operation of noncategorical programs are referred to Hammill and Wiederholt (1972), Blackhurst et al. (1973), Jenkins and Mayhall (1976), and Affleck et al. (1973.)

The Specific Skill Resource Program

Specific skill resource programs are organized around the training of skill areas primarily in reading, mathematics, or speech. (In states where speech disabilities are legally defined as handicaps, this arrangement would be considered a categorical resource program.) Specific skill resource teachers work almost exclusively with normal students and their teachers; only rarely do they provide services to handicapped children.

The availability of special skill programs is desirable in schools that use the categorical and/or cross-categorical resource approaches. These latter programs meet the needs of only the students who are designated as handicapped, whereas the special skill programs serve the non-handicapped problem learners. Teachers in specific skills programs usually are certified in remedial reading, remedial mathematics, or speech and language rather than in special education. Such services are usually provided at local district expense.

The Itinerant Resource Program

The itinerant resource program, which can use a categorical, cross-categorical, noncategorical, or special skills organizational format, is literally a resource program on wheels. The itinerant model often is adopted in areas that have insufficient resources to support a full-time program in each school or that do not have enough students who qualify to warrant a full-time teacher.

The difficulties in operating an itinerant program are quite apparent. First, resource teachers must carry all of their materials and equipment from school to school, a considerable inconvenience. Second, they rarely have a room of their own and frequently must work in the furnace room, in the lunch room, or in the principal's or counselor's office. Occasionally, they share a room with the other itinerant resource staff, such as the speech therapist or the remedial reading teacher. Third, they are rarely able to provide instruction on a daily basis. Fourth, much time that should be spent working with students and teachers is lost by having to drive from school to school. Fifth, the fact that they are in and out of several schools a week makes it difficult for them to develop the social and professional bonds that usually exist between resource teachers and the other teachers in the school. Because of these difficulties, one is not surprised to learn that in a survey of regular and resource teachers, Gickling, Murphy, and Malloy (1979) found that the itinerant program was the least preferred by both groups of teachers.

Selecting an Appropriate Resource Program

Selecting the best resource model for a particular school will depend on the local needs, philosophies, resources, and situations. The possibility of five models merely provides the school personnel with a variety of programs from which to choose.

Conceivably a large school district would use all five approaches in response to varying situations existing within the district. For example, its low-incidence areas might be served by itinerant noncategorical persons. The more severe cases could be transferred to other schools that had special classes and categorical resource programs. In low-incidence schools, noncategorical resource rooms could manage the mild to moderate cases, especially the mentally retarded, learning disabled, and emotionally disturbed, as well as an assortment of regular class pupils with diverse problems. Categorical programs then could handle the speech disordered, the blind, and the deaf students. It is highly unlikely that a single school will need to implement all five types of resource programs; it is equally unlikely that a school district can have its needs properly met by having only one type of resource program. A proposed model for using all five varieties of resource arrangements in a school district is shown in Figure 1-2.

Such a model does not mean that students progress in a step-wise fashion between or among the services. Rather, ad hoc needs may be addressed on a temporary basis in any one of these programs.

ADVANTAGES OF THE RESOURCE APPROACH

While resource teachers and administrators are faced with several knotty and persistent difficulties in operating resource programs, the advantages associated with these programs far exceed any problems that are likely to be encountered. Nine of the most apparent advantages pertaining to using the resource programs are listed below.

1.   Students can benefit from specific resource support while remaining integrated with their friends and age-mates in the school.
2.   The resource teacher has an opportunity to help more students than does a full-time special class teacher. This is especially true when the resource teacher,

FIGURE **1 – 2.**

A model for delivering daily resource program services to students with learning and/or behavioral problems

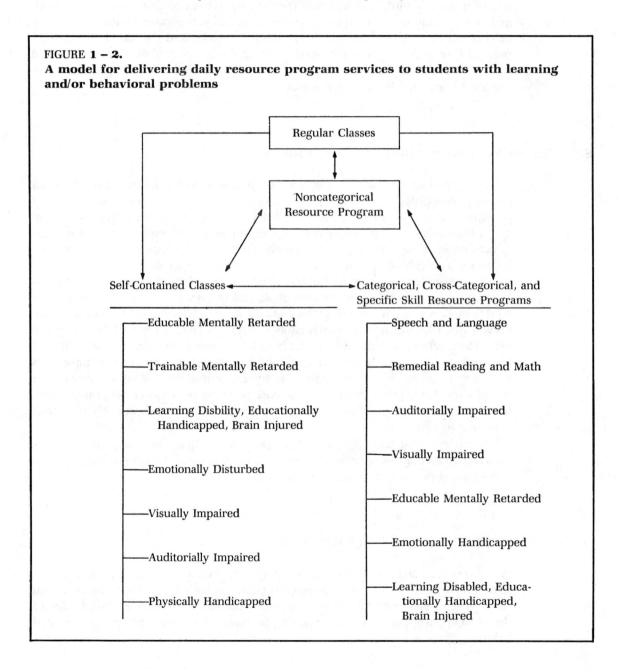

by consulting extensively with teachers, provides indirect services to students with mild or moderate problems.

3. Resource teachers can serve as informational resources to other school personnel, to parents, and to the students themselves.

4. Because young children with mild, though developing, problems can be accommodated, later severe disorders may be prevented.

5. Flexible scheduling means that remediation can be applied entirely in the classrooms by the regular teacher with some resource support or in another room by the resource program personnel when necessary; also, the schedule can be quickly altered to meet the students' changing situations and needs.

6. Since the resource program will absorb most of the handicapped students in the schools, the self-contained special education classes will increasingly become instructional settings for truly and relatively severely handicapped students, those for whom the classes were originally developed.

7. Because resource teachers have broad experience with many students exhibiting different educational and behavioral problems, they may in time become in-house consultants to the school.

8. Resource teachers can serve as ombudsmen for the students they serve.

9. Most handicapped students can receive help in their neighborhood school; thus, the necessity of busing them across the town or county to a school that houses an appropriately labeled class is eliminated or at least reduced.

EFFECTIVENESS OF THE RESOURCE MODEL

A small body of controlled research testing the effectiveness of various kinds of resource arrangements has accumulated over the years. In these studies the researchers have compared the academic and/or affective performance of resourced students with that of similar students who remained in self-contained classes or who were "mainstreamed" in regular classes. The characteristics of these studies and their results are summarized in Table 1 – 1.

For ease of interpretation, the results of each study have been coded +, 0, or +/0. Results favoring the resourced students are indicated by +. In these instances, the differences between the resourced and nonresourced students were tested statistically and were found to exist at the 0.05 level of confidence or less. A 0 in the table indicates that the differences between the groups were not significant. A +/0 means that the researcher performed several tests and that one or more of the analyses significantly favored the resourced students or that one or more were not significant.

Basically, two kinds of students are enrolled in resource programs: (1) handicapped students, for whom the resource programs serve as a mainstreaming alternative to special class enrollment, and (2) low-achieving nonhandicapped students who need remedial or catch-up work. The results of the research have relevance for each type of student.

TABLE 1 – 1.
Investigations That Studied the Effectiveness of Resource Programs

Researcher	Date	Model	Subject	Approach	Contrast	Academics	Affective
Bersoff et al.	1972	Categorical	LD	Direct instruction	Special class	0	0
Bersoff et al.	1972	Categorical	LD	Direct instruction	Regular class	0	+/0
Cantrell & Cantrell	1976	Noncategorical	"Low Achievers"	Consulting	Regular class	+	
Carter	1975	Categorical	EMR	Direct instruction	Special class	0	
Carter	1975	Categorical	EMR	Direct instruction	Regular class	0	
Gerke	1975	Cross-Categorical	EMR/ED	?	Special class	0	0
Glavin et al.	1971	Categorical	Behavior Problems	Direct instruction	Special class	+/0	+/0
Jenkins & Mayhall	1976	Cross-Categorical	EMR/LD	Direct instruction	Special class	+	
Jenkins & Mayhall	1976	Cross-Categorical	EMR/LD	Direct instruction	Special class	+	+
Kerlin & Latham	1977	Noncategorical	"Low Achiever/Problem Students"	Consulting	Regular class		+
Kerlin & Latham	1977	Noncategorical	"Low Achiever/Problem Students"	Direct instruction	Regular class		+
Knight et al.	1981	Noncategorical	"Low Achievers"	Consulting	Regular class	+	
Macy & Carter	1978	Cross-Categorical	EMR, TMR, MBI, ED	Direct instruction	Special class	0	0
Miller & Sabatino	1978	Cross-Categorical	EMR/LD	Direct instruction	Regular class	+	
O'Conner et al.	1979	Noncategorical	"Low Achievers"	Direct instruction	Regular class	+	
Rodee	1971	Categorical	EMR	Direct instruction	Special class	+/0	0
Rodee	1971	Categorical	EMR	Direct instruction	Regular class	0	0
Rust	1978	Noncategorical	"Learning Problems"	Direct instruction	Regular class	0	
Sabatino	1971	Categorical	LD	Direct instruction	Special class	+/0	
Sabatino	1971	Categorical	LD	Direct instruction	Regular class	+	
Schiff et al.	1979	Categorical	LD	Direct instruction	Special class	0	0
Tilley	1970	Categorical	EMR	Direct instruction	Special class	0	0
Walker	1974	Noncategorical	EMR	Both	Speical class	+/0	+/0

*See Glavin (1973) and Ito (1980) for results of follow-up studies.

LD = Learning Disabled
EMR = Educable Mentally Retarded
ED = Emotionally Disturbed
MBI = Minimally Brain Injured
TMI = Trainable Mentally Retarded

For the most part, the collective results of this research indicate that handicapped students who receive resource services do as well as handicapped students who remain in special, segregated classes. Given the current acceptance of the idea that students should be taught in the least restrictive school environment, it would seem that in general resource programs are preferable to special classes, especially since the students appear to profit from instruction in both settings.

In cases where those receiving resource help are nonhandicapped, normal students who merely need remedial work, the collective results of the research are quite clear. Such students consistently do better than their peers who stay in the regular class and receive no additional supplemental help.

The results of the noncontrolled research (Hammill et al., 1972; Affleck, Lehning, and Brow, 1973; Ito, 1980; Weiner, 1969; Barksdale and Atkinson, 1971) have uniformly and significantly favored the resource program. These studies should be viewed as providing only tentative or supplemental support for the resource program. Their results should not be given the same weight as those reported in Table 1 – 1 because of the absence of control subjects.

This discussion is intended to provide only a brief overview of the state of the research concerning the resource model. Our conclusions and observations should be accepted judiciously, for by combining the results of studies for group analysis, as we have done, some significant aspects of individual studies may have been lost. Those who are interested specifically in the topic of efficacy should consider our conclusions to be gross statements and should read the individual studies to learn the subtleties of the research.

WHAT THE RESOURCE PROGRAM IS NOT

Although we advocate resource programs as one of several alternatives that should be provided in the schools, we are aware also that the model can be abused. The teacher or administrator who is responsible for resource programs must be alert to ensure that they do not become tutorial programs, study halls, or dumping grounds.

The resource program is not intended as a tutorial service to keep students up with their daily lessons. Such a service may be needed, but it is not a primary function of the resource program. Instead, a program of peer tutoring, cross-age tutoring, or volunteer services can be set up, perhaps through the resource program. Readers interested in implementing such programs are referred to Ehly and Larsen (1980).

Current interest in teaching independent study behaviors has served as a rationale for turning some resource programs into supervised study halls where students can work under adult supervision. This is a misuse of the resource program; for although study behaviors can be taught in the resource program, they should be used in the classroom or at home doing homework.

There are several ways that resource programs can become known as dumping grounds. First, teachers may send troublesome students to the resource teacher simply to remove an aversive stimulus or an annoyance from their classrooms. If such students are accepted, the classroom teacher may be so reinforced that he or she will send other students quickly. A second dumping ground practice occurs when the resource program is characterized solely as a small-group remedial program. (What difference will a few more students make?) The resource teacher in these circumstances soon has so many students that he or she can do only a superficial job. A third dumping practice can occur where the resource program has been sold as the new alternative to special class placement. It may become a semi-self-contained program for students across inappropriate ages and handicapping conditions. Abuses of the resource program model can be avoided, usually through appropriate cooperative planning such as we describe in Chapter 3.

Occasionally, resource programs have grown too rapidly and are inappropriately large. Consider a school where the curriculum is focused so narrowly that it is inappropriate for a considerable portion of its student body. In such cases, growth in the resource program is not positive, for it suggests that the resource services are serving as a safety valve for the regular classes. In fact the presence of the resource program helps to obscure the school's real problem: the shirking of its responsibility to consider the actual needs and characteristics of its students by revising its curriculum. As a rule, where 5 percent or more of a school's students are being referred for resource help, serious questions might be raised about that school's ability or willingness to meet realistically the educational needs of its students.

In summary, we believe that the resource program can be an effective instructional arrangement for helping many students who have learning and behavior problems. We recognize, however, that for any model to work successfully, resource teachers must be proficient in performing their duties, notably those duties relating to assessing individual needs, planning and implementing instructional programs, and consulting with principals, teachers, and parents. Resource teachers also must be able to manage daily details, such as scheduling and grading. In addition, resource teachers must possess considerable knowledge in many areas, including reading, spelling, writing, arithmetic, spoken language, classroom behavior, and independent study habits. The rest of this text is devoted to discussion of these topics.

2

The Resource Teacher: Role Definition

The resource teacher is expected to perform three basic types of services for referred students: (1) assess their educational needs, (2) prepare and implement instructional programs for them, and (3) consult with their teachers, parents, and others about matters that relate to their education.

ASSESSING INDIVIDUAL NEEDS

At least five ideas about assessment are used consistently in this book. First, the assessment procedures we recommend are intended primarily for the purpose of planning instructional programs for individual students. Second, the assessment will include at least four sets of activities that range from planning the assessment to evaluating it. Third, the resource teacher may need to become competent in the assessment of an extremely wide variety of areas. Fourth, the measurement procedures or tools used in assessment can be interpreted in either a norm-referenced or a criterion-referenced manner. And fifth, there are at least seven basic tools or procedures that the teacher can use to collect information that will assist with instructional planning for an individual student. Each of these ideas will be discussed in this section.

The Purpose of Assessment

As used in this book, the term *assessment* refers primarily to all activities that resource teachers use to develop instructional programs for individual students. Assessment can also refer to the entire process by which students are differentially diagnosed and categorically labelled — for example, as mentally retarded or emotionally disturbed. This type of assessment is done usually by psychologists, physicians, and other nonteaching personnel, although often in conjunction with teachers. Some of the information gleaned in the process of differential diagnosis can be helpful in educational programming. However, the topic itself is better considered separately and at length in a categorically based book on assessment. The focus of this book is assessment for instruction

The Assessment Process

We believe that evaluation is a process that includes at least four sets of activities, regardless of the purpose for the assessment. Further, these activities are rarely the complete responsibility of one person only; usually a team of persons is involved, often including the parent(s) and the student as well. The responsibility for coordinating the activities of team members does, however, often fall to the resource teacher; and it is for this reason that the resource teacher should be well aware of each phase of the process.

The first step in assessment actually occurs before any additional information is collected. The teacher or the team must give thought to the student, the system, and the situation. The purpose of this thinking is to generate appropriate questions, which will be used to organize the assessment. Information should be collected only to answer specific questions about the student and his or her environment (Tull, 1981) and not as a routine measure to create a fat folder of unused data. When relevant questions have been generated and written down, the instruments and procedures of assessment are selected because they are the ones that are most likely to answer the cue questions posed during the planning stage. Although the need for this stage seems self-evident, we cannot overstress its importance. Beginning with Part III of this book, we have used a cue question format to guide the organization of assessment.

The second step is the administration and interpretation of appropriate tools and procedures used to obtain the information that will be used for making informed decisions about the student's educational program. At this stage, responsibilities for the use of specific procedures are assigned to the person(s) who will be best able to administer or interpret them.

After the information is collected, the assessment moves into a third phase where the information obtained is integrated in order to note consistencies and inconsistencies in the patterns of information, to recommend instructional priorities, and to recommend instructional strategies that have a high probability of success with the student. This integration is best accomplished with a transdisciplinary approach so that any team members involved share their information and skills (Sears, 1981).

The fourth phase or set of activities is one that is seldom considered in the assessment process: that of designing procedures that will provide data to validate or to invalidate the recommendations made. Any recommendation made should be considered as a hypothesis to be tested and reevaluated in light of data about its effectiveness with the individual student.

These activities may not occur as separately as they have been described; but however they may occur, it is clear that assessment should involve much more than the information-gathering phase usually associated with the term.

Areas Targeted for Assessment

In order to become competent at assessment, the resource teacher must be prepared to evaluate a wide range of important areas. Academic performance is certainly critical in most cases, but other areas are important too. Attitudes are closely associated with achievement and behavior. Not only should the perceptions of the students toward themselves, their peers, teachers, families, school programs, and problems be investigated, but also the perceptions of others about those students and their problems. The resource teacher will also want to analyze various aspects of the classes or programs that the students attend, especially the climates of those classes, the instructional programs used there, and the teachers' attitudes and expectations. Further, behaviors such as those of independent study habits or vocational readiness may need to be checked. Whatever the area, the types of instruments and/or procedures used are basically the same.

Norm- and Criterion-Referenced Concepts in Assessment

The assessment of individual needs is heavily dependent upon information-gathering tools, which we describe in the next section. We need to preface these descriptions by noting that all of the information eventually obtained will be interpreted in one of two ways: either in a norm-referenced or a criterion-referenced manner. These terms have strong historical associations with tests, but the concepts involved are so important that we apply them broadly.

Norm-referenced applies to any measurement tool, task, or procedure where an individual's relative performance is discussed in comparison with that of a normative group. It does not matter if the group is the original test standardization population or if it is a group of young students in a class whose language patterns were observed, recorded, and then indexed to chronological age. If a student is said to be at the fortieth percentile on a math test; if a three-year-old child does not yet demonstrate the language forms shown by most two-year-olds; if a student is the least chosen by peers; or if a student's "talk-outs" are above the modal number for the class as a whole, then the student has a relative standing, and a norm-referenced interpretation has been made. Norm-referenced interpretation is especially useful where the goal of assessment is to determine whether there is a problem that needs further assessment and intervention, as for screening (Bloom and Lahey, 1978) and where entire programs are to be evaluated (Evans, 1981). Both of these uses are possible because norm-referenced measurement or interpretation allows comparison of the performance of individual students both with that of their peers and with their own aptitudes or abilities.

Criterion-referenced applies to any measurement tool, task, or procedure where we describe the student's performance in somewhat absolute terms — whether the student has met a predetermined criterion and where the student's performance is viewed essentially as a pass or a fail. If 80 percent is needed to pass a math test; if a student must read correctly seventy-five words per minute; if handwriting is noted on a scale from legible to illegible; or if a student must be in his or her seat 90 percent of the time — then the student essentially passes or fails a preset criterion. If the description is without reference either to what any other students do or to how much below or above the criterion the student performed, then a criterion-referenced interpretation has been made. Criterion-referenced interpretation is especially useful where the goal of assessment is to inventory the student's conduct, attitudes, abilities, or performance and to find out if the student has sufficient mastery of whatever is being taught to proceed with a course of instruction.

The differences between criterion- and norm-referenced interpretations can be seen in this example that uses a familiar test. On the Test of Written Spelling (TWS), students are asked to spell sixty words from dictation. The number of words they spell correctly is totaled and converted into scaled scores using norm-referenced tables. If Sally were 7-3 years of age and spelled thirty-one words correctly, her scaled score would be 114. This figure indicates that Sally spells better than 84 percent of the youngsters her age. Although this is useful information for some purposes, such as reporting to parents, it tells the resource teacher nothing about what words or what kinds of words Sally cannot spell. To get the type of detailed information that can be more relevant for planning specific programs for individual students, a criterion-referenced interpretation is required. At this point, the examiner or teacher may either subject the results of the TWS to an item-by-item criterion analysis or administer another test specifically designed for criterion interpretation, such as Kottmeyer's Diagnostic Spelling Test (see chapter on spelling).

Because it implies a close relationship to instruction, the term *criterion referenced* has become a popular adjective in education. The implication is so strong that criterion-referenced testing, mastery learning, and informal assessment have lately become synonymous in the minds of many educators. They are not the same at all, however. A criterion-referenced test is in fact a test that is taken by students. It is subject to the same demands for demonstration of reliability and validity that we ask of any other test, although the nature of the evidence provided will vary with the type of test.

Criterion-referenced tests usually are built around behavioral objectives for a course of study or a content area. One or more items are written for each objective. The items may look like those of any other test, but they are keyed to specific objectives, and they directly reflect the skills of those objectives. As we have noted, a level of mastery is set so that a student who scores, for example, 80 percent or above, is a pass and a student who then scores 79 percent or below is a fail. The purpose of setting such a criterion is an assumption:

> The assumption is that persons performing at this level have mastered enough of the material so that they will be able to complete the next unit in the sequence successfully. Ideally, we would have empirical evidence that the designated proficiency level was, in fact, the minimal level needed to pursue further work in the area. Although there is some evidence that 80 to 90 percent (Bloom, 1971) is an appropriate level, in most cases the level is chosen arbitrarily, rather than on the basis of empirical evidence. [F. Brown, 1976, p. 204]

Most classroom teachers construct, administer, and score many tests with criterion-referenced ideas in mind. For example, a teacher assigns fifteen words on Monday for a spelling test on Friday. The criterion for mastery is set at 80 percent, or twelve words spelled correctly. The students know what the items on the test will be; the criterion for mastery is known; the fifteen items are specifically taught; and every student could potentially achieve a mastery level because neither the range of scores, any other student's score, nor the magnitude of a score either above or below the 80 percent, is important. The test is given, and students A, B, C, and D score as follows:

Student A = 100%
Student B =   80% (missed *percentage, generous,* and *capitol*)
Student C =   60%
Student D =   60% (Each missed the same words, as shown below.)

Expected Word	Student C	Student D
percentage	persentij	percentege
generous	jenerus	genrous
capitol	kapitle	capital
calculate	kalkuelat	calculator
tribute	tribuet	tribut
reliable	relible	reliabel

The relevance of such a test to instructional decision making can be seen in the mastery information it provides. However, it is equally clear that the resource teacher remains in charge of a series of decisions that the test does not address:

> Student A can continue to the next series of words. Did she or he already know how to spell the words prior to the introduction of the lesson?

Student B has passed 12 of 15 words. Are the three misspelled words important?

Why was 80 percent set as an appropriate criterion? Who set the criterion?

Students C and D have both missed the same six words. Will their scores be recorded and the students continued to the next unit?

How long should instruction continue if the students fail again?

Will students C and D be expected to learn fifteen new words in addition to those they missed this time?

Will the remedial instruction differ from the regular instruction?

Does it matter that even though C and D missed the same words, their misspellings were very different from each other?

Which three words should students C and D learn to spell to attain a mastery level?

Were the specific words selected for the test actually appropriate to the educational goals for each?

Is this test the *best* way to determine mastery?

Will mastery of these words ever be checked again?

We could continue to suggest more questions related to the use of criterion-referenced tests that set mastery levels; however, the purpose of raising these questions here is to emphasize the idea that even informal, criterion-referenced, mastery tests merely contribute information that is to be used by instructional decision-makers such as the resource teacher.

Educators are particularly interested in the mastery learning aspect of criterion-referenced testing, primarily because it provides accountability for instructional programs. Teachers wish to inventory what the student knows and does not know. Specific items not known are the items targeted for instruction and then for further mastery testing. Where we are interested in mastery of specific items or behaviors, the pass-fail criterion is applied to each item. The items are usually listed in a checklist fashion.

The term *informal evaluation* is often used synonymously with *criterion-referenced assessment*. The resource teacher may read in a report about a student that tests and informal assessment were used in evaluating educational needs. Frequently, this means that the teacher observed the "passing" or "failing" of daily tasks. But, one can never be sure just what is meant by a term such as *informal evaluation*. When information about a student is based upon informal evaluation, the resource teacher should interview carefully to find out what was actually done. Further, the resource teachers who use assessment techniques other than tests (and we hope and expect that they do so) should describe the actual techniques used. For example, "The analysis of permanent products showed that . . ." is less ambiguous than "Informal evaluation showed that . . ."

We have described the differences among criterion-referenced assessment, mastery learning, and informal assessment so that the resource teacher can both use the terms correctly and be sensitive to the communication problems that can occur when they are used interchangeably.

Tools or Procedures of Assessment

This section describes eight major tools or procedures that are used systematically by resource teachers and others who gather information for assessing individual needs. We recognize that some specific procedures, such as performance tests, may also be used for assessment. They are not described here, however, because they are more likely to be used with special populations and situations; therefore they have less applicability to the general role of the resource teacher. The tools or procedures we describe are: (1) reviewing and analyzing records; (2) observing and recording behavior(s); (3) administering standardized tests and rating scales; (4) developing and using checklists; (5) conducting interviews; (6) using rigorous educational technology; (7) conducting analytic or diagnostic teaching sessions; and (8) analyzing permanent products made by students.

Reviewing and analyzing records. The analysis and review of records made about the student is one of the most important of assessment activities, and it is also one of the most overlooked sources of information. Review of records is relatively unobtrusive, is inexpensive, and is one of the major sources of information for generating assessment questions.

Records are often in disarray and may be poorly organized because no one may have taken or been given the responsibility of records collection and organization. When they are not organized, it is impossible to evaluate the relevance of information gathered. People may continue to collect information superstitiously, believing that it is of value when it is not, or they may understandably complain about collecting information that is never used. People rarely mind collecting information that can be shown to be helpful to a student. Especially where the resources for data or information collection are limited, the resource teacher, usually in conjunction with others in the school, will want to make a careful study of the records system.

The kind of information we can expect from a review and analysis of records is reflected in the following questions:

1. What is the nature of the information provided? The information should be relevant to any presenting problems. It should also be comprehensive enough to describe the problem or the student adequately. Both positive and negative information are important. We will also want to know if information that should be there is missing. This is especially true of information that is needed to rule out possible causes of problems or certain instructional methods. Instructional records often lack enough detail to permit a real analysis of the instructional history of the student.

2. How current is the information? There is no need to duplicate information that is already available. On the other hand, if people are making decisions on old information, there should be an updating to be sure that the information used is currently valid.

3. How reliable and valid is the information? The data base for any statements made about the student must be known. The data base is then evaluated literally as to its goodness. Some statements, such as "John has a central auditory processing

disorder, because he mispronounces words such as *chimney* as *chimley* and *came* as *come*," are clearly in need of further interpretation. In addition, statements based upon a one-time observation, or upon only a single setting may be suspect. Observable fact must be separated from professional fiction.

4. What discrepancies about the student or his or her behavior are apparent from the records? These discrepancies may be between one time and another, between one setting and another, or between an expectation and an actual performance. The sudden onset of social, emotional, or academic problems, as well as gradual declines (as in IQ scores) are signals either of invalid information or a serious adverse change in the student or in his or her environment.

5. What consistent patterns of behaviors, comments about the student, or test scores are noted? Consistencies provide some evidence of reliability in information and evidence for the chronic nature of a problem. On the other hand, we would be concerned about the effectiveness of the instructional program if records showed a consistent pattern of no change during any time of remedial effort.

6. How is the information in the records organized? Although this question is not about the student, it has implications both for the wise use of the resource teacher's time and energy and for public relations with those who will be asked to gather information on behalf of the student. When records are not organized, it becomes impossible to evaluate the relevance of the information recorded, and people continue to collect information that is irrelevant or unused.

In addition to the need for organizing records, the form of the organization is important. While there is an apparent advantage in having a purely chronological account of a student, eventually the information should also be reorganized around presenting problems as well. The problem-oriented record described by Weed (1971) is often used in settings where more than one person works with a student or is to observe the student or where the problem is persistent across time and settings.

Observing and recording behaviors.   There are a variety of reasons for observing a student in both classroom and nonclassroom settings. First, observation can confirm or disconfirm statements or hypotheses made about the student. Second, patterns of student participation and interaction with people, with tasks, and with objects (such as trading cards, marbles, or furniture) can be noted and documented. A third purpose for observation is to note consistencies and inconsistencies in patterns of behavior, both over time and from setting to setting. Fourth, factors that appear to influence the student's behavior can be identified. And fifth, any student behaviors of concern may be described more accurately as the observer sees what the student actually does.

When observations are highly standardized, it is necessary to determine the interobserver reliability, to specify the particular skill or behavior to be observed, and to predetermine the method of observation, the notation system, and the allowable interpretations of the data. Techniques for such observations are presented by Hall (1971) and by Sulzer-Azaroff and Mayer (1977).

Observations of ongoing behavior or vignettes of behavior require yet a different kind of framework for observation and recording. Prescott (1957) suggests that a good anecdotal record gives the date, place, and situation in which the action occurred; describes the action(s) of the student and the reactions of other people involved (including the student's reactions to the reactions); quotes what is said by the student and to the student; supplies mood cues; and provides a description that is extensive enough to cover the episode.

Observations traditionally have included only the student's actual behavior and immediate transactions. Observations should also describe the setting in which the behavior(s) occur, sometimes giving diagrams. For example, a floor plan drawn of the classroom may include the seating arrangement and note the target student's seat location in comparison with peers and with that of the teacher.

Bloom and Lahey (1978) have noted that the technology of observation is important, but even more important is the knowledge of the observer. Having both an appropriate focus to the observation and a credible interpretation of what was observed depends upon the presence of a well-informed observer. Consider an example that is far from education. Two people, a winning jockey and a casual appreciator of horses in general, may view a particular horse. Although both see the same horse, the jockey will bring more relevant information to bear on an observation than will the horse appreciator, because of accumulated knowledge and experience. So, too, can two people observe the same reading lesson. The more knowledgeable and experienced teacher will often provide a more focused description and a more appropriate interpretation of that lesson. The resource teacher will have to become knowledgeable in many areas of assessment and therefore in areas in which observations are to be made.

Administering standardized tests and rating scales.   Tests and rating scales are said to be standardized when they have a common item content administered to those who take the test or make the rating and when they have standard administration and scoring procedures (including standard meanings for the scores). These tests and scales[1] may be interpreted in either a norm-referenced or a criterion-referenced manner when there are appropriate statistical data to support the interpretation.[1]

Since the topic of standardized tests is so familiar, this section is organized around two topics that need special comment: interpreting standardization information and guidelines for the appropriate use of tests.

The resource teacher can learn a great deal about a test merely by reading the manual. For example, one popular test manual notes that the test is not to be used with "provincial subpopulations," whatever that means. Caution must be used in choosing, recommending, and/or interpreting these measurement devices. When selecting any standardized test, the teacher should find out and report how the manual treats the following questions:

1. *Are the instructions for administering and scoring the test clearly stated?* If the instructions are ambiguous or subjective, the examiners will have to improvise.

The use of this test then becomes idiosyncratic to the individual tester, and the benefits of standardization are lost.

2. *Are the reliability data adequate?* Any test that will be used to measure the abilities of individuals must be highly reliable. Of what value is knowing a student's test score if it varies widely on a day-to-day basis? In norm-referenced measurement, internal consistency and stability are the two most common types of reliability data reported, and estimates of at least one of these should be reported in the test manual. Estimates of reliability are reported as correlation coefficients; they must reach a certain level if the test is to be clinically useful. Generally a coefficient of 0.80 (Anastasi, 1982) is suggested as the minimally acceptable figure for the diagnostic uses of tests.

For criterion-referenced tests, we need to know how likely it is that students will respond in the same way each time the test is given and with whether any observers or scorers will score the test consistently. We will also want to know how likely it is that students who either pass or fail on one administration of the test will fall into the same category of pass or fail on a second administration. If the pass or fail decision is not reversed on a substantial number of cases, then the test is believed to be reliable. Test-retest and interscorer reliability provide evidence for this kind of reliability.

3. *Are any validity studies reported to show that the test measures what its authors say it measures and to show that the test has some practical uses?* A test is valid when it is demonstrated experimentally to measure the skill or trait it is presumed to measure. To demonstrate validity, the common practice in norm-referenced measurement is to correlate the test of unknown validity with a test of known or accepted validity (concurrent validity). For example, a new intelligence test might be correlated with the Revised Stanford Binet Test of Intelligence (Terman and Merrill, 1961). If the correlation between the two tests is statistically significant (0.05 or greater) and is reasonably high ($r = 0.35$ or greater), one can assume that they each measure to some extent the same construct: intelligence. The resource teacher must also become familiar with the characteristics of construct, face, and predictive validity, most of which are associated with norm-referenced tests.

Both content and face validity are important for criterion-referenced tests because the test items should reflect relevant or nontrivial objectives. Further, since these tests are used extensively in decision making, their validity will depend to a great extent upon the proportion of correct decisions they yield. In terms of assessment for instructional purposes, then, resource teachers will need to know that students who fail the criterion need further instruction and students who pass the criterion do not. This is true whether the criterion involved relates to passing a number of items (at the 80 percent level, for example), or whether it refers to passing or failing a single item of interest for instructional purposes. Such an index of correct decisions usually involves the use of a predicted criterion performance. One paradigm and formula for an index of decision-making accuracy of such tests is described by F. G. Brown (1976, pp. 109–110).

In addition to these three questions, both norm- and criterion-referenced tests each have a question that should also be addressed in the manual. In the case of norm-referenced tests that question is: *Are adequate normative data available?* Standardized tests usually are given to compare students' peformance with that of peers. To facilitate this comparison, most test developers provide tables that include normative information, which concerns the typical performance of typical students. These tables are used to convert a student's raw scores on a test into standard scores, age or grade equivalents, or percentiles. Norms can be based on the test performance of samples of students drawn from the nation as a whole; or from one state or province, region, or locality; or from one racial, ethnic, or linguistic group. In general, the resource teacher should select tests that have norms based on large nationwide samples of children whose social class, age, ethnic background, and sex characteristics adequately reflect the country's population.

For criterion-referenced tests, the manual should provide some information about the question, *How was the criterion established?* Where there is some reported data base for setting the criterion, it is more likely that the criterion recommended is truly appropriate.

To be able to select good tests, resource teachers need to have a basic understanding of the principles involved in test construction and in test use. These principles and their relation to special and remedial education are discussed quite clearly by Salvia and Ysseldyke (1981), Wallace and Larsen (1978), and McLoughlin and Lewis (1981). Where more detailed information is desired, we recommend Gronlund (1981) and Nunnally (1978).

The primary sources for critical reviews of most available tests are Buros (1974) and *The Eighth Mental Measurements Yearbook* (1978). Although comprehensive, the material about tests that is provided in Buros's volume is often subjective.

Resource teachers with school experience probably have administered and scored the standardized achievement batteries that are given routinely at the beginning and end of the school year. These teachers will recognize the similarity between the procedures for that task and for administering norm-referenced tests in the resource program. Resource teachers with a background in special education probably received some orientation to testing in their preservice training. Additional skill can be obtained through inservice training or by enrolling in an educational measurement course at a nearby college.

The resource teacher does not give norm-referenced tests in order to obtain information with which to plan an instructional program. Again, let us stress that it is not recommended that a resource teacher ever plan a school program for a student based primarily on information derived from this type of evaluation. Better procedures for planning programs are described in the following sections of this chapter.

Teachers who wish to use the principles of test construction to develop their own tests are referred to additional sources, such as Thorndike and Hagen (1977, pp. 198–272) or to Scannel and Tracey (1975).

Much of the recent educational activity surrounding test construction and use has been focused on the test user. Many of the abuses found in testing come about because we do not keep testing in its proper perspective insofar as decision making about individuals is concerned. We agree with Thorndike and Hagen (1977) that significant positive advantages are to be gained from testing. Their guidelines for the constructive use of test results can be adopted. This means that the test user should:

> *Examine and become clear about all the values involved.* Most decisions, whether they relate to one single individual or to a whole class or category of individuals, involve a complex of interacting and competing values . . . . Only as the competing values are recognized and weighed can one decide whether or how tests can contribute to better decisions.
>
> *Recognize that test scores are only indicators or signs of the underlying reality that one is interested in.* A score on a reading test is an indicator of reading ability, not the reading ability itself . . . . But the underlying reality is only accessible to us through the signs that it gives. We become aware of fever through the clinical thermometer, or more crudely through a hot and flushed face. However, when distorting physical, cultural, or social factors intervene, the significance of the indicator may become modified or blurred.
>
> *Recognize test results as only* one *type of* descriptive *data.* The key words in this statement are *one* and *descriptive.* Thus in relation to any decision there are many other types of information that are relevant in addition to test scores . . . . And the . . . test score can do no more than *describe* one aspect of the person's current functioning. By itself, it does not tell *why* he performs as he does, nor make clear what causal relationships that performance bears . . . to the difficulties that he is having . . . .
>
> *Relate test results to whatever else is known about the person or group.* No test score exists in a vacuum. The score gains meaning in proportion as the constellation of information into which it is fitted is complete and comprehensive.
>
> *Recognize the possibilities of error in* all *types of descriptive data.* . . . . The user of test results needs continuously to be aware of the approximate nature of any score, and to bracket the score with a band of uncertainty . . . . But it is equally true, though perhaps less explicitly recognized, that all the other kinds of information we have about a person are also subject to error . . . . Our decisions are always arrived at on the basis of partial and fallible information, test scores being fallible along with everything else.
>
> *In the light of the above, acknowledge the limits of human wisdom, and maintain tentativeness in decisions, to the extent that to do so is realistically possible.* Decisions *do* have to be made. But we make them on the basis of partial and fallible data . . . . But for all decisions, whatever the role that test results may have had in them, let us eternally keep before us the caveat: Maybe we were wrong. [pp. 623–625]

Developing and using checklists.   Basically a checklist is a list of statements (actually inferred questions) of various degrees of specificity about a student's performance in a particular area or areas For example, if the area of interest were penmanship, the items might include:

1.   Size of writing
   a.   Too large
   b.   Too small
   c.   Varying in size
   d.   Appropriate to paper and task

2   Slant of writing
   a.   Too slanting
   b.   Not vertical
   c.   Irregular
   d.   Appropriate

Checklists are second cousins to criterion-referenced tests. Whether the information comes from tests, observations, or analyses of student products, a list of behaviors or skills is checked off as known-not known, or observed-not observed. If an item is not known or not observed, then it is assumed that the skill or behavior should be taught.

Checklists permit a great deal of user flexibility regarding the variety of information that can be determined. They also require considerable practitioner judgment in interpreting the results or even in making a yes-no judgment. Information gathered may be unreliable or of questionable validity, so checklist information should be considered as a basis for forming hypotheses about a student's behavior. These hypotheses then can be recast into forms that can be validated or invalidated using tests or data based teaching procedures.

Conducting interviews.   An interview has been defined briefly as "a conversation directed to a definite purpose other than satisfaction in the conversation itself" (Bingham, Moore, and Gustad, 1957, p. 3). Other authors embellish this definition by emphasizing the use of questions or the need for information exchange, but the need for having a predetermined purpose is always a factor.

Most teachers value the information derived from interviews. They spend a lot of time each year talking with and seeking data from parents, students, and other teachers. The interview approach provides a quick and convenient way of obtaining the perceptions that a person has about a situation or event that is current or historic. For example, by interviewing the parents of a student, the resource teacher can gain some insights as to how the student is perceived and treated at home and what the parents believe is causing or contributing to the problem. These perceptions are usually highly idiosyncratic and subjective and therefore should not be taken at face value. Yet they provide the resource teacher with clues concerning factors that might be influencing a specific situation.

There is a definite art and science to interviewing. Stewart and Cash (1974), Gorden (1969), and McCallon and McCray (1975) are useful how-to books. In the sample interview starters shown below, we have adapted some of the information from these sources to show their application to the resource program.

Sample Interview Starters[2]

1.   *Summary of the problem:* Useful when the person to be interviewed is unaware of the problem or when he or she might not know the details of a problem. *Example*: "Bruce Spencer has been referred this year for resource assistance in reading. Since he was in your room last year, I wanted to get some idea of the materials and techniques you used with him and how he responded to them."

2. *Explanation of how you discovered the problem*: Useful when you can be honest and specific about how you did discover the problem; also requires a summary of the problem.
   Example: "This past week I have been working individually with Sharon Kessler to get some idea of how to help her with math. It seems that she can actually *do* the problems but has trouble with some of the formats used in this new math series. I would like to get your reactions to some procedures that might help her within the classroom, at least until she becomes used to the different way of presenting the problems."

3. *Mention of an incentive or reward for assistance.* May imply that you are a "salesperson"; useful if a real incentive does exist for the teacher.
   Example: "While I was observing Tyrone Johnson and James Brown, I noticed that some of the other children also are rather quarrelsome. I know that you hesitate to refer so many children, but perhaps some of the techniques we plan to try with Tyrone and James could reduce some of the other disruptive behavior. Could you tell me a little more about times of the day that seem to bring on the most problems?"

4. *Request for advice or assistance.* One of the more common interview openings.
   Example: "I have just been studying the referral data on Maria Valdez. I can tell that Maria must have some severe problems. Could we use this referral form as a basis for helping me get a more detailed picture of how these problems show up in your classroom?"

5. *Reference to known position of the interviewee.* May explain why you decided on an interview. Use caution and tact to prevent defensiveness.
   Example: "As a new resource teacher, I need to find out about the kinds of spelling curricula used here in Birchwood School. I understand that you have modified your program because of some of the shortcomings in the Boredom Program."

6. *Reference to the person who sent you to the interviewee.* Be sure that (1) the person really did send you, and (2) the interviewee likes the person you name.
   Example: "Mr. Hafeman suggested that I talk with you about how I might approach Penny DeGraaf's father concerning her hostile attitude toward school. He mentioned that you had worked with the family successfully for some years, but that each year is literally a new one."

7. *Request for a specified period of time.* Perhaps the most overused starter.
   Example: "Janet, when will you have five minutes to discuss Ruth Wright's progress with the Nuffield Math materials?"[2]

Two basic types of interviews are useful for gathering information for planning individual educational programs. The more common is the one in which the teacher wants to find out about perceptions of a problem situation. The interview can also be used to probe a student's cognitive behavior — how the student thinks either about social or emotional events or about academic tasks. In the former case, Morse (1971) provides a classic structure for these interviews. For academic performance, Opper (1977) provides structured guidelines for probing a student's reasoning. In both cases, any information obtained from such a source must be considered hypothetical or tentative.

Using rigorous educational technology (ABA).   Education does have its own technology in which a series of educational experiments are carried out with or on behalf of the student. The use of such a technology makes it more probable that statements made about a student or about what works and does not work with a student are reliable and valid. This technology has become known as applied behavior analysis, or ABA methodology. It is usually associated with behavior modification, but it is an entire system for both assessing and teaching either academic or social behaviors. Lovitt (1975, 1975a) has presented the rationale that underlies ABA and has described how it can be applied to remedial education as well as to curricular research. His discussion of the five ingredients that comprise ABA is important to an understanding of the system.[3]

Direct measurement.   When ABA techniques are used, the behavior of concern is measured directly. If the researcher is concerned with the pupil's ability to add facts of the class 2 + 2 = [   ], or to read words from a reader, those particular behaviors would be measured. This form of measurement is contrasted to more indirect methods that use such devices as achievement tests that measure behaviors not of immediate concern.

Daily measurement.   A second important ingredient of ABA is that the behavior of concern is measured, if not daily, at least very often. If, for instance, the pinpointed behavior is the pupil's ability to add facts of the class 2 + 2 = [   ], he would be given the opportunity to perform that skill for several days during a base-line period before a judgment is made. Averaging data for several days would balance out the possibility that on one day the pupil performed very poorly, the next day better, and so forth. Many times in research, the pretest-posttest methodology is used: a test is given before treatment and another is given after treatment. Judgments or decisions derived from such limited data might be pernicious; the consequences for some children could well be disastrous.

Replicable teaching procedures.   Another important feature of ABA is that generally the instructional interventions are adequately described. In most instances they are explained in enough detail for other interested researchers to be able to replicate their studies. In contrast, other types of research sometime explain general procedures only very casually. For example, one Brand X research study that used a phonics training program as an intervention simply said that "daily phonics drills were conducted." It would be impossible for an interested teacher or researcher to replicate such an investigation. In ABA research, if a phonics treatment was used, the reader would be informed not only about which phonics elements were stressed and how they were presented but also about the amount of time used for instruction.

Individual analysis.   The very heart of the ABA technology is that the data from individuals are presented. For this reason some have referred to this methodology as the "single-subject" method. In an ABA study, if data are obtained on five subjects, a graph of each subject's performance would generally be shown. By this means, all of the idiosyncratic behavioral patterns become obvious. An inspection of these graphs would likely reveal that although the general effects on all five subjects might be the same, no two graphs of pupil performance look exactly alike. Other research systems report the average data of groups — experimental and control. It might well be that these average scores do not represent the scores of any individual.

Experimental control.   In every research study, regardless of the methodology, the researcher is obligated to prove that the effects on the dependent variable are attributed to the scheduled independent variable; we must establish a functional relationship. The reason for establishing such a relationship is extremely important. For if researchers recommend that method C be used by all reading teachers because it was discovered that it improved certain reading skills, the researchers must be certain that variable C and nothing else caused the improvement. [Lovitt, 1975, pp. 433–434]

The precision teaching model offered by Kunzelman (1970), the responsive teaching model advocated by Hall (1972), and the varieties of formalized behavior modification that use baseline procedures and continuous data collection are all forms of ABA. Lovitt (1977) is a particularly good reference. The most comprehensive book that describes the purposes, technology, and ethics of ABA is Sulzer-Azaroff and Mayer (1977). All of these references can be used in conjunction with current case studies that employ ABA procedures. These are found in the *Journal of Applied Behavior Analysis*, published through the Human Development Department of the University of Kansas at Lawrence, Kansas.

Conducting analytic or diagnostic teaching sessions.   Many practitioners have devised various methods for analyzing a student's behavior in dynamic, ongoing instructional situations. Information from these analyses is used to hypothesize about the nature of the problem and/or to determine the next steps in assessment or remediation. In assessment, these methods are used to find out how behavior is produced, changed, or maintained; in teaching, they are used to document student progress or to serve as systematic ways of discovering the elements that need to be changed where expected progress is not evident.

Analytic teaching methods have at least four characteristics in common: (1) the practitioner has to observe the student engaged in the behavior of interest; (2) the student's responses must be noted and analyzed within some constant frame of reference; (3) the selection of future steps to be taken depends on the interpretation of the results of the successive response analyses; and (4) the methodologies are flexible enough to be applied to almost all aspects of a student's school performance, including academic, linguistic, emotional, and social areas. Methodologies that share these characteristics are grouped under the heading analytic teaching.

Analytic teaching methodologies are exemplified by the Piagetian-type interviews of Laurendeau and Pinard (1970), the clinical teaching techniques of Johnson and Myklebust (1967), and the directive teaching approach of Stephens (1970). These methodologies are structured but do not require the degree of measurement needed in ABA. The adaptive testing assessment methodology of Hausserman (1958) also represents techniques that combine behavioral analysis of responses with ongoing instruction.

Perhaps the most popular diagnostic teaching approach used in the schools today is the one set forth by Johnson and Myklebust (1967). They base the choice of remedial goals and activities on the teacher's direct observation of a student's performance and on the interpretation of objective diagnostic information obtained from physicians, parents, educators, and other specialists. Data derived in this manner are used to prepare a totally individualized program for a given student. This program is tried and revised repeatedly in response to the pupil's performance. In all cases, the activities are selected to match the student's characteristics and needs; the student never is forced into conforming to a preselected curriculum.

The whole clinical teaching system advocated by Johnson and Myklebust is superimposed over a medical-psychological-process orientation to the field of remediation. By this we mean that they interpret students' problems and learning behavior in terms of sensory modality preferences, memory and imagery deficits, perceptual impairments, and hypothetical neurological constructs, such as intra- and inter-neurosensory learning. Because our approach is more behavior oriented, we find such conceptualizations to be more philosophical than scientific, more speculative than data based, and more theoretical than practical. We do, however, recognize that the basic procedures used in their approach to clinical teaching have merit and deserve to be studied by resource teachers.

Analyzing permanent products made by students. Permanent products made by students include all academic work done in school or for school purposes. It may also include any nonacademic products that seem important in evaluation, such as art products. These products provide valuable information about the student's approximations to the teacher's expectations and also offer windows to the student's thinking and level of cognitive development. In addition, we have found that many students fail or do poorly in school not because they do not know the content area but because their permanent products do not reflect what they know.

Permanent products are analyzed diagnostically for two purposes: to note patterns of errors, as in mathematics, or to determine how the student structured or interpreted the material, as in the evaluation of compositions. It is more usual merely to be interested in the number of items or units that were right versus the number of items or units that were wrong. Although such analyses do provide measurement information, right-versus-wrong analyses provide no insight or hypotheses about the nature of the student's thinking or motivation. It is this latter type of information that will prove more valuable for instructional purposes.

The information from the analysis of permanent products is highly inferential. For example, we infer the student's understanding of the subtraction process from error patterns such as these:

$$
\begin{array}{ccc}
14 & 12 & 22 \\
-\ 7 & -\ 8 & -\ 7 \\
\hline
13 & 16 & 25
\end{array}
$$

Inferences are confirmed or disconfirmed through diagnostic interviews, diagnostic teaching, or the methodology of ABA.

It is often through improvement in permanent products that student progress is judged by classroom teachers and parents, if not by the students themselves. These products, then, are a major focus assessment activities by resource teachers.

Postscript Regarding Assessment

As the experience of the resource teachers becomes deeper and broader, that is, as they acquire the ability to study students with increasing sophistication and see more students exhibiting a wide variety of problems, they probably will develop a set of internalized norms. That is, the teachers will become aware of the degree of difference in a student's behavior as compared with that of other students. They also will be sensitive to minimal cues — that is, will be alert to the subtleties in the qualities of a student's behavior. Often these two abilities mistakenly are called intuition; we prefer to consider them as examples of clinical judgment, a skill that at least to some extent can be enhanced through continuing integrated experience and training.

One final point needs to be made about assessing students in the schools. Within the past several years, many citizens have become sensitive about violating the rights of privacy and using tests that may be culturally biased. Because of these concerns, many school districts have instituted strict policies regarding the evaluation of students. Resource teachers should ask their supervisors or principals if such policies exist in the district; if so, they should become thoroughly familiar with them in order to behave both ethically and legally. If not, teachers should begin to advocate the consideration of adopting such policies.

PREPARING AND IMPLEMENTING INSTRUCTIONAL PROGRAMS

Preparing and implementing instructional programs that are based on the proficient use of assessment procedures constitute the heart of the services provided in the resource program. Before formulating and executing instructional programs, the resource teacher should consider the following three important questions.

1. Why should the resource teacher have any ongoing teaching duties at all?
2. How do the teaching responsibilities of resource teachers and other teachers differ?
3. What are the basic teaching competencies needed by resource teachers?

Reasons for Maintaining Ongoing Teaching Duties

The statement is made occasionally that resource teachers should restrict their activities to assessment and to consulting with teachers, and forego the delights and frustrations of direct teaching involvement. We strongly disagree with this statement. A resource teacher should participate actively in the direct instruction of students in order to: (1) know the dynamics of a particular student's instructional needs and problems; (2) become proficient in using a variety of educational techniques and programs; (3) demonstrate specific activities to other teachers; (4) become more skillful and insightful in clinical work; and (5) provide a particular student with a particular program.

1. The first purpose for engaging in direct instruction with students is to obtain information that will enable the resource teacher to make valid, accurate statements about the capabilities and needs of youngsters. To do this, one must first have been involved with analytic teaching in order to obtain valid and reliable data about *what* and *how* to teach referred students.

2. The second purpose, to gain proficiency using programs and materials, is based on the assumption that resource teachers should be familiar with the critical features of many instructional programs and approaches. Any teaching systems, new or old, that are potentially useful should be known in the thorough way that can come about only from actual practice with them in a teaching situation. Both experienced and inexperienced resource teachers will need to have ample opportunity to try out many programs and activities in order to see how well they work. Preferably, this will be done before the programs are recommended to other teachers.

3. Direct instruction also may serve as a demonstration or modeling technique. In this situation, the resource teacher may demonstrate a sample lesson in the regular or special class teacher's own room or invite the teacher to the resource room to see the lesson taught there. This procedure may be used to call attention to a unique instructional variable, such as the reinforcement feature of a program such as Distar (Engelmann and Bruner, 1974), or to the motivational principles incorporated into the Fernald (1943) system. When teaching for demonstration purposes, the resource teacher must make sure that the teachers recognize and understand the critical features being shown or emphasized. Demonstration also may be an appropriate way to assist the classroom teacher in assuming an increasing responsibility for implementing recommended programs within their own classrooms. If successful, resource teachers may be able to reduce their assistance to a monitoring function in specific classrooms.

4. Continuing to work directly with students can have an additive effect on the resource teacher's own clinical competence. The critical examination of their continuing teaching experience can make resource teachers sensitive to the infinite variations and nuances of a student's problems, a sensitivity that is often referred to as clinical insight. While working with many students over time, resource teachers also are provided with more substantial internalized norms regarding the range of individual growth and development. Continued direct teaching experience also gives

them a unique opportunity to validate or invalidate previously held assumptions or principles about a particular field, such as reading. Also, ultimate economy and accuracy in formulating educational plans may be effected as resource teachers are able to sort out more precisely which behaviors are more likely than others to be relevant to assessment and to bringing about positive behavioral progress.

5. The final identifiable purpose for engaging in direct instruction is the most widely recognized in the schools today. Direct instruction provides a daily ongoing teaching program for a student. Resource teachers usually are expected to do this when the regular class teacher has neither the time nor knowledge to implement a recommended program. If the reason is time, resource teachers should train an aide or a volunteer to carry out the program under their supervision or to help classroom teachers reorganize their classrooms in order to make more time available. If time is not the factor, such as when the student's responses are extremely erratic, when behavior management is a major problem, or when the regular teacher will not carry out the program, then the resource teacher may be the only one in the school who is able and/or willing to conduct the program.

Teaching Responsibility Differences Between Resource Teachers and Other Teachers

Although regular, special class, and resource teachers all deal with the instruction of students, the nature of the responsibilities, the accountability requirements, and the instructional roles are different. In the regular class, students are usually assigned to a teacher for a single year, after which they are promoted to a higher grade, retained, or transferred to a different teacher. But for one year, the regular teacher has exclusive responsibility for the students in the class. In the special education class, students may be assigned more or less permanently to one room. In each case, the door is closed, and the operation of the program is generally self-contained. Both the teacher and the student function in a relatively segregated environment. Resource teachers, however, never have any students whom they can call exclusively their own; in all cases, the responsibility for the pupils with whom they work is shared with other teachers and specialists.

All teachers are accountable to principals, supervisors, and, to some extent, to parents for the educational progress of their students. Resource teachers are in the unique and frequently uncomfortable position of being accountable to the other teachers in the school as well. This does not mean that the resource teacher should be supervised by other teachers, for he or she is not an aide. Instead, there are identifiable differences in role. The classroom teacher is often responsible for administering the curriculum of the school. The resource program does share the goals of the adopted curriculum, however, the resource teacher may use very different methods, materials, or specific content. For example, it is rare to find independent study behaviors taught as part of the general curriculum because typical students pick up such skills incidentally. Or the methods and materials of a reading program used for most students in a classroom may in fact be detrimental to the reading progress of others. In these cases, the resource teacher may have teaching responsibilities that are independent of the classroom teacher(s). In each case, too, the resource teacher will certainly be in close communication with the teacher(s) who bear the primary instructional responsibility for the students who are also taught by the resource teacher.

Another role difference related to teaching responsibilities is found in the kind of teaching expected in the resource program. The resource teacher uses diagnostic interviews, analytic teaching, and ABA procedures in order to explore and to document what works and what does not work with individual students. These procedural methods are demanding. It is this demanding nature of the kind of instruction that must be mastered by the resource teacher that provides the rationale for the smaller caseload and the one-to-one instruction of the resource teacher.

Basic Teaching Competencies for Resource Teachers

Almost every university training program, state department of education, and local school district in the country has developed lists of instructional competencies that they find useful. Some of these lists relate to teaching regular and special children, and some of them pertain specifically to teaching in the resource program. Competencies appearing on these lists are pretty much the same. It seems that good teaching is good teaching, regardless of whether it is done in the regular class, the special class, or the resource room.

Rather than list all of the individual competencies that we believe the resource teacher should possess, we will discuss the six basic types of competencies that, if mastered, would increase the chances of successful teaching. In short, the resource teacher should be able to analyze curriculum, teach analytically, organize the learning environment, manage that environment, mobilize needed resources, and evaluate the organizational structure of the school. An elaboration of each type of competency follows.

1. *Competency in curriculum analysis* enables resource teachers to "take apart" any given curriculum in order to determine its components or attributes. This skill gives resource teachers information that enables them to:
   a. Compare the relative merits of programs, either between programs, as in knowing that neither the Words in Color method (Gattegno, 1962) nor the Initial Teaching Alphabet approach (Mazurkiewicz and Tanyzer, 1966) require knowledge of capital letters for initial learning, or within a program, as in a mathematics series that purports to emphasize concepts but in fact teaches computation.
   b. Select appropriate content or methodology from a program to use in assessment or instructional activities, such as trying out a lesson with a child, or recommending a particular program for a special purpose —for

example, the Sounds of Language in Reading (Martin and Brogan, 1969) for its value in language and concept development.

c.   Fill in large or small gaps in an ongoing instructional program in order to make it appropriate for a student or group of students, such as when a math program has too few practice materials to help a student shift between vertical and horizontal formats for doing subtraction problems.

2.   *Competency in analytic teaching* refers to the activities discussed on pages 32 – 33.

3.   *Organizing the learning environment* deals with the ability to select, bring together, and arrange properly the physical components (furniture and materials) that are necessary to the successful management of a particular instructional situation or setting. This is the "getting it all together" phase; this phase needs systematic attention to ensure that all possible support is given to the instructional session or situation.

4.   *Competency in managing the learning environment* refers to the daily or ongoing coordination and monitoring of what is happening for the purpose of smooth or efficient operation of the resource program. The importance of management skills becomes obvious when the teacher decides to change any factor previously organized, such as seating arrangements, scheduling, materials location, student movement patterns, grading systems, or record-keeping procedures.

5.   *Competency in mobilizing resources* refers to the abilities involved in getting assistance, such as when a resource teacher helps the classroom teacher document the need for additional services for a student or his or her family, or when a resource teacher helps set up peer tutoring, aide, or volunteer programs.

6.   *Competency in system analysis* is necessary if resource teachers are to understand the formal and informal organizational structure of the school and community in which they work. If resource teachers are to effect change, they must understand what kinds of changes might be possible, the readiness of the system for change, and the attitudes and opinions of individuals who control the avenues by which change is to occur. For example, the fact that a school system currently is providing inservice training in the use of a newly adopted reading series indicates that (1) the system may have made a large financial investment in the series and (2) suggestions about using any alternative might not be appreciated, at least not at the present time.

In addition to being competent in instructional functions, the resource teacher will face some ethical dilemmas often encountered whenever two persons with different perspectives become involved with the same student. One frequent ethical problem occurs when a resource teacher is asked to help a classroom teacher implement a program that she or he believes will harm or at least not help the student. This is especially true when the resource teacher is requested to help a teacher train total compliance behaviors or when the teacher wishes to do perceptual training to improve reading. A careful analysis of the situation may lead the resource teacher to conclude that such training is unnecessary or even undesirable. The resulting dilemma may never be resolved comfortably for all concerned. When these situations arise, resource teachers will have to make good use of their consultation skills in persuading the classroom teacher of the deisrability and feasibility of alternatives.

CONSULTING WITH THE SCHOOL STAFF

Resource teachers are in a unique position because they share their students with the other teachers. They therefore must devote a lot of their time to these activities: (1) discussing the educational problems of specific students with teachers; (2) describing the methodology being used in the resource room; (3) presenting ideas that the teachers can use in their classes to reinforce and supplement the resource effort; (4) acquiring information on how separate resource activities can mesh with the student's regular class program; (5) following up the progress of students who no longer attend the resource program; (6) observing the classroom performance of students who have been referred for resource help; (7) demonstrating techniques by which the teacher can improve the classroom climate, individualize instruction, or manage group behavior; and (8) sharing professional information regarding their respective operations, new programs on the market, and new methods of teaching.

All resource teachers are expected to engage in a lot of continuing communication with other teachers in the school. Resource teachers who have demonstrated their competence by successfully teaching students and whom other teachers see as supportive, interested, and nonjudgmental probably will be consulted often by these teachers. This is a sure sign that the resource program has been accepted in the schools, and resource teachers should grasp the opportunity to use this aspect of their role.

Resource teachers should consult extensively with the school staff for many reasons. First, there are too few people in the schools who are trained or funded to provide direct speicalized services to the many students who need help. This means that increased responsibility for dealing with a variety of instructional problems is being placed upon classroom teachers. The resource teacher is seen as a person who can deliver training or consultation that will be useful in expanding the abilities of classroom teachers to assume this increased responsibility. Since the instructional problems and the solutions addressed by resource teachers are immediately apparent, this type of inservice training is thought to be more relevant to the immediate needs of classroom teachers than course work would be.

Although the activities of resource teachers can be, and often are, confined to a resource room, the impact of their services can be extended considerably by permitting them to teach other teachers a few assessment techniques, some basic classroom and behavior management procedures, and some fundamental curricula adaptation skills. Classroom teachers who have a practical grasp of these and other skills can reach more students than would be possible if all special services had to depend on the exclusive ministrations of the resource teacher. For example, the resource teacher who shows a classroom teacher how to assess instructional reading levels or how to modify disruptive behavior may no longer be needed when such skills are required in the teacher's class.

The second reason that resource teachers should consult with the school staff refers to the phenomenon described by Tharp and Wetzel (1969). They say that the persons who spend most of their time with students are most likely to bring about and maintain desired changes in them than are individuals who are removed from the naturally occurring environment — that is, the regular classroom. If this is true, then the best place for most students to receive help is in the regular classroom, and the best therapists are likely to be their regular teachers. In most instances, therefore, the regular class teacher must help students overcome their learning and behavior problems. This can be done by giving regular teachers enough skills to enable them to provide the intervention for many, perhaps most, of the students who need help; in such cases, the resource teacher can serve primarily in a supportive role. This also can be accomplished by involving the regular teacher in planning and implementing programs for students who attend the resource room for specific instruction. Only the most severe cases should need to be seen exclusively by the resource teacher in the resource room.

Several examples will illustrate the applicability of this concept to the role of the resource teacher. In the case of a student with poor handwriting, the resource teacher may be able to effect a desirable change while the student is in the resource room, but there may be no observable carryover in the regular classroom writing activities. The new skills that have been acquired in the resource room must be reinforced in some way within the regular classroom if they are ever to become generally established and used. To achieve this, the regular teacher must become integrally involved in the remedial effort. In the case of disruptive behaviors that occur frequently in the classroom but are not observed in the resource room, the regular teacher must learn to manage the complexities of that situation in order to avoid the circumstances that bring about the disruptions. It is desirable, then, for someone to teach, through consultation and modeling, the skills required to bring about and maintain behavioral change where it will be necessary — in the regular classroom.

Although the term *consultation* can refer to many activities, as used in this book, its components are primarily *advising* and *instructing* other teachers and *following up* on these activities. Although these components are discussed individually at this point, in practice they cannot be readily separated from each other, just as the consultation function cannot be readily separated from assessment or from the preparation and implementation of instructional programs.

Advising Other Teachers

A considerable part of the resource teacher's consulting time is devoted to sharing professional information with and giving advice to teachers, administrators, and other school personnel. To Newman (1967), this activity is roughly analogous to the medical-practice situation in which a specialist (a resource teacher) is called on to assist in diagnosing a difficult case or prescribing a course of action that is not usually known to the generalist physician (the classroom teacher). In such instances, the patient (the student) is likely to improve; the consultee (the classroom teacher) may benefit in learning to look at the patient (the student) in a different way; and the consultation ends when a specific decision has been made about diagnosis and treatment.

An educational example of this activity occurs when a classroom teacher requests assistance on a problem that a student has in mathematics. The resource teacher, after careful examination of the student's mathematics papers or by observing his or her work, may call attention to a consistent error pattern, such as trying to calculate from left to right instead of from right to left in two-place subtraction problems. In this case, the student is likely to benefit from this consultation; the teacher may or may not be alert to such a problem in the future; and the specific consultation activity will end when the teacher understands the problem and/or how to deal with it, at least in that individual case.

Also analogous to the medical model, the specialist, or in this case, the resource teacher, may serve at times to confirm the soundness of the diagnoses or decisions concerning treatment made by colleagues. Such a situation might occur when a parent or a supervisory person questions the instructional strategies of the classroom teacher.

Resource teachers also are in an excellent position to provide their supervisors and principals with information and advice that they can use to stimulate needed changes in the total school operation. For example, the resource person may notice a consistent pattern of problems in the students being referred for service. Perhaps a disproportionate number of students are being referred because of weakness in comprehension or in elaborative reading skills, such as finding the main idea or anticipating outcomes of stories. If the regular teachers use a strict sound-symbol correspondence system for teaching phonics and word analysis, the resource person may suspect that the students' problems are the direct result of this method rather than of deficiencies within the individual students being referred. In this case, a reevaluation of the approach to reading instruction is desirable; to do this, the principal and faculty must have documented evidence of the possible need for making such a change. Once convinced, the school faculty may decide to augment the word analysis methods with a complementary comprehension program. In this way, many of the students' difficulties can be prevented and valuable resource time is not wasted.

The key ingredients here are that the resource teacher is able to: (1) identify a pattern in the referrals; (2) determine its probable source; (3) formulate a course of action; and (4) effectively communicate both the problem and a potential plan for its amelioration to the faculty.

The use of the intervention-to-prevention model is just one instance in which the resource teacher may have to advise the principal and faculty even though they may not have requested it. On such occasions, advice should be given with considerable care and tact, for resource teachers always should keep in mind that advice is generally received better when it is requested than when it is offered freely. As a rule, therefore, resource teachers should give advice only when their expertise is specifically asked for. As is true of all rules, however, this one is meant to be broken — but judiciously.

Instructing Other Teachers

The instructing that a resource teacher does may be considered a form of inservice training. This is because the aim of the activities is to increase the other teachers' understanding of the difficulties students encounter in school and to develop competence in the teachers' coping with the individual instructional and behavioral needs of their students.

To accomplish these goals, resource teachers may decide from time to time that a formal presentation is called for. On these occasions, they may want to use a prepared inservice package, such as *Teaching Sight Words Using the Kinesthetic Method* (1972, 1976). Packages such as this one are available on a wide variety of topics and formats.

The advantages of using a prepared format are that: (1) the activities are already planned and sequenced; (2) the objectives of the program generally are stated clearly; (3) the evaluation procedures are usually specified; and (4) the materials and additional resources that will be needed are described in detail. Of course, in most instances, the resource teachers will prefer to implement inservice programs that they have planned themselves because of unique local needs. In either case, the chances of having a successful inservice program can be increased considerably by basing its content to some extent on the expressed needs and interests of the people who will attend the workshop or meeting. This necessary participant input can be easily acquired through the use of questionnaires and/or interviews.

Beginning resource teachers probably should postpone conducting formal inservice meetings until they have become firmly established and accepted in the schools. Even then, however, many resource teachers may feel that they lack the particular qualifications necessary to manage a formal inservice presentation. This is regrettable because the benefits associated with this form of inservice training should not be lost. Fortunately, there are many useful sources of help for teachers who feel that they are deficient in the skills and experience needed to hold an effective meeting. For example, a few university training programs now offer courses for resource teachers in how to conduct and evaluate workshops. Attending such courses might be profitable for most resource teachers. For resource teachers who wish to pursue an independent study in the area of organizing and managing formal inservice meetings and workshops, we recommend the book *Planning, Conducting, and Evaluating Workshops* (Davis and McCallon, 1974).

Although inservice training on various topics can be provided using a workshop or formal presentation format, resource teachers will find that the most effective method of instruction is associated with the informal, almost casual, day-to-day interactions that occur between them and their colleagues. These contacts may assume a variety of forms, ranging from informal conversations concerning strategies for managing a particular student's problem to the actual demonstration of new techniques in the teacher's own classroom. In these instances, the teachers will readily see the practical significance of inserve training because it is usually related to a specific student in their classes or to a particular management skill for which they have an immediate need.

Other occasions for which resource teachers may provide inservice training include the frequently held team planning meetings, staffings, and parent conferences. The follow-ups to these meetings offer resource teachers still other promising opportunities to provide teachers with more formalized inservice experiences.

Following Up on Recommendations

Every time resource teachers make a specific recommendation that a teacher use a series of drills, a technique for managing an unwanted behavior, or a training strategy of any type, they should visit the classroom to see that the teacher is willing and able to implement the suggestions properly. For example, the teacher may not know how to translate the recommendations into an actual classroom practice. In this case, the resource teacher may have to show (not tell) the teacher how it is done. This is especially important when working with newly certified teachers because many teacher-training institutions teach the "how-to's" of instructing a student in isolated school subject matter while neglecting teaching dynamics, the means by which all aspects of the curricula are integrated and managed over time.

Another important reason for doing follow-ups is to determine the validity of the recommendations that the resource teacher has made. Resource teachers who assess students, who prescribe programs of instruction for other teachers to use, and who fail to monitor the operation in the classroom will never know the consequences of their suggestions; they are operating in a vacuum and with impunity.

The follow-ups and the demonstrations in the teachers' classrooms are essential features in the resource program. The consultant who merely prescribes to or talks about a student's problem but who avoids offering to pitch in and help classroom teachers ameliorate difficulties loses credibility in at least two ways. First, the teachers will perceive the resource teacher as not being interested enough in their problems to provide much needed support. Second, they may assume that the resource teacher simply lacks the ability to implement his or her own suggestions within a classroom situation. Either way, the credibility of the resource program may suffer.

When engaged in consulting activities, the resource teacher must be very perceptive about sensitivities and possible adverse reaction of regular classroom teachers. Smokoski (1972) has stated that teachers do not want other teachers coming to them and saying, in effect:

> "You have failed with this child and I have some secrets which I'll be glad to share with you which will make you a better teacher and which will better enable you to handle all the children in your classroom." Teachers, it seems, don't want to be considered failures. [P. 6]

Of course, few resource teachers would be so impolitic as to express such opinions to another teacher. Yet, to some extent these sentiments are implicit in the consulting situation. As a result, resource teachers who consult must constantly guard against incipient friction between themselves and the teachers with whom they work or collaborate.

The emphasis that we give to the consulting role in the resource program model is long overdue in special education. Most teacher-training institutions have been slow to include such skills among their competencies; until the advent of the resource programs, public schools had no practical instructionally oriented arrangement that lent itself conveniently to providing consulting services to teachers. In any event, the schools in which the resource teachers are permitted to perform only two duties (to assess and to remediate students' problems) are overlooking a profitable avenue for improving the education of both students and teachers. In fact, in selecting resource teachers, one primary consideration might be their ability to implement tactfully the consulting aspects of the resource program.

The relative proportion of time that resource teachers should spend in consulting functions will depend on their individual competencies in that area and on the number of requests classroom teachers make for such services. In addition, because of the nature of most consulting activities, it is difficult to determine precisely where assessment and teaching stop and consultation begins; this observation reinforces our thesis that the roles cannot and should not be split arbitrarily among three different persons. Readers who want to acquire pertinent and practical information concerning the consulting role in a data-based model are referred to McKenzie (1972). Readers who want practical information on how to consult with teachers are referred to handbooks, such as *The Consulting Process in Action* (Lippit and Lippit, 1978). Heron and Harris (1982) describe the consultant process and provide techniques for consulting with students, teachers, administrators, and parents.

RESEARCH ON THE ROLE OF THE RESOURCE TEACHER

The idea that the resource teacher should assess, teach, and consult enjoys a considerable support among parents and educators. Gickling, Murphy, and Malloy (1979) asked regular and resource teachers about the services that they wanted resource teachers to provide. They reported that both groups of teachers agreed that the resource teachers should offer the three basic services of assessing, teaching, and consulting. In another study of the role of the resource teacher, Dodd and Kelker (1980) investigated the opinions of resource teachers, classroom teachers, and parents about the activities that should be carried out by the resource teacher. They found a substantial agreement among the three groups about the role of the resource teacher, an agreement that included support for the assessing, teaching, and consulting role.

Speece and Mandell (1980) asked 228 regular class teachers about the kinds of services that resource teachers should provide; they also asked them to specify the extent to which the desired services were actually provided. The teachers' responses reinforced the idea that resouce teachers should assess, teach, and consult. Of the three types of service activities, the teachers considered consulting services the most needed and the least available. Speece and Mandell speculated that resource teachers spent so much time in direct instruction that there was little opportunity for interaction with other teachers and that teacher education programs at both the preservice and inservice levels did not give enough emphasis to the consulting role.

The observations of Speece and Mandell are supported by the research of Evans (1980) and Sargent (1981). Evans questioned 48 resource teachers, 144 classroom teachers, and 48 principals about the kinds of activities in which the resource teachers should be engaged and about the kinds of activities that were actually being provided. Her results indicated that 57 percent of the resource teacher's time was devoted to direct instruction, 13 percent to assessment and diagnosis, and 25 percent to program maintenance and miscellaneous activities. All three groups of educators agreed that more time should be allotted to consultation services.

In a similar study, Sargent asked 132 resource teachers to specify the percentage of time spent in different roles. Thirty of these teachers were selected randomly and observed on the job to determine the actual amount of time devoted to various activities. His results indicated that 51 percent of the resource teacher's time was devoted to instruction, 12 percent to consulting, 9 percent to assessment and diagnosis, and 28 percent to maintenance and miscellaneous activities. The resource teachers believed that they needed to allocate more time to their assessing, teaching, and consulting services and relatively less time to other activities.

In conclusion, the research accumulated to date suggests that resource teachers do in fact perform three basic kinds of duties: assessment, instruction, and consultation. Of these, direct instruction with students consumes the majority of the resource teacher's time. Repeatedly parents, classroom and resource teachers, and administrators conclude that the consulting activities in the resource program should be expanded.

ENDNOTES

1. To prevent redundancy, we will use the word *tests* in this discussion, but the term will refer to tests and rating scales.
2. Adapted from C. J. Stewart and W. B. Cash. *Interviewing: Principles and Practices* (Dubuque, Iowa: Brown, 1974) pp. 78–80.
3. Reprinted by special permission of Professional Press, Inc. From T. Lovitt, Part 1: Characteristics of ABA, general recommendations, and methodological limitations. *Journal of Learning Disabilities,* 1975, vol. 8, pp. 34–35. Copyright 1975 by Professional Press, Inc., Chicago, Ill.

ORGANIZING AND MANAGING A RESOURCE PROGRAM

The actual details involved in establishing and operating resource programs are discussed in Part II. The information presented is drawn primarily from our own experiences in implementing and supervising this model in the schools as well as the written observations of others who also have had direct practical experience in resource program operations. Readers can therefore determine how we and other resource administrators and teachers have handled a wide variety of matters associated with the operation of resource arrangements. These matters include enlisting support of school staff and parents for the resource effort, grading student progress, selecting pupils for service, and other activities involved in successfully managing a resource program on a daily basis. This practical information has been organized into three chapters that deal specifically with: (1) implementing the resource program; (2) handling teacher referrals and student selection; and (3) managing the program on a day-to-day basis.

3

Implementing the Resource Program

Administrators who are responsible for establishing a resource program in a school must first decide what kind of program is to be set up: categorical, noncategorical, special skill, or other. Second, they must select teachers to work in the new program who are competent in assessment, instruction, and consultation. They then are ready to take the next steps in actually implementing a resource program: (1) preparing the school staff and parents for the resource program; (2) locating and equipping the resource room; and (3) conducting a public relations effort with local parental and professional organizations. How each step can be handled proficiently is discussed in this chapter.

PREPARING THE SCHOOL STAFF AND PARENTS

Harris and Mahar (1975) have noted that one of the most common problems encountered in starting and maintaining a resource program has been insufficient preparation of school personnel and parents. For example, some teachers, for reasons that may not be fully known or articulated, will be reluctant to work with resource teachers. Also, teachers may be unwilling even to attempt to modify their instruction programs in order to work effectively with resource students. Some administrative and support personnel may have negative attitudes toward resource programs. Perhaps in the past, they were oversold on the merits of innovative approaches and have been disappointed with the results. They may view the resource program as simply another fad that will become obsolete in the near future. Or they may prefer a segregated, self-contained class for students with learning and behavior problems.

Parents have also been known to resist resource programs. A few parents of handicapped students may prefer segregated instructional support because they fear their son or daughter may not receive the quantity of quality of instruction they need in the regular classrooms. Other parents may resist a particular resource model, such as a cross-categorical program, because they prefer a categorical model with the teacher trained in a specific disability area. Finally, some parents of students in the regular classroom may be reluctant to have their children educated with others who have learning and behavioral problems. Or they might feel that too much teacher time may be taken by these latter students, and as a result the quality of instruction to their own children may suffer.

Whatever the spoken or unspoken objections, principals, resource teachers, and other responsible professionals should prepare thoroughly the school staff and parents for the program and make every effort to enlist their support. Some strategies for accomplishing this task follow.

Preparing the School Staff

The major responsibility for preparing the staff of a school in which a resource program is to be established should be assumed by individual building principals and resource teachers. Local education agency personnel probably will assist in this effort in many ways. At the very least, agency personnel should provide principals and resource teachers with written guidelines that describe clearly the rules of the resource operation. These guidelines will help ensure that the operation of the program is consistent with the intent of the funding organization (the local, state, and/or federal agency) and with existing district policies.

We cannot stress enough the importance of these guidelines. Educators are increasingly being held accountable for their activities in providing special services to students. Consequently, principals and resource teachers must be familiar with all regulations that pertain to the resource program.

Once the guidelines are understood, each principal and resource teacher can begin preparing the rest of the school's staff for the program. Together, they should plan the agenda of a faculty meeting called expressly to orient the school staff to the resource program. The specific information that is presented can be drawn from this book, related literature, and the set of written guidelines. The best time to conduct the staff inservice meeting is either during the first several days of the school year or preferably during the school term prior to the actual implementation. Topics that should be included in this session are:

1.   The need for the resource program
2.   The resource program model

3.   The roles of the resource teacher
4.   The roles of the regular and/or special classroom teachers
5.   Referral and pupil selection
6.   Management practices in the program's operation

These topics should be presented to the school staff in as interesting and en-thusiastic a manner as possible. Non-negotiable rules and regulations established by district or state policy should be delineated. If possible, some flexibility should be allowed for an individual school staff to select some of its own operating procedures.

Small group discussions can give the teachers in the school an opportunity to develop some of the negotiable aspects of the program. After familiarizing the facul-ty with the new program, the principal and resource teacher can suggest that small groups be formed and that recommendations concerning the operation of the resource program be suggested by each group. This technique often results in useful suggestions and enlists support for an understanding of the resource program. A suggested discussion guide is presented in Table 3-1.

The left side of the table lists some tentative activities of the resource teacher. The right side of the table lists tentative activities of the regular staff. Both groups should be encouraged to discuss each block of activities and to add to or delete from the list as well as to specify ways in which these activities can be accomplished.

It is important that the principal and resource teacher be sincere in asking for suggestions. They need to consider carefully the recommendations made by the school staff and deal fairly with them. Therefore, the non-negotiable aspects of the resource program should first be carefully stated. Also, the benefits of a resource program should be presented optimistically and realistically. The program should not be over-sold, however.

By the end of this first inservice session, the school staff members should be fairly well informed about the resource program. They also should have made some suggestions about specific activities for resource teachers to follow. These activities should be carefully recorded at the meeting in order for the resource teacher to deal fairly with them in refining their specific responsibilities during the initial months of operating the program in the school. Later, the principal and resource teacher should discuss with the faculty the suggestions that were incorporated into the pro-gram and those that were not. The reasons that some of the suggestions were not implemented should be explained.

Subsequent or periodic inservice sessions are likely to be needed throughout the school year. Resource teachers should not, however, take up too much valuable time at staff meetings discussing the resource program. Small group meetings, writ-ten communications, and consultation on a one-to-one basis are effective ways to deal with changes, modifications, or problems that are likely to occur.

On a few occasions, principals and resource teachers may find a great deal of resistance, which ranges from passive responses (such as apathy or noncommunica-tion) to overt aggressive responses (perhaps verbalized hostility or spoken refusal to cooperate). Almost every resource teacher will find one or two colleagues in the

TABLE 3 – 1.
Discussion Guide for Setting Up Mutual Expectations with Resource Teacher and School Staff

Tentative activities of *resource teacher* *(priorities to be agreed on)*	*Concomitant activities of* *regular staff*

A. *With the Student*
  1. Detailed diagnostic assessment with recommendations for programming
  2. Monitor for validity of recommendations. Assist with implementation if necessary.
  3. Consultation in regard to either:
    a. Intensive programs for resource room students
    b. Modest intervention for students without resource room enrollment
  4. Direct work with a student or a group of students
  5. Observation in regular classroom to determine needs and generalization of resource room behaviors
  6. consultation regarding grades, grade placement, teacher placement and schedules, and related items
	A. *With the Student*
	  1. Try recommendations
	  2. Request assistance with implementation
	  3. Provide feedback on validity or modifications
	  4. Refer new students when questions occur; or
	  5. Request consultation/observation
	  6. Attend staffings
	  7. Modify grading/credit system if necessary
	  8. Encourage observations by resource teacher to determine generalization of behaviors

B. *With School Staff*
  1. Inservice in regard to management, curriculum or organization
    a. By vehicles such as
      (1) Modeling — involves fading out so that teacher can carry on the target techniques independently
      (2) Direct teaching where appropriate
      (3) Participation in team planning
      (4) Literature distribution
	B. *With School Staff*
	  1. Try suggestions
	  2. Provide information in regard to the operation of the total resource room program
	  3. Consider/generate preventive strategies
	  4. Participate in team teaching when new techniques are being introduced

TABLE **3 – 1.** *(Continued)*
Discussion Guide for Setting Up Mutual Expectations with Resource Teacher and School Staff

Tentative activities of resource teacher	*Concomitant activities of regular staff*
(priorities to be agreed on)	

2. Feedback to the total staff of high-frequency problems for consideration of preventive measures

C. *With Parents*
  1. Information about the program
  2. Liaison concerning the individual student home/school program
  3. Teaching: management techniques

C. *With Parents*
  1. Participate in liaison with home/school program for continuity

D. *General*
  1. Schedule or participate in staffings with appropriate personnel
  2. Set up a program evaluation plan
  3. Provide accountability through
    a. Time/activity log
    b. Logs on student progress or interventions tried

D. *General*
  1. Ask questions when you wonder "Why?"
  2. Participate in appropriate staffings
  3. Provide necessary data on curriculum or student

school who respond in such a manner. These cases can be handled on a one-to-one basis with attempts to determine the problem and to delineate and try proposed solutions. In some instances, large numbers of the faculty will be negative toward the program. This negativism may indicate the presence of a serious problem within the school that has little or nothing to do with the resource program itself.

Fox et al. (1975) have noted that some school climates are unhealthy. These schools are characterized by teacher dissatisfaction with their jobs, lack of creativity, complacency, conformity, frustration, and/or poor interpersonal relationships. In these schools, innovations or new programs meet resistance. Healthy schools are high in personal satisfaction by teachers for their jobs, effective learning on the part of the students, good faculty interpersonal relationships, and a willingness by all to incorporate innovations into the school and their classrooms. If resource teachers find themselves in unhealthy schools, they are likely to meet with little success in fulfilling their roles unless something is done to change the school climate.

Many professionals have apporached the modification of school climate through organizational problem solving. Many problem-solving techniques might be used. For example, the nominal group technique (NGT) of Delbecq, Van de Ven, and Gustafson (1975) has been used in many school and mental health organizations to provide a highly structured and effective means of conflict resolution. The NGT meeting elicits a greater flow of ideas than would be found in traditional meetings. Further, it brings the problem or the task to closure and also ensures the satisfaction of participants. It eliminates the domination of a group by high-status or verbally aggressive members and provides a fair method of mathematically ranking ideas or tentative solutions. The NGT process is explained at length in Delbecq, Van de Ven, and Gustafson (1975). The book also describes the use of NGT in various planning situations that could be useful to the resource teacher.

Filley's *Interpersonal Conflict Resolution* (1975) suggests methods for separating problems from persons in order to turn conflict into creative problem solving. Goal attainment scaling (Garwick, 1978) is a technique that focuses staff efforts on improving the school climate and on measuring progress toward this goal. Goal attainment scaling is a problem-focused set of procedures and a measuring device to be used over time where people from different disciplines, roles, or persuasions must work together.

Strategies for organizational problem solving are becoming an important part of the consulting aspect of resource teaching. Most resource teachers, however, have not been trained in these techniques. Even those who have may have limited success unless the other teachers and the administrators are willing to cooperate. Most formal techniques are adjuncts or crisis tools to use along with the informal but powerful political process. Further, resource teachers are not responsible for the school operations as a whole. This is the responsibility of the building principal, and that person should assume the leadership in the use of organizational problem solving. Resource teachers, however, might point out the need for organizational problem solving and actively support principals in the use of formal techniques in the effort.

Preparing the Parents

In some schools, all parents are automatically advised of any new programs about to be implemented in the school and of any major changes or improvements in existing programs that might affect the education of their children. In other schools, only those parents who are actively involved in the operation of the school are notified, such as officers in the local parent-teacher association. Some schools have no policies about notifying parents of program or curricular modifications. The resource teacher should ask the principal if there are any policies governing this matter, and together they should decide what information will be transmitted to parents and how this will be accomplished.

Communication with parents is almost always advisable. For example, if the resource program is to replace a self-contained special education class, the parents of the students to be affected by the change must be consulted. The goals of the new program should be described to them carefully; they should be told just how the changes will enhance the education of their children; and their approval should be obtained. In cases where the noncategorical or specific skills resource model is being implemented, the initial notification of parents may not be necessary, though it would certainly be desirable.

Marion (1981) has suggested several other points that teachers should tell parents. Teachers should explain why a particular resource model was selected; discuss the source of funding; describe the ages and types of students to be served in the program; and discuss the certification(s) of the teachers as well as their preparation for the position. Finally, the parents' involvement in decision making, program planning, evaluation, and classroom instruction should be agreed upon.

Problems occasionally arise from working closely with parents; however, we believe that a comfortable working relationship between teachers and parents of students with learning and behavior problems is desirable. Consequently, this book offers throughout many recommendations concerning parental involvement. Some suggestions are mandated by recent court decisions; others are based on the idea that parental involvement in the educational process is a necessity if the difficulties of certain students are to be ameliorated.

In sum, resource teachers will need to spend considerable time preparing the school staff and parents. This will include informing them on pertinent matters regarding the programs, as well as mutual planning of ways in which all parties concerned can work together.

OUTFITTING THE RESOURCE ROOM

Matters relating to selecting and outfitting a suitable resource room are discussed in this section. In particular, the resource teacher should consider such matters as: (1) the physical facilities that are available; (2) the equipment and materials that are required; and (3) the budgetary limitations. There are books available that deal with the first two of these topics. For example, the one by Loughlin and Suina (1982) provides excellent suggestions that are useful at both elementary and secondary levels.

Physical Facilities

Most resource teachers will be assigned a classroom of their own — the resource room. The physical attributes of this room will necessarily vary from school to school. For example, room size, furniture, lighting, storage space, ventilation, and expansion possibilities will be different for each resource room in the school district.

Unfortunately, special services, of which the resource program is but one, often are given a low priority in the allocation of space. We know of some resource teachers who have been assigned to the furnace room, to a part of the library, to share a classroom with another special teacher, to the storage closet, to the stage in the auditorium, to a part of the hallway, to the cafeteria, to the teachers' lounge, or to a portable trailer parked outside the school. Occasionally, resource teachers are given no space at all and are expected to carry their materials from room to room.

In many instances, the resource teacher will have to make do with what space is available. In a few cases, however, the initial space designated for the resource room may not be the only place available, and new and more appropriate quarters can be acquired. Where inadequate facilities are allocated, it may be possible that some remodeling can be done. For example, new paint, room dividers, portable chalkboards, and better lighting and ventilation can increase the suitability of a given space as a resource room. State or province regulations about per-pupil classroom space always should be kept in mind as a guide to judging needed space.

To avoid any unnecessary stigma, the resource teacher should not be given a room that has been a special education class. For example, if the room were formerly a self-contained classroom for educable retarded children, the other students in the school may continue to consider that room to be a setting for slow children. This is likely to be the case even if the name is changed from the mentally retarded class to the resource room. We suggest that the principal and the resource teacher enlist another teacher's support in changing rooms. In most instances, if the room is similar to other classrooms in the school, a teacher of a regular grade will be willing to move into the special room.

The location of the room also is important. The resource teacher should have a room that is in the center of the school. A central location makes it easier for students to get there and reduces the time they are in transit in the halls. Wings of the building reserved for special services should be avoided; a classroom out of the way of regular school traffic should not be considered; and high traffic areas, like a room across from the cafeteria, should be avoided at all costs. However, a high traffic area, such as a materials center, often may be very appropriate because of its association with independent study.

Once a suitable room has been obtained, the resource teacher should attend to its physical characteristics. First, lighting and ventilation should be in accordance wtih guidelines provided by the state or province department of education. Second, the room should be large enough to permit student movement. In other words, the room should not be so small or crowded that the resource teacher and the students have difficulty in moving about. Third, sufficient space should be available for the storage of materials. Fourth, an office space for the resource teacher (and possibly an aide as well) should be present, though often this office is limited to the teacher's desk. Fifth, space should be available for students to work individually, as well as in small groups.

Where the amount of space allotted to the resource room is insufficient and does not allow for each of these factors properly, the teacher will need to consider carefully the efficient use of horizontal and vertical space in the room, as well as expansion possibilities. For example, in the vertical use of space, higher cabinets may be installed for storage of materials. If room for a teacher's office is not available, a large closet attached to the classroom may be converted for that purpose. In some cases, the resource teacher may ask to use the space immediately outside of the classroom (the hall) for storage of equipment.

Consideration should also be given to the arrangement of the furniture. Three floor plans with furniture arrangements are shown in Figures 3-1, 3-2, and 3-3. Figure 3-1 represents a large room; it contains three learning centers, two round tables, three carrels, a teacher's desk and filing cabinet, a room divider, and two portable chalkboards. The learning centers relate to specific content areas or to types of instruction under one content area. The materials used by the resource teacher and students are stored in these centers. This room also has a space available for small-group instruction in various components of the program. Another round table is available for a tape recorder, and headsets and carrels are placed out of the way for students who are easily distracted. A room divider, filing cabinets, and teacher's desk round out this particular resource room floor plan.

Figure 3-2 illustrates the use of the hall and the closet. This room would be too small to be used as a resource room if the closet were not so large or if the hall were too narrow to allow for storage cabinets.

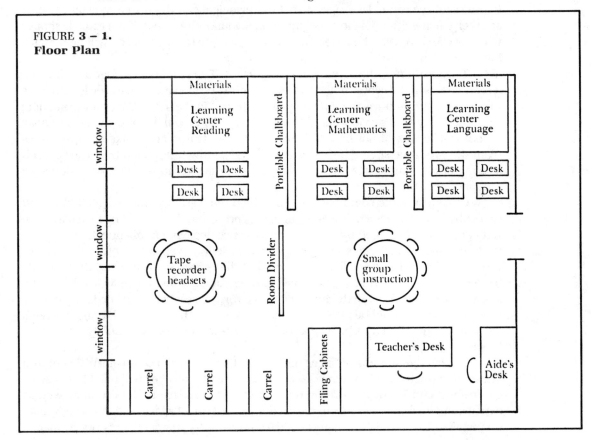

FIGURE 3 – 1.
Floor Plan

FIGURE 3 – 2.
Floor Plan

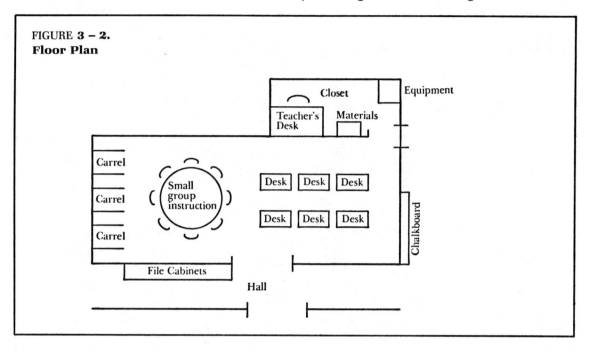

In Figure 3-3, the resource room is part of an open classroom. In this situation, the resource teacher is given a space rather than a traditional classroom with four walls. Many schools are now built in such a manner, and the resource teacher will be expected to function in such a setting. This type of space arrangement has many advantages. First, students are really not segregated to the extent that they would be if they were required to go to a separate room. Second, the resource teacher has ready access to other teachers, their materials, and their equipment. Third, unsupervised travel from room to room is also not a problem in these schools. Finally, the relaxed and informal nature of this arrangement can be highly conducive to learning.

Figure 3-3 is also an example of a floor plan in an instance when a resource teacher is required to share a room with another teacher. In some cases, several special services operate out of one large room. For example, the speech therapist, the reading teacher, and the resource teacher may share a room. As in the open classroom, the resource teacher is given a space rather than a room.

Most physical facilities will vary from these three examples. The figures were presented to stress the importance of the resource room's physical setting as well as to give some general guidelines to the reader. We have visited resource rooms in which a creative use of space and furniture arrangement has made them very functional. Teachers are encouraged to expend the energy and time to make the most effective use of whatever space is available.

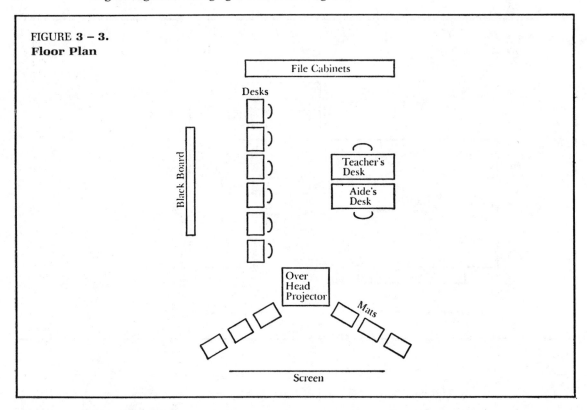

FIGURE 3 – 3.
Floor Plan

Equipment and Materials

In addition to the basic furniture requirements noted in the floor plans, specific types of equipment also are helpful for the successful operation of a resource program. At the very least, a tape recorder, headsets, and an overhead projector should be acquired. The tape recorder can be used with commercially available tapes or teacher-made tapes. This particular piece of equipment greatly enhances individualized instruction. For example, let us say that a resource teacher is providing remedial instruction to a group of students using the Merrill Linguistic Series. One of the skills a student must be able to perform in the program, *I can,* is to write certain words and sentences from dictation. The words include "cat," "bat," "tag," "wag," "jam"; the sentences are "Dan sat," "Nan can bat," and so forth. The resource teacher may dictate these on tape, allowing sufficient time periods for the student to complete each task. At the end of the session, the child may be given the correct responses on a sheet of paper and allowed to monitor his/her own errors and to receive quick feedback.

The resource room also needs other materials. First, a complete set of the regular classroom's standard educational programs that relate to the problems for which students have been referred should be available in the resource room. This usually includes the reading, mathematics, spelling, handwriting, language, and/or content area series. Of particular importance and use will be the teacher's guides that accompany most programs. These guides often provide a wealth of information regarding means for individualizing and supplementing instruction for students using the series.

Second, the resource teacher will need additional materials that relate to the specific types of problems the resource students are encountering. For example, if most students are being referred for reading and behavior problems, then special materials dealing with these areas will need to be purchased. The materials that we recommend for these and other areas of difficulty are described in Part III of this book. We suggest, therefore, that when reading these chapters, teachers make special note of materials that they believe will be useful in their resource rooms.

We cannot help but reflect here on the type of materials found in some of the resource rooms that we have visited. Often there is no evidence that the materials used in these rooms are geared to teaching the skills necessary to do well in the programs used in the regular class. For example, parquetry sets, flash cards containing nonsense symbols, walking boards, specialized faddist language approaches, eye exercise activity sets, perceptual materials, trampolines, and other questionable apparatus are on occasion found in great abundance in some resource programs. Surprisingly, these special education/process types of materials and equipment are being used by resource teachers with students who are referred because they need help in reading, writing, spelling, calculating, behaving, and/or talking.

We, among others, have concluded that the educational value of such techniques has not been established sufficiently to warrant their continued use, especially when their purpose is to teach academics or language. A careful review of the current research literature is likely to lead the reader to the same conclusion. Rather than belabor this point here, we emphasize the programs and materials that we *do* recommend; these are described amply in Part III of this book.

The decision concerning which materials resource teachers should purchase is difficult. We suggest that they follow the same procedures in selecting educational materials that they would use in their own personal shopping. That is, they should: (1) prepare a list of types of materials needed; (2) arrange the items from highest to lowest priority; (3) compare prices on materials; (4) evaluate and compare the ingredients of each material; and (5) determine if it might be possible to make cheaper and equally good materials from scratch.

In order to aid the resource teachers in this often tedious task, we suggest that they follow the guidelines developed by V. Brown (1975). Brown has proposed using a basic questioning approach, which she calls a Q-Sheet. The Q-Sheet approach lists several questions that provide a framework for the teacher to analyze materials so that appropriate evaluations can be made. The questions that Brown suggests need answering are:[1]

1.   *What is the stated rationale for developing the instructional program?* Look for one or more statements of: (a) Definition of the content area under study, e.g., reading,

mathematics, language, etc., (b) Philosophy regarding instruction in the area; or (c) Dissatisfaction with specific aspects of other programs, or perhaps a previous program by the same publisher.

2.   *What is the rationale for selection of program elements or content?* Look for comments on: (a) Tradition; (b) Experimental determination (always check this out in greater detail); (c) Logic of the subject matter; (d) Survey of other programs and their elements; or (e) The assumptions made concerning the content area, such as the linguistic base in a reading program.

3.   *How can the quality of the content be checked?* This question is difficult. Usually some credence is given to the reputations of authors and publishers, as well as to supporting reference material. Usually "expert" opinion is needed as well as a determination of the internal consistency of *all* program elements.

4.   *What is the scope of the program?* Scope tends to characterize the comprehensiveness or the breadth of the program. It determines how much of what is possible to teach has been included in the program at hand. A program of limited scope may be desirable for teaching a specific skill, or as a supplement to an existing program which is weak in a particular area or variable.

5.   *What is the sequencing of skills or items or units?* Sequence determines in what order the subject matter or elements are to be taught. Some materials are sequentially dependent so that success at each level is required for continuing on to the next. Sequentially dependent curricula leave little room for flexible use or the pulling out of components. Other materials are "spiralled" so that the topic may be left and then returned to later. Paradoxically, spiralling may be helpful or detrimental. Sometimes leaving an area of difficulty for a while has the effect of desensitization. However, it may also be possible that mastery is never actually accounted for in a spiralled curriculum except when the particular topic disappears from "mention." The problem of sequence may also be based upon several factors other than the sequential/spiral question. Logical organization of the subject matter may be a determiner; the curriculum may proceed from immediate to remote life experiences; or it may move from concrete to abstract symbolism.

6.   *How is the curriculum paced?* Control of pacing is presently one of the major ways of controlling individualization of instruction. Several bits of information provide clues to intended and actual pacing of the materials or program:

    (a)   Are there differing starting times for various groups or individuals, and then essentially the same pacing along the way? If so, the modification is not in "pacing" but in "readiness" for the program.

    (b)   Are "mastery" suggestions made along the way for those who need more or different experiences at various points? How is it suggested that such modifications be managed if in a group situation?

    (c)   Do suggested instructional time-lines presented elsewhere in the program mitigate against modifications in the pacing of instruction?

7.   *Are there listed or evident any psychological principles of instruction which are content-free?* Look for reference to the systematic use of notions such as stimulus control, reinforcement, rate of introduction, set induction, *et al.*

8.   *What are the specific techniques of instruction for each lesson?* The more highly structured the lessons, the less likely it is that the success of the program depends upon teacher experience and previous training. More highly structured programs may also lend themselves to use by aides and volunteers under the supervision

of the teacher. It may also happen that if little teacher variation is allowed or encouraged, the lesson may not be readily modifiable.

9. *What are the specific modifications suggested for individualization?*
   (a) Is the individualization on a 1:1 basis, or intended for instruction within the group situation?
   (b) What are the bases for the suggestions made?
   (c) What range of suggestions is made, or are they all pretty much alike?
   (d) What range of differences is accounted for?
   (e) Are the suggestions general, or are they specifically tied to potential instructional problems?

10. *Is a prerequisite skill level or information base needed to administer the program?*
    (a) Is there a formalized, separate "package" of instruction available?
    (b) Is the training continuous as an integral part of each unit or lesson?
    (c) Are there suggestions for determining instructional competency of personnel who would work with the program?

11. *Are there "readiness" behaviors specified which are prerequisites for the student?*
    (a) Are assessment strategies included?
    (b) How are the behaviors to be acquired or taught?

12. *How is reinforcement used in the program?*
    (a) If mentioned at all, note the definition well. In the majority of nonspecial education programs there is a tendency to equate reinforcement with repetition.
    (b) What kinds of reinforcement are suggested, e.g., social, tangible, edible, visual . . .?
    (c) Are there suggestions for how to determine what is reinforcing to an individual child?
    (d) Is there any consideration of schedules of reinforcement?
    (e) Are there specific examples, or generalized suggestions?
    (f) Is there a procedure recommended for fading from tangible to social?
    (g) Is there any discrepancy between notions of reinforcement and practices such as paper-grading or marking?

13. *What is the format of the material to be presented?*
    (a) Is the material in kit, book, worksheet, chart, or some other form?
    (b) How are the units organized?
    (c) What kind of type is used? Size? Style? Compactness?
    (d) If pictures are included, what kinds are there, and what are their purposes?
    (e) Are the page arrangements likely to make any difference to the learners?

14. *How independently can the material be used?*
    (a) If independence of use is recommended, is there a systematic program to teach the child *how* to use the materials independently?
    (b) How is progress in work habits or independence to be monitored?

15. *Has any effort been made to assess or control the complexity of the language of instruction, either receptively or expressively?* Does the teacher have any way of assessing the appropriateness? For example, in materials for young children, which "Wh____ questions" are introduced and in what sequence? Do these correspond with the developmental sequences in language and cognition?

16. *What is the developmental interest level of the materials?* Materials which are obviously intended for younger children are likely to be inappropriate for older

students. On the other hand, it may be necessary for the teacher to actually develop or provide background experiences, information or interests for some students. It should be noted that statements of "mental age" do not necessarily correspond to the "interest age" or to the "social age" or stage of the child.

17.   *Are there behavioral objectives for the program or for the lessons?*
   (a)   Is there any attempt to justify the objectives or to determine their value?
   (b)   Are the objectives linked in any way to prior or to subsequent objectives?
   (c)   Are the statements complete in the sense of meeting behavioral criteria?
   (d)   What are the consequences of objectives assessment in terms of future instructional procedures?
   (e)   Is the program built on predetermined objectives, or do the objectives follow from the nature of the program?

18.   *What is the nature of diagnostic assessments provided?*
   (a)   Type?
   (b)   Frequency?
   (c)   Pre/post, or continuous during instructional sequences?
   (d)   Feedback mechanisms to the learner and to the instructional program?
   (e)   What are the consequences of assessment feedback?

19.   *Is this program coordinated with any other programs?*
   (a)   Is the program part of a series or a unified approach by the same publisher? Can it be readily separated from other components?
   (b)   Are there recommendations for companion programs, or for previous and subsequent programs?

20.   *Have there been any attempts to determine readability or learner interest?* What processes have been used, and are the results available?

21.   *What is the comparative cost of the program?* Some attempt should be made to estimate the cost-effectiveness of the program. Where similar materials are available, comparisons may be made. Also, try to determine the feasibility of using "homemade" alternatives that may be made in a workshop or by volunteers.

22   *What is the realistic availability of the instructional components?* If the program is desirable because of the variety or specific inclusion of certain components, it should be determined that these are actually available from the publisher or with funds allocated. This is vital for hardware and computer software needs. The budget factor should also be considered as critical when considering the use of consumable materials.

23.   *Are testimonial, research, author claims, and publisher claims clearly differentiated?*
   (a)   Evidence of formative evaluation?
   (b)   Evidence of summative evaluation?
   (c)   Is there congruence between the program objectives and activities?
   (d)   Are the program development processes specified?

24.   *What are the target populations for whom the materials were developed?* If the population characteristics are stated it is easier to assess the potential relevance of the materials to a population of interest.

25.   *Is it possible to foresee, and does the author describe, any potential problems which might be encountered in using these materials?*
   (a)   How surmountable are the problems?
   (b)   How readily can the materials be modified to account for the problems?

26.   *Are any of the features of this material or program adaptable or incorporatable into*

other programs? Features such as self-correctional procedures, reinforcement techniques, etc., may be noted for use in other instructional situations.

27. *Are any significant modifications in the organization and management of the instructional situation required?*
    (a)   Are there special space and/or equipment requirements?
    (b)   Will the time/event schedule of the day need to be replanned?
    (c)   Will present child groupings be significantly affected? How?
    (d)   Are the descriptions of how the program is to be organized and managed stated clearly enough so that the program may be readily implemented? . . .
29. *How durable are the materials?* Items that require a great deal of handling should be made of strong materials with protected surfaces. Storage or carrying of materials in kit or package form should also be considered in terms of convenience and sturdiness of the packaging materials.
30. *Is there any apparent or subtle bias toward or against a particular target group, e.g., Women, Blacks, Chicanos, or Indians?* Many states or local school districts will have guidelines available for this kind of analysis.

Most individuals who use a Q-Sheet approach in analyzing materials find that the time required is formidable. In addition, the competence of inexperienced professionals to use such a sophisticated approach often is questionable. Brown has suggested that if the process of dissecting materials is new to the teacher, he or she might employ the following techniques. First, he or she might take at least two programs that purport to teach the same skills and analyze them simultaneously. Second, several professionals might work together on analyzing material and then compare their perceptions. Third, the teacher might write down the specific examples in the material that cause him or her to make a judgment and have another person check these perceptions. Fourth, specific experts in one area, such as reading or mathematics, may be requested to evaluate the material. Fifth, only one component of an instructional area, such as teaching addition facts in real life situations, may be evaluated in several different series. Sixth, the teacher may develop a different Q-Sheet that relates to specific content knowledge. Finally, the material under study may be tried with a few students, and various modifications in instructing may be attempted. In this last example, the material is experimented with to determine the conditions of use within a specific program.

Wiederholt and McNutt (1977) have stressed several points that should be considered when evaluating materials for older students. For example, they have noted the importance of the experiential background of the students as it relates to the topics represented in the material. Specifically, the students in most cases should have had either real or vicarious experiences with the topics in order to understand and relate them to their own lives. They also encourage the use of interviews to obtain the students' own perceptions of the materials being considered.

Wilson (1982) also provides guidelines for selecting educational materials and resources. Various professional organizations have also worked together under the leadership of Daniel Stufflebeam to develop a common, detailed handbook, *Standards for Evaluations of Educational Programs, Projects, and Materials* (1981). Its content should be useful to the resource teacher in materials evaluation or in the provision of inservice sessions related to the topic.

Budget

Most resource programs are allocated a certain amount of money for equipment, supplies, and materials. The particular amount varies greatly from one state or province to another and often even among schools within the same district. It is important for the resource teacher to understand the budget policies and processes of the state or province and of the district and even more important to seek out personally and actively all those who have a hand in the budgeting, ordering, or distribution of budgeted items.

In ordering, priority should be given to ordering items that have value across ages, time, and subjects. Very specialized, novel, or consumable materials are usually not as well regarded as more universally applicable items because of their high cost. However, a high-cost item of proven effectiveness may be the better choice in the long run if it helps teach a student to read, write, or calculate.

Before ordering specialized materials, the teacher should check to see if they are already available someplace within the district. Novel items or difficult-to-use programs may have been relegated to the back of a closet after brief use. Or perhaps a new teacher who has no interest in or understanding of a complex material may have discarded it. For these reasons, some districts hold sales or materials exchanges each fall in order to increase the useful life of high-cost, low-use materials.

The new teacher who is looking for materials should check to find out if it is the district's policy to collect all materials at the end of the school year and redistribute them again in the fall. Further, the resource teacher should find out if the district makes an inventory of all equipment, supplies, and materials. Such a list is useful in locating items.

Students in special education programs are entitled to the basic materials, supplies, and equipment that are budgeted and provided for every other student. This is especially important at the secondary level, where supplies are often allocated by departments such as English or math. The special education department should have its own allocation or else work out a mutually agreeable arrangement to be sure that the special materials, supplies, and equipment are indeed over and above those to which the student is normally entitled.

Gallagher (1979) has also noted other matters regarding budget. Some budgets specify the allocation of funds to specific categories, such as equipment or instructional materials. In addition, some schools provide consumable items to students, others do not. Finally, some schools require teachers to complete requisitions for supplies, and in other buildings, teachers can simply take materials as needed.

In any event, a budget for all special programs, including the resource operation, usually has been decided on, and resource teachers should ask their administrators and supervisors how much money has been allocated for use in their program. They also should determine when and how this money can be spent. In some cases, materials may be ordered only at the beginning of the school year. This restriction causes some difficulty in that most resource teachers do not know which materials are needed until they have become familiar with the requirements and problems of the referred students. If they are unsure as to how much money is available and when they can order materials, they should request specific materials and see what happens.

In requesting materials, professional behavior usually pays handsome dividends. A typed, formal request to the principal in which the materials, publisher, and cost are listed and a written statement about the need and usefulness of the instructional package for a specific student or students are more likely to result in a positive response than is a haphazard verbal request. If the teachers also can state how they have used the material in the past or how other teachers have used it with success, the probability that the request will be honored is further enhanced.

Finally, resource teachers should set some money aside in their own personal budget to be used in building a professional library. The actual dollar amount will depend on the financial status and interests of the teacher but generally will range from $50 to $200 a year. In three or four years, the teacher can acquire a comprehensive and useful collection of books, journals, and materials. (The money spent on this professional library is tax deductible.) In addition to their private libraries, resource teachers can always use the facilities of the public library system, instructional materials, and/or media centers, and they can tap the small budgets that most schools keep to buy selected books for teacher use.

PUBLIC RELATIONS

As noted in Chapter 2, one role of the resource teacher is consultant. Specifically, we referred to the teacher's working with regular classroom teachers. In essense, this consulting activity can be referred to as one type of public relations. In these instances, no matter how trivial the communication might seem, resource teachers may improve another persons's attitude toward the program by their statements.

While day-to-day public relations with other personnel in the school is critical, the importance of public relations with community and professional organizations should not be ignored. These community and professional organizations include the Parent-Teachers Association (PTA), the Junior League, the Kiwanis Club, the Rotary Club, the Lions Club, the Council for Learning Disabilities, the National Association of Retarded Children, the International Reading Association, the American Speech-Language-Hearing Association, the Council for Exceptional Children, the Orton Society, and local special education advisory groups. These organizations are rich sources of support for the resource program. This support includes one or more of the following: (1) lobbying for money to support the program; (2) providing volunteers to work as aides in the program and/or small donations of monies to purchase materials and equipment; (3) supporting inservice training; (4) delineating competencies for teachers; and (5) ethical standards of practice. Each of these points is discussed below.

Resource programs often are viewed as ancillary services in the schools. Therefore, when money becomes tight or scarce, the financial support for these programs is among the first to be pared down or eliminated altogether. No matter how loud and long resource teachers may complain about the injustice of this action, they alone have little clout in changing or escaping budget reductions; however, local parental, civic, and professional organizations frequently do have a lot of influence in such matters. If they support the resource program strongly, then local school administrators may be careful when considering any budgetary cuts in these programs.

Funding is particularly a problem for the noncategorical and specific skill resource programs. The financial base for special education programs, the categorical and cross-categorical resource models, is usually more stable. However, regardless of the resource model being used, all resource teachers may find that from time to time special lobbying for money to support the program is necessary. They should be prepared for such an eventuality by having already established good public relations with important local organizations.

The second point concerns the provision of volunteers to work as aides or the allocation of monies for special materials and equipment. Many of the organizations mentioned have set up volunteer programs; each volunteer spends a few hours a week in the schools. For example, members of the Junior League often offer their services in this capacity. In other cases, some organizations have varying amounts of monies that they spend on special materials and equipment for the schools. This is particularly true of the Kiwanis, Rotary, and Lions clubs. Donations may be made by these organizations to the resource program — if good public relations have been established.

Professional organizations often provide inservice training to their members. Local and state chapters of the International Reading Association, the American Speech-Language-Hearing Association, the Council for Exceptional Children, and the Orton Society, among others, schedule many meetings each year that deal with interesting and relevant professional topics. Parent and civic organizations, such as the Council for Learning Disabilities and the Junior League, also sponsor speakers on a variety of subjects.

The final point, the delineation of competencies and ethical standards of practice, relates to the professional organizations. Resource teachers should be members of their professional organizations. Many of the organizations have listed the competencies their members should have; some give certificates for demonstrated competency; a few have delineated ethical standards of practice to which their members must adhere, almost all have professional journals and newsletters that keep members informed on new developments in practice. It is professionally indefensible for a resource teacher not to be an active member of one or more of these organizations.

The question remains as to how resource teachers establish public relations with these organizations. In terms of the professional organizations, the answer is quite simple. Resource teachers will need to contact the membership chairperson of those organizations with which they wish to affiliate and pay their dues. The next step is to start attending local and state meetings and to become actively involved in the business and benefits of the organizations.

The problem of establishing public relations with parent and civic organizations requires more attention. Resource teachers should contact organizations that are the most active in their areas and offer to discuss the resource program with members of these organizations at an upcoming meeting. Most of these organizations will gladly welcome such a presentation.

Preparations for such a meeting will have to be considered carefully. Resource teachers will have to describe clearly the objectives of the presentation. Is it just to familiarize the participants with the resource program? Is it to enlist their support in some specific way? Once the objectives have been determined, the manner of presentation will need to be decided. Is it going to be a short lecture? Will any audio or visual presentations be utilized? Will handouts be given to those attending the meeting? How will questions be handled?

At first, some resource teachers may feel uncomfortable about presenting to a group of adults; however, they must recognize that these presentations are an important aspect of the public relations effort and that they will have to engage in many during their career as a resource teacher. Many teachers have found that a slide presentation is helpful. It serves as a guide for the speaker and usually is more interesting to the audience than simply a straight lecture. Some teachers tape an audio presentation to accompany the slide presentation. Resource teachers from several schools often will get together and select one teacher to give the presentations, even though all of them share equally in preparing for the meetings.

There are, of course, some slide and movie presentations of the resource concept. These usually are available from the local special education resource center for short checkout periods. While these commercially made materials are beneficial in some cases, we feel it is much better for resource teachers to prepare their own presentation using both the local teachers and students as participants (with appropriately secured permissions to take and show pictures). Those who view the presentation then can see the relevance of the resource program to their own school and students more clearly.

This chapter has offered specific suggestions for implementing the resource program in the schools. Readers will note that even though the main focus of the discussions pertained to activities that are of the most value during the initial stages of the development of the resource program, many of the suggestions are equally applicable for use throughout the school year. In other words, resource teachers continually need to direct some of their attention and energies to seeking more support and understanding of the model; to improving the daily operations of the program; and to increasing the quality and amount of materials that they use in working with students who have learning and behavior difficulties.

ENDNOTES

1.   Reprinted by special permission of Professional Press, Inc. From Brown, V. A basic Q-Sheet for analyzing and comparing curriculum materials and proposals. *Journal of Learning Disabilities*, 1975, 8, 407 – 416. Copyright 1975 by Professional Press, Inc.

4

Referral and Selection Procedures

Questions about identifying the students who will receive resource services and the procedures by which they will be declared eligible for those services must be answered before a resource program can be implemented in a school. This chapter will assist resource teachers in the important tasks of managing referrals and selecting students for their programs. First, some comments are made regarding the qualifications of students for the program. Second, some recommendations are offered regarding procedures to be followed in seeking and processing referrals. Third, the resource teacher's role in multidisciplinary staffing is discussed because the final decision concerning placement often is made in such staff meetings.

STUDENT SELECTION: WHO QUALIFIES?

Before implementing any kind of resource program the resource teacher should clearly understand the rules and regulations governing the identification, selection, and qualification of students for resource help. These rules and regulations usually are found in official state and local guidelines or in other policy statements. In most instances, copies of these guidelines can be obtained from state or local education agency personnel, the director of special education, and/or the building principal. When the program is supported financially by an agency of the federal government, the regulations of that organization also will have to be obtained. It should be noted that even when the guidelines are available, they may be: (1) out of date and consequently inconsistent with current thinking; (2) lacking in specificity; (3) in the process of being modified; and/or (4) inappropriate for a given school implementing an experimental type of resource program.

We will not attempt to establish a set of criteria that could be used to qualify students for the various types of resource programs. The criteria that any teacher uses must be consistent with the policies of the particular area, state or province, district, and school; and it should be mentioned that these rules and regulations vary widely across the country. For example, in most places, "normal intelligence" is specified as a necessary criterion for eligibility in a learning disabilities resource program. Yet there is little agreement among professionals or policies as to what constitutes "normal" or as to how intellectual status is to be determined for placement purposes. In some parts of the country, normal intelligence is defined in regulations as being a score on an intelligence test that is within two standard deviations of the mean. In other regions, it is a score that is within one standard deviation of the mean. In at least one state, examiners are not allowed to use any standardized tests of intelligence at all and are required to diagnose normal intelligence on the basis of their clinical judgment.

Another area in which the rules vary significantly pertains to the amount of underachievement or nonachievement that students must manifest in order to qualify for resource help. In some locales, performance that is one standard deviation or one grade level below expected achievement will suffice; in other areas, two standard deviations or two grade levels below expected achievement is required. There also is no consistency regarding the procedures by which poor school achievement is to be documented. Different tests that purport to measure a particular ability often assess quite different aspects of those skills. In the case of reading, for example, one test might measure the student's ability to recognize sound blends and to identify words, whereas another test of reading might measure oral reading and comprehension. Yet both tests yield a score for reading.

In addition, many professionals have noted that the average performance of students on achievement tests varies markedly from school to school; consequently, some guidelines specify that resource students must be severely underachieving in relation to their school peers. For example, if Sally, an underachieving sixth-grade student of normal intelligence who is enrolled in a school district that is characterized by high academic achievement moves to another part of town, her educational status might be changed. Sally might suddenly find that she is doing better than her new peers and therefore would no longer be regarded as underachieving. Even more surprising, it is possible that she may now be seen as a good student.

Regardless of the criteria used to select pupils who qualify for placement, principals and resource teachers frequently find that more students have been referred than can be served adequately. When this occurs, the people responsible for operating the program should be sure that the resource teachers are not overburdened by the enrollment of unrealistically large numbers of students into their programs. This situation can be avoided easily.

For example, let us say that a given state's regulations specify that students are eligible for a special service if they fall within the normal ranges of intelligence and are significantly underachieving. In this state, normal intelligence is defined as an intelligence quotient that falls within two standard deviations of the mean. Underachievement also is defined as an educational quotient in reading, arithmetic, and so forth, that falls two standard deviations below the mean on a standardized achievement test. Let us further speculate that using these criteria, a resource teacher finds that approximately ninety students in the school fall within these ranges. Yet money for only one resource teacher has been allocated. Not all of those students who qualify under these rules can be served. If this situation should arise, we suggest that the principal and resource teacher apply the following two rules.

Rule Number 1. Of the students who meet the guidelines, the most severe cases should
     be given priority in placement.
Rule Number 2. Only the numbers of students that can be served effectively should
     be taken into the program. Usually, the case load should be no fewer than ten
     and no more than twenty. Reger (1973) has recommended a maximum of fif-
     teen students at the elementary level; twenty students at the secondary level.
     Gickling, Murphy, and Malloy (1979) have recommended that twenty students
     be served through direct services but that ten more could be served through
     consultation to their teachers.

If fewer than ten students are enrolled in a resource program, the principal should consider: (1) the competence of the resource teacher to teach realistic numbers of students; (2) the financial feasibilty of the program; and (3) the severity of the students' problems (they might be so severe that some of the pupils who are enrolled in the program may need a more intensive instructional environment such as a part- or full-time special class).

Returning to the example of the ninety students who qualify for service, we can see that at least seventy would not receive resource service if rules 1 and 2 are followed. We know of some cases where resource teachers have yielded to pressure from administrators, other teachers, and parents and have taken on more students and of other instances where resource teachers on their own volition have agreed to work with forty to sixty pupils a day in a resource program. Not only is enrolling so many students a questionable professional practice, but it also is often an actual violation of state guidelines regarding the numbers of students that an individual resource teacher is allowed to serve.

Resource teachers who find themselves in the position of having to serve too many students should stand firm. It has been our experience that when a resource program is opened up to more than twenty students per each qualified resource teacher, the service provided is insufficient to help *any* of the referred students.

We would like to make one final point relative to the situation where an overwhelmingly large number of students are referred for resource help. This occurence may suggest that the instructional program in the regular classes is not meeting the needs of a sizable percentage of the student body. It is also likely that overreferring in a school occurs because the criteria for selecting eligible students have not been explained carefully to the teachers. Regardless, a flood of referrals should be viewed by the principal and the resource teacher as an indication that some inservice training is required.

The outcome of this training should be that the classroom teachers better understand the operation of the resource program and that their skills in adapting curricula more effectively to accommodate those students who are having difficulty in school have been sharpened. Of course, before providing any inservice experience, a careful assessment of teacher needs should be undertaken to determine factors that cause or contribute to the overreferral of pupils in the school. The content of the inservice training sessions would then be planned to focus on the identified factors.

SEEKING AND PROCESSING REFERRALS

Before beginning to seek and deal with referrals, resource teachers should have accomplished the three tasks mentioned in the previous section: they should know the local regulations governing eligibility; they should be committed to serving first those students who qualify for service and have the most severe problems; and they should have clearly in mind the maximum number of students to be served. Resource teachers (in conunction with the building principal) then are ready to develop their own referral and placement procedures.

The referral and placement procedures that are prepared must be in accordance with the regulations; they also must take into account the due process guidelines, any legal mandates, and the needs of the individual personnel within a given school. It also is true that various states or provinces and local agencies differ markedly regarding their referral and placement processes. Resource teachers therefore will need to investigate carefully these matters before beginning to develop their own procedures. This section gives the reader examples of three different approaches to processing referrals.

The first referral and identification approach to be discussed was developed in South Carolina for use in a model resource program (Hawisher, 1975). The process is presented in flowchart form in Figure 4 – 1. In this program, referrals are made to the building principal, who in turn passes them on to the resource teacher, who initiates the screening procedure. The results of this screening procedure are analyzed and a decision is made. This decision could be to keep the student in the regular classroom and specifying the adjustments to be made in that setting or to ask the student's parents for permission to conduct a psychological evaluation in order to determine the possibility of placement in the resource program. Upon completion of the evaluation, individual students may be declared eligible for the resource program or a special class, or they may be referred to agencies outside the school for service.

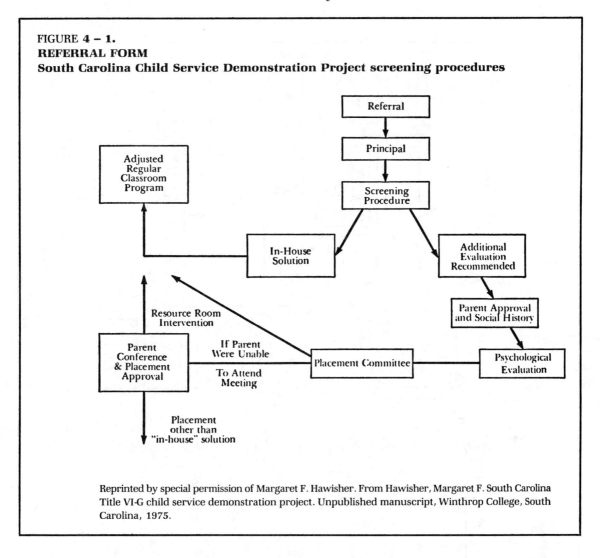

FIGURE 4 – 1.
REFERRAL FORM
South Carolina Child Service Demonstration Project screening procedures

Reprinted by special permission of Margaret F. Hawisher. From Hawisher, Margaret F. South Carolina Title VI-G child service demonstration project. Unpublished manuscript, Winthrop College, South Carolina, 1975.

Figure 4 – 2 presents another example of a referral procedure system. Although this particular referral scheme was used to qualify students for learning disability services, it can be easily modified for use in any kind of resource program. This particular approach is more complex and detailed than the one used in the South Carolina project; however, similarities do exist. First, school personnel evaluate the referral prior to seeking outside help; second, parents are involved early; and third, at any step the student may be classifed as ineligible for special services and returned to the regular classroom. It is different from the South Carolina model because the student may be placed temporarily in a diagnostic class as part of the assessment process and because periodic reevaluation is called for within the model itself.

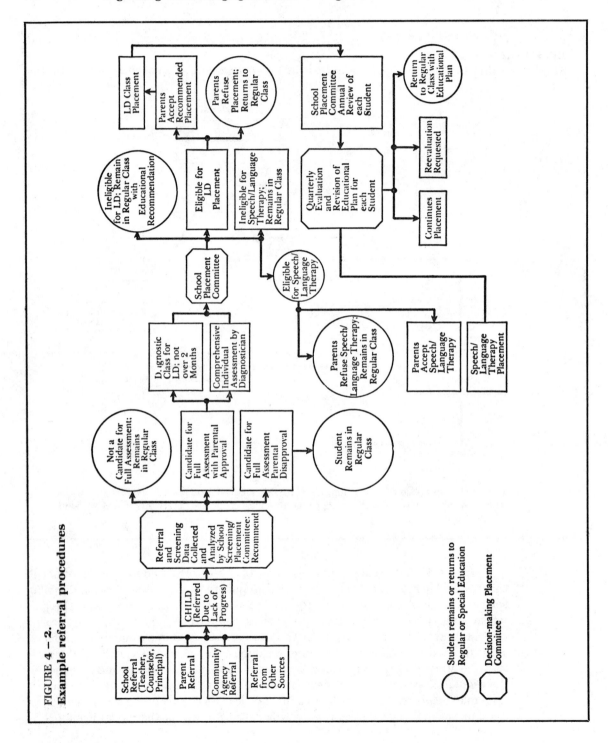

FIGURE 4 – 2.
Example referral procedures

Both the South Carolina and the second referral sequences require that a student be identified as handicapped before categorical resource or other special education services can be provided. In Chapter 1, we noted that not all resource programs are categorical special education services. The referral and placement process presented in Figure 4 – 3 is designed to fit any kind of resource program, including a categorical, cross-categorical, noncategorical, or specific skill program. A description of the activities undertaken by the resource teacher at each of the eight steps in this referral follows.

Step 1. At the first step, the principal and the resource teacher tell others about the nature of the program and the procedures to be followed in referring students. This is usually done at a general faculty meeting at the beginning of the school year. (The reader is referred to the section in Chapter 3, "Preparing the School Staff and

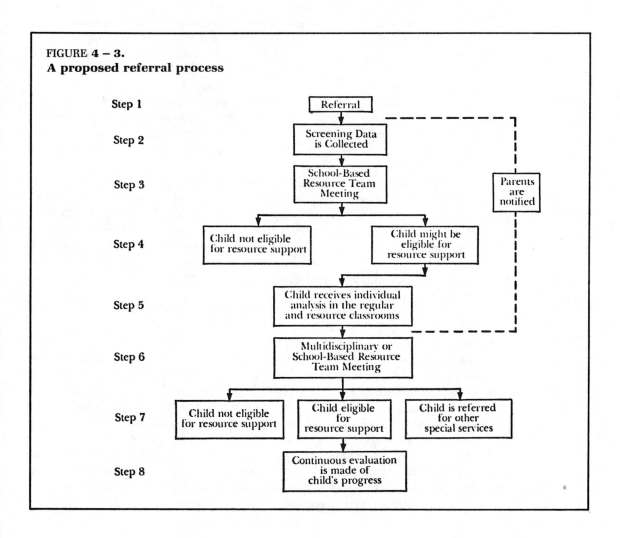

FIGURE 4 – 3.
A proposed referral process

Parents," for more details regarding the planning and operation of this faculty meeting. We limit our comments here to the portion of the meeting that deals with the referral process.) At this faculty meeting, the principal and/or resource teacher: (1) states as clearly as possible who will and who will not qualify for resource services; (2) specifies and justifies the number of students to be served; (3) explains the process to be used in referring a student; and (4) distributes referral forms to the teachers.

The content and format of the referral forms will vary, depending in part on the type of resource program being implemented. If a categorical resource program for the mentally retarded is being established, the referral form would be different from that of a resource program in reading. Three different referral forms are shown in Table 4 – 1, 4 – 2, and 4 – 3. The form in Table 4 – 1 is for use in programs in which the students must be classified as handicapped to qualify for help. Table 4 – 1 could be adapted for use in any categorical or noncategorical program. The second form, Table 4 – 2, is designed for use by a teacher operating a noncategorical resource program. The third referral form, Table 4 – 3, might be appropriate for any type of resource program. This third referral form has the advantage of assuming that the regular staff has been concerned about the student and that available resources have been exhausted.

As with other suggestions in this chapter, these samples are offered as a point of departure for resource teachers who will want and need to develop their own forms. Designing their own forms allows resource teachers to account for the unique features of their program, as well as the sophistication of the teachers who will be making the referrals.

We recommend that resource teachers keep their referral forms as direct as possible, that they avoid the use of complex formats, and that they try to develop a form that is short and easy to complete. The information requested should be of two major types: (1) information that is legally required and (2) information that is useful for program analysis or planning. In time, the resource teacher may wish to modify or change the forms if some of the information is not used or if some desired information is consistently missing. When change is being contemplated, suggestions from other faculty members should be solicited.

Step 2. All referral forms should first be sent to the building principal. The principal thus can keep a record of the referring teachers, the names of the students, and any other information that is desired.

Having reviewed the referral, the principal passes it on to the resource teacher. The resource teacher then initiates a meeting with the referring teacher at which they discuss the problem. In addition, any pertinent information that is readily accessible should be accumulated, such as school records, test results, and a history of a problem. The purposes of the activities at this step of the screening are to determine what the problems might be and to gather already available information.

Step 3. At Step 3, selected personnel meet to discuss the referred student. Those who attend this school-based resource team (SBRT) meeting include the building principal (chairperson), the resource teacher, the referring teacher, and any other members of the school faculty who might be able to make significant suggestions regarding services for the student, such as the nurse, counselor, and/or special education self-contained classroom teacher.

Because these meetings are to be held frequently and regularly, some of the team members may initially resist the idea. The first reason usually cited against regular meetings is the problem of freeing teachers during the school day. Resource teachers are encouraged to counter with the suggestion that the meetings can be held one-half hour before school, after school, or during the lunch period. If other people, including principals, classroom teachers, other teachers, and counselors, are willing to commit some time to this program, then those who are resisting generally

---

TABLE **4 – 1.**
Resource Program — Mental Retardation

Referring Teacher:_____

Student's Name: _____

Criteria for Placement: Low Intellectual Functioning
                             Maladaptive Behavior

1. Why do you suspect the student is of low intelligence?

	YES	NO
A. An intelligence test score	____	____
B. Poor functioning in: Reading	____	____
Arithmetic	____	____
Spelling	____	____
Handwriting	____	____
Spoken language	____	____

2. Is the language of the home standard English?

YES	NO	UNCERTAIN
____	____	____

3. In what areas does the student demonstrate maladaptive behavior?

	YES	NO
A. Socialization with: Adults	____	____
Peers	____	____
B. Attention	____	____
C. Self-Control	____	____
D. Self-Concept	____	____

E. Other (specify): _____

4. What can the student do that is 'normal' for his or her chronological age?_____

_____

_____

5. Additional comments: _____

_____

_____

_____

TABLE 4 – 2.
REFERRAL FORM
Resource Program — Noncategorical

Referring Teacher:_____
Student's Name: _____

1. In what areas does the student perform inadequately?

	YES	NO	UNCERTAIN
Reading	_____	_____	_____
Arithmetic	_____	_____	_____
Spelling	_____	_____	_____
Handwriting	_____	_____	_____
Spoken language	_____	_____	_____

2. Does the student have appropriate independent study habits?

	YES	NO	UNCERTAIN
	_____	_____	_____

3. Does the student demonstrate appropriate classroom behavior?

	YES	NO	UNCERTAIN
Socialization with: Adults	_____	_____	_____
Peers	_____	_____	_____
Attention	_____	_____	_____
Self-control	_____	_____	_____
Self-concept	_____	_____	_____
Other (specify) _____			

4. Additional comments: _____
_____
_____
_____

will go along. Since many states require these meetings by law or policy for placing a student into any type of special education program, organizing a SBRT may not present a problem.

Two points need to be considered in establishing a SBRT. First, the meetings should be short and to the point. Inconsequential irrelevant information often is discussed, or the participants go off on tangents. When this happens, the resource teacher will have to insist that the agenda be strictly adhered to. Administrators and other teachers are busy people; they do not want to attend meetings that are too long, poorly organized, wasteful, and/or indecisive.

The second point deals with the question of who is to comprise the SRBT. Only members of the school staff should be on a team on a regular basis. To include outsiders, such as district personnel and community specialists, generally is not helpful. Since the faculty members of the school have to deal with the referred students, they should be primarily responsible for making decisions about placement and pro-

TABLE 4 – 3.
REFERRAL DATA

THIS IS A REFERRAL FOR: (Check appropriate)

_____ Reading	_____ Spelling	_____ Social Behavior
_____ Mathematics	_____ Writing: Mechanics	_____ Other:
_____ Oral Language	_____ Writing: Composition	_____

Student Name   Student No.   D.O.B.   Grade   School

Parent   Address and Zip Code   Phone   Home School

Date Referral Received   Date Parent Permission Was Received

1. What is the presenting problem?
   SOCIAL BEHAVIOR   ACADEMIC BEHAVIOR

2. Give available data (std. or informal testing, interview, school history, etc. — include date of testing and tester)

3. What are the student's strengths?
   BEHAVIORAL   LEARNING

4. What resources have been used?   5. Effectiveness of resource:

6. What has been done by regular staff to meet the student's needs?
   BEHAVIORAL   LEARNING

7. What has worked?
   BEHAVIORAL   LEARNING

TABLE **4 – 3.** *(Continued)*
REFERRAL DATA

8. What hasn't worked?

BEHAVIORAL	LEARNING
_____	_____
_____	_____
_____	_____

9. What might work?

BEHAVIORAL	LEARNING
_____	_____
_____	_____
_____	_____

Adapted from the Madison, Wisconsin, Public Schools, Division of Specialized Educational Services, 1976.

---

grams. However, when additional help is needed or when specific rules and regulations have to be satisfied, the necessary outside personnel must be contacted.

Step 4. At Step 4, there are two options. The SBRT might decide for any number of reasons that the student is not eligible for resource support. For example, on inspection, the problems may not appear severe enough; the regular classroom teachers might wish to try some suggestions made by the team before putting the student through the rest of the referral and placement process. At this point, the students also might be transferred to another regular classroom that is better suited to his or her temperment and needs. If the student appears to be a possible candidate for resource support, the referral process continues to the next step.

Step 5. An analysis of the student in the regular classroom and an individualized supplemental analysis of the student are undertaken. How these are to be accomplished is described in Part III of this book.

If the student needs to be certified as handicapped before being declared eligible for resource support, then a certified district employee probably will have to make the diagnosis. Resource teachers should recognize that such an assessment is necessary primarily for administrative and funding purposes and should proceed with their own educational-based assessment, as outlined in Part III of this book.

Step 6. This step calls for another meeting. If the student is suspected of being handicapped, the meeting will probably be a multidisciplinary staffing, including specialists who are required by the regulations to examine and to label students — school psychologists, psychiatrists, and/or neurologists. Physicians rarely attend these meetings, although their reports frequently are read into the record. On the other hand, if the regulations do not require any special professionals to certify eligibility for service, then only the original members of the SBRT will need to attend the meeting.

Step 7. The placement decision is made at Step 7, either by the multidisciplinary team or the SBRT. Three options are possible. First, the student may not be eligible for resource support. In this case, the regular classroom teacher should be given suggestions for helping the student in the classroom. Special resource support ends at this point. If the student *is eligible for support,* the resource teacher and the regular classroom teacher will begin to implement the recommendations generated at Step 6. The third option is that the multidisciplinary team or the SBRT may decide that the student probably could profit from other than resource services. These cases often are students whose problems are so severe or complex that a special education self-contained class placement is considered desirable.

If the decision is made at this step that a student is eligible for resource support, then a written educational program should be prepared. Federal regulations under Public Law 94-142 have provided guidelines for preparing these written educational programs for students identified as handicapped. We believe these guidelines are equally relevant to programs for nonhandicapped students receiving any type of resource services. According to Section 121a.346, "Content of Individualized Education Program," in the *Code of Federal Regulations* published August 23, 1977, at 42 *Federal Register* 42474-42514, the individual educational program for each student must include:

1. A statement of the student's present levels of performance.
2. A statement of long-term goals, including short-term objectives.
3. A statement of the specific types of educational and related services to be provided, including the extent to which the student will participate in both the resource and regular educational programs.
4. The projected dates for initiating the services and the anticipated duration of the services.
5. Appropriate objective criteria and evaluation procedures and schedules for determining whether the short-term objectives are being achieved.

We will not elaborate further on the specific nature of individualized educational programs. For those interested in further discussions and descriptions, we refer them to the Council of Exceptional Children, 1920 Association Drive, Reston, Virginia 22091. This organization keeps abreast of current court decisions and legal mandates regarding these programs. As a result they have timely publications on the subject. We would, however, make some cautionary statements.

First, administrators and teachers are becoming increasingly concerned about the amount of paperwork and time involved in writing individual programs for each student. As a result, short-cuts are being explored. For example, some resource teachers have begun to rely almost exclusively upon one or two published lists of arbitrary objectives and/or curricula. Although these objectives and curricula often lack empirical support, resource teachers too often simply transpose them into written programs for individual students. Little, if any, attempt is made to individualize the program from student to student. As a result, all programs are the same or similar for every student receiving support from the resource unit. Other professionals are considering the use of computers in writing the individualized program. In these instances, the student's educational deficit is "fed" into the computer, which provides a list of instructional objectives and teaching strategies.

We find both practices highly questionable and believe they violate the spirit and nature of an individualized educational program. We believe that the number of instructional and human variables that must be accounted for in comprehensive instructional program planning can never be accommodated by consulting one or two lists of arbitrary objectives or curricula or from a computer bank.

Second, many administrators and teachers are also concerned over the number of regulations regarding any special services, particularly those relating to handicapped students. The problem here can be solved to some extent by separating the wheat from the chaff. In other words, the professional has to determine what regulations are required by law and what are elaborate recommendations regarding the implementation of the legislation. Much misinformation abounds in this area. In addition, laws are being reinterpreted constantly and regulations are modified.

Third, we strongly support the idea that an individualized educational program should be written for each student receiving resource support, regardless of whether the program is mandated. As Myers and Hammill (1982) have noted:

> The process of individual educational planning . . . is not a burdensome task nor would it require a great deal of paperwork — the bane of those who operate under numerous state and federal guidelines. It is a sad illusion, however, to think that the education of handicapped students can proceed in a systematic, efficient fashion without a high degree of planning. Saddest of all is the illusion that *only* handicapped students need individual educational planning. Thousands, if not tens of thousands, of nonhandicapped students in our schools would profit from the implementation of such planning. [P. 81]

Step 8. At this point, students have been placed in a resource program and their educational plans have been implemented. The results of these plans will need to be carefully and critically monitored. This monitoring must be continuous in order to ensure that any program continues to be as beneficial as possible for the students and their teachers. Of course, good teaching (as noted in Chapter 2) requires continuous evaluation.

One additional point needs to be made about seeking and processing referrals. In Figure 4 – 3, a space on the right side refers to the notification of parents. This is an extremely important component of a referral and selection process. In most cases, parents must be notified, and usually their permission must be obtained before any type of assessment or programmatic services can be provided to the student. If the resource program is a specific skill program or a noncategorical program, the parents *may* or *may not* need to be notified; but if students being considered as possible candidates for special education, that is, if they might be labeled as handicapped, then the parents or guardians *must be notified*. This point is addressed specifically in Public Law 93-380 (the Educational Amendment of 1974). The language of this act mandates that in providing special education support, the state must

> provide procedures for insuring that handicapped children and their parents or guardians are guaranteed procedural safeguards in decisions regarding identification, evaluation and educational placement of handicapped children including, but not limited to (A) (i) prior notice to parents or guardians of the child when the local or state educational agency proposes to change the educational placement of the child, (ii) an opportunity for the parents or guardians to obtain an impartial due process hearing, examine all relevant records with respect to the classification or educational placement of the child and obtain an independent educational evaluation of the child, (iii) procedures to protect the rights of the child when the parents or guardians are not known, unavailable, or the child is a ward of the State including the assignment of an individual (not to be an employee of the State or local education agency involved in the education or care of children) to act as a surrogate for the parents or guardians, and (iv) provision to insure that the decisions rendered in the impartial due process hearing required by this paragraph shall be binding on all parties subject only to appropriate administrative or judicial appeal. [Public Law 93-380, Title VIB, Sec. 612(d) (13 A)]

We purposely have not designated the exact point in the referral and placement process when parental permission should be secured. It will vary from place to place. Resource teachers must ascertain the local policies relative to securing parental agreements and involvement. Regardless of the local rules, the resource teacher should make sure the due process is followed with regard to the labeling and placement of handicapped students. If resource teachers are unfamiliar with their due process responsibilities, we strongly urge them to consult *A Primer on Due Process* by Abeson, Bolick, and Hass (1976). This publication will provide a suitable background on the legal aspects of due process, the sequence of procedures that must be followed, an overview of the structure and operation of hearings, the role of the surrogate parents, and sample forms.[1]

The referral and selection process often is a complex, cumbersome, time-consuming, and law-governed procedure. Consequently, care must be taken to ensure that all local and state rules and regulations that relate to providing special services to students are followed to the letter. The rights of children and their parents probably will be drawn more sharply in the future as more court cases are decided. Resource teachers are strongly encouraged to keep abreast of any changes in these legal rights and to alter their procedures to comply with pertinent court decisions.

MULTIDISCIPLINARY STAFFING

Historically, the multidisciplinary staffing model was developed in clinical settings where severe physical, social, and/or emotional cases were involved and where complex and highly restricted treatment procedures were employed. For example, a child with severe problems might need medication, very specialized individualized educational programming, and/or highly specific psychiatric treatments. The multidisciplinary staffing model was created to meet the need of communication among the relatively specialized professionals who generally worked independently with these cases. Such a model allowed professionals to determine interrelated treatment possibilities, to establish treatment priorities, and to discuss or monitor the progress of severely impaired persons over time.

We view the multidisciplinary model as a necessary and valuable component of treating these severe cases. For most students referred to the resource program, however, we question the value of using such a multidisciplinary approach.

During their preservice training, resource teachers have likely been told about the importance of multidisciplinary work with individuals who have learning and behavior problems. Consequently, these teachers may be inclined to enlist the aid of psychiatrists, social workers, psychologists, guidance counselors, curriculum experts, and other specifically trained personnel in the resource program effort. For most students referred for resource help, this is an inefficient and unrewarding practice. Most of these referred students will have mild to moderate learning and/or behavior problems and will require academic and behavior treatments that the resource teacher should be able to implement without any assistance other than that of the regular classroom teacher and the students' parents. A competent resource teacher should have had sufficient training and experience to manage most referred students quite successfully.

In a few cases, some other specially trained individuals occasionally may be called on. For example, some resource students may need medication, and a properly trained physician may be consulted on the matter. In other cases, the home life of the student may need intensive attention, and a social worker may be asked to investigate this problem. In all cases, however, the resource teacher should be intimately involved and informed and should participate to the extent feasible.

Occasionally, a resource teacher will be unfamiliar with techniques for dealing with a student who has a particular problem. For example, an individual student with a speech and/or language disability may have been assigned to a resource teacher who knows little or nothing about such cases. In these instances, the resource teacher will have to call on a speech therapist for assistance. However, resource teachers should always attempt to increase their competence so that they have to rely on others less and less. Further training, reading, and practice are needed on a continuing basis to round out the resource teacher's skill. Part III of this book presents information relative to the skills a resource teacher needs in various content and behavior areas.

In sum, we suggest that multidisciplinary staffing for most resource students is unnecessary but may be undertaken occasionally when needed. Specifically, we feel that individuals other than those housed in the school in which the resource program is located generally should *not* be part of developing and implementing programs for referred students. Only when a student's problem is outside the domain of authority or skill of a resource teacher should ancillary professionals be called on. Although rules and regulations specify that specialists other than the resource teacher must certify a student as eligible for special support, the resource teacher should recognize that this labeling process will relate very little to the daily instructional program of an individual student in a specific school and classroom. The planning, implementing, and evaluation of daily programs for the resource teachers must be the responsibility of the resource teacher and local school staff.

In this chapter, we have given an overview of the referral and selection procedures relative to the resource concept. In addition, guidelines regarding the development of an individual educational plan and suggestions on multidisciplinary staffings were included. The legal requirements, the detail and scope of the referral process, the specificity of the individual educational plan, and the sheer amount of talent and competency needed by professionals to adhere to these matters may be somewhat overwhelming at first. However, there are few shortcuts to defensible professional practices, and resource teachers will usually find, after a period of study and implementation, that these matters can be smoothly and efficiently incorporated into their own personal skills and competencies.

ENDNOTES

1.   This primer is available from Publications Sales, CEC, 1920 Association Drive, Reston, Va. 22091.

5

Managing the Program

As with most other educational enterprises, a great deal of attention must be directed toward planning and managing the daily operations of the resource program. Without careful planning and management, even the most instructionally competent resource teachers will find that their programs are disorganized and ineffective. The information in this chapter will help resource teachers develop a management system applicable to the unique requirements of operating resource programs. The suggestions in each section of this chapter are not comprehensive enough to solve all the problems that arise in the day-to-day operation of resource programs. Instead, we have attempted to deal pragmatically with management difficulties that usually crop up in any resource program. The areas discussed are: (1) elementary and secondary schools; (2) start-up procedures; (3) scheduling; (4) movement between classes; (5) grading; (6) individual instructional plans; (7) parent or guardian involvement; (8) peer tutoring; and (9) evaluation of the program.

ELEMENTARY AND SECONDARY SCHOOLS

Up to this point in the book, we have described the resource program concept, resource teacher roles, methods for initial implementation of the program, and referral and selection procedures. Little attempt has been made to differentiate these descriptions for elementary and secondary schools.[1] This is because there is not much differentiation on the topics discussed. The concept of resource programs does not change from elementary to secondary; the same categorical programs, cross-categorical programs, and the others exist at all levels in schools. Nor do the roles of the resource teacher change. At both they are expected to assess, teach, and consult. The procedures employed for initiating a program and selecting students for both systems are also very similar. The organization and curricula of both systems are somewhat different, however and, as a result, different management strategies are sometimes needed at the two levels. In this section, the major differences in organization and curricula are described.

The person responsible for the entire operations of an individual school is the building principal, who in turn is responsible to the district superintendent and a board of education. There is considerable variation of titles and line authorities throughout school districts. For example, some districts employ a great number of directors, supervisors, assistant or associate superintendents, and other administrators, and their relationship to principals may be somewhat different from locale to locale. All teachers, including resource personnel, should become very familiar with their district's administrative structure. Knowing who makes decisions and who is responsible for certain aspects of the educational endeavor is useful information.

There is considerable difference between elementary and secondary principals in their day-to-day relationship with teachers. In a typical elementary school, the principal relates directly to teachers on administrative and instructional matters. Secondary schools, however, are traditionally much larger than elementary schools. Consequently, secondary-level principals often do not deal directly with each teacher; instead they delegate responsibility to guidance personnel, athletic directors, and department heads. Resource teachers need to determine who within their own school is responsible for specific administrative tasks.

There is considerable variation between elementary and secondary resource teachers in their relationship to other teachers. At the elementary level, resource teachers share major responsibility for an individual student with only one other teacher — the regular classroom teacher — because in most elementary schools, each classroom teacher is responsible for all of his or her students throughout the school day. Auxiliary personnel, such as gym teachers, art teachers, and counselors, are usually available to assist classroom teachers for a period or two a day, but for the most part, the regular classroom teacher bears the major responsibility for each child's instruction throughout the school day.

At the secondary level, however, resource teachers are likely to find that students assigned to their program see as many as five or six different teachers per day — homeroom teachers, mathematics teachers, history teachers, vocational education teachers, science teachers, and so forth. Each of these teachers may have a department head who is also vitally interested in what is happening with each student in their area. Resource teachers therefore must consult with many more professionals in the secondary schools. As a result the management of each student's program will take more effort.

Another difference between elementary and secondary schools relates to the curricula. At the elementary level, teachers focus on the development of basic reading, writing, and computational skills. At the secondary level, teachers focus on content-area subjects such as science, distributive education, history, and foreign language. This is not to say that content is not taught at the elementary level or that basic skills are not taught at the secondary level. Rather, there is a shift in emphasis between the two systems. Management will require more effort at the secondary level because of greater variety of course offering for students.

That there are differences between elementary and secondary schools should not imply that these organizational structures are discontinuous. As far as the individual student is concerned, the program begun in the elementary years should account for transitions between school levels. For example, during the last year of the elementary program, the primary emphasis of the resource program should shift to assessing and teaching the skills that will be needed in the next environment. Whether a sixth grader reads at level 10 or level 11 in a particular series is likely irrelevant to the real demands of the junior high school.

Serious considerations must be given by the district and especially by the resource teacher to the transition needs of students who move from one major program structure to another. (This is also the case when students move horizontally from one school to another rather than vertically through the grades.)

In order to provide transition programming, resource teachers at both ends of the transition must know each other's structure. The elementary teacher must understand the structure and demands of the secondary program to prepare students, and the secondary teacher must understand better the extent to which students have been prepared at the elementary level for realities of the secondary school.

In sum, the basic differences between elementary and secondary resource programming relate to administrative organization and curricula. Resource teachers will need to devote some time to investigating their own school's unique organization, as well as the course offerings. In addition, teachers should consider the offerings of the schools their students come from, as well as those they might eventually attend.

START-UP PROCEDURES

If possible, no students should be assigned to a new resource room during the first two or three weeks of its operation. There are several good reasons for this delay.

1. The delay gives the resource teacher ample time to reassess and plan programs for students who were in the resource program the previous year, many of whom will still need special resource services.

2. The delay allows regular and special teachers an opportunity to implement their own programs and to identify students in their classes whom they may want to refer.

3. The time interval can give the resource teacher, especially a new one, a chance to meet the other teachers in the building, to learn about the curricula used in the school, and to prepare the resource program for the coming year. Resource

teachers can accomplish this by visiting selected classrooms, and doing some short-term teaching demonstrations in order to try out new teaching techniques, familiarize themselves with the regular class curricula, and/or maintain their classroom teaching skills. On these occasions, resource teachers can become acquainted with regular teachers on a professional and perhaps personal basis, can get to know some of the students, and can learn first hand about the curricula used in the classes. Also, if done well, demonstration teaching is good for public relations. To ensure success, however, the resource teacher should be thoroughly prepared for these demonstrations.

4. If resource teachers are seasoned, and if time permits, they might want to devote part of this initial period to helping inexperienced teachers adjust to the first few weeks of school. The new teacher may need assistance in understanding the scope and sequence of particular programs used in the school, grouping the students for instruction, and establishing discipline. Any help that the resource teacher can provide would probably be most appreicated, for the first week or two of school can be a harrowing experience for a beginning teacher.

5. New resource teachers also should use this time period to become familiar with any other aspects of the school situation that might affect the resource effort, such as pertinent school policies and procedures, the instructional programs used throughout the school, the demographic characteristics of the community, record-keeping practices, and any special programs operating in the building. Some information that it might benefit the resource teacher to know is presented in Table 5 – 1.

This initial period should not get the reputation of being free time for resource teachers. Classroom teachers become justifiably concerned when other school personnel appear to have nothing to do. Resource teachers, therefore, should take the time to explain quite carefully to the school staff the purpose of the period and what activities are being conducted during the interval. In all probability, the activities will relate to planning and organizing the resource program and to assessing pupils who are likely to need resource support during the school year. The resource teacher should be visibly busy at all times, especially during this initial start-up period.

After the first two or three weeks of school, resource teachers should be fairly well organized regarding the program and well informed about the school. They will have assessed and assigned a few students to the resource program, organized their classrooms, meet all of the teachers, developed an understanding of the school policies, noted the potential trouble spots that might exist in the school (such as the teachers who are likely to refer too many or no students), and located a few students who might need special support but who have not yet been referred. The time has now come for the resource teacher to begin providing direct and indirect services.

Before discussing the preparation of student and teacher schedules, one additional point should be made. In some situations, the new program may not be allowed a two- or three-week grace period, the resource teacher may be given a list of students the first day of school and expected to begin the instruction program immediately. We believe that this type of placement procedure should be avoided if possible because it places an undue burden on the resource teacher. It is difficult, if not impossible,

TABLE **5 – 1.**
Specific Information That a Resource Teacher Should Have about School and Community

A. **GENERAL SCHOOL AND DISTRICT POLICIES AND PROCEDURES**
 1. School organization, including grade levels and sections
 2. School hours
 3. Use of secretarial services
 4. Ordering and use of supplies and materials
 5. Meeting attendance
 6. Social amenities and customs
 7. Duty schedules
 8. Workroom use
 9. Lunchroom schedules and policies
 10. Substitute teacher policies and preparation
 11. Student transportation
 12. Field trips
 13. Required permissions
 14. Liability questions
 15. Schedules of special personnel, such as art, music, or physical education instructors
 16. Aide policies
 17. Schedules of special support personnel, such as school psychologist; social, speech, and language therapist; and reading teacher
 18. Committee purposes, memberships, meetings, and processes
 19. Emergency procedures, such as medical, fire, and disaster
 20. Library or instructional materials center use and personnel
 21. Floor plan of the school
 22. General achievement levels and expectations
 23. Playground policies, schedules
 24. Parking
 25. Restroom locations and use policies
 26. Parent organizations and involvement
 27. School history
 28. Faculty evaluation, rationale, procedures, and schedules
 29. Bus schedules and routes
 30. Professional organizations: structures; influence; regulations
 31. Supervisory personnel: authorities and responsibilities
B. **INSTRUCTIONAL PROGRAM**
 1. Mandatory curriculum content or methodologies
 2. Scope and sequence of curriculum offerings
 3. Series or curriculum guide names and editions
 4. Grouping practices
 5. Standardized testing program: schedules and use
 6. Record keeping

TABLE **5 – 1.** *(Continued)*
**Specific Information That a Resource Teacher Should Have about School
and Community**

      7. Grading practices
      8. Accountability expectations
      9. Availability of required resources
    10. Supplemental assistance available
    11. Supervision patterns for instructional improvement

C. INDIVIDUAL STUDENT INFORMATION
      1. Rationale for current teacher assignment
      2. Cumulative records: form, function, accessibility, confidentiality
      3. Parent contacts and attitudes
      4. Reporting policies and practices
      5. Retention policies
      6. Behavioral expectations

D. CLASSROOM INFORMATION
      1. Specific curriculum scope, sequence, content, and methodologies
      2. Time/event schedule
      3. Floor plan with potential distractors identified
      4. Seating chart with student names
      5. Policies or customs idiosyncratic to that classroom
      6. Resources available for individualization
      7. Teacher preference in organization and management of the instructional
         program
      8. General experience and training history of the teacher
      9. Assessment procedures: academic and sociometric
    10. Discipline policies
    11. Independent work expectations and evaluation practices

E. COMMUNITY
      1. School boundaries and adjacent schools
      2. Names and locations of schools to which students are promoted, either
         middle schools or junior high schools; or those schools students have
         previously attended
      3. General community characteristics, such as housing appearance, open
         space, street lighting
      4. Community landmarks, such as stores, laundromats, parks, churches, and
         fire station
      5. Community health and social services, such as recreation facilities and
         programs, mental health centers, hospitals, and clinics
      6. Transportation system
      7. General attitude toward school and education

to begin relevant instruction without first completing a proper assessment of the
type described in Chapter 2. If resource teachers are expected to provide educa-

tional support on the first day of school to a full case load of children, they should arbitrate the matter with the school building principal or special education administrator. If a student's program is provided legally through special education, then permission must be obtained from parents or guardians to change any ongoing program that has been provided. Usually this permission is obtained during a spring meeting that deals with the student's yearly progress summary. Of course, seeking any alteration should be approached in a professional manner; the rationale for a two- or three-week planning period should be carefully spelled out, and the resource teacher's activities during this period should be clearly specified. The resource teachers also can point out that each teacher's load would be five or six students at the end of the first two weeks of school and that additional students would be added on a weekly basis until the full load had been reached. This process should take no more than six weeks. By phasing new students into an ongoing, operational program, difficulties in scheduling can be managed easily and ample time for assessment can be found.

SCHEDULING

One tedious and time-consuming task confronting the resource teacher is preparing and keeping student schedules. Included in this task are arrangements with individual teachers in order for students to receive assistance in the resource room. Resource teachers also must schedule their own time so as to include sufficient time each school day for planning, assessment, and consultation.

Careful consideration and deliberate planning are necessary for developing a schedule that will work agreeably in a given school. The following example will illustrate one difficulty in developing a suitable schedule.

Let us say that an elementary-level resource teacher has ten students who are severely impaired in reading ability. These children vary markedly in mental ability, type of reading disorder, age and temperament. How are they all to be grouped for instruction and scheduled to come to the resource room? To complicate matters further, some teachers want the students to attend the resource room during periods specified for reading in the regular classroom; other teachers refuse to release the student during that time; others prefer to have the resource teacher provide instruction in the regular classroom. It is obvious from this example that attaining a proper, agreed-on working schedule requires serious attention. To help, this section presents several example schedules that have been found useful in some schools.

The first schedule is the *staggered procedure.* In this schedule, students report to the resource room for no longer than one-half hour at a time; however, they may return to the resource room two or even more times during the school day. A schedule of this nature may look like this:

    8:30 – 9:00   Preparation
    9:00 – 9:15   Reading (3 students)

9:15 – 9:30	Reading (3 students)
9:30 – 9:45	Independent study skills (3 students)
10:00 – 10:15	Reading (3 students)
10:15 – 10:30	Mathematics (4 students)
10:30 – 10:45	Mathematics (2 students)
11:00 – 11:30	Consultation
11:30 – 12:00	Lunch
12:00 – 12:30	Lunchroom duty
12:30 – 12:45	Spelling (3 students)
12:45 – 1:00	Handwriting (5 students)
1:00 – 2:30	Assessment and consultation
2:30 – 3:00	Social studies (5 students)

In this staggered schedule, the resource teacher is emphasizing direct teaching, independent seat work, and reinforcement. Each student spends one-half hour at a time in the resource room on a school activity in which he or she is experiencing difficulty.

Here is an example illustrating this schedule. Steven is an eleven-year-old boy with pronounced problems in reading, writing, and attention. He reports to the resource room at 9:00 A.M. The resource teacher works directly with Steven and two other children for ten minutes on a reading lesson. Steven and his two schoolmates are then sent to another desk for fifteen minutes of independent exercises on the material covered during the direct instruction. Five minutes later, three other students enter the resource room for help in reading. At the end of their ten-minute direct instruction, they also go to another part of the room for a back-up exercise, and Steven and his schoolmates return to the teacher's desk so that the teacher can check and reinforce their work. Once this is completed, they return to their regular classrooms, and two other pupils enter the room for resource instruction. This procedure is repeated with various students in reading and mathematics until 11:00, when the teacher begins to consult with other teachers or parents. Steven returns to the resource room at 12:45 for help in handwriting.

Proceeding in this manner, the resource teacher may wish to provide the regular classroom teacher with back-up activities for use with Steven or even to give the boy additional work to be done at home. In any event, Steven has had one hour of resource support each day devoted to correcting a specific problem he is experiencing in school.

Other suggestions for scheduling in secondary schools include the following. (1) Study hall time could be used for resource room instruction. (2) Release time for course supplantation or shared instruction should be employed. Course supplantation refers to those instances where a student attends the resource room for special instruction in a subject area when he or she cannot function in the regular class. Shared instruction refers to those instances where the student may attend a regular class on a periodic basis, coming to the resource room on other days. (3) Resource students may elect to take a reduced load and extend their schooling for another year or so.

Barksdale and Atkinson (1971) suggest a different type of scheduling sequence that they find helpful in dealing with students in a resource program. Their schedule is as follows:

8:30 – 9:00	Planning and Preparation
9:00 – 10:15	Instructional Session, Group I
10:15 – 11:30	Instructional Session, Group II
11:30 – 12:00	Lunch
12:00 – 1:15	Instructional Session, Group III
1:15 – 2:30	Instructional Session, Group IV
2:30 – 3:15	Conference time with students, parents, regular teachers, other personnel [P. 14]

They report that this schedule was markedly aided by the presence of a full-time supportive person (an aide) in the resource room. Because of the aide's presence, the resource teacher could briefly visit the regular classrooms from which the pupils were referred. In addition, the presence of an aide gave the resource teacher plenty of opportunity to conduct adequate individual assessment, thereby allowing the resource teacher to fulfill all three roles.

Another schedule has been proposed by Hawisher (1975). She reported that this schedule was popular in South Carolina in learning disabilities resource programs:

8:00 – 9:00	Pre-School Planning
9:00 – 9:45	Group A
9:30 – 10:15	Group B
10:00 – 10:45	Group C
10:30 – 11:15	Group D
11:15 – 11:45	Planning Time
11:45 – 12:30	Lunch
12:30 – 1:15	Group E
1:00 – 1:45	Group F
1:30 – 2:15	Group G
2:15 – 3:10	Post-School Planning [P.39]

In this schedule, the resource teacher can work with two or three students for thirty minutes of individualized instruction. Students in this group would then work independently for fifteen minutes after the arrival of the next group. Hawisher noted that some resource teachers scheduled students on an alternative basis. For example, Group E can be divided into two subgroups, E^1 and E^2. E^1 may visit the resource room on Mondays, Wednesdays, and Fridays, whereas E^2 attends only on Tuesdays and Thursdays. The drawback is that this schedule allows no time for individual assessment and observation or for consultation in the regular classroom. Dropping one group and substituting these activities during that period rectifies the problem.

These schedules do not allow sufficiently for classroom observation and consultation during prime instructional time within the classroom. Therefore, daily schedules that include constant direct supervision of students should be modified so that resource consultation and observation can be conducted appropriately within the classrooms when it is most relevant — during instruction and independent study times. That is, direct instruction may occur two or three or four days each week, and alternate days should be spent within classrooms. The exact proportion of days spent in each setting would depend on the degree of classroom involvement desired or possible within the local situation.

Some resource teachers may wish to develop a schedule similiar to the ones presented but use it on alternate days. For example, a teacher may use a Hawisher schedule on Monday, Wednesday, and Friday. On Tuesday and Thursday, time may be allocated in this way:

8:00 – 8:30	Pre-School Planning
8:30 – 10:00	Implementing or monitoring programs within classrooms
11:00 – 11:45	Individual student conferences
11:45 – 12:30	Lunch
12:30 – 2:00	Classroom visitation and consultation
2:00 – 2:30	Student, parent, or teacher conferences
2:30 – 3:10	Preparation of data summaries and replanning

Schedules will likely change during the year as student needs change. This aspect of scheduling should be explained to parents and teachers early in the year. The idea of flexible scheduling allows grouping for temporary needs. Resource programs should not become a fixed alternative program unless it is impossible to modify the regular classroom to accommodate students' instructional needs.

These example schedules should provide resource teachers with models from which to select, modify, or build upon. Most teachers probably will never find a perfect schedule. But resource teachers may wish to try each schedule until they find one that is best suited to their talents and to the needs of the students in their school. Although a usable schedule may have been found, teachers should consider changing its portions from time to time to accommodate changing needs.

MOVEMENT BETWEEN CLASSROOMS

In any resource program operation, students have to move back and forth between the regular classroom and the resource room throughout the school day. It is inefficient and too time-consuming for a resource teacher to supervise movement by dropping students off and picking them up. Resource teachers who do this spend an inordinate amount of time walking around in the school halls. Consequently, students must be required to walk unsupervised between the classrooms. In some schools, and with most students, this provides no difficulty. In other schools and with a few students, this unsupervised movement is potentially harmful to the resource program operation and occasionally also to the resource student.

Consider, for example, a secondary school in which discipline is a serious problem and/or where Kim, the student coming to the resource room, is a conduct problem. If other students are in the halls unsupervised at the same time, Kim could verbally or physically abuse them. Also, she may stop off in the bathroom and/or other supervised rooms of the school and cut class. In addition, she may disturb other classrooms by looking in the doors, making faces at the other students or teachers, or any number of other activities available to any unsupervised teenager.

Chronic tardiness in reporting to the resource room or back to the regular classroom can adversely affect the quality of a child's instruction. For example, let us say that three students from three different classrooms in the school are to report to the resource room at 9:45 A.M. The needs of the students are similar so they receive instruction in the resource room as a group. But student 1 reports at 9:40, student 2 at 9:45, and student 3 at 9:50. Ten minutes have been wasted by one or more of the students and the resource teacher while the group has been getting organized. Readers to whom this tardiness seems insignificant should consider that this situation may go on group after group and day after day in both the resource room and regular classroom. The amount of time wasted yearly can be quite considerable, to say nothing of the problem it presents to teachers.

No magic formula or management system can entirely erase this movement problem. Rules, however, can be: (1) established with care and with the teachers' agreement; (2) frequently explained to both the regular classroom teachers and to the resource students; (3) monitored carefully; and (4) modified whenever appropriate for either an individual student or for all students who are required to move independently between classrooms.

One system for managing the behavior of the emotionally disturbed student in the classroom (Hewett and Taylor, 1980) was modified by one of the authors of this book in his supervision of resource programs. Hewett and Taylor recommened that the check marks be given for every work period. In these instances, the students were given two checks for starting their task on time, three if they followed through on the assignment, and five if they were respecting the rights of others, the limits of time, space, and activity, and the classroom rules. Using a management system such as this one, the resource teacher can give checks or points for reporting on time for class. Reinforcing a student for reporting on time stresses the significance of being punctual and increases the likelihood that she or he will be on time each day.

An example of this procedure will help to clarify its usefulness. If a student is to report to the resource room at 9:45 A.M., the resource teacher should calculate the amount of time needed to walk from the regular classroom to the special program. Three to five minutes usually is sufficient for a student to walk, not run, the distance. If a five-minute period were decided on, the student would be told to leave the classroom at 9:40 and to be in the resource room at 9:45. A student leaving the resource room at 10:15 would be expected to be back in the regular classroom at 10:20.

In this example, the student might receive five check marks for reporting on time to the resource room and five more for being on time back in the regular classroom. When a previously specified number of these check marks have been earned, they can be traded in for some reward. (The principles of reinforcement are discussed in Chapter 12 on classroom behavior.) In any event, a management system that allows the teachers and the student to focus specifically on movement between classes should be established.

As with any new system, however, problems will occur during the first months of its implementation; this will be especially true of the procedures used to control student movement to and from the resource room. Teachers and students may not be used to such a tight schedule and both may forget from time to time. Also, the students are going to test the system to see what happens. Persistence on the resource teacher's part can help students get used to a schedule. A drawing of a clock on their desks may help some students keep track of the time to report to the resource room.

For the student who tests the schedule, we, like most other teachers, prefer to approach this matter positively rather than negatively. That is, we prefer to emphasize the reward for punctual arrival rather than the punishment of tardiness. A student therefore should receive something that he or she values as a reward for meeting the time requirements.

Chronic tardiness should not be viewed as totally a student's problem. The problem could be in the program being offered in either the resource or regular classroom. One way to decrease lateness or absenteeism is to make the program interesting and relevant to each student.

Some regular classroom teachers may oppose the tight schedule and/or may not want to keep track of the resource student's movement. These teachers probably will have problems in dealing with other aspects of the resource program as well. Resource teachers must find the source of the difficulty and use their consulting skills to reach an agreeable solution.

Resource teachers must be patient during the first few weeks or even months of any movement management system that they have set up, and they must consistently follow through on the system that is implemented. Where this consistency is adhered to, the resource teacher can expect that after a period of time, the problems associated with travel between classrooms will be fewer.

GRADING

As mentioned in Chapter 1, the resource teacher must share with other teachers (usually the regular classroom teacher) the responsibility for the students who receive resource help. One shared responsibility relates to grading students' progress. In the regular class, grading generally is done by assigning a letter grade in various school subjects and in providing comments or check marks for social behavior. Resource teachers should be prepared to deal with some problems that may arise

when this type of grading is used. The following sections discuss some of these problems and make some recommendations about quarterly and daily grading.

Quarterly Grading

Many teachers base their grading of students' school performance on some arbitrary
criterion of proficiency. For example, if progress in reading is to be measured, the
teacher will analyze their accomplishments roughly in terms of grade-level achievement. As a result, fourth-grade students who read at the second-grade level often
are assigned flunking grades by their teachers.

Many educators are dissatisfied with this method of grading. Part of their
dissatisfaction is based on the premise that this type of grading does not account
for individual differences in ability or opportunity — differences over which students
have little control. Thus many students are punished by receiving low grades even
though they may be doing the best they can do. In many cases, the effect is punitive
and will likely dampen their enthusiasm for future learning. Critics of the traditional
grading system consider it destructive to the accepted goals of education.

In some schools, teachers have implemented a grading system that accounts
for the student's ability, performance, and progress. In these classes, children receive
high grades if they are viewed as doing as well as they are able. Sometimes no grades
are given at all; instead teachers either hold periodic conferences with the parents
or provide parents with descriptive reports concerning the pupil's school
performance.

In schools where a student's individual abilities, performance, and progress
are considered in assigning grades and/or where parent conferences or descriptive
reports are employed, there is little problem in grading students who receive resource
support. These approaches to grading are so individualized that any resource pupil
can be accommodated easily. During conferences, both parents and the students will
want to know the student's academic and/or social standing relative to that of peers.
Such information is critical to planning. Nevertheless, this kind of information need
not be used to grade the actual progress the student makes.

In schools where students are measured in terms of deviation from their
expected grade-achievement levels, problems will arise. The regular classroom
teachers, the principals, and/or the parents may be opposed to giving a report that
reflects variables other than this expected achievement level. For example, even
though Wayne may be receiving special reading instruction in the resource room
and doing very well, his achievement may be so low when compared with that of
other students his age that some teachers might give him a flunking grade.

In some schools where regular classroom teachers use traditional grading, some
resource teachers prepare their own report cards. Thus two grades are received —
one from the regular classroom teacher and one from the resource teacher. Another
variation is to give a student two grades for each subject area. One grade is based
on the child's progress relative to himself or herself, and the other grade reflects

his or her standing relative to grade-level achievement. On the report card, the grades appear like this: "A/D." The "A" stands for the student's achievement over the past few weeks. The "D" stands for the student's standing relative to the norm. In still other cases, the resource teacher may assume the sole responsibility for grading the pupil. When this occurs, an asterisk often is put beside the grade, and a footnote indicates that this is a resource grade.

Inherent in all these approaches, however, is the belief that even though the students are doing as well as they can, they *are still inadequate.* Consequently, we much prefer that: (1) students be graded only in relation to themselves; (2) parent conferences be employed; and/or (3) descriptive reports of progress be used. We believe that parents should be involved in the development and interpretation of the local grading system. Because the parents are responsible for the student's longitudinal lifetime planning, they are entitled to the most realistic information available to help with the planning process.

Professional concern about the detrimental effects of pass-fail grading systems has stimulated many conferences and publications about alternative grading systems. The book *Wad-ja-get?* (Kirschenbaum, Simon, and Napier, 1971) presents the rationale for nontraditional grading systems and includes an extensive annotated bibliography of references. Vasa (1981) has presented some alternative procedures for grading handicapped students in the secondary schools. His suggestions include alternative methods of assessing student progress through the use of verbal tests, shortened tests, modifying questions on tests by using more concrete items, increasing the amount of time allowed for a student to complete a test, employing checklists, and assessing mastery of content through a student's participation in class discussion or class projects. Resource teachers who are dissatisfied with the grading system used in their school should read these and other publications and then try to modify, where appropriate, the reporting format employed in their school.

Finally, secondary resource teachers will need to become familiar with their school district's policies regarding student credit hours and competency requirements for graduation. As with many other educational endeavors, there is some variation on these between school districts and/or state and provinces. In the case of credit hours, the number and types are usually specified that are needed to obtain a high school diploma. In addition, many districts have recently mandated a certain level of achievement in such areas as reading, mathematics, and written expression that is necessary before a student can obtain a high school diploma (Wiederholt, Cronin, and Stubbs, 1980). Both requirements need to be carefully considered when planning courses of study and grading of students in resource programs.

Daily Grading

A second type of grading considers the evaluation of students on a daily basis. In these instances, a student is graded every time he or she is asked to complete an assignment. These daily grades are helpful: (1) for teachers, students, and parents in keeping systematic and daily track of the achievement of individual students; (2) in motivating a pupil's continual effort; and (3) for indicating to teachers when they need to modify their teaching strategies. This last point often is overlooked. Daily grading systems can serve very well as an evaluation device for the effectiveness of the instructional programs.

Unfortunately, many teachers judge the daily achievement of a student almost solely upon performance on paper and pencil tasks, that is, they evaluate the student on a teacher-developed test or program worksheets. However, as Kim and Kellough (1978) have noted, many other types of activities furnish information on students' progress and development. These include the questions they ask during and after class, the responses they make to questions, the way in which they explain ideas to others, the manner in which they listen, the way in which they work in laboratory or workshop situations, the degree of their involvement in class discussions, as well as the kinds of challenges they seek out or accept. The authors note that "although these activities do not fit into a numerical grading system, they may be more significant than the results of some formal, written exam (p. 209)."

Jones (1980) has stressed the importance of involving students in the grading process, and he points out several ways that they can participate. First, teachers can discuss grading procedures with a student or with an entire class. Jones notes that it is important in these discussions that students have a clear understanding about grading policies and the reasons behind teachers' decisions on grades. During these discussions, students may also provide teachers with helpful ideas concerning the grading process. Second, Jones suggests that individual conferences between teachers and students be employed. In these conferences, teachers can discuss the student's concern regarding testing and grading. These conferences can provide students with a feeling that the instructional goals are realistic and attainable. Third, students can help to evaluate their own work, a process that often increases motivation and also provides the student with meaningful feedback. Students can evaluate their own learning in several ways. For example, students can express in their own words what they have learned; they can keep a notebook in which they record in some manner what they are learning; class discussions can be held that focus upon what has been learned and how it can be applied. Jones has stated that when students participate in the grading process it becomes obvious that it

> provides students with better understanding, a greater sense of worth and more control over their environment. Also, it seems obvious that [this practice] has much greater potential for increasing students' skills in such areas as critical thinking, personal responsibility, and self-evaluation. [P. 146]

It is not uncommon to find resource students who have consistently received bad or unsatisfactory grades over a period of time. From our point of view, continued bad or unsatisfactory daily grades represents a failure of the program to provide adequately for the student. After all, the purpose of resource programming is to help students find both academic and social success. Consequently, poor performance is an indication to teachers that they need to modify the program's materials,

methods, arrangements, and/or contingencies. We recommend that any grades imply-
ing inappropriate performance be supplemented with suggested program modifications. Various means to modify most instructional programs are provided in Part
III of this book.

INDIVIDUAL EDUCATIONAL PLANS

Resource teachers most likely will need to prepare educational plans for each student in the resource program. These plans usually are based on a thorough assessment of the specific problems that the student is experiencing in school. These plans
also specify the intervention strategies designed for both the resource room and the
regular classroom. In general, most educational plans formulated by resource teachers
include certain information. First, the plan specifies what the student will be taught.
For example, if Linda is to be taught to spell a list of words, these words will be
recorded.

Second, the plan delineates the specific information or skill that will be taught
at each step in the instruction. If, for example, Linda is expected to be able to spell
forty words, not all words would be given to her at once to learn. Perhaps only five
words would be presented each day. The resource teacher often writes the words
taught at every step into performance objectives; for example, "Linda will be able
to spell the following five words in sentences and on request: *city, street, address,
sign, number."*

Third, most daily records specify the methods and materials to be used to teach
the information or skill. Using the example of Linda, the teacher may plan to use
Fernald (1943) steps in teaching spelling: the word to be learned is written on paper
by the teacher; the teacher and child pronounce each word; the word is erased; and
the student writes it from memory. The word is again written from memory, arrangements are made for the word to be used in sentences, and so on.

Fourth, most daily plans also specify the motivational component of the instruction. To try to teach almost anything to a student who has a learning or behavior
problem without including some motivation component probably will not be pro-
ductive. Consequently, the rewards that the resource teacher has discovered to be
motivating for Linda are included as part of the plan. The evaluation of Linda's performance each day, or periodically, also should be noted on the record. Where
improvement is not made, plans for reteaching or curricular adaptations are made.

Using a standard form for each individual plan facilitates record keeping; and
once explained to parents, teachers, administrators, and students, these forms can
be easily interpreted by them. To help resource teachers develop their own forms,
we have included an example in Table 5 – 2. Another form for an individual educational plan in mathematics is found in Chapter 7 on mathematics.

Table 5 – 2 contains five major sections. Section I gives an overall picture of
the student and the plan. The six items in Section II allow the resource teacher to
keep detailed records of the various services provided to the pupil. Section III is for

TABLE 5 – 2.
Individual Educational Plan

SECTION I

Student's Name _____

Assigned Classroom _____

Date of Program Entry _____

Prioritized Long-term Goals:

_____

_____

_____

_____

Summary of
Present Levels of Performance.

_____

_____

_____

_____

_____

SECTION II

Short-term Objectives	Specific Educational and/or Support Services	Person(s) Responsible	% of Time	Beginning and Ending Date	Review Date

SECTION III

% of Time in Regular Classroom: _____
Short-Term Objectives
1.
2.
3.
4.

% of Time in Resource Classroom: _____
Short-Term Objectives
1.
2.
3.
4.

SECTION IV

Specific Procedures/Techniques, Materials, Motivation, etc.

SECTION V

Criteria and Evaluation Procedurs for Each Goal Statement

a delineation of the pupil's short-term objectives in both the regular and resource classrooms. Additional settings may be added where appropriate. For example, if a child is also receiving speech therapy, the short-term objectives for the child in this program should be listed in Section III.

The categories in Section IV also can be divided into the various classrooms. In this manner, the instructional strategies used in each setting can be specified.

Finally, Section V is for the definition of the criteria and evaluation procedures for each goal statement. The goal statements are broader than the objectives. Learning the objectives should result in the pupil's successful achievement of the goal. The evaluation criteria should deal with how effectively the objectives are in helping a student reach the predetermined goal.

The form presented in Table 5 – 2 in addition to other examples found in this book, should provide resource teachers with sufficient information on preparing educational plans. Using these examples, they should be able to formulate their own format for an individual instructional plan that relates specifically to their own resource program. By adhering to the plan and the evaluation criteria, resource teachers should be able to monitor very closely the progress of their pupils and to document the effectiveness of the plan.

Some instructional plans developed by the resource teacher may not fit easily into one of the samples. For example, when the teacher and student are involved in analytic teaching and/or in the language experience approach, the method of instruction rather than the specific content to be learned is emphasized. Another situation that does not fit occurs when the teacher is attempting to decrease disruptive behavior. In these cases, baseline charting or other techniques discussed in Chapter 12, "Classroom Behavior," might be a more appropriate form of record keeping. A student working in a programmed text also does not fit into the sample In this case, the resource teacher has to specify in the individual instructional plans only what activities the student is to accomplish during each work period — the name and page number of the text. The teacher would wish to specify, however, the motivational techniques that are used and the techniques for evaluating the student's progress.

PARENTAL OR GUARDIAN INVOLVEMENT

Most parents or guardians of students with problems tend to be enthusiastic about the resource program from the beginning, so there is little problem in enlisting their support and involvement. A request by telephone or letter usually will bring these parents to the school for a meeting that will explain how they can help. Occasionally, however, a few parents or guardians will resist the program and/or the resource teacher and will avoid becoming involved.

Resource teachers should seek out parents or guardians and ask them to help implement and maintain the resource efforts. Parental help is important because it can: (1) minimize any parental criticism about the program (people are hesitant to criticize programs they participate in or have had ample opportunity to provide input for); (2) seek their approval to provide resource support to their child; (3) enlist their support and possibly active involvement in implementing the instructional plan; (4) obtain their constructive comments regarding program improvements; and (5) help the resource teacher maintain current information about the student's life and changing needs. This section makes some suggestions for seeking parental and guardian involvement and makes some recommendations about how to communicate effectively with parents.

Seeking Parental or Guardian Involvement

The first step in seeking parental or guardian support and participation is to notify them that their child is being considered for resource services. The procedures involved in the initial contact will vary from school to school. In some schools, principals, home-and-school coordinators, guidance counselors, or other staff make the initial contact with parents by telephone or by visiting in the home. The resource teacher will need to ask the building principal about the local policies regarding this matter.

The resource teacher usually is responsible for notifying parents. The initial contact with parents might be by telephone with a conference following or by letter requesting a conference. The letter should be typed on school stationery and bear the principal's signature as a co-signer.

Before writing the letter, the resource teacher should consult both the school records and other faculty members to obtain some information about the parents or guardians, including their awareness of the student's problem and their past experiences with the school. An example will illustrate the importance in getting information about the parents. Let us say that a child, Margaret Farnan, is living with an aunt who has a different surname. A letter sent to Mr. and Mrs. Farnan could be embarrassing for all involved. Another undesirable situation to avoid is sending a letter in English to parents who cannot read that language. In preparing a letter, the resource teacher should keep several points in mind. First the letter should be individually written; form letters should never be used.

Second, the use of esoteric or pseudo-professional jargon should be avoided in the letter. For example, if Margaret is having trouble in arithmetic, the resource teachers should say so; he or she should not write that the child has trouble in conceptualizing multiplication as union of sets or in mastering the role of zero. If the student is misbehaving in class, the resource teacher should give examples of the undesirable behavior rather than writing that "Margaret is suspected of being emotionally disturbed because of her hyperactivity." The reason a student has been referred for resource help should be stated simply, accurately, and in plain language.

Third, fear-provoking words should not be used. Such ill-defined terms include *serious, severe, critical, mentally retarded, brain damaged, emotionally disturbed,* and *dyslexic.* Instead the letter should contain a clear statement that the student is having some difficulty in school and that a special program is available.

Finally, the letter should be friendly in tone, short in length, clear in purpose, and contain some mechanism whereby the parents or guardians may respond. A sample letter about Margaret Farnan, who was referred to the reading resource program is shown in Table 5 – 3.

In most cases, a letter such as this will produce the desired results — the parents

TABLE **5 – 3.**
Letter to Parents or Guardians

(School letterhead)

(date)

Ms. Attie Lyles
(Address)
(City, State, Zip)

Dear Ms. Lyles:

Your niece, Margaret, is having some difficulty with her reading. Fortunately, we have a program in our school that we believe will provide her with the help she needs.

In order to provide Margaret with the best possible program, we need your cooperation and permission. Could you please come to the school for a short visit, at which time you can talk about the program with Ms. Ruth Angel? Any day during the week between 8 a.m. and 4 P.M. will be fine. If you have questions before that time, please call 494-3765, asking for Mr. Goff.

Please specify the time that you are available to attend the meeting on the form that is at the bottom of this letter, place the form in the attached envelope, and return it to Ms. Angel by mail or by Margaret. Thank you very much. We're looking forward to meeting you in person very soon.

Sincerely,

_____

John Goff, Principal

_____

Ruth Angel, Resource Teacher

- -

Dear Ms. Angel:
   I can come to the school on _____ *(date)*
at _____ *(time).*

                _____

                Ms. Lyles

Comments if any:

- -

or guardian will visit the school to discuss the child. Occasionally, however, this will not happen. The form may not be returned, the parents or guardian may work during the school hours, or they may not be able to leave the home due to health problems or because there are small children in the home. If the form is not returned, another letter should be sent. If there is still no response, a telephone call to the home is in order. Finally, if neither strategy works, the matter should be turned over to the principal, the special education administrator, a social worker, or other appropriate school personnel for a home visit.

Whenever someone other than the resource teacher is to make the contact with the parents or guardians, the resource teacher should tell him or her all that is known about the student and acquaint him or her thoroughly about the resource program. This information will enable the contact person to speak knowledgeably about both the program and the student. The resource teacher also will want to stress that he or she must eventually meet with the parents or guardians and to request that the contact person arrange such a meeting. Finally, the resource teacher will have to state specifically, perhaps in writing, what he or she wants to be accomplished during this initial meeting.

Communicating with Parents and Guardians

Teachers often view a meeting with parents or guardians as an opportunity to tell them what is "wrong" with their child and what progress the child has or has not made recently. In other words, teachers frequently talk to the parents in a grade card fashion — "Here is what your child is doing in math and here is how your child behaves in school." The parents want this information. But such a meeting also should give the parents a chance to contribute their observations and feelings about their children. They often have valuable information that the resource teacher can use to understand the student better and to develop a more appropriate instructional plan. The resource teacher therefore should plan carefully for the meeting and prepare to be an active listener.

Preparing for the meeting. In the first meeting, the parents or guardians probably want information about five topics: (1) what specific problems their child is having in school; (2) why it is believed the problems exist or the source of the problems (it is often hard to pinpoint a specific reason for the problems of concern to teachers; nevertheless, parents will want to know how the problems have come about and what the prognosis is for cure. Will temporary help be needed, or is the problem one that will require lifelong accomodations? Any statements made in this regard should be tempered both with truthfulness and with knowledge of our fallibility); (3) what the resource program is; (4) what type of help will be provided for their child and how long it will last; and (5) what they can do to support the resource effort. Resource teachers should have this information available when the meeting is held

When discussing the student's specific problems, the resource teacher should let the parents or guardians see assessment results, samples of the student's work, history data on the problem, and so on. The resource teachers also should include examples of what the student does well in school. It is important to give a fair picture of the whole student and not just focus on the negative aspects of performance.

Parents or guardians also will want to know what the resource program is and what type of help it will provide their child. Since the need for such information will be frequent, resource teachers probably should prepare a small handbook or paper describing the program. (This handbook also can be given to other members of the school staff and to community agencies.) The resource teacher should go over each point in the handbook with the parents or guardians. This procedure allows plenty of opportunity for discussion and clarification of points that may be unclear.

Finally, most parents or guardians want to know what they can do to help their child. The resource teacher should know what kind of support she or he wants from them. Does the teacher want them to help in the educational plan? (It is usually wise to consider any instructional plan as tentative until it has been discussed with parents. Their insights and their experience with their child may provide data that will change the best-laid plans. Further, it is hard for parents to believe a request for their help when plans are already cast in school district forms.) How does the teacher want them to reinforce positively the student for work efforts? How does the resource teacher want to schedule regular meetings with the parents or guardians? How often will these be held and for what purpose? Does the teacher want to set up some other type of communciation system with the parents or guardians? If so, what type of system? Some answers to these questions are discussed in Chapter 12, "Classroom Behavior."

As is evident, resource teachers will need to plan carefully for the meeting with parents or guardians. Specific information should be readily available and plans for future interactions should be made. Of course, the resource teacher should listen to and consider the parents' ideas throughout the meeting. Resource teachers should be prepared to deal with parents or guardians who claim no responsibility for helping the child and who lay the problems squarely on the school. These parents might assert, often with some hostility, that the school is at fault and that nothing is wrong with their child. Others might blame the child for being lazy, and/or no-good. Occasionally, a few parents or guardians even blame other adults, such as their spouses, grandparents, and teachers. In such cases, resource teachers must call on their consulting skills to the fullest and must be patient, calm, and flexible.

Active Listening. In conducting parent-teacher conferences, the resource teacher should assume the role of an active listener. The importance of being a good listener when communicating with parents or guardians has been stressed strongly by Kroth (1975) and Lichter (1976), among others. Good listening involves accepting (but not necessarily agreeing with) and interpreting what another person is saying in a nonjudgmental manner while still actively participating in the conversation.

In order to listen effectively, we suggest that resource teachers develop the four basic attitudes recommended by Gordon (1970). A good listener must: (1) really want to hear what the parent has to say and take sufficient time to listen; (2) be able to accept the parents' or guardians' feelings even when these feelings are different from his or her own; (3) trust the parents' ability to find some solutions to the problem their child is having; and (4) have a genuine desire to help. A resource teacher who does not have these basic attitudes probably will not be successful in dealing with parents or guardians.

What are active listening skills? Lichter (1976) presents the following guidelines for being an active listener. First, teachers should listen carefully for the basic message the parent is trying to convey. Second, teachers should restate what the parents say in a simple and concise summary. Third, teachers should observe or ask the parent if their interpretation of what the parent is saying is correct. Finally, the parents should be allowed to correct the restatement by the teacher if it is incorrect.

Two examples of how a teacher might respond to a parent follow. In the first example, the teachers is *not* being a good listener. Instead, he or she is lecturing the parent. In the second example, the teacher *is* being an active listener. In this latter case, he or she is simply restating what the parent was saying.

EXAMPLE I

Parent: Johnny has always been a problem. He is not like his brother at all. His brother never has had any problem with school.

Teacher: You should not compare Johnny to his brother. All children are different from one another.

EXAMPLE II

Parent: Johnny has always been a problem. He is not like his brother at all. His brother never has had any problem with school.

Teacher: You feel that Johnny has always had problems with his school work?

Good listening involves more than just restating what another person has said. The possible meaning of the statement also must be interpreted. For example, from the conversations just cited, it appears that the parent is comparing Johnny negatively to his brother. But the parent might be trying to convey that he or she is a good parent; after all, the other son does not have any problems. Teachers always should be attentive to these nuances.

Resource teachers who have not had training in active listening may want to read further on this subject. We recommend Kroth (1975), Gordon (1970), and Lichter (1976) as rich sources of information. We also suggest that two or more teachers role play several meetings with parents before scheduling a parent-teacher conference.

PEER TUTORS

Resource teachers will likely find themselves in need of support staff to implement the program efficiently. We highly recommend that every resource teacher be assigned an aide; however, we recognize that while aides are provided as a matter of course in some districts, in others funds are not available for such support personnel. Regardless of the availability of an aide, we recommend the use of peer tutors. Not only can this practice be extremely helpful to the resource teacher, but an abundance of studies indicate positive success with such programs (see Ehley and Larsen, 1980, for a current review of the studies).

Many teachers resist using peer tutoring in their classrooms. They believe that such an approach is misusing students, and that the tutors should be learning new information rather than teaching others what they already know. We disagree. Students helping other students are learning appropriate social behaviors, as well as reinforcing and elaborating on their own skills and knowledge. What better way to teach the necessity of helping other members of society than by actually having people do so? Other teachers object to the use of peer tutors on the basis that these students are not trained to teach. We concur with this statement. Any effective peer tutoring program must have tutor training component, supervision, and evaluation. Simply putting two students together, one who has information and skill and the other who does not, probably will not result in significant improvement of the one needing help.

Ehly and Larsen (1980) have provided a practical guidebook and resource text on peer tutoring programs. They discuss techniques for establishing goals for tutors and learners; strategies for training tutors, selecting students, and pairing students with tutors; methods for structuring peer tutoring programs; examples of content of instruction; guidelines for organizing large-scale programs; techniques for setting up programs for students with physical, emotional, or learning problems; methods for using adults as peer tutors; and activities associated with peer tutoring programs.

Since resource teachers will likely want to train tutors, we paraphrase here seven steps recommended by Ehly and Larsen in training sessions.

1. The tutor should be trainined to put the tutee at ease. Resource teachers should emphasize that tutoring can be fun and that tutors should be friendly at all times.
2. The tutor should be able to clarify the required tasks and delineate the required behaviors.
3. Part of the tutoring should be geared toward helping the tutor learn ways to show the tutee how to verify answers.
4. The tutor should be trained in the appropriate use of forms, worksheets, marking or recording responses, and/or tutor logs.
5. A large segment of training should be upon teaching the tutor to avoid any form of punishment.
6. Tutors should be trained in the use of both verbal and tangible rewards.
7. Training should include what constitutes mastery of the subject being taught.

The organization and supervision of a peer-tutoring program calls for a great number of management skills, particularly during the initial operation of such an effort. For the resource teacher to serve as a tutor is much too limited for the possibilities and responsibilities we advocate. As a result peer tutors will need to be located, trained, and supervised by resource personnel.

EVALUATION OF THE PROGRAM

The word *evaluation* often arouses some fear in the minds of those whose programs are going to be examined. Clichés such as "Nobody likes to have their work evaluated" and "People don't like to be told what they are doing wrong" are frequently heard in an institution that soon will be evaluated. Yet evaluation can be a rewarding and helpful experience, and it is a necessary, desirable, and ongoing process in any program. Consequently, resource teachers should expect to be evaluated, should be well prepared for it, and on many occasions will want to conduct their own evaluations. This section discusses types of evaluation procedures: (1) program components; (2) program outcomes; (3) administrator perceptions; (4) consumer satisfaction; and (5) colleague evaluations.

Program Components

In a program evaluation, all elements that play a part in the successful operation of the resource model are assessed periodically. These components include: (1) physical environment; (2) curriculum; (3) time allocated for specific activities; (4) factors that relate to the resource pupils; (5) personnel involved in the resource effort; (6) planning and monitoring process; (7) reporting procedures; (8) record keeping; (9) materials used in the program; and (10) public relations activities. Other components also might be included for evaluation by resource program personnel.

Table 5 – 4 contains a suggested format for the program evaluation. This sample form elaborates each component listed above. For example, the component Physical Environment includes room size, horizontal use of space, and vertical use of space. By each component, the resource program personnel can note the current status of these points as S – Satisfactory or NS – Not Satisfactory. Suggested corrective steps can be listed beside each NS item along with the person(s) responsible for constructive action. NS items are of two types — those readily fixed and those requiring substantive or collective effort. These latter NSs can be numbered in terms of priorities, and realistic timetables can be set for their accomplishment. A specific time also should be scheduled for periodic review and modification.

Table 5 – 4 is presented as a guide for administrators and teachers who want to undertake a program evaluation. We encourage these professionals to develop their own format that directly relates to the program under consideration. The evalua-

TABLE **5 – 4.**
Program Evaluation

Components	Status S/NS	Suggested Corrective Action	Personnel	Priority	Timetable
A. Physical environment					
1. Room size					
2. Horizontal use of space					
3. Vertical use of space					
4. Light					
5. Materials storage					
6. Flexibility					
7. Pupil movement					
8. Furniture: nature/ arrangement					
9. Teacher role in					
10. Pupil space requirements					
11. Areas: work, play, storage, individual, group					
12. A-V aids					
13. Office space for teacher and aides					
14. Expansion possibilities: other room, hall; etc.					
15. Restroom distance					
16. Ventilation					
17. Sound level					
18. Room location					
B. Curriculum					
1. Definition					
2. Topic selection: academic, social					
3. Materials available					
4. Selection procedures					
5. Administration/super-vision					
C. Time					
1. Planning: group; individual					

TABLE **5 – 4.** *(Continued)*
Program Evaluation

Components	Status S/NS	Suggested Corrective Action	Personnel	Priority	Timetable
2. Accounting for: monitoring					
3. As a manipulatable instructional variable					
4. Pupil self-timing					
5. Devices: stopwatches, clocks, stamps					
6. For planning/ communication					
7. In a time/event/transition schedule					
D. Pupils					
1. Screening processes					
2. Selection for service criteria					
3. Placement for service rationale					
4. Academic assessment					
5. Social assessment					
6. Records					
7. Task					
8. Responsibility for					
9. Scheduling in/out					
10. Pre/post program monitoring					
11. Reentry plans					
12. Data sources					
13. Contingency management					
14. Stimulus considerations					
15. As instructional personnel					
16. Grouping bases					
17. Role in staffings; program development					

TABLE **5 – 4.** *(Continued)*
Program Evaluation

Components	Status S/NS	Suggested Corrective Action	Personnel	Priority	Timetable
E. Personnel 　1. Parents 　2. Colleagues: special ed.; general ed. 　3. Aides 　4. Other school personnel: principal, secretary 　5. State department 　6. Local administrators and supervisors 　7. University personnel 　8. Sources of assistance: aides, peer tutors, etc. 　9. Psychologist 　10. Speech and language therapist 　11. Counselor 　12. School social worker 　13. Community agency personnel					
F. Planning/monitoring 　1. Purposes 　2. Formats 　3. Revisions 　4. Types: system; pupil; group; emergency; routines, pupil-teacher, etc. 　5. Time for 　6. Events in a time/event/ transition schedule 　7. As a means of suggesting system changes/ needs					
G. Reporting 　1. Purposes					

TABLE **5 – 4.** *(Continued)*
Program Evaluation

Components	Status S/NS	Suggested Corrective Action	Personnel	Priority	Timetable
2. Timing					
3. Frequency					
4. Storage/retrieval; protection (confidentialities)					
5. Formats					
6. Targets: parents, pupils; administrators/supervisors; colleagues; self					
7. Self: teacher; pupil; parents					
H. Record Keeping					
1. Formal/informal					
2. Continuous/pre-post					
3. Format: graphics; organization					
4. Selection					
5. Keeper: pupil; peer; teacher; parent; other					
6. Storage/retrieval/ confidentiality/use					
I. Materials					
1. Manipulative devices					
2. Self-assessment features					
3. Self-correcting features					
4. Self-recording features					
5. Audio-visual considerations					
6. Multilevel teaching materials					
7. Modifications					
8. Sources of materials/ creators and makers					
9. Analysis dimensions					
10. Horizontal/vertical use					
11. Storage and accessibility					

TABLE **5 – 4.** *(Continued)*
Program Evaluation

Components	Status S/NS	Suggested Corrective Action	Personnel	Priority	Timetable
12. Commercially prepared/ teacher prepared					
J. Public relations Target groups or persons					
1. Parents: individually; organizations					
2. Administrators/super-visors					
3. public					
4. Legislators					
5. School board					
6. Colleagues: special/ general					
7. Other curriculum personnel					
8. Universities					
Plans for informing re:					
1. Nature of program					
2. Successful aspects					
3. Self-training/ competencies					
4. Availability for further communication					
5. Willingness to share ideas					
6. Accountability procedures					

tion then should be done by administrators, teachers, or other personnel on a periodic basis.

This type of program evaluation procedure has two major strengths. First, what is to be evaluated is predetermined. That is, the people involved in the resource program know what components of the model will be evaluated. Individuals usually are more comfortable when they know specifically what is going to be evaluated. Second, the focus of the evaluation is directed more toward the program than toward the resource teacher. This type of evaluation does not interpret the program as the role responsibility of one individual. Because the responsibility for the program's effectiveness is shared by all who are involved in it, it is evaluated in that way.

We prefer the program evaluation format for the reasons specified above. However, the resource teacher also can use other evaluation procedures, which include different strategies. In these procedures, care must be taken to avoid making the resource teacher rather than the resource program the focus of the evaluation.

Program Outcomes

The increasing trend toward accountability for special programs will likely affect the resource programs. Often this is called an evaluation of program outcomes, or "what kinds of growth can we expect from students who receive resource support?" Specific questions usually asked by superintendents and school boards include: (1) How much progress have resource students made this year? and (2) How much progress can be expected in the future based upon the past history of the students? These questions and others, are predicated upon the reasonable assumption that achievement will be improved as a result of having been in a resource program.

The information needed to answer program outcome questions sometimes will be gained by standardized achievement tests adopted by the district. In these cases, all students in the district, including those in resource programs, are tested annually. Figure 5 – 1 demonstrates how the resulting data may be reported. The vertical axis gives grade level, the horizontal axis the year. Both the average achievement of regular class students and resource programming are reported. The resource program in this example was implemented in 1983, showing a marked increase in achievement of the students, even though it remains less than regular class students. By extending the lines, one can predict with some certainty increased achievement as a result of the program.

Other options for evaluating program outcomes include annual testing of all resource pupils and a representative sample of regular program students. Achievement tests may be administered annually to all resource program students and on alternate years to regular program students. Or achievement tests may be administered annually to resource program students only. In many districts, program evaluation personnel will be available to help the resource teacher analyze the data. In analyzing the data, teachers should be attentive to the nuances of testing, a topic discussed in Chapter 2.

Administrator Preceptions

Resource teachers may want to know what their principal and district supervisor think about the resource program. Most likely, this evaluation will be done formally to distinguish it from the day-to-day feedback that the resource teacher probably

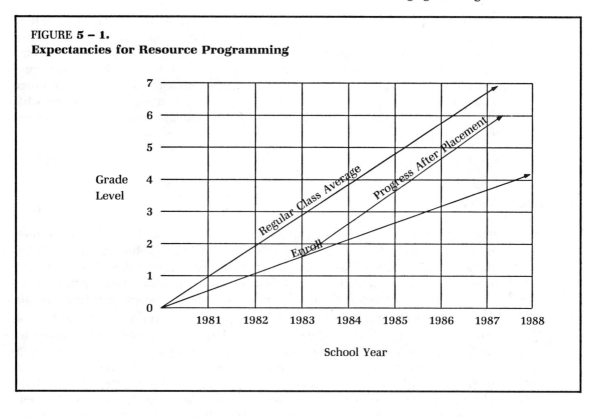

FIGURE 5 – 1.
Expectancies for Resource Programming

gets from the administrators. For this formal type of evaluation, we prefer the interview technique. In these interviews, the resource teacher first asks the principal and supervisor what they think are the strengths and weaknesses of the program and then elicits some suggestions from them as to how the effort can be improved. The resource teacher takes notes on the responses to the questions asked and later analyzes them.

The resource teacher can prepare for this interview by listing some questions to use as a guide. However, the questions should not be followed slavishly. The resource teacher may want to probe some areas in more depth and allow the administrators the latitude to divert into areas that they wish to discuss.

As in the case of communicating with parents, resource teachers will want to listen carefully. When perceived weaknesess are pointed out, they should not become defensive or try to blame others for the problem. Instead, resource teachers should ask the administrators for the reason that they think a particular component is weak and also solicit suggestions for rectifying the situation.

Resource teachers should be aware that some administrators may approach this formal interview with some uncertainty. They may not be sure how honest they should be with the resource teacher; they may feel uncomfortable making negative statements about the program; a few may be hesitant to make positive comments about the program. In addition, some may get off the subject of the resource program entirely and discuss their other concerns about the school. The resource teachers should set the ground rules for the interview; they should specify what they expect from the meetings and keep the discussion relevant to an evaluation of the program.

Consumer Satisfaction

The consumers in a resource program are the students in the program and their teachers and parents. The formal interview is a good way to obtain evaluation information from students. Throughout the year, the resource teacher should ask each student what he or she likes and dislikes about the program and suggestions for improving it. The teacher should take notes on their responses for future analysis.

Some teachers may feel that resource students are too young or immature to participate in an evaluation of the program. Think again! Young children often are quite aware of and influenced by the opinions of others in their environment. Consequently, their answers to questions will reflect in part their perceptions of what their classmates, teachers, and parents feel about the resource program. Also, most of them can give good suggestions for improving the program. Resource teachers may be surprised at what they can learn from their students about the program.

For teachers and parents, we prefer a questionnaire approach because it is not as time-consuming as an interview. When one or two responses are negative, however, the resource teacher will want to follow up the questionnaire with a formal interview.

In the questionnaire, resource teachers should ask specific questions rather than open-ended questions such as, "What do you like about the resource program?" Specific questions are important because most consumers will not be sure of what points they should respond to. The questions should focus on the benefits the consumers feel that they and their children are receiving from the program. Some questions will relate to whether they have noticed any improvements in the resource students since they were enrolled in the program. Other questions will be directed toward whether the teacher has received any useful help from the resource program in dealing with problems. The questionnaire also should solicit suggestions from improving the program. The questionnaire should ask only a few questions. Esoteric or lengthy questionnaires are inappropriate and take too much time. Whenever a responder specifies any problem, the resource teacher should follow up with a formal interview. Resource teachers may want to develop separate questionnaires for the teachers and for the parents. A sample questionnaire is presented in Table 5 – 5.

TABLE 5 – 5.
Sample Questionnaire for Parents and Teachers

Name: _____

	YES	NO	UNSURE
1. I feel that my resource child (student) is improving because of the program.	___	___	___
2. I have some recommendations that I would like to make for improving the program for my child (student) that I have not made.	___	___	___
3. The information provided me on my child (student) has been helpful.	___	___	___
4. I feel I need additional information on helping the child (student).	___	___	___
5. Overall, I believe the resource program is meeting the objectives that were outlined	___	___	___

Any additional comments:

Strengths:

Weaknesses:

Recommendations:

Colleague Evaluation

One of the most practical and useful evaluations is the one done by colleagues of the resource teacher — other resource teachers in the district. The evaluation is accomplished by a site visit. That is, resource teachers from other schools visit a program, observe it in operation, interview administrators, parents, other teachers, students *and* the resource teacher. They then give a written and/or oral evaluation along with some recommendations. If the resource teacher has been evaluated by administrators and consumers, these results should be given to the site visitors. After reading and reviewing these evaluations, they may or may not wish to interview these other people.

We cannot stress strongly enough the value of this type of evaluation. Other resource teachers have many of the same problems and often have found practical solutions to some of these difficulties. We heartily encourage that this peer evaluation be done at least once a year in each school in a district with a resource program. This is not a difficult task to arrange administratively. Observation days usually are built into any teacher's contract so that a teacher can take a day or two off without any loss in pay or in allowed absentee days. However, pressure to use observation days in this way should not be undue. In addition, resource teachers often can cancel their classes for half a day in order to serve as a peer evaluator. When resource teachers are the evaluators, they usually learn a lot that they can use in their own programs.

Resource teachers may encounter some difficulties with the teacher's union if they use free days to evaluate a colleague. They should check with union officials before proceeding. If the union objects, then perhaps resource teachers from one district could visit specific programs in another part of the district and then meet as a large group to formulate the entire district's resource program development. This type of activity could easily serve as inservice training for all resource teachers in the district.

Using the Results of the Evaluation

The resource teacher will need to take the results of the various evaluations and compile them into some usable form. The compilation should include a list of the program's strengths, weaknesses, and recommendations. All redundancies should be removed, although the number of times one point was referred to should be noted. For example, if six teachers, one administrator, three students, and four peers all said that two strengths of the program were the management system used to move students between classes and the positive attitudes of the students toward the program, these responses would be recorded in the following manner:

NUMBER

POSITIVE	NEGATIVE	
14	0	1. Management system for movement between classes.
14	1	2. Positive attitude of students for the program.

The next step is to provide feedback on the evaluation to those who participated. By using the format suggested in Table 5 – 6, this report is almost self-explanatory. The next step is for the resource teacher and others to analyze those "Weaknesses with Recommendations" and to make some decision as to which suggestions will be integrated into the current operations of the program. Feedback should be made to the appropriate individuals on these changes or modifications.

The most difficult step in using the evaluations relates to the "Weaknesses

TABLE **5 – 6.**
Sample Resource Program Evaluation

Date _____
Type of Evaluations
_____ 1. Administrators
_____ 2. Consumers
_____   A. Students
_____   B. Parents/guardians
_____   C. Colleagues
_____ 3. Peers

STRENGTHS
NUMBER
_____ 1.
_____ 2.
_____ 3.
_____ 4.
_____ 5.

WEAKNESSES WITH RECOMMENDATIONS
WEAKNESS   RECOMMENDATION
_____ 1.   1.
_____ 2.
_____ 3.   2.
_____ 4.
_____ 5.   3.

                            4.

                            5.

WEAKNESSES WITHOUT RECOMMENDATIONS
_____ 1.
_____ 2.
_____ 3.
_____ 4.
_____ 5.

ADDITIONAL COMMENTS FROM RESOURCE TEACHER

without Recommendations." There are several ways to deal with these weaknesses. First, resource teachers may survey the literature relative to the problem area to find if other teachers have found ways to deal with a particular difficulty. They may ask experts for some recommendations; such experts include state department personnel, local supervisors, district personnel, university professors, and/or other teachers. A second approach would be to ask several members of the school staff and some parents to serve on a problem-solving committee. The purpose of this committee would be to come up with recommendations for the resource teacher. These two approaches may be integrated in that the resource teacher may compile some information to bring to the problem-solving group for their analysis and comments.

The most important thing that the resource teacher must do is to use the evaluation to improve the program. Unfortunately, we have found that too often the evaluation results are used simply to justify continued existence of a program. If resource teachers use the evaluation results for making improvements, they will find that after a few years their programs are indeed efficient and effective operations.

Chapter 2 of this book described in some detail the resource teacher's roles: assessing, teaching, and consulting. In Chapters 3, 4, and 5, we described another critical role: program management. Such matters as preparing the school staff and parents for the program; public relations; pupil selection; processing referrals; serving on multidisciplinary staffings; scheduling; grading; involvement of peers, parents, or guardians in the efforts; and evaluation of the program have been overviewed. A resource teacher who does not manage well will likely fail. Conversely, effective attention to management will pay high dividends and make the resource activities much easier for all concerned.

It is appropriate here to mention one other management area: the resource teacher's management of her or his personal mental health. The demands of the job are extensive and may include some stress. DeShong (1981) has recently detailed some strategies for stress management. Although writing primarily to special educators, her comments are applicable to all who work with students experiencing difficulty: "Accomplishing management of job stress in . . . education means moving beyond the process of merely coping with situations and events. A stress-managed workstyle involves a changed relationship with self, others, and the . . . education environment. Such changes do not come easily or quickly" (p. viii).

ENDNOTES

1.　Middle schools and junior and senior high schools are grouped together in this section as secondary schools. This is because the differences between these subcomponents of secondary schools are minor. Marsh, Gearheart, and Gearheart, 1978.

PLANNING APPROPRIATE
INDIVIDUAL PROGRAMS

The first two parts of this book discussed many critical issues concerning the nature of the resource program, the competencies of resource teachers, and the methods by which the model can be implemented and managed in the schools. The third part of the book focuses on a more fundamental topic: How does the resource teacher plan and execute effective educational programs for individual children? This question is at the very heart of the entire resource effort. If the needs of the referred student are not met, then it does not matter that a suitable resource model has been selected; that the principal, teachers, and parents are supportive; that materials are available; or that the room is large and well equipped.

To plan and implement effective programs for referred students, resource teachers will have to apply diligently and simultaneously all of the competencies described in Chapter 2. That is, they must use successfully their assessment, teaching, and consulting skills in a dynamic, integrated, and ongoing fashion; this is good teaching. The eight chapters in Part III will help resource teachers master this integrative process.

Because students who are referred for resource help usually manifest problems in one or more of seven areas (reading, arithmetic, spelling, handwriting, written expression, spoken language, classroom behavior, and study skills), each chapter in Part III deals with one of these common complaint areas. Each chapter provides: (1) a brief overview of the subject area being considered; (2) a guide for collecting pertinent data about the dynamics of the problem; the teacher's expectations, attitudes, and teaching techniques; and the classroom 'climate'; (3) several ways of analyz-ing the specifics of the difficulty through individual assessment; (4) alternatives for selecting promising intervention strategies; and (5) some information about particular approaches to assessment and intervention that we think will succeed. Studying these chapters will help the resource teacher plan programs for specific students in the subject areas covered. We view all of this valuable information as minimal, at best, and recommend that resource teachers consider the chapters as points of depar-ture for their continued study of the topics involved.

6

Reading

Most students who are referred for resource help probably have difficulty in some aspect of reading. Although a lot has been written about reading and reading problems, the information available is often redundant, conflicting, and limited. This is especially true in regard to assessing and treating reading problems. It is beyond the scope of this chapter to examine all literature on the complex issues, problems, and procedures related to acquiring and improving reading competence. Instead, our comments and recommended procedures are based on two considerations. The first is our belief that some courses of action are more critical and/or promising than others. We therefore advocate the approaches that now are thought to be the most instructionally relevant and professionally defensible. Our second consideration relates to the unique role of the resource teacher in the school — responsibility for assessing, teaching, and consulting. Information relating directly to these three functions is emphasized.

ANALYSIS OF THE LEARNER IN THE CLASSROOM

The answers to the questions discussed below will give the resource teacher a broad perspective on the instructional practices of the classroom from which a student has been referred. These answers should be used to obtain clues for working on an individual basis with the referred student and also to determine what measures might be taken to involve that student in a more appropriate program within the regular classroom.

1. *What does the referral information look like, and why?* Referral forms are intentionally brief because they are used primarily as a way of indicating that a potential problem needs further attention. Because their information is either introductory or sketchy, it must be elaborated on in order to: (1) understand the specific behaviors that led to the students' being referred; (2) clarify any inexact terms; and (3) gain clues about the experience, training, and attitudes of the teacher(s) making the referral. This elaboration usually is obtained by interviewing the teacher, often using the completed referral form as the basis for the discussion.

2. *What are the intended meanings of any special terminology used on the referral form?* The field of reading contains an overabundance of terminology. Because definitions and interpretations of many terms vary widely, the resource teacher must obtain an exact behavioral description of the referred problem from the teacher. Statements such as "Marianne has a perceptual problem" are meaningless. To one teacher, it could mean that she could not name the letters of the alphabet. To another, it might suggest inattention during instruction. To a third teacher, it might mean that her penmanship was poor. Even when an apparently direct description is given, such as "She can't do consonant blends," the resource teacher must determine if this means that the child cannot use blends in spoken words, cannot read isolated blends presented on flash cards, cannot do workbook tasks, or just choose not to "do" consonant blends. Clarifying ambiguous terms will improve communication and thus will help the resource teacher analyze the problems more quickly.

3. *What additional information does the teacher provide about the instructional problem(s)?* The necessary briefness of the referral form means that classroom teachers cannot provide sufficient details about the reading problem itself. Therefore, in an interview with the resource teacher, the referring teachers should describe the unique aspects of the problem, such as how the difficulty differs from similarly observed problems and how the student seems to view the difficulty. The resource teacher uses this information to confirm or disconfirm the presence of a problem, to identify gaps in the information provided, and to obtain a more complete picture of the circumstances that have produced the reading problem.

4. *What influence might the referring teacher's impressions of the student or of the problem have on long-range instructional planning?* Information volunteered by the classroom teacher about the problem is critical for two reasons. First, whether valid or not, the teacher's perceptions are an important part of the instructional environment. Often in helping a student, a resource teacher must deal with both the reading problem and the expressed beliefs of the teacher. For example, the classroom teacher saw dramatic improvement in the reading behavior of an eight-year-old boy, but his reading grade moved only from an "F" to a "D." The teacher's reason was that "he has an emotional block and only seems to be doing better. He will not really be improved until that block is discovered and removed." The resource teacher's failure to heed and deal with this teacher's original referral statements about the child's emotional problem must now be rectified.

There is another reason for attending to teacher perceptions: if the classroom teacher does not think that a recommended course of treatment will ameliorate the problem specified in the initial referral, then she or he probably will not carry out that recommendation (Lovitt, 1967). For example, the classroom teacher may think that a student having trouble reading science or social studies may need reading instruction. Subsequent analysis, however, might suggest that a wiser course would be for the classroom teacher to spend more time building the conceptual background necessary for dealing adequately with these curricular areas. In the referral interview, the resource teacher can discover clues about how the teacher's experience, training, and attitudes might affect one recommended course of action over another.

5. *What is the nature of the standardized test information available?* Historical and current standardized test information should be examined to document the nature of tests administered and the interpretations that have been made of the results. If the student has been in a special program, tests administered there also should be reviewed.

In some schools, only tests that accompany an instructional program are given. Although such tests may be good indicators of how a student has progressed in the program, they may not reflect reading achievement in general. Therefore, some valid and reliable measure outside the local program may need to be administered to determine measured progress or achievement in reading.

Any testing that has been completed as part of a minimum competency assessment should also be examined. Scores from these tests are often used for making major instructional decisions about students. Further, the resource teacher may eventually be placed in the position of having to verify or discredit these test scores. And it may also be an assigned responsibility of the resource teacher to make sure that the student passes the test, regardless of the contribution of such instruction to the student's actual reading abilities.

The resource teacher should look at test scores already available for the age and the kinds of scores reported. If test scores are old, they will not represent the current status of the student's reading. A new test may need to be administered in order to make any valid inferences about how the student's reading compares with that of peers.

Reading tests are so numerous and varied that the test manual and the forms should be examined to determine the nature of the content and the technical information about validity, reliability, and the normative populations used to standardize the test. If the technical information is not given or if it does not show that the test has adequate validity and reliability, a note to that effect should be placed by the scores.

Even if statistical information about a reading test is adequate, its theoretical base is often questionable. Because of this, we emphasize the need for a careful examination of construct and content validity. It is one thing to say that a student failed to "read" a test that required knowledge of technical items such as the schwa, digraphs, and diphthongs and quite another if he or she failed to read story or informational material.

6. *What methods and materials are used and have been used with the student?* It is a rare student who cannot learn to read. Some have not learned to read because of the methods and materials used with them so far. When encountering nonreading students, therefore, the resource teacher probably will recommend modifications in the present approach. To determine the nature and extent of these changes, the resource teacher must know the reading materials and methods currently being used.

Occasionally the resource teacher will want to know which programs were used in the earlier grades. For severe reading disability problems, it is wise to compile a list of techniques used previously. These can be discussed with the student to find out how he or she perceived their use. These techniques should not be repeated unless there is good reason, and then any emotional residue the student has should be taken into consideration before recommending them.

Historical information about methods and materials can also be important because many family moves or many different reading programs can contribute to a reading disability. Because reading programs differ in content, methodologies, and skill sequences, the resource teacher must make a careful, detailed analysis of the curricular history in reading.

Many sources are available to teachers who want discerning information about reading programs. For example, the Educational Products Information Exchange (EPIE) has produced several reports dealing with reading materials (1973, 1974). Further, their EPIE PRO/FILES offer point-by-point descriptions of thirty or more basal reading series. Updates are available during the school year in which purchase of the FILES is made. These profiles are intended to assist with textbook selection, but they are ideal for the curriculum analyst. (EPIE also provides a similar service in various content areas.)

Frequent articles on the analysis of reading materials also appear in such journals as *Reading Teacher* and *Language Arts*. Finally, we also recommend that resource teachers consider applying the generalized curriculum analysis guide found in this book.

Regardless of the program to be analyzed or the procedures used to conduct an analysis, the resource teacher initially looks for general features that can be modified. Ten of these general considerations are discussed below.

a. To what extent does reading instruction occur within the program? Durkin (1978 – 1979) has reported that classroom observations that were originally intended to analyze the methods used for teaching reading comprehension turned up the surprising fact that little instruction in reading comprehension ever occurred. One of the reasons given by teachers for the lack of comprehension instruction was that teachers were working on skills as a precursor to comprehension. Yet observation failed to substantiate this claim. Durkin noted that in most cases, workbooks and work sheets substituted for the direct instruction that these materials were originally designed to supplement. In short, the children were not instructed within the classroom programs, and we cannot assume that the learner will intuit skills or strategies from worksheet materials.

Even more problematic insofar as the resource teacher is concerned is the belief held by teachers that they were teaching, when they were in fact merely passing out and grading worksheets. In such cases, the resource teacher may need to model appropriate instructional techniques within the classroom or else provide the direct instruction where it is lacking.

b. Within the program's planned experiences, how much can the individual student respond, and can the teacher monitor interactions with the materials and with the teacher? Sometimes these opportunities are too infrequent to support progress, suggesting that a better means must be found to insure active involvement in the program.

c. How amenable is the program to the imposition of a management system that will help structure the student's tasks and will help the teacher monitor progress? Superimposed management systems help with motivation, task analysis, and record keeping. (The discussion of analytic teaching in Chapter 2 describes a management system.)

d. How does the reading program relate to other language arts subjects? This consideration can have good or bad consequences for an individual. For example, great differences in the instructional approaches confuse some students but provide others with more than one way to approach language-related learning in school.

e. How repetitive or boring are the tasks? The resource teacher should try to make both independent work and the instructional activities more attractive. Ideas for modifications are found in many books on Open Education and in magazines such as *Reading Teacher, Learning,* and *Instructor,* or publications such as *Reading Aids through the Grades: A Guide to Materials and 501 Activities for Individualizing Reading Instruction* (Mueser, Russell, and Karp, 1981).

f. How appropriately are the materials being used? If a program has been carefully prepared to be delivered in a specific way and if these procedures are not followed conscientiously, then the student will not have had a fair chance to master the content of the program. For example, perhaps the teacher has neglected to do the preparatory language or vocabulary development work that may be specifically called for in the manual of the program being taught. The resource teacher should not depart capriciously from the procedures recommended by the reading program's authors; any departure should be for the expressed purpose of providing a better way to help an individual.

g. How does the classroom teacher use the supplementary activities and materials that may accompany a particular program? The program often provides additional experiences designed to supplement the core materials and to make them more meaningful. Too often, these enrichment experiences are ignored, or are unavailable. Most students with reading problems can benefit greatly from listening to tapes, reading supplementary stories, engaging in creative drama and art, writing, and similar activities. These activities can provide the student with other avenues for learning and with an experiential base for later reading activities.

h. How does the program "tell" the teacher to interpret the learning-to-read process? A program's philosophy of how children learn to read greatly influences how the teacher perceives and accounts for students' abilities and disabilities. Reading defined as "words read aloud, correctly and sequentially" is different from reading defined as "comprehending and using the meanings intended by the author." Each definition has different implications for the instructional activities that the teacher will emphasize.

i. How was the material chosen? A classroom teacher who does not understand or like the program will not convey much confidence in or enthusiasm for it to the student. The resource teacher can help the classroom teacher understand the rationale and techniques of the program. But if the classroom teacher does not like the program, then the only remaining action is to work together to make modifications for individual students.

j. How firm is the administrative commitment to using the program? Adopting a reading program usually involves a substantial financial and professional investment for a school district; it therefore will be necessary to clear any major changes with the supervisory and administrative staff. It has been our experience that administrators and supervisors seldom fail to support a program change that can be shown to be in the best interests of a student.

7. *What specific language of reading instruction is used in the classroom?* The "language of instruction" refers to all of the vocal and written directions and explanations, the gestures, and the media such as pictures or films that are used to teach. The resource teacher should watch for any problems that arise from a mismatch between the language of instruction and the student's ability to interpret and deal with it. The language of reading instruction is very specialized and often uses difficult patterns and concepts (Clay, 1967). Whether the instruction is given by the teacher or by the material, it should be reviewed carefully. For example, it is not unusual to find that directions to a young student include several potentially difficult and frustrating instructions: (1) placing a finger *beside/lower/*or *on* a picture that shows the *front/back/*or *top* of a picture of an object; and (2) asking what the object is called.

8. *What does an analysis of independent work samples show?* The assignment of independent written work, usually accompanying group lessons, accounts for a lot of reading "instruction." In fact , 'progress' in a reading program usually is judged entirely by how students complete workbooks and worksheets (V. Brown, 1967). The resource teacher, however, should be careful not to equate reading ability with workbook performance. Instead, workbook performance should be analyzed primarily for its contribution to the teacher's perceptions of the students' reading ability and the information it provides about study skills.

When evaluating independent work, the resource teacher should look at many samples in order to note all relevant aspects of the student's reading performance. Consistent errors usually indicate an incomplete understanding of how to do the task. Inconsistent errors may be explained in many ways. The student may be careless, in which case a simple contingency management system could be used to reward consistent performance. Inconsistencies also may indicate that a student is in a transitional or growth state in acquiring a skill. In this case, the continued use of corrective and positive feedback should help. Inconsistent performance also is a characteristic of boredom, and the cure is to increase the variety and interest level of the tasks.

Studying work samples gives the resource teacher useful knowledge about the classroom teacher's marking system. For example, red checks noting errors (measle marks) do not motivate most children, nor do they suggest how a student could change behavior to get fewer marks and more correct responses. If the classroom teacher treats each worksheet as a minitest rather than as an opportunity for supervised practice to aid learning, then the resource teacher should question its educational value.

The common practice of counting unanswered items as wrong gives an erroneous picture of what students know and do not know. Some students are slow workers rather than slow learners; they may not be able to judge time well, or they may simply decide not to complete the assigned tasks. Incompleted tasks do not necessarily mean that they do not know *how* to perform the skill, only that they did not perform it.

The resource teacher also will want to apply task analysis in order to evaluate further the difficulties that a student is having in completing independent work in reading. Task analysis is helpful in finding specific variables. Myers and Hammill (1982) provide an overview of task analysis and Becker, Engelmann, and Thomas (1971) give in-depth, how-to-do-it directions.

9. *How do classroom grouping practices affect the student?* Educators concerned with reading agree that one important component of a good reading program relates to adequate provisions for grouping. A comprehensive program uses more than one basis for grouping; that is, students may read together because of common interests, specific content area assignments, social choices, or sequenced achievement levels reflected in basal readers.

When achievement is used as the basis for grouping, the resource teacher should determine the student's status within the classroom reading group structure. This information is critical because parents and peers often judge success in terms of assignment to the high, middle, or low achievement group. In addition, teachers often refer a student for resource assistance because he or she does not fit into any of the achievement groups. It is not always possible to have the student fit comfortably into existing groups, nor is it always possible to change the student's status within the achievement group structure. However, some negative effects of limited achievement grouping can be alleviated by modifying both the type and number of groupings.

Using various reasons for grouping (such as common interests and social choices) prevents undue attention from being given to achievement grouping alone. Placement in more than one kind of group can maintain or renew interest in reading as a pleasurable and purposeful activity.

The number of groups a classroom teacher establishes often is as important as the types. If the entire class is the *only* group, then the resource teacher should help the teacher develop subgroups or move to an individualized program. Organizing and managing various groups are discussed extensively in basic textbooks of reading methods such as Farr and Roser's *Teaching a Child to Read* (1979, pp. 370 – 421) and Spache and Spache's *Reading in the Elementary School*, 4th ed. (1977, pp.

462 – 475). An excellent source of alternative prescriptions for managing both the elementary and the secondary reading program are found in *Making Reading Possible through Effective Classroom Management* (Lapp, 1980).

10. *How does the referred student behave during group reading?* Reading achievement groups often are managed so that individual students must attend quietly while waiting for their turn to recite. If the amount of time is overly long, the temptation for disruption may be too great to resist. Yet, the student who does not attend will find it difficult to learn and may bother others. The techniques of behavior management, such as providing positive consequences for attending, may find ready application here. In addition, the resource teacher may need to help the classroom teacher better adjust how time is used for the group or to reorganize the grouping practices.

11. *Will any of the classroom's assessment procedures limit the recommendations that can be made for the student?* Assessment at a gross level is available in the form of standardized test results (See Question 5), but these results seldom influence the daily instruction within the classroom. It is more likely that performance on mastery reading tests and on the teacher's own evaluation criteria will affect curriculum planning.

Some commercial reading programs provide their own tests to determine whether the learner is ready to move along within a program. The teacher should remember that these tests are seldom standardized or validated. In addition, even though these mastery tests are called criterion-referenced, they rarely satisfy the rigorous item-selection demands of true criterion-referenced test construction. In any case, the use of publisher-constructed tests should be supplemented by analyses of daily work, as well as through more direct observation of actual reading behavior.

Some recommendations cannot be used in a classroom because the administration restricts the instructional practices to those that match a monitoring or measurement system already in use in the school or district. These systems, such as the sophisticated Wisconsin Reading Design (Otto and Askov, 1974), or the less commercialized Precision Teaching system described by Starlin (1971), provide continuity to the district's reading instruction. The use of such a system, however, often becomes a programming guide; that is, only procedures amenable to that kind of measurement are encouraged. It becomes difficult then to recommend practices that are not directly measurable in terms of the system being used.

For example, the Wisconsin Design specifies all word analysis and comprehension skills considered to be relevant to reading instruction. Measuring reading progress depends on passing successive mastery tests of these skills. Precision teaching uses rate data only, so that a skill that is not readily measurable by rate data, such as the quality of story retelling, would not usually be considered for teaching. Figure 6 – 1 shows an example of a precision teaching measurement of sound blending.

12. *What other persons are involved in the reading instruction?* When other persons also provide direct reading instruction, the resource teacher will need to know: (1) who is directly involved and responsible; (2) the exact nature of the assistance being provided; (3) when and where the assistance occurs; (4) how the

FIGURE **6 – 1.**

Identifying Letter Sounds Blended in Seqeuence as a Blending Project Pinpoint

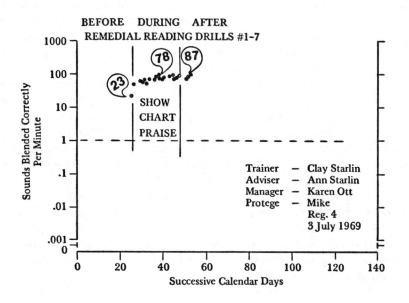

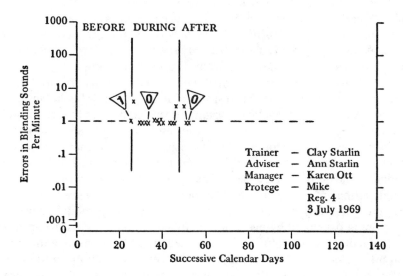

From C. Starlin, Evaluating Progress toward Reading Efficiency," in B. Bateman, ed., *Learning Disorders vol. 4: Reading* (Seattle: Special Child Publications, 1971) p. 433.

student is responding; (5) how the student, the parents, and the classroom teacher view the assistance; and (6) how the various plans and activities are coordinated. Such efforts should be identified and coordinated so that they can complement each other rather than work at cross-purposes to the disadvantage of the student. The resource teacher should observe the student when he or she is being given assistance. If this is not possible, then the resource teacher should schedule routine conferences and records review with the people involved. Several common sources of supplemental reading instruction are discussed below.

Special reading teachers may have collected extensive records about a student, including accounts of his or her previous work. They also may be conducting the kind of thorough assessment that we recommend be done by the resource teacher; in this case, the special teacher's efforts should probably not be duplicated. If this is not the case, however, the two teachers, working with the classroom teacher, should coordinate assessment and treatment efforts while considering each person's unique professional talents.

The *speech and language therapist* may be working independently with the student who has severe speech or language problems. The therapist can alert the resource teacher to any special articulation, language, or concept problems that might be related to reading instruction. The resource teacher should know of any developmental articulation problems and of regional or social dialect patterns, which, of course, are *not* reading errors.

Tutors may be adult volunteers, paid instructional assistants, or peers. Knowing how frequently they work, what they do, and how well they are supervised can indicate how useful and how flexible tutorial services can be in that setting. Publications such as *Partner Learning: A Practical Guide for Teachers and Teacher Trainers* (Stahlbrand, Pierce, and Armstrong, 1983) can help in developing or evaluating tutor programs. (See the earlier section on the peer tutoring.)

13. *How do the parents regard the student's reading abilities?* The importance of parental involvement has been stressed throughout this book. Most parents respond well to inquiries about reading assistance provided outside the school and can describe the impact of reading problems on the family. Parents also can give the resource teacher a view of the student's interests and behaviors that is not evident in school. Much of this information can be used for instructional purposes. For example, some students who do not read at school may be voracious readers at home or in the functional settings of everyday life. The boy who does not care for the Level 4 reader may enjoy *Playboy* or the directions for constructing model airplanes.

Some parents, however, may be placing undue pressure on the student. For example, one six-year-old boy had to read aloud for forty-five minutes both before and after school each day. Also, parents frequently compare the referred student unfavorably with their other children or with children of neighbors and friends. The potentially harmful effects of these comparisons should be pointed out to parents.

The following references can help parents provide positive support to their children's reading development: *Parents' Guide to Children's Reading* (Larrick, 1975) and *Parents and Reading* (C. Smith, 1971). Specialized publications about specific problems parents encounter also are available from the International Reading Association, including *How Can I Help My Child to Read English as a Second Language?* (Garcis and Deyoe, 1974). At the secondary level, "Home Remedies for Reluctant Readers" (Childrey, Jr., 1981) offers many suggestions for parents of adolescents.

14. *What should the resource teacher note when students are referred because they are considered high risk?* The resource teacher may be asked to suggest a program for a young student who has not yet been exposed to formal reading instruction but who is not doing well in the regular reading readiness program. In this case, the clinical judgment of the experienced primary teacher has provided the basis for a referral. Observing the student's behavior in areas such as language use, perceptual motor tasks, general information, social skills, and self-help often forms the basis for such a teacher judgment. Yet it has not been demonstrated that any one of these behaviors is a useful predictor of reading success.

Students may also be classified as high risk because of their performance on tests. Yet many of the readiness tests commonly used for this purpose are poor predictors of future reading ability. Their use, therefore, is potentially dangerous because their results may cause undue alarm on the part of the parents and the teacher.

Reid (1981) has taken issue with pervious concepts of reading readiness. She joins Gibson (1976) and Y. Goodman (1980), who believe that childen learn to read in an evolutionary fashion that begins long before the child starts school. The evolutionary position, as opposed to the readiness position, suggests that there is no definable period of reading readiness. Instead, the experiences of the child lead to abilities for (1) finding meaning in print, (2) learning the alphabet and its uses, after having some idea of the meaning in print, and (3) discovering the arbitrary conventions employed in reading and writing English. Reid, Hresko, and Hammill's *Test of Early Reading Ability* (1981) focuses on the child's development in these areas rather than on deficits in specific reading readiness skills.

The resource teacher who observes in the regular classroom should focus on the opportunities the young student has for finding meaning in print, learning the alphabet and its uses, and discovering the arbitrary conventions employed in reading and writing English. A great deal of this kind of understanding comes from experiences planned by the teachers and not from workbooks. Even young students who already read may flunk workbooks. Determining the understanding that the classroom teacher has of the reading process is the critical task of classroom observations by the resource teacher.

Current practices in kindergarten reading are described in the *Handbook for Administrators and Teachers: Reading in the Kindergarten* (Ollila, 1980). An annotated bibliography that deals with both practical and theoretical issues in early reading has been prepared by Teale (1980). We also recommend a thorough study of Reid's review, "Child Reading: Readiness or Evolution?" (1981).

15. *What additional information should be considered for the older student who must read in the content areas?* Students who are failing to read and achieve in content materials such as science, social studies, and mathematics are often referred for resource assistance as remedial readers. Around third grade, when the emphasis

on content areas is beginning, there is usually an upsurge in referrals for reading. Rather than sudden declines in reading, these referrals mean that the classroom teacher has realized that the students could not cope with the transition from story to more factual materials.

Poor grades in content areas may be a reflection of reading disability and not of the student's ability to learn the material itself when it is presented through media other than print. On the other hand, some students who are referred for reading in the content areas may read other materials satisfactorily. This is because of the density of concepts, the style of writing, and the amount and nature of the background information needed for success in content area reading. One of the major diagnostic tasks in content areas is to discriminate the student who *could* read the material if background information were there from the student who may (or may not) have the appropriate background information, but who lacks basic reading skills.

Allington and Strange (1980) have noted that there are two basic differences between developmental and content area reading: the style (story versus informational material) and the source of the skills to be taught. In a developmental reading program, a scope and sequence chart proceeds along more or less independently of the story content. In content areas, the material itself determines the skills or strategies that must be brought to bear if the student is to read with comprehension.

Since the material determines the strategies needed to comprehend it through reading, it is important to observe while the material is being presented within the classroom. Classroom observations include analyses of instructional sessions, of the methods and materials being used, of the independent work required, and of the concepts that the student must bring to the materials. If the classroom teacher is not using reading strategies to help the students, then much of the remedial effort will need to be focused on consulting with the teacher. The purpose of consultation will be to help structure daily lesson materials so that strategies and skills for teaching students how to read and study in the content areas are incorporated into those lessons.

There are many useful sources of information that will guide the resource teacher in learning more about reading in the content areas and therefore about what to look for in the classroom. These sources also suggest alternatives to reading and writing as a means of learning and transmitting the content itself. The alternatives are to be used diagnostically as well as remedially, for if the student does not comprehend the content when it is presented in a medium other than print, it is highly likely that the problem is not one of reading.

Many of the resources for content area reading contain the words *adolescent* or *secondary level*. The resource teacher who works at the elementary level should not be put off by these words. The literature provides suggestions that are easily adaptable to younger students who face the same situations. The same is true, in turn, of the secondary-level teacher who may find a wealth of material in the college book store.

As basic resources, we recommend a wide array of informational sources. Alley and Deshler's *Teaching the Learning Disabled Adolescent: Strategies and Methods* (1979) suggests strategies that can be brought to bear within the content area classroom, as well as with individual students. *Learning through Reading in the Content Areas* (Allington and Strange, 1980) deals with emerging ideas of the teaching aspect. As supplements to these two books, several sources contain numerous specific examples that can be used without much modification by the classroom or the resource teacher. These books are: *Teaching Reading in the Content Areas* (Herber, 1978), *Reading Strategies for Secondary School Teachers* (Burmeister, 1974), *Improving Reading in Every Class*, (Thomas and Robinson, 1982) and *Reading and Learning in the Content Classroom* (Estes and Vaughan, 1978).

The literature of secondary education offers many ideas for dealing with reading in the content areas, such as *Reading in the Science Classroom* (Bechtel and Franzblau, 1980). This rich literature also presents many ideas for the use of alternatives to print.

Periodicals available from professional organizations deal with content areas, such as the National Association of Teachers of Mathematics. In addition, the printed resources available from the International Reading Association (IRA) deal with this topic. IRA publications include the secondary-oriented *Journal of Reading*. It consistently presents materials reviews, new products, methodology, and research in reading in the content areas.

The resource teacher is not expected to become an expert in every content area taught in schools. Instead, the role of the resource teacher is one of supporting content area instruction by teaching both students and teachers how to structure the study, and therefore the reading, of these materials. Where students cannot read the materials because of poor reading ability, then the task is to ensure that the content is presented using media other than print. Where students cannot read the materials because of inappropriate background, then the direct or indirect role of the resource teacher is to change the material to accommodate the background that *is* there or, alternately, to see that the background material is taught prior to reading.

SUPPLEMENTAL INDIVIDUAL ANALYSIS

Many of the reading problems referred to the resource program can be understood and helped readily as the result of interpreting information obtained from the anlaysis of the learner within the classroom, however, it may be that classroom analysis is not enough, and supplemental individual analysis is called for. Working on an individual basis with a student enables the resource teacher to determine:

1. Whether the student does indeed have a reading problem
2. The nature of any problems that do exist
3. A better understanding of the strategies the reader-student uses
4. The student's understanding of reading and of reading instruction
5. How well the student reads in materials intended for reading instruction
6. Factors that seem to affect the student's reading

7. The student's interests, especially in books and reading materials
8. The student's attitude toward reading and toward his or her own reading abilities
9. Which of various methods and materials are likely to be effective with the student
10. The amount of responsibility the student is likely to assume for learning to read.

Placing intraclassroom and supplemental individual analysis one after the other does not imply that this is a necessary sequence. The resource teacher may in fact work with both at once or back and forth as clues to the individual are obtained in the classroom, and conversely, clues to the nature of the classroom are obtained from the work with an individual student.

Since the previous edition of this book was published in 1978, there have been many advances in our understanding of the act of reading and how we learn to read. Although much of the information is at a theoretical level, a great deal can now be used to improve the kind of individual assessments made in reading. To a great extent, the improvement lies in the nature of the questions that are asked about a student and his or her reading. These questions replace the routine administration of diagnostic tests and interviews, whose results are seldom used for instructional planning.

This section presents many of the questions that might be asked about the reading of an individual student. Not every one is relevant to the individual case. Further, other questions may be more relevant in the local situation. In this case, the resource teacher and those who are responsible for the reading program may use the same format for cue questions to serve as guidelines for resource personnel.

1. *Does the student have a measurable problem in reading?* Standardized test scores offer evidence of a problem in reading when standard scores are used to make comparisons between one student and peers. In general, performance that is one or more standard deviations from the norm for the age group should be of concern.

When a new test must be given to document a problem, we recommend that the reading core of the *Test of Reading Comprehension* (TORC) (V. Brown, Hammill, and Wiederholt, 1978) be used because it is a silent reading test based upon current ideas about reading comprehension. (See Figure 6 – 2.)

The TORC yields a reading comprehension quotient (RCQ) that is composed of three subtests, each based on a different aspect of reading comprehension. These aspects are: (1) relational vocabulary, (2) syntactic similarities, and (3) paragraph reading for elementary students or paragraph idea construction for secondary students. The RCQ is a more reliable indicator of the student's comprehension abilities than any single measure considered alone. The RCQ is a standard score with a mean of 100 and a standard deviation of 15.

Tests that measure skills such as word attack should not be used to determine whether a student has a measurable reading problem because these skills are not reading as it ever appears in the world outside of schools. The appropriate occasions for analyzing or cataloging word analysis skills are described on pages 156 – 160.

FIGURE 6 – 2.
Summary and Profile Sheet for TORC

TORC

TEST OF READING COMPREHENSION:

A Method for Assessing the Understanding of Written Language

Virginia L. Brown, Donald D. Hammill, J. Lee Wiederholt

Female ☐ Male ☐ _____ Name

	Year	Month	Day
Date tested	_____	_____	_____
Date of birth	_____	_____	_____
Age	_____	_____	_____
School			

Examiner's Name: _____
                               (FIRST)   (LAST)
Examiner's Title: _____

SECTION I   TORC SUBTESTS

GENERAL COMPREHENSION CORE

	Raw Scores	Scaled Scores
General Vocabulary	_____	_____
Syntactic Similarities	_____	_____
Paragraph Reading or		
(Sentence Sequencing)	(_____)	(_____)
Total Reading Comprehension Core		_____
Reading Comprehension Quotient (RCQ)		_____

DIAGNOSTIC SUPPLEMENTS

	Raw Scores	Scaled Scores
Mathematics Vocabulary	_____	_____
Social Studies Vocabulary	_____	_____
Science Vocabulary	_____	_____
Reading Directions	_____	_____

SECTION II   TORC PROFILE

SECTION III   INFORMATION RELEASE RECORD

Date: Test results released or interpreted to: By:

1. _____ _____ _____
2. _____ _____ _____
3. _____ _____ _____

© Copyright 1978, by Virginia L. Brown, Donald D. Hammill, J. Lee Wiederholt

Additional copies of this form are available from PRO-ED,
5341 Industrial Oaks Blvd., Austin, Texas 78735
512-892-3142

FIGURE **6 – 2.** *(Continued)*

SECTION IV
TORC DESIGN

Rationale: The TORC is a silent reading comprehension test based upon current psycholinguistic and cognitive theories.

Item Selection: Items were built using reviews of current content area textbooks and graded word lists. The final roster of items was selected experimentally on the basis of analysis of item difficulty and discriminating power.

Reliability: Internal consistency was determined for the entire standardization sample using the Kuder-Richardson method. With few exceptions, coefficients were greater than .80. Studies of test-retest yielded subtest reliabilities ranging from .64 to .86; while that for RCQ was .91.

Validity: Validity is supported by subtest correlation with SAT-Reading (Mdn. r = .46), SRA Reading (Mdn. r = .41) and PIAT Reading (Mdn. r = .72). Additional studies dealing with criterion-related, and construct validity are found in the TORC Manual.

Normative Data: Norms are based on the test performance of 2,707 students aged 6-6 to 17-11 living in 10 different states. Scaled Scores and Grade Equivalents are provided.

SECTION V
ADMINISTRATION CONDITIONS

A. TORC administered in:

    One session _____

    Two sessions _____

    Three sessions _____

    Four or more _____

B. Tested individually _____

    or

    Tested in group.

    Size of group _____

C. Administered by

    experienced examiner _____

    By other:

    Specify (aide, trainee, etc.) _____

D. Departure from directions in Manual. Explain. _____

_____

_____

_____

_____

_____ (Add sheet if necessary)

SECTION VI
ENVIRONMENTAL CONDITIONS

A. Place tested _____

_____

	Interfering			Not Interfering	
B. Noise level	1	2	3	4	5
C. Interruptions	1	2	3	4	5
D. Distractions	1	2	3	4	5
E. Light	1	2	3	4	5
F. Temperature	1	2	3	4	5

G. Notes and other considerations _____

_____

_____

SECTION VII
STUDENT RELATED CONDITIONS

	Poor				Good
A. Energy level	1	2	3	4	5
B. Attitude toward test	1	2	3	4	5
C. Rapport with examiner	1	2	3	4	5
D. Perseverence	1	2	3	4	5
E. Visual Acuity	1	2	3	4	5
F. Hearing Acuity	1	2	3	4	5
G. State of Health:					
General	1	2	3	4	5
During Testing	1	2	3	4	5

H. Notes and other considerations _____

_____

_____

SECTION VIII
INTERPRETATION AND RECOMMENDATIONS

_____

_____

_____

_____

_____

_____

_____

_____

_____

_____ (Add sheet if necessary)

The information derived from test scores is not used for program planning but to document the existence or nonexistence of a problem. Many students who fail the daily tasks of reading are in fact good readers outside the classroom. If the student does not appear to have a significant problem with reading abilities, then the resource teacher must examine again the questions in the Classroom Analysis section of this chapter. In addition, the student may need to be motivated or rein-forced for completing daily tasks correctly. In this case, the resource teacher would likely serve as a consultant to the classroom teacher to implement such a program within the classroom itself. Or monitoring and reinforcement for appropriate classroom work can be provided within the resource program.

2. *How does the student's reading achievement compare with his or her other cognitive abilities?* Many students who are referred to the resource program are reading as well as can be expected in view of their general thinking and reasoning abilities. Measures of cognitive abilities should be compared with those of reading to determine if there is a statistically significant discrepancy between the two. We have noted elsewhere (V. Brown, Hammill, and Wiederholt, 1978):

> The relationships between reading comprehension and cognitive abilities are quite complex and not always as pleasing to our "sense of possibility" for human potential as we might wish. Cognition appears to provide some "ceiling" to what we can realistically and reasonably expect in terms of student performance. However, the poorer the cognitive abilities seem to be, the more we need to help the student make the most of these. Whether cognition is considered as "good" or "poor," it is unlikely that we have stretched those abilities to their limits in terms of their application to reading. . . .
>
> To assist the student in the application of his or her cognitive abilities to reading comprehension, we would recommend the use of any strategies that require reasoning rather than matching and direct "memory" tasks. We are not suggesting here that we "train" reasoning. Instead, we believe that traditional techniques simply do not elicit or challenge the comprehension capabilities of most students. Also, higher order responses are not brought out through low level questions or purposes (e.g., Lowery, 1973; Smith, 1977; Taba & Elzey, 1964). [P. 39]

The report of Phi Delta Kappa's Commission on the Teaching of Thinking Skills constitutes the entire issue of PDK's newsletter, *Practical Applications of Research* (1980). The commission's report deals with issues and problems that face the teacher and reviews currently recommended programs such as *The Basic Thinking Skills* (Popp, Robinson, and Robinson, 1974). The works of Russell Stauffer offer excellent sug-gestions for incorporating thinking abilities into the reading process during instruc-tion. Primary-level teachers who believe that thinking comes after skills would profit from two older but still cogent booklets: *Critical Reading Develops Early* (Lee, Bingham, and Woelfel, 1968) and *Teaching Critical Reading at the Primary Level* (Stauffer and Cramer, 1968). We also recommend the use of Piaget-based programs in mathematics, such as *Mathematics . . . A Way of Thinking* (Barrata-Lorton, 1977) and in science, such as *Developing Teacher Competencies* [in science] (Weigand, 1971).

3. *How does the student's reading compare with other language abilities?* It has been traditional in reading education to think of other language abilities as speak-

ing, listening, and writing. Yet current ideas about language suggest that these domains are merely the media through which language is understood and communicated. The language abilities of concern to the resource teacher are primarily those of semantics and syntax, especially as they are represented in vocabulary and grammar.

In cases of reading disability, we would expect measures of vocabulary and syntax that involve speaking and/or listening to be above those in reading. The relationship of reading and writing is more complex (see Chapter 10). If listening, speaking, and reading are relatively even, then a general language disability is more likely a diagnosis for the student than one of specific reading disability.

We also expect a reader to understand language ideas and relationships with which he or she is familiar *when they are presented through other language forms.* If the student does not comprehend language through other means, then we would not expect reading to be a surpassing strength.

The previous comments imply a holistic view of language. This does not mean that a student must be a good speaker, listener, and writer in order to read. For example, deaf and mute people learn to read. Speakers of regional or social dialect learn to read the standard forms of written English. In fact, some people with listening or speaking disabilities or dialectical differences learn standard English through reading. The use and understanding of the underlying propositions of language are more critical than errors or disabilities in its surface structure or forms. The differences between the surface structure of language and the underlying propositions involved can be illustrated in these examples:

1. The sentence has one surface structure, but two underlying propositions can be understood, depending upon the context.
    Visiting relatives can be boring.
2. One general set of propositions can be represented by several surface structures.
    Don gave the pie to Steve.
    Don gave Steve the pie.

Whether in listening, speaking, reading, or writing, students whose vocabularies are impoverished are not likely to bring enough *to* the communication situation to get much *from* it. In grammar, students must in general understand the underlying propositions of adverbial clauses, word order, anaphoric relations, and so forth before they can be expected to understand them in reading.

The resource teacher can use checklists, discussion with the student, or standardized tests such as the *Test of Adolescent Language* (Hammill et al., 1980) to make some of the intraindividual comparisons among language abilities (see Figure 6 – 3).

Weaver's *Grammar for Teachers: Perspectives and Definitions* (1979) provides background information as well as assessment and instructional strategies that deal with grammar specifically as it relates to reading. Johnson and Pearson's *Teaching Reading Vocabulary* (1978) provides many suggestions for strategies and exercises in vocabulary development.

FIGURE **6 – 3.**
Summary and Profile Sheet for TOAL

TOAL

TEST OF ADOLESCENT LANGUAGE:

A Multidimensional Approach to
Assessment

Donald D. Hammill, Virginia L. Brown, Stephen C. Larsen &
J. Lee Wiederholt

Name _____ Female ☐ Male ☐

	Year	Month	Day
Date tested	___	___	___
Date of birth	___	___	___
Age	___	___	___
School:			

Examiner's Name: _____
(FIRST)   (LAST)

Examiner's Title: _____

SECTION I TOAL SUBTEST SCORES

	RAW SCORES	SCALED SCORES			RAW SCORES	SCALED SCORES
I. Listening/Vocabulary	___	___	V. Reading/Vocabulary		___	___
II. Listening/Grammar	___	___	VI. Reading/Grammar		___	___
III. Speaking/Vocabulary	___	___	VII. Writing/Vocabulary		___	___
IV. Speaking/Grammar	___	___	VIII. Writing/Grammar		___	___

SECTION II TOAL SUBTEST PROFILE

Additional copies of this form are available from PRO-ED,
5341 Industrial Oaks Blvd., Austin, Texas 78735

FIGURE **6 – 3.** ***(Continued)***

Summary and Profile Sheet for TOAL

SECTION III WORKSPACE FOR ANALYSIS OF COMPOSITE SCORES

AREAS OF ANALYSIS	L/V	L/G	S/V	S/G	R/V	R/G	W/V	W/G		SUM OF SCALED SCORES	QUOTIENTS
ADOLESCENT LANGUAGE QUOTIENT (ALQ)	☐	☐	☐	☐	☐	☐	☐	☐	=	☐	( )
LISTENING	☐	☐							=	☐	( )
SPEAKING			☐	☐					=	☐	( )
READING					☐	☐			=	☐	( )
WRITING							☐	☐	=	☐	( )
SPOKEN LANGUAGE	☐	☐	☐	☐					=	☐	( )
WRITTEN LANGUAGE					☐	☐	☐	☐	=	☐	( )
VOCABULARY	☐		☐		☐		☐		=	☐	( )
GRAMMAR		☐		☐		☐		☐	=	☐	( )
RECEPTIVE LANGUAGE	☐	☐			☐	☐			=	☐	( )
EXPRESSIVE LANGUAGE			☐	☐			☐	☐	=	☐	( )

SECTION IV TOAL PROFILE OF COMPOSITE SCORES

Test used: ______

Scaled Scores	CONCEPTUAL ABILITIES	ALQ	Scaled Scores	LISTENING	SPEAKING	READING	WRITING	SPOKEN LANGUAGE	WRITTEN LANGUAGE	VOCABULARY	GRAMMAR	RECEPTIVE LANGUAGE	EXPRESSIVE LANGUAGE	Scaled Scores
150	•	•	150	•	•	•	•	•	•	•	•	•	•	150
145	•	•	145	•	•	•	•	•	•	•	•	•	•	145
140	•	•	140	•	•	•	•	•	•	•	•	•	•	140
135	•	•	135	•	•	•	•	•	•	•	•	•	•	135
130	•	•	130	•	•	•	•	•	•	•	•	•	•	130
125	•	•	125	•	•	•	•	•	•	•	•	•	•	125
120	•	•	120	•	•	•	•	•	•	•	•	•	•	120
115	•	•	115	•	•	•	•	•	•	•	•	•	•	115
110	•	•	110	•	•	•	•	•	•	•	•	•	•	110
105	•	•	105	•	•	•	•	•	•	•	•	•	•	105
100	—	—	100	—	—	—	—	—	—	—	—	—	—	100
95	•	•	95	•	•	•	•	•	•	•	•	•	•	95
90	•	•	90	•	•	•	•	•	•	•	•	•	•	90
85	•	•	85	•	•	•	•	•	•	•	•	•	•	85
80	•	•	80	•	•	•	•	•	•	•	•	•	•	80
75	•	•	75	•	•	•	•	•	•	•	•	•	•	75
70	•	•	70	•	•	•	•	•	•	•	•	•	•	70
65	•	•	65	•	•	•	•	•	•	•	•	•	•	65
60	•	•	60	•	•	•	•	•	•	•	•	•	•	60
55	•	•	55	•	•	•	•	•	•	•	•	•	•	55

4. *What is the student's rate of reading?*[1]   Measures of the speed of reading are often incorporated into reading tests such as the *Durrell Analysis of Reading Difficulty* (Durrell, 1955). Not only must the student's reading be acurate, but it must also be fast, or the result will be a lowered score or reading level designation. On the other hand, tests such as the TORC are deliberately untimed because they are designed to measure how well the student can read, not how quickly. Yet we recognize that most good readers can combine a high degree of comprehension with a rapid rate. We also know that reading rates vary, both among individuals and within the same individual who adjusts both purpose and rate of reading to suit the materials at hand. One of the characteristics of mature reading is the ability to adjust rate and purpose to material.

This section deals with the importance of reading rate, factors that may cause a slow rate, and how to collect rate data, as well as ways to improve reading rate.

There are at least four major reasons that reading rate is important in individual assessment. First, excessively slow reading is currently assumed to be a result of poor comprehension abilities — and not their cause. That is, the slow reader does not use a minimum number of cues to get the maximum amount of information from the text. Efficient comprehenders may skip redundant words, phrases, and passages or may scan the text for main ideas or for the thread of an argument. They can also project much of the meaning of a sentence or a passage when the eyes are stopped before having completed visual scrutiny of the material. Further, eye movements of the good comprehender are associated with meaningful clusters of words or phrases. Inefficient comprehenders skip nothing; they rarely project meaning beyond the last word read; and their eyes are fixed upon each word separately, regardless of its relative weight in the sentence or the passage. All of these reading behaviors of the poor comprehender serve to slow the reading rate considerably.

The relationship between slow rate and poor comprehension is always a hypothesis to be disproved in the individual case, however. It may be that the student reads very slowly and is able to comprehend very well. The task of the resource teacher is to find out if this is indeed the case. And as in other matters, *comprehension* is always the criterion of the appropriateness of any reading rate.

A second reason that reading rate is important lies in the nature of reading instruction, particularly in the elementary school and in remedial reading programs. In these settings, there is a long history of using oral reading both diagnostically to analyze a student's reading errors and rate of reading and also evaluatively during the reading lesson to make a gross judgment about the quality of the student's reading. In each of these cases, the slow reader is perceived by the teacher as being a poor reader simply because of a slow rate. Often the parents, peers, and the student share this perception. Rate improvement is seen, then, as reading improvement. To read fluently and quickly when called upon may become a teacher-pleasing behavior, and the pleasure of the teacher is reflected on to others who judge the student.

Rate improvement may also be needed because reading speed is such an integral part of tests, not only in reading but in content areas as well. The slow-reading student may have a decidedly lowered score on any reading test in which speed is a factor. On a content area test, as in social studies or mathematics, slow-reading students may not be able to show the extent to which they have actually mastered the content because they never get to all the items within the time limits provided.

Finally, readers who are habitually slow may never finish independent study assignments that they could otherwise do. Where time limits are imposed on independent study such as seatwork, grades suffer as a consequence of not completing assignments, whether the reason is slow reading, slow working, or not comprehending the material.

A slow reading rate may be the result of poor comprehension, but there are several other reasons for an excessively slow rate. First, it is often the school's emphasis on reading aloud correctly that has fostered a habit of slow reading. As a result, may poor readers have learned to read aloud in a halting, word-by-word fashion. They often seem intent upon pronouncing every word, hopefully correctly, and appear to recognize no apparent connection between or among the words themselves. Furthermore, these habits begun in oral reading may well be carried over to silent reading. They are certainly carried into the remedial reading situation, where many teachers of older students comment on the habit but rarely attempt to change it.

Another reason for slower rates, both in oral and in silent reading, may be that the material the student is asked to read is too difficult. This is often the case in reading achievement groups where the material is not geared to the abilities of all the students within the group. It also happens in remedial instruction when the teacher gives the student difficult material to read because she or he wants to make an ongoing record of how the student attacks new or difficult material. If the material is deliberately difficult, then a slow rate would be expected.

A final reason for slower rates in oral reading may be that the student is shy or nervous when reading in any audience situation, and especially when being timed. Such a situation is like a test.

In assessing rate, the resource teacher must consider both the materials and the methods. Contrary to tradition, the assessment of rate should not be combined with other assessment, such as that of oral reading errors. The materials to be used for initial rate assessment should be already familiar to the reader. It may have been practiced before so that the student knows the material. Hopefully, it will also be material the student enjoys. Later, rates under these conditions may be compared with those obtained under other conditions, such as those suggested in Figure 6 – 4.

Rates may be determined for both oral and silent reading. These rates will differ, of course, especially as the student becomes a more proficient reader. Further, silent reading is the preferred condition for reading because it is usually more natural, unless there is a specific audience for oral reading, and it is usually more efficient because the reader need not deal with every word.

The basic practical method for calculating reading rate is to divide the number of words read by the number of minutes it took to read them:

$$\frac{400 \text{ words}}{10 \text{ minutes}} = 40 \text{ words per minute (wpm)}$$

FIGURE 6 – 4.
Initial Reading Rate Data Sheet

INITIAL READING RATE DATA SHEET   NAME _____

WORDS PER MINUTE

CONDITIONS

CONSIDERATIONS   WPM   A B C D E F G H I J K

Type of Reading
   1. Oral
   2. Silent
Timed by:
   1. Other person
   2. Self
   3. Mechanically
Time Frame
   1. Finish time
   2. Finish passage
Type of Material
   1. Practiced; familiar
   2. Unpracticed; new
   3. Recreational
   4. Specialized
   5. Directions
   6. Other: _____
Directions or Incentives
   1. None
   2. "Read faster"
   3. "Read more carefully"
   4. " — 2 & — 3 above"
   5. Improvement in wpm
   6. Praise
   7. Material reward
   8. Other: _____

WPM scale: 100, 95, 90, 85, 80, 75, 70, 65, 60, 55, 50, 45, 40, 34, 30, 25, 20, 15, 10, 5, 0

	CONDITION DESCRIPTORS		EXAMINER	DATE
A.	1 min. timing; familiar material; no directions	(25)	K. Armstrong	3-12-82
B.	3 min. " ; " " ;Read fast + corr".	(50)	"	"
C.	Passage completion;" " ; 400 words/10 min.	(40)	"	3-15-82
D.	1 min. timing; familiar material; Read quickly"	(45)	"	3-16-82
E.	Same as D	(51)	"	3-17-82

FIGURE 6 – 4.
Initial Reading Rate Data Sheet *(Continued)*

	CONDITION DESCRIPTORS	EXAMINER	DATE
F.	*Same as D*	(50) *K. Armstrong*	*3-18-82*
G.	*1 minute; self-timed; familiar material*	(49) *K.A + Alysa*	*3-18-82*
H.			
I.			
J.			
K.			

COMMENTS

Seemed unaware of need for more rapid rdg. Re-   K. Armstrong   3-18-82
sponded well to direction to speed. Can self-chart + time.

© Virginia L. Brown, 1982   From V. Brown, 1982.

A set time may be used instead, such as three minutes. At the end of that time, the number of words read are again divided by the number of minutes. The use of one minute as the measure of time means that no division is needed. One need only count the number of words read before the timer sounds. This latter method is especially useful when teaching students to time themselves.

Both in silent and in oral reading, an additional measure is needed for using rate data: comprehension. Usually a general retelling of the material in the student's own words is enough for this purpose. Comprehension questions may also be used.

Where oral reading is used to determine rate, several points should be remembered. First, many students get off to a slow start in oral reading when they read in front of people. After several pages, the rate speeds up as the student either gets into the material or becomes more comfortable in the situation. This common factor should be considered for any student with a slow oral reading rate.

For initial rate assessment using oral reading, we do not recommend commenting on or examining errors at all — errors are simply counted as words read. Repetitions count for as many words as are repeated correctly. *For this purpose,* we are not interested in words read correctly but only in the rate of whatever the student reads with ultimate comprehension.

Additionally, any student who is sensitive about a speech problem, one who is extremely shy, or one with a problem in speaking English may need silent reading and rehearsal before the teacher attempts to collect any oral rate data.

If slow rate is due to poor comprehension, then rate improvement should not be of great concern until the student is taught comprehension skills or strategies such as reading for main ideas, understanding the role of aids to meaning, such as parenthetical expressions, or developing a schema, or general idea, of the material to be read. The student should also be made aware of the nature of reading — that it is not a question of word-by-word accuracy but a participatory venture in which the reader must sample enough of the text to understand the ideas the author is trying to convey.

For the shy or nervous student, behavior rehearsal, in this case in oral reading, may prove effective. This is especially important where the student will be expected to read orally during instructional sessions. Even if the resource teacher shares our belief of minimizing the role of oral reading in the instructional program, the practice will not likely die soon. Since the student will not be with the resource teacher forever, the student should learn to read orally at an appropriate rate, if only as a coping skill for school survival.

The usual remedy for improving reading rate, especially if slow rate is the product of habit, involves competition with self or with peers to improve over the previously recorded words-per-minute index. Charts or graphs provide visual aids for this purpose, and praise or other incentives may be supplemental. Often merely the act of charting is enough to improve rate. To equalize differences in materials, some teachers average rates over five sessions. Regardless of the methods used, the material for building rate should be easy and familiar.

Eventually, attention should be given to promoting flexible reading rates to accommodate purposes and materials. Most of this instruction can be readily incorporated into the reading materials themselves, as in social studies or history. For the secondary or young adult reader, we recommend Raygor and Schick's *Reading at Efficient Rates* (1970). It can be used relatively independently, and it emphasizes concurrent comprehension strategies as well as rate improvement.

5. *Does the student have a sufficient grasp of the concepts that are necessary to deal with the instruction being attempted?* What appears to be a reading problem may be only a reflection of a learner's limited conceptual ability to handle the content of the text. To determine if this is the case, the resource teacher should be able to separate skill at reading words from the ability to comprehend the intended meaning of those words. A program to develop word analysis or sound blending skills in a student who does not understand the significance of the words or phrases he or she reads is not a good program.

There are several methods for obtaining information about how well the student's concepts match the instructional activities being presented. For example, the teacher can discuss a wrong answer with the student to determine how much he or she really understands. The teacher also can examine and discuss vocabulary, phrases, and the context within which high frequency words occur in an effort to determine how well they are understood. For example, *on* often is considered a simple, basic word denoting a relative position in space. However, this word is used in many contexts: *wish on, take on, keep on, on the nose,* and *on and on,* for example. A broad program of concept development may be more important than belaboring the visual identification of *on* as a sight word with no supporting context. The teacher also can obtain information about concepts by asking the student to retell information he or she has seen, read, or heard. Listening to the student's own words helps the teacher detect an erroneous or an incomplete informational background.

6. *What are the student's attitudes toward his or her reading abilities? Are these*

attitudes obvious? Being treated differently from peers will adversely affect the student's motivation to read. For example, many students are reluctant to participate in situations that call attention to their reading problems. The resource teacher will want to learn about the student's attitudes and self-concept as a reader and about how these are affected by the classroom environment. A total reading program may involve changing the behavior of classmates and teacher, as well as changing the student's responses to any inappropriate attention.

In the classroom, the teacher can assess a student's attitudes toward reading by noting any of the relevant effective factors suggested by Krathwohl, Bloom, and Masia (1964), including "Completes reading assignments" and "Makes an effort to understand what is read." Powell's "Attitude Scale for Reading" (1972) is a useful structured teacher-observation checklist. Outside the classroom, *The Estes Attitude Scales* (Estes et al., 1981) include a reading component that allows comparison with other school subjects. Versions are available for both elementary and secondary levels.

7. *Is the student appropriately placed in reading materials?* The question of an appropriate match among the student's reading abilities, the purpose for reading, and the material to be read is a major diagnostic concern of the resource teacher. This section deals with (1) the need to consider reading purpose in the matching of materials to student abilities, (2) customary methods of determining placement, and (3) current alternatives for finding an appropriate match.

a. *The importance of purpose.* In at least several instances the reader should not have to worry about many unknown words, and the material's difficulty could interfere with instruction or proficiency. Comfortable reading should be used when:

Focusing on one or more aspects of comprehension
Building very low reading rates
Learning to read for an audience situation
Working independently, especially where accuracy is important
Practicing reading, such as for pleasure or for future discussion

When the purpose of the reading is to find out how the student attempts to read unknown words or material, the text should contain more difficult vocabulary and concepts so that the teacher can analyze errors and plan instruction accordingly. More difficult material may also be appropriate when it contains instances of a skill that has been taught and when the teacher wants to find out if the student can now apply the skill in new situations. More difficult material is useful for instructional purposes or when the student is extremely motivated to comprehend it.

Much of the reading students are expected to do in content areas is too difficult for them, and one of the major problems of the resource teacher is trying to obtain an appropriate match of materials and students in the regular classroom. It is primarily because this task is so difficult that resource teachers are often so involved in tutoring and in finding media other than print to teach the content.

b. *Customary practice in matching student to print.* It is common practice to place students in reading material, especially in reading textbooks, by coordinating a measured reading level — from a test or from an individual reading inventory (IRI) — with the readability score of the passage or text. This method for matching has two problematic subtasks: (1) finding the score that correctly reflects the student's reading abilities, or reading level, and (2) determining the correct grade-level designation of the materials that best match the student's abilities. These subtasks are problematic because in each case the scores used may not be valid, and the criteria used to generate the scores are not specified, or else they are incomplete for this purpose.

The grade equivalent score from a standardized test should not be used to match a material bearing the same grade-level designation. Using such a score in this manner is rarely recommended by test constructors, and it is not viewed by the International Reading Association as good professional practice (International Reading Association, 1981).

When IRIs are used to determine a reading level for the student, there are actually three levels that are of interest to the teacher or diagnostician: (1) frustration level, (2) instructional level, and (3) independent level. These levels are obtained from the administration of an IRI. Basically, this instrument is a series of graded passages that the student reads aloud in sequence, until he or she makes a certain number of errors. Predetermined comprehension questions are asked and scored for correctness after each passage is read. Then the number of oral reading errors and the percentage of comprehension questions answered correctly are translated into scores that are said to represent three reading levels for the student: frustration, instructional, and independent. If the IRI is standardized, these scores are based upon norms. If the IRI is teacher made from the local series, then the scores are based upon either the publisher's designation of levels or upon the results of application of a readability formula.

The usual criteria for determining the three reading levels are taken from Betts (1946), even though these criteria are often considered rather stringent:

	WORD RECOGNITION (%)	COMPREHENSION (%)
Independent	99	90
Instructional	95	75
Frustration	90	50

Any passage where errors total ten in a sample of one hundred running words, and comprehension questions are answered at the 50 percent level is considered too difficult for the student. Any passage where few errors are made and comprehension is good is considered as an independent level, suitable for comfortable reading. Between these two levels is an area where the student is assumed to be able to read with some comprehension but still makes enough errors to permit instruction *based upon an analysis of these errors or others taken under the same circumstances.* Rarely, however, does instruction based upon error analysis actually occur. The most common use of the information from an IRI is to place students in material that is assumed to provide generally appropriate instructional experiences. This practice continues in spite of widespread criticism by professional reading educators (such as Powell, 1974). The arguments against its continuation center on the basic validity or invalidity of the criteria; on the need for different criteria for different reading levels; and upon the fact that its most desirable features — the opportunity for qualitative error analysis and instructional planning based upon error analysis — are obscured by its least desirable feature, an invalid score. For a review of currently available commercially produced IRIs, see "Test Review: Commercial Informal Reading Inventories" (Jongsma and Jongsma, 1981).

The second problematic concept involved in matching reader to print lies in the validity of the grade-level designation of the material. Publishers are notorious for their lack of criteria on which to base their grade-level designations. The usual practice is to increase the new vocabulary load at each successive level and to reduce the number of repetitions of these new words. Some materials are subjected further to the administration of a readability formula. These formulas primarily take into account the factors of sentence length and vocabulary difficulty.

Current critiques of using readability formulas are based upon the fact that changes in difficulty levels as measured by the readability formulas do not correspond to difficulty in the real world of reading. Factors that are now being studied include the syntactic structure of sentences, the logical connections between sentences, and the way topics of a text are organized (that is, their coherence). Of particular concern in terms of matching students to print is the recent research that examines the practice of reducing sentence length to reduce measured readability and therefore, difficulty. Irwin (1980) has shown that shorter sentences that reduce readability may actually make the message more difficult for the reader, especially where inferences are required of the reader. Davison et al., (1980) also present data to show that reduced sentence length does not necessarily make the material easier, a comment on readability with implications for the use of the instructional levels assigned to high interest-low vocabulary books often used with older students. It may be that the high interest is more valuable than the low vocabulary and the reduced sentence lengths. Many clinicians have observed that older students with mature language patterns often have problems, especially in oral reading, with material that uses stilted, too-simple sentences. Now we have some idea of why this phenomenon might occur.

c. *Current alternatives for matching student to print.*   If the indexes for the student's reading level and the reading level of the materials are not defensible as a means of matching the reader to print, what methods are recommended? The variables involved include not only an analysis of the student's reading but also the background of the student and his or her intrinsic interest in the material.

Either silent or oral reading may be used for assessing the appropriateness of materials to the student. Each involves certain diagnostic trade-offs. Silent reading is weighted heavily toward clinical judgment and is short on countable data. Oral reading is weighted toward countable, or accountable, data but is not the "natural" condition of independent reading.

If silent reading is used, the teacher can ask the student to mark unknown or uncertain words, fuzzy ideas, or anything the student wants to question. Postreading retelling of the ideas of the passage, as well as the teacher's specific probings of items of interest, can clarify the extent to which the material is fruitful for instruction or for independence.

Where oral reading is used, Lovitt and Hansen (1976a) have shown that the direct assessment of a student's oral reading with a specific passage, being read for the first time, is a reliable and valid method of assessing the best fit of materials to an individual. They recommend the use of comprehension checks and oral reading rate data. The rates they calculate are both words read correctly per minute and errors per minute. Rate data are used because they can show qualitative differences between the student who takes ten minutes to complete a passage, and the student who takes fifty minutes. The rate of words read correctly indicates accuracy, and the rate of words read incorrectly (the error rate) is used as a quality check since these rates can vary independently of each other. This type of measurement shows status only; it does not yield a qualitative description of errors. Qualitative analysis must be superimposed on their methodology for determining best fit.

Proponents of rate data recommend daily measurement. In most cases, however, a weekly direct measurement should be sensitive enough. Measures may also be averaged over time to account for variations inherent in materials and within the student. Qualitative judgments of oral reading can supplement the collection of rate data if the teacher uses daily oral reading lessons.

The methodology described by Lovitt and Hansen (1976a) can also be used to decide when to advance students from one book level to another rather than allow time spent getting through be the determiner (Lovitt and Hansen, 1976b). This means that the assessment must occur at intervals more frequent than just at the end of the book or workbook.

Whatever measures are used to match reader to print or to advance the student, they are not sufficient to account for other variables that enter into the final or tentative decision about whether the match is good. For example, the background the student brings to the material may be a deciding factor in the difficulty of that material for that person. Further, the interest value must be considered because it alone may make the difference in engaging or not engaging the reluctant reader in any instruction at all — interest *nearly* conquers all.

Quite often, the more difficult part of being a resource teacher lies in explaining why traditional assessments and practices do not well serve the student for whom they were originally designed. For example, when Lovitt and Hansen's contingent skip and drill procedure (1976b) is used to advance students in reading material, they may skip an entire book level because they read at an acceptable rate and with no loss of comprehension at the higher level. This practice of skipping material is unheard of in many schools. The "Yes, but . . ." deals primarily with the need to learn the accompanying skills (which rarely have an empirical base) in order to read better. Yet if the student already reads at the better level, perhaps the skills are already being used where they belong — in reading books or magazines rather than in workbooks.

In summary, we have noted that problems exist in determining the appropriate placement of students in materials. These problems center around the use of scores for determining reading levels for students and readability levels for materials. Better matches are made through qualitative assessment of the student's relative success with materials to be used. Further, the kind of assessment suggested depends upon how the materials are to be used. We have also noted a more objective procedure for the direct assessment of oral reading, both to place and to advance students in reading materials. Finally, we have called attention to several factors other than difficulty that should be taken into account when selecting materials for students.

8. *What are the student's reading interests?* Fitzgerald (1977) has noted that "the challenge in teaching reading is in turning out children who will read for information and enjoyment, not in perfecting each child's ability to sound out letters" (p. 9). Reading educators have never stopped advocating having students read. However, the recent trend toward skills-first programs has had the effect of making many teachers feel guilty if the student is "reading" rather than "working." Some teachers do not know the student well enough to become aware of reading interests or interests that could lead to reading.

To find out what a student wants to read or does read, the resource teacher can simply ask the student or observe what he or she chooses to read. More formal techniques can also be used. Summers (1979), for example, suggests a forced choice method that provides a gross numerical index of the category of material the student would prefer to read (Figure 6 – 5). The teacher merely asks if the student would prefer a mystery or a sports story? a mystery or a science story? a mystery or a history story? A plus sign is recorded in each cell if the student prefers the first-named category (the vertical list, to the left of the matrix), and a zero sign if not. Students who read and understand the procedure may complete the form alone and discuss its results later with the teacher.

Measures of interest are usually readministered within a short period of time to determine the reliability of the choices made. They can also be used from time to time to determine the changing interests of the student. If the measure is easily administered, as is the case in the Summers's matrix, the general interests of the classroom or peer group can be determined so that students may be grouped on the basis of reading interests.

In general, guides to the development of reading interests and tastes can be found in books that deal with literature for juveniles. These sources help the teacher select material related to current interests, assignments, or problems that the student may be experiencing. They are also sources of materials that can be read *to* the students who are not yet reading. Literature should find its way to the student even if the student does not do the actual reading.

We especially recommend Glazer and Williams's *Introduction to Children's Literature* (1979) because it gives so many suggestions for the teacher who is just

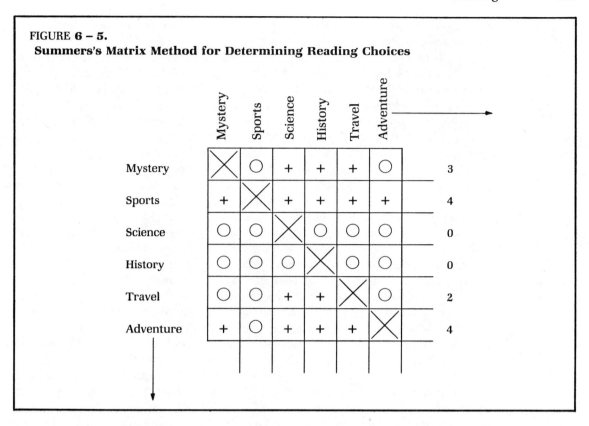

FIGURE **6 – 5.**

Summers's Matrix Method for Determining Reading Choices

discovering the uses of literature. Both White's *High Interest Easy Reading for Junior and Senior High School Students* (1979) and Walker's *Your Reading: A Booklist for Junior High School Students* (1975) are excellent guides for teachers of adolescents.

The resource teacher might want to become aware of the market research that relates to the sale of various reading materials. For example, Kline (1980) reports interesting data about the sales of reading materials in the United States during 1979. Of 12,000 magazines published, thirteen aimed specifically at juveniles are among the top 1½ percent in circulation: *Mad Magazine, Boy's Life, Seventeen Magazine, Highlights for Children, Teen, Hot Rod Magazine, Co-ed, Sesame Street, American Girl, National Lampoon, Jack and Jill, Tiger Beat,* and *Teen Beat.* Each edition of the following four magazines tops 1 million copies: *Mad Magazine, Boy's Life, Seventeen Magazine,* and *Highlights for Children.* In terms of books, there are 40,000 children's book titles in print and therefore available for circulation. One best-selling author, Beverly Cleary, has more than a million copies of her books in print. Kline's comments underscore the need for teachers who work with reading to be aware of the empirical data about choices made by reading consumers, including juveniles: "Beyond all market research, the greatest need remains that every good teacher recognize the right moment, the right text, the right person, and bring them together — moment, text, person — in one miraculous stroke of genius" (p. 286).

9. *What is the extent of the student's understanding of the nature of reading?* One of the differences between good and poor readers lies in their understanding of the nature of reading. Much of this understanding remains at the unconscious level, much as riding a bicycle does *after* one has learned how. Yet understanding the nature of reading is at the heart of current efforts in the direct instruction of comprehension. A great deal of the content of such instruction is intended to bring the student's covert understandings to his or her conscious attention.

The teacher who has worked with a student over time may, in turn, have an unconscious idea of what the student understands about reading. The assessment task is partially to bring these insights about the student to the *teacher's* conscious awareness. V. Brown's Reading Profile Chart (undated a) may be used to inventory various behaviors and understandings that can be checked with the student at different times and under prompted and unprompted conditions (see Table 6 – 1). The strategies noted below are representative of direct and indirect methods the teacher can use to find out what the student understands about reading.

First, the teacher may simply ask the student to describe the way he or she gets meaning from print or goes about reading. Since this question may be akin to asking how one goes about driving, the teacher may need to probe or say, "Tell me more." If the student does not respond, then more indirect methods can be used.

A second method is more indirect. It uses questions that are involved in daily reading tasks. For example, when the student answers comprehension questions in class or on a test, the teacher may also ask how the student came to select that particular answer given, whether the answer itself is correct or incorrect.

A third procedure is more direct. There are various programs designed to teach comprehension strategies (such as Wong, 1980). The teacher can try these materials with the student and discuss with the student how they seem to relate to reading.

Another procedure can be used after the student reads a story or passage. As the teacher discusses the content with the student, the teacher can ask about the story or passage structure, why the author might have written the story, and similar questions.

Finally, when an error analysis is made of oral reading, these errors may be discussed with the student. Does the student understand the concept of miscue? Does the student understand both reader and author contributions to errors made by the reader?

Knowledge of the student's understanding of reading will help focus instruction on key understandings that will give the student independence in learning to read.

10. *Which specific phonic and word analysis skills does the student need to learn?* Traditional remedial and developmental reading assessments place heavy emphasis upon inventorying skills in phonic and structural word analysis. Through the use of specific test items, various skills are listed as deficient and in need of instruction. This emphasis is misplaced. It is not that students may not need to be taught skills; it is the data base for making the judgment that is problematic. For various

TABLE **6 – 1.**
Individual Reading Profile Chart

Name	Unprompted	Prompted	Instructional Ideas	Date
During Oral Reading				
1. Uses context cues				
2. Uses picture cues				
3. Uses intraparagraph cues				
4. Uses interparagraph cues				
5. Uses word analysis cues				
a. phonic				
1) linear				
2) comparative				
3) checking				
b. structural				
1) linear				
2) comparative				
3) checking				
6. Uses cues flexibly				
7. Phrases meaningfully				
8. Rereads to get meaning				
9. Uses self-correction				
a. Aware of need				
b. Attempts				
c. Checks for meaning				
10. Fluency/speed				
11. Expression suits material				
12. Dialect				
a. syntax				
b. pronunciation				
13. Experience/maturity				
a. syntax				
b. pronunciation				
14. Shows evidence of practice				
Awareness of Sources of Miscues				
1. Author				
a. vocabulary				
b. clarity				

TABLE **6 – 1.** *(Continued)*
Individual Reading Profile Chart

Name	Unprompted	Prompted	Instructional Ideas	Date
c. organization				
d. style				
e. syntax				
f. audience gauge				
2. Self				
a. carelessness				
b. background information				
c. depth of vocabulary				
d. range of vocabulary				
e. knowledge of appropriate cues				
f. material gauge				
g. syntax				
h. attention/interest				
3. Other:				
a.				
b.				
Postreading Probes (Oral or Silent)				
1. Telling/Retelling				
a. main idea(s), theme(s) or plot(s)				
b. genre				
c. characterization				
d. details to support ideas or judgments				
e. sequence of events/ideas				
f. structure/story syntax				
g. relationships among people, ideas, events				
h. inferential extensions				
2. Apparent interest				
3. Knowledge of related materials				
4. Knowledge of related ideas				
5. Background brought to reading				
6. Background extended by reading				

TABLE **6 – 1.** *(Continued)*
Individual Reading Profile Chart

Name	Unprompted	Prompted	Instructional Ideas	Date
7. Knowledge of language structures				
8. Specific concepts/vocabulary				
a.				
b.				
c.				
d.				
e.				
f.				
g.				
h.				
9. Rate: words per minute				
Rate: charted				
10. Other				
a.				
b.				
c.				

Specific comments, questions, or instructional plans

reasons, students may fail test items that are designed to test the use of a specific skill, such as the following:

1. Circle the words in which a secondary accent on the first or second syllable is followed by one unstressed syllable before the primary accent.

    hippopotamus   peninsula   Portugal   originality

    or

2. I don't know _____ he lives.

    (where, there)

Failure on items such as these does not necessarily mean that the student misses the same element during actual reading of text material. Students who are characterized as not knowing *bl* blends are often caught reading words with *bl* blends, and often without specific instruction.

A further problem with using tests or inventories of skills is that the skills assessed in a particular set may not be the ones the student actually needs for reading tasks or pleasures. Rarely does the skill-of-the-day match the reading-of-the-day.

If the skill items of reading are not reliably assessed with tests and if the skills taught from tests or from inventories may not meet the reading needs of the individual, then how can the resource teacher obtain valid and reliable information about the skill needs of individuals? The answer is compatible both with behavioral approaches to reading and with individualized reading as it was advocated, if not implemented, during the past several decades.

From a behaviorist point of view, baseline data are required to show a need for instruction. Behaviorists prefer to obtain baseline samples from the naturally occurring context of the behavior of interest. The naturally occurring context for obtaining baseline data in this case comes from listening to the student read various kinds of reading material. As the student reads orally, errors are noted, and *if the errors recur across contexts* — that is, if there are enough baseline data to indicate that the data supporting the existence of a skills problem are valid and reliable (for example, if the student continuously misses *-ble* endings or cannot pronounce *-ou* words) — then instruction in these elements is certainly justified.

From the perspective of individualized reading proponents, students should not be taught skills that they have already induced and mastered enough to use routinely in their reading, regardless of what tests may show. Further, groupings for skills instruction should be based upon mutual need for learning the skill and not upon some gross assignment to a reading group. Although the rationale is different, the procedures used for deciding what to teach in individualized reading are essentially the same as those described for the behaviorists.

If the student does not yet read well enough to make a skills assessment from oral reading, then skills instruction should be postponed. At this stage of reading, attention should be given to getting meaning from print and to understanding the nature of the reading process.

11. *What are the qualitative aspects of the student's reading?* Most of the assessment in reading is qualitative, even when the instrument used is individually admin-

istered and purportedly diagnostic in nature. The lower the student's score in comparison with that of age or grade peers, the poorer the quality of reading is assumed to be.

During the past decade, there has been a growing emphasis on the need to make some qualitative assessment of reading, especially in remedial situations. By qualitative, we mean that judgments are made about various aspects of the student's reading. The judgments made are derived from analyzing and probing (1) the student's discussion of what he or she has read and (2) errors made during reading, usually oral reading. The discussions about the reading content are intended to determine how well the student comprehends the material and, to some extent, how well the student goes about comprehending. The analysis of errors involves making judgments about the relative importance of each error in terms of its relationship to comprehension. Errors that are judged as important, because they interfere significantly with comprehension are targeted for instruction. Those that are not viewed as interfering with comprehension are ignored or subjected to further analysis to determine if they might be potentially problematic. This section deals with the two methods of choice for making these qualitative judgments.

Student-teacher discussion: The use of comprehension questions after silent or oral reading is a good technique to use when quantitative information is needed. This procedure may be adequate for a test situation or for a quick check of comprehension. It is insufficient for finding out how well the individual student understands the various aspects of comprehension.

For qualitative assessment, the resource teacher selects passages, stories, or books that are long enough to permit the student to use a relatively full range of comprehension strategies. It is unlikely that any one passage is adequate for this purpose. The assessment of comprehension should be made over time with a variety of materials.

Silent reading should be used whenever possible because it is the more naturally occurring mode of reading and is more likely to focus the student's attention on comprehension abilities rather than those of reading words correctly. The student should be told to read carefully because he or she will be expected to discuss the material with the teacher.

When the student has completed the silent reading, the teacher may first ask the student to tell about what was read. Depending on the kind of information the student volunteered, the teacher may then use probes or questions to check the student's understanding of:

The main idea(s), theme(s), or plot(s)
The kind of story or passage it is — that is, its genre, such as fairytale, sports report, adventure tale, or mystery
Characterizations
Details (only those needed to support any statements or judgments made about the material)
The sequence of events or ideas
The structure of the material, often called the story syntax

Relationships among ideas, people, or events
Indirect information or inferential material
Specific language structures such as simile, metaphor, or anaphora

In addition, the teacher will want to probe the student's:

Knowledge of related ideas
Inferential extensions of the material (for example, how information can be applied
     or what might happen next)
Background brought to the reading situation
Background extended by the reading situation
Specific concepts or vocabulary items (for example, "What exactly is a *lob*, a *globe*,
     or a *sarcophagus?*")
Knowledge of related material
Use of interparagraph and intraparagraph links
Apparent interest in the material

Not every bit of information need be wrung from the student each time she
or he reads. Most material is unsuitable for assessing everything we might want to
know about comprehension.

After analyzing the student's comprehension abilities and strategies over an
extended period of time, the resource teacher can plan a more individualized program than would be possible merely by following a scope and sequence chart, which
may not have relevance to the student's present needs. Instructional resources for
teaching comprehension are noted throughout this chapter.

For most purposes, the kind of comprehension assessment just described will
be sufficient for instructional planning. It is especially important to use for students
who experience problems with oral reading. The results of silent reading comprehension can be used to show that they are better readers than they have probably been
led to believe.

Analysis of oral reading: A more detailed assessment may be needed when problems in comprehension are not readily solvable from probing silent reading comprehension abilities. In this case, oral reading errors are used as the basis for judging the qualitative aspects of ongoing reading behavior. When the student does not
read the exact words of the text, he or she has deviated from the text. These deviations are usually called *errors*, if only by definition of the term. Until the advent of
the reading miscue inventory (RMI) (Y. Goodman and Burke, 1972), there was no
formal framework for making judgments about the relative importance of errors
made during oral reading. Whether or not one uses the RMI as a formal diagnostic
tool, the concepts on which it is based permeate the literature of diagnosis in reading.

The word *miscue*, as in the RMI, is the term used to refer to qualitative analyses
of reading. To describe miscue, we must compare it with the word *error*, which means
a deviation from a standard — in this case, from each word of the reading text. The
implication of this term is usually noted in dictionary — that these deviations are

due either to carelessness or to ignorance of the standard (the text). It is possible to continue to use the word *error* instead of *miscue,* since deviations from the text are indeed errors in the basic sense of the term. But it is the connotation or assumption of carelessness and/or ignorance that makes the term *miscue* necessary in reading analysis. *Miscue* refers to an assumption about the nature of reading itself: that it is largely a matter of authors and readers using the respective linguistic *cues* available to them to aid the comprehension of printed text.

Writers use many strategies to clarify their meanings. For example, they may use redundancy; they may choose traditional or untraditional language patterns, depending on the audience for whom the communication is intended; they try to select their words carefully; and they try to present their thoughts in a logical sequence. Readers usually respond predictably to these cues and also use some of their own. For example, they anticipate what the author is going to say and how he or she will say it; they relate what the author says to their own experiences and thinking; and they use what they know about language to comprehend the real meaning of structures such as metaphor or simile.

The use of the word *cue* is appropriate for describing strategies used by authors and readers because it is consistent with the dictionary meanings of cue which refer to signals to begin an action; hints, intimations, or suggestions as to what course of action to take or when to take it; or items or features acting as indications of the nature of an object or situation perceived. A reader who has missed the more salient signals, hints, or features of the author is assumed to have missed the cue(s), or *miscued.* Whatever the person reads instead of the text as it was written is called a *miscue.*

Miscues are not always the fault of the author. The reader who miscues may not know how to use all of the linguistic or cognitive information available during reading. Perhaps the student who is reading lacks the appropriate background for the material. For whatever reasons, it is clear that the contributions that the author *and* the reader make to the act of reading create essentially two potential sources of miscues.

There are three basic purposes for miscue analysis: (1) to identify the nature of the cues that have been missed or misused; (2) to judge their relative importance to comprehension; and (3) to decide the likely source of each miscue, the consistency with which the student misses it, and how likely it is that the cue will be used again in wide reading. Instruction is planned around important miscues that are consistently experienced by the student and for cues that are likely to reappear often in reading.

The resource teacher who has been counting the number of times we have used the word *cue* may be wondering why we are explaining the concepts of miscue analysis at such length. It is partly because of the importance we attach to qualitative analysis and also partly because of widespread misuse of the term. In remedial work, the reports of reading assessment may contain phrases such as, "The results of miscue analysis showed that the student was reading at a 3.0 level," or, "The student missed the words *September, holiday, Labor, summer, and, of,* and *the.*" Statements such as these merely reflect the fact that the term *miscue* has largely replaced the word *error* in reading education materials; however, the terms are not interchangeable. Where deviations from the text are simply counted and summed, then there is no reason to discuss or even to think about cueing systems. This counting of errors is characteristic of all IRIs, even where the errors are first noted as repetitions, omissions, and so forth. Ultimately, these categories make no difference to the end product, a score, and they carry no implications for instruction, except to use easier material. The term *miscue analysis* should be reserved for instances in which deviations from the text are evaluated in terms of (1) their help or hindrance to the reader's comprehension of the text; (2) the cueing system that has been used or has not been used; and/or (3) the probable source of the miscue.

Consider the sentence, "The dog ran down the dusty road." Jennifer reads the sentence as, "The dog runned down the dus road." An analysis would correctly show 1 substitution + 1 missed word element = 2 errors. From a miscue standpoint, additional analysis would be required. If Jennifer were then instructed to read the sentence very carefully, she might still say, "The dog ran down the dust road." If we know Jennifer's oral language patterns well enough, we might conclude that "run-ed" is her usual way of saying the past tense of *run;* yet she can correct the pattern to conform to the visual characteristics of *ran* in standard written English. The deviation was not critical, or even relevant, to her comprehension. Since she used an alternative form of *ran,* we can assume that she did comprehend the meaning. Since she missed the -y of *dusty,* even though she had an opportunity to self-correct, it may be that she is not aware of the adjective form of words such as *dust-dusty* or *trust-trusty.* If this is the case, then instruction in this type of change might be based upon the more likely understood word set of *luck-lucky.*

Some reading analyses yield only scores or lists of words that the reader has missed. These scores or lists are unaccompanied by evaluative judgments or descriptive statements. Where this kind of analysis is reported, then no qualitative analysis of the student's reading has been made. Certainly no miscue analysis has been made, for it is somewhat correct to say that miscue analysis is a form of error analysis. It is *not* correct to say that the word *miscue* is just a more positive term to use for a reading *error.*

Since the framework for miscue analysis is found in the RMI, a summary of the questions involved in making judgments about deviations from the text is summarized below.[2]

Each miscue is analyzed into nine major categories to call attention to how well the student functions with the given text. The analyses require evaluator judgment. These judgments are made in response to a series of questions:

1. *Dialect.* Is a dialect variation involved in the miscue?

EXAMPLES	READER	TEXT
Sound variation	idear	idea
Vocabulary variation	goed	went
Grammatical variation	two boy	two boys

2. *Intonation.* Is a shift in intonation involved in the miscue (pitch, stress, or pause from what is expected)? Coded as a miscue only when changes in the grammatical structure or the meaning of a passage occur. Usually this is a complex miscue.

EXAMPLES	READER	TEXT
Word level	an original pro ject'	an original project
Phrase level	. . . after *he cut in* his allowance	. . . after *the cut in* his allowance
Sentence level	Clairbel got *nosey* when we hid her sometimes.	Claribel got *noisy* when we hid her. Sometimes . . .

3. *Graphic similarity.* How much would the miscue look like what is expected? Coded: high, some, or none.

4. *Sound similarity.* How much does the miscue sound like what is expected? Coded: high, some, or none.
Examples:

READER	TEXT	GRAPHIC SIMILARITY	SOUND SIMILARITY
our	your	high	some
the	a	none	high

5. *Grammatical function.* Is the grammatical function of the miscue the same as the grammatical function of the word in the text? Coded: identical (Y), different (N), or not possible to determine (P).
Examples:

	READER	TEXT
(Y)	Claribel always got nosey when we hid her.	Claribel always got noisy when we hid her.
(N)	She likes to wear pretty *colors* dresses.	She likes to wear pretty *colored* dresses.
(P)	Harry did . . . (reader stops and corrects, then goes on.)	Harry *was* playing ball.

6. *Correction.* Is the miscue corrected? Coded: corrected; unsuccessful attempt, or correct response abandoned; or no attempt at correction.

7. *Grammatical acceptability.* Does the miscue occur in a structure that is grammatically acceptable? Coded: acceptable; acceptable as read, but not in relation to prior and subsequent sentences in the text; or not acceptable.

8. *Semantic acceptability.* Is the whole sentence meaningful within the dialect system of the reader?

9. *Meaning change.* How much of the message of the text is altered by the reader's miscues? Does the miscue result in a change of meaning? Coded: extensive (Y), minimal (P), or no change (N).

RETELLING OUTLINES

STORY MATERIAL	*INFORMATIONAL MATERIAL*
Character analysis	Specifies
Recall	Generalization
Development	Major concepts
Events	
Plot, theme	

The actual miscue analysis coding sheets often are too cumbersome for most purposes; many teachers construct modifications of the analysis sheets. Kathy Wingert has used a simple format (see Figure 6 – 6) in which each departure from the text is numbered as it occurs. The reader's exact response is compared with the text word it represents. A series of questions is then used to make qualitative judgments of the relative importance of the discrepancy.

The RMI offers several advantages over more traditional approaches to reading analysis. The major advantage is that the RMI approach is more consistent with current research on language learning, of which learning to read is a part. This point as stated by K. Goodman (1971) can be applied to oral language learning as well as to reading:

> The skill of riding a bicycle comes with riding a bicycle. We do not offer a child lectures, diagrams, and drills on the component skills of bicycle riding — we set him on the saddle and use a guiding hand or training wheels to make sure he does not fall off while he teaches himself the precarious art of keeping balance. Forcing him to worry about laws of motion and centers of gravity would obviously confuse him.
>
> Making learning to read easy means ensuring cues at the time a child needs them, ensuring feedback of the kind he requires at the time he requires it, providing encouragement when it is sought. Making learning to read easy requires an understanding of the reading process, and of what the child is trying to do. [P. 195]

The disadvantages of miscue analysis lie primarily in its complexity. It is difficult to conduct such an analysis, to interpret the results, and to communicate them to people who do not understand the rationale underlying the approach. Despite this disadvantage, various forms of miscue analysis are finding their way into traditional reading evaluation. For example, Page and Barr (1975, pp. 101 – 110) have suggested how to recast the IRI into a form of miscue analysis; their detailed description of how this can be done should be helpful to teachers familiar with IRIs. Williamson and Young (1974), who have been interested in the problems of content area reading, have also suggested how these two procedures can be synthesized. Teachers who may be contemplating combining these techniques first should read V. Brown's (1975b) comparison of the IRI and RMI approaches.

FIGURE **6 – 6.**
Wingert Example of Reading Miscue Modification

EXAMINER ___Wingert___   READER ___Danny Metcalf___

# IN SEQ.	READER RESPONSE	TEXT WORD	SUCCESS-FULLY COR-RECTED?	RETAINS MEANING OF THE TEXT?	MAKES SENSE IN PASSAGE TO THAT POINT?	RESULTS IN GRAM-MATICAL ENGLISH UTTER-ANCE?	HOW DOES IT RESEM-BLE TEXT WORD IN SOUND OR SPELLING?
1	a	the	No	Yes	Yes	Yes	No
2	tank	mask	No	No	No	Yes	No - follows "oxygen" in exp.
3	woods	forest	No	Yes	Yes	Yes	OK meaning
4	– o –	little old	No	Yes	Yes	Yes	Omits a continuing text redundancy
5	Claba	Claribel	Eventually	Yes	In sense of a name	Yes	Initially, both

RETELLING

CHARACTERS: (Names, traits, descriptions, etc.)
_____
_____
_____

PLOT-EVENTS: (Mention, sequence, significance, etc.)
_____
_____
_____
_____

INFERENCES: (Relationship to personal or vicarious experience; elaborative
           ideas, etc.)
_____
_____
_____
_____
_____
_____
_____

Reprinted by special permission of Wingert, K., and Geissal, M.A. *Reading miscue modification.* Un-published manuscript, Northeastern Illinois University, Chicago, Illinois, 1975.

Both Kenneth Goodman and Yetta Goodman give more detailed descriptions of the rationale and procedures involved in miscue analysis; see the chapter "Twelve Easy Ways to Make Learning to Read Difficult" (K. Goodman, 1973, pp. 183 – 196) and the article "Using Children's Miscues for Teaching Reading Strategies" (Y. Goodman, 1970, pp. 455 – 459). Frank Smith's works, "Understanding Reading" (1978), *Psycholinguistics and Reading* (1973), and *Comprehension and Learning: A Conceptual Framework for Teachers* (1975), continue to reinforce our opinions about the close relationship between current conceptualizations of psycholinguistics and reading instruction. In their book, Y. Goodman and Burke (1980) offer many ideas for helping teachers who are limited in their approaches to remediation. Allen and Watson's *Findings of Research in Miscue Analysis: Classroom implications* (1976) also offers practical suggestions for teaching. We especially recommend the extensive how-to prescriptions of Gillespie-Silver in her *Teaching Reading to Children with Special Needs* (1979).

12. *How much responsibility is the student likely to assume for learning to read?* The best person to teach the student to read is the student. Teachers may facilitate, encourage, and structure, but the student must assume the responsibility for learning. Students may not believe that they *can* learn to read, attributing any problems they have to labels such as "dyslexia," "learning disabilities," or "dumbness." They may also believe (too often correctly) that they have been instructed poorly.

Schools, on the other hand, are likely to attribute failure to the student or to the family background. Yet rarely do teachers make an effort to deal realistically with the degree of responsibility the student can reasonably be taught and expected to assume for learning.

Students may also be involved with many teachers who have differing points of view and who provide inconsistent instruction and feedback. Often there is no real instruction at all. Students, then, may be the only sources of possible continuity in reading development. They must be encouraged and specifically taught to pursue this development independently of any one instructional program or teacher.

Students can take over much of their own instruction, and they can certainly learn to record behaviors and progress. Many teachers teach students to do their own miscue analyses.

During evaluation, the resource teacher picks up clues about the nature and degree of responsibility the student can assume. In a more structured way, various procedures can be tried and evaluated before formulating the student's program. This element of individual responsibility should be considered in the recommendations for any instructional program to be suggested.

13. *Which of various approaches to reading are likely to be effective with the student?* Part of assessment deals with determining what does work with the student. After planning the methods and materials that are likely to succeed, whatever is recommended should be tried out, and at this stage, daily data recorded to judge its effectiveness. The form of the data will depend upon the methods selected. Perhaps it will involve observations back within the regular classroom. In any case, effectiveness data should accompany any programing recommendations made on behalf of the student.

DEVELOPING INSTRUCTIONAL PROCEDURES

Dividing this chapter into three sections is a device for giving individual focus to analyzing the learner within the classroom, providing supplemental individual analysis, and developing instructional procedures. In practice, however, these three aspects of remedial planning are not easily separated, nor should they be. The resource teacher who studies the students in the classroom and works with them individually should develop and test out instructional procedures while doing so. Therefore, many of the suggestions that are about to be made for instructional procedures have been mentioned briefly in other sections of this chapter in conjunction with their relationship to assessment. Also, some of the topics mentioned previously, such as parent involvement, self-concept, motivation, and the coordination of services, must be accounted for regardless of the instructional approach chosen. Since these topics are discussed both in the preceding sections of this chapter and in other parts of the book, we will not deal with them here. The suggestions summarized below are more directly related to reading instruction and deal specifically with (1) instruction within the classroom; (2) individualized instruction; and (3) alternatives to reading.

Instruction within the Classroom

This section describes four general procedures that are useful when dealing with altering reading instruction within the classroom. These procedures involve: (1) superimposing a management system on the program; (2) changing selected program elements; (3) changing to an alternative program; and (4) modifying reading-related tasks for: (a) independent work; (b) the content areas; and (c) other language arts areas.

1. *Superimposing a Management System on the Program.* Some individual sessions show that a classroom program is appropriate in the sense that the student can do the tasks and can profit from doing them. The problem is that he or she does not try or does not attend to instruction. Classroom observation also might show that the teacher is distracted from good management practices. In these cases, a management system will help keep the reading program on target by breaking the program down into its component steps, providing consequation to the student for correct performance, and setting up a system of record keeping that will chart progress. This kind of structure is likely to insure that both teacher and student attend to relevant aspects of the reading instruction (see appropriate sections in Chapters 2, 5, and 11 for discussion of management systems).

A lot of time for planning and for monitoring is required to initiate a management system with a reading program. Many resource teachers work with classroom teachers to find a new program that is already well defined in terms of instructional sequences or in terms of behavioral objectives. In this way, some of the major tasks of creating such a system are already accomplished before attending to the other factors. Any new program should, of course, be tried out with the referred student to see if he or she responds to the proposed program.

It should be remembered that a management system does not improve the nature of a program; it merely ensures its correct and systematic implementation and allows for ongoing assessment of the student's responses to it. Durkin (1981) reports the results of an analysis of the manuals for five basal reading programs in regard to their suggestions for comprehension instruction. She concluded that "the manuals give far more attention to assessment and practice than to direct, explicit instruction. When procedures for teaching children how to comprehend *are* provided, they tend to be brief" (p. 515). Thus, while a management system seems logical as a means of improving instruction, it may in fact serve to make a poor system more efficiently poor.

2. *Changing Selected Program Elements.*   Only certain portions of the reading program used may need to be modified for a particular student. For example, supplementary lessons might provide additional practice with troublesome skills, enrichment activities can help the student apply what is learned, or the instructions given might need to be made simpler. The resource teacher usually makes these modifications or teaches the classroom teacher to do so. In either case, *monitoring* should be done by a designated person to determine how long the assistance is needed.

3. *Changing to an Alternative Program.*   Sometimes a complete departure from the classroom method of instruction is needed in order to desensitize the reader to a program associated with failure or to accommodate particular reading characteristics. For example, programs such as *Rebus* (Woodcock, 1967) or the *Initial Teaching Alphabet* (Mazurkiewicz and Tanyzer, 1966) may be so different that the student is motivated to learn to read. They also may account for the unique language problems or for the capacity for initial learning of individual students.

The resource teacher usually will administer programs that are very different from the classroom methods and materials in use. If the student is working with an alternative series or program, he or she should not be allowed to continue with the inappropriate program in the classroom setting. This means that the resource teacher must try to schedule the alternative instruction during the reading time in the classroom or else must provide work for the student while others are reading. The resource teacher also should work with the rest of the class to help them develop positive attitudes toward the student(s) who needs special help.

4. *Modifying Reading-Related Work.*   Independent work such as homework or seatwork can be modified to make them more appropriate. The task presented in Table 6 – 2 shows some modifications that could be made for a single task and what each modification may accomplish.

For the young student, the resource teacher should move away from convergent answer and paper-and-pencil tasks, such as workbooks in which only the answer wanted is acceptable. Instead, the independent work should emphasize creative, divergently oriented activities that are related to language and cognition, such as science, artwork, dramatics, creative writing, or mathematics concepts.

TABLE 6 – 2.
Variations on an Exercise
(Originally intended for a seatwork exercise)

Directions: Underline any word in each line that is opposite in meaning to the one
already underlined.

(a) tree	bottom	top	line
(b) light	sun	heavy	dark
(c) watch	stand	sit	fence
(d) owl	take	please	give
(e) all	green	none	time
(f) always	ever	every	never
(g) summer	late	winter	early
(h) cold	hot	bring	upon

VARIATIONS

1. Instead of marking right and wrong, ask about how each response was arrived at.
   (To prove any misinformation)
2. Type on a large index card to be filed with others under *Opposites*; with answers
   provided on card backs. (To promote self-correction; to be more teacher independent; to make more individually useful)
3. Have the student number a paper from 1 – 8 and write each pair or group of anto-
   nyms; or the antonym of the underlined word. (Independence; combine with handwriting and/or spelling practice)
4. Change directions to: Underline the two words that are opposite in meaning in each
   line — where none has yet been underlined. (To cause the student to do more thinking by removing a cue — the underlined word)
5. Use the direction: If the first four are completed correctly, do not complete the last
   four. (Motivation for attending and for accuracy)
6. Use the direction: Complete any four of the eight examples. (Motivation by allowing
   the student choice; to analyze choices made)
7. Use the direction: Underline the examples you are pretty sure of in red, and the
   ones you aren't so sure of with erasable pencil. (To gain insight into thinking, and
   to focus on the idea that independent tasks are for learning — not testing)
8. Put a pool of items, each on one small card, in a box from which items may be drawn
   at random. Change the directions for various students or on various days. A master
   direction sheet may be made, and the appropriate directions checked for the student. (To increase individualization and independence possibilities for the teacher)

In order to implement the suggestions made by many authors who work with
reading in the content areas (mathematics, science), the resource teacher may have
to work very hard to gain the cooperation of the classroom teacher. Often once the
classroom teacher has used some modifications in presenting tasks or in specific

teaching strategies, he or she quickly sees their advantages when used with other students. The payoff is so great that the classroom teacher usually becomes increasingly receptive to making these changes. If, however, the classroom teacher is not receptive to modifying the content area tasks and strategies, then the resource teacher must arrange for tutoring the student who has trouble. For a student with impoverished concepts or experiences, the resource teacher should discuss any supplemental enrichment activities with that student so that he or she understands how the new experiences relate to the old ones.

Poor readers often have difficulty with the other language arts — writing (both penmanship and composition), spelling, listening, and speaking. The resource teacher is referred to Chapters 8, 9, and 11 of this book to learn how to develop any of these programs.

Individualized Instruction

Individualized instruction occurs when the resource teacher or aide: (1) uses tutoring to supplement classroom instruction; (2) uses one of the clinical reading systems; (3) engages in direct teaching; or (4) uses individualized reading.

1. *Tutorial Work.*   In some cases, regular classroom teachers and administrators may expect the resource teacher to supply some extra tutoring in reading in order to "keep the learner up" with the rest of a particular group. We believe that unless a student has missed instruction, there rarely is any justification for establishing a tutoring program over a long period. If tutoring must be continued for an extended period, the basic instructional program probably is inappropriate, and alternatives such as a superimposed management system should be explored.

To see the resource teacher as a tutor is much too limited for the possibilities and responsibilities we advocate. The use of peer tutors in certain instances is highly recommended, however (see Chapter 11).

2. *Use of Clinical Systems.*   Well-administered one-to-one approaches such as those of Fernald (1943) or Gillingham and Stillman (1966) vary widely, and the secret of their reported clinical success is not known; yet they appear to work. Clinical systems have common characteristics that they all require or provide: (a) the attention and involvement of the learner; (b) planned success experiences, including immediate restructuring of an inappropriate task; (c) consistent and continuous positive reinforcement for appropriate responses; (d) immediate feedback to the learner; (e) overlearning of basic response units; (f) multisensory stimuli and/or the learner in the methodology (V. Brown and Botel, 1972, p. 47). These characteristics are similar to the characteristics of analytic teaching.

All clinical systems and their derivatives have the disadvantages of being extremely time-consuming and of requiring a lot of supervised practice to learn. Despite these teaching disadvantages, they should be used when necessary; it is difficult to continue to suggest that students *cannot* learn to read because we are unwilling to put the effort required into teaching them. Often, clinical approaches need not be continued indefinitely. Once the reader has gained confidence that he or she *can* read and is learning to read through practice, the approaches may be modified and often discontinued.

3. *Direct Teaching.* For students who have not learned to read or who have very specific problems that require direct teaching, the resource teacher may need to become the reading teacher. Some of the methodologies and materials to be used in direct instruction are offshoots of applied behavioral analysis. Others come from a variety of research and curriculum sources. They all share the characteristics of involving direct instruction of the student(s) by a teacher.

Jenkins and Heliotis (1981) describe the characteristics of the behavioral approach to direct instruction:

> The direct instruction approach focuses not only on the content of the material presented — the selection of skills and teaching examples — but also on the initial introduction and sequencing of those skills and examples, the frequency with which practice items are introduced and reviewed, and the development of specific instructional strategies. Certain teacher presentation variables are also characteristic of a direct instruction approach, such as simple, clear, and usually scripted teacher directions; error corrections; and use of both group and individual responses. [P.27]

Characteristic of behavioral approaches to direct instruction are programs like DISTAR (Engelmann and Bruner, 1974) and *Thinking Basics: Corrective Reading Program: Comprehension A* (Engelmann, et al., 1978). This type of material is difficult for one teacher to produce, even from such models. It is likely that the decade of the 1980s will see the emergence of more behaviorally oriented programs of direct instruction. Jenkins and Heliotis (1981, pp. 29 – 31) report a variety of goals for which programs are now being formulated. They include training in inferencing and in making overt what are usually the covert strategies used in reading comprehension.

Other approaches to direct teaching are more eclectic. Even though they may include one or more of the characteristics noted by Jenkins and Heliotis, they cannot be characterized as behavioral in their sense of the word. They are, however, direct. The following strategies or programs provide the methodologies for true individualization.

For the instruction of specific word analysis skills, Gray's classic, *On Their Own in Reading: How to Give Children Independence in Analyzing New Words* (1960), has never been superseded in terms of its comprehensiveness. It presents the role of word analysis in reading; provides an extensive account of the scope and sequence of a word analysis program; and for each skill provides how-to lessons that may be used to teach the skill, independently of any program the student may be currently using. The primary methodology is one of leading students to induce a generalization and apply it to a new situation. This book is an excellent handbook to use for students who need direct instruction in skills.

Programs such as the *Essential Sight Words Program* (Sundbye, Dyck, and Wyatt, 1979, 1981) can be used to teach the identification of basic sight words. This approach uses a combination of sight word drill and the actual reading of sight words in context. It is an excellent model, geared to the interests of the elementary-age student. At this time, no comparable program exists for the older student.

There are an infinite number of ways to teach comprehension. Pearson and Johnson's *Teaching Reading Comprehension* (1978) offers instructional suggestions and also provides explanations of the ideas and skills they address, such as anaphoric relations. Their book, *Teaching Reading Vocabulary* (1978), presents such a meaningful approach to vocabulary development that it can truly be described as assisting with comprehension too. In each case, the authors present samples of exercises that may either be copied by the teacher to adapt at the local level or be used as guides when seeking materials from publishers, school bookstores, or instructional materials centers.

One of the more newly prominent techniques for comprehension instruction is the cloze procedure. This procedure has long been associated with assessment and recently has become an important technique for instruction. Originally the cloze procedure involved the deletion of words from a passage, usually on a random, every *n*th basis. Students then generated the missing word from the context and their expectations, and the word filled in the blank. The term *cloze* has since been widely used to refer to almost any procedure in which the reader must fill in the blank, even if the student did not generate the word but selected from multiple choices.

Jongsma (1980) summarizes the research on the use of cloze for instructional purposes. He reports that of the instructional strategies that appeared in the literature, ony that of Samuels, Dahl, and Archwamety (1974) has been validated. Their procedures are intended to teach sight word identification and meaning in the primary grades. He also reports other recommended procedures, such as Rankin's prescription for sequencing cloze instruction. These are procedures that can be used readily by the resource teacher.

The approaches noted above are somewhat fractionated and directed toward specific skills or strategies. They are only a *part* of a comprehensive reading program, even one of remedial reading. The framework for a complete individualized reading program is found in, ironically enough, the Individualized Reading literature.

4. *Individualized Reading.* Individualized Reading, in this capital-letter sense, is based upon the use of both text and trade book material to interest and encourage learning to read by reading. Unlike recreational reading, Individualized Reading places an emphasis on skills instruction that is directly related to the student's current reading needs. It is ideal for use with content area material because the instructional needs can be taken from the naturally occurring demands of the school environment. Seatwork activities focus upon the uses of reading, for example, with materials such as *URICA: Using Reading in Creative Activities* (Sunflower and McNutt, 1981). The use of an individual reading conference allows the teacner to come to know the student and his or her reading better than is possible with traditional instruction. In this way, the teacher can note not only ongoing skills needs but also trends in the student's reading interests.

For the nonreader, programs such as a basal series (through the preprimer level), DISTAR I (Engelmann and Bruner, 1974), or the language experience approach to beginning reading, can be used to get students started. Once students are reading at a minimal level of some basic sentences, Individualized Reading can be started. Veatch's *Individualizing Your Reading Program: Self-Selection in Action* (1959) is especially helpful during the transition from more traditional programs. It is geared toward the elementary level. For postelementary programs, Fader's *The New Hooked on Books* (1976) will help in starting a program of Individualized Reading. For application specifically to the remedial situation, V. Brown's *Remediating Remedial Reading* (undated a) provides more how-to detail.

Alternatives to Reading

If all options discussed in this chapter have failed and if the student is approaching adolescence, the resource teacher must consider the appropriateness and desirability of continuing remedial programming. This is true in terms not only of the financial costs of continuing such an approach but also of the social and emotional cost to the student. It is bad enough that such individuals will be illiterate; they need not be ignorant as well. There are many alternatives to reading and writing, and resource teachers will need to become familiar with these various approaches and use them to their fullest.

ENDNOTES

1. This material has been adapted from V. Brown, *Remediating Remedial Reading* (1983).
2. Reprinted by special permission of Professional Press, Inc. From Brown, V. Reading miscue analysis. *Journal of Learning Disabilities*, 1975, 8, pp. 605 – 611. Copyright 1975 by Professional Press, Inc.

7

Mathematics

Except for students with reading or behavior problems, those who have difficulty acquiring a functional mastery of math concepts and computational skills constitute the largest group referred for resource help. This chapter gives resource teachers useful information about: (1) evaluating the students' learning environment, including the curriculum, the attitudes of teachers and students, and other aspects of the classroom that might relate to math instruction; (2) assessing abilities and needs in mathematics in a qualitative manner; and (3) teaching students effectively.

ANALYSIS OF THE LEARNER IN THE CLASSROOM

A classroom teacher may refer a student for resource assistance if the student: (1) performs relatively poorly on a standardized test; (2) shows evidence of specific problems in diagnostic testing situations; (3) fails mastery tests; and/or (4) has consistent trouble with daily work, during either instruction or independent study periods. The answers to the questions presented in this section provide a comprehensive view of how a particular context can either help or hinder a student's progress in math. The resource teacher must consider the referred student in relation to the classroom setting in order to plan and evaluate modifications in the daily instructional program. In addition, such an analysis will provide clues to the kind of intensive, one-to-one work needed so that students can learn both the computation and the concepts of mathematics.

1. *What information in school records might be relevant to mathematics achievement?* Historical patterns of test scores should be examined carefully to determine the chronicity of math problems. The resource teacher also will want to note factors that might be involved in low achievement, such as patterns of absence or high mobility. Students who are absent frequently may have missed instruction or practice on specific concepts or procedures. In a sequential math curriculum, these topics or opportunities are not often repeated. Further, in math the topics may be sequentially dependent. A missed topic may also mean a missing component that is critical to later instruction or learning.

If a student is mobile, he or she may have been placed in different programs that have different sequences for the topics. One student we know went from daily A's to D's and F's because the family moved and the student was placed into a different math program without any connection being made to his previous program. The same student scored at the ninety-fifth percentile on standardized math tests but received a D on two quarterly reports that year. The boy was placed in a non-accelerated math class although the parents continued to receive congratulatory letters concerning their son's achievement.

Discrepancies such as the one described can be seen in school records of grades and test scores. Failing grades do not necessarily signal a problem in actual math achievement. Supplemental analysis in the classroom and with the individual will be needed in order to separate real learning problems from those of chance circumstances.

2. *What kind of useful information can be gained from achievement or diagnostic testing?* There are at least three distinct ways that a resource teacher can interpret the results of standardized achievement tests to obtain helpful information: (1) norm-referenced analysis; (2) discrepancy analysis; and (3) item analysis.

NORM-REFERENCED ANALYSIS. A resource teacher must often document a need for service by showing that a student's scores are widely discrepant from some norm. Requests for this kind of information are straightforward. It is critical to administrative or supervisory use because it provides data for program evaluation and for continued funding. We recommend that standard scores rather than grade or age equivalents be used for this purpose.

DISCREPANCY ANALYSIS. If achievement scores are at variance with other information about the student's performance, the resource teacher should find out why. If the student's test score indicates higher-level mastery than is observed in daily performance, perhaps the formats or the language of daily instruction are troublesome. The problem then can be dismissed as accounted for. The student can be taught to deal more effectively with aspects of the program that cause him or her to accommodate his or her way of working. If the discrepancy is motivational — the student can do but does not do — the assessment and the remediation are the same. A program of stimulus control can make the work so attractive that the student will want to do it for its own sake, or a contingency management system can be used to reward succcessful task completion. Stimulus control and contingency management (see Chapter 2) are the primary techniques used to sort out the can-do/does-not-do student from the one who cannot do the work.

If low standardized-achievement test scores highlight a problem not otherwise evident, perhaps the student did not understand the format or the specific content of the test. Carefully observing the student while working examples that are similar to test items as well as daily assignments and discussing the examples with the student can help the resource teacher determine whether a discrepancy does exist. Perhaps, too, the poor academic performance of one who is socially adept or whose general achievement otherwise is high has been overlooked or discounted. In this case, the halo must be removed and an objective analysis made of ability in mathematics.

TEST-ITEM ANALYSIS. The results of standardized achievement tests in mathematics also can be interpreted to provide diagnostic information that may be useful in planning a program. The two principal means of transforming achievement test data into diagnostic (instructionally useful) information are by a conventional analysis of the items passed and failed and by sampling the procedures the student uses to solve the problem.

Often, agencies that score the results of group-administered tests include an item-by-item computer printout of the performance of a school, a classroom, or any instructional group of interest. The resource teacher also can obtain an item-analyzed profile that indicates each student's areas of strength and weakness. Items also may be keyed to appropriate pages in the student editions of leading mathematics textbooks so that teachers may find additional practice pages to use with individual students.

Although this approach has been hailed as a revolutionary solution to evaluation and remediation, it has several obvious drawbacks. First, the reliability of individual items in a lengthy achievement test is questionable; that is, the limited sample size of each problem type may allow chance or carelessness to enter unduly into individual item performance. Additional diagnostic work is needed to check the test results for each individual case. Another problem relates to matching *student* text editions to the test. A better practice would be to key test items to the instructional techniques described in the *teacher* editions; a student who does not understand the problem usually needs additonal *instruction* rather than more practice. Perhaps, however, the primary value of this diagnostic approach is keying instructional techniques and materials to the kinds of weaknesses or gaps found in the local curriculum.

Sampling of procedures is a different approach to the diagnostic use of performance on mathematics achievement test items. For a teacher, the technique involves "observ[ing] the student performing each computation and . . . record[ing] the approach, algorithm, or method being used by means of a standard observation schedule" (Carpenter et al., 1976, p. 217). Schedules from an addition and a division example (Figure 7 – 1) show the major alternatives actually used to solve problems.

Sampling of procedures is a technique that can be adapted to both classroom and resource programs. Teachers can use it to see if answers to computational prob-

FIGURE 7 – 1.
NAEP Observation Schedules in Mathematics

ADDITION	DIVISION
1. Do the item mentally—no other numbers written but the answer.	1. Do the exercise mentally—no other numbers written but the answer.

ADDITION

1. Do the item mentally—no other numbers written but the answer.

$$3 + 4 + 16 + 7 = 30$$

2. Add 3, 4, 6, and 7; put 2 above 16.

$$\overset{2}{3} + 4 + 16 + 7 = 30$$

3. Add 3, 4, and 7. Add sum (14) to 16.

$$\overset{14}{3} + 4 + 16 + 7 = 30$$

4. Rewrite in vertical format; do in head.

$$\begin{array}{r} 3 \\ 4 \\ 16 \\ 7 \\ \hline 30 \end{array}$$

5. Rewrite in vertical format; indicate carrying.

$$\begin{array}{r} 3 \\ 4 \\ 2\;16 \\ 7 \\ \hline 30 \end{array}$$

6. Rewrite in vertical format; add 3, 4, 6, 7, and then add 10.

$$\begin{array}{r} 3 \\ 4 \\ 6 \\ 7 \\ \hline 20 \\ 10 \\ \hline 30 \end{array}$$

7. Any other variation.

DIVISION

1. Do the exercise mentally—no other numbers written but the answer.

$$37604 \div 7 = 5372$$

2. Work in this form but record intermediate steps.

$$37604 \div 7 = \overset{5372}{}$$
$$251$$

3. Rewrite problem, no recording of intermediate steps.

$$\overset{5372}{7\overline{)37604}} \quad \text{or} \quad 7\overline{)37604} \;\; 5372$$

4. Abbreviated long division.

$$\overset{5372}{7\overline{)37604}}$$
$$251$$

5. Long division

$$\begin{array}{r} 5372 \\ 7\overline{)37604} \\ 35 \\ \hline 26 \\ 21 \\ \hline 50 \\ 49 \\ \hline 14 \\ 14 \end{array}$$

6. Repeated subtraction algorithm.

$$\begin{array}{r|r} 7\overline{)37604} & \\ 35000 & 5000 \\ \hline 2604 & \\ 2100 & 300 \\ \hline 504 & \\ 490 & 70 \\ \hline 14 & \\ 14 & 2 \\ \hline & 5372 \end{array}$$

7. Any other variation.

Adapted from T. P. Carpenter, T. G. Coburn, R. E. Reys, and J. W. Wilson, "Notes from National Assessment: Processes Used on Computational Exercises," *Arithematic Teacher* 23 (1976): 217 – 222.

lems are correct or incorrect and to determine how the problems were solved. Here, we recommend the sampling of procedures as a means of demonstrating to both teachers and students that flexibility in computation procedures is (1) an individual matter, regardless of the instructional program; (2) normal; and (3) to be encouraged.

A more formal approach to the assessment of strategies used in mathematics is found in the *Diagnostic Test of Arithmetic Strategies* by Ginsburg and Mathews (1983). DTAS is unusual in that it focuses on both weaknesses and potential strengths. It identifies the incorrect strategies employed to solve calculational problems and also describes informal skills which can be used to facilitate instruction.

3. *What does an analysis of the child's daily work samples show about instructional expectations?* The resource teacher should collect and analyze the referred student's daily written work or permanent products after they have been graded or marked. These papers will include textbook or boardwork copied by the student, and worksheets, workbook pages, and homework.

The analysis of this work is of limited but critical value. It is limited because it deals only with the end product; the teacher must continue to observe and interview to see how the child has arrived at these particular products. However, written work in math often is the best indicator of the nature and expectations of the instructional program. This feature carries two major implications. First, if a student is to be integrated, reintegrated, or even maintained in a particular instructional group, the papers from the entire group can be checked both for the range and the modal performance. Such an analysis enables the resource teacher to estimate the parameters of acceptable work in that class. This information can be used to determine the student's readiness for joining or for staying in a particular group. Conversely, the resource teacher also may obtain some idea of how much and in what directions the range and the content for the group must be changed in order to accommodate the student. Written work also provides a base line of daily response patterns in the natural instructional environment. Details of this feature are discussed in Question 3 of this section.

The resource teacher will have specific ideas about what to look for. The points listed below suggest the kinds of information for a minimally acceptable body of working knowledge about a student's completed work in math.

a. In classrooms where a lot of written work is expected, there is often not enough instruction for learning math skills and concepts. Even where concrete materials are available, their use may not be evident or encouraged by the classroom teacher. Instead, brief oral explanations and written drill may form the heart of the instructional program. In this case, the resource teacher should try various instructional approaches with the individual student. It may be that if he or she is merely taught, learning will occur. It also may be necessary to demonstrate within the classroom how to conduct group lessons using appropriate methods and materials. Documenting progress for the resource teacher's consultant role often can come from noting the changing amount of direct teaching instruction compared with the amount of written independent seatwork within a particular classroom.

b. Math requires a certain amount of drill or repetition at the proficiency stage. If no attempt has been made to make practice work more interesting or to vary it, the student may be so bored that the work is not completed, or if completed, only carelessly so. Attempts to provide interesting drills are well illustrated in materials such as *Individualized Arithmetic Instruction: Arithmetic Drill Sheets* (Taylor, Artuso, and Hewett, 1970) and in the monthly column "Let's Do It!" in *Arithmetic Teacher.* The resource teacher should organize and file these and other interesting materials so that they can be readily retrieved, either for use by students or for use in inservice or consultation sessions with the classroom teacher.

One of the best "drill" programs to use *as directed* is the *Computational Arithemtic Program,* or CAPS (D. Smith and Lovitt, 1982). This program is comprehensive, and is based upon years of extensive research with normal and remedial populations.

Paper-and-pencil drill tasks are not as necessary as they once were because there are several alternatives for practice work. Classroom computers such as the Classmate 88 (Monroe Education Center) generate an unlimited number of skill exercises with immediate feedback for the student. However, computerized practice may become as boring as any other kind and usually is only one of many avenue to drill. Furthermore, drill is necessary only where there is a dearth of naturally occurring practice situations. The recently available abundance of applications cards and ideas makes meaningless repetition obsolete. In applications activities, the practice becomes the means of solving interesting problems rather than an end in itself.

If the teacher cannot provide more interesting material, we recommend a contingency management system. Such techniques are described in books with behavioral approaches to academic achievement, such as *Analysis and Modification of Classroom Behavior* (Haring and Phillips, 1972) and *Measurement and Analysis of Behavioral Techniques* (J. Cooper, 1974).

c. Practice work that is massed rather than distributed loses its interest and value. To many students, fifty or a hundred problems of the same type are an overwhelming task. In fact, an early curriculum modification in special education was reducing the number of problems to be done at one sitting. Now teachers can make an individual determination of the number of practice units appropriate for a given student. The use of correct *and* error rate data provides a sensitive daily measure. The data collection is readily made in the classroom setting.

Some teachers work out ingenious ways to distribute practice, such as setting a timer at specified or at periodic intervals and allowing only five minutes of practice or making it possible to check and reward smaller sets of problems.

If teachers use lengthy, massed practice sessions, they may suggest modifications such as these to students: (1) Do the problems you know and leave the rest blank; (2) If you do half correctly, then you may skip the rest; (3) Do only the first row (or any ten problems, or the last two rows); or (4) See how many you can do in three minutes. These modifications should make the assignment more intriguing.

d. A cursory examination of papers will reveal if the classroom teacher already is modifying assignments for the student. If so, then he or she probably will be amenable to other relevant changes. Occasionally, however, a teacher may resist variations that alter the major program substantively. Nevertheless, the resource teacher should note whatever modifications exist; and the classroom teacher should be reinforced for interest in the student. The resource teacher also can gain some insight into the experience or training of the teacher by asking how he or she learned the modifications used. The learning relationship between the classroom and the resource teachers is not a one-way street.

e. An analysis of the marking and grading system that the classroom teacher uses in mathematics can show if each assignment is treated as a minitest to check mastery, or if the written work fulfills its ostensible purpose — to assist with learning. The resource teacher should pay particular attention to: (1) the form of the marking; (2) the person responsible for doing the marking; (3) the availability of answers; (4) the consequences of the marking; and (5) how any incomplete assignments are marked. Each of these points is discussed below.

(1) The form of the marking system tells a lot about the degree of perfection expected and about how the purpose of the assignment is viewed. For example, marks that cannot be erased imply that there are no nonpunitive opportunities available for self-correction and that the teacher sees the assignment as requiring perfect performance. Light notations and comments in erasable pencil are more likely to permit and encourage self-correction.

Perfection also seems to be expected when marks are translated into percentages correct or incorrect. If 100 percent is always the expectation, then there might be no challenge or growing room for the student. On the other hand, percentages correct that are consistently well below 100 seem intended merely to confirm the problem and to be sure that both student and parent(s) are aware that a low semester grade is forthcoming. We question the appropriateness of the program when consistently low marks are made on daily assignments. If a student's percentage consistently is below 100, the teacher should consider these three options. First, the work can be adjusted so that a 100 percent score is possible some of the time. Second, if the question is one of motivation rather than difficulty, then stimulus control or contingency management can be used. A third approach is to adjust the basis for the 100 percent. For example, if the child consistently does correctly ± 20 out of 25, then the 20 should be used to calculate the 100 percent.

The use of stamps or stamp substitutes, such as smiling and sad faces, and printed or stamped comments such as "poor work," "sloppy," "careless," and "good," may have some motivational value for some students. However, stamps and comments often are noted briefly and forgotten. The negative comments certainly carry no suggestions for changing the direction of the smile or the nature of the comment.

Some marking systems involve points for each problem correct. These are often graphed or noted cumulatively, and an ultimate grade is derived from the total number of points. However, if the points are given for only the final answer, a great opportunity is being lost for helping and motivating the child. For example, one teacher[1] had assigned five problems of the type: $21\overline{)4362}$ with six points possible for each correction solution. The teacher encouraged one reluctant worker by giving one point for correct copying, another point for correct number alignment, and another for correct multiplication. In no time, the youngster announced that he could easily get "all six points now!" A variation of the point system can reinforce certain behaviors of interest; bonus points may be given for writing numerals legibly, copying correctly, appropriate spacing, care with subtraction, or whatever is relevant.

The location of the negative marks made on papers can be of some assistance. Instead of putting one overall checkmark beside the answer, the teacher can lightly circle or arrow any trouble spot. Caution should be taken, however, in using the desire to be helpful as an excuse for requiring all work to be shown — a not uncommon dictum in mathematics. This practice is wearisome and time-consuming. Scratch paper can be kept for awhile or paper-clipped to the final paper. Or, the teacher may ask the student to choose a certain number of problems on which to show the work so that a check can be made for errors in following the algorithm.

(2) Papers usually are marked by the teacher, by an aide, by the student, or by classmates. When the teacher marks each paper, the student often must wait to know how well he or she did on the assignment. In addition, constant teacher checking tends to keep students dependent; they have no opportunity to learn self-evaluation or correction. Grading math papers is time-consuming and may become the teacher's busywork. Further, the teacher who uses paper grading as an excuse for not having time for working individually with children is doing just that — using an excuse.

Some way must be found for shortening the time spent grading papers. Teachers may let tutors, aides, or the students themselves do most of the marking and then spot check certain problems, certain students, or students only on certain days. In addition, any information the teacher obtains from grading all papers he or she can obtain in other ways. For example, high frequency errors can be found by having students tally difficult problems on a master problem sheet.

Paper marking by aides is subject to the same problems as when the teacher does it and includes the added disadvantage of removing the teacher from discovering what is happening with the class or with individuals.

When classmates grade math papers, trouble, from pettiness to mismarking, ensues. Students do not enjoy having classmates notice their mistakes. Their time is better spent in working together as partners or in small groups to solve the assignments rather than in checking the work of others. In some classrooms, the fact that math problems can be readily checked against the answer list encourages the teachers to let a good student check all the class papers. This practice is a questionable use of the good student's time in school and may affect his or her social relationships.

The student is the logical person to mark most of the written work in math. This practice enables him or her to learn responsibility and independence. There is a chance to check and self-correct one's own errors and to note and report any persistently troublesome areas. Students who learn that daily work helps them perfect skills they already have acquired are on their way to becoming successful in mathematics. Explanations, demonstrations, role playing, and constant reinforcement for appropriate behavior are the means by which students are taught to check their own work. The target of reinforcement must be correct checking rather than problems correct. Periodic monitoring and intermittent reinforcement will help maintain self-checking until it becomes intrinsically reinforcing to the student.

(3) If the student receives no feedback until the teacher returns the papers, he or she may view math work as busywork rather than as learning activities. If, however, the student can see the answers soon after working the problems, then he or she is more likely to see the benefits of doing the work. The following suggestions are some of the alternatives to teacher-provided answers. (a) Some teachers go over the problems with the class as a whole, checking the examples together and discussing or working through each problems. The chalkboard of the overhead projector usually is used to focus group attention on each problem. (b) In some classes, each student writes a different problem on the chalkboard for the rest of the class to check. The teacher can save a student from embarrassment by first checking the problem for accuracy. If the teacher lets the student's error show in an effort to help him or her, then the resource teacher should help the teacher find another way of helping that student, such as asking the class what kinds of problems the chalkboard example might present and discussing the possible error points. (c) Two students who have completed their assignments can check each other's work, and when they are in agreement, the teacher can give them an answer sheet. (d) The teacher's edition of the text can be given to students who have finished their work. (e) The teacher can place answers in a retrievable file, can duplicate them, or can place them on a master assignment sheet for checking. (f) The answer key on seatwork can be written at the bottom of the sheet and folded back or cut off for later use. (g) Finally, using pocket calculators to check computation exercises now is sanctioned by most math educators, who consider them an acceptable method for providing feedback to students.

(4) If the only result of marking is a grade in the teacher's gradebook or in the student's records, then the value of the written work has been lost. Errors provided an excellent diagnostic opportunity. Even though error analysis is discussed elsewhere in this chapter, we should note here that errors not due to carelessness require some direct intervention. A few written problems that are well monitored, well analyzed, and well understood are preferred to many problems that allow the student to practice erroneous procedures and responses.

Unfortunately, the grading or progress report systems used to record pupil performance in mathematics often are based on the student's deviations from some norm such as class performance, grade-level expectation, textbook pages completed correctly, or a predetermined behavioral objective. Fortunately, however, the nature of mathematics offers some alternatives to the norm-deviation method that are not feasible in other subjects. For example, a teacher can give two grades, one for the correct answers and one for using reasonable procedures for working the problems. This practice is defensible only if the student has a reasonable grasp of the process and is working toward proficiency. In some classrooms, the teachers have adjusted instruction for students so that they may all earn A's or 100 percent each day. The final grade then depends on the class of problems the student can solve or on a deviation-from-norm basis. If behavioral objectives are used to set the math curriculum, then progress often is stated in terms of whether a certain objective has been met. Any reference to not having met a predetermined objective implies that the objective was poorly chosen. Any discussion of the objective should contain some hypotheses about why it was not met or adjusted, and some plans to change either the objective or the instructional means of attaining it. Objectives are better thought of as trial objectives for any individual. We have discussed grading problems in Chapter 3; in most cases in elementary math, we deplore the constant giving of grades, preferring instead a good behavioral description of what the student can do.

(5) Incompleted problems should not be marked as wrong. They are, in fact, neither wrong nor right. A slow worker is routinely penalized twice — once by a poor grade on the assignment and again when the error evaluation causes him or her to be judged poor in mathematics. We recommended using rate data if incomplete assignments must be accounted for and if problems and response units are equivalent, such as in single column addition with three integers. A readable paper that makes extensive use of math examples to describe the rationale and procedures of collecting rate data is "Rate per Minute as an Academic Measure" (Lovitt, 1971).

f. The teacher should determine reading, conceptual, and language levels involved in any written math problems. Even at the primary stages, math work frequently requires a mastery of reading levels of around sixth grade, as measured by standard readability formulas. In addition, the language of directions can be very ambiguous to some youngsters. For example,[2] on an exercise where the children were to "Circle the larger number," one child was in tears because he had done as directed, and yet many of his problems were marked wrong:

$\checkmark$1.   1 yard or ②feet
2.   2 pints or ③quarts
$\checkmark$3.   ⑤feet or 2 yards
$\checkmark$4.   ⑦cups or 4 pints

These examples indicate that a student must have a certain level of understanding before he or she can deal successfully with the abstractions of most written math problems. Although written materials will be used with the referred student during the supplemental individual analysis to determine specific capabilities in dealing with the reading, conceptual, and linguistic aspects of math, the resource teacher should note how the classroom teacher demonstrates, explains, and accounts for these parameters in the materials to be taught.

g. The level of difficulty may be too high. If the problems clearly are beyond the pupil's capabilities, then an obvious adjustment is in order. Many modifications are possible, such as using achievement or skills groupings. Some teachers adjust by using multilevel instruction to make a variety of responses to a base problem equally satisfactory:

Given: 2   6   4
          +3   +1   +3
         ____   ____   ____

Different students may:

1. Put each example on a card, pasting the correct number of beans, or buttons beside the integers to be added.
2. As above, but draw pictures instead.
3. Do the examples as shown.
4. Make a different example from each, as:

$$\begin{matrix} 2 \\ +3 \end{matrix} \text{ may become: } \begin{matrix} 5 \\ -3 \end{matrix} \text{ ; or } \begin{matrix} 5{,}000{,}000 \\ +3{,}000{,}000 \end{matrix} \text{ ; or } \begin{matrix} 2 \\ 3 \\ +5 \end{matrix}$$

Adapting multilevel techniques is difficult for older students. Instead, the teacher may choose to have the student go through an old workbook completing just enough problems of each example type to show understanding and skill. Then, when the student finds a troublesome place, the teacher can help. This technique is both practical and motivational because the student can see a logical purpose in the work — trying to find specific areas of difficulty. In addition, the student does not waste time on unnecessary practice; rapid progress through the book emphasizes what he or she can do. Teachers using this approach usually keep the student in the regular instructional program while he or she completes this process. They do not expect the student to do work that is too difficult within the regular program.

4. *What does an analysis of written work show about the student's response patterns?* In addition to instructional demands, examining daily work samples provides information about consistencies and inconsistencies in the student's performance and shows any problems with important nonmath factors, such as legibility and neatness, and provides the material for analyzing error patterns. These topics are discussed as a part of Supplemental Individual Analysis in this chapter. While in the classroom, the resource teacher should note the teacher's views of these topics and any interactions with the student in relation to them.

5. *What multisensory instructional aids are available and encouraged?* Both mathematics educators and remedial clinicians agree that the use of multisensory manipulative and instructional aids should be actively encouraged. These materials often are erroneously limited to a math-lab approach or to the primary grades. Fortunately, they are fast becoming an integral part of modern textbook-based instruction at all levels.

Manipulative devices are used to obtain the data from which hypotheses are made, confirmed, or disconfirmed and to give concrete expression to abstract ideas. They are the sensory avenues to developing mathematical concepts; they also function as an evaluation tool to help determine the level of abstraction used by an individual student. The wide variety of aids may be classified as:

1. Demonstration boards and devices
2. Place value devices
3. Colored beads, blocks, rods, and discs
4. Number boards
5. Cards and charts
6. Measurement devices
7. Models of geometric relationships
8. Games and puzzles
9. Special computational devices [Jackson and Phillips, 1973, p. 304]

Some critics think that these devices discourage abstract thinking. We suggest, however, that continued overdependence on concrete aids usually is due to the failure to pair concrete and more abstract representations and then gradually to fade the concrete representation. Even remedial clinicians note that overdependence on prosthetic aids is the result of poor methodology (see Strauss and Lehtinen, 1947, pp. 166 – 167).

Some critics also discourage prosthetic devices such as pocket charts and calculators because they think that the student must know number facts and processes without any extraneous support. We consider such an expectation unrealistic and punishing to anyone who has problems with mathematics. A student who spends math time in frustrating and futile attempts at memorizing cannot learn the appropriate use of socially acceptable means of assistance. This is especially true for the older student, who may have developed a real antipathy toward mathematics.

The Instructional Affairs Committee of the National Council of Teachers of Mathematics has issued guides to encourage the use of minicalculators in the classroom. In the full report, each of the justifications noted below is accompanied with application ideas from a wide range of grade levels. The minicalculator can be used to:[3]

1. Encourage students to be inquisitive and creative as they experiment with mathematical ideas
2. Assist the individual to become a wiser consumer
3. Reinforce the learning of the basic number facts and properties in addition, subtraction, multiplication, and division
4. Develop the understanding of computational algorithms by repeated operations
5. Serve as a flexible answer key to verify the results of computation
6. Provide a resource tool that promotes student independence in problem solving
7. Solve problems that previously have been too time-consuming or impractical to be done with paper and pencil
8. Formulate generalizations from patterns of numbers that are displayed
9. Decrease the time needed to solve difficult computations.

If commercial purchase of minicalculators is not feasible, teacher-, aide-, or volunteer-made devices can be used. There are some data (Harshman, 1962) and a lot of opinion that teacher-made materials that address ad hoc problems or needs are more effective for instructional purposes. A set of buildings in the public schools of the City of Los Angeles contains hundreds of games made by classroom teachers for specific instructional problems. All raw materials and packaging for game construction are available to any area teacher at cost per item used. Staff members convert the completed and tried games to directions and to kits that then are available to any teacher who needs them. The Math Center also is used for inservice training and as housing for other kinds of math teaching resources. Dr. Viggo Hansen of California State University at Northridge initiated and monitored this project which is now part of the local school system. Although few school districts could afford such an operation, the cooperative development of such a center or some adaptations of the center functions could be implemented locally. The resource teacher will want to explore such possibilities with persons responsible for the math program.

The resource teacher should become familiar with the construction, use, evaluation, and sources of instructional aids. Comprehensive, basic information can be found in these four resources:

a. *Instructional Aids in Mathematics* (NCTM, 1973) is intended primarily to give teachers: (1) reliable, organized information regarding the range of possibilities of acquisition and utilization of instructional aids in mathematics; (2) a basis for evaluating their quality and utility; and (3) suggestions for their effective use. The chapter by Jackson and Phillips (1973, pp. 299 – 344) in the NCTM volume provides guidelines for and discussion of the use of aids in the elementary math program.

b. *The Fabric of Mathematics (K – 9)* by Laycock and Watson (1975) is a comprehensive source of objective-keyed lists of manipulatives, games, activities, visuals, children's references, and teacher's references. It also provides publisher's names and addresses. Objectives and materials are further coded by five levels of difficulty.

c. *Teacher-Made Aids by Elementary School Mathematics*, edited by Smith, Jr., and Backman (1974), is a compilation of readings from *Arithmetic Teacher*. The articles are grouped according to: (1) what, how, and why; (2) whole numbers; (3) numeration; (4) integers; (5) rational numbers; (6) geometry and measurement; and (7) multipurpose aids.

d. "Designing Instructional Games for Handicapped Learners" by Thiagarajan (1976) is not directly intended for mathematics, but many of the examples are from math. It concisely presents the advantages, disadvantages, and evaluative criteria for games. Of special note, the concept of the game frame allows almost unlimited applications of a basic game structure.

Other sources of multisensory materials information are found in math texts and journals and in magazines such as *Learning* and *Instructor*.

6. *What is the source and the nature of the curriculum?* The resource teacher must know the source of the curriculum in order to determine how readily it can be modified. Large expenditures for materials, inservice, and supervision of a program usually mean that changes will be difficult to effect. The nature of the curriculum, both as intended and as practiced, becomes the baseline for determining what elements must be systematically changed so that the student can find success

in learning math. (Remember: this is not necessarily the same as finding success "in the curriculum.")

Scope and sequence charts often provide an overview of the math curriculum across levels, but more careful analysis is required to obtain a working knowledge of a program. The curriculum analysis guide suggested elsewhere in this book can be used to analyze and compare programs. We also recommend that the resource teacher become thoroughly familiar with the analyses of leading commercial programs found in the *EPIE Report No. 69/70* (Educational Products Information Exchange, 1975). This publication provides an excellent discussion of criteria for determining the quality of mathematics programs. In general, commercial programs in mathematics have the disadvantages of encouraging large group instruction, locking in the pacing of the program, and limiting the range of teaching techniques to those of the program. However, they also have the advantage of providing structure to teachers who are uncertain about math or about their teaching capabilities.

Behavioral objectives in math are of two kinds: descriptions of problem types to be learned and growth expectations. Growth expectation objectives are not sources of curriculum. For example, the objective that "at the end of the school year, each student in the class will have gained one grade level as measured by the BLANK Achievement Test" commonly is used in many schools as the basis for evaluating student or teacher performance. This practice rarely is accompanied by the curriculum support systems that would make attaining such an objective remotely approachable; it puts unprofessional pressures on teachers, and it discounts what is known about normal child development and growth.

A better practice would be to examine individual students' characteristics, the kinds of curriculum support that are available, and the experience and training of the teachers for the purpose of setting and monitoring realistic and modifiable expectations. Another alternative would be to abandon the practice of using such unindividualized behavioral objectives in favor of descriptions that tell what each student can do, what types of activities have been effective with him or her, and what the next steps in his or her instruction might be. In any case, the resource teacher should be alert to the expectation-objective when a behavioral objective based program is used.

If behavioral objectives are used to describe problem types, many math educators would agree with Swart (1974) that

> the mathematics teacher has understood his objectives in behavioral terms for as long as there has been the subject of school mathematics. When the teacher makes an assignment, the behavior expected for the stimulus "24 × 38" is not ambiguous. And the notion that instruction will be improved by writing it in the jargon of the day ("given two two-digit numbers the learner will find the product") is absurd. [P. 9]

This negative viewpoint arises when undue energies are spent in writing objectives at the expense of thought and time for instructional planning and interaction.

Mastery tests often accompany a behavioral objectives approach. They originally were intended as diagnostic in the sense that the teacher could replan instruction to help an individual achieve mastery. There are unresolved problems in determining what mastery really is or should be (Meskaukus, 1976). More basically, in some classrooms, students are allowed to fail one objective and continue to the next. This means that the criterion-referenced intent has been subverted, and no advantage over textbook or standardized achievement testing approaches is gained. There are positive ways of using instructional objectives in the development of a math program. If such an approach is used or planned, we recommend that the teacher study *The Unit Leader and Individually Guided Education* (Sorenson, Poole, and Joyal, 1976).

If curriculum construction is left to the discretion of the classroom teacher, the source of the scope and sequence of skills should be determined, as well as the record-keeping system in use. Erratic approaches to instruction are usually confusing. However, the teacher may be so competent at individualizing that no prestructured program is needed. For the resource or classroom teacher who needs some idea of what constitutes a sound noncommercial curriculum in math, descriptions of developmental math tasks and the basic methodologies for teaching them are available. *Primary Mathematics Today* (Williams and Shuard, 1970) extends from preschool through secondary levels and is based on Piagetian descriptions of normal child growth and development. *Mathematics and the Elementary Teacher* (Copeland, 1976) is the third edition of a classic teacher text that provides less pedagogy and more theoretical background.

7. *Does the teacher attempt to relate math to daily living or to vocational demands?* Whether in preschool or high school, math can be related easily to daily living or to future needs. Especially for students who see math as meaningless drill, connections should be made to the real world. Figure 7 – 2 and Table 7 – 1 show examples of classroom activities at two levels. These activities are designed to make math more relevant to the student's life.

8. *What grouping practices are in evidence?* In classrooms where textbooks are used, teachers rarely attempt to form a variety of instructional groups. Yet achievement-, interest-, skills-, and social-based grouping also are relevant here. If grouping is used extensively in reading, however, the organization and management of math groups becomes a burden. Cross-grade groupings are useful in accounting for the level of difficulty in practice materials but rarely are used for actual instruction or reteaching. The major alternative to grouping is the math-lab or center approach, in which the teacher provides the overall structure according to a scope and sequence and keeps records of individual progress. The student then works with task cards or assignments at his or her own level. Flexible groupings are determined by skill and concept development needs, interests, and social choices. Organizing a math center is quite complex and requires planning and preparation. We recommend that if such centers are operational or are planned, then the resource teacher consult basic materials, such as *The Laboratory Approach to Mathematics* (Kidd, Myers, and Cilley, 1970), *Freedom to Learn* (Biggs and MacLean, 1969), and the many slim books of the *Nuffield Mathematics Project* (Nuffield Foundation, 1967 – 1974). The developmental math books referred to in the previous section also are valuable in this regard. These sources recommend many materials that are suitable for math

FIGURE **7 – 2.**
Relevant Math in the Classroom (Primary Level)

Name _____

What Time Is It?

8:00

1. Cut out the pictures.

2. Paste them in order, from the first to the last activity of the day.

3. Show the correct times by drawing in the clock hands or writing in the time.

6:00

| 1 | 12:00 | 5 |

| | 3 | |

| 2 | | 6 |

| | 4 | |

From *Arithmetic Teacher* 29 (1981): 29.

TABLE 7 – 1.
Relevant Math in the Classroom (Secondary Level)

SAMPLE MATHEMATICS SURVIVAL UNIT — BANKING AND FINANCE

SKILLS AND APPLICATIONS	*VOCABULARY*	*ACTIVITIES*

SKILLS AND APPLICATIONS

MATHEMATICAL SKILLS

Students will have to use the four basic whole-number operations — addition, subtraction, multiplication, division —in working with a checking account. They will use interest, percents, and decimals with savings accounts.

PRACTICAL APPLICATIONS

1. Opening a checking account
— Filling out the necessary forms for opening an account
— Making a deposit
— Making a withdrawal
— Writing a check

2. Maintaining a checking account
— Balancing the monthly statement — posting canceled checks and recording outstanding checks
— Understanding service charges
— Handling overdrawn accounts

3. Investigating ways to save
— Finding out how commercial banks, savings banks, credit unions, and savings and loan associations are alike and/or different
— Finding out how a savings account works. What is principal? What is the rate of interest? How long does it take for an account to gain interest?
— Finding out about other ways to invest money — U.S. saving bonds, investments

VOCABULARY

checking account
checks
checkbook
canceled checks
outstanding
　checks
overdrawn
deposit
service charge
bank statement
outstanding
balancing
withdrawal
commercial bank
savings bank
savings and loan
　association
U.S. savings
　bonds
savings account
rate of interest
principal
time accounts
compound
　interest

ACTIVITIES

1. Take students on a bank visit to discuss the bank's services with an official.
2. Back in the classroom, investigate the services and skills necessary for maintaining a checking account, including a list of the mathematical skills involved.
3. Using forms obtained from the bank, have the class set up mock accounts, write checks, record them, and balance sample statements.
4. Since there are various ways of saving money, have students divide into committees, each one investigating a different savings institution. Be sure specific questions about each kind are identified. Then each group might visit the type of institution they are studying and bring back items for discussion and further investigation. Finally, debate the pros and cons of each type.
5. Have students solve problems using different principals and interest rates to see how daily compound interest varies from interest compounded twice a year, quarterly, etc.
6. Have students report on alternate ways of investing money such as U.S. savings bonds, and mutual funds.
7. A student committee might want to study bank Christmas clubs. How safe are they, and why do people use them? Students can collect brochures from several banks and compare the benefits.
8. If time allows, discussion and activities on the stock market could be included at this point.

From A. Wilderman, "Math Skills for Survival in the Real World," *Teacher Magazine*, 94 (1977): 68 – 70.

centers. Other sources are noted in the section that discusses instructional aids, and other sources are analyzed in *Materials for Individualizing Math Instruction* (EPIE, 1974). Together, these resources constitute the body of information needed by the resource teacher to modify classroom instruction.

9. *What are the teacher's attitudes, capabilities and expectations regarding math instruction?* In teaching math, many teachers depend unnecessarily on the directions included in the textbook because their own grasp of math skills and concepts is shaky. Some teachers are weak in math due to a longstanding dislike or even fear of math. For the resource teacher and for the student in the classroom, there are two major implications of this phenomenon. First, the classroom teacher's preservice preparation may not have taught him or her how to teach math; math educators spend a lot of time dealing with adult dread, improving understandings of persons with minimal skills, and helping prospective teachers understand the kinds of learning possible from students when their instruction is appropriate. The resource teacher must find tactful ways of dealing with teachers who are minimally prepared or insecure in teaching mathematics. Some teachers with fearful or unfavorable attitudes toward math may transfer these emotions to the student, making remedial efforts doubly difficult.

The resource teacher will find the overview of the research on affective variables in mathematics that deals with both teachers and students (Aiken, Jr., 1976) to be particularly interesting. Of special interest in this review are the consistent findings of sex differences (with females more unfavorably inclined toward math than are males) and the effectiveness of behavior modification technique as a means of changing attitudes. In a more humorous vein, *The I Hate Mathematics! Book* (Burns, 1975) should interest teachers as well as the children for whom it was written.

10. *What is the student's attitude toward the math instruction?* Attitudes toward mathematics in general and certain topics or assignments in particular can be measured in several ways in the classroom. Written attitudinal devices are somewhat unreliable, yet they can provide clues for individual follow-up The revised Attitude Scales (Estes et al., 1981) provide both elementary and secondary levels of attitude measurement. These scales allow comparison between the attitude of the student and those of classroom peers.

Daily or periodic attitudes measurement can be designed to accompany daily work samples for primary grades. Or problems can be sampled with faces to accompany each problem type. The student may crossout the face that represents his or her feelings about working that kind of problem (see Figure 7 – 3).

Direct observation also can indicate the student's interest as time-on-task (TOT) data are collected (see pp. 308 – 310). TOT is either an open-ended or an interval recording technique that usually is considered a measure of attention and choice in the sense that the student chooses to spend time doing the task. TOT procedures produce a percentage of available time spent on the task at hand. Of course, time and task expectations should be closely calibrated in the classroom so that a student is not considered inattentive or disinterested because he or she does not spend thirty allotted minutes on a task that requires only a few minutes to complete.

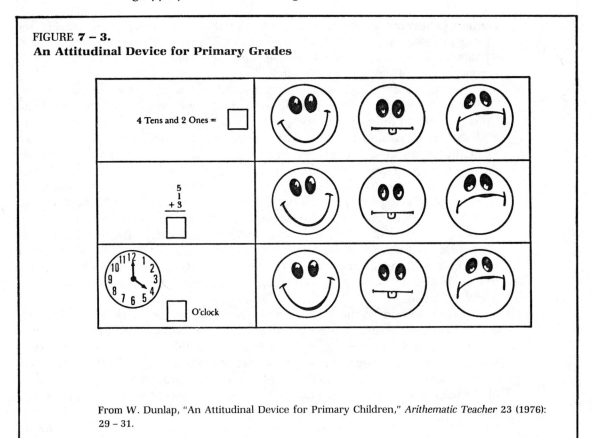

FIGURE **7 – 3.**
An Attitudinal Device for Primary Grades

From W. Dunlap, "An Attitudinal Device for Primary Children," *Arithematic Teacher* 23 (1976): 29 – 31.

11. Is the student penalized for related errors of a nonmath nature? Some students have no major problems with computational or conceptual abilities but are perceived as poor workers because of the appearance of the math paper. These errors involve format or how the teacher expects the problems to be arranged on the page, and neatness and legibility. Various prompts can be used to help with format. For example, having the student use graph paper, putting heavily lined paper with problem boxes under the work, and arranging for spacers between problems can improve page arrangement. Perhaps the teacher must explain correct numeral formation and reinforce it as an objective in itself. The younger student may need to use number stamps until legibility can be taught. Clean erasing is not difficult to learn; a contingency management program may be needed to see that it is maintained. The function and use of scratch paper should be taught. The teacher should explain the need for meeting reasonable expectations of appearance in the student's work. If the expectations are unreasonable, the counseling should be undertaken with the classroom teacher.

SUPPLEMENTAL INDIVIDUAL ANALYSIS

It is extremely important for the resource teacher to conduct supplementary individual analysis in mathematics. Unlike reading, where one *can* learn to read through the self-selection of books or materials of interest, students rarely self-select activities that will bolster their abilities in math. A group of students are not as likely to be discussing equilateral triangles as they are to be discussing news from a teenage magazine. It is not uncommon, then, to find students in the junior high school who cannot tell time or who believe that a pie can be divided into thirds by cutting it into three pieces of varying sizes. Basic problems such as these are rarely uncovered within the classroom setting.

There are two basic sources of supplementary information about a student's mathematical abilities: product analysis and clinical interviews. Products of interest are test responses and daily work samples. These products are analyzed to find: (1) present success or failure in regard to specific kinds of problems, such as long division or story problems with extraneous information in them; and (2) the difference between those errors that are largely the result of carelessness or slow working and those that are the result of inadequate understanding of the task or of its components.

Clinical interviews are designed to find out how the student thinks in relation to mathematics, using logical reasoning, comparision, one-to-one correspondence, rule learning, and seriation. This kind of information is needed before trying to remediate specific difficulties. Math instruction that is not based solely upon drill will need to account for the nature of the student's thinking. Clinical interviews are also used to supplement error analysis of products, for the teacher needs to find out the kind of thinking or literal misunderstanding that has led to the error.

The diagnostic questions posed in this section rely heavily upon product analysis and clinical interviewing. *Clinical teaching*, which is often considered as a separate technique, is considered here as an applicaiton of continuous product analysis and clinical interviewing.

1. *Does the student really have a math problem?* Students with test scores one or more standard deviations from those of their age peers have a measurable problem in math. This does not necessarily mean that the student has trouble with learning mathematics or arithmetic. It does mean that his or her achievement is not what we would normally expect. Factors discussed in the previous section, such as poor instruction, as well as others we will discuss in this section, may well contribute to low achievement.

The existence or nonexistence of a measurable problem in math achievement should be determined early in assessment. Norm-referenced, standardized tests such as the *Test of Mathematical Abilities* (TOMA) by V. Brown and McEntire (1983), the *Test of Early Mathematics Ability* by Ginsburg and Baroody (1983), or any other well-constructed test that reports standard scores can be used for this purpose.

2. *What can diagnostic tests in mathematics tell about the student's performance?* Diagnostic tests in mathematics are of three general types. One provides information about relative performance in regard to broad diagnostic questions; another

inventories an extensive range of items to differentiate known from unknown items; and the third type is used to place students appropriately in a particular instructional program.

For example, the TOMA provides information about questions such as how well informed the student is about the general uses of math in the course of daily living or how well the student understands the vocabulary associated with mathematics. On the other hand, the *Kraner Tests of Mathematics Mastery* (Kraner, 1979) or the *Maryland Diagnostic Arithmetic Test and Interview Protocols* (J. Wilson and Sadowski, 1976) provide comprehensive inventories of concepts and skills. Placement tests such as that used with the *Computational Arithmetic Program* (CAP) (D. Smith and Lovitt, 1982) are also inventory-like, except that their results are translated directly to a specific instructional program. Few programs provide data concerning the reliability with which such placement decisions are to be made. CAP is unusual because it does provide reliability data for its placement test.

Resource teachers can make their own sets of diagnostic cards or tests based on local scope and sequence charts. It is important to consider that the small sample size of each kind of item in typical diagnostic tests provides only a gross estimate of true abilities. Often, too few examples are present to be of value in detecting error patterns, and unless error patterns are evident, there is no way to determine how the student reached the answers given. Diagnostic tests can be made more instructionally useful by increasing the sample size of each problem type so that error patterns can emerge. It is also possible to supplement these tests with observations of the student as he or she works the examples.

Our primary reservation about diagnostic tests in arithmetic or mathematics is primarily that diagnosticians jump too quickly from testing to teaching. Regardless of the type of diagnostic test used, the information yielded is merely status information, telling us what the student does and does not do. The test does not provide a great deal of insight into the student's thinking.

Despite our reservations about the true diagnostic merit of "diagnostic" tests, we believe they can be used to:

1. Compare scores among students or for one student over time.
2. Try out the student's performance under varying conditions.
3. Determine a starting point for more detailed analyses.
4. Observe test-taking behaviors.
5. Provide an entree to discussion about mathematics.
6. Provide documentation that the student does or does not have a math problem.
7. Provide standard material to use in observing the working patterns of referred students in order to detect any commonalities that might be due to faulty instruction.
8. Provide materials for error analysis, if sample sizes of each problem type permit.

3. What computation error patterns can be found in work samples? Detecting one error is never interpreted as a call to instruction or to prescription. It is merely a signal that the teacher should monitor the student's work carefully to see if the error recurs. Recurring errors *are* of concern, not necessarily because they prevent good grades but because they represent systematic rules that are being used inappropriately. The longer these rules continue to misserve the student, the more difficult it will be to replace them with appropriate ones. Students do learn what they practice. In addition, the rule used by the student may become incorporated into more complex problems, causing extended difficulty in areas outside the original problem.

The diagnostician who analyzes errors is interested in two basic questions: (1) What is the nature of the error? (2) What are the most likely causes of the error? This information is used for instructional planning.

Error patterns in computation usually can be detected by inspecting the student's written responses. To find out about the nature of the error made, the teacher first uses several problems to form a hypothesis or hunch about what it is that the student does. For example:[4]

$$\begin{array}{r} 2\,0\,6 \\ \times \quad 6 \\ \hline 1386 \end{array} \qquad \begin{array}{r} \times\,4\,0\,9 \\ \times \quad 8 \\ \hline 3762 \end{array} \qquad \begin{array}{r} 5\,0\,4 \\ \times \quad 7 \\ \hline 3648 \end{array}$$

In this case the teacher hypothesized that the student replaces the zero in ten's place with the number of tens involved in the first multiplication product — for example, $6 \times 6 = 36$, $8 \times 9 = 72$, and $7 \times 4 = 28$. This ten's number is used in the second multiplication to produce the products of the second multiplication, as $6 \times 3 = \underline{18}$, $8 \times 7 = \underline{56}$, and $7 \times 2 = \underline{14}$. The student appears to use this strategy only for replacing the zero. The teacher would then construct similar problems:

$$\begin{array}{r} 3\,0\,7 \\ \times \quad 6 \\ \hline \end{array} \qquad \begin{array}{r} 2\,0\,3 \\ \times \quad 4 \\ \hline \end{array}$$

If the student made the same kinds of errors here, then the original hypothesis would receive support. The teacher may also wish to have the student talk the problem through while working it. For this diagnostic purpose, the teacher does not interrupt or correct but listens and considers.

Once the nature of the recurring error has been noted or the nature of the student's rule has been uncovered, the teacher will usually want to find out some of the causes for the error. In the previous example, the student may have remembered "You can't multiply a zero," and looked for something else in its place.

Some causes of errors are rather obvious. Perhaps the student was never taught the rule. Other reasons should be explored, particularly those that relate to the student's thinking. Radatz (1979, pp. 165 – 170) has noted several categories of possible error causes. He notes that the error types may be interactive and that the categorization is not exhaustive. Nevertheless, it provides a beginning framework for thinking about possible causes of errors.

1. *Errors due to language difficulties.* Since terms in mathematics are precise and unambiguous, there may be interference from using natural language in math situations. Kane, Byrne, and Hater's *Helping Children Read Mathematics* (1974) provides extensive description and examples of specific problems with the language of mathematics.

2. *Errors due to difficulties in obtaining spatial information.* Radatz is particularly concerned with misreading the various picture or iconic representations characteristic of math textbooks. These pictures are not always interpreted by students in the manner intended by the author or the text illustrator.

3. *Errors due to deficient mastery of prerequisite skills, facts, and concepts.* Included here are knowledge of appropriate algorithms, mastery of basic facts, knowledge of necessary symbols, and concepts.

4. *Errors due to incorrect associations or rigid thinking.* Courtis (1911) noted that some students had practiced borrowing in subtraction for so long that they borrowed even when it was not necessary. Pippig (1975) provides a more detailed classification system for this kind of error, noting factors such as perseveration, association, and interference (reported in Radatz).

5. *Errors due to the application of irrelevant rules or strategies.* This kind of error is more closely related to traditional error analysis such as that of Ashlock in his *Error Patterns in Computation: A Semi-Programed Approach* (1976). His booklet provides many examples of error patterns at the various computational levels used with conventional algorithms introduced in the elementary schools. His purpose is to engage teachers in the process of error pattern detection, in hypothesizing about a thought process that could have produced the error pattern, and in developing instructional strategies to eliminate the error. We recommend this book as a source for inservice training with teachers in the classroom and as a critical skill to teach the students themselves.

We emphasize the analysis of error patterns as a primary diagnostic technique that should be followed with appropriate instruction. Humphrey (1981), who studied error patterns in relation to performance on Piagetian tasks, has made the following comments about her current data and its predecessors in the literature of error analysis in diagnostic mathematics:

> . . . the error patterns identified in this study were identified as early as the Buswell and John (1926) study and also as recently as the Cox (1974) and Graeber and Wallace (1977) studies. Error patterns such as addition of digits in horizontal addition problems, smaller minuend digit subtracted from subtrahend digit, using digits from multiplicand and multiplier for product, and would not attempt any division problems suggest failure to comprehend the symbols of mathematics and number concepts (e.g., 12 = 10 + 2, and not 1 + 2). Persistent errors such as regrouping across 0 in the minuend, multiplying by an amount carried over 0, and subtracting differences in long division where the differences were greater than or equal to the divisor, indicate learned procedures without understanding the relationships among the digits being computed. Instructional programing to remediate these errors should include activities to develop concepts of

"numberness" as well as activities to develop appropriate computational procedures. [PP. 156 – 157]

4. *What kinds of errors occur in problem solving and in story problems?* The terms *problem solving* and *story problems* are often used interchangeably in math classrooms; however, they are not the same at all. Story problems are presented in order to encourage the use of previously learned skills in a somewhat realistic situation that requires those skills (LeBlanc, 1977). For example:

> Carolyn wanted to make a half recipe of chocolate cake. The recipe called for ¾ cup of sugar. How much sugar will she use for the half recipe?

Problem solving is intended to increase the student's ability to think mathematically. Problems in this area are often called challenge problems because they are unfamiliar in the sense that there is no standard algorithm for their solution. They take effort, thought, and perseverance (McKillip et al., 1978). For example:

How many line segments are needed

to connect every point to every

other point by a line segment?

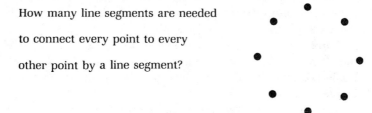

For both types of problems, it is necessary for students to: (1) understand the problem; (2) devise a plan for its solution; (3) carry out the plan; and (4) go back to check the results and evaluate the plan used in the solution. Diagnostic techniques center around questions that students learn to ask themselves as a means of self-help and self-analysis. The questions are organized around the four steps noted previously.[5]

UNDERSTANDING THE PROBLEM

a. Can the student retell the problem in his or her own words? If the student cannot read the problem, it should be read to him or to her so that the student can then paraphrase the problem. Misunderstandings can be probed at this time.

b. What information does the student glean from the problem? Are there related pictures that might be misinterpreted? Can the student discriminate relevant from irrelevant information?

c. Does the student know exactly what to look for or find out? Does he or she understand the question? Can the student indentify the information that is relevant to the question? Can useless information be discarded?

d. Can the student identify other information needed to solve the problem or story? For example, to find out how many feet above sea level one might be, the student must know that sea level is the zero or beginning point in such measures; or that 2 *boys* and 3 *girls* are 5 *children.*

DEVISING A PLAN FOR THE SOLUTION

a. Can the student call to mind any related problems? A great deal of problem solving is through analogy, or recognizing familiar elements among problems.

b. Can the student draw a picture of the problem? In drawing, the student must organize the information in some manner. The drawing will reflect the organization used.

c. Can the student solve any part of the problem? Perhaps the problem can be broken down to single, simpler elements. Success in one area might provide insight for the remaining portion(s).

d. Can the student solve a similar but easier problem? Perhaps the computation loading is too great or the problem is too complex.

e. Can the student organize the information available? If the information is organized, then a plan for solution may become apparent from the relationships shown.

f. Can the student see patterns or regularities in the information? Perhaps a rule can be induced from the pattern, and the pattern may be extended to test the rule.

g. Can the student tell or write *an* appropriate mathematical sentence for the plan? There may be more than one solution. If *a* solution can be planned, eventually the plan can be compared to other plans in order to find the one that is most efficient.

h. Can the student stop a frustrating problem situation by leaving it but returning later to work again? Perseverance need not be compressed in one sitting. A fresh look often does wonders. Students need to learn this strategy. Teachers may therefore provide time for fresh looks at old problems.

CARRYING OUT THE PLAN

a. Can the student keep records of trials and errors to use in evaluating the strategy used? Even if the plan is not a correct one, the records made in trying may provide clues to a correct solution.

b. Can the student solve the mathematical sentences? The computation is often familiar enough to the student to be reinforcing.

c. Can the student finish any drawings begun or tables started in the planning stage? In this case, the student may have an intuitive understanding of the problem but lack the mathematical forms to use in its solution.

d. Can the student carry out any fully developed plan? This is a test of the planning stage, as well as one of the specific plan for the problem of immediate interest.

CHECKING THE RESULTS AND EVALUATING THE PLAN

a. Can the student verify the answer? Are all the conditions of the problem satisfied?

b. What *is* the answer to the question? If the result does not answer the question, it is usually incorrect. The student should be able to reask the question, providing the answer. The student should be able to pick up on any obviously wrong answers to the question stated in the problem.

c. Can the student find another answer or another solution to the problem? There is usually more than one way to solve problems. Flexibility of method eventually will be important to the student's success in problem solving.

d. Can the student identify and solve similar problems? Once a problem is solved, it is no longer a problem. Similar problems should be provided at intervals to build confidence for the student. Further, if the student can create similar problems, there is good evidence for mastery of the structure of the problem type.

5. *Does the student understand about the uses of math in daily life?* For diagnostic purpose, there are two questions of interest here. First, how does the student use opportunities to learn and to use mathematical thinking in his or her daily environment? For example, can he or she handle money appropriately, make comparative measurements, or tell time?

A second kind of understanding is that of general information that is related to mathematics, such as the significance of zip codes or telephone area codes, how tire air pressure is measured, or what it means to leave a tip at a restaurant. This kind of general information is measured by a subtest of the TOMA, or the teacher can devise questions related to the topic.

Literacy skills also reflect the kinds of information needed for daily living. For example, Negin and Krugler (1980) used the printed materials that were essential to effective functioning in Milwaukee, Wisconsin, to identify the math-related skills shown in Table 7 – 2.

Where choices are to be made about what to teach, it would seem that the math needed for daily living in society would be of higher priority than topics of less relevance. Further, students who are having problems in math need motivation. Real-life or general information situations are a better vehicle for instruction than drill or esoteric explanations.

6. *What is the student's attitude about math?* We have described assessment techniques related to this question in the section about the student within the classroom. For any individual, however, the teacher should also discuss the results of any attitude scales or inventories that have been administered. The student may elaborate on responses made or provide examples of behavior that relate to expressed attitudes. It is not necessary for the resource teacher to press for a reasonable explanation of the feelings the student has expressed; however, when reasons are given, they should be received without evaluative comment.

It should not be surprising if girls express somewhat more negative attitudes toward math than boys do. For whatever reasons, the older the girl, the more likely it is that she will have a poor attitude toward math. Sex difference in attitudes toward math are well documented, although they receive little attention in school programs.

For boys or girls with poor attitudes toward math, attempts should be made to make it more relevant, to cut down on busywork, to provide a diet of success,

TABLE **7 – 2.**
Essential Math Literacy Skills

Symbols

° (degrees)	$ and
F (Fahrenheit)	¢
″ (inches)	#
%	

Numbers

Fractions
measuring (1/2, 1/4, 1/8, 1/3, 3/4, 2/3)

Two-place digits
miles per hour (1 – 55)
minutes (1 – 60)
hours (1 – 24)
pieces
capsules
measuring units
age
month/day/year designation

Three-place digits
price and total weights (1 – 100)
hours
temperatures (200 – 450)
street numbers (1 – 999)
route numbers
distance signs
mile markers
measurement of areas

Computational skills

Addition
add money amounts for prices, bills, deposits, incomes,
    assets and debts
add years in school, years at previous address, years
    with present bank, years of experience
add hours to find times for taking medication
add minutes to time for cooking or baking

Subtraction
figure change in financial transactions
subtract outstanding checks from bank statement

Multiplication and division
convert ounces, pounds, pints, quarts, and gallons
convert salary from an hourly to a weekly basis
reduce or expand amounts of a product
figure hours worked per week
figure time between administrations of medicine
compute price per unit when total price and weight
    are given

Negin and Krugler, 1980, p. 115

Abbreviations

acc't	mo.
bus.	no.
dept.	orig.
Dr.	oz.
fl.	qt.
ft.	R.R.
gr. pt. or g.p.a.	Rx
hr.	soc. sec.
in.	U.S.
lb.	Wis.
lbs.	wt.
min.	Xing
mtg. or mtge.	yr.

Writing skills

Personal data
name
address
phone number
social security number
birthdate
driver's license number
signature
credit account numbers
educational background
schools
addresses
military record
conviction record
medical information
position sought
qualifications and skills
interests and ambitions

Money amounts
value of assets
income
amount being paid on bills

Other information
employer's name, address, and phone
    number;
references' names, addresses, positions, and
    phone numbers;
relative's name, address, and phone number;
co-applicant's name, address, and phone
    number

and to make it more interesting. The *Nuffield Mathematics Project* (1967 – 1974) provides many suggestions in this regard, as do materials used in math labs.

7. *What are the math-related language abilities shown by the student?*   In assessing language abilities in relation to mathematics, we are interested in special applications of language to mathematics instruction and learning. Some of these applications are described below: vocabulary, syntax, story grammar or structure, reading, writing, and speaking.

Vocabulary.   The meanings of terms in mathematics may involve complex concepts, but they are always consistent and very precise. Kane, Byrne, and Hater (1974) have noted that there are several types of vocabulary items in mathematics. One is reserved exclusively for mathematical meaning; *isosceles* is an example. Others are used in natural language but also have special meanings in math, such as *difference.* Still other vocabulary items have no phonographic or sound-symbol base to help the student with pronouncing them or to use as clues to their meaning; *percent* is an example.

The student's understanding of math vocabulary can be measured in a reading format with the TORC (V. Brown, Hammill, and Wiederholt, 1978) and in a written format with the TOMA (Brown and McEntire, 1982). Resource teachers may also have students explain terms encountered in the math text being used in class.

Math terms are taught basically through teaching the concepts and procedures with which they are associated. Books dealing with reading in the content areas also provide instructional plans related to math vocabulary. *Helping Children Read Mathematics* (Kane, Byrne, and Hater, 1974) also provides teaching suggestions that may be used with or without reading. In addition, the authors provide a concise description of the classifications of mathematical words and symbols.

Syntax.   The syntax of mathematical sentences and stories is somewhat unique. The structure of questions asked in story problems is usually found in no other kind of content material. In computation, the algorithms themselves are a kind of syntax that must be interpreted if the problem is to be understood correctly — for example, $4 \times 36 = $ _____, or $3 (4 = 3) - 2 (5 - 2) = $ _____. Error analysis, talking about the problem with the student, having the student read the problem, or having the student explain the problem are easy ways to find out how well the student understands this aspect of mathematical language. Instruction involves the same procedures, with the teacher inserting actual instruction where it is needed to clarify the relationships involved.

Story grammar or story problem structure.   Differences in perceiving the structure of story or challenge problems are strongly related to competence in problem solving (Kruteskii, 1976; Silver, 1979; and Cohen and Stover, 1981). Good problem solvers are hypothesized to have schemata, or an understanding of various problem structures that allows them to see similarities among problems and their solutions. This phenomenon is well accepted in the field of reading, where mysteries, fables, and directions for making something all have predictable, differentiated structures. This idea is now being studied extensively in mathematics education.

Unlike computation, where certain combinations recur frequently, each story problem is likely to be unique except for structural elements. Attention to structural elements of problems has now become an integral part of instruction in problem solving.

Teachers who are unaware of the need to approach problem solving from the perspective of problem structure may be teaching students in ways that do them great disservice. For example, they may tell students to look at *key words* in the question to find out which algorithm to use. One of these key associations is the word *left*, which is supposed to signal subtraction. Yet some problems use the word in a different sense:

> Lee has 40 cupcakes.
> He puts them in bags of a dozen each.
> How many cupcakes are left?

Unless the student sees the entire problem structure, he or she might initially subtract instead of divide.

Instruction in problem structure involves the careful construction of problems that are structurally related in some way. They are solved *with* the student so that various relationships might be discussed. Eventually the student should be able to sort problems according to their structural similarities (see Table 7 – 3).

Reading. Reading and math specialists have called attention to a number of factors that characterize reading in mathematics. McEntire (1981, pp. 44 – 47) has described twelve such factors, which are paraphrased below. The implications of each for individual assessment by the resource teacher are also noted.

a. Reading speed. Mathematics requires careful attention and a relatively slow rate of reading because of the way symbols are compacted and because one must read for inferred meanings. Rereading is often necessary. *Implication:* The student who tries to read mathematics as if it were a novel will not likely be able to understand the problem or explanation. Students must learn to differentiate reading rate according to the purpose of reading. Further, some students may need to be told that it is acceptable to reread.

TABLE **7 – 3.**
Problems That Involve Similar Structures

A. Death Valley, California, is 282 feet below sea level. Mt. Whitney, California, is 14,494 feet above seat level. What is the difference in feet between these two points?

B. The record low temperature in Alaska for a January was – 79° F. The lowest January temperature in Hawaii was 14° F. How much warmer was the Hawaii low temperature than that of Alaska?

b. Reading symbols in varied arrangements. Mathematics is written from left to right, diagonally, vertically, or a mixture of all. The direction of reading is critical to understanding and solving the problems. *Implication:* Students who are accustomed to progressive reading from left to right and returning to a starting place will have to learn to vary their eye search according to the material. Resource teachers may have students talk through where they are looking or perhaps even number the consecutive places they look during problem reading. Some teachers have drawn lines on the chalkboard as they read or solve problems to call attention to the differences in eye movements during mathematics.

c. Reading with paper and pencil. Often the translation from reading to writing is in the form of symbols of number and relationships. Diagrams may also be considered a form of note taking in mathematics. *Implications:* The resource teacher may ask the student to take math notes while working on a problem. The notes may be computations or diagrams. The idea of math notes can be introduced by reminding the students that they often show their work during long division and that these notes serve to help with organization, as well as provide a record to which the student can refer back if necessary.

d. Reading graphic materials. Graphs help organize and display concepts and facts. Students need special abilities to read these materials, which are so prevalent in modern life that they may be taken for granted. Most mathematics programs now pay special attention to the development of what is termed *graphicacy*. *Implications:* Students may be asked to interpret various kinds of graphs, such as, pie, bar, pictorial, or line formats. They should also learn to construct them with data given. Since the construction of graphic materials reflects the organization of information, this procedure is an excellent diagnostic technique, as well as a worthwhile task for the student.

e. Reading to comprehend relationships among objects, ideas, words, and symbols. Words and symbols are used interchangeably at times. Further, a reading passage might contain different kinds of forms or symbols, as well as words. All of them are related to complex ideas. *Implications:* The resource teacher will want to find out if the student understands the relationships among ideas, symbols, objects, and words. This is true in primary grades as well as in high school. Pictorial material may be as misleading as it is helpful. Simply asking the student to tell about his or her understanding is the easiest and most fruitful diagnostic technique.

f. Reading sparse, concise information with few context clues. Mathematics reading contains virtually no descriptive or extraneous information that could be related to other information on the page. *Implications:* Students must learn to focus on other clues to aid in their understanding. Even math vocabulary is easier to read in context, but the context is contained solely within the problem. This means that the student must bring a great deal of background to the problem to compensate for the lack of other contexts. Students should be observed to find out if they do indeed use all the cues or clues available to them, such as rereading, note taking, and pulling together related information.

g. Reading a variety of number languages. Numbers appear not only in the familiar decimal base but also in other bases. Further, the language of place value notation must be comprehended. Roman numerals present unique problems of reading both place value and numerical value. *Implications:* Math programs that are based primarily on textbooks may not have made these languages clear to the student. For example, the failure to understand place value is one of the primary problems in remedial mathematics. In most cases, the students have not been taught place value. Diagnostic interviews are usually needed to tap the student's understanding of this kind of reading.

h. Reading for relationships between pieces of information in problem solving. The ability to discriminate relevant from irrelevant information requires the detection of logical relationships between the pieces of data given in the problem. *Implications:* Many story problems use extraneous data. Some students are accustomed to accounting for every piece of information in a problem, a practice that leads to erroneous conclusions. As teachers work through such problems with students, one of the first questions is to find the relevant data.

i. Reading to understand the best form of algorithm to be used in computation. Mathematics reading requires translation into symbols and operational signs. *Implications:* Since the setting of purpose is important in any reading, students may be taught to read specifically with these translations in mind. It is part of the unspoken part of solving story problems. Students should also become familiar with alternate translations from words and numerals in problems. There is often more that one way to translate any problem.

The last three factors have been described previously in this section:

j. Reading to find the main idea. In the mathematical sense, this is very much like trying to find the story or problem structure.

k. Vocabulary forms.

l. Reading specific types of grammatical forms. In addition to characteristics we have noted, McEntire emphasizes the language structures of one-to-one correspondence, the noun phrase, and comparative constructions. Those who work with specific language problems may wish to check the student's use of such forms to the content of mathematics.

Writing. Writing includes both handwriting and the expression of ideas. Numerals must be legible, both for the student and for the teacher. Further, the placement or format of written material is often crucial in mathematics. Teachers can detect misunderstandings merely by examining the written product.

Writing is also used in the sense of language experience to help students write about their math experiences. As they do so, they clarify their thinking and reinforce the math concepts involved (See the sample from *Nuffield* math.).

Speaking. Although speaking ability is not closely related to competence in mathematics, the importance of having paraphrasing or retelling as a diagnostic tool makes speaking about math a valuable skill. Some math educators have advocated that the use of oral explanation of a math concept or procedure be used as a test of readiness for written expression of the same ideas (for example, Hamrick, 1979).

8. *What cognitive understandings or thought processes are related to the student's performance in mathematics?* There are two approaches to tapping a student's thinking abilities in relation to mathematics. One is to uncover thinking about a particular problem or problem type, as is done in error analysis. Through clinical interviews, the resource teacher can extend this approach to probe the level of the student's understanding. Ginsburg (1977) provides a brief example of such an interview:

> Kathy was asked to compare 6 + 6 with 6 × 6.
> I: Which one do you think will give you the biggest number for an answer?
> K: Times.
> I: Why?
> K: Well, 6 × 6 is more than 6 + 6 'cause you have to count 6 times instead of only two times.
> Kathy interpreted both addition and multiplication in terms of counting by sixes. To get 6 + 6, you count by sixes two times. To get 6 × 6, you count by sixes six times. By interpreting both addition and subtraction in terms of common language — counting by sixes — Kathy was able to make the required comparison. She may be said to have understood both addition and multiplication in terms of a simpler calculational routine. [P. 76]

The interview situation is used to force the student to clarify and focus mathematical thinking. The teacher usually has some relevant manipulative materials, such as paper, pencils, and crayons, so that the student may tell and/or show some aspect of a problem-solving procedure. If she or he can only *tell* and not *show*, then additional manipulative work may be necessary until the teacher can confirm that the student does understand what the language means. If the student can *show* and not *tell*, then additional work with vocalizing or writing should accompany math activities to be sure that language and cognition are developing in a parallel fashion.

Interview questions often are general enough to accommodate any content at hand. Initial questions are open-ended to lessen the chance that the student can pick up a cue to an expected response and also to reinforce the idea that the teacher is not even looking for a right answer. More specific questions can follow as more refined information is needed.

Lankford (1974) describes an oral interview technique specifically useful for computation. We think, however, that these ten questions will help the resource teacher get started with mathematics interviewing in almost any situation. Note that a *question* in a math interview is not necessarily cast into an interrogative form but involves any means of probing the student's thoughts or ideas:

1. "Tell me about how you . . ."
2. "Why did you . . .?" (But, not in a chastising voice!)
3. "How else could you . . .?"
4. "As I do this problem, you tell me what you think I'm doing for each step."
5. "You work this problem. As you do it, tell me out loud what you are doing."
6. "How did you happen to . . .?"
7. "How can you be sure that . . .?"

    8. "How can you find out if . . . ?"
    9. "Show me how . . . ."
  10. "If . . . , then . . . ?"

A second approach to tapping cognitive skills that are assumed to underlie mathematical concepts, operations, and logical reasoning is based upon the developmental theories of Piaget. This position is stated succinctly by Hendrickson (n.d.):

> . . . *counting* and *comparing* and *transforming* are the basis for development of competence in *classifying, ordering, seriating,* and knowledge of *number*. These are used along with *patterning, combining, grouping, separating,* and *distributing* to develop understanding of the *arithmetic operations, fraction,* and *place value.* Upon these foundations are constructed *algorithms* for computations, *application* of mathematics to *"real world"* problems and *logical arrangements* and sequences.

The task of the resource teacher is to be aware of the relationship these basic understandings bear to the learning of mathematics. Background for the teacher is found in two excellent books: *The Learning Theory of Piaget and Inhelder* (Gallagher and Reid, 1981) and *The Piaget Primer: Thinking, Learning, Teaching* (Labinowicz, 1980). More specific application to math is described by Copeland (1976), Williams and Shuard (1970), and by Ginsburg (1982).

As students experience difficulty in mathematics, interviews that deal with basic thinking skills for math can be structured to determine if the task is within the present developmental level of the student.

DEVELOPING INSTRUCTIONAL PROCEDURES

Many resources for instructional procedures have been mentioned in connection with comprehensive analysis of the learner and his or her environment. Here we want to emphasize five important considerations that should be taken into account as the resource teacher develops plans for organizing and managing an instructional *program* in mathematics education. These considerations are relevant to both classroom and clinic:

1.   The readiness of the resource teacher to deal with mathematics.
2.   The centrality of language and thinking to mathematics.
3.   The need for systematic options for instruction.
4.   The need to develop long-range instructional plans that are central to the student's thinking and readiness.
5.   Needed changes within the ongoing classroom program.

The readiness of the resource teacher to deal with mathematics

The resource teacher eventually must accumulate a store of understandings and instructional strategies to allow for both developmental and remedial teaching of a particular skill or concept. The continuing education of the resource teacher can be accomplished not only through courses in mathematics education but also through the study and use of the many fine books that deal with instruction. In addition to the resources suggested throughout this chapter, we recommend the following professional references, which are immediately applicable to any teaching situation:

Today's Mathematics: Concepts and Methods in Elementary School Mathematics, 4th ed. (Heddens, 1980)
Teaching Mathematics to Children with Special Needs (Reisman and Kauffman, 1980)
Mathematics Their Way (M. Baratta-Lorton, 1976) (for younger students)
Mathematics . . . A Way of Thinking (R. Baratta-Lorton, 1977) (for older students — a companion volume to *Mathematics Their Way*)
The Math Teaching Handbook for Teachers, Tutors, and Parents (Herold, 1978)
Workjobs II (M. Baratta-Lorton, 1979) (for early childhood)

In addition to the suggestions already provided, the resource teacher also may wish to acquire a basic repertoire of clinical approaches to teaching mathematics. The accounts of clinicians in the field of learning disabilities often reinforce those of mathematics educators. See, for example, the articles or books of Fernald (1943, pp. 213 – 255), Freidus (1966, pp. 111 – 128), Strauss and Lehtenin (1947, pp. 147 – 167), Johnson and Myklebust (1967, pp. 244 – 271), and Cruickshank et al., (1961, pp. 206 – 234).

For resource teachers more comfortable with a written curriculum for teaching mathematics, we recommend *Project Math* (Cawley et al., 1976). A sample instructional guide from that program is shown in Figure 7 – 4. Even a program so carefully constructed as this one is must still be used with a clinical eye to see situations that need modifications for a specific student. However, the structure of this program does account for many of the variables discussed in this chapter and also presents multiple instructional options.

The centrality of language and thinking to mathematics

The overiding centrality of language to mathematics instruction has been noted throughout this chapter. The resource teacher must take every opportunity to explore the student's understanding of each item of language used. *The Child's Conception of Number* (Piaget, 1965) is a good book on the importance of language. Articles dealing with language and cognition include "The Primitive Nature of Children's Relational Concepts" (Clark, 1970) and "Less Is More: A Study of Language Comprehension in Children" (Donaldson and Balfour, 1968). In addition, we recommend that instruction be designed to maintain a constant relationship between oral language, pictorial

FIGURE 7 – 4.
Level 1: Project Math Instructional Guide

STRAND	Measurement
AREA	Height
CONCEPT	Tall/Short

	INPUT	OUTPUT

	INSTRUCTOR	LEARNER
BEHAVIORAL OBJECTIVE	State directions in terms of tall/short.	Constructs a representation of different heights.

ACTIVITIES

1. Towers of Blocks. Construct two towers of blocks, one six blocks high and the other three blocks high. Point to the taller one and say, "Here is something that is tall." Point to the shorter one and say, "Here is something that is shorter than the tall tower. Here are some blocks. Please use them to construct a tall tower and a shorter one like mine." Construct a ten-block tower and a five-block tower and say, "Here is a tall tower and here is a shorter tower." Dismantle the towers and give some blocks to each learner. Ask them to construct a tall tower and a shorter tower.

2. Using Lego Blocks. Construct two walls of Lego blocks (or any blocks with interlock), one three blocks tall and one twelve blocks tall. Give each learner a pool of blocks and ask each to construct a tall wall and a shorter wall.

    Construct a tower ten blocks high and another tower twelve blocks high. Point to the first tower and state, "This tower is tall, but this one is taller." Construct another tower which is fourteen blocks tall and state that this is the tallest of the three. Dismantle the towers and build a tower which is twelve blocks high. Ask the learners to build a tower that is taller than yours and then build one that will be the tallest of the three. Repeat the words *tall, taller,* and *tallest* when referring to the corresponding tower. Repeat the above procedure substituting the words *short, shorter,* and *shortest.* Construct a tower six blocks high and state that the tower is short. Build another one four blocks high and state that this one is shorter. Build a third towr which is two blocks high and state that this is the shortest one.

MATERIALS

Plain or colored blocks; Lego blocks or other blocks which interlock.

SUPPLEMENTAL ACTIVITIES   M54; 1, b, c, d.

EVALUATION

Construct a pile of books. Ask the learner to construct one pile of books taller than the model and one pile shorter than the model.

From J. F. Cawley, H. A. Goodstein; A. M. Fitzmaurice, A. Lepore, R. Sedlak, and V. Althaus, *Project Math: A Program of the Mainstream Series* (Wallingford, Conn.: Educational Sciences, 1976). Used by permission of Educational Development Corporation, Tulsa, Okla.

and symbolic representation as well as real-life situations. This is shown in Figure 7 – 5.

The need for systematic options for instruction

As a format that can be used to observe and note both error and success during analytic teaching, we recommend the "Interactive Unit" described by Goodstein (1975)[6]: "The Interactive Unit focuses independently upon instructor and learner behaviors. The four instructor behaviors are construct, present, state, and graphically symbolize. The four learner behaviors are construct, identify, state, and graphically symbolize" (p. 6). These behaviors form the framework for sixteen possible instructional interactions for a specific bit of content; if the student does not get it one way, then fifteen options are left to try. The unit is presented in Figure 7 – 6.

The need to develop long-range instructional plans that are central to the student's thinking and readiness

It is tempting to ignore all that is known about the development of mathematics abilities in children and youth and all that is known about such development in an individual student. The pressure to tutor the student for the "next page" in the classroom is great. Although short-term maintenance is served through assignment tutoring, the student is placed in the ultimately difficult position of having basic problems that are never attended to systematically. For example, one of the authors recently worked briefly with a third grader who counted words in reading with no understanding of a one-to-one correspondence between each word and the number he said. Further investigation showed problems with seriation and place value as

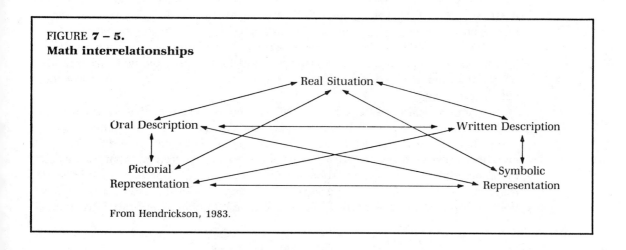

FIGURE **7 – 5.**
Math interrelationships

From Hendrickson, 1983.

FIGURE **7 – 6.**
Matrix Formed from Interactional Unit

INSTRUCTOR (DOES)	STUDENT (DOES OR DOES NOT)			
	Construct	Identity	State	Graphically Symbolize
1. Construct (active manipulation)	1.	2.	3	4.
2. Present (fixed stimulus; nonvocal)	5.	6.	7.	8.
3. State (orally)	9.	10.	11.	12.
4. Graphically symbolize (written, pictorial, etc.	13.	14.	15.	(Diagnostic Tests) 16.

well. The resource teacher was allowed to attend to these matters in a minimal fashion as they came up in daily assignments. There was no attempt by any teacher to anchor these ideas in the child's thinking.

If instruction in basic math matters cannot be provided in the classroom, it must be provided by the remedial educator, in this case, the resource teacher. It may even be necessary to remove the competing expectations of classrooms for a period of time for the student. Since students are quite divergent in their readiness for the classroom program, we urge the resource teacher to promote the reorganization of any rigid instructional programs in the classroom to accommodate those individual differences.

In any case, the resource teacher will want to be sure that analysis and instructional plans are not limited by local custom or convenience. The framework suggested here for an individual instructional plan in mathematics (see Table 7 – 4) is a way of seeing that an appropriate evaluation has occurred and that the instructional plans are related to the problems. The plan must, of course, be based on data that are: (1) comprehensive in the sense of covering all relevant facts of math instruction; (2) valid and reliable; and (3) related to modifiable aspects of instructional situations.

TABLE **7 – 4.**
Format for Individual Instructional Plan

A. *Data Sources* (Reports available or attached)
☐ Specific tests   ☐ In-classroom observations
☐ Analysis of permanent products   ☐ Analytic teaching
☐ Other:

B. *Skill or Concept to Be Taught*
☐ Expanded Strategy   ☐ Replacement strategy   ☐ New

C. *Prerequisite Math Skills:*   *Evidence of Competence*
   1.   1.
   2.   2.
   3.   3.
   4.   4.

D. *Materials to Be Used*
   Manipulatives: Activities:
   Models: Games:
   Visuals: Audio Materials:
   Practice Work: Other:

E. *Procedures to Be Used*
   Sources: Procedures:

F. *Special Instructional Considerations*
   1. Mode of presentation: 2. Mode of response:
   3. Language/mathematics   4. Language/instructional:

G. *Nonmath Considerations and Plans*
   1. Behavior management:
      a. Academic behaviors:
      b. Social behaviors during instruction:
   2. Format assistance:
   3. Legibility:
   4. Neatness:
   5. Other:

H. *Evaluation of Instructional Progress*
   1. Error analyses of permanent products:

   2. Error analyses of analytic instruction:

I. *Instructional Replanning*

Needed changes within the ongoing classroom program

For other academic areas, we have suggested that a management system often can be superimposed on the commercial program with good effect for many students. In mathematics, this is rarely the case because: (1) the instructional group (the class) is too large to allow for the individualization usually needed by students who have not mastered prerequisite skills; and (2) many commercial math programs give too little attention to the extended use of manipulative materials and to mediated language experiences. We suggest that if the teacher must use a commercial program, then he or she should supplement it with appropriate manipulative and language experiences. This is certainly the case for the resource teacher.

A math lab that spans several grades should eventually be considered as a means of accommodating the range of mathematical abilities in the elementary school. Such an approach also helps ensure that expensive manipulative materials will not need to be purchased in duplicate as the math lab will be available to all teachers and students.

If major program changes are not possible, the resource teacher should try to introduce some of the modifications we have suggested. The choice of a particular modification and the reason for its introduction will come from interpreting the data obtained about the capabilities of the referred students.

ENDNOTES

1. Reported by Vern Simula.
2. Example supplied by Roger Kroth.
3. NCTM Instructional Affairs Committee, "Minicalculators in Schools," *Arithmetic Teacher* 23 (1976): 72 – 74.
4. Example supplied by Jack Cawley.
5. The questions in this section are adapted from material described by McKillip, Cooney, Davis, and Wilson in *Mathematics Instruction in the Elementary Grades* (1978), pp. 87 – 107.
6. H. A. Goodstein, "Assessment and Programming in Mathematics for the Handicapped," *Focus on Exceptional Children* 7 (1975): 1 – 11.

8

Written Expression

Although writing, along with reading and arithmetic, is often called one of the three basics of education, relatively few students of lower elementary age are referred for resource help because of problems with written expression. The number of students referred for writing difficulties increases during the upper elementary and postelementary years. Regardless of when the problem is identified, both regular and resource teachers tend to spend a lot of time evaluating and remediating the surface skills of writing (spelling and handwriting) but devote little attention either to the quality of the ideas expressed or to how they are formulated.

The purposes of this chapter are: (1) to alert the resource teacher to the problems of teaching written language; (2) to suggest a framework for analyzing relevant aspects of both the instructional environment and the student's present abilities; and (3) to recommend preventive and corrective steps that the resource teacher can use to give the student an opportunity to learn to write and perhaps even to enjoy writing!

ANALYSIS OF THE LEARNER IN THE CLASSROOM

Resource teachers who intend to work with students on their written expression should observe and evaluate more than just the activities that occur during writing class because written language is an integral part of most school work. Therefore, for resource teachers to have a comprehensive picture of a problem in writing, they first must determine the role that written expression has in the daily activities of the school. Then the resource teacher can study students' performance in those activities. The following questions will help resource teachers discern factors within the classroom that are likely either to foster or inhibit growth in written expression.

1. *Is there evidence that written expression is being taught in the classroom as an integrated, multipurpose ability?* Students should be taught to write. A certain level of proficiency in writing ability is necessary: (1) to do well in many academic subjects; (2) for adequate social communication; (3) for success in many vocations; and (4) for the enjoyment derived from its creative or literary value.

The reasons for teaching written expression are specified and illustrated in many basic language arts textbooks, such as *Children and Language* (Lee and Rubin, 1979), *Language and Thinking in School, 2nd ed.* (Smith, Goodman, and Meredith, 1976), *Student-Centered Language Arts and Reading, K – 13: A Handbook for Teachers* (Moffett and Wagner, 1976), and *Easy in English* (Applegate, 1960).

An overview of a broad, well-balanced curriculum in written expression can provide evidence that the teacher is considering all of these reasons for teaching writing. For example, the resource teacher should note the different opportunities that a student has to practice meaningful writing, especially as these opportunities relate to the four purposes mentioned above.

Many teachers attempt to integrate the teaching of writing with other subjects. For example, they often incorporate writing with science and mathematics instruction by requiring the students to write down their structured observations (see Figure 8 – 1). Writing also can play a major part in learning to read, especially when a language experience approach is used to teach reading.

Descriptions of language experience methods in reading are found for all ages. Veatch, et al. (1973, notably pp. 56 – 95) and Brogan and Fox (1962) write specifically about the young child; Stauffer (1970) shows how the approach is applied to all ages; and Fernald (1943) deals with the clinical applications of language experience methods for use with severe reading and writing cases.

Activities that integrate written expression instruction with social studies instruction include question answering, report writing, and creative writing of plays and stories. Creative aspects of written expression may be found within academic areas; more often, however, they are encouraged by separate attention through using the techniques found in books such as *They All Want to Write* (Burrows, Jackson, and Saunders, 1964), *Easy in English* (Applegate, 1960), *Slithery Snakes and Other Aids to Children's Writing* (Petty and Bowen, 1967), and *Wishes, Lies and Dreams* (Koch et al., 1970).

Resource teachers may want to systematize their observations of teachers' classroom operations by using a checklist that specifies when instruction in written expression does or could take place. A starter checklist is presented in Table 8 – 1. For this example to be used most effectively, it should be modified to meet individual and local situations. Such checklists also may be used as premeasures and postmeasures to evaluate the effects of the resource teacher's consultations in helping referring teachers increase classroom opportunities for teaching written language.

FIGURE 8 – 1.
Writing in the Content Areas

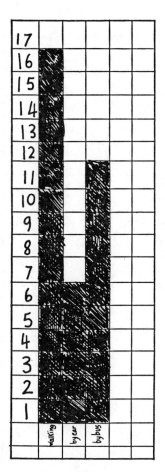

Richard   7 Years.

The graph tells us that most people Walk home from school. It tells you that eleven people come by bus. It tells you that 6 people come by car. It tells you that there are 33 people in the class. It tells you that 10 more people walk home than go by car. And 5 more people come by bus than by car and it shows you that 5 more people walk home from school than go by bus.

Reproduced by special permission of John Wiley & Sons, Inc. From Nuffield Mathematics Project. *Pictorial Representation, I.* New York: John Wiley & Sons, Inc., 1967.

2. *What opportunities does the academic curriculum provide for students to express their ideas in writing?* Classroom requirements and opportunities for written language vary both by grade level and by type of classroom. For younger students, writing may be confined to answering questions from academic areas, such as reading

TABLE **8 – 1.**
Situations in Which Written Language Can Be Encouraged and/or Taught

SITUATION	ENCOURAGED	HOW	TAUGHT	HOW
I. *Academic situations* A. Reading B. Mathematics C. Spelling D. Social Studies E. Science F. English				
II. *Letters* A. Personal: contact, thanks; appreciation; sympathy; congratulations apology; invitation; acknowledgement; request or offer of service; explanation; praise or commenation. B. Business: requests for materials, help, advice, or information; orders for materials; acknowledgement; complaint, explanation; apology; appreciation; furnishing information; answering requests. C. Gift tags and greeting cards.				
III. *Records* A. Observations in academics B. Plans C. Class activities D. Minutes E. Room histories, diaries.				
IV. *Filling Out Forms* A. Registration slips; examination blanks; applications; checks; receipts.				
V. *Publicity* A. Advertisements, notices, or announcements B. Articles for school or local newspaper				

TABLE **8 – 1.** *(Continued)*
Situations in Which Written Language Can Be Encouraged and/or Taught

SITUATION	ENCOUR-AGED	HOW	TAUGHT	HOW
V. *Publicity* C. Headlines for newspaper D. Legends and labels exhibits E. Duties to be performed				
VI. *Requiring* A. Reports by individuals or groups B. Directions and recipes C. Lists D. Dictation or copying of information or directions E. Bibliographies				
VII. *Stimulating Original* A. Riddles, puzzles, jokes B. Poems, stories, myths, fables, news stories C. Scripts for plays, TV, radio D. Songs E. Descriptions: Games, recipes, people, places F. personal accounts, e.g., diaries, biographies				

Adapted in great part from and reprinted by permission of the publisher, from Ruth G. Strickland: *The Language arts in the elementary school.* Lexington, Mass. D. C. Heath and Company, 1957. 2nd edition.

or spelling, and from copying stories, poems, and letters. Exercises from English textbooks often appear around Grade 3, along with written social studies, science assignments, and compositions such as "What I Did during Summer Vacation."

Opportunities available for expressing ideas cannot be separated from the expectations of the general curriculum. The student's responses can seldom be better than the questions or problems posed there. If the written responses built into the curriculum require only convergent or narrow, recall thinking, then the student will not have experience with planned opportunities to engage in the divergent, evaluating thinking that can be expressed in writing. Consider, for example, the differences in quality of response for these two questions for the older student:

1.   Where is the city of Chicago?
2.   Why would you or wouldn't you like to live in the city of Chicago? [Cunningham, 1971, pp. 101 – 102]

And for the younger child:
1.   Maria was _____. (happy, sad)
2.   Tell about two things Maria could do next. [To be written, drawn, or told to teacher, aide, or recorder; if drawn or told, to be written eventually by teacher or aide to show written expression of the ideas.]

The resource teacher should obtain samples of any written products from academic work. The resource teacher analyzes these samples to determine the relative proportion of opportunities for doing higher-order thinking and responding, whatever the grade level. The chapter "Developing Question-Asking Skills" (Cunningham, 1971) and Sander's book, *Classroom Questions: What Kinds?* (1966), are especially helpful in determining or changing the quality of expected written responses in academic areas.

In addition to contributing to the overall level of cognition expected in written expression, the kinds of responses required in academic areas may have several other effects. First, if written activities are limited to filling in blanks or to paraphrasing the text, writing may be viewed as an unpleasant task with but one purpose — showing right answers. Neither of these kinds of responses encourages the student to develop fluency and flexibility of style. Limiting written expression to a responsive mold in academics also may mean that the student is prevented from seeing writing as something he or she can initiate.

3. *What kind of standards are expected and how are they taught?* If perfection of mechanics and the use of standard English content and structures are always required, the student may think of writing as an adverse activity. This statement does *not* mean that mechanics and standard English should never be taught and expected. It *does* mean that:

a.   Instruction should precede or accompany evaluation
b.   Such instruction is developed slowly and carefully with the students.
c.   The student is not expected to know usage and mechanics of written expression simply because they were in last year's curriculum guide
d.   Instructional opportunities in mechanics and usage arise from naturally occurring occasions and from occasions that the teacher deliberately creates within the classroom, and not from a textbook or curriculum timetable.
e.   Standards are reasonable; for example, adults often disagree about the correct punctuation of a sentence or paragraph.
f.   Constructive assistance is provided to help the student with rewriting before a final, evaluatable draft is handed in.

FIGURE 8 – 2.
Example of Teacher Focus on Form of Student Writing

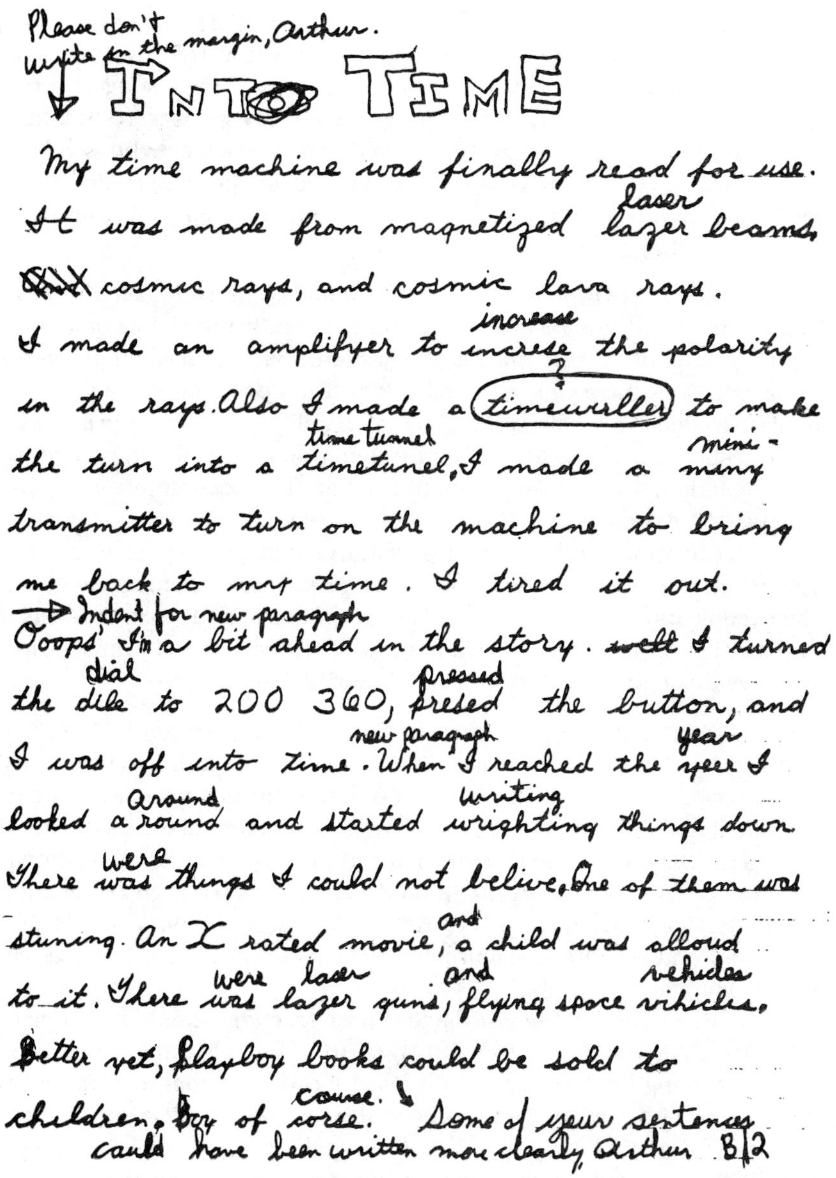

Please don't write in the margin, Arthur.

↓ INTO TIME

My time machine was finally read for use.
It was made from magnetized ~~lazer~~ *laser* beams,
~~XXX~~ cosmic rays, and cosmic lava rays.
I made an amplifyer to ~~increse~~ *increase* the polarity
in the rays. Also I made a (timewriller?) to make
the turn into a ~~timetunel~~ *time tunnel*, I made a *mini-* ~~many~~
transmitter to turn on the machine to bring
me back to my time. I tired it out.

→ *Indent for new paragraph*
Ooops' I'm a bit ahead in the story. ~~well~~ I turned
the ~~dile~~ *dial* to 200 360, ~~fresed~~ *pressed* the button, and
I was off into time. *new paragraph* When I reached the ~~year~~ *year* I
looked ~~a round~~ *around* and started ~~wrighting~~ *writing* things down
There ~~was~~ *were* things I could not belive. ~~One of them was~~
stuning. An X rated movie, *and* a child was alloud
to it. There ~~was~~ *were* *laser* lazer guns, flying space *vehicles* ~~vihicles~~.
Better yet, Playboy books could be sold to
children. Boy of ~~corse~~ *course.* Some of your sentences
could have been written more clearly, Arthur   B/2

From D. Searle and D. Dillon, "Responding to Student Writing: What Is Said or How It Is Said,"
Language Arts 57 (1980), p. 774.

g.   Content is considered separately from other factors and is also evaluated differently from those factors.

Searle and Dillion (1980) have noted that teacher responses to student writing continue to focus predominantly on elements of form or surface structure rather than content, as seen in the example in Figure 8–2. They suggest that teacher reactions to student writing be varied according to the role that the teacher assumes as a respondent and by the focus of the response. They suggest a framework that can be used to evaluate the range of the teacher's responses to student writing (Table 8 – 2). This format will be useful to the resource teacher who is collecting information about how student writing is evaluated in the classroom and also how it is evaluated by the resource teacher if the student is in a writing program within the resource setting.

4. *What provision is made for the student who is not yet able to write?* Written expression is but one means of communication. If the classroom teacher places too high a premium on this means, the student may be prevented from showing that he or she does have the required information or cognitive skills. Penalizing a student in academic areas because of a real inability to use appropriate written language is a questionable if not an outright unfair practice. Talking, recording, oral discussion, dictation, drawing, or dramatization are fast becomming acceptable substitutes for written responses.

Overemphasis on producing written language may have the further effect of removing the student from needed writing readiness activities. These activities include the organization of ideas, the expression of ideas, and various facets of vocabulary and concept development. Readiness experiences are found primarily in oral language, in dramatic activities, and in reading and being read to.

5. *What assistance is provided for written expression within the classroom?* In addition to providing a clasroom that is rich in stimulating experiences, many tangible experiences can contribute to growth in written expression. The categories and specific items listed below suggest how a classroom might be outfitted for writing.

a. Ideas for getting started or for improving an existing writing program. See, for example, *What Can I Write About? 7000 Topics for High School Students* (Powell, 1981), *Writing Aids through the Grades* (Carlson, 1970), *The Whole Word Catalog* (Teachers' and Writers' Collaborative, 1972), and the other references cited previously in this chapter.

b. Helps for finding words. Resource teachers should consider the class-made thesaurus suggested by Tiedt (1975, p. 10). They also might want to (1) give each child a spelling book of commonly used words, numbered consecutively for extra convenience (the teacher can refer to the number while mentioning the word, and the student can look it up that way if the spelling is unknown); (2) prepare individual word lists, dictionaries, or word-card boxes; and (3) have available a variety of dictionaries with their use unrestricted by any level of competence designation.

c. Guides to form and format. Individual handwriting charts with both cursive and manuscript forms should be accessible to students. These may be placed

TABLE 8 – 2.
Classification of Teachers' Responses to Children's Written Work

TYPE	CONTENT	Focus		
		FORM		
EVALUATION		STYLE	STRUCTURE	MECHANICS
INSTRUCTIONAL a) didactic/correction b) encouragement c) attitude				
AUDIENCE a) clarification b) elaboration c) reaction d) taking action				
MOVING BEYOND a) extention b) addition				
GENERAL COMMENT a) Grading b) Impressiong				
UNCLASSIFIED				

From D. Searle and D. Dillon, "Responding to Student Writing: What Is Said or How It Is Said," *Language Arts 57* (1980), p. 778.

in individual notebooks or kept in desks for handy reference. Proofreading guides developed in class, models of standard formats for letters, reports, and paper headings also should be within easy access for all students. Some of these are idiosyncratic to the classroom; others, especially those found in language arts textbooks, can be guides for class development.

d. Access to writing supplies and supplementary materials:

paper (in great variety)	staples
puppets	chalk
picture-type magazines	paper clips
various colors, sizes, and styles of	overhead projector
pencils, pens, crayons, and felt pens	envelopes
rulers	stamps (real)
typewriter	Ditto masters for sharing products
tape recorder	Ditto paper
drawing papers	paper clips
graph paper (various sizes)	colored and textured papers
stationery and stationery-making	extra "writing" paper
supplies	chalkboard
card and picture files	printing supplies[1]
punches	bookbinding materials (see art guides)
	computer with wordprocessing soft-
	ware, perhaps with a spelling correcter
	program

6. *What are the attitudes of the teacher(s) toward writing, and how knowledgeable is each teacher about instruction in writing?* The teacher's attitude has been called the most important part of any writing program. Attitude is usually obvious from noting the extent and the manner in which writing is encouraged within the classroom. In secondary schools, the resource teacher should note the attitudes of content area teachers, as well as those of teachers of English. Writing, like reading, is often expected, but rarely taught in these classrooms.

Teachers at any level may have noncommittal attitudes toward writing because they have had little background or few resources available to them to encourage interest in writing. In addition, although many states and teacher-training programs require at least one course in reading for teachers, no such requirement has ever existed for courses in writing theory and practice (Walmsley, 1980). Now that there is active professional interest in writing instruction, perhaps there will be more balanced attention to reading and writing.

Teacher attitudes may also be influenced by administrative expectations. For example, perhaps thirty minutes a day are allocated to spelling instruction and fifteen minutes for handwriting, but no such requirement may be expressed for the teaching of writing. Time expected is a good indication of the school district's relative emphasis on writing; time spent is a good indication of the teacher's interest.

7. *How is writing integrated in the content area classrooms of the adolescent?*

In the content areas, students may be asked to write reports, to synthesize readings from various sources, or otherwise to report their independent work. Quite often students copy verbatim from sources such as encyclopedias, scarcely stopping to perceive relationships among pieces of information or ideas.

Content area teachers who are interested in the development of students' thinking in regard to school subjects are more likely to have students write and revise, based upon teacher comments about how the ideas are woven together or the arguments presented. Other teachers merely grade and return papers.

Content area teachers who are interested in writing and thinking are also likely to provide modeling or instruction in the inter-relationships of ideas in their subject domains. Writing reports, summaries, and evaluative statements is based upon the *thinking* activities promoted within the classroom, and not necessarily upon the writing assignments.

Writing and "study skills" are irrevocably related. Books such as *Notemaking* (D. Brown, 1977) provide excellent instructional formats both for teachers and students who wish to incorporate writing-thinking-studying into the content area curriculum.

8. *Does the teacher of younger students show awareness of current professional information about the beginning stages of writing?* Advances in the study of the beginnings of writing behavior in young children are the outgrowth of the explosion of knowledge about language development in general and spelling and reading in particular. For example, the reading abilities of young children appear to develop naturally from their interest in and knowledge of the forms and functions of writing. Children often wish to learn to write before they want to learn to read. Clay (1975) has noted the importance of writing to reading. Her view is in contrast to those who support the primacy of oral language to reading. She makes the case for writing instead:

> The child who engages in creative writing is manipulating the units of written language — letters, words, sentence types — and is likely to be gaining some awareness of how these can be combined to convey unspoken messages. The child is having to perform within the directional constraints that we use in written English. The child is probably learning to generage sentences in a deliberate way, word by word. He makes up sentences which fit both his range of ideas and his written language skills. Fluent oral language may permit the young reader to depend almost entirely on meaning and the eye may overlook the need for discriminating details of letters and words. Creative writing demands that the child pay attention to the details of print. To put his messages down in print he is forced to construct words, letter by letter, and so he becomes aware of letter features and letter sequences, particularly for the vocabulary which he uses in writing again and again. These words become part of his writing vocabulary, the ones that he knows in every perceptual detail. [P. 2]

The identification of predictable patterns in the normal development of spelling competence in young children has been based upon the spontaneous writing of young children themselves. As a result, certain developmental patterns in children's written spelling are now viewed as indicators of growth rather than failure. This means that teachers, who have been accustomed to evaluating writing negatively because of what they perceive as failure with the surface forms of writing (in this case, spelling) now have a basis for more valid assessment of writing growth. Teachers of young students — and some older ones as well — now have access to information about how *most* children begin writing and spelling and what should come next from one particular developmental point or stage to another. For example, Zutell's Spelling Strategy Rating Scale (1980) shows the normally developing spellings that children systematically "invent" during writing activity (Table 8 – 3).

TABLE 8 – 3.
Spelling Strategy Rating Scale

Category	Strategy	Score	Examples of Children's Spellings
Short Vowel	unclassifiable	0	krof (craft), scod (skid)
	vowel omitted	1	krft, scd
	closest tense vowel	2	crift, sced
	transitional	3	creft, scad
	vowel correct, incorrect form	4	kraf, scid
	correct form	5	craft, skid
Long Vowel	unclassifiable	0	crop (creep), slom (slime)
	letter-name	1	crep, slim
	transitional	2	crip, slam
	vowel correct, marking incorrect	3	creyp, sliym
	vowel correctly marked, incorrect form	4	creap, sime
	correct form	5	creep, slime
Past Tense	unclassifiable	0	rake (raked), cet (cheated)
	letter-name	1	rakt, chetd
	d-marker	2	rakd, cheatd
	vowel (not e, not o +d	3	racid, cheatud
	marker correct, incorrect form	4	raced, cheeted
	correct form	5	raked, cheated

TABLE **8 – 3.** *(Continued)*
Spelling Strategy Rating Scale

Category	Strategy	Score	Examples of Children's Spellings
Consonant	unclassifiable	0	flop (flopped), wad (wading)
Doubling	letter-name	1	flpt, wadn
	lax, undoubled	2	floped
	tense, doubled	3	wadding
	doubling correct,		
	incorrect form	4	floppid, weding
	correct form	5	flopped, wading
Derivational	unclassifiable	0	xpln-xplntn (explain-explanation)
Pairs	letter-name	1	xplan-xplnashon
	vowel present,		
	unextended	2	explain-explinashon
	vowel incorrectly		
	extended	3	explain-explaination
	vowel correctly		
	extended, incorrect		
	form	4	explain-xplanashon
	correct form	5	explain-explanation

From J. Zutell, "Children's Spelling Strategies and Their Cognitive Development," in E. H. Henderson and J. W. Beers, eds., *Developmental and Cognitive Aspects of Learning to Spell: A Reflection of Word Knowledge* (Newark, Del.: International Reading Association, 1980), p. 68.

The development of various spelling features in the writing of children has been shown to be tied to their understanding of the concept of a *word,* so that at various times different features of the concept are predominant. As children develop different phonological, morphological, syntactic, and semantic features of words, their ability to spell the words changes accordingly.

We will not dwell on this aspect of writing but refer those interested to Henderson and Beer's *Developmental and Cognitive Aspects of Learning to spell: A Reflection of Word Knowledge* (1980), and to Nathan and Burris' *The Beginnings of Writing* (1982). The importance of the topic to early writing is that teachers of young students, just like those of older students, may tend to judge writing by surface forms rather than content or stage of the student's development. Hopefully, with the research moving quickly into application, teachers of young students will be seen to encourage writing in students who were once believed to be unready.

SUPPLEMENTAL INDIVIDUAL ANALYSIS

Knowledge of the classroom situations gives the resource teacher some idea of the extent and nature of any writing program within those classes It also allows a cataloging of the required uses for writing, as well as those that are intended for nonschool situations, such as personal writing or writing related to functional living or occupational needs. The resource teacher should also have some idea about the possibilities for consulting with school personnel about any changes that should be made within classrooms. And finally, factors that inhibit or encourage the student will have been identified.

Individual analysis is needed in order to begin instructional planning with the student and others who might be involved. We recommend that the resource teacher begin to collect various samples of the student's writing and keep individual folders for documenting student progress in this area.

The cue questions listed below are intended to guide further description of the student's writing and to begin focusing on instructional strategies.

1. *Does the student have a serious problem with written expression?* Standardized tests of written expression can be used to determine if the student's writing is significantly discrepant from that of age peers. The *Test of Written Language* (TOWL) (Hammill and Larsen, 1983) can be used with students in grades 2 through 12. Its purpose is to identify students who have problems in written expression, to pinpoint specific areas of deficit, and to conduct research. The TOWL yields information about six areas of writing competence, including:

1. *Word Usage,* the use of standard verb tenses, plurals, pronouns, and other grammatical forms;
2. *Style,* the use of generally accepted conventions regarding punctuation and and capitalization;
3. *Spelling,* the ability to spell both phonetically regular and irregular words;
4. *Thematic Maturity,* the ability to construct a meaningful story on a given theme;
5. *Vocabulary,* the level of words used in a written story;
6. *Handwriting,* the legibility of the written story.

Part of this information is derived from the analysis of an elicited sample of continuous writing and part from subtest performance. A TOWL profile sheet is shown in Figure 8 – 3.

For older students, two subtests of the *Test of Adolescent Language* (Hammill et al., 1980) are especially relevant. These subtests are writing/vocabulary and writing/grammer. Information obtained from these subtests is described in comparison with other language abilities measured by the test.

2. *To what extent does the referred student write?* Teachers often complain that the student does not write very much. They usually mean that he or she hesitates to write even when encouraged to do so, avoids situations requiring writing, and expresses a dislike for writing. Teachers also can mean that the student's written products are too brief and sparse in content. Table 8 – 4 specifies the more common

FIGURE 8 – 3.
Summary and Profile Sheet for TOWL

TOWL

TEST OF WRITTEN LANGUAGE

Donald D. Hammill & Stephen C. Larsen

Name: _____ Male ☐ Female ☐

	Year	Month	Day
Date tested	____	____	____
Date of Birth	____	____	____
Age	____	____	____

School: _____ Grade: _____

Examiner's Name: _____
(FIRST)   (LAST)

Examiner's Title: _____

SECTION I RECORD OF SCORES

SUBTESTS	Raw Scores	% iles	Std. Scores
I Vocabulary	____	____	____
II Thematic Maturity	____	____	____
III Spelling	____	____	____
IV Word Usage	____	____	____
V Style	____	____	____
VI Handwriting	____	____	____

Sum of Standard Scores = _____

Written Language Quotient (WLQ) = _____

SECTION II OTHER TEST SCORES

NAME	DATE	STD. SCORE	TOWL EQUIV.

SECTION III PROFILE OF SCORES

SECTION IV OBSERVATIONS

© Copyright 1983 by Hammill & Larsen

Additional copies of this form are available from PRO-ED, 5341 Industrial Oaks Blvd., Austin, Texas 78735
512-892-3142

reasons for students' negative reactions to writing. Table 8–1 also contains evaluation techniques and suggestions for alieviating a student's low writing production.

TABLE 8 – 4.
Potential Factors Involved in Low Production of Written Language

FACTOR	HOW DETERMINED	POSSIBLE ASSISTANCE
1. Few, or restricted opportunities for learning and practicing written expression	1. a. Classroom observations b. Examination of expectations and the student's written work	1. Increasing instructional and practice opportunities
2. Student knows the content, but does not know how to organize and express ideas	2. a. Examination of written work b. Oral discussion with planned opportunities to organize and express ideas c. Analysis of other forms of communication	2. a. Readiness work with aural/oral aspects of language b. Dramatics c. Work with organization through other means of visual expression, such as picture story order
3. Student lacks the essential content required to meet requirements of written expression	3. Oral discussion with probing questions designed to elicit depth of knowledge	3. a. Conceptual development relevant to content at hand, or related topics b. Concurrent oral discussion c. Evantually, concurrent written expression of content

4. Student hesitates to write because judgmental standards are too high:
(a) self-imposed by student
(b) school-imposed
	4. (a) Self-imposed:
	  a. Comments made by student
	  b. Contingency management
	(b) School-imposed:
	  a. Examination of evaluation system
	  b. Discussion with student
	  c. Classroom observation
		4. (a) Self-imposed:
		  a. Teach self-modification of behavior
		  b. Reinforcement of acceptance of reasonable standards
		  c. Counseling
		(b) School-imposed:
		  a. Made more realistic
		  b. Teacher reinforcement for modifying standards appropriately
		  c. Redeveloping with teachers and students

TABLE **8 – 4.** *(Continued)*
Potential Factors Involved in Low Production of Written Language

FACTOR	HOW DETERMINED	POSSIBLE ASSISTANCE
5. Student knows how to write; does not choose to do so	5. a. Talk with student b. Provide motivational experiences related to student's interests c. Contingency management	5. a. Couseling b. Provide motivational experiences related to student's interests c. Contingency management
6. Problems with subskills such as spelling, handwriting, and grammar	6. a. Examine permanent written products b. Examine evaluation system to determine if undue emphasis is being placed on subskills c. Analyze student's competence in subskills out of their natural environment	6. a. Teach separately b. Teach or use compensatory tactics c. De-emphasize some of these skills during writing d. Teach subskills in more personalized way to meet individually determined writing requirements
7. Student is a slow worker	7. a. Baseline rate data collection b. Check Item 4 above c. Setting time/production requirements d. Contingency management	7. a. Contingency management b. If standards are too high, see Item 4 above c. Pairing with faster worker

3. *What extraneous factors are involved in the student's perceived problems with written expression?* As in other areas, factors such as neatness, cleanliness, and page arrangements can contribute to a teacher's perceptions of a student's ability. When analyzing writing, the resource teacher may want to separate these elements from the writing itself. Of course, these factors should receive separate attention through counseling or through a program of systematic positive reinforcement for improvement.

4. *What is the student's attitude toward writing?* It is often hard to have an attitude about something you do not do. Many students are indifferent to writing, for they have been in schools where they have never *had* to write at all, except for daily homework assignments. Further, evaluation practices in schools do not always lend themselves to building the self-concept of any student experiencing problems. A conference with the student can set the occasion for discussing the student's feelings

and attitudes about writing. If the attitudes are negative, changes will accompany a program that values writing and the writer.

5. *What is the parent's involvement with the student's writing?* Many parents are concerned about the decline of writing as a basic skill. Yet they may not themselves provide any opportunities for their child to see the value and use of writing, for example, the telephone call to a great extent has supplanted the letter in communication. Further, parents may not always be the primary care givers as children are placed in day schools or sitters' homes.

On the other hand, it may be up to parents to provide a *program* of writing if it is not to be provided at schools. We highly recommend as a virtual mine of suggestions to use with parents or primary care givers, Wiener's *Any Child Can Write: How to Improve Your Child's Writing Skills from Preschool through High School* (1978). The reource teacher might wish to use such a book as the basis for a meeting with parents or recommend it for parents who wish to help with writing at home. Table 8 – 5 shows pointers for parents to use in helping with writing. These suggestions might also be discussed with classroom teachers and modified for the local school situation.

6. *How well does the student command the mechanics of written expression?* Since mechanics (spelling, penmanship, puncuation, and so forth) play such an important part in how the student's written expression is judged, the resource teacher should analyze samples of the referred student's written work to see how the student uses these aids to conform to standards and for clarity. Mechanical skills such as spelling and penmanship are treated in other chapters.

Puncutuation is a difficult subject to evaluate because there is so little agreement about standards of correctness. The use of conventions such as those governing the use of capital letters and letter greetings can be accepted easily, although exceptions are found constantly in everyday life; but other puncutation is chancy at best. Puncutuation tests are relatively useless because the punctuation of written expression depends on context, author style, and oral interpretation. To check this assumption, we suggest that the resource teacher ask several colleagues to punctuate the comment shown below. Responses then can be compared with Mellon's original.[2]

> And suppose too that one interpreted the decline of writing ability as evidence of a reduction in the amount and intensity of in-school writing instruction over the past half-decade a likely interpretation since of all the language skills that of writing is uniquely dependent for its acquisition upon the kind of overt teaching that in youth occurs only in school. [P. 73]

Tables 8 – 6 and 8 – 7 may help determine what could have been presented to the student in regard to mechanics. The resource teacher also can adapt charts such as these into checklists for noting areas of success or problems for each student. However, specific items for individual instruction should *not* be taken from scope and sequence charts but from an analysis of the student's needs.

FIGURE 8 – 6.

Tips and Pointers: How Parents Can Help with Writing for School

Stage	Do's	Don'ts
Before Writing	1. Encourage the child to explain the assignment made by the teacher. Ask questions so that you're sure he understands it.	1. Don't interpret the assignment. Don't *tell* him what the teacher wants. Ask questions so the child can figure it out for himself.
	2. Let the child discuss what he wants to write about. Ask questions to make sure he can offer details to support any idea he wants to develop.	2. Don't respond to questions like, "What should I write about?" without making a wide range of suggestions from which the child can choose without feeling obliged to follow your ideas.
	3. Encourage the jotting down of words or ideas as the child thinks the topic through.	3. Don't add details for the child. Ask questions: What color? What size? and so on.
Rough Copy	1. Remind the youngster of how writers write. Show a page of "rough writing" from this book or better still, a page of your own writing before you turn it into something you'd like to show someone.	1. Don't worry yourself or the child about neatness or correctness.
	2. Ignore mistakes. Encourage cross-outs. Encourage skipped lines for information to be added later.	2. Don't push too hard. If the child draws a blank, let him turn to other things. Come back to the writing after a glass of milk, or a game.
	3. Spell out words only if the child asks you. Write them down for the child to copy. Better, help him sound out the words.	3. Don't let spelling get in the way of the writing effort. Let youngsters *guess* at spelling until later on.
	4. Keep an eye on errors so that you can direct the child's learning about some of them later on.	

TABLE 8 – 5.
Tips and Pointers: How Parents Can Help with Writing for School

Stage	Do's	Don'ts
Reading the Rough Copy	1. Ask the child to read the work aloud. Praise it!	1. Don't interrupt the reading no matter how many suggestions you can make for improvement.
	2. Ask questions: "What color was the house?" "What sound did the door make?" "Would you like to put those words in to give a better picture?"	2. Don't correct the errors.
	3. Show sensitivity to word choice in general. "You've said, 'The shoe *crunched* the glass on the pavement!' What wonderful word!" or "You wrote, "My sister *walked* to the door.' Why don't you try to find a word that shows a better picture of how she moved?"	3. Don't add any details.
	4. Explain the use of the caret ($\wedge$) to insert omitted words. Draw arrows out to the margins, if necessary.	4. Don't show any disappointment about poor writing or about errors.
	5. When you see a glaring mistake, help the child find it and correct it hmself. After you're both satisfied with the ideas expressed, say, "Oh, oh, I see a place in the first three lines where a sentence should end. Can you find it?" Or, "You have six spelling mistakes. See if you can find them." You'll want to use proofreading techniques here (see the next section in this chapter). You might suggest that the youngster use a different color pencil so that corrections will stand out clearly.	5. Don't make any reference to neatness or sloppiness.

TABLE 8 – 5. (Continued)
Tips and Pointers: How Parents Can Help with Writing for School

Stage	Do's	Don'ts
	6. Encourage sentence diversity. Say, "Why don't you put together two sentences toward the end? You can use *and* or *because* or *since* to join them together." Or, "You've used *and* so many times to join sentences. Can you put them together in another way?"	6. Don't expect correctness in areas that the child does not understand or has not yet learned. Again, it's your judgment: If the first few letters of a difficult word tell you what the child means, you may want to ignore the error completely. However, don't allow an attitude of carelessness or indifference to the writing process to develop.
	7. Given the age and attention span of the child, with especially thorny topics or especially hard-to-read rough copies, suggest another draft written from the first.	
Copying Over: the Final Draft	1. Encourage the preparation of a careful final copy. Ask about the teacher's instructions on how the page should look. Where does the name go? the date? the title? May the child write on both sides of a page? What margins does the teacher require? Offer hints about good handwriting. Periods at ends of sentences should be clear and firm: the child should leave enough space between the period and the next word. Capital letters should be clearly capitals. With cursive writing, ask that the *i* be dotted directly over the letter and not between the *i* and *e.* Discourage circles as dots for *i*'s.	1. Don't type or write the paper over for the child no matter how "sloppy" he claims his handwriting is.

TABLE **8 – 5.** *(Continued)*
Tips and Pointers: How Parents Can Help with Writing for School

Stage	*Do's*	*Don'ts*
	2. Answer questions about spelling. Spell out the toughest words, writing them down on a separate sheet for the youngster to look at and to copy over. Encourage his use of the dictionary. Look up words toegether.	2. Don't hang over the child as he copies his paper over. Answer questions if he has any — but this is his effort so don't make him nervous. Welcome questions. You can decide whether or not to answer them after they are asked!
	3. Listen as the chid reads the paper aloud. Ask him if words sound smooth together, if sentences make sense to him	3. Don't be embarrassed if the child asks you to spell a word and you cannot. That's what dictionaries are for! A youngster who sees his mother or father reach for a dictionary when a word stumps her or him develops good habits.
	4. See that the child proofreads his final draft carefully. Using what you know of previous kinds of errors the child makes, you can help focus the proofreading activity: "Ramón, last time you misspelled *disappoint* and *already*. Let's see if you've spelled those words correctly this time" or "Last time you had trouble with sentence endings. Let's check the paper over so you put in all the periods where they belong."	4. Don't be ashamed if you can't help straighten out problems that both you and your child perceive. Reach for a book if you can, or ask the teacher about a particular sentence (a note attached to the writing when handed in will be fine).
		5. Given the child's age, no teacher should expect an absolutely correct paper, especially not for the very young, so don't be overly zealous. The child should apply what he has already learned and what you feel he should know.

TABLE 8 – 5. *(Continued)*
Tips and Pointers: How Parents Can Help with Writing for School

Stage	Do's	Don'ts
		6. Don't be reluctant to refuse to help in places when you believe it might be ethically unsound. Say gently but firmly, "Beverly, I don't think Mrs. Wilson would want me to help you with that one. After all, it's your word and you'll get the grade for it. But let's see how you can find out the answer yourself."
The Graded Paper Returned	1. Read the teacher's comments together. Make sure the child understands what's said.	1. Don't complain about the grade or the effort. The attitude must be, "Let's see what the teacher says so that you can do better next time."
	2. Talk about discouragement. Explain how in writing people learn by trying and by making mistakes. Tell about how professional writers often have their work severely criticized and refused for publication.	2. Don't challenge the teacher's judgment. It's all right to disagree, but remember that many responses to writing are subjective. The question is, do the instructor's comments explain her evaluation of the paper?
	3. See that the child works carefully on correcting errors even if the teacher does not require it – and this comes before any revision (see 5, below). Suggest a different color pen or pencil as the youngster makes corrections according to the teacher's comments or symbols in the margin.	3. Don't tell the child how to correct errors the teacher points out. Help him find out how to make corrections on his own.
	4. Help the child keep a record of his usual errors. This is especially valuable: first, by giving practice not to make	

TABLE **8 – 5.** *(Continued)*
Tips and Pointers: How Parents Can Help with Writing for School

Stage	Do's	Don'ts

error; and, second, if the child consults his errors before he writes the next paper, he can signal himself about mistakes he often makes.

5. Insist that the child copy misspelled words – correctly spelled – onto a list of individual spelling errors. If the mistakes fall into patterns (that is, *plurals, -ie* mistakes, *suffixes,* and so on), help the child group the errors on index cards or on small sheets. When you can identify patterns, the task of learning about correct spelling is not overwhelming. Make sure the young writer consults the list before each writing assignment.

6. Many instructors (especially in junior and senior high) will ask for a revision – that is, they expect students to rewrite papers based upon class suggestions for their improvement. Encourage revision along the lines the teacher suggests *after the child corrects the errors.* Otherwise, in revision, youngsters may avoid the words or structures that caused the problems and thereby lose the opportunity to learn how to correct mistakes.

Wiener, H. *Any child can write: How to improve your child's writing skills from preschool through high school.* New York: McGraw-Hill Book Co., 1978, pp. 65 – 71.

TABLE 8 – 6.
Capitalization Chart

WORDS TO CAPITALIZE	K	1	2	3	4	5	6	7	8
First word of a sentence	*	*	+	'	'	'	'	'	'
First and last names of a person	*	+	'	'	'	'	'	'	'
Name of street or road	*	*	+	'	'	'	'	'	'
The word *I*	*	+	'	'	'	'	'	'	'
Name of city or town		*	+	'	'	'	'	'	'
Name of a school or special place	*	*	+	'	'	'	'	'	'
Names of months and days	*	*	+	'	'	'	'	'	'
First and important words in titles	*	*	*	+	'	'	.	'	'
Abbreviations: Mr., Mrs., St., Ave.	*	*	+	'	'	'	'	'	'
Each line of a poem			*	+	'	'	'	'	'
First word of salutation of a letter		*	+	'	'	'	'	'	'
First word of complimentary close		*	+	'	'	'	'	'	'
Initials		*	*	+	'	'	'	'	'
Titles used with names of persons		*	*	+	'	'	'	'	'
First word in an outline topic			*	*	+	'	'	'	'
Names of organizations			*	*	+	'	'	'	'
Sacred names			*	*	*	+	'	'	'
Proper names generally: countries, oceans			*	*	*	+	'	'	'
Proper adjectives				*	*	+	'	'	
Titles of respect and rank and their abbreviations			*	*	+	'	'	'	'

* Introduction
+ Suggested teaching
' Maintenance

From: W. T. Petty, D. C. Petty, and M. F. Becking, *Experiences in Language: Tools and Techniques for Language Arts Methods.* Boston: Allyn and Bacon, Inc. 1973, p. 195. Reprinted by permission of the publisher.

7. *Is the student able to prewrite, write, and rewrite?* The student may have become accustomed to turning in papers without proofing and may never have thought about or been taught how to revise. Since most writing involves three phases—prewriting, writing, and rewriting (Weaver, 1979)—the resource teacher should observe the extent to which the student prepares for writing through scribbling, drafting, and writing notes or phrases, considering ideas, and so forth. We also want to find out if the student can proofread or have someone help with this aspect of writing. Further, does the student consider the first draft as the final draft,

TABLE 8 – 7.
Punctuation Chart

ITEM AND USE	K	1	2	3	4	5	6	7	8
				GRADE					
Period									
At end of a statement	*	*	†	'	'	'	'	'	'
After initials	*	*	†	'	'	'	'	'	'
After abbreviations	*	*	*	†	'	'	'	'	'
After numerals in a list	*	*	†	'	'	'	'	'	'
After letters or numerals in an outline				*	*	†	'	'	'
In footnotes and bibliographies						*	*	†	'
Question Mark									
After interrogative sentence		*	†	'	'	'	'	'	'
After a question within a larger sentence			*	†	'	'	'	'	'
Comma									
Between day of month and year	*	*	†	'	'	'	'	'	'
Between city and state	*	*	†	'	'	'	'	'	'
After salutation in a friendly letter		*	†	'	'	'	'	'	'
After complimentary close			*	†	'	'	'	'	'
To separate parts of a series			*	†	'	'	'	'	'
To set off words of direct address				*	*	†	'	'	'
To separate a direct quotation					*	†	'	'	'
Before and after appositives					*	*	†	'	'
After introductory clauses					*	*	†	'	'
After introductory words: yes, no; interjections						*	†	'	'
Before the conjunction in a compound sentence						*	†	'	'
Before and after a nonrestrictive clause						*	*	†	'
Before and after parenthetical expressions						*	*	†	'
In footnotes and bibliographies							*	†	'
Apostrophe									
In contractions		*	*	†	'	'	'	'	'
To show possession		*	*	*	*	†	'	'	'
To show plurals of figures and letters					*	*	*	†	'
Quotation Mark									
Before and after a direct quote		*	*	†	'	'	'	'	'
Before and after titles (other than of books)					*	*	*	†	'
Exclamation mark									
At the end of an exclamatory word or sentence					*	*	†	'	'

TABLE **8 – 7.** *(Continued)*
Punctuation Chart

ITEM AND USE		GRADE								
	K	1	2	3	4	5	6	7	8
Period									
After the salutation of a business letter				*	*	+	'	'	'
To separate the hour from minutes			*	*	*	+	'	'	'
Before a long series or list					*	*	*	+	'
To denote examples						*	*	*	+
Hyphen									
At end of line to show divided word	*	*	*	+	'	'	'	'	'

* Introduction
+ Suggested teaching
' Maintenance

From: W. T. Petty, D. C. Petty, and M. F. Becking, *Experiences in Language. Tools and Techniques for Language Arts Methods*. Boston: Allyn and Bacon, Inc. 1973, pp. 196 – 197. Reprinted by permission of the publisher.

or does he or she work on the manuscript to revise it for the intended audience? It is at the rewriting stage that attention to surface details becomes most important.

Whether writing needs to be revised depends upon the importance of the communication, the intended audience, and the purpose for communicating. Ultimately, the decisions about rewriting are those of the writer. However, in her article, "Revising Writing in the Upper Grades," Haley-James (1981, pp. 564 – 566) provides these suggestions for helping the student:

1. Both purpose and meaning must emerge before the student can see a need to revise.
2. The teacher can provide reams of scratch paper in order to symbolize the tentativeness of the first writings. This stage should be considered a natural part of writing.
3. Scratch paper may also be cut into smaller pieces for jotting down notes, ideas, or phrases.
4. When the student begins to draft, the focus should be kept on meaning rather than surface structures.
5. The teacher's guideline, to be communicated to the student, is that form follows function, and that both follow meaning.
6. The teacher may read silently what the student has written, and paraphrase it back to the student to see if the meaning expressed was the meaning intended.

7.   If the student has trouble sensing what is needed in a piece of writing that has been drafted, the teacher may ask the student to reduce the information to its simplest statement in order to give focus. The student may add supporting details later.

8.   The writer may need distancing before revising. What seems fine at the time of writing may have lost its meaning even to the writer when time has passed.

9.   The draft may be read aloud to ensure that punctuation is helpful rather than hindering in terms of intended meaning.

10. The teacher can teach students to help each other with the rewrite stage, as professional writers often do.

11. Older students may come into the classroom to reinforce the idea of revising. They may help the students learning to revise, or they may discuss the ups and downs involved in writing for personal or professional purpose. Further discussion of revising is provided by Graves (1979).

The current availability of wordprocessing software makes revising "fun" for many students because computer revision allows the results to be seen clearly and quickly.

8. How are the student's writing products evaluated or judged? Both classroom and resource teachers look for fair, valid, and reliable methods for evaluating the writing students produce in school. They are interested both in the student's development and in the evaluation of any interventions they might make to encourage development.

This section is organized around two ways of looking at writing evaluation. The first is from a language perspective to identify elements of interest. The second is from the measurement standpoint to describe various schemes used for evaluation.

Writing, from a language point of view. As a form of language, writing fits nicely into the overall framework of Bloom and Lahey (1979), who describe language as an interaction among:

Content: Having something to say.
Form: Having a way to say it, and
Use: Matching the communication to the situation.

Of these dimensions, *use* is probably the easiest to measure — whether the student's writing is appropriate to the occasion — in addition, the resource teacher will want to create occasions to be sure that the student is being exposed to the range of writing uses. An inventory of writing uses will serve as a checklist to note the student's growing competence in adjusting writing to purpose.

Content or *form* are somewhat more difficult to evaluate. Content refers to having ideas that may be arranged in ways appropriate to the writing purpose. This aspect of writing is much like tapping the student's cognitive development. If the student cannot draw upon personal or vicarious experience and/or intellectual understanding of specific topics, then writing will be difficult.

Ideas themselves are judged on the basis of characteristics such as originality, insight into the topic, rationality or logic, and clarity. Characteristics such as these are often incorporated into more holistic[3] writing scales.

In elementary schools, teachers who encourage wide reading (or who read widely *to* students) and who encourage or provide broad experiences for students are enriching the base for writing. In the upper grades and postelementary school, teachers assign reports, for which students are expected to look up background material. Students might be reminded of the background searches in the nonschool world needed by reporters investigating various topics for stories; or more personally, they might be reminded of people sharing new experiences and ideas with friends.

Reflections of the content range of student writing may be tapped by looking at the range of content the student addresses over time, the difficulty of the content, and the vocabulary the student uses. We have mentioned that a test of written vocabulary is available as a subtest of the TOAL (Hammill et al., 1980) for the adolescent. Clay (1975) describes a test for young children's written vocabulary. She encourages the student to write down all the words he or she knows how to write, starting with the child's own name and including basic vocabulary and words personal to the child. She notes that such a test has good test-retest reliability and that it correlates with word reading scores (p. 67).

The *forms* of writing are mechanical, syntactic, rhetorical, and organizational. Mechanics have been noted previously. We would also mention that this aspect of form is also included within holistic scoring protocols.

Growth in syntactic control is usually measured with the T-unit of Hunt (1965). The T-Unit consists of a main clause and any subordinate clauses attached to it. The "T" means "terminal" because each unit can be started with a capital letter and terminated with a period. The following composition written by a fourth-grade boy is shown as written (A), and then as analyzed into measurable T-Units (B).[4]

A

> I like the movie we saw about Moby Dick the white whale the captain said if you kill the white whale Moby Dick I will give this gold to the one that can do it and it is worth sixteen dollars they tried and tried but while they were trying they killed a whale and used the oil for the lamps they almost caught the white whale.

B

1. I like the movie/we saw about Moby Dick, the white whale. (M)
2. The captain said/if you kill the white whale, Moby Dick,/I will give this gold to the one/that can do it. (L)
3. And it is worth sixteen dollars. (S)
4. They tried and tried. (S)
5. But/while they were trying/they killed a whale and used the oil for the lamps. (M)
6. They almost caught the white whale. (S) [Hunt, 1965, p. 21]

T-Units are categorized by length: short T-Units consist of about eight to ten words (*S* above); middle-length T-Units are from nine to twenty words (*M* above); and long

T-Units contain more than twenty words (*L* above). For norms and for additional information about using the T-Unit as a measure of maturity, the resource teacher should consult Hunt (1965). Additional normative and research data are provided in the comparative measure study of O'Donnell, Griffin, and Norris (1967), and comparative discussions of other measures are found in the recent critique of indexes of syntactic maturity (O'Donnell, 1976).

Syntax encompasses not only the use of grammatical forms that are appropriate to the piece of writing, but the way the student connects sentences (for example, Garber, 1980) in order to provide cohesion to the writing:

Reference — On Saturday evening *Marvin's parents* left to go out to dinner. As *they* left, *his* mother said, "Don't let anyone in the house and don't speak with strangers."
Substitution — My sister and brother always *refuse to clean up their room. So does* this boy.
Ellipsis — If I were him I wouldn't want to clean the room even though it would be in my house. If I had to (　) I would feel awful.
Conjunction — There was popcorn, candy, potato chips . . . hanging from the ceiling and from the lamp. *Finally*, Joey gathered up his courage and asked, "What did your mother say?"
Lexical Cohesion — There was probably a *party*. Usually at a *party* the room where the *party* is gets all messed up because of balloons. [P. 317].

Connectors of this kind are meaning-related ties. This use of connectors is also related to the basic idea of sentence combining (for example, Cooper, 1973), in which a series of short sentences are combined into one sentence with appropriate clauses and embeddings. For example, there are several ways to combine the following ideas:

Jenny is a girl.	Jenny lives next door.
Jenny is nice.	Jenny goes to school every day.
Jenny lives in a house.	Jenny goes to school with Jerry.

Rhetoric may be considered part of form because the style used to say something may be more important than what is said. Courses in high school and college composition often focus on rhetoric. The considerations of audience, word choices, and structures center around rhetoric.

Beyond the forms of sentences, intersentence connections, and rhetoric, there must be some organizing structure to the writing. Here we are interested in such characteristics as theme, idea subordination, plot, and sequences of ideas. For example, a plot for a detective story might be organized around a description of the crime, a description of the detective, a discovery of clues, a solution, and an explanation of how the detective figured it out (Wilde and Newkirk, 1981).

Writing, from a measurement point of view. Measurement almost always includes some consideration of the features described above, however, the primary means of evaluating the writing of students in English classes is the use of *holistic scoring.* Cooper (1977) defines holistic evaluation as a guided procedure for sorting or ranking written pieces. The rater takes a piece of writing and either (1) matches it with another piece in a graded series of pieces or (2) scores it for the prominence of certain features important to that kind of writing or (3) assigns it a letter or a number grade. The placing, scoring, or grading occurs quickly, impressionistically, after the rater has practiced the procedure with other raters . . . . Holistic evaluation is usually guided by a holistic scoring guide which describes each feature and identifies high, middle, and low quality levels for each feature [P. 3]

Cooper also describes the many kinds of holistic evaluation scales that may be used by teachers. The samples in Table 8 – 8 are of an analytic and a dichotomous scale for evaluating a personal narrative. The analytic scale has high, low, and midpoints. The dichotomous scale is answered only as yes or no. More detailed description of the construction and use of holistic evaluation devices is found in *Evaluating Writing: Describing, Measuring, Judging* (Cooper and Odell, 1977).

TABLE 8 – 8.
Holistic Scales for Personal Narrative Writing

Analytic Scale

Reader _____   Paper _____

	Low		Middle		High
I. General Qualities:					
A. Author's Role	2	4	6	8	10
B. Style or Voice	2	4	6	8	10
C. Central Figure	2	4	6	8	10
D. Background	2	4	6	8	10
E. Sequence	2	4	6	8	10
F. Theme	2	4	6	8	10
II. Diction, Syntax and Mechanics:					____
A. Wording	1	2	4	5	5
B. Syntax	1	2	4	5	5
C. Usage	1	2	4	5	5
D. Punctuation	1	2	4	5	5
E. Spelling	1	2	4	5	5
					____
			Total		____

TABLE 8 – 8. *(Continued)*
Holistic Scales for Personal Narrative Writing

Dichotomous Scale

Reader _____   Paper _____

	YES	NO	
I.	_____	_____	Author's role consistent
	_____	_____	Interesting personal voice
	_____	_____	Theme clearly presented
	_____	_____	Background rich and supportive
	_____	_____	Sequence of events clear
	_____	_____	Central figure fully developed
II.	_____	_____	Wording unique and developed
	_____	_____	Syntax correct and varied
	_____	_____	Usage errors few
	_____	_____	Punctuation errors few
	_____	_____	Spelling errors few

Total   Yes _____

From C. R. Cooper, "Holistic Evaluation of Writing," in C. R. Cooper and L. Odell, eds., *Evaluating Writing: Describing, Measuring, Judging* (Urbana, Ill.: National Council of Teachers of English, 1977), p 24.

For the younger child, Clay (1975) has suggested a relatively simple rating technique for observing early progress in writing. See Table 8 – 9. The components of her scale are more fully described in her book, *What Did I Write?* (1975).

DEVELOPING INSTRUCTIONAL PROCEDURES

Some educators believe that writing proceeds deductively from learning the rules and structures, whereas others believe that writing cannot be taught — it can merely be motivated (Ezor and Lane, 1975). We believe that these two approaches should not be made separate. We prefer the view that motivation is critical and that improvement can be effected through careful guidance and some specific instruction. The recommendations below reflect both the importance of motivation and the possibilities of gentle instruction.

1. Creating an environment that is conducive to writing is the first step to take for instruction. If such an environment is not provided within classrooms, the resource

TABLE **8 – 9.**
A Rating Technique for Observing Early Progress in Writing

To estimate the level of a young child's written expression in the first six months of instruction take three samples of his written work on consecutive days, or over a period. The child's behavior must develop in each of three areas and he should receive a rating for each aspect of the writing task. This is an arbitrary scale and should be taken only as a rough guide to a child's instruction needs.

LANGUAGE LEVEL: Record the number of the highest level of linguistic organization used by the child.
1. Alphabetic (letters only)
2. Word (any recognizable word)
3. Word Group (any two word phrase)
4. Sentence (any simple sentence)
5. Punctuated story (of two or more sentences)
6. Paragraphed story (two themes)

MESSAGE QUALITY: Record the number below for the best description of the child's sample.
1. He has a concept of signs (uses letters, invents letters, uses punctuation.)
2. He has a concept that a message is conveyed (ie he tells you a message but what he has written is not that message).
3. A message is copied, and he knows more or less what that message says.
4. Repetitive, independent use of sentence patterns like 'here is a . . .'
5. Attempts to record own ideas, mostly independently.
6. Successful composition.

DIRECTIONAL PRINCIPLES: Record the number of the highest rating for which there is no error in the sample of the child's writing.
1. No evidence of directional knowledge.
2. Part of the directional pattern is known
    Either Start top left
    Or   Move left to right
    Or   Return down left
3. Reversal of the directional pattern (right to left and/or return down right). A sample with one lapse should be rated at this level.
4. Correct directional pattern.
5. Correct directional pattern and spaces between words.
6. Extensive text without any difficulties of arrangement and spacing of text.

TABLE 8 – 9. *(Continued)*
A Rating Technique for Observing Early Progress in Writing

| | A | B | C |
	Language Level	Message Quality	Directional Principles
Not yet Satisfactory	1 – 4	1 – 4	1 – 4
Probably Satisfactory	5 – 6	5 – 6	5 – 6

From M. M. Clay, *What Did I Write?* (Exeter, N.H.: Heinemann Educational Books, 1975), pp. 66 – 67.

teacher may wish to set up a writing center within the resource room itself. The suggestions provided in the books we have cited, both in the teaching of writing and in the language arts, will help the novice get started and the experienced teacher gain additional insight into helping students write.

Gonzales (1980) describes and illustrates such a center. Shown in Figure 8 – 4 is a note sent to parents when children complete books in the author center. The note refers to an author party day, just as commercial authors may experience. Such a note may also be sent to best friends in the school, to the principal, and to any others who might attend.

Bookmaking instructions are provided in several books, among them Purdy (1973), Weiss (1974), and D'Angelo, Korba, and Woodworth (1981).

2. For the beginning writer, the techniques of group story writing, dictation, and copying can be of value (see Veatch et al., 1973, pp. 65 – 71; and Strickland, 1957, pp 275 – 283). These early experiences, no matter at what chronological age they occur, should be accompanied by a rich variety of readiness experiences.

3. Assignments made in writing, especially those for the older student, should be considered in terms of the criteria suggested by Moffett.[5]

1. Is it given for punitive reasons? . . . If we wish to kill writing, setting up such negative associations is a splendid way to do it.
2. Is it given essentially as a check to prove that something was read? I have in mind here such tasks as reporting on a book or paraphrasing reference books.
3. Is motivation intrinsic to the kind of writing assigned?
4. Does it have, at least potentially, an authentic audience besides the teacher?
5. Does it require cognitive abilities too advanced for the age?
6. Is it given mainly as a vehicle for teaching something extraneous to itself?

The work of the resource teacher may be made more difficult if these criteria are violated too often.

FIGURE **8 – 4.**
A Note to Parents

Mr. and Mrs. _____ .

_____   _____'s Author Party will be on Tuesday,

9:00 A.M. in Room 5. This will be a great day for _____
since he/she has completed a book. Hope you can be here to celebrate! If possible
please bring:

    cookies or cupcakes
    cups   } for 30 children
    punch
    napkins

    *a camera, if you wish

If you wish to contact me, please call _____ .

                                 Thank you.

                                  _____

(Gonzales, 1980, p. 283)

---

4. Standards are developed with students, or else they are taught indirectly through application to the writing of others. For example, Sager's project for improving the quality of writing through the use of a rating scale that students are taught to use for evaluating supplied compositions has been shown to be effective (1975). Group or partner writing also can help create the need for agreeing on standards.

5. Creating an audience for the products of written expression provides motivation for original writing and also shows the need for rewriting. Newspapers, plays, literary magazines, and bookmaking are stimulating if the student knows that his or her work might be used. Such stimuli are especially crucial for students who do not speak standard English. *A Day Dream I Had at Night and Other Stories: Teaching Children How to Make Their Own Readers* (Landrum, 1971) is a good example of creating a product with and for such children.

6. Ideas for helping the older elementary student often are found in the literature dealing with writing for adolescents. Most of the suggestions can be used

as they appear or can be adapted. See, for example: *On Righting Writing* (Clapp, 1975), Moffett's book (1968), and *They Really Taught Us How to Write* (Geuder et al., 1974). Kits and commercial programs are listed in catalogs available from publishers, such as Science Research Associates of Chicago or Developmental Learning Materials (DLM) of Dallas. Materials for teaching written English as a second language are distributed by Oxford University Press of New York. Both kits and second language materials are primarily of value for the older student in the elementary grades.

7. Fluency in writing may be encouraged by using the techniques of copying and journal writing. Timed writing activities and application of a contingency management system that reinforces a higher rate of production also may be tried. Since slow rate may be related to the teacher's placing too high a value on standards, either self-imposed or school imposed, these areas also might require attention.

8. Thorndike's comments about the teaching of punctuation (1948) are still cogent today. Unlike spelling, punctuation is not so fixed by convention that creative use cannot be tolerated or encouraged. Thorndike suggested, and we agree, that punctuation does not begin with marks but with the thoughts and feelings to be conveyed to or aroused within the reader. Punctuation should be taught through careful examination of the author's intent, no matter what the age of the author. Punctuation, then, can help the words cause feelings or thoughts within the intended audience. More conventional approaches to punctuation instruction are found in the language arts textbooks.

9. Clinical procedures for students with severe problems are well illustrated by Fernald (1943). Of particular interest is her account of application to content areas such as geography, social science, and mathematics (pp. 93 – 102). We also recommend materials developed for teaching students with problems in written language. For example, *Written language instruction* (Phelps-Gunn and Phelps-Teraski, 1982) describes and evaluates various systems for teaching written aspects of language.

10. More direct instruction in various aspects of writing can be provided through lessons and assignments that deal with target areas. For example, *sentence combining* (Cooper, 1973; Weaver, 1979) can be used to stimulate intellectual growth, as well as to improve the quality of writing. The combining of sentences is not an exercise to be completed and graded. Its primary value lies in the discussion of various imbedding and subordination strategies, perhaps trying out more than one. The value of the technique is also in the analysis of the idea relationships that underlie the various components of sentences that are, or are to be, combined.

Story structure can be taught with various devices such as the circle story (Jett-Simpson, 1981) (Figure 8 – 5) or with the basic story maker (Rubin, 1980) (Figure 8 – 6). In each case, the story is planned prior to writing. In one instance, illustrations are used to help the student with organization; in the other, relationship trees are formed. The directed writing activity of Blake and Spennato (1980) is a good example of the specific techniques that are beginning to appear in resources such as *Language Arts*. This technique is described in Table 8 – 10. We also recommend the books and other resources we have mentioned previously.

FIGURE 8 – 5.
The Circle Story for *Millions of Cats*

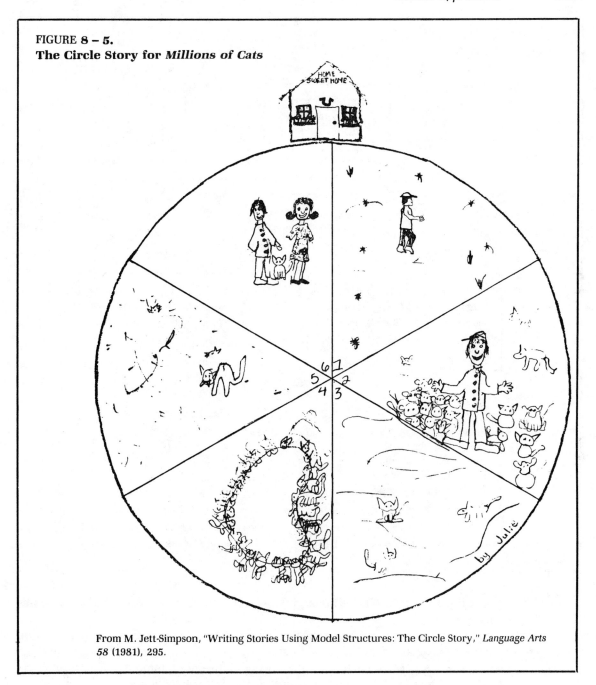

From M. Jett-Simpson, "Writing Stories Using Model Structures: The Circle Story," *Language Arts* *58* (1981), 295.

11. Journal writing has become one of the major ways to promote personal writing. It is also used to get writing started and to get to know the student. No

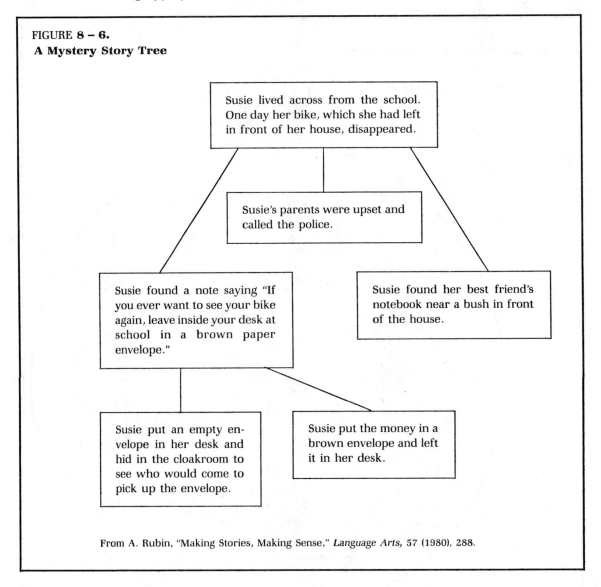

FIGURE 8 – 6.
A Mystery Story Tree

Susie lived across from the school. One day her bike, which she had left in front of her house, disappeared.

Susie's parents were upset and called the police.

Susie found a note saying "If you ever want to see your bike again, leave inside your desk at school in a brown paper envelope."

Susie found her best friend's notebook near a bush in front of the house.

Susie put an empty envelope in her desk and hid in the cloakroom to see who would come to pick up the envelope.

Susie put the money in a brown envelope and left it in her desk.

From A. Rubin, "Making Stories, Making Sense," *Language Arts*, 57 (1980), 288.

evaluative comments should be placed on journal entries – only those of a communicative nature.

12. Older students who are learning to write in the content areas may benefit from the suggestions of Alley and Deshler (1979). Their chapters on writing and on study skills are relevant to writing. In addition, books intended for the college freshman, such as *A Laboratory Approach to Writing* (Lague and Sherwood, 1977), provide step-by-step methods for beginning young adult writers. The second reference is especially helpful because of its emphasis on self-evaluation for the student.

TABLE **8 – 10.**
Directed Writing Activity Technique

STEP I — PREWRITING

To prepare pupils to write with a purpose, there are many types of activities the teacher might consider. The most practical appear to be those which help pupils select a topic, collect information, organize and sequence information, personalize the topic, develop a useful vocabulary list, and experiment with the structure and syntax of language.

STEP II — FRAMING THE WRITING ASSIGNMENT

A) Once the writing topic is selected, pupils find it helpful to develop questions which are relevant to it. For example, if a boy decides to write about his baseball team, he might ask before he writes: 1) What is the team's win-loss record? 2) Who are the team's best pitchers, batters and fielders? 3) What other teams will provide the stiffest opposition? 4) What are the team's chances of making the play-offs and winning the championship?

B) Having developed a list of questions, pupils then decide which ones interest them most. They reflect on which questions seem related. Next the authors think about how they are going to organize the questions. Finally, the writers conduct an inventory to decide how much information they have and how much more is needed to answer the questions selected.

STEP III — WRITING THE ASSIGNMENT

A) The pupils organize their information by selecting, adding, and deleting from the information already collection. They then answer the questions, tying the bits of information (words and phrases) into sentences.

B) The writer next reads the draft aloud to a classmate or to the teacher who listens for clarity of thought and fluidity of language.

C) The listener makes suggestions and recommendations which the author may use later to revise the initial draft.

STEP IV — REVISING THE DRAFT

The author, noting the suggestions and recommendations made by the listener, proceeds to revise the draft. At this time, the revisions relate solely to the substance and syntax of the draft — not to its mechanics.

STEP V — EDITING

A) For editing purposes, we suggest that all pupils at all grade levels have a handbook which includes punctuation and capitalization rules, a list of working symbols (*c* — needs capital letter; *m* — margin; *ns* — not a sentence, etc.) and a proofreading checklist.

TABLE **8 – 10.** *(Continued)*
Directed Writing Activity Technique

B) As the teacher, another pupil, an aide, a lay reader or an administrator reads the draft, the author is referred to a specific section of the handbook if there are mechanical errors. The writer edits the paper, referring to the handbook as needed.

STEP VI — FINAL DRAFT

Using the information received from all sources, the author edits the writing, proof-reads it, and submits a finished draft to the audience for whom it was intended. The audience should not always be the teacher.

The DWA may take several days to complete: The pre-writing activities should be viewed as a warm-up for the more formal writing activities which follow. Just as pitchers need to loosen-up their arms by throwing the baseball before a game, so pupils usually need some time to "loosen" their minds and their pens through reflection and stream of consciousness writing of their thoughts. Once writers have engaged in intro-spection and reflection and have done some preliminary writing, they need time to frame questions related to the topic which will assist in transforming sentences into paragraphs. If students frame three questions, they will probably write at least three paragraphs for the interested audience. Time to write an initial draft and to read it aloud to a resource person is essential if writers are to have feedback which they can use in subsequent drafts. In preparing the final draft (and at times the draft to be published), young writers, as do all adult writers, need time to proofread and edit, if the draft is to be considered their best effort.

From H. Blake and N. A. Spennato, "The Directed Writing Activity: A Process with Structure," *Language Arts 57* (1980): 317 – 318.

ENDNOTES

1. For example: The "Printing Press," available from the Workshop for Learning Things, Inc., 5 Bridge St., Watertown, Mass. 02172, is used from preschool through elementary grades.

2. Mellon, J. C. Round two of the national writing assessment – Interpreting the apparent decline of writing ability: A review. *Research in the Teaching of English*, 1976, *10*, 66 – 74. Mellon's original version reads as follows: And suppose too that one interpreted the decline of writing ability as evidence of a reduction in the amount and intensity of in-school writing instruction over the past half-decade – a likely interpretation, since of all of the language skills, that of writing is uniquely dependent for its acquisition upon the kind of overt teaching that in youth occurs only in school.

3. Holistic tests are based upon the idea that a valid test of discourse depends upon the examination of a sample of discourse as a whole, not merely as a collection of parts" (Lloyd-Jones, 1977, p. 36).

4. Hunt, K. *Grammatical structures written at three grade levels*. NCTE, Research Report No. 3, NCTE, 1965, pp. 20 – 21.

5. Moffett, J. *A Student-Centered Language Arts Curriculum, Grades K – 13: A Handbook for Teachers*, first edition. Copyright © 1968 by Houghton Mifflin Company, p. 253.

9

Spelling

Spelling, or orthography, is the proper arrangement of letters in words. Spelling can be done orally, as in a traditional spelling bee where words are spelled aloud, or graphically, as in writing words in an essay or for a spelling test. Of these, teachers today consider written spelling to be the more important skill for a student to master. When oral spelling is done now, it is usually justified, perhaps mistakenly, on the belief that any ability developed by the activity will extend to the written form.

Before the invention of the dictionary, which imposed a rigidity on spelling, individuals spelled words as they pronounced them; the single criterion for acceptability was that the reader understand the writer's intended meaning. Thus a person who said /bar/ for "bear" might spell the word b-a-r and not be considered particularly untutored by a reader. Any confusion in meaning was resolved by interpeting the context clues. Unfortunately, how words are pronounced varies significantly from generation to generation and from place to place, whereas the spellings that appear in dictionaries are set and do not change much over long periods of time.

This situation is complicated further because English orthography now has only twenty-six letters, even though English speech uses many more phonemes. As a consequence, the difference between words spelled and words pronounced widens with each passing decade.

The general procedure in schools is to introduce formal spelling instruction at the end of the first grade or at the beginning of the second. One of several commercial programs usually is used. Occasionally, the student merely is taught to spell words from lists supposedly geared to grade levels, or spelling instruction is individualized completely and integrated into an experience story reading program. Regardless of which approach is used to teach spelling, students who do not acquire an expected proficiency level are marked by their teachers as being poor spellers and may be referred to the resource teacher for help.

When this occurs, the resource teacher will have to obtain certain information about the students and their problems in order to prepare an appropriate teaching program for them. The resource teacher can secure some information by observing the student in the classroom and by interviewing the teacher; some information may have to be obtained from individual assessment sessions.

ANALYSIS OF THE LEARNER IN THE CLASSROOM

The resource teacher should determine answers to the following questions relating to the teacher's instructional approach to spelling and to the nature of the student's problem.

1. *Does the teacher use a commercial program?* If so, what are its characteristics? Many publishing companies have developed comprehensive spelling series that are sold to individual teachers or to entire school districts. Each series is organized into specific teaching units more or less according to grade levels; each also has been developed according to a particular frame of reference; for example, the authors of Lippincott's *Basic Spelling* (Glim and Manchester, 1977) maintain that their series has a multisensory orientation, and the authors of Silver Burdett's *Spell Correctly* (Benthul et al., 1980) say that their series is a linguistic approach. Most of these series include supplemental lessons for teaching dictionary use and study skills. They also differ markedly one from the other as to the words included and the sequence in which the words are presented – a specific word might be introduced in book 2 of one series and in book 5 of another series.

Resource teachers must know thoroughly the theoretical underpinnings, formats, drills, and other distinguishing characteristics associated with the series being taught in the regular class if they are to understand the nature of the pupil's problem in that program and to prepare special instruction for the pupil.

To understand a series fully, the resource teacher should acquire and study a scope and sequence chart of the spelling program being used. This chart also can serve as a guide for determining where the student is in a particular program and which skills he or she has not mastered properly.

If a classroom teacher has referred several students for poor spelling, has little appreciation of the spelling process, uses no consistent approach to teaching the skill, and is unable or unwilling to adopt a systematic, individualized approach, the resource teacher may recommend the use of a commercially available program. On the other hand, spelling can readily be taught without any formal commercial program.

2. *What is the teacher's position on teaching spelling generalizations?* Since the resource teacher may want to error analyze the student's spelling performance later

during the individual evaluation, he or she must ascertain the nature of the spelling instruction to which the youngster has been exposed in the regular classroom. To some extent, the kind of instruction used will be governed by the teacher's attitude toward the importance of teaching phonological and morphological spelling rules. For example, if the teacher emphasizes sound-to-symbol relationships (phonological rules) in instruction, the student might spell irregular words (words that are not linguistically predictable) rather poorly. This occurs because some teachers, to lessen confusion, avoid introducing the student to unpredictable words such as *eight, knew,* and *enough.* However, if the teacher believes that English spelling is basically irregular, he or she will teach each word separately, emphasizing revisualization and drill and minimizing the teaching of linguistic generalizations or rules. As a result, the student may miss some words that are spelled as they are pronounced *(bed, that)* or that are spelled according to set rules *(able, forty).*

Our position is that a successful spelling program should be well balanced on this issue. Although English orthography is far from regular, it is not completely random either. Many general rules work more than 75 percent of the time. Knowing these rules gives the student a rational means for trying to spell unfamiliar words. Teachers who do not teach any rules should be encouraged to introduce rules that are helpful for spellers; teachers who pretend that English slavishly follows consistent linguistic patterns should be enlightened as to the true nature of the language.

3. *How does the teacher use spelling-related activities?* This question relates to the procedures that the teacher actually uses to teach students to spell. Many teachers give their students a list of words on Monday and test their ability to spell them on Friday. If this is the case, the resource teacher should determine if the students are left to learn the words on their own or if they are formally taught to spell them. If drills are undertaken in class, the resource teacher should observe the referred students while they are actively engaged in doing drill work in order to evaluate their attitudes and work habits.

Often a student will execute an activity improperly, thereby negating its value; for example, a student who has been told to write *cat* five times may do so by first printing a column of *C*'s, then a column of *A*'s, and finally a column of *T*'s. Such situations can be remedied by having the teacher monitor the student more closely. The resource teacher should pay special attention to the format of the drills used; some drills may need to be incorporated later into analytic teaching or remedial activities. Also, the resource teacher should note the relationship of oral to written practice to ensure that written spelling drills predominate the teaching effort.

4. *What provisions, if any, has the classroom teacher made to accommodate the poor speller?* The teacher who has identified a student as needing help in spelling may have tried to deal with the problem before making a referral. The resource teacher should find out what remedial techniques have been attempted, how systematically they were used, and what the outcomes of their use has been. Usually these efforts involve no more than recycling the student through previously failed lessons, providing more verbal support, and using a few additional drills. When little or no special corrective help is offered to the student in the classroom, the resource

teacher should encourage the teacher to institute remedially oriented sessions with the content based in part on error analysis or to individualize the spelling program by reducing the number of words to be learned and by adding more useful and interesting words.

SUPPLEMENTAL INDIVIDUAL ANALYSIS

Having acquired sufficient information about the classroom situation through observation and interview, the resource teacher is ready to evaluate the student's spelling performance in detail. This evaluation is done in order to obtain the answers to the following specific questions.

1. *Does the student actually have a problem in spelling?* If so, then at what level should special instruction begin? The resource teacher can answer this question by interpreting the results of a standardized test of spelling or by checking the student's written work. A student whose performance on such a test is from one to two standard deviations below the mean for stuidents his or her age is said to have a borderline problem; the student whose scores are two standard deviations or more below the mean has serious difficulty. The resource teacher should share this information with the classroom teacher, who may use it to adjust the poor speller's program to that level.

For these purposes, we recommend that the teacher use *The Test of Written Spelling* (Larsen and Hammill, 1976). This test yields a standard score, a grade level, and an age equivalent on the student's ability to spell rule governed words and unpredictable words (demons). It also provides an index of overall spelling proficiency. The test requires only twenty or thirty minutes to administer to an individual or to groups, has demonstrated reliability (coefficients exceeeding 0.80) at every grade level between three and nine, and has normative information based on 4,544 subjects from twenty-two states. A unique feature is that the test is criterioned to the leading spelling series used in the country today. This added feature should be useful for resource teachers when they consult with regular class teachers about adapting their curriculum to meet individual needs.

If the *Test of Written Spelling* is unavailable, the resource teacher can use the results of the spelling subtests from the *Wide Range Achievement Test* (Jastak and Jastak, 1965), the *Metropolitan Achievement Tests* (Durost et al., 1959), the *Iowa Tests of Basic Skills* (Lindquist and Hieronymus, 1956), or any other standardized achievement battery.

2. *What kinds of spelling errors does the student make?* It is not enough to document that the student has a problem or even to know where to begin instruction. The teacher also should want to identify the specific errors that the poor speller makes consistently. Presumably when these errors are recognized and corrected, the pupil will be able to progress to a higher level of spelling proficiency. Edgington (1967) has suggested that teachers doing error analysis in spelling should be especially sensitive to the following types of errors:

Addition of unneeded letters (for example, *dresses*)
Omission of needed letters (*hom* for *home*)
Reflections of child's mispronunciations (*pin* for *pen*)
Reflections of dialectical speech patterns (*Cuber* for *Cuba*)
Reversals of whole words (*eno* for *one*)
Reversals of consonant order (*lback* for *black*)
Reversals of consonant or vowel directionality (*brithday* for *birthday*)
Reversals of syllables (*telho* for *hotel*)
Phonetic spelling of nonphonetic words or parts thereof (*cawt* for *caught*)
Wrong associations of a sound with a given set of letters, such as *u* has been learned
    as *ou* in you
"Neographisms," or letters put in a word which bear no discernible relationship with
    the word dictated
Varying degrees and combinations of these or other possible patterns.

Spelling errors can be analyzed in two ways: informal evaluation of written samples or interpretation of criterion-referenced tests. Most resource teachers will use both approaches. In conducting an informal evaluation, the teacher can use work samples already available or can ask the student to write a story or essay. Writing from dictation also can be used if the teacher wants to control the words used. The sample of written work should be three or four pages long. The teacher can ask the student to write several paragraphs each day for as long as is necessary to obtain a representative sample of spelling ability. When the teacher has the sample, he or she identifies the misspelled words and transcribes them onto a piece of paper exactly as they were spelled. Each misspelled word is then analyzed according to the criteria specified by Edgington.

One difficulty with this method is that many students avoid using words they cannot spell. The samples, therefore, will not be representative, and many troublesome errors will go undetected. To guard against this possibility, the teacher may want to administer an error-oriented test, such as Kottmeyer's (1970) *Diagnostic Spelling Test*. Kottmeyer provides two tests, one for students in second and third grades and one for students in the fourth grade or above. The tests are designed so that each item is supposed to measure a particular spelling element. The two tests and the norms that accompany them are shown in Figure 9 – 1.

Using several of the procedures mentioned in this section will help the teacher inventory the student's spelling errors. The resource teacher needs this inventory if he or she is to prepare an educational corrective program for the poor speller.

3. *What proficiency has the student in spelling the 100 most frequently used words?* Horn (1926) studied 10,000 words and found that 100 of them accounted for 65 percent of all words written by adults (see Table 9 – 1). He reported that only 10 words (*I, the, and, to, a, you, of in, we,* and *for*) accounted for 25 percent of all words used. It seems reasonable, therefore, that many students are referred for poor spelling because they cannot spell correctly the words on Horn's list. It also seems plausible that their spelling would improve noticeably and quickly if they were syste-

FIGURE **9 – 1.**
Diagnostic Spelling Test

DIRECTIONS FOR DIAGNOSTIC SPELLING TEST

Give list 1 to any pupil whose placement is second or third grade.
Give list 2 to any pupil whose placement is above Grade 3.
Grade Scoring, List 1;

    Below 15 correct: Below second grade
    15 — 22 correct: Second grade
    23 — 29 correct: Third grade

Any pupil who scores above 29 should be given the List 2 Test.
Grade Scoring, List 2:

    Below 9 correct: Below third grade
     9 — 19 correct: Third grade
    20 — 25 correct: Fourth grade
    26 — 29 correct: Fifth grade
    Over 29 correct: Sixth grade or better

Any pupil who scores below 9 should be given the List 1 Test.

LIST 1

Word   *Illustrative Sentence*

1. not — He is *not* here.
2. but — Mary is here, *but* Joe is not.
3. get — *Get* the wagon, John.
4. sit — *Sit* down, please.
5. man — Father is a tall *man*.
6. boat — We sailed our *boat* on the lake.
7. train — Tom has a new toy *train*.
8. time — It is *time* to come home.
9. like — We *like* ice cream.
10. found — We *found* our lost ball.
11. down — Do not fall *down*.
12. soon — Our teacher will *soon* be here.
13. good — He is a *good* boy.
14. very — We are *very* happy to be here.
15. happy — Jane is a *happy* girl.
16. kept — We *kept* our shoes dry.
17. come — *Come* to our party.
18. what — *What* is your name?
19. those — *Those* are our toys.
20. show — *Show* us the way.
21. much — I feel *much* better.
22. sing — We will *sing* a new song.
23. will — Who *will* help us?
24. doll — Make a dress for the *doll*.
25. after — We play *after* school.
26. sister — My *sister* is older than I.

LIST 2

Word   *Illustrative Sentence*

1. flower — A rose is a *flower*.
2. mouth — Open your *mouth*.
3. shoot — John wants to *shoot* his new gun.
4. stood — We *stood* under the roof.
5. while — We sang *while* we marched.
6. third — We are in the *third* grade.
7. each — *Each* child has a pencil.
8. class — Our *class* is reading.
9. jump — We like to *jump* rope.
10. jumps — Mary jumps rope.
11. jumped — We *jumped* rope yesterday.
12. jumping — The girls are *jumping* rope now.
13. hit — *Hit* the ball hard.
14. hitting — John is *hitting* the ball.
15. bite — Our dog does not *bite*.
16. biting — The dog is *biting* on the bone.
17. study — *Study* your lesson.
18. studies — He *studies* each day.
19. dark — The sky is *dark* and cloudy.
20. darker — This color is *darker* than that one.
21. darkest — This color is the *darkest* of the three.
22. afternoon — We may play this *afternoon*.
23. grandmother — Our *grandmother* will visit us.
24. can't — We *can't* go with you.
25. doesn't — Mary *doesn't* like to play.
26. night — We read to Mother last *night*.

FIGURE **9 – 1.** *(Continued)*
Diagnostic Spelling Test

27. toy — I have a new *toy* train.
28. say — *Say* your name clearly.
29. little — Tom is a *little* boy.
30. one — I have only *one* book.
31. would — *Would* you come with us?
32. pretty — She is a *pretty* girl.

27. brought — Joe *brought* his lunch to school.
28. apple — An *apple* fell from the tree.
29. again — We must come back *again*.
30. laugh — Do not *laugh* at other children.
31. because — We cannot play *because* of the rain.
32. through — We ran *through* the yard.

LIST 1

Word	*Element Tested*
1. not	
2. but	
3. get	Short vowels
4. sit	
5. man	
6. boat	Two vowels together
7. train	
8. time	Vowel-consonant-*e*
9. like	
10. found	*ow-ou* spelling of *ou* sound
11. down	
12. soon	long and short *oo*
13. good	
14. very	final *y* as short *i*
15. happy	
16. kept	*c* and *k* spellings of the *k* sound
17. come	
18. what	
19. those	*wh, th, sh, ch,* and *ng*
20. show	spellings and ow
21. much	spelling of long o
22. sing	
23. will	doubled final
24. doll	consonants
25. after	*er* spelling
26. sister	

Word	*Element Tested*
27. toy	*oy* spelling of *oi* sound
28. say	*ay* spelling of long *a* sound
29. *little*	*le* ending
30. one	
31. would	Nonphonetic spellings
32. pretty	

LIST 2

Word	*Element Tested*
1. flower	*ow-ou* spellings of *ou*
2. mouth	sound *er* ending, *th* spelling
3. shoot	Long and short *oo, sh*
4. stood	spelling
5. while	*wh* spelling, vowel-consonant-*3*
6. third	*th* spelling, vowel before *r*
7. each	*ch* spelling, two vowels together
8. class	Double final consonant, *c* spelling of *k* sound

FIGURE 9 – 1. *(Continued)*
Diagnostic Spelling Test

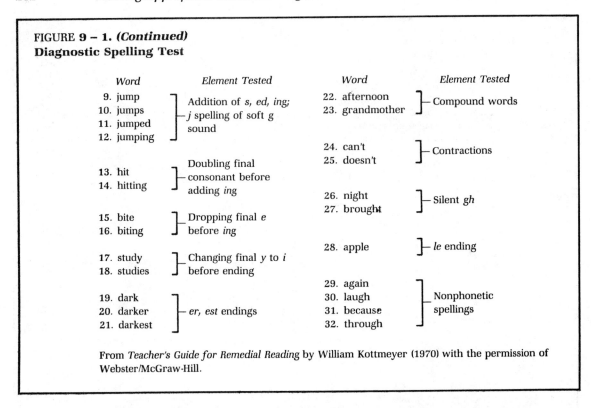

Word	Element Tested	Word	Element Tested
9. jump 10. jumps 11. jumped 12. jumping	Addition of *s, ed, ing;* *j* spelling of soft *g* sound	22. afternoon 23. grandmother	Compound words
13. hit 14. hitting	Doubling final consonant before adding *ing*	24. can't 25. doesn't	Contractions
15. bite 16. biting	Dropping final *e* before *ing*	26. night 27. brought	Silent *gh*
17. study 18. studies	Changing final *y* to *i* before ending	28. apple	*le* ending
19. dark 20. darker 21. darkest	*er, est* endings	29. again 30. laugh 31. because 32. through	Nonphonetic spellings

From *Teacher's Guide for Remedial Reading* by William Kottmeyer (1970) with the permission of Webster/McGraw-Hill.

matically taught the words on the list. Because many of these words are meaningless outside of a specific context, they probably should not be taught in isolation.

A review of five leading commercially available spelling programs, including Kottmeyer and Ware (1964) and Benthul et al. (1974), indicates that between 85 and 90 percent of these high-frequency words are introduced to students in the first book of the series. The exceptions usually are the words *about, order, think, please, received, send, could,* and *dear.* The teacher therefore should evaluate students' ability to spell the words that are commonly presented at the beginning of spelling instruction before testing their proficiency on the words that are exceptions.

4. *How much difficulty does the student have with the spelling demons?* Many English words seem to dare people to spell them correctly. For the most part, these words are linguistically irregular — they adhere to no obvious rules are are characterized by the presence of silent and/or double letters. The 100 most often misspelled words (the orthographic demons) appear in Table 9 – 2.

Teachers of older students may want to see which of these words their poor speller cannot spell. The list should not be used with students below the fourth or fifth grade because most teachers do not introduce these words until at least the third grade.

TABLE **9 – 1.**
Words of Highest Frequency Use

FIRST 100 WORDS IN ORDER OF FREQUENCY

1. I	21. at	41. do	61. up	81. think
2. the	22. this	42. been	62. day	82. say
3. and	23. with	43. letter	63. much	83. please
4. to	24. but	44. can	64. out	84. him
5. a	25. on	45. would	65. her	85. his
6. you	26. if	46. she	66. order	86. got
7. of	27. all	47. when	67. yours	87. over
8. in	28. so	48. about	68. now	88. make
9. we	29. me	49. they	69. well	89. may
10. for	30. was	50. any	70. an	90. received
11. it	31. very	51. which	71. here	91. before
12. that	32. my	52. some	72. them	92. two
13. is	33. had	53. has	73. see	93. send
14. your	34. our	54. or	74. go	94. after
15. have	35. from	55. there	75. what	95. work
16. will	36. am	56. us	76. come	96. could
17. be	37. one	57. good	77. were	97. dear
18. are	38. time	58. know	78. no	98. made
19. not	39. he	59. just	79. how	99. glad
20. as	40. get	60. by	80. did	100. like

From Ernest A. Horn, *A Basic Writing Vocabulary 10,000 Words Most Commonly Used in Writing.*
University of Iowa Monographs in Education, First Series, No. 4, Iowa City, Iowa, 1926.

TABLE **9 – 2.**
100 Commonly Misspelled Words

ache	families	neither	sandwich
afraid	fasten	nickel	scratch
against	fault	niece	sense
all right	February	ninety	separate
although	forgotten	ninth	shining
angry	friendly	onion	silence
answered	good-bye	passed	since
asks	guessed	peaceful	soldier

TABLE **9 – 2.** *(Continued)*
100 Commonly Misspelled Words

beautiful	happened	perfectly	speech
because	happily	piano	squirrel
beginning	here's	picnic	stepped
boy's	holiday	picture	straight
buried	hungry	piece	studying
busily	husband	pitcher	success
carrying	its	pleasant	taught
certain	it's	potato	their
choose	kitchen	practice	there's
Christmas	knives	prettiest	through
clothes	language	pumpkin	valentine
climbed	lettuce	purpose	whose
course	listening	quietly	worst
double	lose	rapidly	writing
easier	marriage	receive	yours
eighth	meant	rotten	
either	minute	safety	
enemy	neighbor	said	

From Kuska, A., Webster, E. J. D., and Elford, G., *Spelling in Language Arts 6. Ontario, Canada: Thomas Nelson & Sons (Canada) Ltd., 1964. Reprinted by permission of the publisher Thomas Nelson & Sons (Canada) Limited.*

DEVELOPING INSTRUCTIONAL PROCEDURES

The activities described in the previous two sections of this chapter discuss gathering information about a student's spelling problem in order to decide what changes should be made in the regular classroom situation and what the content of any remedial effort should be. Activities described or referred to in this final section relate to how the content might be taught.

Remediating Specific Errors

Having used the assessment techniques described previously to determine the types of errors the student is making, the resource teacher's attention shifts to locating suitable activities. The resource teacher can select remedial spelling activities from many sources. Otto and R. J. Smith (1980) provide instructions for handling careless spellers, students troubled with the "demons," and those who lack phonic ability. Burns (1980) and Wallace and Kauffman (1973) provide lists that match activities with spelling errors. Arena (1968) is rich in ideas concerning the remedial use of color coding, linguistic and visual techniques, and informal methods for managing reversals, motivation, and other aspects important to teaching spelling.

We should point out, however, that the effectiveness of these activities has never been confirmed through objective research and that the often-made etiological statements about spelling errors (for example, that in some cases poor spelling is caused by deficits in auditory discrimination, visual imagery, memory, attention, and/or phonics ability) are based mostly on speculation. Therefore, when the resource teacher deems it necessary to remediate specific spelling errors, we recommend the careful, systematic use of the techniques of applied behavioral analysis, such as those described by Lovitt (1975, 1975a) among others, and described briefly here in Chapter 2.

Remediating Severe Cases

More severe and/or resistant cases may need highly structured approaches. The most structured method for remediating spelling is recommended by Fernald (1943) and by Johnson and Myklebust (1967). The resource teacher should thoroughly study Fernald's chapter on spelling before attempting to implement any of her teaching procedures. Fernald insists that the method be applied according to her specifications regarding how words are selected for teaching, how tracing is used, how recall is reinforced, and how motivation is attained. Her approach to teaching children to spell is divided into these eight steps:

1. The teacher writes the word to be learned on the blackboard or on paper.
2. The teacher pronounces the word very clearly and distinctly. The students pronounce the word.
3. Each student is given time to study the word. (Finger tracing is done during this step.)
4. When every student is sure of the word, the teacher erases or covers the words and the student writes it from memory.
5. The student turns the paper over and writes the word a second time.
6. Some arrangement should be made so that it is natural for the student to use the word he or she has learned often in his writing.
7. Finally the student should be allowed to get the correct form of the word at any time when he or she is doubtful of its spelling.
8. If spelling matches (spelling bees) are desired, they should be written instead of oral.

Resource teachers are referred also to the useful book by Shaw (1971), *Spell It Right*. He suggests that an individualized course of study in spelling should attempt to teach six basic skills: (1) to visualize words as well as to hear them; (2) to pronounce words correctly; (3) to use a dictionary; (4) to learn a few simple rules of spelling; (5) to use recall devices; and (6) to spell carefully to avoid errors. The resource teacher should remember these points and incorporate them into an individualized spelling program.

Older students with spelling problems that affect their grades in content areas should be taught strategies to compensate for poor spelling. For example, a "spelling checker" could be enlisted to help before a paper is turned in. Where feasible, a computerized spelling-corrector can be added to word-processing software.

We conclude this discussion by summarizing F. Smith's (1983) recently formulated theories about developmental and remedial spelling. First, he points out that individuals have acquired the spellings for an incredibly large number of words —at least 50,000 in most older students — and that all of these many spellings could not possibly have been learned as a consequence of direct instruction in school. Only a few of these words are troublesome to spell, and the difficulty lies in the fact that poor spellers often have learned two possible spellings for the problematic words and cannot recall which is correct. Thus, Smith speculates that the problem is not that we do not have enough spellings, but that we have too many. Second, he questions the effectiveness of traditional approaches to remediation, including some of the activities mentioned earlier in this chapter. For example, he asserts that students actually learn to spell relatively few words in response (1) to writing activities where teachers circle misspelled words on their paper, (2) to frequent trips to the dictionary to look up the spellings of words they cannot spell in the first place, and (3) to learning to write down letters representing the sounds of words that we hear in speech. Third, he speculates that students learn to spell from reading.

> I am not asserting that anyone who reads will become a speller because that is not the case. But anyone who is a speller must be a reader. Reading is the only possible source of all the spelling information you have in your head. [p. 193]

If he is right, the instructional implications of these statements are evident — poor readers are likely poor spellers as well and any success derived from direct remediation of their spelling errors will be limited by the severity of the student's reading problem. Conversely, as they learn to read better, their spelling should improve commensurately. F. Smith's ideas about the relationship of reading to spelling receive support in the work of Hammill and McNutt (1981), who performed a meta-analysis on the results of 322 correlational studies. They reported that of all the variables studied, spelling ability was the single best short- and long-term predictor of reading competence.

For these reasons, in remediating spelling, resource teachers should consider the reading status of the referred student and the role that reading might play in instruction. This is especially the case where the students evidence spelling difficulties in the mild to moderate range of severity.

10

Handwriting

Handwriting (penmanship) instruction usually begins in kindergarten or first grade. A readiness program emphasizes the development of pencil and crayon use through scribbling, tracing, and copy activities. During the first grade and continuing approximately to the third grade, students are taught to form letters, numbers, and words using commercially available programs or exercises designed by their teachers. After the third grade, formal penmanship instruction is minimized or omitted.

The classroom teacher can easily recognize students who do poorly in handwriting activities and often tries to give them extra support. When this effort fails, the teacher may refer the students to the resource program. The resource teachers institute the usual information gathering and program planning procedures; they interview the classroom teacher about the students' difficulties, observe them in the classroom, assess their problems on a one-to-one basis, and prepare a specific plan of instruction for each student.

ANALYSIS OF THE LEARNER IN THE CLASSROOM

Before they can plan appropriate individualized programs, the resource teacher needs information about the students' handwriting performance. He or she can obtain such information by asking the teacher or by observing referred students in the regular classroom while handwriting is being taught.

This kind of information can help the resource teacher determine that aspects of the classroom environment are contributing to the student's problem and identify areas that will be probed later during the individualized evaluation. In particular, the resource teacher should try to answer the following kinds of questions when working with a student with poor handwriting.

1. *What is the precise complaint about the student's handwriting?* In making referrals, teachers often describe the student's problem in vague terms: "Billy's handwriting is very poor for his age." Such descriptions lack definitive meaning and therefore are of little value to the resource teacher. On these occasions, the resource teacher must determine what the classroom teacher really believes is the specific difficulty in handwriting. For example, the resource teacher may discover that the teacher is concerned about the student's slow writing speed, improper pencil grip, sloppiness, messiness, and/or illegibility.

The teacher's opinions should be noted and checked out thoroughly during the individual evaluation. If the resource teacher ignores the areas that the classroom teacher has identified as problems, then the resource and the regular programs will run along parallel tracks, never intersecting.

2. *What approach do referring teachers use to teach handwriting?* Do they use a system of sequenced, teacher-designed activities, a commercial program (which one?), or a series of random activities? Handwriting is learned best when it is taught systematically on a regular basis under motivating conditions. A teacher who uses a hit-or-miss approach probably will have several students with problems in learning to write. The resource teacher may suggest that the teacher implement a comprehensive handwriting program, such as *Writing With Look and See* (Skinner and Krakower, 1968) or *Better Handwriting for You* (Noble, 1966). Using these programs will add needed sequence, structure, and regularity to teaching handwriting in the classroom and may help prevent handwriting difficulties.

It may be that a much simplified approach to handwriting is needed. In this case the resource teacher should recommend *D'Nealian Handwriting* (Thurber and Jordan, 1979). This system uses lower case manuscript letters that are the basic forms of the corresponding cursive letters.

3. *How many minutes a day or week are devoted specifically to teaching handwriting?* Some teachers do not believe that handwriting is important and devote little time to its instruction. Consequently, many of their students eventually are referred for help because of illegible handwriting. As a general rule, teachers in the primary grades should allocate a minimum of fifty to seventy-five minutes a week (ten to fifteen minutes a day) specifically to teaching handwriting. Teachers who spend less time should be encouraged to give the skill more direct attention.

4. *Is cursive or manuscript being taught?* Which particular style is being used? Most researchers believe that cursive and manuscript are about equally effective and that it does not matter which is taught first. Most schools introduce manuscript during the first grade and shift to cursive around the third grade. The resource teacher also should determine which publisher style is being taught; differences exist in the styles used in the programs offered by Zaner Blozer, Lectroleain, and other

companies. The resource teacher needs this information to plan a program that will be consistent with the expectations of the regular class teacher.

Some teachers report that a few students who had difficulty with a particular kind of writing (manuscript, for example) did much better after being switched to another kind (cursive). If a student is shifted from one kind of writing to another, the resource teacher should be sure to tell the regular teacher that the conversion has been made and why.

5. *Is the student's pencil grip comfortable and flexible?* In writing, the pupil should hold the pencil in a free, comfortable fashion. Awkward grips often cause unnecessary strain and contribute markedly to illegibility, errors, and slowness. Teachers consider two grips to be the most acceptable: the *standard* and the *stenographer's* grip. However, they usually allow considerable latitude for individual preferences in the choice of a grip. Figures 10-1 and 10-2 illustrate the standard and the stenographer's grips. Other grips do exist. In most cases, however, their use generally results in a loss of flexibility and control. It is probably useless, however, to try to convert older students who have firmly established atypical grips to a more desirable one. In teaching younger students to write, the teacher should stress one of the standard grips.

FIGURE **10 – 1.**
Standard grip for right- and left-handed writers.

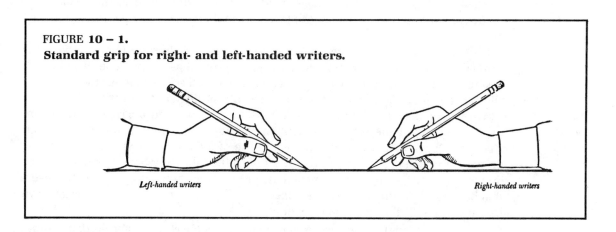

Left-handed writers   Right-handed writers

6. *Is the student right- or left-handed?* What specific provisions does the classroom teacher make relative to grip, posture, and paper position for the left-handed student? The grips that result in comfortable and legible writing usually are different for right- and left-handed people. The teacher should consider this distinction. In the past, some teachers tried to make all students right-handed; this practice certainly is not recommended today. Teachers should try to teach left-handed pupils to use postures that contribute to comfort and legibility. For example, Enstrom (1962) provides convincing evidence indicating that left-handed writers who keep their hands below the writing line and who slant their paper write more legibily than those who

FIGURE **10 – 2.**
The stenographer's grip.

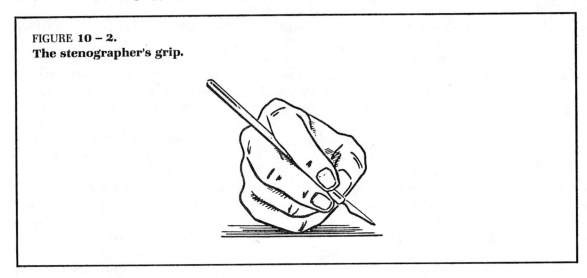

hook or keep the hand above the writing line. We do point out, however, that it is usually inadvisable to try to change a student who has developed a firmly established hook; yet, for beginning writers, the teacher should try to develop a more standard grip.

7. *Does the student have a physical problem that might contribute to writing difficulties?* The effects of such conditions as mild cerebral palsy and general awkwardness on handwriting are obvious; yet many teachers still refuse to make the necessary allowances for mildly to moderately involved physically handicapped students or to recognize the need to adapt both their expectations and their curriculum for them. Certain aspects of the school curriculum should be modified or omitted for such students. Occasionally, typewriting or the use of a computerized word processing program can be substituted for handwriting, although many handicapped students do not have sufficient motor control to do either. One should not assume, however, that because children are physically impaired, they cannot learn to write or improve that writing skill they may have acquired.

8. *Are writing models displayed prominently in the room?* Some students forget how to form letters and numbers properly and need models to which they can refer frequently. These models usually are written on strips of poster board and are attached to a classroom wall. Of course, to profit fully from such a model, a student must sit close enough to see it clearly. The resource teacher may suggest that a special model be prepared for a particular student and be taped directly to his or her desk.

9. *Is the student's chair the correct size?* Trying to write while sitting in an uncomfortable chair or in one that is an improper height can lead to early fatigue and illegibility, especially when the student has to do a lot of writing. For most students, a chair on which they can sit with their hips near its back, knees forming a right angle, and feet resting flat on the floor is usually the most conducive for

writing. If a poor writer and his or her chair are mismatched, the resource teacher might suggest to the regular teacher that a different chair be found.

10. *Is the student's desk or writing table an appropriate height?* The question here is one of comfort. A table that is too high forces students to raise their arms to an awkward level in order to write and often brings the paper too close to the eyes; an unusually low table requires them to bend their backs to an uncomfortable degree in order to write. The table is of an optimal height if when the student leans forward slightly, the forearms rest comfortably on the desk without having to raise the shoulders. For left-handed writers, the desk should be a little below the normal height.

11. *Where does the student position his or her paper when writing?* Most teachers recommend that the right-handed person place the paper squarely on the desk with its lower edge parallel to the lower edge of the desk and directly in front of the student. Both forearms should rest on the desk for approximately three-quarters of their length. The nonwriting hand is placed at the upper left-hand side of the paper to hold it steady or to move it both horizontally and vertically as needed. Some teachers advocate slanting the paper for the right-handed manuscript writer; this position is an acceptable variation.

There are two points of view about the proper position of the paper for the left-handed writer. Some teachers believe that the paper should be placed squarely on the desk as it is for right-handed individuals. Other teachers recommend slanting the paper to varying degrees. Those who suggest a slanted position agree that the top of the paper should be slanted to the right (clockwise) for the left-handed writer.

12. *When writing, do referred students hold their heads disordinately close to or far from the paper?* When copying from the chalkboard, do they squint? These questions relate to visual efficiency. If the answer to either question is yes, then the student should be referred to the school nurse for a visual screening evaluation. The legibility of the teacher's handwriting may also cause students to squint or try to move closer to the writing.

13. *What is the student's attitude during the writing exercise period?* Attitudinal factors are important in teaching a student to write; good motivation is critical. The resource teacher can get some hints about how the student feels about writing by watching his or her behavior during a writing lesson. Is the student enthusiastic (not likely), bored, disruptive, and/or moody? Is his or her attitude negative because handwriting is inadequate or because the lessons are dull and unimaginatively taught?

14. *Does the classroom teacher supply the student with any additional individualized support?* Students with handwriting problems need extra help from their regular teacher. This help may take the form of additional verbal encouragement, individual attention during the lessons, and/or extra lessons scheduled later in the day. If the regular teacher provides special help, the resource teacher should note: (1) the kinds of support provided; (2) the teacher's attitude (warm, critical, punitive); (3) the pupil's reactions (appreciative, hostile, embarrassed); (4) the amount of time spent on special help; and/or (5) the types of special exercises and techniques used that differ from

those employed with the rest of the class. If the teacher provides little or no support, the resource teacher may tactfully suggest that some be given.

15. *Is there ever any handwriting audience besides the teacher?* If the teacher gives no reasons for legible writing, then it will be difficult to motivate a student to write legibly.

SUPPLEMENTAL INDIVIDUAL ANALYSIS

Having gathered essential background information from talking with the teacher, reviewing any available records, and observing in the classroom, the resource teacher now can begin the individual assessment of the student's handwriting performance. To do this the resource teacher must have samples of the student's work to analyze. He or she can get samples from young students by asking them to copy a paragraph or more from the chalkboard or a book. Older students can be requested to write a paragraph or two describing a picture, or they, too, may be asked to copy passages. In either case, samples should be collected under two conditions. In the first, students are asked to write or copy the paragraph; in the second, they are asked to write the selection using their very best handwriting. A comparison of the two samples is interesting because many students can write legibly but for some reason do not unless specifically asked to do so. The resource teacher also should collect and analyze samples of the student's writing from the classroom teacher. The writing samples should be evaluated to determine the exact kinds of difficulties that are representative of the student's handwriting.

Unlike the other subject areas discussed in this book, no standardized tests are available for handwriting; therefore, there is no clear-cut established criterion for adequacy. Resource teachers therefore must depend on their own judgments about whether a particular aspect of a student's handwriting is acceptable. To judge properly, resource teachers should calibrate their clinical opinions by reviewing samples of handwriting from many different students with good and poor ability. In addition, they should evaluate informally both cursive and manuscript ability.

In assessing a student's *manuscript performance*, the resource teacher determines the correctness of the following skills by analyzing samples of the students' written work and by directly observing the students while writing.

1. Position of hand, arm, body, and/or paper
2. Size of letters: too small, large, and so forth
3. Proportion of one letter or word to another
4. Quality of the pencil line: too heavy, light, variable, and so forth
5. Slant: too much or irregular
6. Letter formation: poor circles or straight lines, lines disconnected, and so forth

7. Letter alignment: off the line, and so forth
8. Spacing: letters or words crowded or too scattered
9. Speed: too fast or too slow

In assessing a student's *cursive writing*, a resource teacher should analyze the following:

1. Position of hand, arm, body, and/or paper
2. Size of writing: too large, small, and so forth
3. Proportion of one letter or word to another
4. Quality of the pencil line: too heavy, light, variable, and so forth
5. Slant: too much slanting, too nearly vertical, or wild
6. Alignment of letters: off the line in places
7. Letter formation: angular letters, too round or thin, illegible, beginning or ending strokes poorly made, downstrokes not uniform, letters disconnected, looped letters weak, and so forth
8. Spacing: margins uneven, letters or words crowded or scattered
9. Connecting lines between letters: improperly executed or placed

Occasionally, resource teachers will want to compare a student's handwriting with that of age peers or to document the degree of discrepancy between the two in terms of deviation scaled scores. For these purposes, we recommend the handwriting subtest of the *Test of Written Language* (Hammill and Larsen, 1983). This is the only norm-referenced test of handwriting that we know of. The subtest is a series of cursive paragraphs of varying degrees of legibility (see figure 10–3). The teacher collects representative samples of the referred student's written work and matches their quality to one of the paragraphs in the series. The number that corresponds to the paragraph is the student's score. The value is converted into a standard score or a grade equivalent using tables in the test manual. The test is suitable for students ranging in age from 8½ to 18½. Stability and interscorer reliability have been explored thoroughly; reported reliability coefficients range from 0.76 to 0.89.

Resource teachers can either design their own checklists based on the above item analysis or can use those already prepared by Freeman (1965). In evaluating a student's ability to form cursive letters, the teacher should pay special attention to the letters *a, e, r,* and *t;* more than half of all the illegibilities in cursive writing are associated with these four letters. The teacher also should remember that the four most common errors, (the writing demons) in cursive writing are: (1) failure to close letters (such as, *a, b,* and *f,*); (2) inappropriately closing loops (*l* like *t, e* like *i*); (3) looping unlooped strokes (*i* like *e*); and (4) using straight up strokes rather than rounded strokes (*n* like *u, c* like *i*).

FIGURE 10 – 3.
Scoring guide for cursive handwriting.

Rating 10

Rating 9

Once upon a time there was a Mars club
around the corner where every day most
of the people in my class went to after
school at three o'clock every. Soon later on
in the year five people had joined. Soon

Rating 8

Rating 7

The first picture is about science-
tist have notice that the earth is starting to explode. Because the earth is crack-
ing. They got all of the people together
because they have notice that there

Rating 6

Rating 5

Once upon a time in a galaxy far
away the planet of Qunbee. Qunbebeen sharkin
by a series of Qunbee quacks. This planet
has a very well advanced science department it clains the planet will be

Rating 4

Rating 3

Once upon a time some space ships
landed on some planet were there was
elephants, mice, ducks, turtles, pegs and
hipptalpatimas and the peaple
started digging halls in the the

Rating 2

Rating 1

onet a time that was is popued fonae
meme and the try and try
to git the aila forn aut paped
and the was mot art con
foune poypome ders was not

Rating 0

DEVELOPING INSTRUCTIONAL PROCEDURES

After obtaining the necessary information about the student's handwriting problem, the resource teacher is ready to formulate a program for remediation. Many students, especially those with mild or moderate difficulties, require only direct instruction in letter formation. The resource teacher also can give the regular teacher some ideas to implement in the classroom, such as: (1) changing the student's chair and desk if they are an improper size; (2) starting a systematic handwriting program; (3) allowing more time for handwriting instruction; (4) providing for left-handed students; and (5) teaching a student a more confortable grip. Basic information relating to these and other points have been discussed earlier in this chapter. This section develops instructional procedures based primarily on data obtained from the supplemental individual evaluation.

Before beginning a remedial program with a student, the resource teacher considers the principles that underlie effective programming in handwriting. Graham and Miller (1980) list the following twelve principles and conditions that should be incorporated into a comprehensive handwriting program.

1. Handwriting instruction is direct and not incidental.
2. Because handicapped students exhibit a diverse range of handwriting achievement, instruction is individualized.
3. The handwriting program is planned, monitored, and modified on the basis of assessment information.
4. Successful teaching and remediation depend upon the flexible use of a wide variety of techniques and methods.
5. Handwriting is taught in short daily learning periods during which desirable habits are established.
6. Skills in handwriting are overlearned in isolation and then applied in meaningful context assignments.
7. Teachers stress the importance of handwriting and do not accept, condone, or encourage slovenly work.
8. Effective handwriting instruction is dependent upon the attitudes of both student and teacher.
9. The instructional atmosphere is pleasant, and motivation is promoted through incentives, reinforcement, success, and enthusiasm.
10. Teachers practice lessons prior to presentation and are able to write a "model" hand.
11. Students are encouraged to evaluate their own handwriting and, when appropriate, actively participate in initiating, conducting, and evaluating the remedial program.
12. Although students do develop personal idiosyncrasies, the teacher helps them maintain a consistent, legible handwriting style throughout the grades. [Pp. 5–6]

Having considered the above principles, the resource teacher is ready to begin selecting training activities. Training activities usually relate to correcting two broad kinds of difficulties: letter illegibility and problems of spacing. Students with poor handwriting usually need work in both areas.

When the goal is to improve *legibility*, (the clear formation of letters in words), the lessons should be consistent with the following sequence, at least at the start.

1. Finger tracing of the letters is a good place to begin, especially if the student is inexperienced in pencil use.

2. Tracing letters and/or words using pencils, and/or crayons, is introduced next.

3. Copying letters and words from models is popular activity with many variations. Most remedially oriented teachers begin by having the student copy isolated letters and introduce words as soon as possible. Copying meaningless letters is boring, whereas reproducing words is not. Also, because most students think of copying words as a sign of growing up, they are motivated to participate in copying exercises that use words to improve the skill.

For younger children, the words to be copied should be presented one at a time in fairly large print. The fewer extraneous markings on the page, the easier it will be for them to focus on the word. In the beginning, the teacher may want to write the word to be copied directly on the student's paper. Later, the teacher should put the stimulus word on a card that can be placed on the student's desk.

Most teachers require students to copy material from the chalkboard as well as from cards. On these occasions, the model should be written large enough for all students to see clearly. Lowercase letters should be approximately four inches high, and capital letters should be twice that size. As the student's skill increases, the size of the letters is decreased. Also, no student should sit within four feet of or farther than fifteen feet from the chalkboard from which he or she is to copy. Lined chalkboards should not be used in the beginning; the parallel horizontal lines can be confusing. If lined boards are the only ones available, then colored chalk should be used to make the lines of the letters readily distinguishable from those on the board.

4. Writing letters and words from dictation.

When the goal is to correct problems that the student has in letter and word *spacing*, the following activities can be used.

Some children have problems in spacing because they are trying to write too small too soon; they should be encouraged to write larger until they have acquired sufficient control. Also, the proper spacing of letters can be facilitated by using a top and middle line on the writing paper in addition to the base line. If the students are shown only a bottom line, their letters will likely vary a great deal in height.

If the student has trouble with both letter size and staying on the line, a cardboard frame with a rectangular piece cut out can be used as an aid. The student writes within the cut-out area, using the lower limits of the cardboard as a baseline. In this way, he or she has a barrier that stops downward movement. Three separate frames are needed: a frame for words comprised of letters that are two spaces high but have no letters extending beneath the base line, (*b, f, h*); one for words that contain letters only one space high (*a, e, o*); and one for words that contain some letters that are two spaces high and others that go under the base line (*b, g, h, j*). The resource teacher should be prepared for difficulties related to the five letters that go beneath the base line (*g, j, p, q,* and *y*) because many young students tend to place them so that they do not extend beneath the baseline. The teacher will have to explain and demonstrate repeatedly to the student that a few letters go under the line — that "their tails hang down."

A few students run their words together when writing or copying. This practice is remediated easily by teaching them to place the index finger of their nonwriting hand at the end of each word and to leave this space before writing the next word. Usually they get the idea quickly, and the activity does not have to be used long.

Throughout all remedial handwriting exercises, the resource teachers should maintain an accepting, warm attitude and should keep their expectations regarding the quality of student's writing consistent with realistic goals. Gross errors can be corrected and self-correction can be encouraged; but too much criticism should be avoided because it can cause the student to lose interest in the activity and eventually may contribute to a deep dislike for writing.

From time to time, the resource teacher will encounter students who cannot do any of the handwriting activities mentioned in this section. These students should be given considerable opportunity to perfect the skills associated with very early writing before being introduced to a remedial handwriting program. These early skills involve the mastery of pencils and crayons through scribbling, coloring, gross tracing and copying, line-to-line drawing, free-style drawing, and templates. When successful in these activities, the student will likely be able to profit from a developmental or remedial handwriting program. To the extent possible, these early writing activities should involve letters, numbers, and words. From the beginning of instruction, the idea that letters and words play a major role in meaningful communication should be made clear to the learner. And as soon as possible, handwriting instruction should be integrated into the general language arts program.

The remedial procedures described are merely examples of those available to resource teachers. To prepare a complete program, the teacher should read widely in the area of handwriting and should accumulate many ideas and activities in addition to those few mentioned in this chapter. We suggest that teachers begin their independent study by reading the chapters on handwriting by Hammill (1982), by Wallace and Kauffman (1973), by Burns (1980), by Cohen and Plaskon (1980), and by Otto and Smith (1980). The material in these chapters deals specifically with assessing and correcting handwriting difficulties. Teachers who are interested in a particularly thorough investigation of handwriting are referred to Herrick (1963).

11

Spoken Language

Language is a system of arbitrary symbols, whose proper use enables students to understand and to generate an infinite number of meaningful sentences. The presence of language ability makes communication through speech possible.

Bloom and Lahey (1978) have identified three dimensions of language — content, form, and use — that are viewed separately but that in fact are highly interrelated. These dimensions refer to having something to say (content), having a way to say it (form), and having a reason and occasion to say it (use). *Content* refers to the understanding and expressing of language and includes knowledge of vocabulary items and conceptual categories, their classification, and their relationships to one another. *Form* refers to the manner in which oral communications are structured and includes the ability to use the sound system that carries the vocal message (phonology); to enlist the smallest meaningful units of language, such as inflections, suffixes, and root words (morphology); and to create sensible sentences (syntax). *Use* refers to the purposes of language, to the employment of language to achieve personal goals, and to the selection of appropriate means of expression in response to changing environmental situations.

Language disorders (difficulties involving aspects of content, form, or use) can be either developmental in nature (present from birth) or acquired (occurring after language has been fairly well established).

Developmental problems are fairly common occurences in young children and usually have an obscure or unknown etiology. These deficiencies have been evident throughout the child's life and do not seem to be associated with any particular trauma or injury. Frequently, parents and professionals say that these children have baby talk, delayed language, immature speech, developmental aphasia, or retarded language development.

Acquired language problems are caused by brain injuries occurring after the child has already mastered language. They are called *aphasias* or *dysphasias*. Such cases are characterized by a loss of or a noticeable impairment of language function while the use of the speech mechanism (the tongue, jaw, and/or lips) remains relatively unaffected. Aphasias are comparatively rare. Language disorders, acquired or developmental, often are complicated by the presence of hyperactivity, distractibility, emotional hypersensitivity, acting out behavior, voice problems, and severe articulation difficulties.

Most students referred to the resource teacher because of oral language problems are between four and nine years old and exhibit only mild or moderate difficulty. Resource teachers who have had sufficient supervised training in this area should try to handle the problem; if they have not had the necessary training, they should refer the student immediately to someone who has. Generally this individual will be another resource person, such as a speech therapist or language clinician. Severe cases of language disorder probably will be placed in a special class in which the teacher may be a specialist in either learning disabilities or speech/language. Moderately involved cases may be served by the resource teacher, by the speech/language therapist or jointly by both. Mild cases will receive special help from the regular class teacher working cooperatively with the resource personnel. Local school policies probably will dictate the type of professional who is to serve students with language problems; we suggest that the student be assigned to the person who is the most qualified to handle the difficulty, regardless of job title.

ANALYSIS OF THE LEARNER IN THE CLASSROOM

To obtain a true picture of a student's problems with spoken language, the resource teacher should observe the student in actual speaking situations. If evaluation occurs only in a testing room or in some other sheltered place where there are no distractions, students may not exhibit the kinds of behaviors that prompted the teacher(s) to refer them. Therefore, the resource teacher should arrange to visit the class on two or three occasions when the teacher has scheduled oral expression activities — when the student is expected to "show and tell," discuss topics, tell a story, read orally, engage in creative dramatics, or play.

The information that the resource teacher obtains from the classroom deals not only with the language of the individual but also with the language context within which the student communicates. Through talking with classroom teachers and observing the student during periods when oral language is used, information about the content, form, and use of language can be collected. Further, one can note the parameters that might affect how the student uses language, such as physical problems that might impede communication or limited bilingualism.

The school or classroom is only one setting in which language is used for interpersonal communication and learning. We will focus primarily on the classroom setting, although we recognize and recommend assessment and programming across settings. The questions that follow are designed to help resource teachers focus on the appropriate information that is needed as part of a comprehensive assessment in language.

1. *What topics does the student talk about, and what is the quality of the vocabulary used?* In class, students often have the opportunity for sharing experiences with others. On these occasions, resource teachers can learn much about a student's understanding of topics by attending both to the maturity of the ideas expressed and to the quality of the vocabulary used. It would be significant to note kindergarten and first-grade students who are not using the personal pronoun, *I;* who have limited, shallow vocabularies of fewer than two hundred to three hundred words; who lack the capacity to describe objects or actions in detail; and who, when called upon for show and tell, have nothing to say.

For older students, the real and vicarious experiences they have had should influence their range of topics and the quality of their vocabularies. Students with a limited range, both of topics and of vocabulary, will be at a disadvantage in dealing with the expanding content of postelementary schools.

It is also important to note how the learner picks up and uses the technical vocabularies introduced in content areas such as math, social studies, and science. Of course, if these vocabularies and topics are not observed to be taught in a deliberate fashion, we know that it is unlikely for a student to acquire them as incidental learning.

Since part of the purpose of education is to expand students' awareness of topics for discussion and related vocabularies as well, it is also desirable to find out how the student's range of topics and vocabulary has changed over the years.

In addition to the range of topics and vocabulary, we are also interested in specific topics discussed by the student so that they can be used as entrées to instruction and/or further assessment.

2. *Does the child speak a nonstandard variation of English that conforms to his or her social, ethnic, or regional background?* The term *standard English* refers to the particular variety of English spoken by most Americans today, especially those who reside in a geographic band stretching across the Middle Atlantic, Midwestern, and Western states. In general, it is the language of the television, the radio, and the movies.

Many teachers become concerned when a student speaks English in a markedly nonstandard fashion. Especially irritating is the inappropriate use of tenses (*seen* for *saw*), pronouns (*him played* for *he played*), and negatives (*haven't no* for *haven't any*). The use of illiteracies, such as *ain't, his'n, our'n* is particularly distasteful to many teachers. We should point out, however, that even though such nonstandard speech may exasperate some teachers, it does not necessarily constitute a defect in language. That is, in most instances, an individual who uses nonstandard English is merely speaking correctly the language that is characteristic of and socially acceptable in his or her present or past neighborhood, region, and/or social class.

Although resource teachers may be tempted to remediate nonstandard English in a student, we recommend that they consider the matter thoroughly before beginning. In our general culture, it is no advantage to speak a nonstandard form of English; but it is no real handicap either. The days when 'Liza Doolittle was "condemned by every syllable she uttered" are over. Today, many groups that previously might have felt ashamed of their nonstandard speech think of it with pride. As a result, many people are suspicious of teachers' attempts to improve or refashion their children's language, and often they resist the effort. So unless the student expresses a strong interest in altering speech patterns and unless the parents are willing to support the undertaking, we suggest that the resource teacher forgo the opportunity to play Henry Higgins to a school full of little 'Lizas.

Where remediation efforts do occur, we cannot emphasize too strongly the need for listening and speaking activities. Some classroom teachers attempt to remedy nonstandard English with written tasks such as:

The boy ＿＿＿＿＿＿＿＿＿＿ the big dog.
(seen, saw)

In this case, the student has a 50 percent chance of a correct response merely through copying one of the words. No real oral language pattern need ever be used. We recommend instead the use of listening and speaking drills, such as those designed for teaching English as a second language. It is even more important for the teacher to arrange communication situations in which appropriate language will be modeled for the student and in which the student will have an opportunity to practice the language desired in a nonthreatening situation. We also recommend frequent reading aloud to students so that they might hear both standard oral language patterns and the literary patterns that they will be expected to read without benefit of a listening and speaking model, such as "Laughing loudly, the friends ran down the hill."

Even the resource teacher who has worked with students with nonstandard dialects should seek a more formal understanding of ethnic language or dialect. We recommend highly the book and accompanying records of *The Sounds of Children* (Williams, Hopper, and Natalicio, 1977). The program is intended for people without backgrounds in language development or linguistics and is easy to read. An excellent second book, which provides more technical background, is *Children's Speech: A Practical Introduction to Communicative Development* (Hopper and Naremore, 1978). The latter book provides many practical and immediately implementable suggestions for classroom instruction.

3. *How well does the student appear to accommodate to the language requirements of the classroom?* This question is related to the use of language, although form and content are also included as a matter of course. In the classroom, the resource teacher should observe factors such as these:

a. Staying on the topic at hand
b. Bridging from one topic to another
c. Attending to or being aware of the nonlinguistic aspects of the communication situation, such as feelings, time frame, and the roles of people present
d. Asking appropriate questions
e. Answering questions appropriately, even if the answer itself is incorrect
f. Asking for repetition or clarification as needed to understand the message
g. Providing repetition or clarification as needed to make the message understood by others
h. Understanding proxemics, or body positions and the locations of speakers, as well as the way speakers and listeners use their bodies in communicating
i. Using the voice itself appropriately, which encompasses the volume or speed of speech and qualities such as stridency or whininess
j. Using prosodic features — stress, pitch, intonation, or pauses (juncture) — appropriately
k. Using an appropriate style of speech and language to fit the occasion and the people present, such as the principal, strangers, family members, peers, close friends, or the teacher
l. Using eye contact as expected, even where cultural differences suggest that eye contact is disrespectful of authority. Cultural difference should be noted as a possible reason for lack of eye contact.

Factors such as these just suggested eventually may become more important to the speech and language program than specific items or forms, for we tend to teach the forms and content that are needed to support appropriate use.

4. *How does the student react during classroom activities in which he or she is required to communicate verbally?* The reactions of the student to the language expectations of the classroom are noted for several reasons. First, if the student's own language disability causes withdrawal, aggression, or fear, then the emotional component of language use must be accounted for in further assessment and in programming. It is especially important to note any periods of silence or withdrawal from a topic or a class session. During later evaluation, the resource teacher may want to try to elicit language behavior that would have been appropriate. In this way, it is possible to differentiate the shy student from the one who does not have language skills relevant to the situation.

The resource teacher will also want to identify environmental factors that might cause an adverse reaction on the part of the student. These factors often may be the attitudes of teachers or peers to the student or a communicative context that is too advanced — or too simple — for the student.

5. *What is the attitude of the teacher and/or the other students toward the student's spoken language?* Occasionally, other students will laugh and make fun of a person whose language is noticeably different. Such inconsiderate actions cause a sensitive student to suffer. There may, however, be more subtle indicators of unfavorable attitudes toward the student's language. Whether through speech, looks, or gestures, any unfavorable attitude toward the student's speech or language should be noted.

Williams, Hopper, and Natalicio (1977, pp. 118–133) suggest that two dimensions of language are especially critical to attitudes toward the student and his or her language. These dimensions are:

1. Eager to speak ◀——► Reticent to speak

2. Standard, nonethnic ◀——► Nonstandard, ethnic

The resource teacher may wish to obtain more formal indicators of the attitudes of teachers and other adults who work with the student, especially in regard to these dimensions. From listening to the student's speech, the resource teacher can make several kinds of ratings that incorporate these dimensions or any others that seem indicated. In this way, it is possible to develop a more concrete picture of attitude toward the language of the student. It should be kept in mind that these measures are subjective perceptions and should be reported as such. Judgments concerning four students are shown below as examples of the kinds of data that can be collected during an interview with the teacher(s).

Judgment 1. Is the student's language closer to standard, nonethnic, or to nonstandard, ethnic?

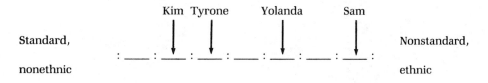

Judgment 2. Is the student reticent to speak or eager to speak?

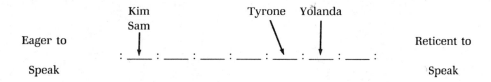

The data from these judgments can be combined to locate perceptions of one student or a group of students in one of the quadrants, as shown below.

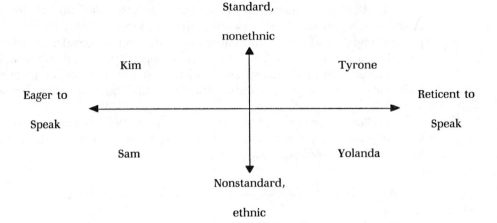

In addition, Williams, Hopper, and Natalicio also ask:

Judgment 3. How different will the student's language likely be in varying contexts and times?

The examples we show are of two teachers who rated Sam as a reticent speaker of nonstandard English. (We have adapted their coding system to a simple check mark for the teacher or observer to use in recording.)

Teacher I

Eager to   Reticent to

Speak   : ___ : ___ · ___ : ___ : ___ : ___ : ___ :   Speak

Teacher 2

Eager to   Reticent to

Speak   : ___ : ___ : ___ : ___ : ___ : ___ : ___ :   Speak

Teacher I

Nonstandard,   Standard,

ethnic   : ___ : ___ : ___ : ___ : ___ : ___ : ___ :   nonethnic

Teacher 2

Nonstandard,   Standard,

ethnic   : ___ : ___ : ___ : ___ : ___ : ___ : ___ :   nonethnic

It is clear that teacher 1 is more certain that Sam will be less reticent to speak and will be able to use standard English in certain other situations. Teacher 2 does not view Sam's language as being that flexible.

6. *What specific aspects of the student's use of the forms of language call attention to themselves?* It is not likely that the student will have an occasion to use every phonological, morphological, or syntactic form that might eventually be inventoried. As the resource teacher observes the student's spoken language, however, he or she should be alert to any inappropriate forms that are obvious enough to draw an observer's attention. It is also important to note any repetitions of the same inappropriate form and also to plan follow-up individual assessment to be sure that the problem heard or observed was not a situational accident.

7. *What kind of language is used by teachers during instruction?* It is difficult for students to deal with the content, forms, and use of language if it is highly technical and if the students have not had many language experiences with the material at hand. The language of instruction and the way the teacher carries on instruction are major aspects of the classroom milieu. The teacher's language may, of course, be complex simply because it is read from a Teacher's Manual. Labinowicz (1980), for example, notes several contrasts in teachers' use of language for instructional purposes:

A. Find out if the set of cookies is equal in number to the set of children.

Find out if there are just enough cookies for all the children. [P. 203]

B. A leaf is a projected growth from a stem which functions in food manufacture by photosynthesis.

A leaf is a part of a plant that is seen above the ground, is usually attached by a stem, is flat or needlelike, and many of them make shade from sunlight. [P. 202]

The work of Pollack and Gruenewald (1983) provides a structured program for analyzing the teacher's language interactions, both in content and in complexity.

8. *What is the language environment in the classroom?* Some classrooms are rich in language experiences to promote positive growth in students, and others are impoverished. If the use of spoken language is discouraged, perhaps as a means of behavior control, then intervention procedures for the target student will have to deal with the teacher and other students in this regard. Also, the importance attached to language by teachers and peers may influence the student's attitude toward any intervention planned.

The language models available to the student should be observed, too, for the student may need teacher and peer models in order to understand the appropriate uses of language, to hear appropriate forms, and to encourage attention to content. A strategy to use when it is necessary to intervene in a total class is one of engaging the teacher in a project that requires the use of appropriate forms and communications situations. In this way the teacher and the class are not singled out as inappropriate.

Special attention should be paid to the teacher's use of questions. Questions are critical to the instructional situation because it is through the language of questions that cognitive development and further language development are stimulated. Sund and Carin's *Creative Questioning and Sensitive Listening Techniques: A Self-Concept Approach* (1978) is especially helpful for resource teachers.

9. *What cognitive demands are reflected in the language used in the classroom?* The cognitive demands or the level of thinking and reasoning expected in the classroom may be inappropriate for the student. This means that the problem may not be one of language at all but may be a question of the student's inability to think at the levels of abstraction or reasoning required. Furthermore, older students — especially those who have been highly mobile in their school careers — may not have the appropriate cognitive background needed for the concepts and the relational thinking used in a particular classroom.

The mismatch between the student's background of experiences and the resulting cognitive abilities and the background he or she is expected to have in a particular class is readily apparent with students who have lived their school lives in one school, only to be moved abruptly to another. It is also characteristic of students entering junior high, middle school, or high school. Content area teachers are particularly aware of the variation in backgrounds and therefore in readiness for the use of language in their areas.

There are also limitations imposed from within the individual in regard to his or her ability to deal with the cognitive level of the classroom. Such a determination can be made through observation if the disparity is great or through supplemental individual analysis if there is a question. We recommend that any judgment made in this area be confirmed or disconfirmed through more objective standardized tests.

10. *Is the student bilingual? Does he or she speak little or no English? Is a foreign language spoken in the home?* From time to time, teachers will refer students who speak either a foreign language or English with a pronounced accent. They reason that since these students have difficulty speaking English, they must need language therapy. If there are only a few referrals of this kind, if the resource teacher has the required training and experience, and if the case load permits, the students might be enrolled in the program. Referrals of this nature, however, can present a large problem for the resource teacher who works in areas with large minorities or even majorities of non-English speaking people. In south Texas, for example, the resource program easily could become inundated with such students to the exclusion of other students who need help. Also, few resource teachers are bilingual; and if they are, they generally have received no specific training in the skills necessary to teach English as a second language.

The resource teacher should set some criteria for deciding on which of these students will qualify for resource help. A general rule is that referred students who are linguistically competent in their own language or dialect should not be enrolled in the resource program. On these occasions, it should be pointed out to the referring teacher that these pupils have no phonological, syntactic, or semantic problems when speaking their own language; if they speak English poorly, it is probably due to a lack of exposure to that language.

Most teachers will accept this explanation and even agree that the student does not really qualify for the resource program, but they also will insist that the student still has a problem that they cannot handle. If there are many of these students, the school might establish a special resource program specifically designed to help them to acquire English and to ensure that they are not penalized in meeting the requirements of the school curriculum because they speak English poorly. If there are only a few such students, the resource teacher may want to recommend that special tutors, either adults or older students, be assigned to assist them with their school activities.

When either approach is recommended, the resource teacher can consult EPIE publications such as *Selector's Guide for Bilingual Education Materials:* volume 1, *Spanish Language Arts* (Educational Products Information Exchange, 1976) for materials in bilingual education. In addition to providing detailed descriptions and evaluations of appropriate programs that are commercially available, the guides describe how the curriculum in this area was developed and also provide criteria for evaluating the quality of bilingual materials.

The state or province education department will also have rules and guidelines for the education of bilingual students or for those who are fluent only in one language that is not English.

The teacher who *does* work with programs for teaching English can consult Dever's *TALK: Teaching the American Language to Kids* (1978) and also various other publications related to teaching English as a second language.

SUPPLEMENTAL INDIVIDUAL ANALYSIS

Having obtained sufficient information by observing the student in the classroom, interviewing the teacher, and reading the school records, the resource teacher may decide that an individual evaluation of the student's language is desirable. The purpose of this evaluation will be to document the existence of the problem, if necessary, and to identify specifically the nature of the language problem. To do this properly, the resource teacher may have to use one or all of the assessment approaches described in Chapter 2.

To use most of the specific assessment procedures presented here, resource teachers should understand the area of language and have had training in language evaluation. If they do not have this background and experience, they should refer students with language problems to another resource person such as a speech pathologist or to a clinic that specializes in language disorders. Regardless of who does the evaluation, however, the resource teachers will have to answer some or all of the questions that follow.

1. *Does the student actually have a problem in language?* The answer to this question is not as simple as it sounds. Some language problems are serious enough that they are obvious to parents, peers, and to any observer; however, the problem usually must be documented as to its existence and its severity. In other cases, it is difficult to tell if the student's language is actually different from that of normal peers. Nor is it easy to determine the specific area(s) in which problems exist. When the answer to the basic question is needed for qualifying a student for services, the question relates to valid and reliable information that compares one student's performance or abilities with those of peers and which also allows intraindividual comparison of relative strengths and weaknesses. The information needed is nearly always obtained from the administration of a standardized test.

Many suitable tests are available from which the resource teacher may choose. Of these, we prefer the *Test of Early Language Development* (Hresko, Reid, and Hammill, 1981) for children aged two through seven; the *Test of Language Development — Primary* (Newcomer and Hammill, 1982) for students aged four through eight; the *Test of Language Development — Intermediate* (Hammill and Newcomer, 1982) for students aged seven through twelve; and the spoken language sections of the *Test of Adolescent Language* (Hammill et al., 1980) for students aged eleven through eighteen and a half.

These tests have been normed on large representative samples of the nation's student population. The research associated with the tests is considerable and highly supportive of both their internal consistency and stability reliabilities (reported coefficients predominately above 0.80) and their content, concurrent, and construct validity. All four tests measure many different aspects of content and form in both receptive and expressive modes. The dimension of use is not measured, for it is a concept best evaluated through informal methods. The Summary and Profile Sheet for the *Test of Language Development — Primary* is illustrated in Figure 11–1.

Other comprehensive, norm-referenced test batteries can be used to obtain initial information about students' language, and resource teachers may wish to become familiar with them, as well as with those we recommended above. Among the other suitable tests are the *Carrow Elicited Language Inventory* (1974), the *Test for Auditory Comprehension of Language* (Carrow, 1973), and the *Clinical Evaluation of Language Functions* (Semel and Wiig, 1980).

The results derived from these tests can document the existence of a language problem, document the severity of a language problem, identify major areas of language that deviate significantly from norms, and distinguish between receptive and expressive problems. They may also be used to specify the general areas for analytic teaching and for inventorying items known and items to be taught. Programmatically, they serve as screening devices to identify problems in need of verification (or nonverification) and also serve as measures for assessing the status or the progress of groups of students in a program.

FIGURE 11 – 1.

Summary and Profile Sheet for TOLD-P.

TOLD-P

TEST OF LANGUAGE DEVELOPMENT PRIMARY

Phyllis L. Newcomer & Donald D. Hammill

Name _____ Female ☐ Male ☐

	Year	Month	Day
Date Tested	____	____	____
Date of Birth	____	____	____
Age	____	____	____

School: _____ Grade: _____

Examiner's Name: _____
(FIRST)   (LAST)

Examiner's Title: _____

SECTION I   RECORD OF SCORES

SUBTESTS:

		Raw Scores	Ages	% iles	Standard Scores
I	Picture Vocabulary	____	____	____	☐
II	Oral Vocabulary	____	____	____	☐
III	Gram. Understanding	____	____	____	☐
IV	Sentence Imitation	____	____	____	☐
V	Gram. Completion	____	____	____	☐
VI	Word Discrimination	____	____	____	☐
VII	Word Articulation	____	____	____	☐

COMPOSITES:

	PV	OV	GU	SI	GC	Sum of Std. Scores	Quotients
Spoken Language (SLQ)	☐	☐	☐	☐	☐	= ☐	( )
Listening (LiQ)	☐	☐				= ☐	( )
Speaking (SpQ)		☐		☐	☐	= ☐	( )
Semantics (SeQ)	☐	☐				= ☐	( )
Syntax (SyQ)			☐	☐	☐	= ☐	( )

SECTION II   TOLD-P PROFILE:

SECTION III   NOTES:

Additional Forms Available from PRO-ED   5341 Industrial Oaks Blvd., Austin, TX 78735   512/892-3142
© Copyright 1982 by Phyllis L. Newcomer & Donald D. Hammill

In using standardized tests to document the existence or severity of a language problem, we encourage the resource teacher to use appropriate scores for making such decisions. Norms are often reported in terms of age equivalents or grade equivalents, both of which are inappropriate statistics to use in the identification of students whose scores are different from our expectations. Vexing as it sounds, finding students whose scores are significantly different from age or from grade peers is *not* accomplished well through the use of either age or grade equivalents.

2. *If the child's problem is speech articulation, which phonemes are deficient?* Even an untrained person can detect poor articulation; but it takes a good ear and a little training to be able to identify the specific sounds and their positions in syllables that are defective in speech. Therefore, the comprehensive analysis of misarticulation and needs is best left to the speech pathologist (though occasionally other resource teachers may have sufficient training and experience to do this kind of assessment).

For this evaluation, we recommend the Test of Articulation Performance-Diagnostic (Bryant and Bryant, 1983). This instrument permits the examiner to learn which phonemes are defective and in need of training. It also allows the examiner to study the child's speech in terms of discriminate phonemic features, deep testing, and stimulability. Other commonly used tests include the Tests of Articulation (Templin and Darley, 1960), the Goldman-Fristoe Test of Articulation (1969), A Deep Test of Articulation (McDonald, 1964), and Laradon Articulation Scale (Edmonston, 1963).

The items of these tests can easily be subjected to a criterion-referenced interpretation. The resultant information can be used to determine: (1) the precise phonemes that are defective; (2) the syllable positions in which they are deficient; (3) the particular kinds of errors made (distortions, substitutions, or omissions); and (4) if the errors relate to any particular place of articulation (labial, dental, alvelor, and so forth) or manner of emission (nasal, plosive, fricative, and so forth). These data are used for planning an articulation program.

Whether from tests or from observations, the clinician should ask the following questions before establishing a program of articulation training. These questions are based upon the incorrect production of /s/ and /z/ sounds in conversation:

a.   Are the /s/ and /z/ sounds produced incorrectly in isolated words?
b.   What is the degree of consistency of the articulation errors?
c.   What are the phonetic substitutions? Errors should be transcribed precisely and the missing phonetic features should be noted.
d.   Are the missing distinctive features available in the sounds the child produces correctly?
e.   Can the child produce the sound when an auditory representation is provided by the clinician?
f.   Are there underlying rules that jointly account for the mispronunciation of /z/ and /s/? Frame a rule and test it out by examining additional words and phonetic contexts.

g. Finally, what is the child's discrimination between /z/ and the error sound, and between /s/ and the error sound? [Winitz, 1975, p. 114]

Most moderate to severe cases of articulation disorders will be the exclusive responsibility of the speech and language pathologist. The resource teacher and the regular class teacher(s), however, can work with the clinician on mild cases. Working with the speech clinician is also necessary to help modify the reactions of other students, as well as to help the target student learn to cope with unkind reactions.

Articulation deficits are very common in students referred to the resource program. Resource teachers therefore must have more than a superficial knowledge of articulation, although other people may be responsible for the assessment and for most of the instruction. We recommend that resource teachers read the appropriate chapters in Van Riper (1972) and other books on articulation or general speech therapy.

3. *If the student's difficulty seems to center in the area of syntax and/or morphology, what specific kinds of grammatical errors does he or she make?* Many methods are available for pinpointing specific items of syntax or morphology in need of remediation. Geffner (1981) has tabulated those that use spontaneous language analyses (Table 11 – 1). We describe several of these below and also recommend the study of *Clinical Language Sampling: A Handbook for Students and Clinicians* (Barrie-Blackley, Musselwhite, and Rogister, 1978).

TABLE **11 – 1.**
Measures of spontaneous language analysis procedures.

MEASURE

Mean length of utterance (MLU)
Length-complexity index
Developmental sentence types (DST)
Linguistic analysis of speech samples (LASS)
Co-occurring and restricted structure procedure (CORS)
Developmental sentence scoring (DSS)
Tyack and Gottlesben's language analysis system
Grammatical analysis of language disability
Trantham and Pederson's Modified DSS
Case relation analysis
Language sample analysis
Assigning structural stage (ASS)

D. S. Geffner, "Assessment of Language Disorders: Linguistic and Cognitive Functions," *Topics in Language Disorders 1* (1981): 5.

Lee (1974) and Lee, Koenigsknecht, and Mulhern (1975) provide the procedures for developmental sentence analysis, a useful clinical tool for assessing this area. In this technique, a tape recording is made of a conversation between the teacher-therapist and a child, using toys or pictures to stimulate spontaneous utterances. Their transcribed utterances serve as the basis for the analysis. The analysis itself contains two parts: (1) developmental sentence types, an evaluation of incomplete sentences (presentence utterances), and (2) developmental sentence scoring, an inventory of the specific components of grammar used in forming the complete sentences.

In the first analysis, which requires interpreting one hundred utterances, the incomplete subject-verb sentences are sorted according to five categories of emerging sentences (noun, designator, descriptive item, verb, vocabulary item) and three types of constructions (one-, two-, and multiword). For example, the utterance *pretty* is interpreted as a fragmented sentence and is classified as a descriptive, one-word type of presentence. Since the child's performance is plotted on a 5 × 3 scope and sequence chart, the teacher can tell at a glance the types and variety of grammatic structures that he or she does or does not use.

TABLE 11 – 2.

Part of the developmental Sentence Scoring Chart (Revised to Emphasize the Sequence of Pronoun Development)

SCORE	INDEFINITE PRONOUNS OR NOUN MODIFIERS	PERSONAL PRONOUNS	MAIN VERBS
1	—	1st and 2nd person: I, me, my, mine, you, your(s)	—
2	—	3rd person: he, him, his, she, her, hers	—
3	—	A. Plurals: we, us, our(s), they, them, their B. these, those	—
4	—		—
5	—	Reflexives: myself, yourself, himself, herself, itself, themselves	—

Revised material from: L. Lee, R. A. Koenigsknecht, and S. T. Mulhern. *Interaction Language Development Teaching* (Evanston, Ill.: Northwestern University Press, 1975).

The second analysis also uses a chart to facilitate interpretation but requires only fifty complete sentences for analysis. In analysis, the grammar components (noun modifiers, pronouns, main and secondary verbs, negatives, conjunctions, interrogative reversals, and Wh- questions) are presented at the top of the chart, and the developmental order of each category is listed at the side. For example, in the pronoun category, the order of development is hypothesized to begin with the mastery of the first- and second-person pronouns; next comes the third-person pronouns, followed by the pronoun plurals. Table 11 – 2 is an example of part of the developmental sentence scoring chart as revised to demonstrate the sequence of pronoun development. Points are assigned and an overall mean score per sentence is computed. Reliabilities and rough norms based on a sample of 200 children between the ages of two and seven are available.

A system similar to Lee's but broader in scope is offered by Miller (1981) in *Assessing Language Production in Children: Experimental Procedures.* He has adapted the analysis-of-free-speech-samples procedure so that it can be used to measure semantic as well as syntactic and morphological qualities. He advises computing and interpreting the mean length of utterance in morphemes (MLU) in a speech sample. This value, which is an estimate of morphological ability, is the total number of morphemes that the child used divided by the total number of utterances made. The MLU is interpreted in terms of age norms presented in his book. Syntax is measured by evaluating the kinds of simple sentences the child uttered and comparing them to developmental stage norms. Semantic ability is estimated by the type-token ratio (the number of different words used divided by the total number of words used) and by classifying the words according to the kinds of meaningful relationships they represent. The type-token ratio is interpreted by comparing it to age norms. Our handling of Miller's techniques is of necessity cursory. Teachers who are interested in assessing the language of students eight years or younger will profit greatly from a careful study of his work.

These evaluation systems are particularly useful for teachers and therapists because their results demonstrate the level of grammatical development and indicate in which order the unmastered forms should be introduced in a training program. They also can determine the success or failure of any intervention program that might be proposed and implemented. Their major shortcoming is that considerable study and training is necessary to use them well. The individual who plans to assess and remediate spoken grammar and syntax will find it worthwhile to learn techniques based upon the analysis of spontaneous language samples.

However the analysis of forms is made, differentiation should be made between those that have not yet appeared and those that are of a nonstandard nature. These distinctions must be checked by a clinician who is experienced and trained in language development. Further, some "errors" are good ones; they are to be expected during the course of normal language development. For example, the use of *runned* for *ran* may indicate an appropriate sequence of language development that should be left alone. Only relevant knowledge about other aspects of a student's language development will enable the clinician to make the decision about whether instruction is necessary.

4. *If the student's language problems relate to vocabulary, which words should he or she be taught to understand and use appropriately?* Unlike the other areas of language, we know of no completely satisfactory procedures or tests that can inventory vocabulary ability. Tests are available, but their content is not comprehensive; results cannot be used to prepare individualized remedial programs. There are, however, several informal ways to determine a body of words that a child should have mastered by a given age.

The most practical approach is to analyze the school setting and curricula in order to identify the words and concepts that are presented and required at each grade level. For example, after interviewing the teacher, looking at the curriculum guides, and reviewing the classroom materials, the resource teacher might conclude that the kindergarten teachers expect their students to learn the basic colors, farm animals, simple geometric forms, the names of other students, letters, and numbers. The resource teacher also should ascertain the vocabulary used by the regular teacher when giving instructions. Criterion-referenced tests or checklists that reflect the classroom's vocabulary requirements could be prepared and administered to referred students. The resource teacher can use the resulting information to identify the precise words and topics that need to be taught.

A second approach is to use the Wepman and Hass (1969) spoken word list or a similar compilation. This list is a collection of words that children use in their daily speech. The words are grouped by age (five through seven) and by parts of speech. The list also gives a frequency count for each word. The most commonly used nouns, verbs, adjectives, and pronouns used at each age also are provided. The resource teacher can assess the student's mastery of these words and design a specific vocabulary development program based on the words that the student does not know or use.

5. *Does the student understand the uses of oral language in the school setting?* Individual interviews and role playing can be used to find out how well a student interprets the expected uses of oral language in the classroom setting. These uses may be social as well as academic. The language of friendship for behavior-disordered students or the language of asking for help for learning-disabled students have their own content and form. It is primarily their use that will be of interest to the resource teacher.

DEVELOPING INSTRUCTIONAL PROCEDURES

Students with language problems tend to be: (1) completely nonverbal; (2) significantly delayed in language development; or (3) deficient only in one or two aspects of language, such as phonology, syntax, semantics, or morphology. Having used assessment procedures to determine the general pattern to which a particular student conforms, the resource teacher can select an appropriate remedial or developmental program or strategy.

Developing Language in Nonverbal Students

Students who have developed little or no speech and language even though they have had ample opportunity to do so are seriously handicapped. They may be mentally retarded, deaf, or language disordered. These students probably will profit from a highly structured, systematic, and individualized language development program. Many programs and teaching systems have been designed for use specifically with nonverbal children; programmed conditioning for language (Gray and Ryan, 1973) and the association method (McGinnis, 1963) are two examples.

The programmed conditioning for language, called the Monterey Program, focuses on teaching oral grammar forms, such as nouns, pronouns, verbs, negatives, conjunctions, adjectives, prepositions, and adverbs. The curriculum itself is divided into three parts, each of which contains several instructional programs. The first part, the core curriculum, is the most essential for nonverbal students to master because it includes many fundamental skills, such as naming nouns and using correctly forms such as *is*, "is verbing," basic pronouns and prepositions, and present tense nouns. Behavioral (programmed conditioning) principles are used extensively in teaching this curriculum. This curriculum also gives the teacher: (1) a test to help decide which training programs the student should be taught and (2) a series of criterion tests that can serve as premeasures and postmeasures for each program.

·The results of a few uncontrolled studies apparently support the use of the program, but the authors themselves suggest that these results should be considered cautiously. The program looks promising, and hopefully conclusive research will be forthcoming. To use programmed conditioning for language well, the resource teacher should have a basic understanding of linguistic development and some specific training. Individuals who expect to teach oral language to nonverbal children should become familiar with this system.

The association method's goal is to enable students with severe language problems to enter regular schools at as near their appropriate age and grade level as possible. Therefore, academic subjects are an integral part of the program, along with speech and language skills. To achieve this goal, a student begins by learning to say individual sounds and to associate them with the appropriate written letter-symbol. Next, he or she is taught to combine sounds into words and words into sentences of increasing syntactic complexity. Examining the seven steps used for teaching nouns reveals the association method's emphasis on repetition, retention, and recall. The seven steps for teaching nouns are:

1. To produce in sequence from the written form the sounds composing a noun.
2. To match the picture of the object represented by the word to the written form of the word.

3.   To copy the word and to articulate each sound as he/she writes the letter(s) for it.
4.   To repeat the word aloud after watching the teacher say it and to match the object or picture to the written form of the word.
5.   To say the name of the object from memory.
6.   To write the word for the object from memory, articulating each sound as he/she writes the letter(s) for it.
7.   To repeat the word spoken into his/her ear and to match the picture to the written form of the word. [McGinnis, Kleffner, and Goldstein, 1956, p. 242]

Classes are composed of six or seven students, one teacher, and an aide. The teacher handles both the academic and the language training. The aide may be a regular employee, a student teacher, or a parent. McGinnis suggests that parents should work under the teacher's direction and conduct some of the lessons. The physical arrangement of the room should be similar to a normal classroom.

In addition to these approaches, resource teachers should be familiar with the works of Fitzgerald (1966) and Pugh (1947), who also have designed procedures for teaching language to children with little or no oral communication ability. Generally, these and similar programs are implemented on an individual-planned basis in settings other than the regular classroom (the speech room, the resource room, or a special class).

Stimulating Language in Language-Delayed Students

Unlike the systems that are highly individualized and usually used with nonverbal students, the systems discussed here are designed for students who have some degree of language ability but who appear to be generally depressed in most or all aspects of language. These students need broad-based, general, language instruction.

The recommended teaching systems should be used with groups rather than with individuals and originally were conceived of as stimulation programs for the mildly mentally retarded, socioeconomically deprived, and language delayed. These programs usually are implemented in classrooms by regular or special education teachers; they also are used frequently by resource teachers and speech therapists. Three popular programs are the Peabody Language Development Kits (PLDK), the DISTAR Language Program, and the Learning Staircase.

There are actually four Peabody kits: a primary version (Dunn, Horton, and Smith, 1981), level 1 (Dunn, Smith, and Dunn, 1981), level 2 (Dunn, Dunn, and Smith, 1981), and level 3 (Dunn, Smith, and Smith, 1982). These kits were prepared to stimulate spoken language and increase verbal intelligence, and thereby to affect school achievement positively. Peabody's rationale is based on certain aspects of Osgood's and Guilford's models; the program therefore attempts to teach many visual-motor skills in addition to language. The program, which is divided into four kits, is used best with children whose mental ages range from three to nine-and-a-half-years. The lessons become increasingly more conceptual; by the seven-and-a-half-year age level, concept formation and creativity are stressed predominately.

The DISTAR Language Program (Englemann and Osborn, 1970) is highly structured; its lessons must be presented in a prearranged order and prescribed manner. It also emphasizes the use of reinforcement techniques. Some training in how to administer it therefore is desirable. DISTAR's basic assumption is that language rules can be externally imposed through drill. The authors assert that their content selection reflects the linguistic demands or criteria actually existing in the schools; they do not try to justify the lessons in terms of the concepts of Osgood, Guilford, and Chomsky. DISTAR is appropriate for preschool and elementary-aged students and usually is presented daily in thirty-minute sessions to small groups.

Resource teachers needing a general language program for students who are developmentally between the ages of one-and-a-half and seven will find *Learning Staircase* (Coughran and Goff, 1976) suitable. This curriculum is designed primarily for teaching oral language and oral language-related abilities, though some of its lessons deal with body image and fine motor skills as well. *Learning Staircase* is a set of materials including a teacher's manual, instructional modules (568 activity cards), an assessment instrument, a parental report form, and record-keeping materials. As yet, no research has been done testing the effectiveness of the program; regardless, it is potentially useful and worthy of the resource teacher's consideration.

Remediating Specific Problem Areas

Often teachers, especially teachers of young students, encounter students whose difficulties seem to center in only one area, such as articulation, grammar, or vocabulary. These students need their specific errors noted and an individualized remediation program planned for them. The resource teacher will find that using applied behavioral analysis has many advantages in remediating these specific language problems. This technique easily applies to teaching highly defined elements relating to articulation, grammar, and/or vocabulary. McReynold's (1974) monograph, *Developing Systematic Procedures for Training Children's Language*, is useful for resource teachers interested in this approach. Other approaches are discussed below.

If the difficulty is *articulation* and if it is relatively mild, the resource teacher might encourage the regular teacher to implement in class a speech improvement program similar to that suggested by Scott and Thompson (1951). These authors believe that most speech problems can be easily corrected by regular class teachers using specified drills according to a few simple recommended principles. They provide a simple method for determining the sounds that need correction by analyzing how the student says the numbers one through twelve and the basic colors. Another source for training stories and lessons for correcting articulation errors is Nemoy and Davis's book (1954). Most school districts have prepared curricula dealing with speech improvement; and, if available, resource teachers should study and adapt these for use in the resource program. Students who do not respond fairly quickly to such instruction should be referred to a person in the schools (usually a speech therapist) with experience in treating articulation defects.

Problems in *syntax* usually are manifested by inappropriate word order, omission of articles, difficulty with verb tenses, failure to generalize rules governing plurality of nouns, and subject-verb disagreements. In their book, *Effective Intervention with the Language Impaired Child,* Cole and Cole (1981) recommend many specific training activities to correct each of these problems. Teachers who prefer a systematic, structured approach to developing syntax are referred to the Fokes Sentence Builder (1976). This kit consists of two hundred picture cards divided into five boxes labeled "Who," "What," "Is Doing," "Which," and "Where"; an apparatus on which sentences are constructed by placing the picture cards in meaningful sequence; forty-five sentence markers; fifteen sentence inserts; one question-mark card; and a teacher's guide. "Who" cards depict people and occupations; "What" cards, animals and objects; "Is Doing" cards, human figures involved in actions of various kinds; "Which" cards, adjectives; and "Where" cards have an X or an arrow on them to indicate a particular position or location. The use of these cards gives the student ample practice in forming differing kinds of sentences and in mastering both the syntactic and morphological aspects of the language. The program is appealing to teachers, who usually can use it without much difficulty.

For students with mild *semantics* problems, the resource teacher may supplement their regular classroom curricula with special vocabulary building and word classification activities. Ample material for these activities can be found in many trade books. For example, many beginning picture and story books that deal with word meanings and word history are valuable, especially with very young students. For older students, a more direct, formal approach is possible; books such as *Words and What They Do to You* (Minteer, 1953) can be employed. This useful book deals with the differences between surface and deep structure and with cultural relativity. Students with more severe semantics problems may profit from one of the Piaget-based programs, such as Lavatelli (1973), that emphasizes concept formation and categorization ability. Materials designed for deaf children are also useful, such as the programmed text, *The Language of Classification: Animals* (Rush, 1975).

The general language programs mentioned in the previous section can be studied to locate additional activities emphasizing word, phrase, or story meaning. They are rich sources of suitable activities. For example, the divergent thinking word games of the Level III Peabody Language Development Kits are designed to teach various semantic aspects of language.

The resource teacher who wants an unusually clear explanation of the role of semantics in teaching academic subjects should read the works of Frank Smith (1971, 1973, 1975). Give special attention to the chapter "The Identification of Meaning" (1971, pp. 185–211) and to his book *Comprehension and Learning* (1975).

We know of no general language programs for postelementary students. Many of the techniques for language improvement or correction are found in language arts materials. The National Council of Teachers of English has an extensive collection of materials that may be ordered for the secondary level. If the problems of secondary-age students are severe, however, they will benefit from programs that are commensurate with their developmental levels of language as long as the content is not too discrepant from their interests.

We end this chapter by reproducing Weiss and Lillywhite's "101 Ways to Help the Child Learn to Talk" (1981, pp. 146–171). In their book, each of the 101 ways is discussed in detail; the rationale as to why each way is important is explained carefully; and an abundance of related instructional activities is presented. Attending to their list would go a long way toward making a language resource program both a pleasant and a rewarding experience for a student.

1. Spend more time with the child who is not talking or who is talking very little
2. Be a good model
3. Make certain that speech and language learning are fun
4. Make certain that the communicative activities are rewarding
5. Make certain that the communicative activities are appropriate
6. Make certain that the communicative activities are meaningful
7. Provide the child with many experiences in listening
8. Verbally bombard the child
9. Discourage others from talking for the child
10. Provide a need to talk
11. Do much labeling
12. Determine an effective reward system
13. Play games that stress basic, key words
14. Tell stories to the child
15. Read aloud to the child
16. Give the child an old catalog or some other picture book to play with
17. Do narrative or parallel talking
18. Do self-talking
19. Do interrogative talking
20. Start where the child is
21. Start early
22. Use language that the child is likely to understand
23. Make certain that the child has adequate attending behavior
24. Accompany your words with gestures
25. Teach specific physical gestures
26. Teach tonal gestures
27. Teach understanding by being consistent
28. Become familiar with normal communication development
29. Carefully plan each activity
30. Consult periodically with a speech-language pathologist
31. Eliminate contributing problems
32. Set aside at least one 10-minute talking time each day
33. Plan ways the child can use words meaningfully
34. Avoid criticizing imperfection
35. Do not ask too much talking of the child
36. Limit baby talk to the first 9 months
37. Speak clearly
38. Speak slowly

39. Encourage the child to look at you when you are talking
40. Provide the child with a compatible, communicating playmate
41. Break up longer words into syllables, if you must use them at all
42. Encourage the child to imitate your language
43. Establish realistic, short-term goals
44. Teach language according to the developmental hierarchy
45. Teach articulation according to the developmental hierarchy
46. Improve the quality of your interaction with the child
47. Provide a favorable emotional atmosphere
48. Do not interrupt vocal play, jargon, or self-communication
49. Provide a wide range of experiences
50. Vary your play activities as needed
51. Chart progress daily
52. Occasionally use a tape recorder
53. Occasionally use a mirror
54. Teach receptive language
55. Remember the M's; maturation, motivation, and mother
56. Be certain the child understands what is expected
57. Do not try to teach too much at once
58. Play "say it right" games
59. Sing to and with the child
60. Teach the child nursery rhymes
61. Name objects within the home
62. Play sentence completion games
63. Teach the child to categorize
64. Teach speech through differential reinforcement
65. Practice good timing
66. Identify objects by sound
67. Find pictures to accompany the words in a basic vocabulary list
68. Practice intraoral awareness exercises
69. Teach sentences
70. Make the child feel part of what is going on
71. Become more animated when talking
72. Supply the child with appropriate words as the need arises
73. Correct grammatical errors by rephrasing
74. Expand the child's responses
75. Provide opportunities for the child to interact with adult males
76. Refrain from putting your child on exhibition
77. Provide a good setting for daily lessons
78. Have the child tell you stories
79. Encourage the child to make rhymes
80. Take time to listen
81. Do finger plays
82. Choose appropriate materials
83. Play rhythm games
84. Engage the child in voice gymnastics
85. Know when to go to a new task
86. Select a variety of games

87. Use the objects that you are teaching
88. Provide a relaxed learning environment
89. Do role-playing
90. Consider taking courses or workshops
91. Encourage good vocal hygiene
92. Play "What's in the bag"
93. Provide everyday experiences
94. Avoid labeling a child a stutterer
95. Build a scrapbook
96. Help the child analyze phonemes
97. Teach conjunctions
98. Use pictures and objects to teach sequence
99. Explain new words
100. Discuss events
101. Counsel parents and other adults

12

Classroom Behavior

Today, classroom teachers are expected to cope with the vast majority of students' behavior problems. In most cases, the principal and/or the counselor are the only support available. For example, students who misbehave usually are sent to the principal or vice-principal for disciplinary action. The administrators might punish the students, send a note home to their parents, and/or suspend them from school. The counselor might work with some who are very withdrawn, socially rejected by their peers, or chronic discipline problems. If a student's problems are severe and persistent, the teacher might refer him or her to be tested as a possible candidate for special education — to be diagnosed as emotionally disturbed or behaviorally disordered. The students so identified usually are placed in special classes or remain in the regular classroom and receive resource support.

Identifying and managing the situational variables that might be associated with or contribute to perceived classroom behavior receives little attention. Such matters as the referring teacher's skill in coping with disruptive behaviors, the social climate of the classrooms, the demands of the curricula, the student's relationship with peers, the parents' support for the educational program, and even the interactive nature of all of these variables must be considered if a comprehensive approach to dealing with unacceptable classroom behaviors is to be tried. Often changes in situational aspects of behavior will ameliorate or at least minimize a student's problem, whether it is perceived or real.

Since resource teachers are expected to assess the students in the regular classrooms and to consult with both parents and teachers, they are in a unique position to observe, document, and deal effectively with these situational variables. Therefore, regardless of the type of resource model implemented, teachers assigned to such programs must be able to prepare instructional programs that consider the affective as well as the academic needs of referred students. Techniques for assessing the behaviors of students in regular classrooms, for undertaking supplemental individual analyses, and for developing strategies to deal with behavior problems are discussed in this chapter.

ANALYSIS OF THE LEARNER IN THE CLASSROOM

More than any other aspect of school experience, the criteria for appropriate classroom behaviors tend to be idiosyncratic to a given teacher and classroom. All teachers vary in their expectations for and tolerance of students relative to attention, motivation, conduct, study skills, and independent work habits. Classrooms also differ in their organization, climate, amount of student movement permitted, classroom rules, and structure. In addition, all learners react differently to the requirements of and interactions among teachers, peers, classrooms, and curricula. Because one important goal of the resource teacher is to maintain students in the regular classrooms, careful attention must be directed toward managing their behavior in these settings. To accomplish this, resource teachers must first obtain valid information about a referred student's classroom behavior and interactions. Some of the data required are discussed below.

1. *What is the school district's policy regarding discipline of students?* Most school districts have prepared a written document that spells out in some detail the policies and procedures regarding discipline of its students. In many cases, the document has been prepared by administrators, teachers, parents, and student representatives. Legal counsel is often sought to ensure that the practices of the district conform to federal and state mandates, as well as recent court decisions. If a district does not have such a document, it should. In fact, the district may be out of compliance with federal and individual state mandates if such a document does not exist. Also, it simply makes good sense for teachers, administrators, parents, and students to have their rights and responsibilities spelled out clearly and in writing.

In certain cases, students who have been labeled as handicapped may be treated under a separate special education discipline policy. Again, as in the case of nonhandicapped students, federal and state laws, as well as court rulings, have recently more clearly defined the rights of special populations in regard to discipline. For example, if a special education student's behavior problem is related to the handicapping condition, he or she may in some instances not be eligible for long-term suspension or even short-term supervision as a form of discipline.

As noted in Chapter 4 of this book, policies regarding the education of the handicapped are undergoing changes almost daily. New court decisions are being handed down and then challenged; repeal of existing legislation is being considered; the federal role in education is being diminished. Consequently, resource teachers must be ever attentive to policies regarding discipline.

2. What are the school practices regarding students who are inattentive, withdrawn, or poorly socialized? District and individual school policies regarding behavior are primarily directed toward aggressive or conduct-problem students. Our experience is that it is indeed rare for policies to be defined for students with behavior problems that are not disruptive to the day-to-day functioning of the schools. Nevertheless, students who are withdrawn, truant or excessively absent, friendless, or chronically sad and unhappy are equally in need of special attention. As is the case with disruptive students, teachers need to determine what services are available in their schools for these individuals, how to refer appropriate students for such services, and how to evaluate the availability of other services in the community, such as mental health and community centers and church groups. Parental or guardian approval for referring students for special help is in most cases necessary and always recommended. In addition, resource teachers need to be competent in the teaching of behaviors that minimize or lessen such problems.

3. What is the referred student's previous record regarding behavior? The school's cumulative records will show if the student has a history of long-term behavioral problems. Of special interest would be documented instances of truancy, suspensions, special counseling, poor grades in classroom behavior, and/or fighting. If the records indicate that the behavior of the referred student has not been a problem up to this time, the resource teacher should consider that the current problem may be situational; that is, it may be due to the student's inability to cope successfully with some current difficulties in the home, with the personality and demands of the regular classroom teachers, and/or with peer relationships.

4. What is the precise nature of the student's classroom behavior as noted by the referring teachers? In their referrals, many teachers describe students in vague, general terms, such as "he doesn't behave," or "she doesn't do her work." The resource teacher should request more specific information to determine precisely what misbehaviors are occurring: talking out (when?), fighting (with whom?), disrespectful (to whom?). If the classroom teachers have many complaints about the student, the resource person should help the teachers isolate and identify the one or two most bothersome behaviors. By pinpointing the more troublesome behaviors, teachers can reduce the problems to a manageable number for making an initial intervention. For example, if the most troublesome behavior appears to be a student's lack of attention, the teachers may want to deal with that problem before moving on to other difficulties.

5. *Is the reason for referral confirmed by the resource teacher's direct observation?* By observing the student several times in regular classrooms, the resource teacher may notice problems that the referring teachers did not detect, fail to see evidence of the behavior that precipitated the referral, or confirm the teacher's observation. Through direct observation, the resource teacher might also determine factors that seem to precipitate the referral behavior — for example, the curriculum demands are too great for the student's ability or functioning level, or the referred learner is no worse than the rest of the class. Resource teachers must employ considerable tact when dealing with teachers whom they think are wrong in their perceptions of the student and their problems.

6. *What is the general classroom climate?* The resource teacher should note such matters as the classroom teacher's apparent comfortableness in working with students, the perceived attitudes of the students toward teachers and the curricula, and the students' seeming relationship to one another. In some classes, the interactions among individuals may appear to be hostile, nonsupportive, or tinged with fear. Where this is the case, the atmosphere is not conducive to learning, and the resource teacher may need to plan intervention strategies.

7. *How are the classrooms organized?* The resource teacher should learn how the classrooms are structured. Some classrooms appear highly organized; others appear to be minimally so or even chaotic. The appearance of very little structure (the presence of excessive noise and movement) does not always indicate that the teacher has lost control of the class, however. Instead, some teachers may be encouraging self-directed student work or may have a high tolerance or even a propensity to such a classroom climate. Knowing how the classroom is organized and run is necessary when planning a program for a referred student in that setting. With older students who attend several classrooms per day, it is helpful to compare the organization of classrooms where the student is experiencing no difficulty to those where she or he is experiencing considerable difficulty.

8. *What are the classroom rules for behavior?* In most classes, teachers and students together have developed a few basic rules of behavior. The resource teacher should know these rules and make sure that the referred student also understands them. The resource teacher must know if the incidents that precipitated the referral (fighting or talking out, for example) were covered in the rules. Of course, some reasons that prompt teachers to refer a student will not be noted in the rules. For example, it would be ludicrous for teachers to have a rule forbidding withdrawn behavior.

The resource teacher must determine the minimum criteria that teachers will accept as adequate performance. Are the rules always to be followed? Are students always expected to remain in their seats unless permission is granted for them to leave? Must the students always raise their hands before talking out?

Resource teachers should be very attentive to the ethical aspects of rules. For example, if a teacher has rules that are unrealistic, demand total compliance, or violate legal rights, the resource teacher should consider whether she or he should help enforce these standards. In this case, the resource teacher should try to change the teacher's attitude toward certain rules. If this fails, the resource teacher may have to refuse to help enforce such questionable rules of behavior. Even if the resource teacher cannot sanction certain rules, she or he should continue to give other kinds of resource help to the referring teacher. Resource teachers should never feel that they are obligated to help an administrator or teacher accomplish any task that violates their ethics.

9. *Are the consequences of misbehavior and good behavior specified?* Requiring students to conform to behaviors without specifying either why they should or what the consequences of noncompliance are is a poor practice that should be avoided. Consequently resource teachers should know if the referred students understand why they should comply with the rules. In addition, they should learn exactly how the referring teachers deal with students who do and do not comply with classroom rules. Particularly they should know if the teachers have set any rewards for adhering to rules, a practice that some teachers regrettably do not establish. If the students do not understand the rationale behind the rules and do not think that there is any reason for complying with them, then the referring teacher probably will not be able to enforce them to any appreciable degree.

10. *In the past, how have the teachers dealt with the classroom behavior of a referred student?* Not only is it necessary to find out what methods have not worked but also the methods that *have* worked, either with a referred student or with any other students with similar problems. Especially in dealing with misbehavior, it is easy to overlook positive aspects of behavior management as a place to start program development. We need to find out, then, what does work as well as what does not work in the particular situation.

The resource teacher will want to find out from previous teachers the methods of behavior management that have worked with the student. Students' behaviors are often the same from teacher to teacher, but the methods of successful behavior management may not have been passed on to the next teacher(s).

11. *What are the subgroup dynamics within the classroom?* Some referred students may be members of a subgroup of students who continually cause problems for teachers and administrators. Other students may be disliked or feared by their peers. The resource teacher should understand the student's relationships with other students before developing an educational plan.

12. *What is the student's physical location in the classroom?* Some referred students may be seated as far away from teachers as possible, perhaps an indication of teacher rejection. Others may be in high traffic areas or placed close to other stu-

dents who also demonstrate poor classroom behavior. Moving a student to another area of the room may partially diminish some of the negative behaviors. A floor plan of the room, with the student's location noted, will be helpful at conferences. The map should also note any distractors available to the student. A sample of such a map is shown in Figure 12–1.

13. *What is the student's behavior during direct instruction?* The resource teacher should observe the student while teachers are presenting a lesson. In this manner, he or she can gather data on whether the student understands what the teacher is saying, asks questions, daydreams, acts out, and/or is disruptive. One quick way to observe some of these behaviors is to note what the student does when the teacher gives the class a specific direction. For example, if the teacher tells the students to open their books to page 24, the referred student may do so immediately or may observe what others are doing and follow their lead. In this instance, he or she may not be paying attention or may not understand the directions.

14. *What is the student's behavior during independent study and work?* Many students behave admirably when the teacher is involved in direct instruction with them. These same students, however, may become disruptive or inattentive when

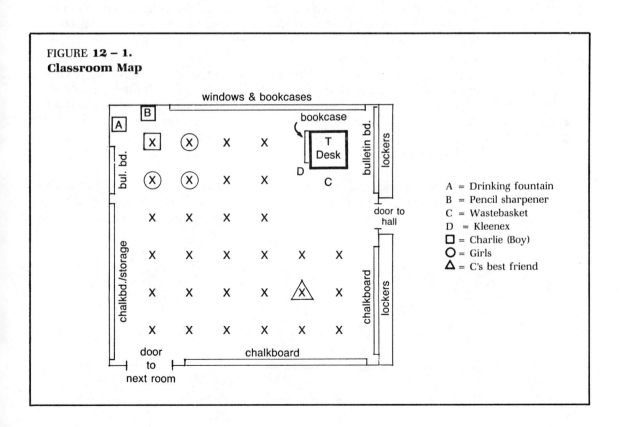

FIGURE **12 – 1.**
Classroom Map

they are required to do independent study or work. The assignment may be too difficult or boring, or the students may not have sufficient self-control to work unsupervised. Comparing his or her behavior during both direct instruction and independent work might yield some information that would be helpful in preparing the instructional program.

For observation during instruction and work sessions, we recommend the use of a time-on-task (TOT) format adapted by V. Brown (undated b) from Balla (1967). It is an open system of descriptive observation that is easy to learn to use, and it provides a way to restate behavior that would otherwise be possible only through the use of video equipment. Traditional TOT systems, such as that of Hall (1974), yield information such as the following:

1. Percentage of time on task
2. Percentage of time off task
3. Ratio of on-task to off-task behaviors

The Brown-Balla system provides the information shown above and also allows for the description of:

4. Patterns of work: work evenly paced over the time allocation; sporadically paced over the time allocation; initially on task but progressively off task; on task when time allocation nears the end; rarely on task; and/or on task at teacher or other request
5. Behaviors that are incompatible with working — going to the wastebasket, daydreaming, or talking (these are the incompatible behaviors that must be accounted for when trying to increase the student's attention to the task)
6. The percentages of time spent in each off-task activity
7. What specifically seems to be distracting to the student — peers, self, objects, or atmosphere

Continuous recording of what the student does during a particular work or class time period is written by an observer (the resource teacher, usually) on paper divided into four columns, with each section representing fifteen seconds or one minute for each line:

Curriculum input or teacher directions and/or expectations:

	15'	15'	15'	15'
1.				
2.				
3.				

Any coding system that the teacher can read back in order to restate the behavior (much as in shorthand) can be used. Brown, for example, uses the following:

T = teacher

S = student

P = peers

O = objects

W = walks

OT = on task

$\dfrac{T}{S}$ = teacher/student interaction

$\dfrac{S}{P}$ = student/peer interaction

T – = negative teacher attention

T + = positive teacher attention

——▶ = code continues

—⋀— = change in code

Other categories are invented as needed. The lines and codes are combined to provide the behavioral description, as in the five-minute minirecord shown in Figure 12–2. This record shows that within a five-minute period, Gary appeared to be on task for 40 percent of the time. The time was sporadic. The rest of the time was spent in a teacher interaction about a noise he was making; pencil sharpening; going

---

FIGURE **12 – 2.**
Time on Task for Gary

Curriculum input or teacher directions and/or expectations: Complete spelling assignment alone at own desk. 20 minutes allocated.

	15 sec.	15 sec.	15 sec.	15 sec.
1.		T– (noise)	OT	
2.		W / PS		
3.	OT	P (David)		Waste basket
4.		OT		S / P (Jim)
5.		day / div ... OT	S / P (Sally)	

to the wastebasket; daydreaming (apparently); and interacting with peers. The interpretation of this record is made in conjunction with other information obtained through interviews or through subsequent observations in the same or in different settings.

This type of TOT system is used to generate hypotheses about the student's work patterns; to confirm or disconfirm statements made about the student's behavior in the classroom; and to find out what *does* engage his or her attention. Observer judgment is required, and some of these judgments cannot be verified, even with interobserver reliability. For example, it is difficult to distinguish between daydreaming and task concentration. Nevertheless, this kind of data base is helpful to the resource teacher because it allows an ongoing record of *all* behavior and not just what the resource teacher is looking for. This characteristic is important when depersonalizing observations away from the teacher.

15. *What does the referred student appear to like to do in the classroom?* Almost all learners have something that they enjoy doing in school — an academic task (arithmetic or handwriting, for example), an administrative activity (helping the teacher hand out papers), a housekeeping chore (sharpening pencils), or working with others on a project. The resource teacher should discover what the student likes, as it may be helpful in preparing a workable and practical educational plan.

16. *How does the student's behavior compare with that of classroom peers?* We have noted several times that a student's behavior might not be as different from that of peers as we initially are led to believe. It is important, then, to collect data about how the student's behavior compares with that of peers. *Modal* information deals with which behaviors are most common among students or which are characteristic of most students. We may want to know the mean, or *average*, behavior in the classroom — for example, how many talkouts a student actually commits during a period of time. Usually, however, we will want to know the *range* of behavior tolerated or reinforced by the teacher. It may be the case that the student's behavior is well within the range, but other factors cause this student to be singled out for attention. For example, the student may engage in multiple negative behaviors, or the student may simply be nearer to the teacher than others are. Whichever comparison is made, it is important to note how the student's behavior(s) compares with those of classmates.

By now, the resource teacher should have a good idea of the student's problems in the regular classroom. He or she also should have gathered a great deal of information regarding the practices of the classroom teacher relative to this particular student as well as to the class as a whole. He or she now may want to undertake a more specific individual analysis of the referred student's behavioral problems. Hopefully, most resource teachers will feel they have enough information about a student after analyzing the learner in the regular classroom and can begin to plan and implement an educational plan without delay.

SUPPLEMENTAL INDIVIDUAL ANALYSIS

This section discusses seven assessment techniques that provide information on various aspects of classroom behavior. For the most part, these assessment techniques can be administered in the regular classroom and/or account for situational variables in that setting. Therefore, they are particularly useful in a resource program operation. The techniques discussed are: (1) ecological assessment, (2) teacher-devised checklists, (3) sociometrics, (4) the *Behavior Rating Profile*, (5) teacher-student interaction analysis, (6) baseline data, and (7) self-assessment.

Ecological Assessment

Ecological assessment is a way of looking at an individual that considers the many environments in which he or she operates, as well as his or her interactions in those various environments. The major environments studied in most ecological assessments are the school, home, community, and peer interactions. We suggest that resource teachers limit their investigations to environments existing within the school: the regular classrooms, the resource room, the gym, and the music room, for example. Comprehensive ecological assessments of environments outside the school are too time-consuming and should be done by the school psychologist, social worker, or other professional persons.

The concept of in-school ecological assessment is relevant to the resource teacher. First, it gives the teacher the opportunity to observe a referred student in several environments. This analysis may yield significant information regarding the pervasiveness of the student's behavior problems. For example, a student may present or experience problems in only one environment in the school, such as a regular classroom, and not in other settings, such as the gym, the playground, the lunchroom, the resource room, and the music room.

Ecological assessment also yields information on both the positive and negative factors in the student's environment. Resource teachers may isolate particular aspects that appear to facilitate appropriate behavior (students are allowed movement, can work with their peers, appear to enjoy what they are doing, have a warm relationship with the teacher in charge, attend a highly structured class), or that appear to thwart appropriate behavior (students are required to remain seated for extended periods of time, are not allowed to interact with peers, do not act as if they enjoy doing specific tasks, appear to dislike the teacher, misbehave only in loosely structured environments).

Ecological assessment relates directly to situational variables and to the student's interactions with these variables in different environments. The resource teacher must evaluate the student, especially if he or she is evidencing any type of behavior problem, in different environments in the school and make adjustments in the environments in which the student is having difficulty, adjustments with the student, or adjustments in both.

Laten and Katz (1975) have developed a structure for undertaking an ecological assessment. They divide this technique into five phases:

1. Referral.
   A. Individuals within the student's environment are acquainted with ecological assessment and their support is enlisted.
   B. Information is gathered from the specific environment from which the pupil is referred.
   C. Information is gathered from other environments that support the referral.
   D. Information is gathered from other environments that do not support the referral.
2. Expectations.
   A. Information is gathered about the expectations of the environments in which the learner is having problems.
   B. Information is gathered about the expectations of the environments in which the student is not having problems.
3. Behavioral Descriptions.
   A. Data is collected on the interactions and skills of the people involved in the environments in which the student is having problems.
   B. Data is collected on the interactions and skills of the people involved in the environments in which the student is not having problems.
   C. An assessment of the skills needed by the student in specific environments is undertaken.
4. Data is summarized.
5. Reasonable expectations are set for the student, for teachers in the referring and supporting environments, and for the resource teacher.

The ecological map in Figure 12–3 illustrates this assessment technique. Phyllis has been referred for disrespectful behavior toward the regular classroom teacher. On completion of the ecological assessment, it is apparent that Phyllis demonstrates this problem in only one school environment: the regular classroom. A broken line in the ecological map indicates that the problem exists in the regular classroom. Unbroken lines in the map indicate no problems in the other environments. By gathering information as noted in phases 1, 2, and 3 of the ecological assessment, the resource teacher also has determined that Phyllis cannot perform many of the teacher's expectations in the regular classroom. She does, however, experience success in the other school environments where the expectations are more realistic for her ability, skills, and interests. The plan of action, phase 5, has been to lower the referring teacher's requirements for Phyllis in the regular classroom and, through resource support, to strengthen Phyllis' skills in specific areas.

The data collected will be more detailed and complex than in this simplified hypothetical example. A few attempts at this process by the resource teacher will quickly illustrate this point. The resource teacher should follow the specific rules

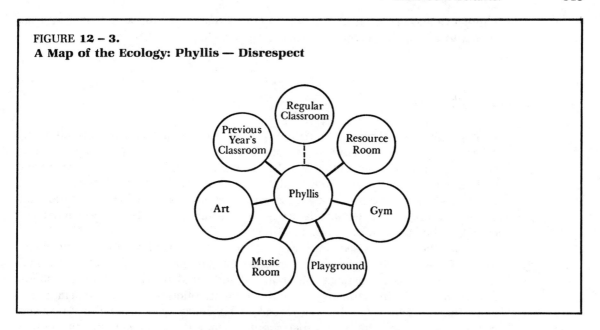

FIGURE 12 – 3.
A Map of the Ecology: Phyllis — Disrespect

listed by Wright (1967). From his list, we mention several that are especially critical for the resource teacher to employ:

1. The resource teacher should focus on both the student and the environment during data gathering.
2. The teacher should report on these two variables in as much detail as possible.
3. The resource teacher should objectively record data and avoid making personal interpretations of the information.
4. Whenever possible, the information should be stated positively rather than negatively; for example, the statement "Phyllis can attend to an academic task for a short period" is better than "Phyllis doesn't attend to an academic task for very long."
5. The resource teacher should try to be as specific as possible in describing the student and the environments.

It may appear on first inspection that an ecological assessment would be too time-consuming to consider. This is not true. As noted throughout this book, we have stressed the importance, indeed necessity, of having resource teachers always clearly understand the practices and dynamics operating in regular classrooms. Certainly they cannot effectively consult with regular classroom teachers unless they have this understanding. Teachers will find that after a few trials, an ecological assessment is indeed an efficient methodology.

Readers who are interested in undertaking an ecological assessment should consult the works of Baker and Wright (1955); Wright (1967); Marjoribanks (1972);

Randhawa and Lewis (1973); Freedman (1974); and Laten and Katz (1975). We particularly recommend Laten and Katz.

Teacher-Made Checklists

Perhaps the easiest, most straightforward, and efficient technique for obtaining information about students' classroom behaviors is the use of teacher-devised checklists. After becoming familiar with the literature on behavior management and with the problems most often exhibited by students in their schools, resource teachers should develop their own assessment checklists. After observing the pupil in the classroom, the regular classroom teacher and/or the resource teacher can complete the checklist on referred students.

Many teacher-devised checklists overlook some critical variables. Some checklists note only the obvious and most troublesome (to some teachers) behaviors. Such matters as profane language, fighting, defiance, and poor attention are almost always included. Unfortunately, they pay little attention to equally important variables such as withdrawn behavior, teacher behaviors, peer behaviors, and classroom climate. The resource teacher should include these items in any checklist.

Some resource teachers, with the support of the building principal, have helped regular classroom teachers develop useful behavior checklists. This excellent practice should be attempted by all resource teachers. To devise a checklist, a group of teachers list the problems they most frequently encounter in dealing with their students' behavior. The resource teacher should structure the development of such a list by making sure that all important variables that assess classroom behavior are included. Generally the checklist should cover at least three categories of behavior: (1) student behaviors, (2) teacher-student interactions, and (3) student-student interactions.

The number of specific behaviors that can be itemized under these three categories is almost infinite. As a result, unless the resource teacher is very careful, the checklist might be so long that it would take hours to complete. Most checklists should be limited to as few questions as possible. Once the problem in a specific category has been determined, a more in-depth probing can be made of that area. It is too inefficient, tedious, and time-consuming to go through a checklist and note a pupil's behavior on variables that have little relevance to the major problem.

One behavior checklist is included here (see Table 12 – 1). This checklist was developed for a middle or junior high school. It includes building-related, schedule-related, material-related, classroom-related, and task-related behaviors. The behaviors are stated in a positive fashion — for example, "has pass when in hall" instead of "does not have pass when in hall" — and the behaviors evaluated relate to many separate ecological or environmental factors. We do not necessarily recommend that this specific checklist be used by teachers. It is offered as a guide to follow in developing a checklist relevant to a particular school and age group.

TABLE **12 – 1.**
Behavior Checklist for Middle Schools

Student Name _____ Grade _____ Date _____
School _____ Class _____ Teacher _____

Code: 3 — essential
       2 — important
       1 — helpful
       0 — not required

Behaviors	Required	Rarely Shown	Below Class Standards	Meets Class Standards
A. Building Related: 1. Walks in halls				
2. Appropriate noise level in hall				
3. Has pass when in hall				
4. Shows pass when in hall				
5. Does not peer or shout into classrooms or office				
6. Moves from one room to another within a reasonable time limit				
7. Appropriate peer interaction a. verbal				
b. physical				
8. Responds appropriately to adult initiated interaction.				
9. Able to sit quietly in office				
10. Talks appropriately to building personnel				
11. Stays in middle school areas				

TABLE **12 – 1.** *(Continued)*
Behavior Checklist for Middle Schools

Behaviors	Required	Rarely Shown	Below Class Standards	Meets Class Standards
12. Leaves building within reasonable time limit a. when instructed				
b. when bell rings				
B. Schedule related 1. Attends regularly				
2. Knows what to do when a. late				
b. absent				
3. Know which class to attend a. room				
b. time				
4. Attends class on time				
5. Attends school on time				
C. Material related: 1. Has pencil				
2. Has colored pencils				
3. Has notebook				
4. Has paper				
5. Has books				
6. Has misc. materials specific to day's task				
7. Has completed assignments				

TABLE **12 – 1.** *(Continued)*
Behavior Checklist for Middle Schools

Behaviors	Required	Rarely Shown	Below Class Standards	Meets Class Standards
D. Classroom related 1. Sits in desk				
2. Raises hand				
3. Enters room appropriately				
4. Responds to bell by being in the classroom and attending to teacher				
5. Appropriate interaction with peers within classroom				
6. Able to deal with praise appropriately				
7. Able to deal with criticism appropriately				
8. Reacts to peer provokes appropriately a. verbal				
b. physical				
9. Reacts appropriately to teacher statements				
10. Reacts appropriately to teacher directives				
11. Able to deal with teacher expectations for the classroom				

TABLE **12 – 1.** *(Continued)*
Behavior Checklist for Middle Schools

Behaviors	Required	Rarely Shown	Below Class Standards	Meets Class Standards
12. Able to attend to class activity for 55 minutes				
13. Treats material with proper care				
14. Puts material away				
15. Directs eyes (attention) toward teacher-directed activity				
16. Listens to lectures				
17. Listens to discussions				
18. Participates appropriately in classroom discussions				
19. Able to copy notes or other information a. from board				
b. from overhead				
c. from books				
d. from misc. sources				
20. Has appropriate voice level				
21. Able to work in small group (less than 10)				
22. Able to work in large group (more than 10)				
23. Able to work individually				
24. Able to work with one another				

TABLE **12 – 1.** *(Continued)*
Behavior Checklist for Middle Schools

Behaviors	Required	Rarely Shown	Below Class Standards	Meets Class Standards
25. Able to ask for help when needed				
26. Leaves room appropriately a. when directed				
b. at end of class				
E. Task related: 1. Asks appropriate questions				
2. Responds appropriately to questions				
3. Starts task within reasonable time limit				
4. Completes task on time				
5. Remembers assignments as given				
6. Able to volunteer information appropriately				
7. Able to deal with grades received				
8. Writes or prints clearly				
9. Does assignments neatly				
10. Completes assignments as given by teacher				
11. Is responsible for work missed				
12. Able to take tests				

TABLE **12 – 1.** *(Continued)*
Behavior Checklist for Middle Schools

Behaviors	Required	Rarely Shown	Below Class Standards	Meets Class Standards
13. Able to use free ur unstructured time well				
14. Hands in completed work				

Additional Comments Relevant to the Student's Performance in Class:

Dawson, L., McLeod, S. and Mathews, S. *Behavior checklist for middle schools.* Madison, WI: Madison Metropolitan Schools, 1976.

Sociometrics

One important factor in students' adjustment to school is the extent to which they are accepted by their peers. Because of their maladaptive classroom behaviors, many pupils are socially rejected, withdrawn, and find few rewards in the social aspects of their school experience. Other behavior-problem students become leaders of small classroom revolts and encourage their peers into breaking rules and fighting. Students with social problems need help if they are to adapt successfully to the demands of the classroom and the school. The resource teacher thus may want to analyze a pupil's social position.

One method of determining social standing in a classroom is through sociometric analysis (Moreno, 1953). In this technique, each pupil in the classroom is asked to choose two other students with whom they would like to play, eat, work, or perform any other type of classroom or social activity. By studying the results of such a questionnaire, the resource teacher can determine the social status of the problem student as viewed by his or her peers. For example, do any of the students pick the problem pupil to play with? Who are they? Who does the referred student pick to interact with?

Figure 12–4 shows a sociometric analysis. In this example, the students were asked, "Who would you like to eat lunch with?" Don, the referred student, was never chosen. The most popular student was Virginia.

The responses of the students should be secret; that is, the questions should not require the students to give a verbal response in front of the entire class. For example, consider Don's feelings if the students were asked to respond verbally and not one of them wished to eat lunch with him. For students who cannot write the names of other pupils, numbers can be put on the desks so that they need only respond with a written number. A shortcut to doing a sociogram on the entire class is to ask Don the questions without involving the entire class. This approach, however, does not give any data on how the rest of the class feels about him; it reveals only how he feels about other classmates.

The information from the sociometric evaluation can have direct implications for remediation. A totally friendless pupil can be paired with others of her or his

FIGURE **12 – 4.**
Sociogram — Eating Lunch

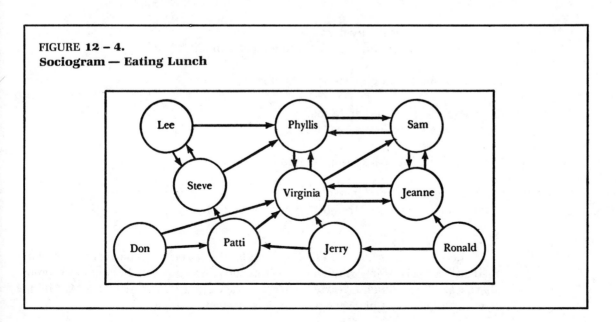

choosing for social activities or work. If the class terrors all want to work together, perhaps they can be paired instead with good students. Peer tutors can be selected on the basis of this kind of information, and social situations between students can be arranged and monitored to some extent.

Behavior Rating Profile

The Behavior Rating Profile: An Ecological Approach to Behavioral Assessment (L. Brown and Hammill, 1983) combines the ecological, checklist, and sociometric formats. It considers the student's behavior in several environments; requires teachers, parents, and the targeted student to respond to a checklist of specific behaviors; and gathers data on the social status of the student as viewed by peers. In addition, *the Behavior Rating Profile* (BRP) is well standardized, highly reliable, experimentally validated, and norm referenced. As a result, resource teachers can use the BRP with confidence when they desire a more formal and objective measure of a student's behavior and social status.

The BRP is comprised of four major components. First, a student rating scale is provided that allows pupils to note their perceptions of themselves in (1) the home, (2) at school, and (3) with their peers. This scale includes sixty statements to which the student responds true or false. Examples from the questions that relate specifically to home behaviors are:

"I often break rules set by my parents."
"When at home, I spend too much time daydreaming."

Two questions relating to school behaviors are:

"Teachers are often unfair to me."
"I can't seem to concentrate in class."

Two questions that relate to peer interactions are:

"I get teased a lot by other children."
"I am rarely invited to a friend's home to eat or play."

The second checklist is to be filled out by the parents or guardians of the targeted student. The thirty statements on this form are responded to on a four-point Likert scale: "Very Much Like My Child," "Like My Child," "Not Much Like My Child," "Not At All Like My Child." Two example statements are:

"My child is shy; clings to parents."
"My child is verbally aggressive to parents."

The third checklist is to be filled out by teachers who work consistently with the targeted pupil. This checklist also includes thirty statements that are responded to in the same four-point Likert scale as the parent or guardian form. Two example statements here include:

"The student lacks motivation and interest."
"The student argues with teachers and classmates."

The fourth component of the BRP is a peer rating scale, which follows the sociometric format. To derive scores in this component, the teacher asks the targeted student and classmates questions like:

"Which of the girls and boys in your class would you most like to work with on a school project?"
"Which of the girls and boys in your class would you least like to work with on a school project?"

The resource teacher may elect to give all of the scales or just selected ones. After they have been administered and scored, the scores may be entered on a profile sheet. An example of one student's profile is found in Figure 12–5. The profile on the left side indicates that the student is falling outside the average for his age level. Joey appears to view himself as having behavior problems in home, school, and with his peers. The teachers have ranked Joey within the average ranges in school behavior. His mother ranked him below average, his father as within the average range. Joey's peers ranked him in such a way as to indicate some interpersonal difficulties.

The BRP combines the strengths of the ecological format, the efficiency of checklists, and the critical information derived from a sociogram in a reliable, valid, and norm referenced manner. Resource teachers desiring these points in their supplemental individual analyses will find the BRP helpful.

We end this section by reiterating two points made consistently throughout this book. First, the interpretation of norm-referenced tests, like the BRP, should always be backed up by other data. In other words, the resource teacher should ensure prior to program planning or implementation that the individuals who responded to the BRP do in fact feel the way they indicated. This can be done through observational and interviewing techniques. Second, parental permission, and if at all possible student permission, should be solicited before administering any test, particularly ones that deal with such sensitive and personal areas as the BRP. Confidentiality of the results should be assured.

FIGURE 12 – 5.
Summary and Profile Sheet for BRP

B R P

BEHAVIOR RATING PROFILE SHEET

LINDA L. BROWN & DONALD D. HAMMILL

Name _Joey Stewart_

Parent's Name _David & Ellen Stewart_

Address _110 Allen St._

School _David Brewer_

Teacher (Grade) _Ms. Brooks_ (_3_)

Examiner _Dr. J. Brothers-School Psch._

Referred by _Ms. Brooks_

	YEAR	MONTH
Date Tested	82	10
Date of Birth	74	1
	YEARS	MONTHS
Age	8	9

BRP Scales	Raw Scores	Standard Scores	Percentile Ranks
Student Rating Scales			
Home Scale	8	6	10
School Scale	6	5	5
Peer Scale	2	3	1
Teacher Rating Scale			
Teacher = 1	47	7	16
Teacher = 2	79	11	64
Teacher = 3	—	—	—
Parent Rating Scale			
Mother	54	6	10
Father	66	9	36
Other	—	—	—
Sociogram			
Question #1	27/27	3	1
Question #2	25/27	5	5
Question #3	26/26	4	2

Standard Scores: Mean = 10, Standard Deviation = 3

COMMENTS:

Additional copies of this form are available from PRO-ED, 5341 Industrial Oaks Blvd., Austin, Texas 78735 512/892-3142

Teacher-Student Interactional Analysis

After observing the referred pupil in the regular classroom, the resource teacher may suspect that some of the problems relate to the types of interactions between the teacher and student. For example, regular classroom teachers may ignore referred students, be overly critical of them, or deal with them in a strained or uncomfortable manner. In turn, students with behavior problems may react in a hostile, passive-aggressive, and/or fearful fashion. Because a respectful, accepting, if not warm, relationship between a student and the teacher is highly conducive to learning, many professionals have developed procedures for measuring the quality and quantity of teacher-student interactions; see Medley, Schluck, and Ames (1968) and Brophy and Good (1974), among others.

Several observational systems have been designed to assess the teacher-pupil interaction objectively. Because resource teachers who want to measure a student's interactions with a teacher can use these systems, three are discussed in this section: (1) Flanders's interaction analysis categories; (2) the dyadic interaction system; and (3) the observation schedule and record.

Flanders (1970) has developed an approach to measuring the interactions of a teacher with the entire class. He divides the possible kinds of interactions into ten categories. Seven categories relate to the teacher's verbalizations, and two relate to the students' verbalizations. One category is for silence or confusion. These categories are presented and described in Table 12 – 2. Flanders recommends that an observer (here, the resource teacher) record the type of interaction that occurs every four seconds during a short, specified period over an interval of several days. For example, 5,5,5,5,5,5,5,5,5,4,8,5,5,5,5, means that in a one-minute period, the teacher lectured approximately fifty-two seconds and spent four seconds asking a question to which a student gave a four-second response. By measuring the verbal interaction over several twenty-minute periods, the categories of interaction most adhered to in a given classroom can be determined. The categories that are never used become obvious. Flanders is careful not to make any judgments as to which categories should or should not be used. He believes that given the available research, it appears that each category has merit in given situations at certain times.

A resource teacher may find the Flanders approach helpful in specific instances. Occasionally, the regular classroom teacher may request such an analysis if he or she is having difficulty with the entire class. In other cases, the resource teacher may want to use the Flanders scale as a guide in talking to regular classroom teachers about verbal interaction in the classroom. The system, however, focuses on the class as a whole rather than on a teacher's interactions with a specific student. Information on specific teacher-pupil interactions usually is more relevant for the resource teacher.

An approach that might be more useful to a resource teacher was developed by Brophy and Good (1969). Unlike Flanders, they developed a system that applies only to the teacher's interactions with an individual student or specific students. Their approach, the Dyadic Interaction Analysis, measures five different types of

TABLE **12 – 2.**
Flanders' Interaction Analysis Categories (FIAC)

TEACHER TALK	*Response*	1. *Accepts feeling.* Accepts and clarifies an attitude or the feeling tone of a pupil in a nonthreatening manner. Feelings may be positive or negative. Predicting and recalling feelings are included. 2. *Praises or encourages.* Praises or encourages pupil action or behavior. Jokes that release tension, but not at the expense of another individual; nodding head, or saying "Um hm?" or "go on" are included. 3. *Accepts or uses ideas of pupils.* Clarifying, building, or developing ideas suggested by a pupil. Teacher extensions of pupil ideas are included but as the teacher brings more of his own ideas into play, shift to category five.
		4. *Asks questions.* Asking a question about content or procedure, based on teacher ideas, with the intent that a pupil will answer.
	Initiation	5. *Lecturing.* Giving facts or opinions about content or procedures; expressing his own ideas, giving his own explanation, or citing an authority other than a pupil. 6. *Giving directions.* Directions, commands, or orders to which a pupil is expected to comply. 7. *Criticizing or justifying authority.* Statements intended to change pupil behavior from nonacceptable to acceptable pattern; bawling someone out; stating why the teacher is doing what he is doing; extreme self-reference.
PUPIL TALK	*Response*	8. *Pupil-talk — response.* Talk by pupils in response to teacher. Teacher initiates the contact or solicits pupil statement or structures the situation. Freedom to express own ideas is limited.
	Initiation	9. *Pupil-talk — initiation.* Talk by pupils which they initiate. Expressing own ideas; initiating a new topic; freedom to develop opinions and a line of thought, like asking thoughtful questions; going beyond the existing structure.
SILENCE		10. *Silence or confusion.* Pauses, short periods of silence and periods of confusion in which communication cannot be understood by the observer.

Reprinted with permission of the publisher from N. Flanders. *Analyzing teaching behavior,* Menlo Park, California: Addison-Wesley Publishing Company, Inc., 1970.

interactions: (1) response opportunities — the pupil attempts to answer a teacher's question; (2) recitation — the student reads aloud or makes an extended oral presentation; (3) procedural contacts — the interaction deals with classroom management or the student's individual needs; (4) work-related contacts — the interaction concerns written or other type of work completed by the student; and (5) behavioral contact — the pupil is disciplined or the teacher makes an individual comment concerning his or her behavior.

Using a coding system to note the interactions, Brophy and Good (1969) state:

> In addition to this physical separation of the coding for the five types of dyadic contacts, coding distinctions are also made concerning the nature and sequence of the interaction observed. For every interaction, coders note whether the initiator was the teacher or the child and also code information concerning the teacher's message or response to the child during the interaction. In addition, the coding of response opportunities and recitation turns also includes information concerning the type of question asked and the quality of the child's response, both of which are coded before coding the nature of the teacher's feedback. The latter coding also includes preservation of the sequential order of events, so that the chain of action and reaction sequences within these interactions is maintained. [P. 5]

The third system discussed here is the Observation Schedule and Record (OSCAR 5) developed by Medley, Schluck, and Ames (1968). Their system studies six categories of interaction: (1) student behaviors; (2) teacher's questions; (3) teacher's response to student behavior; (4) problem structuring; (5) feedback provided; and (6) teacher's behavior in managerial and procedural matters.

The importance of each of these three measures of teacher-pupil interaction is their objectivity. The resource teacher can use the information derived from this type of analysis to describe the interactions in the classroom to a referring teacher. Resource teachers should be sufficiently familiar with at least two or three of these techniques for two reasons. First, familiarity with these approaches will give him or her information on observational skills. Second, the unique behaviors examined in each system can help resource teachers focus on relevant and specific interaction variables while they are observing in classrooms.

A final word of caution about using these systems. Some teachers' unions are opposed to this type of measurement, particularly if it is used to evaluate the competencies of teachers. Also, many classroom teachers are opposed to having anyone measure their behavior. The resource teacher therefore should make sure that no union agreements would be violated by using one of these systems and should secure the classroom teacher's permission before undertaking any formal assessment of teacher-student interactions. Finally, we suggest that resource teachers be formally trained to use these approaches. These complex systems are difficult to understand alone or to use without some supervised training.

Baseline Data

Few, if any, teachers, have not been trained in the use of behavior modification, of which the collection of baseline data is a critical component. The use of baseline data is a valuable tool for resource teachers who wish to evaluate the effects of intervention. Let us say that regular classroom teachers are concerned that a referred student, Judy, is frequently out of her seat during instruction and is disturbing other students. Analyses of the learner in the classrooms by the resource teacher indicate that this is indeed a significant behavior which needs immediate attention.

The judgmental statements of "frequent" and "significant" are verified by presenting baseline data, or frequency counts of Judy's behavior. They might show, for example, that she is out of seat twenty-five times during the class period and that twenty-five is twenty-four more than the classroom average. Therefore it is indeed frequent and significant. By comparing the number of these inappropriate behaviors occurring during the treatment period with the number occurring during the baseline period, the teacher can objectively evaluate the effectiveness of the intervention strategy.

More detailed discussions of this approach by Hall (1974, 1975) appear in two clearly written booklets: *The Measurement of Behavior*, on measurement, and *Basic Principles*, on basic principles of behavior modification. These booklets should give the resource teacher an adequate introduction to this measuring approach. We also recommend *Behavior Modification for the Classroom Teacher* (Axelrod, 1977) and *Applying Behavioral Analysis Procedures with Children and Youth* (Sulzer-Azaroff and Mayer, 1977).

Self-Assessment

Baseline data traditionally have been gathered by a teacher or another observer on a targeted individual. Self-assessment is a relatively recent addition to the behavior modification literature and is usually a component of a technique known as behavioral self-control (Glynn, Thomas, and Shee, 1973).

Workman (1982) has compiled a practical step-by-step method for implementing these self-assessment procedures. First, teachers select one target behavior that they would like to see occur or not occur. Second, they devise a rating system, which the student uses as a yardstick of the appropriateness of behavior. A Likert scale of 0 to 5 or 0 to 2 (depending upon the age and ability of the student) is usually employed. For example, if on-task is the target behavior, the student would rate a 0 when not on-task, 1 if somewhat on-task, and so on during a specified period of time.

The third step is to determine the interval in which the students will self-rate themselves — every five minutes, every fifteen minutes, and so on. The final step is to decide upon the mechanics of the rating systems. Workman has provided an example of a rating form in Figure 12–6.

FIGURE **12 – 6.**
Measurement Schedule

	Monday	Tuesday	Wednesday	Thursday	Friday
9:15					
9:30					
9:45					
10:00					

Each time I instruct you to do so, I want you to rate yourself on how well you've been paying attention. Give yourself a "0" if you haven't been paying attention very well at all, a "1" if you've been paying attention fairly well, and a "2" if you've really been paying attention extremely well.

Reprinted with permission of the publisher from Workman, E., *Teaching Behavioral Self-Control to Students*, Austin, Tex.: PRO-ED, 1982.

A resource teacher will likely find this technique to be extremely efficient for use in regular classrooms (and in resource rooms). Let us take the case of Judy described in the previous section on baseline data. Judy was frequently out of seat during instruction, which resulted in her disturbing other students and the teachers. Using the steps Workman outlined, the target would be to decrease out-of-seat behavior. The second step would be to devise a rating system. In this case, a 0 to 5 scale is used because Judy is thirteen years old and of normal intelligence. Zero would be out of seat all of the time; 1 would be out of seat most of the time; 3 would be out of seat about one half of the time; 4 would be in seat most of the time; 5 would be in seat all of the time. The third step would be to determine the interval, which in this case was set at twenty-minute intervals. The final step, the mechanics, was to tape a rating scale to Judy's desk so that she could mark it herself at the appropriate times.

The advantages of self-assessment are fairly obvious. It frees the teacher from what is sometimes cumbersome work, such as gathering baseline data. It encourages students to attend to their own behavior. Self-assessment can be used with individual students or the entire classrooms. It is objective in that data are gathered on the targeted behavior. Finally, as noted by Workman (1982), research indicates that self-assessment actually works.

Workman (1982) is a prime reference for resource teachers interested in more detail regarding self-assessment. Additional references are found later in this chapter under "Behavioral Self-Control." Self-assessment is one part of the behavioral self-control strategy.

In this section on Supplemental Individual Analyses, we have overviewed several assessment approaches that we believe are relevant for resource programming: (1) ecological assessment, (2) teacher-devised checklists, (3) sociometrics, (4) the *Behavior Rating Profile*, (5) teacher-student interaction analysis, (6) baseline data, and (7) self-assessment. Additional assessment strategies can be found in the chapter by L. Brown (1982), "Evaluating and Managing Classroom Behavior," by Hewett and Taylor (1980) in *The Emotionally Disturbed Child in the Classroom*, by Newcomer (1980) in *Understanding and Teaching Emotionally Disturbed Children*, and by Long, Morse, and Newman (1976) in *Conflict in the Classroom*.

DEVELOPING INSTRUCTIONAL PROCEDURES

By using one or more of the assessment techniques discussed in the previous two sections, resource teachers will likely have gathered enough data to have pinpointed problems needing intervention. These problems usually fall under one or more of the following five categories: (1) the curriculum category, (2) the student category, (3) the peer category, (4) the teacher category, and/or (5) the parent category.

Before examining some intervention strategies in each of the categories, it should be noted that in a few cases, a particular student's problem may be too complex or difficult for resource and regular classroom teachers to handle alone. On these occasions, the resource teacher should seek the assistance of specialists in mental health, teachers of the emotionally disturbed, school district supervisory personnel, clinical psychologists, counselors, and/or social workers. In most instances, however, teachers will proceed with an intervention program on their own. Only after several different strategies have been tried, evaluated, found not to work, and documented in writing will they request additional help.

The Curriculum Category

In many cases, resource teachers will find through their assessment that the curriculum being taught in the regular classroom is inappropriate for a given student. The inappropriateness of the curriculum may contribute significantly to the behavior problem. Jones and Jones (1981) have noted that classroom misbehavior is dramatically decreased when students: (1) understand the teacher's goal, (2) are actively involved in the learning process, (3) can relate instructional content to their own lives, (4) are allowed to follow their own interests, (5) experience success, (6) receive immediate and realistic feedback, (7) are provided opportunities to integrate what is learned, and (8) receive instruction appropriate to their needs and level of functioning.

Our agreement with these eight points can be noted readily throughout this book. For example, the chapters on reading, oral language, mathematics, and other subject areas include sections on the analysis of the student in the regular classroom. Data derived from this source will provide the resource teacher with information on the appropriateness of the curriculum with individual students. The sections on developing instructional procedures provide ways in which instruction can be adjusted to meet the interest and needs of the students.

Consequently, one of the first steps in planning intervention programs would be to ensure that instructional techniques and content are appropriate for the learner. A hypothetical example will stress the importance of this step. A student named Steve did not attend during the mathematics period and was disrupting the entire class and the teacher. The resource and regular classroom teachers decided to reward Steve for on-task behavior, and a systematic program was implemented. The behavior modification program did not increase Steve's on-task behavior to any appreciable extent. Further assessment indicated that he found the material too difficult, boring, and not related to anything of interest to him. With this in mind. adjustments were made in the mathematics lessons and the behavior modification program again instituted. Steve's on-task behavior increased significantly as well as his math achievement.

Recently, Thompson and Quinby (1981) have developed a series of individualized interest area contracts. These contracts are designed to motivate students and are built around a central theme or interest, such as getting a driver's license, looking into the life of a motorcycle stunt driver, or learning about sewing. The authors state that they can be used with students who are having difficulty in the regular school curriculum, have little or no interest in traditional school subjects, display negative attitudes and behaviors, or are at an impasse with their teachers.

Jones and Jones (1981) have described several methods for facilitating positive behavior through curriculum modifications. These include techniques for planning interesting lessons, methods for implementing disruptive-free learning sessions, and other preventative techniques for encouraging positive classroom behavior. In addition, each chapter in this section of the book contains specific recommendations and several additional references for modifying instruction in specific content areas.

The Student Category

In many cases, the resource teacher will find through assessment that a student has a behavior or set of behaviors that is particularly bothersome to the teacher or in some way interferes with learning. Three techniques with demonstrated effectiveness that can be applied easily in regular classrooms are traditional behavior modification, behavioral self-control strategies, specific skill approaches, and contracts.

Behavior Modification.   There are few, if any teachers, who have not been trained on the use of behavior modification (see section on Baseline Data). As a result, we will not describe these procedures in detail in this chapter. We will, however, give one example of how this technique can be used by resource and regular classroom teachers. For this illustration, we again will use Judy as an example. Judy was frequently out of her seat in class and disturbing other children, especially after lunch. The number of times that she behaved inappropriately between 1:00 and 1:30 P.M. had been counted and recorded; that is, baseline data had been collected.

Both the resource teacher and regular classroom teacher decided to use behavior modification on Judy to decrease her inappropriate behavior. They met with Judy and asked her what she liked to do best in school. She replied that she liked to work with Esther on assignments. The teachers then told her that she could work with Esther after 1:30 if she decreased her out-of-seat behavior. For every five minutes she went without inappropriately leaving her desk, she received five minutes equivalent time with Esther. Therefore, if she was not out of her seat at all during this period, she would earn one-half hour with her friend.

Judy's progress is reported in Figure 12–7. The first day she was out of her seat inappropriately six times. Each of these behaviors was in a different five-minute

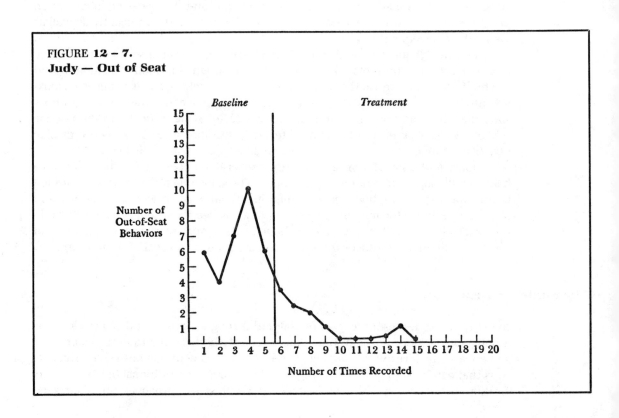

FIGURE **12 – 7.**
Judy — Out of Seat

block so she earned only five equivalent minutes with Esther. The next day she earned ten minutes, the next day twenty minutes, and so on. After a two-week treatment period, the regular classroom teacher decided to extend Judy's behavior modification program throughout the school day. The teacher then set up another plan on her own and reported continued satisfaction with Judy's progress.

This example illustrates how a behavior modification program can be implemented. In this case, both the regular and resource teachers planned the treatment program. By continuing to measure the behavior over a two-week period, they could see progress objectively. Such a systematic procedure also served to convince the regular classroom teacher that behavior modification can work if implemented systematically and appropriately.

Educational literature contains many studies that demonstrate effectiveness of this popular technique when used with individuals who have learning, mental, and/or behavior problems. Excellent references on the rationale and procedure for implementing a traditional behavior modification program include Hall (1974, 1975), Axelrod (1977), and Sulzer-Azaroff and Mayer (1977). In addition, almost every book that includes strategies for dealing with behavior presents an overview of this technique.

Behavioral Self-Control.   In a previous section, self-assessment was overviewed as a strategy for gathering data on the behavior of the learner in the regular classroom. In these cases, the student is charged with the responsibility of measuring how well he or she conforms to a specified behavior. Self-assessment is one component of a behavioral self-control program. Additional information on this relatively new form of behavior modification follows.

Once the students have determined their level of performance on a specified behavior using self-assessment techniques, they are then encouraged to use self-monitoring and self-reinforcement techniques. In self-monitoring students are taught to keep a record of how often they engage in a specified behavior. They do so using either frequency counting or interval recording. Frequency counting refers to counting the total number of times a given behavior occurs. Interval recording requires the student to record her or his behavior at specified intervals of time. In this instance, the students note every five minutes, ten minutes, and so on whether they were engaged in a behavior during that period of time (similar to the techniques described in self-assessment).

Self-reinforcement is similar to reinforcement strategies used in traditional behavior modification programs, with one exception: the students rather than the teacher administer their own reinforcers. It is recommended that the students pick their own rewards. Workman (1982) has recommended that teachers list potential rewards that are available in a "reinforcement menu." An example reinforcement menu is found in Figure 12–8.

The advantage of behavioral self-control over traditional behavior modification programs is obvious. First, students learn to observe, count, and monitor their own behavior. Second, it is less time-consuming for the teachers. Finally, Workman

FIGURE 12 – 8.
Reinforcement Menu

Here is a list of several activities that you can earn for doing good work in class. I want you to look at each activity and tell me how much YOU like that activity. If you don't like an activity, put a check in the "DON'T LIKE" space. If you feel that the activity is OK, but not really exciting, put your check in the "OK" space. If you really like an activity, put a check in the "REALLY LIKE" space. Put only one check beside each activity.

Activity	Don't Like	OK	Really Like
10 Minutes Extra Recess			
Getting to Talk with a Group of Friends during the Last 10 minutes of Class			
Reading Comic Books During the Last 15 Minutes of Class			
Getting to Sit Beside Whomever I Want to at Lunch			
Playing Game Y During the Last 10 Minutes of Class			
Winning a "Star Student" Button to Wear			
Having a Note Sent Home Telling My Parents What Good Work I've Done			

Reprinted with permission of the publisher from Workman, E. *Teaching Behavioral Self-Control to Students*, Austin, Tex.: PRO-ED, 1982.

and Hector (1978) found in their review of the research that behavioral self-control was equally as effective as traditional behavior modification in strengthening appropriate classroom behaviors.

More information regarding the use of behavior self-control can be found in Meichenbaum (1977, 1980) and Stuart (1977), among others. We highly recommend the book by Workman (1982), which contains a practical step-by-step method for implementing these programs in addition to a review of the research and a comparison to more traditional behavior modification programs.

Behavior modification programs are extremely popular in the schools today, probably because they almost always work. Undoubtedly they are the most powerful techniques available to educators in changing a student's behavior. It is not surprising, therefore, to find this technique under close scrutiny by society at large. As Harris and Kapache (1978) noted, "Behavior modification has recently come under a veritable barrage of attacks from the popular press, civil rights groups, and politicians — at both the state and federal levels. The bases of the attacks involve the issues of the ethics and legality of behavior modification programs." (p. 25). For the most part, the concerns are based upon the selection of (1) students for whom behavior modification is appropriate, (2) behaviors to be changed that would benefit the student, (3) procedures that should be tried prior to implementing a behavior modification program, (4) specific change procedures to be employed (token economy, contingency contracts, or aversive controls), and (5) personnel with demonstrated competencies to implement such a program.

We also are concerned about these five issues. In the case of resource programming, we have found in many cases that many teachers who use these approaches appear to lack sufficient training and/or competencies in these strategies. In addition, sometimes the behaviors being changed are questionable — for example, seeking total compliance to situational demands that bear little or no observable benefit to the pupils. In some instances, no other behavioral change strategy has been employed prior to implementing a behavior modification program. Finally, we have observed that aversive control has been selected when token economy or contingency contracts may have been more appropriate.

It is strongly recommended that teachers become familiar with the ethics and legality of the use of behavior modification programs. Harris and Kapache (1978) is an excellent reference for familiarity with these points. In addition, it is likely that the current educational and legal literature will increasingly contain several treatises on these matters. Our concerns should not be taken as an indictment of behavior modification; we are supportive of its use when implemented properly. Unfortunately, this is not always the case in our schools.

Specific Skill Approaches. Many of the approaches geared to the individual are focused on the decreasing of inappropriate behavior. Following the tradition of social learning theorists such as Bandura, there have been excellent recent programs developed to teach specific social skills to aggressive, withdrawn, or "immature" students. One of the readily useable programs designed specifically for adolescents is *Skillstreaming the Adolescent. A structured learning approach to teaching social skills* (Goldstein, Sprafkin, Gershaw, and Klein, 1980). The methods described in this booklet are quite appropriate to the elementary level as well. Rose's

Treating of children in groups (1973) is essentially the same type of approach, but with more of an orientation to the supporting- or non-supporting peer group.

Contracts. One technique for motivating students to learn is through the use of contracts. Resource teachers can use contracts to specify: (1) a task to be completed (usually in the regular classroom); (2) a time limit for completing the task; (3) how others are involved (teachers, aides, peers); (4) the reward for completing the task; and (5) the individual's responsibility for recognizing the completion of the task.

Kohfeldt (1974) and Kaplan, Kohfeldt, and Sturia (1974) have compiled booklets of contracts to cover many situations. Figure 12–9 illustrates two of these contracts. Resource teachers can order inexpensive, commercially available contracts or prepare their own contracts. Contracts help develop proper classroom behavior in many ways and likely will stimulate interest in learning specific regular classroom content.

Jones (1980) has noted that contracts vary considerably and range from written contracts that stress immediate, tangible reinforcement to verbal agreements that stress self-reinforcement and social reinforcement. He has noted that older adolescents sometimes view written contracts as childish and unnecessary. As a result, he recommends that in developing contracts, it is best to employ consequences directed toward self-management and lesser amounts of external control. The various types of consequences that can be employed in contracts are those that stress: (1) social reinforcement and self-reinforcement, (2) activity reinforcement, (3) combined token and activity reinforcement, (4) activity curtailment, (5) tangible reinforcement, and (6) combined token and tangible reinforcement. Jones suggested that number 1 above be applied if feasible prior to attempting the others.

Contracts can be used on specific regular classroom content and behavior or on outside areas of interest to students. Hopefully, through their use, students will be less likely to demonstrate inappropriate behavior and will learn appropriate behaviors.

The Peer Category

Often resource teachers will find in their analysis of the learners in the classroom that a student has problems relating appropriately to peers. In some instances, the student may be aggressive or hostile; in other instances withdrawn or fearful. As a result, classroom peers may reject or even ridicule the student with problems. This is an intolerable state of affairs, and interventions should be tried. The resource teacher might consider using one of the structured programs that have been recently developed to help remedy problems in the affective areas. These programs usually contain a teacher's guide and often several pieces of equipment and materials. Their use calls for the creation of a warm, accepting environment in which students are encouraged to express their feelings about themselves and others. These

FIGURE **12 – 9.**
Contracts

From Kohfeldt, J. *Contracts*. Kernersville, N.C.: Innovation Education Support Systems, 1974. Reprinted by permission of the publisher.

discussions hopefully increase the pupil's self-acceptance and others, as well as develop appropriate interaction skills among students.

The regular classroom teacher can use structured program approaches to facilitate affective growth in students. For example, the resource teacher may feel that the referred student is not accepted or understood by other pupils in the regular classroom. Therefore, she or he may suggest that the regular classroom teacher adopt one of these programs as part of the daily instruction. As a result, resource pupils may become more accepted by the other pupils and may develop a better understanding of how their behavior affects social interactions.

In a few instances, the resource teacher may want to use these programs in the resource room. When this is done, she or he will have to ensure that any positive affective change in pupil behavior or attitude is transferred into the regular classroom situation. Improved behavior that is confined to the resource room is of little practical value and must be considered only as an initial phase of the intervention effort.

The affective programs are good because many teachers are not trained in social skill teaching and thus are unsure about how to proceed. The teacher's guides in these packages often contain detailed information about proper teacher behaviors during training sessions with pupils. Thus, practice, rather than specific training, may be enough to develop the appropriate skills in some teachers.

To acquaint the reader with these approaches, this section will look at four widely used programs: *Developing Understanding of Self and Others* (Dinkmeyer, 1982); *Magic Circles* (Palomares and Ball, 1974); *Social Skills in the Classroom* (Stephens, 1978); and *Building Interpersonal Relationships Through Talking, Listening, Communicating* (Bormaster and Treat, 1982).

Developing Understanding of Self and Others (DUSO).   DUSO was prepared to stimulate feelings of personal adequacy and self-acceptance in oneself. The DUSO kits contain specific directions for the teacher and planned experiences and materials that encourage students to talk about their feelings, goals, values, and behavior. DUSO, a puppet, is a wise and understanding dolphin who serves as a central character in this program. The DUSO kits contain colorful posters, unit stories and songs, hand puppets, puppet activity cards, and supplementary music, art, and game activities. There are two kits, one for kindergarten and one for lower-primary-aged students. Kit 1 has eight major unit themes:

1.   Understanding and Accepting Self
2.   Understanding Feelings
3.   Understanding Others
4.   Understanding Independence
5.   Understanding Goals and Purposeful Behavior
6.   Understanding Mastery, Competence and Resourcefulness
7.   Understanding Emotional Maturity
8.   Understanding Choices and Consequences

Kit 2 also has eight major unit themes:

1. Towards Self-Identity
2. Towards Friendship
3. Towards Responsible Interdependence
4. Towards Self-Reliance
5. Towards Resourcefulness and Purposefulness
6. Towards Competence
7. Towards Emotional Stability
8. Towards Responsible Choice Making

Magic Circles. This program was developed on two key concepts: (1) positive student interaction can be a powerful force in making life meaningful and (2) certain structured situations can be used as guides to improve the quality of interaction among students. The program's format contains teacher-guided discussions, which take place in a circle of approximately seven to twelve pupils. The circle sessions usually last from twenty to thirty minutes and should be carried out daily. The program includes a teacher's manual, activity guides for preschool and kindergarten-aged pupils, and other guides for grades 1 through 6. Also included are additional guidebooks for institutionalized teenagers and a supplementary idea guide. The teacher's guide contains suggestions for managing the sessions in a typical classroom of twenty-eight to forty-eight students. For each student, the teacher prepares a developmental profile that helps make the program more individual. Each developmental profile contains the pupil's awareness of self, sensitivity to others, self-confidence, effectiveness, interpersonal comprehension, and tolerance. Table 12 – 3, the overview chart of the magic circle (human development program), further illustrates the components of this curriculum.

Social Skills in the Classroom. Stephens (1978) has developed an extensive curriculum, which is appropriate for use by the resource teacher. In this social skills curriculum, four subcategories of behaviors are taught: (1) environmental behavior, (dealing with emergencies, lunchroom behavior, and so forth), (2) interpersonal behaviors (such as coping with conflict and making conversation), (3) self-related behaviors (such as expressing feelings and ethical behavior), and (4) task-related behaviors (such as classroom discussion and independent work. Each unit contains the skills to be taught, assessment strategies, evaluation of the assessments, and teaching strategies, which include social modeling, social reinforcement, and contingency management.

The social skills curriculum, in addition to having units on a large number of behaviors, also contains directions for consulting resource teachers. Stephens recommends that resource teachers follow these steps in assisting regular classroom teachers:

TABLE 12 – 3.
Overview Chart: Human Development Program: Levels, Group Arrangement, Strategies, and Objectives Grades Preschool through 6

Level	Grade	Age	Groupings	Strategies	Objectives
Pre-School		4	Single Circle 5 – 10	Encouragement to talk, listen, succeed.	Improve self-control and ability to listen and express; develop self-confidence and understanding of inter-personal interaction. Tolerance for individual differences. Understanding of universalization principle — emphasis on common human traits.
Kinder-garten		5	Single Circle 8 – 12	As above. Deal with negative as well as positive topics.	Increase self-acceptance and listening skills. Begin coping with mixed feelings.
I	First	6	First one circle 8 – 14; then add self-controlled children to outer ring until whole class is in two concentric rings. Teacher and child leaders alternate.	As above. Discuss: 1) ambivalence in feelings, thoughts, behaving; 2) effective and ineffective behavior; 3) reality and fantasy. Discuss variables of inclusion, warmth, coldness, making of decisions. Begin leadership experiences.	As above. Effective self-control, ability to comfortably experience ambivalence, improve reality testing, self-confidence, effective meeting of needs, increase responsibility, tolerance, empathy, skill in making helpful suggestions. Sharing in decision making and recognition of leadership abilities.
II	Second	7	As above.	As above. Continued presentation of methods of awareness, coping, social interaction. Character development is fostered by challenge, commitment, and direct interpersonal communication with peers. Continued decision-making and child leadership.	As above. Articulation of wide range of experiences in positive and negative feelings, thoughts, and behavior. Self-confidence and positive self-concept. Ability to distinguish between reality and fantasy. Motivation to be responsible, productive, kind. Share in decision-making. Leadership as service, not exploitation. Ability to make helpful suggestions to guide leaders to better functioning.

III	Third	8	As above.	As above. Self-control as a matter of personal pride. Verbal facility, skillful and tolerant listening. Ability to tolerate ambivalent feelings in self and others. Skill in observing differences between verbalization and performance. Wise decision-making and responsible, constructive leadership. Courage in taking the initiative to build good social relationships.
			As above. Further challenge to self-sufficiency, integration, honesty. Emphasize responsibility in social interaction, keeping commitments.	
IV	Fourth	9	As above.	As above. Accepting and reflective listening. Deeper self-awareness and understanding of social relationships. Fuller acceptance of responsibility for their own behavior.
			As above. Challenge to recognize psychological similarities and differences between the sexes. Role playing. Micro Lab. Experiences with authenticity and duplicity and problem solving. Exploring dreams and practice at problem solving.	
V	Fifth	10	Three general plans for articulation, presented.	As above. Increased understanding of how trusting relationships are developed. Awareness of the complexities in social situations. Development of a sense of identity. Dealing with Role Expectations, such as sex role demands. Increasing awareness of one's own capabilities and likeable qualities.
			As above. Focus on importance of flexible outlook and behavior. Units no longer assigned to a certain number of days of the week. Supplemental affective activities presented in a variety of subject areas.	
VI	Sixth	11	As above.	As above. Increased self-confidence through validation of self and others. Increased sense of self-identity and group identification. Increased practice at problem solving and decision-making. Exploring the complexities in conflict resolution.
			A above. Focus on responsibility for one's own behavior. Increased supplemental affective activities presented in a variety of subject areas.	

Reprinted by permission of the publisher. From Ball, G. (Ed.). *Magic circle: An overview of the human development program.* La Mesa, California: Human Development Training Institute, 1974.

1. Have teachers identify the target students and the social behavior they fail to demonstrate.
2. Ask the teachers to describe the social behavior.
3. Have teachers indicate conditions under which they wish to increase or decrease the social behavior.
4. Have teachers rate the frequency and/or quality of the behavior.
5. With the teachers, select a strategy to change the social behavior.
6. Teach or suggest methods to continue increasing or decreasing the behavior.
7. Develop a way for teachers to report progress.
8. Maintain follow-up contact with the teacher.

In addition, Stephens outlines four short-term in-service training sessions for resource personnel to conduct with classroom teachers. The social skills curriculum can be used with all school-aged students although some units appear more appropriate for older students.

Talking, Listening, Communicating. Bormaster and Treat (1982) noted that the primary focus of building *Interpersonal Relationships Through Talking, Listening, Communicating* is to develop a positive regard in students for individual differences, to foster a sense of belonging, to build nonauthoritative relationships, and to maximize development of students' potential. Both Bormaster and Treat have served for several years as consultants to regular classroom teachers in implementing this affective curriculum in their classrooms.

In the first chapter, the authors overview strategies for helping teachers become effective group leaders. They then present several modules for use with students that focus on developing self-understanding, the ability to work and relate with others, and how to function as a group leader. The second section focuses on the development of creativity and problem-solving and decision-making skills. Many of the modules are appropriate for elementary students, but overall, they appear more appropriate for students in the middle and high schools.

DUSO, Magic Circles, the *Social Skills Curriculum,* and *Talking, Listening, Communicating* are four commercially available programs for teachers. Other programs on the market or currently being developed also can help teachers who wish to implement a component of affective education. We encourage each resource teacher to locate and learn from other teachers, counselors, psychologists, and/or college faculty members who have been trained in affective training techniques. This learning may take place before implementing any type of curriculum approach. The resource teacher should observe some actual sessions in process, discuss with experienced professionals the strengths and weaknesses of various approaches, and seek some training before implementing a curriculum with students or helping other teachers implement such an approach.

Implementing any affective approach does not necessarily mean that peer relationships will be improved. Teachers must carefully, critically, and objectively evaluate the effectiveness of the program employed. L. Brown (1982) noted that there was little empirical evidence to support the efficacy of commercially available affective programs. Consequently, evaluation of their success in individual cases is mandated.

The Teacher Category

In some cases, resource teachers, through their analysis of the learner in the classroom, will determine that the problem may be due totally or in part to the lack of skill or a poor attitude of a regular classroom teacher. If the problem is one of skill — for example, teachers do not know how to adjust the curriculum, implement a behavior modification or affective program, or maintain discipline — resource personnel can usually deal with this problem in their role as a consultant or through inservice training.

One of the major problems in schools today, one that most resource teachers will likely encounter and has not been discussed up to this point, is that of discipline. This problem has reached such proportions that police or guards patrol the halls in some schools. Many regular classroom teachers have been poorly prepared to deal with discipline of students with learning and behavior problems. As a result, they need specific help in disciplining the targeted students.

Since discipline is such a problem, it is not surprising that several books are available on strategies for dealing with inappropriate behavior. These include, but are not limited to, *How to Discipline without Feeling Guilty* (Silberman and Wheelan, 1980), *Discipline in the Classroom* (Howell and Howell, 1979), *Solving Discipline Problems* (Wolfgang and Glickman, 1980), *Responsible Classroom Discipline* (Jones and Jones, 1981), *Adolescents with Behavior Problems: Strategies for Teaching, Counseling, and Parent Involvement* (Jones, 1980), and *Teaching Discipline: A Positive Approach for Educational Development* (Madsen and Madsen, 1974).

Several theories and models exist on discipline. Wolfgang and Glickman (1980) have described the supportive model, the communication model, the valuing model, the social discipline model, the reality model, the behavior modification model, and the behaviorism/punishment model. The authors recommend that teachers develop discipline strategies using these in accordance with both student needs and teachers' personal beliefs. This text is an excellent practical and comprehensive book, which includes a self-test for determining teachers' attitudes toward discipline, as well as recommendations for writing individualized educational plans for special education students in the regular classroom. Resource teachers unfamiliar with discipline strategies should seek competence in this area by studying this and the other books cited.

It is not unusual for resource personnel to encounter a teacher who is unwilling to modify instruction, use behavior modification techniques, implement an affective training program, or attempt different strategies for maintaining discipline even though the situation calls for change. This resistance could be due to any number of factors. These include burn-out, the teacher's belief that students who do not appear to want to learn or who will not conform to expected standards should not be in their classroom, dislike for the resource teacher, or lack of faith in their ability. If repeated attempts to work with such teachers fail to achieve results, the resource teacher should seek help from the building principal, the department head, the counselor, or the district supervisor. If these professionals do not become actively involved or if their assistance does not result in improvement, the resource teacher is faced with a serious dilemma. Placing a student in a setting that does not account for his or her needs is not helping and may well be exacerbating the behavior problem.

In these instances, the resource teacher may want to work around the situation by transferring the student to another classroom, or help might be provided the student in the resource room. If the problem is one of an interpersonal nature between the resource teacher and the regular classroom teacher, the resource teacher may need to modify her or his own behaviors. Unfortunately there are sometimes no easy solutions, or any solutions, to these problems other than getting the teacher fired (almost an impossible task) or transferring to another school (something many resource teachers are unwilling to attempt).

The Parent Category

We have already stressed earlier the importance of parental or guardian participation in the educational process with students assigned to resource programs. At times resource teachers may want to work with parents to develop an intervention program geared to altering a pupil's behavior. This is particularly true in cases where the student does not respond to an appropriate curriculum, behavior modification techniques, positive peer interaction, and typical discipline procedures.

Several programs have been effectively used with groups of parents as well as individuals. These include filial therapy (Guerney, 1969), parent counseling groups (Keppers and Caplan, 1962; McCowan, 1968), parent effectiveness training (Gordon, 1970), the parent "C" group (Dinkmeyer and Carlson, 1973), and behavior modification (Kroth, 1975).

Kroth's (1975) *Communicating with Parents of Exceptional Children: Improving Parent Teacher Relationships* is an example of a rather comprehensive program that is based upon behavioral principles. Kroth describes ways in which to prepare for individual parent conferences, how to listen to parents, and techniques for comparing student-teacher-parent perceptions. Also strategies are presented for preparing information for parents, reporting progress to parents, and parent group meetings. Problem-solving techniques in defining the problem, selecting and applying reinforcers, and setting up a reinforcement menu are also included.

Kroth provides eight points on what research and experience have told us about working with parents:

1.   Parent conferences held before school starts reduce student absenteeism and discipline problems and increase academic growth.
2.   Parents serve as powerful reinforcers if they have daily or weekly reports.
3.   Parent sharing groups are useful in helping them to consider long-term goals, feel less alone, and help each other in problem solving.
4.   Parent conferences held immediately after a problem occurs often actually increase rather than decrease the frequency of occurrence of the problem.
5.   Parents also need reinforcement.
6.   Parents need specifics, not generalities, if change is to occur.
7.   Teachers should not present the problem to the parents without a solution to propose.
8.   Parents should not be blamed for the occurrence of the problem; many students react differently at home.

In a similar vein, Jones (1980) in his book *Adolescents with Behavior Problems: Strategies for Teaching, Counseling, and Parent Involvement* has defined the steps in developing a collaborative home-school behavior intervention program.[1] The ten steps are:

Step 1.   Reinforce the parents for their willingness to attend the conference.
Step 2.   Outline the goal of the conference.
Step 3.   Describe the problem.
Step 4.   Indicate what the school has done to alleviate the problem.
Step 5.   Display the data to indicate that an additional type of intervention is needed.
Step 6.   Present the anticipated consequences should the behavior remain unchanged.
Step 7.   Indicate that the school has exhausted its available resources and suggest that a collaborative home-school program appears most likely to help the student.
Step 8.   Outline the proposed program.
Step 9.   Negotiate a final agreement.
Step 10. Plan a follow-up.

In this chapter, we have overviewed techniques for helping students with learning and behavior problems adjust to regular classroom standards of behavior. This will call for the analysis of situational variables in addition to the assessment of the student's own needs and interests. Comprehensive and effective interventions may require modification of the curriculum, modification of student behavior, modification of social peer interactions, modification of teacher behaviors, and parental involvement. The overview of strategies has not been exhaustive, nor was it intended to be. The purpose was to acquaint resource teachers with a wide scope of procedures from which they might select. Proficiency in using any of the methods described, or others, will require more reading and study and in a few cases formal training.

ENDNOTES

1.   Reprinted by permission of the publisher. From Jones, V. F. *Adolescents wtih Behavior problems: Strategies for teaching, counseling, and parent involvement.* Boston: Allyn and Bacon, 1980.

13

Independent Study

Many of the students referred for various academic and behavior problems will also be characterized as poor studiers who do not work well independently. Their report cards may have check marks showing "Needs Improvement" in areas related to studying or working independently. Their apparently poor study habits are of concern to: (1) teachers as they mark report cards; (2) parents who believe that their children either do not seem to "apply themselves" or do not show all that they really know; and (3) the students themselves, because they are constantly admonished — but rarely taught — to study.

Students with learning or achievement problems may not view themselves as responsible for their own learning or behavior. They may have been taught indirectly that their problems are not their fault, attributing them to factors such as "bad luck," "The teacher doesn't like me," "I'm hyperactive," or "I forgot to take my pill." Further, they may have had the undivided attention of parents, volunteers, tutors, or special teachers who have helped them on demand. These are the kinds of circumstances that are referred to as "learned helplessness," thus creating a need for direct attention to increasing the student's self-responsibility and independence as a learner.

Classroom teachers often note that many of their students do not know how to study or to work independently. Yet rarely are students referred to the resource teacher for problems in these areas. It is more likely that the resource teacher will have to explain the need for such assessment as an adjunct to whatever assessment is made in the areas for which the student is referred, including both academic and social behaviors.

This chapter deals with study behaviors and also with teaching students to find the necessary expedients for maintaining themselves within the complexities of school situations — that is, to cope with school. Coping skills allow the student to be well perceived *as a student.* In working to become perceived as good students, many youngsters become good students.

ANALYSIS OF THE LEARNER IN THE CLASSROOM

Accountability for independent study begins and ends within the classroom. Assignments originate there, and regardless of where study occurs, the results of study or independent work are evaluated there. It is within the classroom that we will find many of the clues that will help the student, and perhaps the classroom teacher(s) as well, in regard to improving the independent study behaviors of students.

1. *What is the nature of information already available about study or independence behaviors?* Most of the information about the student's independent study is evaluative rather than descriptive. The resource teacher who interviews the classroom teacher(s) about the student can use the current report card and the permanent records as entreés to discussion. For example, one rather typical intermediate report card (Figure 13–1) shows the characteristics that are graded with checks if improvement is needed.

Whether or not one agrees with the categorization of characteristics, these are the realities of a school district's assessment framework for both students and teachers. Usually the discussion of these items is designed to determine the basis for a teacher's perceptions of the student. "Tell me about . . . ," "Tell me more about . . . ," and "What does/did Johnny do that is related to this category?" are some of the question forms used during the teacher interview.

In examining historical information it is important to note the chronicity of poor work habits and the nature of any assistance that has been provided. In addition, any sudden changes from one teacher, class, or school to another should be investigated.

The student's records may be used as the basis for discussion with the parent(s) and with the student. Here, the resource teacher is interested in comparing perceptions and in determining the differences from one study environment to another — that is, from school to home.

2. *What are the products of independent study?* The usual products of independent study are homework, seatwork during class, various tests, class discussions, and oral recitation. Each of these products will have to be examined independently to determine factors relevant to their success.

a. *Evaluation criteria.* How clearly are the criteria for evaluating the product perceived and communicated by the teacher? Are the criteria largely objective or

FIGURE 13 – 1.
A Typical Intermediate Report Card

	Periods			
	1	2	3	4
WORK HABITS (Effort)				
Listens				
Follows directions				
Is neat and orderly				
Works indenpendently				
Completes assignments				
Uses materials well				
Uses time wisely				
Works near capacity				
SOCIAL GROWTH (Behavior)				
Dependable				
Self-controlled				
Obedient				
Confident				
Thoughtful of others				
Accepts criticism				
Courteous				
Cooperative				
PHYSICAL GROWTH				
Neat appearance				
Good health habits				
Well rested				
Coordination				

subjective? Has the student seen any available models of a completed product? Does the student understand the criteria involved?

    b. *Consequences involved.* Is every product a minitest — that is, are grades always recorded? Is the material used diagnostically for reteaching, or is it merely graded, recorded, and forgotten? Must students redo poor work? Is a student *allowed* to correct the work? Does the student receive poor grades in content areas because of incompleted assignments? Are some products weighted more than others — for example, tests more or less than daily work?

c. *Time allotment.* Some assignments are task bound; they must be completed however long they may take. Others are time bound; the student completes as much as possible within the time period specified. Incompleted material is usually graded as wrong or in error.

d. *Content.* Is the content an extension of classwork, or is the student expected to self-instruct through studying independently? How well does the student understand the content, including the directions? Is the student interested at all in the content? Does he or she have an appropriate background to deal with it?

e. *Assistance permitted.* Does the teacher permit group or partner work or tutorial assistance? How independent must the work actually be? May mechanical assistance — such as, reference charts or hand-held calculators — be used? May the student have spelling checked before turning in an essay or a written report? May parents help with homework?

f. *Format.* What is the format of the product, even of discussion? The rules of format are often implied, and they must be derived from teacher comments or from the marking system used. For example, written work may have to be spelled correctly, have margins, be clean, or have the name and date in a certain place, even though these factors are not made clear in the criteria. Oral discussion may include hand raising, turn taking, and complete sentences.

g. *Motivation.* What attempts are made to motivate the student to complete the work? For example, is it made fun or attractive? Are reinforcers used for successful completion? What attempts have been made to capitalize on the student's intrinsic interests?

h. *Instruction.* What is the nature of instruction given to the student(s)? Is the assignment handed out or written on the board? Are examples shown or worked? Must the student instruct himself or herself?

i. *Monitoring and checking.* Since independent study is usually undertaken in schools to show *someone* that the student was indeed working, and hopefully learning as well, who will actually check or monitor the work: the teacher, the student, the resource teacher, aides, peers, or tutors?

3. *What is the teacher's understanding about the nature of independent work?* The resource teacher will need to find out what the teacher(s) perceive as study and independence and what it is they expect in this regard. Any differing perceptions and expectations from teacher to teacher should be noted, for it may be necessary to teach the student to make discriminations of these variations among people in terms of their expectations and perceptions.

4. *How clear is the classroom instruction related to independent study?* Some of the problems with independent work and study have their origin in the instructional milieu of the classroom. For some years, there has been a growing body of

research to indicate that the clearer the instructional presentations, the more students will achieve (for example, Rosenshine and Furst, 1971).

Phi Delta Kappa's Center on Evaluation, Development, and Research (1981) provides a summary of items that have been validated as indicators of instructional clarity within the classroom (see Figure 13–2). These items may be used by the resource teacher as cues to examining instructional clarity in the classroom. Such observations should be made over time. Not every item will be relevant to every case referred; however, they provide good focus to classroom observation. A companion checklist to be used by students is shown in Figure 13–5 in this chapter.

5. *How much self-discipline does the student show during times of independent study?* Independent study is usually a lonesome job, requiring a high degree of self-discipline. The use of time-on-task (TOT) observations usually shows the work patterns of the student within the classroom. In addition, TOT will show what appears to distract the student. The resource teacher who collects these data will also want to observe factors such as:

a.   Whether the student appears to know how to do the assignment
b.   The voluntary comments the student makes about the work
c.   If and how the student asks for or obtains assistance
d.   How legitimate any requests for assistance might be

6. *How do others in the class appear to handle the assignments?* The resource teacher wants to know if any problems with independent work are unique to the student or characteristic of the school or the class. If the entire class is involved, then instruction should include this entire group. If the student appears to be quite discrepant from the group, then instruction will be individually planned.

This question is important also because if there are students who are good independent studiers, then these students may be used to focus the student's observations of good student behaviors.

7. *What is the apparent intention or value of the assignment?* Teachers often need to provide busywork for one group of students while they are engaged with another group. They may also wish to provide genuine opportunities for skill practice or for the independent study of a topic. A preponderance of busywork tasks will tax even the most avid student. Assignments with a purpose that is perceived both by the teacher and the students as worthwhile are more likely to engage the student.

8. *What instruction is provided within the classroom about how to study or work independently?* Rarely are students actually taught how to study or work independently. Often teachers at each successive grade believe that these behaviors were (or should have been) taught before they reached the grade they are in. Since these behaviors have not been taught, it is important to stop wherever the student may be to attend to them. It is especially important for students who are leaving the elementary school or the junior high or middle school to learn to study independently. It is likely that whatever content of the day they might miss can be taught later, or

FIGURE **13 – 2.**
Items Listed in Studies of Instructional Clarity

1. Explains the work to be done and how to do it. ☆
2. Asks students before they start work if they know what to do and how to do it. ☆O
3. Explains something then stops so students can think about it. ☆
4. Takes time when explaining. ☆
5. Orients and prepares students for what is to follow. □O
6. Provides students with standards and rules for satisfactory performance. □
7. Specifies content and shares overall structure of the lectures with students. O
8. Helps students to organize materials in a meaningful way. □
9. Repeats questions and explanations if students don't understand. ☆O
10. Repeats and stresses directions and difficult points. □O☆
11. Encourages and lets students ask questions. O
12. Answers students' questions. ☆O
13. Provides practice time. □
14. Synthesizes ideas and demonstrates real-world relavancy. □
15. Adjusts teaching to the learner and the topic. □
16. Teaches at a pace appropriate to the topic and students. ☆
17. Personalizes instruction by using many teaching strategies. □

18. Continuously monitors student learning and adjusts instructional strategy to the needs of the learner. O
19. Teaches in a related step-by-step manner. □O
20. Uses demonstrations. □O
21. Uses a variety of teaching materials. □
22. Provides illustrations and examples. □
23. Emphasizes the key terms/ideas to be learned. □
24. Consistently reviews work as it is completed and provides students with feedback or knowledge of results. □
25. Insures that students have an environment in which they are encouraged to process what they are learning. O
26. Makes clear transitions. O
27. Reduces mazes. O
28. Avoids vague terms. O
29. Avoids fillers (uh, ah, um). O
30. Reduces nonessential content. O
31. Communicates so that students can understand. □
32. Demonstrates a high degree of verbal fluency. □

Source
□ Cruickshank, Myers, and Moenjak 1975
☆ Bush, Kennedy, and Cruickshank 1977
O Land 1979; Land and Smith 1979a, 1979b

Items listed in "Studies of Instructional Clarity," *Practical Applications of Research. Newsletter of Phi Delta Kappa's Center on Evaluation, Development, and Research* 3 (1981): 3.

perhaps ignored. It is unlikely that study behaviors will be taught outside a special program.

9. *What is the difficulty level of the assignments?* Students who spend time on tasks they can complete correctly tend to have higher achievement than those who

must always work on too-difficult assignments (for example, Stallings, 1978). The idea of the difficulty of an assignment is largely one that involves an interaction between the task and student abilities, much as we have noted in the chapter "Reading" in this book.

Rather than go through complex procedures, the resource or the classroom teacher can tell if an assignment is generally too difficult by looking at the proportion of right and wrong answers to written assignments or during oral recitation or discussion. Quick checks may be made to be sure that the proportion of incorrect responses is not inflated by unanswered questions counted as wrong or by carelessness. Reviewing the items missed can help make this determination.

Brophy and Evertson (1976) have suggested that an 80 percent accuracy level was needed for students in Title I schools to have higher achievement, while in non-Title I schools the percentage could be somewhat lowered. One consultant provided a feedback sheet (Figure 13–3) to the teacher to let her know how difficult the assignments were for students assigned to her special education class.[2]

Since students do not spend time on tasks they believe are too hard for them, the difficulty level of the assignment may inhibit good studying behaviors and contribute substantially to behavior problems that occur because the student cannot do the work. A review of the issue of task difficulty is presented by Powell (1979).

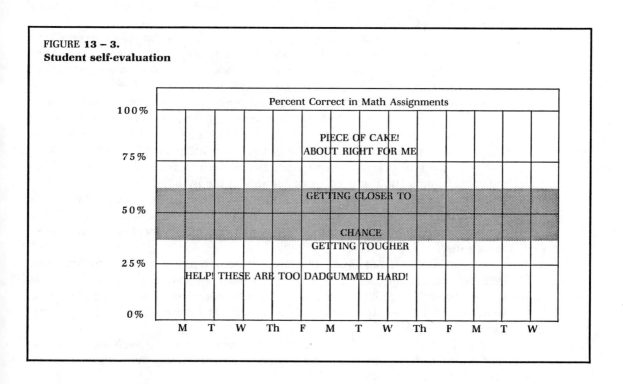

FIGURE 13 – 3.
Student self-evaluation

10. *What are the physical conditions in areas where students are expected to study?* The conditions under which people can study may be somewhat idiosyncratic; however, it is unlikely that if there are many distractions that are attractive to the student, study will win out over competing distractions. Further, whether at home or at school, noise level, interruptions, lighting, and temperature will play some part in making the environment conducive to study.

SUPPLEMENTAL INDIVIDUAL ANALYSIS

One of the major purposes of supplemental individual analysis is to separate the behaviors that the student knows how to do and does not choose to do from those that are not within his or her repertoire. The methods for making this determination are behaviorally based. The teacher uses either *contingency management* to make rewards contingent upon appropriate performance or *stimulus control* to make the assignment so attractive that it will be intrinsically motivating to the student. This kind of assessment is crucial in the area of independent study, for many students know *how* to study; they simply do not choose to do so, thereby earning the label "poor student."

In situations where it appears that the student does not know how to engage in appropriate independent study behaviors, additional assessment will be needed. This section suggests areas that should be checked before planning an instructional program for the individual student.

1. *How does the student view herself or himself as an independent studier?* Some students respond well to open discussion of their study habits. Others need a more structured approach to use as an opener for discussion. V. Brown (undated b) has shown (Figure 13–4) how the Q-Sort pyramid used often in behavior disorders (Kroth, 1972) can be adapted for determining perceptions about independent study. The Q-Sort format is desirable because it forces a relative evaluation of the behaviors of interest. Items for the Q-Sort may be generated to suit the circumstances. Those shown are only representative of the factors that might need to be considered. The sort may be lengthened or shortened by expanding or reducing the number of items and the number of squares in the pyramid.

The resource teacher may also have the student(s), teacher(s), parents, or peers fill out the same scale. It is then possible to make comparisons among all who complete the scale to find out if there are widely differing perceptions of the student as a studier.

Q-Sort data are not always objectively based, so they are subject to fluctuation over time and in need of validation. The teacher may already have observational data to be used to validate or invalidate the perceptions expressed. In addition, most students can be taught to collect data in support or contradiction of their self-reports.

2. *Does the student understand the general nature of the assignments and the content on which they are based?* If the student does not understand the assignments

FIGURE 13 – 4.
Independent Study Q-Sort

Item Suggestion Pool

A. Finish assigned work
B. Do as well as I can
C. Usually understand assignments
D. Don't understand purpose of most assignments
E. Collect all materials needed
F. Budget time for study
G. Can explain what "studying" means
H. Can't stand studying
I. Check over completed assignments
J. Concentrate well
K. See little real value in studying
L. Use textbooks well
M. Study with tests in mind

N. Learn a lot from assignments
O. Take notes well
P. Begin assigned work
Q. Prefer to study alone
R. Study as well as my friends do
S. Take notes well
T. Keep "study" records
U. Easily distracted from study
V. Ask for help with studying
W. Organize study time well
X. (Your own idea) _____
Y. Can outline study materials
Z. Study only subjects I like

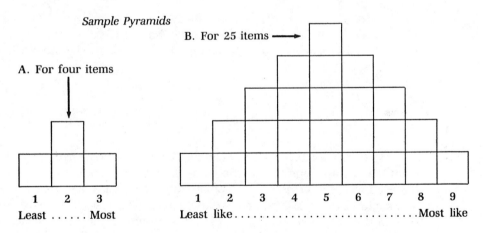

Sample Pyramids

A. For four items

1   2   3
Least . . . . . . Most

B. For 25 items ➝

1   2   3   4   5   6   7   8   9
Least like . . . . Most like

1. Select the number of items to correspond to the size of the pyramid.
2. Number or letter each item.
3. Working from the ends, place the numbers or letters of the items that are "most like me," and "least like me."
4. Work toward the center to select items that are relatively neutral for the student.
5. Discuss the reasons for the placements made. If others have filled out the Q-Sort, note any major discrepancies in perceptions.

V. Brown, undated.

or the content on which they are based, independent study will become an unrealistic expectation. The resource teacher may use the "retell" technique associated with reading miscue analysis to find out how the student understands the assignments. In addition, discussion of errors can take place after the assignment has been completed.

3. *Is the assignment too difficult?* We have noted the primary diagnostic techniques associated with this question as we discussed the student within the classroom, where the assignments originate. Supplemental analysis in this area has several purposes. The first is to make sure that the student cannot, rather than will not, do the work. A second purpose is to determine the level of difficulty that *is* appropriate for the student. It is one thing to say that assignments are too hard and another to state positively the nature of an assignment that *would* be appropriate. Variations that are often recommended to modify the difficulty level of assignments include factors such as these:

a. Sheer number of items
b. Readability of the content for the student
c. Provision of background needed for the content
d. Medium through which the content is communicated, both to the student and back to the teacher
e. Format changes

4. *Does the student know how to ask for appropriate assistance?* If the assignment is truly appropriate for the student, assistance should not be needed much. But even with good students, the ability to ask for assistance when it is needed, and to ask appropriately, is a positive study behavior. Further, teachers may be heard to remark that they would be happy to help a student "if only he or she asked for help." Students who are observed not to ask for assistance under appropriate conditions may not understand how to go about it.

The usual methodologies for teaching students to ask for assistance use behavior rehearsal or role playing in combination for reinforcing the student for asking for help. Often the classroom teacher is enlisted as a cohort when students are learning this kind of behavior.

Some students do not want assistance with assignments. For whatever reason, they must be made to understand the critical role that assistance seeking plays in being perceived as a good student — perhaps even in *becoming* a good student. Whether in kindergarten or graduate school, many teachers view the student who asks for help — appropriately — as one who is trying. He or she is perceived as a better student than one who simply fails.

Students who are given appropriate assignments but who seek assistance constantly become annoying to teachers. In most cases, reinforcing the student for completing work without asking for inappropriate assistance will remedy the problem. The general procedures are to make teacher praise contingent upon working without asking for help. Teachers are also taught to praise students who are working appropriately. Reinforcement can be based upon a specific number of minutes, or upon reductions in the number of times the student asks for help. This technique can also be used with parents who are available to assist with homework.

5. *Does the student understand the real nature of the teacher's expectations?* It is fairly obvious to those who have ever been to school that some of the expectations for students are indeed "Mickey Mouse," and others are truly conducive to learning. It is perhaps unrealistic to expect every assignment to be meaningful for every student throughout his or her school career. Students need to understand this reality about schools. Further, the expectations that teachers have about assignments, how they should be done, and the criteria for their successful completion will vary considerably from teacher to teacher. Most good students see this aspect of school much like a game. They make the necessary discriminations and go along with it. Many of the poor independent studiers in the resource program fall into one of two categories in this regard: (1) they do not understand that it is a game and therefore do not know the "rules" or (2) they know the game, know the rules, and do not want to "play."

This game-playing aspect of school — the question of meeting expectations even when these expectations may not be contributing to learning — poses one of the major ethical dilemmas of the resource teacher, and for the student as well. This dilemma will need to be addressed by the individual resource teacher according to the constraints of the personal and professional situation of that individual.

We believe that "game playing" in school is indeed preparation for the "game playing" in jobs and in many relationships throughout life. We may wish that it were not so, but it is. Students who do not understand this state of life's affairs should be taught *how* to play the game. Whether they choose to do so is ultimately a personal decision. The techniques of values clarification (Simon and Kirschenbaum, 1973) and moral education (Galbraith and Jones, 1976) may be applied to the life-supplied problems in values and morality involved in game playing.

For students at the secondary level, the material usually found in college bookstores will provide a rich supply of ideas for dealing with the realities of teachers' expectations. For example, *The Student's Guide to Good Grades, or Surviving the Undergraduate Jungle* (Crafts and Hauthner, 1976) offers advice about how to get into closed courses, what to do after failing a class, and the etiquette of classrooms, in which this piece of advice is provided:

> Try to get to class on time. Professors do not like people waltzing in late and leaving early on a regular basis. . . . If you do show late and disrupt your seminar or small class, then always apologize after class. [P. 70]

Some resource teachers have had high school students compare the advice given in this book with the local situation at the secondary school. Very few differences were found, and the students were delighted with the honesty of the approach. As paradoxical as it seems, the students who use techniques such as those recommended *do* become better students.

While the expectation dilemma is most apparent in the secondary school, we have experienced the same situation with first graders who refused to complete assignments well within their capabilities and who were "failing" first grade because they saw no reason to "please the teacher" by doing the work. Again, a mixture of honesty, values education, and behavior modification can work.

6. *Which of the tasks of independent study behavior are problematic?* An analysis of the student's competence with actual subtasks of independent study must be made with the assistance of the student. Quite often it is the student who must supply specific data about his or her own behaviors, such as time management. The tasks that cut across most independent study situations are described below. They may be cast into a checklist format for the resource teacher to show the factors that the student already considers during independent study.

a. *Criteria of acceptability* should be known to the point that the student can discuss these criteria with someone else. Having the student work with another student can be an informal way of finding out how the student sees these criteria. Or the resource teacher may ask the student to explain the assignment(s) to him or her. If the student cannot uncover unstated criteria, he or she should be taught directly how to do so.

b. *Task analysis* and *subtask ordering* are often taught to teachers. However, the students themselves must know how to separate the components of tasks so that they can budget time appropriately and find further troublesome spots that will need special care or assistance.

c. *Knowledge of the product format* is needed in order to help the student select the best methods of study for the task. Oral reports, true-false tests, and written compositions, among others, all have special formats. Millman and Pauk (1969) and Feder (1979) provide resources for mastering these methods of study.

d. *Aids to memory* may be needed at any stage of study. In general, the more socially acceptable the aid is, the more likely it is that the student will use it. A handheld calculator is more socially acceptable than a table of multiplication facts carried in a pocket or billfold. Even first-graders can be taught to use reference books that relate to schoolwork. Some teachers have students make notebooks that show the forms for various kinds of work and have basic spelling lists, color charts, and number charts. Reference material can also be placed in a special section of the high schooler's notebook.

e. *Checking or verifying potential answers or products* is one of the more critical skills for the student to learn. Not many people turn in important documents such as income tax statements before double checking the accuracy of their work. In school, too, students must learn to check the work in whatever way they can. Poor spellers may have friends who will serve as spelling checkers for them.

This is one of the areas for which it is difficult to gain acceptance within the regular classroom. The idea of independence in school often means doing the work alone rather than finding the appropriate ways of helping oneself do the work correctly. This skill may be explained as one that is important for future job success as well as present school achievement.

f. *Physical conditions.* We have noted the importance of physical conditions for study. In this case, the student must decide which conditions are most conducive for independent study and how these conditions might be made real.

g. *Time management* is often a high priority for instruction. Further, once taught, these skills require extensive monitoring to ensure that they are maintained.

Time management can be taught in many ways, most of which involve planning and estimations of time needed for the task at hand (V. Brown, undated b). For example, students who learn to estimate optimistic time (the least time the task will take) and pessimistic time (the most time the task will take) and then to calculate the real elapsed time can chart their progress in making better estimations (see Figure 13–5).

h. *Self-monitoring* is becoming a more important part of programs in behavior modification. The techniques used can be applied to monitoring of independent study. Usually some tangible checklists or data sheets are prepared initially. As the student becomes more used to the idea of self-monitoring, these are faded out. They may be reinstated during problem times, just as adults often find checklists in magazines for monitoring preparations before going on a vacation or getting ready for winter.

i. *Self-reinforcement* systems may need to be taught to the student. Workman (1982) presents techniques to use for teaching self-control of study and social behaviors to students. (See the chapter on Classroom Behavior) His methodology includes both self-monitoring and self-reinforcement. Whether the rewards administered are verbal self-acknowledgment or tangible rewards, this part of any assessment and programming will become important to the student's independence in this area.

j. *Grades and grading* become of concern to the student who tries very hard to study but is still doing poorly insofar as grades are concerned. Students who have spent much of their school careers in self-contained special education classes may never have been in a competitive situation before. Accustomed to making A's for effort, they are readily discouraged by grade systems. A great deal of role playing, values discussion, and expectation setting may be needed before placing such students into the competitive grade situation.

Students should also be taught to analyze situations that might have led to poor grades. Barnstorf (1981) shows a self-assessment guide for college students to use when they have failed a test (see Figure 13–6). This kind of data sheet can be used readily with secondary students and adapted to the elementary level. Students may also be taught how to approach teachers if they believe that they have been treated unfairly insofar as grades are concerned.

k. *Revision* of products such as written assignments is related to the idea of verifying. It includes the idea of redoing an assignment as well. This skill is especially

FIGURE **13 – 5.**
Chart Sample for Time Graph

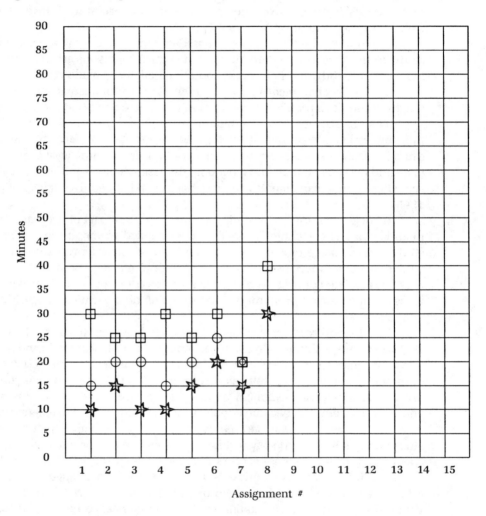

Visual display of Time Card records

☆ or green = optimistic time
□ or blue = pessimistic time
○ or red = real time

V. Brown, undated b.

FIGURE 13 – 6.
Factors Influencing Failure

	Before the test	During the Test	After the Test
Course design: and/or Instructor ▲	____ test expectations unclear ____ instructor presented ideas unclear-ly, examples: ____ inadequate study guides ____ textbook wasn't clear ____ textbook, in-class material not related ____ instructor not available or unwilling to answer questions ____ study sessions not helpful ____ other, specify	____ poor physical conditions ____ inadequate time allowed ____ test questions poorly phrased ____ test did not cover expected material ____ test did not cover significant material ____ test directions were unclear ____ other, specify	____ adequate feedback not provided ____ not enough opportunity to go over test ____ test scored improperly or incorrectly ____ other, specify
Self ▲	____ used study time poorly ____ didn't read text or mark adequate-ly (or hand-outs) ____ didn't review ____ didn't attend 100% ____ didn't participate in class ____ didn't attend study sessions ____ didn't take adequate notes ____ didn't pay attention to class material ____ didn't predict test questions ____ negative attitude ____ other pressures on my mind ____ other, specify	____ my test questions were not good predictors ____ couldn't concentrate ____ didn't follow directions ____ felt tense ____ felt fatigued ____ didn't plan my time well ____ other, specify	____ felt disappointed, angry ____ didn't pay attention to feedback ____ didn't go over my test carefully to learn from my mistakes ____ other

Barnstorf, 1977, p. 133.

important in areas where content, thinking, and the organization of material are important, as in composition.

l. *Actual study skills* such as those suggested by Alley and Deshler (1979), Zifferblatt (1970), Morgan and Deese (1974), and S. Smith (1970) include note taking (e.g., *Notemaking*, D. Brown, 1977), organization of materials, and intensive techniques such as SQ3R (Robinson, 1946). These are the behaviors that have the most chance of being taught by the regular classroom teacher with the assistance of the resource teacher. They do not have a major impact on the curriculum but teach students how to learn the content. For a comprehensive program geared to the post elementary level, we suggest the working book, *A Guidebook for Teaching Study Skills and Motivation*, by Bragstad and Stumpf (1982).

m. *Alternate ways of acquiring information* may need to be learned by students who are having difficulty with the media through which they are expected to learn. For example, the very poor reader is not likely to learn enough about reading to be able to acquire ongoing content in the classroom program. It may be necessary to teach the student how to use materials labs to find films, filmstrips, or tapes of the content.

n. *How to negotiate with the teacher* is an important skill for students who experience problems within the academic setting. On many occasions, modifications of assignments or extra help may be needed. The student who knows how to be pleasantly assertive, to explain the situation, and to suggest some method of remedy or to ask the teacher for an appropriate remedy is more likely to be allowed these modifications. Instruction in these techniques is found in *Skillstreaming the Adolescent* (Goldstein et al., 1980).

o. *Question-asking skills* are useful in class discussion and recitation, both to make the student appear interested in the topic and to focus the student's attention on the topic. Resources in this area are noted in the chapter that deals with Spoken Language. Many curriculum programs that are designed to teach students to get along in the mainstream classroom focus a great deal of attention on asking questions appropriately.

7. *What problems are experienced specifically during homework?* The home is the setting where a great deal of independent study is supposed to occur through the completion of homework assignments. Often the distaste students have for homework is exceeded only by the distaste of parents who are expected to monitor its completion. Since a parent is unaware of what has happened in class to set up the homework assignment, he or she is often placed in a difficult position. Usually it is not a question that parents want homework abandoned; instead, they wish to diminish this area as a source of conflict between them and their children.

The resource teacher should interview the parent(s) if possible to obtain some idea of their attitudes about homework and the degree to which it is an area of conflict. Zifferblatt's *Improving Study and Homework Behaviors* (1970) has been useful as a means of introducing this topic to parents and to parent groups. It may also be used readily with the students themselves.

DEVELOPING INSTRUCTIONAL PROCEDURES

Instructional procedures for the improvement of independent study are to be used through consultation with the classroom teacher if at all possible. Skills such as note taking, previewing material, and preparing for tests should become an integral part of the regular instructional program. Where it is not possible to use this indirect approach to instruction, then the skills or behaviors should be specifically taught and practiced as resource program curriculum but applied and monitored within the settings where independent study is more likely to occur — within regular classrooms, study halls, libraries, or the home.

This section recommends resources for procedures that may be used either as the basis for consultation or with the individual student. The methodologies and materials are essentially the same in each case.

Behavioral Methodologies

The methodologies by which students may be taught the various components of independent study are primarily behavioral. Most of these methodologies are intended to shift the analysis and control of behavior from teachers or parents directly to the student. The specific techniques of interest include: behavior rehearsal (Rose, 1973); modeling and role playing (Sarason and Sarason, 1974; Shaftel and Shaftel, 1967); behavioral counseling (Hosford and DeVisser, 1974); contracting (DeRisi and Butz, 1975; Homme, 1970); and formalized behavior modification (Sulzer-Azaroff and Mayer, 1977).

The methodologies described in these resources are content free and may be applied to problems in independent study. We especially recommend that the resource teacher consider teaching the techniques of behavior modification to the students themselves, so that they can learn to modify the behavior to those to whom they are responsible for products of independent study. For example, an "incorrigible" eighth-grade student in Visalia, California, learned to say to his teacher, "You really help me when you are nice to me," and "It makes me feel good when you praise me." The same boy also learned to come to class early and to stay to chat with the teacher (Gray, with Graubard and Rosenberg, 1974).

Observation and Analysis of the Environment for Students

If students are to become independent of the vagaries of teachers and schools, they must learn to "psych out" the demands of the situation. One project reported by Bowen and Davidson (1977) involved sixth graders who were to enter the seventh grade the next year. Several boys who were in the resource program visited seventh-grade classes and taped interviews with students, counselors, and teachers. They collected samples of books, assignments, and grading and reporting systems;

drew floor plans; and took photographs. The boys analyzed the books and assignments, prepared questions to ask on their return visit, and prepared a slide-tape presentation for the rest of the sixth graders. At that time they fielded questions asked by their classmates and the teachers.

For these boys, the written instructional goal was for them to "raise their reading levels from 10 to 11 in the *XYZ* reading program." The resource teachers had planned to use the remainder of the year in preparation for seventh grade, for several reasons. First, the boys were looking forward to going to the seventh grade but were also somewhat fearful. The exploration of this environment as a means for learning to analyze needed independent study behaviors was reinforcing. The skills they learned would actually be used in the near future. Second, the boys were quite bored with trying for the second year in a row to get from level 10 to level 11 in the reading program. However, the sixth-grade teachers were interested primarily in having the resource teachers tutor the students so that they could keep up with the work in the classrooms.

This kind of situation is typical of the problems faced in trying to implement an instructional program without the cooperation of the classroom and perhaps without the approval of the administration as well. Especially in the area of independent study, we refer the resource teacher to the material in Part I of this book: to recommendations for setting up the program expectations to including behaviors in this critical area.

Additional information about teaching students to observe and identify good student behaviors is presented by Minuchin, Chamberlain, and Graubard, 1967.

Curriculum Development

Resource teachers often have to devise their own curriculum for teaching independent study. Some of these curricula have been written down for sharing. See Figure 13 – 7.

The content of curriculum development in study behaviors is usually the classroom material of immediate importance to the students. We recommend that the resource teacher use easy materials on the same general topic for instructional purposes. The skills can then be applied to the classroom. It is very difficult to attend to learning new behaviors and at the same time learn difficult content material.

Parent Groups

Because homework is important to independent study, this is the area in which parent groups may be started. The topic is of sufficient interest to draw many otherwise disinterested parents to school. This is an area where communication may be opened readily between parent and school. Often monitoring reports are used as formal devices to sustain this communication. The student is reinforced at school

FIGURE **13 – 7.**
Curriculum Examples from Strategies into Nifty Goals

TUNE INTO TWO REAL LIFE EXAMPLES:

(1.) IN ACADEMICS...

PROBLEM/DECISION: "YOU ARE WRITING AND CAN'T SPELL MANY OF THE WORDS. WHAT SHOULD YOU DO?"

NOTE: AS THE KIDS WORK THROUGH THE PROCESS, THEY RECORD THEIR IDEAS IN A NOTEBOOK FOR STRATEGIES.

DEFINE:

EFFECTS ON YOU	EFFECTS ON TEACHER
EMBARRASSED – DON'T LIKE SPELLING	THINKS YOU DIDN'T TRY
DECIDE NOT TO WRITE AT ALL.	THINKS YOU CAN'T DO IT
LIMIT THE AMOUNT YOU WRITE	GIVES YOU A LOWER GRADE
DON'T WRITE THE WORDS YOU WANT	. . .

BRAINSTORM: WHAT CAN YOU DO?   JUDGE: WHEN COULD YOU DO IT?

1.) SOUND WORDS OUT CAREFULLY	1.) ALWAYS – ESPECIALLY WHEN THIS IS ALL YOU CAN DO.
2.) WRITE NEATLY	2.) ALWAYS
3.) USE A DICTIONARY	3.) IF YOU KNOW HOW TO START THE WORDS & DON'T HAVE TOO MANY
4.) ASK SOMEONE: TEACHER FRIEND PARENT	4.) WHEN THE PERSON IS NOT BUSY. DON'T "BUG" THE PERSON
5.) . . .	5.) . . .

FIGURE **13 – 7.** *(Continued)*
Curriculum Examples from Strategies into Nifty Goals

(2.) TALKING ABOUT BEHAVIOR . . .

PROBLEM / DECISION : "YESTERDAY SOMETHING HAPPENED TO INTER-
FERE WITH OUR WORKING EFFECTIVELY IN THIS CLASS.
WHAT HAPPENED ? WHAT CAN WE DO ABOUT IT ?

NOTE : THESE PROBLEMS ARE DISCUSSED WITH THE
STUDENTS SEATED IN A CIRCLE. THE TEACHER TAKES NOTES.

DEFINE:

1. PEOPLE WERE NOT TAKING TIME OUTS PROPERLY...
DISRUPTED EVERYONE.

2. EVERYONE NEEDED HELP AT ONCE ... NO ONE
ENDED UP GETTING MUCH.

3. GENERAL EFFECT: EVERYONE HASSLED ... NOT MUCH DONE.

BRAINSTORM: WHAT CAN WE DO?	JUDGE: WHEN? WHY? HOW?
1.) TIME OUT IN A DIFFERENT CORNER.	1.) TAKE TIME OUT IN BACK SO NO ONE BUT TEACHER SEES.
2.) EVERYONE RAISE HAND WHEN THEY WANT HELP.	2.) TEACHER SHOULD NOT HELP KID UNLESS KID RAISES HAND.
3.) GIVE A REWARD IF WE DON'T FEEL HASSLED.	3.) TEACHER DECIDES IF HASSLED. IF NOT, LEAVE 2 MINUTES EARLY.
4.) . . .	4.) . . .

Sherry et al., 1976.

for work done well at home and reinforced at home for work done well at school. Further, parents can be taught specific techniques such as timing and clarifying assignments. They often appreciate efforts made to assist them in this difficult area.

Endnotes

1   The material in this chapter has been adapted and/or extended from: (1) Brown, V. *Independent study behaviors. Learning Disability Quarterly*, 1978, *1*, 78 – 84, and (2) Brown, V. *How to assess and teach independent study.* Austin, TX: PRO-ED, undated b.

2   Dr. Thomas Caldwell, University of Kansas Medical Center, Kansas City, Kansas. 1966.

References

Abeson, A., Bolick, N., and Hass, J. *A primer on due process.* Reston, Va.: Council for Exceptional Children, 1976.

Affleck, J. Q., Lehning, T. W., and Brow, K. D. Expanding the resource concept: The resource school. *Exceptional Children,* 1973, *39,* 446 – 53.

Aiken, L. R., Jr. Update on attitudes and other affective variables in learning mathematics. *Review of Educational Research,* 1976, *46,* 293 – 310.

Allen, P. D., and Watson, D. J. (eds.) *Findings of research in miscue analysis: Classroom implications.* Urbana, Ill.: National Council of Teachers of English, 1976.

Alley, G., and Deshler, D. *Teaching the learning disabled adolescent: Strategies and methods.* Denver: Love, 1979.

Allington, R., and Strange, M. *Learning through reading in the content areas.* Lexington, Mass.: D. C. Heath, 1980.

American Psychological Association. *Standards for educational and psychological tests.* Washington, D. C.: American Psychological Association, 1974.

Anastasi, A. *Psychological testing.* 5th ed. New York: Macmillan, 1982.

Applegate, M. *Easy in English.* Evanston, Ill.: Row, Peterson, 1960.

Arena, J. (ed.) *Building spelling skills in dyslexic children.* San Rafael, Calif.: Academic Therapy Publications, 1968.

Ashlock, R. B. *Error patterns in computation: A semi-programmed approach.* 2d ed. Columbus, Ohio: Merrill, 1976.

Axelrod, S. *Behavior modification for the classroom teacher.* New York: McGraw-Hill, 1977.

Baker, R. G., and Wright, H. F. *Midwest and its children.* New York: Harper & Row, 1955.

Ball, G. (ed.) *Magic circle: An overview of the human development program.* La Mesa, Calif.: Human Development Training Institute, 1974.

Balla, D. *Class notes.* Lawrence, Ks.: University of Kansas, 1967.

Baratta-Lorton, M. *Mathematics their way.* Menlo Park, Calif.: Addison-Wesley, 1976.

Baratta-Lorton, M. *Workjobs II: Number activities for early childhood.* Menlo Park, Calif.: Addison-Wesley, 1979.

Baratta-Lorton, R. *Mathematics . . . A way of thinking.* Menlo Park, Calif.: Addison-Wesley, 1977.

Barksdale, M. W., and Atkinson, A. P. A resource room approach to instruction for the educable retarded. *Focus on Exceptional Children,* 1971, *3,* 12 – 15.

Barnstorf, T. *Study skills guide.* Minneapolis, Minn.: Burgess Publishing Co., 1977.

Barrie-Blackley, S., Musselwhite, C. R., and Rogister, S. H. *Clinical language sampling: A handbook for students and clinicians.* Danville, Ill.: Interstate Printers and Publishers, 1978.

Bechtel, J., and Franzblau, B. *Reading in the science classroom.* West Haven, Conn.: National Education Association, 1980.

Becker, W. C., Englemann, S., and Thomas, D. R. *Teaching: A course in applied psychology.* Chicago: Science Research Associates, 1971.

Benthul, H. F., Anderson, E. A., Utech, A. M., Biggy, M. V., and Bailey, B. L. *Spell correctly.* Morristown, N.J.: Silver Burdett, 1980.

Bersoff, D. N., Kabler, M., Fiscus, E., and Ankney, R. Effectiveness of special class placement for children labeled neurologically handicapped. *Journal of School Psychology,* 1972, *10,* 157 – 63 (I & II).

Biggs, E., and MacLean, J. *Freedom to learn.* Menlo Park, Calif.: Addison-Wesley, 1969.

Bingham, W. V. D., Moore, B. V., and Gustad, J. W. *How to interview.* New York: Harper & Row, 1957.

Blackhurst, A. E., Cross, D. P., Nelson, C. M., and Tawney, J. W. Approximating noncategorical teacher education. *Exceptional Children,* 1973, *39,* 284 – 88.

Blake, H., and Spennato, N. A. The directed writing activity: A process with structure. *Language Arts,* 1980, *57* (3), 317 – 18.

Bloom, B. Mastery learning and its implications for curriculum development. In E. W. Eisner (ed.), *Confronting curriculum reform.* Boston: Little, Brown, 1971.

Bloom, L., and Lahey, M. *Language development and language disorders.* New York: John Wiley & Sons, 1978.

Bormaster, J. S., and Treat, C. L. *Building interpersonal relationships through talking, listening, communicating.* Austin, Tex.: PRO-ED, 1982.

Bowen, P., and Davidson, K. Transition skills for entering junior high school students. Practicum Report. Duluth, Minn.: University of Minnesota-Duluth, 1977.

Bragstad, B. J., and Stumpf, S. M. *A guidebook for teaching study skills and motivation.* Boston: Allyn and Bacon, 1982.

Brogan, P., and Fox, L. K. *Helping children read.* New York: Holt, Rinehart & Winston, 1962.

Brophy, J., and Evertson, C. *Learning from teaching: A developmental perspective.* Boston: Allyn and Bacon, 1976.

Brophy, J. E., and Good, T. L. *Teacher-child dyadic interaction: A manual for coding classroom behavior.* Austin, Tex.: Research and Development Center for Teacher Education, University of Texas, 1969.

Brophy, J., and Good, T. *Teacher-student relationships: Causes and consequences.* New York: Holt, Rinehart & Winston, 1974.

Brown, D. *Notemaking.* Toronto: Gage Educational Publishing, Ltd., 1977.

Brown, F. G. *Principles of education and psychological testing.* 2d ed. New York: Holt, Rinehart & Winston, 1976.

Brown, L. Evaluating and managing classroom behavior. In D. Hammill and N. Bartel *Teaching children with learning and behavior problems.* Boston: Allyn and Bacon, 1982.

Brown, L., and Hammill, D. *Behavior Rating Profile.* Austin, Tex.: PRO-ED, 1983.

Brown, V. L. Out of the classroom: Reading instruction. *Exceptional Children,* 1967, *34,* 197 – 99.

Brown, V. L. A basic Q-sheet for analyzing and comparing curriculum materials and proposals. *Journal of Learning Disabilities,* 1975, *8,* 409 – 16.

Brown, V. L. Learning about mathematics instruction. *Journal of Learning Disabilities,* 1975a, *8,* 476 – 85.

Brown, V. L. Reading miscue analysis. *Journal of Learning Disabilities,* 1975b, *8,* 605 – 11.

Brown, V. L. Independent study behaviors. *Learning Disability Quarterly,* 1978, *1,* 78 – 84.

Brown, V. L. *Remediating remedial reading.* Austin, Tex: PRO-ED, Unpublished manuscript, undated a.

Brown, V. L. *How to assess and teach independent study behaviors.* Austin, Tex.: PRO-ED, Unpublished manuscript, undated b.

Brown, V. L., and Botel, M. *Dyslexia: Definition or treatment?* Bloomington, Ind.: Indiana University, 1972. ERIC Document Reproduction Service No. ED 058014.

Brown, V. L., Hammill, D. D., and Wiederholt, J. L., *Test of Reading Comprehension: A Method for Assessing the Understanding of Written Language.* Austin, Tex.: PRO-ED, 1978.

Brown, V. L., and McEntire, M. E. *Test of Mathematical Abilities.* Austin, Tex.: PRO-ED, 1983.

Bryant, B., and Bryant, D. *The Test of Articulation Performance: Diagnostic.* Austin, Texas: PRO-ED, 1983.

Burmeister, L. E. *Reading strategies for secondary school teachers.* Reading, Mass.: Addison-Wesley, 1974.

Burns, M. *The I hate mathematics! book.* Boston: Little, Brown, 1975.

Burns, P. C. *Assessment and correction of language arts difficulties.* Columbus, Ohio: Merrill, 1980.

Buros, O. K. *The eighth mental measurements yearbook.* Highland Park, N.J.: Gryphon Press, 1978.

Buros, O. K. (ed.) *Tests in print II.* Highland Park, N.J.: Gryphon Press, 1974.

Burrows, A. T., Jackson, D., and Saunders, D. O. *They all want to write.* 3d ed. New York: Holt, Rinehart & Winston, 1964.

Buswell, G. T., and John, L. Diagnostic studies in arithmetic. *Supplementary Education Monographs, No. 30.* Chicago: University of Chicago Press, 1926.

Cantrell, R. P., and Cantrell, M. L. Preventive mainstreaming: Impact of a supportive services program on pupils. *Exceptional Children,* 1976, *42,* 381 – 385.

Carlson, R. K. *Writing aids through the grades.* New York: Teachers College Press, Columbia University, 1970.

Carpenter, T. P., Coburn, T. G., Reys, R. E., and Wilson, J. W. Notes from National Assessment: Processes used on computational exercises. *Arithmetic Teacher,* 1976, 217 – 22.

Carrow, E. *Test for Auditory Comprehension of Language.* Austin, Tex.: Learning Concepts, 1973.

Carrow, E. *The Carrow Elicited Language Inventory.* Austin, Tex.: Learning Concepts, 1974.

Carter, J. L. Intelligence and reading achievement of EMR children in three educational settings. *Mental Retardation,* 1975, *95,* 26 – 27 (I & II).

Cawley, J. F., Goodstein, H. A., Fitzmaurice, A. M., Lepore, A., Sedlak, R., and Althaus, V. *Project Math: A program of the mainstream series.* Wallingford, Conn.: Educational Sciences, 1976.

Cegelka, W. J., and Tyler, J. L. The efficacy of regular class placement for the mentally retarded in proper perspective. *Training School Bulletin*, 1970, *67*, 33 – 68.

Childrey, J. A. Jr., Home remedies for reluctant readers. In A. J. Ciani (ed.), *Motivating reluctant readers*. Newark, Del.: International Reading Association, 1981.

Christopolos, F., and Renz, P. A. A critical examination of special education programs. *Journal of Special Education*, 1969, *3*, 371 – 79.

Clapp, O. (ed.), *Classroom practices in teaching English 1975 – 1976. On righting writing.* Urbana, Ill.: National Council of Teachers of English, 1975.

Clark, H. H. The primitive nature of children's relational concepts. In J. R. Hayes (ed.), *Cognition and the development of languages*. New York: Wiley, 1970.

Clay, M. The reading behavior of five-year-old children: A research report. *New Zealand Journal of Educational Studies*, 1967, *2*, 11 – 31.

Clay, M. M. *What did I write?* Exeter, N.H.: Heinemann Educational Books, 1975.

Cohen, A., and Stover, G. Effects of teaching sixth grade students to modify format variables of math word problems. *Reading Research Quarterly*, 1981, *16* (2), 175 – 200.

Cohen, S. B., and Plaskon, S. P. *Language arts for the mildly handicapped.* Columbus, Ohio: Charles E. Merrill, 1980.

Cole, M. L., and Cole, J. T. *Effective intervention with the language impaired child.* Rockville, Md.: Aspen Systems Corp., 1981.

Cooper, C. R. An outline for writing sentence-combining problems. *English Journal*, 1973, *62*, 96 – 102, 108.

Cooper, C. R., and Odell, L. *Evaluating writing. Describing, measuring, judging.* Urbana, Ill.: National Council of Teachers of English , 1977.

Cooper, C. K. Holistic evaluation of writing. In C. R. Cooper and L. Odell (eds.), *Evaluating writing. Describing, measuring, judging.* Urbana, Ill.: National Council of Teachers of English, 1977.

Cooper, J. O. *Measurement and analysis of behavioral techniques.* Columbus, Ohio: Charles E. Merrill, 1974.

Copeland, R. W. *Mathematics and the elementary teacher.* 3d ed. Philadelphia: Saunders, 1976.

Coughran, L., and Goff, M. *Learning staircase.* New York: Teaching Resources, 1976.

Courtis, S. A. Measurement of growth and efficiency in arithmetic. *Elementary School Teacher*, 1911, *11*, 528 – 39.

Cox, L. Analysis, classification, and frequency of systematic error computation patterns in the addition, subtraction, multiplication, and division vertical algorithms for grades 2 – 6 and special education classes. Unpublished manuscript. Kansas City, Kans.: Kansas University Medical Center, June, 1974. ERIC Document Reproduction Service No. ED 092 407.

Crafts, K., and Hauthner, B. *The student's guide to good grades, or surviving the undergraduate jungle.* New York: Grove Press, 1976.

Cruickshank, W. M., Bentzen, F. A., Ratzeburg, F. H., and Tannhauser, M. T. *A teaching method for brain injured and hyperactive children.* Syracuse, N.Y.: Syracuse University Press, 1961.

Cunningham, R. Developing question-asking skills. In J. Weingand (ed.), *Developing teacher competencies.* Englewood Cliffs, N.J.: Prentice-Hall, 1971.

D'Angelo, K., Korba, S., and Woodworth, C. Bookmaking: Motivation for writing. *Language Arts*, 1981, *58* (3), 308 – 15.

Davis, L. N., and McCallon, E. *Planning, conducting, and evaluating workshops.* Austin, Tex.: Learning Concepts, 1974.

Davison, A., Kantor, R. N., Hannah, J., Hermon, G., Lutz, R., and Salzillo, R. Limitations of readability formulas in guiding adaptations of texts. Technical Report No. 162. Urbana, Ill.: Center for the Study of Reading, University of Illinois, March 1980.

Dawson, L., McLeod, S., and Mathews, S. *Behavior Checklist for Middle Schools.*Madison, Wis.: Madison Metropolitan Schools, 1976.

Delbecq, A. L., Van de Ven, A. H., and Gustafson, O. H. *Group techniques for program planning. A guide to nominal group and delphi processes.* Glenview, Ill.: Scott Foresman, 1975.

DeRisi, W. J., and Butz, G. *Writing behavioral contracts. A case simulation manual.* Champaign, Ill.: Research Press, 1975.

DeShong, B. R. *The special educator: Stress and survival.* Rockville, Md.: Aspen, 1981.

Dever, R. B. *Teaching the American language to kids.* Bloomington, Ind.: Center for Innovation in Teaching the Handicapped, 1978.

Dinkmeyer, D. D. *Developing understanding of self and others.* Circle Pines, Minn.: American Guidance Service, 1982.

Dinkmeyer, D., and Carlson, J. (eds.). *Consulting: Facilitating human potential and change processes.* Columbus, Ohio: Charles E. Merrill, 1973.

Dodd, J. M., and Kelker, K. A. *The role of the resource teacher: Role conflict and role concensus.* Paper presented at the Montana Council for Exceptional Children Convention. Great Falls, Mt., 1980.

Donaldson, M., and Balfour, G. Less is more: A study of language comprehension in children. *British Journal of Psychology*, 1968, *59*, 561 – 67.

Dunlap, W. P. An attitudinal device for primary children. *Arithmetic Teacher*, 1976, *23*, 29 – 31.

Dunn, L. M. Special education for the mildly retarded — Is much of it justifiable? *Exceptional Children*, 1968, *35*, 5 – 22.

Dunn, L. M., Dunn, L., and Smith, J. O. *The Peabody Language Development Kit: Level 2 Revised.* Circle Pines, Minn.: American Guidance Services, 1981.

Dunn, L. M., Horton, K. B., and Smith, J. O. *The Peabody Language Development Kit: Level P Revised.* Circle Pines, Minn.: American Guidance Services, 1981.

Dunn, L. M., Smith, J. O., and Dunn, L. *The Peabody Language Development Kit: Level 1 Revised.* Circle Pines, Minn.: American Guidance Services, 1981.

Dunn, L. M., Smith, J. O., and Smith, D. D. *The Peabody Language Development Kit: Level 3 Revised.* Circle Pines, Minn.: American Guidance Services, 1982.

Durkin, D. What classroom observations reveal about reading comprehension instruction. *Reading Research Quarterly*, 1978 – 1979, *14*, 481 – 533.

Durkin, D. Reading comprehension instruction in five basal reading series. *Reading Research Quarterly*, 1981, *16* (4), 515 – 44.

Durost, W. N., Bixler, H. H., Hildreth, G. H., Lund, K. W., and Writhstone, J. W. *Directions for administering Metropolitan Achievement Tests.* New York: Harcourt Brace Jovanovich, 1955.

Durrell, D. D. *Durrell Analysis of Reading Difficulty.* New York: Harcourt Brace Jovanovich, 1955.

Edgington, R. But he spelled them right this morning. *Academic Therapy Quarterly*, 1967, *3*, 58 – 59.

Edmonston, W. *Laradon Articulation Scale.* Beverly Hills, Calif.: Western Psychological Services, 1963.

Educational Products Information Exchange. *Report No. 62/63. Selecting and evaluating beginning reading materials.* New York: Educational Products Information Exchange, 1973.

Educational Products Information Exchange. *Report No. 64. Analysis of basic and supplemental reading materials.* New York: Educational Products Information Exchange, 1974.

Educational Products Information Exchange. *Report No. 65. Materials for individualizing math instruction.* New York: Eduational Products Information Exchange, 1974.

Eduational Products Information Exchange. *Report No. 69/70. Analysis of elementary school mathematics materials.* New York: Eduational Products Information Exchange, 1975.

Educational Products Information Exchange. *Selector's guide to bilingual education materials:* Vol. 1: *Spanish language arts.* New York: Educational Products Information Exchange, 1976.

EPIE PRO/FILES. EPIE Institute, P.O. Box 620. Stony Brook, N.Y., 1981.

Ehly, S. W., and Larsen, S. C. *Peer tutoring for individualized instruction.* Austin, Tex.: PRO-ED, 1980.

Engelmann, S., and Bruner, E. C. *DISTAR: An instructional system.* Chicago: Science Research Associates, 1974.

Engelmann, S., Haddux, P., Hanner, S., and Osborn, J. *Thinking basics. Corrective reading program. Comprehension A.* Chicago: Science Research Associates, 1978.

Engelmann, S., and Osborn, J. *DISTAR: An instructional system.* Chicago: Science Research Associates, 1970.

Enstrom, E. A. The realtive efficiency of the various approaches to writing with the left hand. *Journal of Educational Research,* 1962, *52,* 573 – 77.

Estes, T. H., Estes, J. J., Richards, H. C., and Roettger, D. *Estes Attitude Scales: Measures of attitudes toward school subjects.* Austin, Tex.: PRO-ED, 1981.

Estes, T. H., and Vaughan, J. L. *Reading and Learning in the content classroom. Diagnostic and instructional strategies.* Boston: Allyn and Bacon, 1978.

Evans, F. *Rationale for using standardized achievement tests to provide information regarding their gains in academic skills.* Madison, Wis.: Department of Public Instruction, April 17, 1980.

Ezor, E. L., and Lane, T. Applied linguistics: A discovery approach to the teaching of writing. *Language Arts,* 1975, *52,* 1019 – 21.

Fader, D. N. *Hooked on books: Program and proof.* New York: Berkeley, 1968.

Fader, D., et al. *The new hooked on books.* New York: Berkeley, 1976.

Farr, R., and Roser, N. *Teaching a child to read.* New York: Harcourt Brace Jovanovich, 1979.

Feder, B., *The complete guide to taking tests.* Englewood Cliffs, N.J.: Prentice-Hall, 1979.

Fernald, G. *Remedial techniques in basic school subjects.* New York: McGraw-Hill, 1943.

Filley, A. C. *Interpersonal Conflict resolution.* Glenview, Ill.: Scott Foresman, 1975.

Fitzgerald, E. *Straight language for the deaf.* Washington, D.C.: Volta Bureau, 1966.

Fitzgerald, S. Some current problems in language arts instruction. In C. Weaver and R. Duoma eds., *The language arts teacher in action.* Kalamazoo, Mich.: Department of English, Western Michigan University, 1977.

Flanders, N. *Analyzing teaching behavior.* Menlo Park, Calif.: Addison-Wesley, 1970.

Fokes, J. *Fokes sentence builder.* New York: Teaching Resources, 1976.

Fox, R. S., Schmuck, R., Egmond, E. V., Ritvo, N., and Jung, C. *Diagnosing professional climate of schools.* Fairfax, Va.: NTL Learning Resources, 1975.

Frampton, M. E., and Gall, E. D., (eds.) *Special education for the exceptional.* Boston: Porter Sargent, 1955.

Frampton, M. E., and Rowell, H. G. *Education of the handicapped.* Vol 2. Yonkers, N.Y.: World Book, 1940.

Freeman, F. W. *Reference manual for teachers. Grades one through four.* Columbus, Ohio: Zaner-Bloser, 1965.

Freedman, B. J. An analysis of socio-behavioral skill deficits in delinquent and non-delinquent boys. Ph.D. dissertation, University of Michigan, 1974.

Freidus, E. S. The needs of teachers for specialized information on number concepts. In W. M. Cruickshank (ed.) *The teacher of brain-injured children: A discussion of the bases for competency.* Syracuse, N.Y.: Syracuse University Press, 1966.

Galbraith, R. E., and Jones. T. M. *Moral reasoning. A teaching handbook for adapting Kohlberg to the classroom* Minneapolis, Minn.: Greenhaven Press, 1976.

Gallagher, P. A. *Teaching students with behavior problems: Techniques for classroom instruction.* Denver: Love, 1979.

Gallagher, J. M., and Reid, D. K. *The learning theory of Piaget and Inhelder.* Monterey, Calif.: Brooks/Cole Publishing Co., 1981.

Garber, M.D. *An examination and comparison of selected cohesive features found in child-produced texts and beginning reading materials.* Paper presented at the National Conference on Language Arts in the Elementary School, San Antonio, Texas, March 21, 1980.

Garcis, R. L., and Deyoe, R. M. *How can I help my child read English as a second language?* Newark, Del.: International Reading Association, 1974.

Garrison, M., and Hammill, D. Who are the retarded? *Exceptional Children,* 1971, *38,* 13 – 20.

Garwick, G. B. Program evaluation of services for visually impaired persons through individual goal setting. *Education of the Visually Handicapped,* 1978, *10* (2), 38 – 45.

Gattegno, C. *Words in color.* Chicago: Learning Materials, Encyclopedia Britannica, 1962.

Geffner, D. S. Assessment of language disorder: Linguistic and cognitive functions. *Topics in Language Disorders,* 1981, *1* (3), 1 – 10.

Gerke, R. E. *The effects of mainstreaming on the self concept and reading achievement of exceptional children at the elementary level,* Lehigh University, 1975 (Order Number: 76 – 10, 366).

Geuder, P., Harvey, L., Loyd, D., and Wages, J. (eds.) *They really taught us how to write.* Urbana, Ill.: National Council of Teachers of English, 1974.

Gibson, E. J. Learning to read. In H. Singer and R. Ruddell (eds.), *Theoretical models and processes of reading.* Newark, Del.: International Reading Association, 1976.

Gickling, E. E., Murphy, L. C., and Malloy, D. W. Teacher's references for resource services. *Exceptional Children,* 1979, *45* (6), 442 – 49.

Gillespie-Silver, P. *Teaching reading to children with special needs. An ecological approach.* Columbus, Ohio: Charles E. Merrill, 1979.

Gillingham, A., and Stillman, B. *Remedial training for children with specific disability in reading, spelling, and penmanship.* Cambridge, Mass.: Educators Publishing Service, 1966.

Ginsburg, H. P. *Children's arithmetic: How they learn it and how you teach it.* Austin, Tex.: PRO-ED, 1982.

Ginsburg, H. P. The psychology of arithmetic thinking. *Journal of Children's Mathematical Behavior,* 1977, *1* (4), 1 – 89.

Ginsburg, H. P., and Baroody, A. J. *The Test of Early Mathematics Ability.* Austin, Tex.: PRO-ED, 1983.

Ginsburg, H. P., and Mathews, S. C. *Diagnostic Test of Arithmetic Strategies.* Austin, Tex.: PRO-ED, 1983.

Glavin, J. P. Follow-up behavioral research on resource rooms. *Exceptional Children,* 1973, *40.* 211 – 13.

Glavin, J. P., Quay, H. C., Annesley, F. R., and Werry, J. S. An experimental resource room for behavioral problem children. *Exceptional Children,* 1971, *38,* 131 – 37.

Glavin, J. P., Quay, H. C. & Werry, J. S. Behavioral and academic gains of conduct problem children in different classroom settings. *Exceptional Children,* 1971, *37,* 441 – 446.

Glazer, J., and Williams III, G. *Introduction to children's literature.* New York: McGraw-Hill, 1979.

Glim, T. E., and Manchester, F. S. *Basic spelling.* Philadelphia: Lippincott, 1977.

Glynn, E., Thomas, J., and Shee, S. Behavioral self-control of on-task behavior in an elementary school classroom. *Journal of Applied Behavioral Analysis,* 1973, *6,* 105 – 13.

Goldman, R., and Fristoe, M. *Goldman-Fristoe Test of Articulation.* Circle Pines, Minn.: American Guidance Service, 1969.

Goldstein, A. P., Sprafkin, R. P., Gershaw, N. J., and Klein, P. *Skillstreaming the adolescent: A structured learning approach to teaching prosocial skills.* Champaign, Ill.: Research Press, 1980.

Gonzales, D. G. An author center for children. *Language Arts,* 1980, *57* (3), 280 – 84.

Goodman, K. Review of reading tests and reviews. *American Eductional Research Journal,* 1971, *8,* 169 – 70.

Goodman, K. Twelve easy wasy to make learning to read difficult and one difficult way to make it easy. In F. Smith (ed.), *Psycholinguistics and reading.* New York: Holt, Rinehart, and Winston, 1973.

Goodman, Y. Roots of literacy. In M. Douglas (ed.), *44th Yearbook of the Claremont Reading Conference.* Claremont, Calif.: Claremont Reading Conference, 1980.

Goodman, Y. M. Using children's miscues for teaching reading strategies. *Reading Teacher,* 1970, *23,* 455 – 59.

Goodman, Y. M., and Burke, C. L. *Reading miscue inventory: Manual, and Procedures for diagnosis and evaluation.* New York: Macmillan, 1972.

Goodman, Y. M., and Burke, C. L. *Reading strategies: Focus on comprehension.* New York: Holt, Rinehart and Winston, 1980.

Goodstein, H. A. Assessment and programming in mathematics for the handicapped. *Focus on Exceptional Children,* 1975, *7,* 1 – 11.

Gorden, R. L. *Interviewing: Strategy, techniques, and tactics.* Homewood, Ill.: Dorsey, 1969.

Gordon, T. *Parent effectiveness training.* New York: Wyden, 1970.

Graeber, A. O., and Wallace, L. *Identification of systematic errors: Final report.* Philadelphia: Research for Better Schools, 1977. ERIC Document Reproduction Service No. ED 139 662.

Graham, S., and Miller, L. Handwriting research and practice: A unified approach. *Focus on Exceptional Children,* 1980, *13,* 1 – 16.

Graves, D. What children show us about revision. *Language Arts,* 1979, *56,* 312 – 19.

Gray, B. B., and Ryan, B. *A language program for the nonlanguage child.* Champaign, Ill.: Research Press, 1973.

Gray, F., with Graubard, P., and Rosenberg, H. Little brother is changing you. *Psychology Today*, 1974, *7*, 42 – 46.

Gray W. S. *On their own in reading. How to give children independence in analyzing new words.* Rev. ed. Chicago: Scott, Foresman, 1960.

Gronlund, N. E. *Measurement and evaluation in teaching.* New York: Macmillan, 1981.

Gronlund, N. E. *Preparing Criterion-referenced tests for classroom instruction.* New York: Macmillan, 1973.

Guerney, B. G., Jr. (ed.) *Psychotherapeutic agents: New roles for nonprofessionals.* New York: Holt, Rinehart and Winston, 1969.

Haley-James, S. Revising writing in the upper grades. *Language Arts, 1981, 58* (5), 562 – 66.

Hall, R. V. *The measurement of behavior.* Lawrence, Kan.: H & H Enterprises, 1974.

Hall, R. V. *Managing behavior. Part 1.* Lawrence, Kan.: H & H Enterprises, 1971.

Hall, R. V. *Basic principles.* Lawrence, Kan.: H & H Enterprises, 1975.

Hall, R. V. Responsive teaching: Focus on measurement and research in the classroom and the home. In E. Meyen, G. Vergason, and R. J. Whelan (eds.), *Strategies for teaching exceptional children.* Denver: Love, 1972, 403 – 415.

Hammill, D. Handwriting. In D. Hammill and N. Bartel *Teaching children with learning and behavioral problems.* Boston: Allyn and Bacon, 1982.

Hammill, D. D., Brown, V. L., Larsen, S. C., and Wiederholt, J. L. *Test of Adolescent Language. A multi-dimensional approach to assessment.* Austin, Tex.: PRO-ED, 1980.

Hammill, D., Iano, R., McGettigan, J., and Wiederholt, J. Retardates' reading achievement in the resource room model: The first year. *Training School Bulletin,* 1972, *69,* 105 – 107.

Hammill, D. D., and Larsen, S. C. *Test of Written Language.* Austin, Tex.: PRO-ED, 1983.

Hammill, D., and McNutt, G. *The correlates of reading.* Austin, Tex.: PRO-ED, 1981.

Hammill, D. D., and Newcomer, P. *Test of Language Development—Intermediate.* Austin, Tex.: PRO-ED, 1982.

Hammill, D., and Wiederholt, J. L. *The resource room: Rationale and implementation.* New York: Grune & Stratton, Buttonwood Farms Division, 1972.

Hamrick, K. Oral language and readiness for the written symbolization of addition and subtraction. *Journal for Research in Mathematics Education,* 1979, *10* (3), 188 – 94.

Haring, N. G., and Phillips, E. L. *Analysis and modification of classroom behavior.* Englewood Cliffs, N.J.: Prentice-Hall, 1972.

Harris, A., and Kapache, R. Behavior modification in schools: Ethical issues and suggested guidelines. *Journal of School Psychology,* 1978, *16,* 25 – 33.

Harris, W. J., and Mahar, C. Problems in implementing resource programs in rural schools. *Exceptional Children,* 1975, *42* (2), 95 – 99.

Harshman, H. W. The effects of manipulative materials on arithmetic achievement of first-grade pupils. *Dissertation Abstracts,* 1962, *23,* 1:150.

Hausserman, E. *Developmental potential of preschool children.* New York: Grune & Stratton, 1958.

Hawisher, M. F. *The resource room: An access to excellence.* Lancaster, S. C.: South Carolina Region V Educational Services Center, 1975.

Hawisher, M. F., and Calhoun, M. L. *The resource room: An educational asset for children with special needs.* Columbus, Ohio: Charles E. Merrill, 1978.

Heddens, J. W. *Today's mathematics.* 4th ed. Chicago: Science Research Associates, 1980.

Henderson, E. H., and Beers, J. W. (eds.). *Developmental and cognitive aspects of learning to spell.* Newark, Del.: International Reading Association, 1980.

Hendrickson, A. D., *Mathematics the Piaget way.* St. Paul, Minn.: Council on Quality Education, n.d.

Hendrickson, A. D. Prevention or cure? Another look at mathematics learning problems. In D. Carnine et al.*Interdisciplinary voices in learning disabilities and remedial education.* Austin, Tex.: PRO-ED, 1983.

Herber, H. L. *Teaching reading in content areas.* 2d ed. Englewood Cliffs, N.J.: Prentice-Hall, 1978.

Herold, P. J. *The math teaching handbook for teacher, tutors, and parents.* Newton, Mass.: Selective Educational Equipment, 1978.

Heron, T. E., and Harris, K. C. *The educational consultant. Helping professionals, parents, and mainstream students.* Boston: Allyn and Bacon, 1982.

Herrick, V. E. (ed.) *New horizons for research in handwriting.* Madison, Wis.: University of Wisconsin Press, 1963.

Hewett, F. M., and Taylor, F. D. *The emotionally disturbed child in the classroom.* Boston: Allyn and Bacon, 1980.

Homme, L. *How to use contingency contracting in the classroom.* Rev. ed. Champaign, Ill.: Research Press, 1970.

Hopper, R., and Naremore, R. J. *Children's speech. A practical introduction to communication development.* 2d ed. New York: Harper & Row, 1978.

Horn, E. A. *A basic writing vocabulary.* University of Iowa Monographs in Education, First Series No. 4. Iowa City: University of Iowa, 1926.

Hosford, R. E., and DeVisser, L.A. *Behavioral approaches to counseling. An introduction.* Washington, D.C.: APGA Press, 1974.

Howell, R. G., and Howell, M. S. *Discipline in the classroom: Solving the teaching puzzle.* Reston, Va.: Reston Publishing Co., 1979.

Hresko, W. R., Reid, D. K., and Hammill, D. D. *Test of Early Language Development.* Austin, Tex.: PRO-ED, 1981.

Humphrey, J. M. H. Persistent error patterns on whole number computations and scores on Piagetian tasks as they relate to mathematics achievement of adolescents. Ph.D. dissertation, University of Texas at Austin, 1981.

Hunt, K. *Grammatical structures written at three grade levels.* National Council of Teachers of English, Research Report No. 3. Urbana, Ill.: National Council of Teachers of English, 1965.

Iano, R. P. Shall we disband our special classes? *Journal of Special Education,* 1972, *6,* 167 – 78.

International Reading Association Resolution #1 of the Delegates' Assembly: Use of grade equivalents in reading tests. Annual Convention of the International Reading Association, New Orleans, La., April 28, 1981.

Irwin, J. The effects of explicitness and clause order on the comprehension or reversible causal relationships. *Reading Research Quarterly,* 1980, *15,* 477 – 88.

Items listed in studies of instructional clarity. *Practical Applications of Research. Newsletter of Phi Delta Kappa's Center on Evaluation, Development, and Research,* 1981, *3* (3), 3.

Ito, H. R. Long-term effects of resource room programs on learning disabled children's reading. *Journal of Learning Disabilities,* 1980, *13,* 322 – 26.

Jackson, R. L., and Phillips, G. Manipulative devices in elementary school mathematics. In *Instructional aids in mathematics: Thirty-fourth yearbook of the National Council of Teachers of*

Mathematics, Washington, D.C.: National Council of Teachers of Mathematics, 1973.

Jastak, J. F., and Jastak, S. R. *Wide-Range Achievement Test.* Wilmington, Del.: Guidance Associates, 1965.

Jenkins, J. R., and Heliotis, J. G. Reading comprehension instruction: Findings from behavioral and cognitive psychology. *Topics in Language Disorders,* 1981, *1* (2), 25 – 41.

Jenkins, J. R., and Mayhall, W. F. Development and evaluation of a resource teacher program. *Exceptional Children,* 1976, *43,* 21 – 30.

Jett-Simpson, M. Writing stories using model structures: The circle story. *Language Arts,* 1981, *58* (3), 293 – 300.

Johnson, D., and Myklebust, H. *Learning disabilities: Educational principles and Practices.* New York: Grune & Stratton, 1967.

Johnson, D. D., and Pearson, P. D. *Teaching reading vocabulary.* New York: Holt, Rinehart & Winston, 1978.

Jones, V. F. *Adolescents with behavior problems: Strategies for teaching, counseling, and parent involvement.* Boston: Allyn and Bacon, 1980.

Jones, V. F., and Jones, L. S. *Responsible Classroom Discipline.* Boston: Allyn and Bacon, 1981.

Jongsma, E. *Cloze instruction research: A second look.* Newark, Del.: International Reading Association, 1980.

Jongsma, K., and Jongsma, E. Test review: Commercial informal reading inventories. *Reading Teacher,* 1981, *34* (6), 697 – 705.

Kane, R. B., Byrne, M. A., and Hater, M. A. *Helping children read mathematics.* New York: American Book Company, 1974.

Kaplan, P., Kohfeldt, J., and Sturia, K. *It's positively fun.* Denver: Love, 1974.

Kennedy, J., Cruickshank, D. R., Bush, A., and Myers, B. Additional investigation into the nature of teacher clarity. *Journal of Educational Research,* 1978, *72,* 3 – 10.

Keppers, G. L., and Caplan, S. W. Group counseling with academically able underachieving students. *New Mexico Social Studies Education Research Bulletin,* 1962, *12,* 17 – 28.

Kerlin, M. A. and Latham W. L. Intervention effects of a crisis-resource program, *Exceptional Children,* 1977, *44,* 32 – 34.

Kidd, K., Myers, S., and Cilley, D. *The laboratory approach to mathematics.* Chicago: Science Research Associates, 1970.

Kim, E. C., and Kellough, R. D. *Resource guide for secondary school teaching: A planning for competence.* New York: Macmillan, 1978.

Kirschenbaum, H., Simon, S., and Napier, R. W. *Wad-ja-get? The grading game in American education.* New York: Hart, 1971.

Kline, L. W. Market research: What young people read. *Journal of Reading,* 1980, *24* (3), 284 – 86.

Koch, K. and Students of P. S. 61 in New York City. *Wishes, lies, and dreams. Teaching children to write poetry.* New York:; Vintage Books/Chelsea House, 1970.

Kohfeldt, J. *Contracts.* Kernersville, N. C.: Innovative Educational Support Systems, 1974.

Kottmeyer, W., and Ware, K. *Basic goals in spelling.* 4th ed. New York: McGraw-Hill, 1964.

Kottmeyer, W. *Teacher's guide for remedial reading.* New York: McGraw-Hill, 1970.

Kraner, R. E. *Kraner tests of mathematics mastery.* Tigard, Ore.: C. C. Publications, 1979.

Krathwohl, D., Bloom, B., and Masia, B. *Taxonomy of educational objectives: the classification of educational goals. Handbook 2: The Affective Domain.* New York: McKay, 1964.

Kroth, R. L. *Communicating with parents of exceptional children.* Denver: Love, 1975.

Kruteskii, V. A. *The psychology of mathematical abilities in school children.* J. Kilpatrick and I. Wirszup (eds.) Chicago: University of Chicago Press, 1976.

Kunzelman, H. P. *Precision teaching: An initial training sequence.* Seattle: Special Child, 1970.

Kusha, A., Webster, E. J. D., and Elford, G. *Spelling in Language Arts 6.* Ontario, Canada: Thomas Nelson and Sons (Canada) Ltd., 1964.

Labinowicz, E. *The Piaget primer. Thinking, learning, teaching.* Menlo Park, Calif.: Addison-Wesley, 1980.

Landrum, R., and Children from PS 1 and PS 42 in New York City. *A day dream I had at night and other stories: teaching children how to make their own readers.* New York: Teachers' and Writers' Collaborative, 1971.

Lankford, F. G., Jr. What can a teacher learn about a pupil's thinking through oral interviews? *Arithmetic Teacher,* 1974, *21,* 26 – 32.

Lapp, D. (ed.) *Making reading possible through effective classroom management.* Newark, Del.: International Reading Association, 1980.

Laque, C. F., and Sherwood, P. A. *A laboratory approach to writing.* Urbana, Ill.: National Council of Teachers of English, 1977.

Larrick, N. *Parents' guide to children's reading.* 4th ed. New York: Pocket Books, 1975.

Larsen, S. C., and Hammill, D. The relationship of selected visual perceptual abilities to school learning. *Journal of Special Education,* 1975, *9,* 281 – 91.

Larsen, S. C., and Hammill, D. *The Test of Written Spelling.* Austin, Tex.: PRO-ED, 1976.

Laten, S., and Katz, G. *A theoretical model for assessment of adolescents: The ecological/behavioral approach.* Madison, Wis.: Specialized Educational Services, 1975.

Laurendeau, M., and Pinard, A. *The development of the concept of space in the child.* New York: International Universities Press, 1970.

Lavatelli, C. S. *Teacher's guide to accompany early childhood curriculum — A Piagetian program.* Cambridge, Mass.: Center for Media Development, 1973.

Laycock, M., and Watson, G. *The fabric of mathematics.* Rev. ed. Hayward, Calif.: Activity Resources Co., 1975.

LeBlanc, J. F. You can teach problem solving. *Arithmetic Teacher,* 1977, *25,* 16 – 20.

Lee, D., Bingham, A., and Woelfel, S. *Critical reading develops early.* Newark, Del.: International Reading Association, 1968.

Lee, D. M., and Rubin, J. B. *Children and language.* Belmont, Calif.: Wadsworth Publishing Co., 1979.

Lee, L. Developmental sentence types: A method for comparing normal and deviant syntactic development. *Journal of Speech and Hearing Disorders,* 1966, *31,* 311 – 330.

Lee, L. *Developmental sentence analysis.* Evanston, Ill.: Northwestern University Press, 1974.

Lee. L., Koenigsknecht, R. A., and Mulhern, S. T. *Interactive language development teaching.* Evanston, Ill.: Northwestern University Press, 1975.

Lichter, P. Communicating with parents: It begins with listening. *Teaching Exceptional Children.* 1976, *8,* 66 – 75.

Lindquist, E., and Hieronymous, A. *Iowa Test of Basic Skills.* New York: Harcourt, Brace, and World, 1956.

Lippitt, B., and Lippitt, R. *The counsulting process in action.* San Diego: University Associates, 1978.

Long, N. J., Morse, W. C., and Newman, R. *Conflict in the classroom.* Belmont, Calif.: Wadsworth, 1976.

Loughlin, C., and Suina, J. *The learning environment: an instructional strategy.* New York: Teachers College, Columbia University, 1982.

Lovitt, T. C. Assessment of children with learning disabilities. *Exceptional Children,* 1967, *34,* 233 – 39.

Lovitt, T. C. Rate per minute as an academic measure. Unpublished paper, Department of Special Education. Seattle, Wash.: University of Washington, 1971.

Lovitt, T. C. Applied behavior analysis and learning disabilities. Part I: Characteristics of ABA, general recommendations, and methodological limitations. *Journal of Learning Disabilities,* 1975a, *8,* 432 – 43.

Lovitt, T. C. Applied behavior analysis and learning disabilities, Part II: Specific research recommendations and suggestions for practitioners. *Journal of Learning Disabilities,* 1975b, *8,* 504 – 518.

Lovitt, T. C. *In spite of my resistance . . . I've learned from children.* Columbus, Ohio: Charles E. Merrill, 1977.

Lovitt, T. C., and Hansen, C. L. Round one — Placing the child in the right reader. *Journal of Learning Disabilities,* 1976a, *6,* 347 – 53.

Lovitt, T. C., and Hansen, C. L. The use of contingent skipping and drilling to improve oral reading and comprehension. *Journal of Learning Disabilities,* 1976b, *9* (8), 482 – 87.

Lovitt, T. C., and Smith, D. D. *The Computational Arithmetic Program.* Austin, Tex.: PRO-ED, 1982.

Lowery, L. F. *Learning about instruction: Questioning strategies I.* Berkeley, Calif.: University of California-Berkeley, 1973.

McCallon, E. and McCray, E. *Planning and conducting interviews.* Austin, Tex.: Learning Concepts, 1975.

McCowan, R. J. Group counseling with underachievers and their parents. *School Counselor,* 1968, *16,* 30 – 35.

McDonald, E. T. *A Deep Test of Articulation.* Pittsburgh: Stanwitz House, 1964.

McEntire, M. E. Relationships between the language proficiency of adolescents and their mathematics performance. Ph.D. dissertation, University of Texas at Austin, 1981.

McGinnis, M. *Asphasic children.* Washington, D.C.: Volta Bureau, 1963.

McGinnis, M., Kleffner, F. R., and Goldstein, R. Teaching aphasic children. *Volta Review,* 1956, *58,* 239 – 44.

McKenzie, H. S. Special education and consulting teacher. In F. W. Clark, D. R. Evans, and L. A. Hamerlynck (eds.), *Implementing behavioral programs for schools and clinics.* Champaign, Ill.: Research Press, 1972.

McKillip, W. D., Cooney, T. J., Davis, E. J., and Wilson, J. W. *Mathematics instruction in the elementary grades.* Morristown, N.J.: Silver Burdett Co., 1978.

McLoughlin, J. A., and Lewis, R. B. *Assessing special students.* Columbus, Ohio: Charles E. Merrill, 1981.

McReynolds, L. *Developing systematic procedures for training children's language.* Monograph No. 18 of the American Speech and Hearing Association, August 1974.

Macy, D. J. and Carter, J. L. Comparison of a mainstream and self-contained special education program. *The Journal of Special Education,* 1978, *12,* 303 – 313.

Madsen, C. H., and Madsen, C. K. *Teaching/discipline: A positive approach for educational development.* Boston: Allyn and Bacon, 1974.

Marion, R. L. *Educators, parents, and exceptional children.* Rockville, Md.: Aspen, 1981.

Majoribanks, K. Environment, social class, and mental ability. *Journal of Educational Psychology,* 1972, *63,* 103 – 109.

Marsh, G. E., Gearheart, C. K., and Gearheart, B. R. *The learning disabled adolescent: Program alternatives in the secondary school.* St. Louis: C. V. Mosby, 1978.

Martin, B., and Brogan, P. *Sounds of language reading program.* New York: Holt, Rinehart, and Winston, 1969

Mazurkiewicz, A. J., and Tanyzner, H. J. *Early-to-read: i/t/a program.* New York: Initial Teaching Alphabet Publications, 1966.

Medley, D., Schluck, C., and Ames, N. *Assessing the learning environment in the classroom: A manual for users of OSCAR 5.* Princeton, N.J.: Educational Testing Service, 1968.

Meichenbaum, D. *Cognitive-behavior modification. An integrative approach.* New York: Plenum Press, 1977.

Meichenbaum, D. Cognitive behavior modification with exceptional children: A promise yet unfilled. *Exceptional Education Quarterly,* 1980, *1* (1), 83 – 88.

Meskauskas, J. A. Evaluation models for criterion-referenced testing: views regarding mastery and standard-setting. *Review of Educational Research,* 1976, *46,* 133 – 58.

Miller, J. (ed.) *Assessing language production in children: Experimental procedures.* Baltimore: University Park Press, 1981.

Miller, T. L., and Sabatino, D. A. An evaluation of the teacher consultant model as an approach to mainstreaming. *Exceptional Children,* 1978, *45,* 86 – 91.

Millman, J., and Pauk, W. *How to take tests.* New York: McGraw-Hill, 1969.

Minteer, C. *Words and what they do to you.* Evanston, Ill.: Row, Peterson, 1953.

Minuchin, S., Chamberlain, P., and Graubard, P. A project to teach learning skills to disturbed, delinquent children. *American Journal of Orthopsychiatry,* 1967, *37* (3), 558 – 67.

Moffett, J. *A student-centered language arts curriculum, grades K – 13: A handbook for teachers.* Boston: Houghton Mifflin, 1968.

Moffett, J., and Wagner, B. J. *Student-centered language arts and reading, K – 13. A handbook for teachers. 2d ed.* Boston: Houghton Mifflin, 1976.

Moreno, J. L. *Who shall survive? Foundation of sociometry, group psychotherapy, and sociodrama.* New York: Beacon House, 1953.

Morgan, C. T., and Deese, J. *How to study.* 2d. ed. Boston: Houghton Mifflin, 1974.

Morse, W. C. Worksheet on life-space interviewing for teachers. In N. J. Long, W. C. Morse, and R. G. Newman (eds.), *Conflict in the classroom.* 2d ed. Belmont, Calif.: Wadsworth, 1971.

Mueser, A. M., Russell, D. H., and Karp, E. *Reading aids through the grades. A guide to materials and 501 activities for individualizing reading instruction.* 4th ed. New York: Teachers College Press, 1981.

Myers, P., and Hammill, D. D. *Learning disabilities: Basic concepts, assessment practices and instructional strategies.* Austin, Tex.: PRO-ED, 1982.

NCTM. Instructional Affairs Committee. Minicalculators in schools. *Arithmetic Teacher,* 1976, *23,* 72 – 74.

NCTM. *Thirty-fourth yearbook. Instructional aids in mathematics.* Washington, D.C.: National Council of Teachers of Mathematics, 1973.

Negin, G. A., and Krugler, D. Essential literacy skills for functioning in an urban community. *Journal of Reading*, 1980, *24* (2), 109 – 15.

Nemoy, E. G., and Davis, S. F. *The correction of defective consonant sounds: A teacher's manual of ear training stories and motivational lessons for group or individual instruction.* Magnolia, Mass.: Expression, 1954.

Newcomer, P. L. *Understanding and teaching emotionally disturbed children.* Boston: Allyn and Bacon, 1980.

Newcomer, P., and Hammill, D. D. *Test of Language Development — Primary.* Austin, Tex.: PRO-ED, 1982.

Newman, R. G. *Psychological consultation in the schools: A catalyst for learning.* New York: Basic Books, 1967.

Noble, J. K. *Better handwriting for you.* New York: Noble & Noble, 1956.

Nuffield Mathematics Project. New York: Wiley, 1967 – 1974.

Nunnally, J. C. *Psychometric theory.* New York: McGraw-Hill, 1978.

O'Conner, P. D., Stuck, G. B., and Wyne, M. D. Effects of a short-term intervention resource room program on task orientation and achievement. *The Journal of Special Education*, 1979, *13*, 375 – 385.

O'Donnell, R. C. A critique of some indices of syntactic maturity. *Research in the Teaching of English*, 1976, *10*, 31 – 38.

O'Donnell, R. C., Griffin, W. J., and Norris, R. C. *Syntax of kindergarten and elementary school children.* National Council of Teachers of English Research Report No. 8. Urbana, Ill.: National Council of Teachers of English, 1967.

Ollila, L. *Handbook for administrators and teachers: Reading in the kindergarten.* Newark, Del.: International Reading Association, 1980.

Opper, S. Piaget's clinical method. *Journal of Children's Mathematical Behavior*, 1977, *1* (4), 90 – 107.

Otto, W., and Askov, E. *The Wisconsin design for reading skill development: rationale and guidelines.* 3d ed. Minneapolis: National Computer Systems, 1974.

Otto. W., and Smith, R. J. *Corrective and remedial teaching.* 3d ed. Boston: Houghton Mifflin, 1980.

Page, W. D., and Barr, R. D. Use of informal reading inventories. In W. D. Page (ed.), *Help for the reading teacher: New directions in research.* Urbana, Ill.: ERIC Clearinghouse on Reading and Communication Skills: National Conference on Research in English, 1975.

Palomares, V. H., and Ball, G. *Human development program: Magic Circle.* La Mesa, Calif.: Human Development Training Institute, 1974.

Pearson, P. D., and Johnson, D. D. *Teaching reading comprehension.* New York: Holt, Rinehart and Winston, 1978.

Petty, W. T., and Bowen, M. *Slithery snakes and other aids to children's writing.* New York: Appleton-Century-Crofts, 1967.

Petty, W. T., Petty, D. C., and Becking, M. F. *Experiences in language. Tools and techniques for language arts methods.* Boston: Allyn and Bacon, 1973.

Phelps-Gunn, T., and Phelps-Teraski, D. *Written language instruction. Theory and remediation.* Rockville, Md.: Aspen Systems, Corp., 1982.

Piaget, J. *The child's conception of number.* New York: Norton, 1965.

Pippig, G. Rechenschwache in psychologischer sicht. *Mathematik in der Schule,* 1975, *13,* 623 – 28. (Reported in Radatz, 1979).

Pollak, S., and Gruenewald, L. *A manual for assessing language interaction in academic tasks.* Madison, Wis.: Midwest IGE Services, School of Education, University of Wisconsin-Madison, 1978.

Popp, L., Robinson, F., and Robinson, F. P. *The basic thinking skills.* St. Catherines, Ontario, Canada: Niagara Center, Ontario Institute for Studies in Education, July 1974.

Powell, D. *What can I write about? 7000 topics for high school students.* Urbana, Ill.: National Council of Teachers of English, 1981.

Powell, G. C. An attitude scale for children. *Reading Teacher,* 1972, *25,* 442 – 47.

Powell, M. Difficulty level of student assignments. *Practical Applications of Research. Newsletter of Phi Delta Kappa's Center on Evaluation, Development, and Research,* 1979, *1* (3), 1 – 2, 6.

Powell, W. R. The validity of the instructional reading level. In A. Berry, T. C. Barrett, and W. R. Powell (eds.), *Elementary reading instruction: Selected materials II.* Boston: Allyn and Bacon, 1974.

Practical Applications of Research. Newsletter of Phi Delta Kappa's Center on Evaluation, Development, and Research, 1980, *3* (1).

Practical Applications of Research. Newsletter of Phi Delta Kappa's Center on Evaluation, Development, and Research, 1981, *3,* 3.

Prescott, D. *The child in the educative process.* New York: McGraw-Hill, 1937.

Public Law 93 – 380, Title VI B, Sec. 612(d) 13A.

Pugh, B. *Steps in language development.* Washington, D.C.: Volta Bureau, 1947.

Purdy, S. *Books for you to make.* New York: J. B. Lippincott, 1973.

Radatz, H. Error analysis in mathematics education. *Journal for Research in Mathematics Education,* 1979, *10* (3), 163 – 72.

Randhawa, B., and Lewis, L. Assessment and effect of some classroom environment variables. *Review of Educational Research,* 1973, *43,* 303 – 21.

Raygor, A. L., and Schick, G. B. *Reading at efficient rates.* New York: McGraw-Hill, 1970.

Reger, R. What is a resource room program? *Journal of Learning Disabilities,* 1973, *6,* 607 – 14.

Reid, D. K. Child reading: Readiness or evolution? *Topics in Language Disorders,* 1981, *1* (2), 61 – 72.

Reid, D. K., Hresko, W. P., and Hammill, D. D. *Test of Early Reading Ability.* Austin, Tex.: PRO-ED, 1980.

Reisman, F. K., and Kauffman, S. H. *Teaching mathematics to children with special needs.* Columbus, Ohio: Charles E. Merrill, 1980.

Robinson, F. P. *Effective study.* New York: Harper Brothers, 1946.

Rodee, M. W. A study to evaluate the resource teacher when used with high level educable retardates at the primary level. The University of Iowa, 1971 (Order No. 71 – 30, 485).

Rose, S. *Treating children in groups: A behavioral approach.* San Francisco: Jossey-Bass, 1972.

Rose, S. *Treating children in groups.* San Francisco, Jossey-Bass, 1973.

Ross, S. L., DeYoung, H. G., and Cohen, J. S. Confrontation: Special education placement and the law. *Exceptional Children*, 1971, *38* (1), 5 – 12.

Rush, M. L. *The language of classification: Animals.* Washington, D.C.: Alexander Graham Bell Association, 1975.

Rust, J. O., Miller, L. S., and Wilson, W. A. Using a control group to evaluate a resource room program. *Psychology in the Schools*, 1978, *15*, 503 – 506.

Sabatino, D. A. An evaluation of resource rooms for children with learning disabilities. *Journal of Learning Disabilities*, 1971, *4*, 84 – 93.

Sager, C. Improving the quality of written composition through pupil use of rating scales. *Language Arts*, 1975, *52*, 1021 – 23.

Salvia, J., and Ysseldyke, J. E. *Assessment in special and remedial education.* Boston: Houghton Mifflin, 1981.

Samuels, S. J., Dahl, P., and Archwamety, T. Effects of hypothesis/test training on reading skill. *Journal of Educational Psychology*, 1974, *66*, 835 – 44.

Sanders, N. M. *Classroom questions: What kinds?* New York: Harper & Row, 1964.

Sarason, I. G., and Sarason, B. R. *Constructive classroom behavior: A guide to modeling and role playing techniques.* New York: Behavioral Publications, 1974.

Sargent, J. V. *An easier way: A handbook for the elderly and handicapped.* Ames, Iowa: Iowa State University Press, 1981.

Scannell, D. P., and Tracy, D. B. *Testing and measurement in the classroom.* Boston: Houghton Mifflin, 1975.

Schiff, G., Scholom, A., Swerdlik, M., and Knight, J. Mainstreamed vs. self-contained classes: A two year study of their effects on the personal adjustment and academic achievement of children with learning disabilities. *Education*, 1979, *99*, 397 – 405.

Scott, L. B., and Thompson, J. J. *Talking time.* St. Louis: Webster, 1951.

Searle, D., and Dillon, D. Responding to student writing: What is said or how it is said. *Language Arts*, 1980, *57* (7), 773 – 81.

Section 121a 346. "Content of individualized education program." *45 Code of Federal Regulations*, August 23, 1977. 42 Federal Register 42474-42514.

Semel, E. M., and Wiig, E. H. *Clinical Evaluation of Language Functions.* Columbus, Ohio: Charles E. Merrill, 1980.

Shaftel, F. R., and Shaftel, G. *Role-playing for social values: Decision-making in the social studies.* Englewood Cliffs, N.J.: Prentice-Hall, 1967.

Shaw, H. *Spell it right.* New York: Barnes & Noble, 1971.

Sherry, P., Franzen, M., Buch, M., Christopherson, P., Dawson, L, and Mosheim, E. *Zing. (Z) Strategies into nifty goals. Guides to learning strategies for teachers and students.* Madison, Wis.: Madison Metropolitan Schools, 1976.

Silberman, M. L., and Wheelan, S. A. *How to discipline without feeling guilty.* New York: Hawthorn, 1980.

Silver, E. A. Student perceptions of relatedness among mathematical verbal problems. *Journal of Research in Mathematics Education*, 1979, *10* (3), 195 – 210.

Simon, A., and Kirschenbaum, H. *Readings in values clarification.* Minneapolis, Minn.: Winston Press, 1973.

Skinner, B. F., and Krakower, S. *Handwriting with writing and see.* Chicago: Lyons & Carnahan, 1968.

Smith, C. *Parents and reading.* Newark Del.: International Reading Association, 1971.

Smith, C. T. The relationship between the type of questions, stimuli, and the oral language production of children. *Research in the Teaching of English,* 1977, *11,* 111 – 16.

Smith, D. D., and Lovitt, T. C. *Computational arithmetic program (CAP).* Austin, Tex.: PRO-ED, 1982.

Smith, E. B., Goodman, K. S., and Meredith, R. *Language and thinking in school.* 2d ed. New York: Holt, Rinehart, and Winston, 1976.

Smith, F. Understanding reading. *A psycholinguistic analysis of reading and learning to read.* New York: Holt, Rinehart, and Winston, 1978.

Smith, F. (ed.) *Psycholinguistics and reading.* New York: Holt, Rinehart, and Winston, 1973.

Smith, F. *Comprehension and learning: A conceptual framework for teachers.* New York: Holt, Rinehart, and Winston, 1975.

Smith, F. How children learn. In D. Carnine et al. *Interdisciplinary voices in learning disabilities and remedial education.* Austin, Tex.: PRO-ED, 1983, 187 – 214.

Smith, S. *Best methods of study.* 4th ed. New York: Barnes & Noble, 1970.

Smith, S. E., Jr., and Backman, C. A. (eds.) *Teacher-made aids for elementary school mathematics. Reading from the Arithmetic Teacher.* Washington, D.C.: National Council of Teachers of Mathematics, 1974.

Smokoski, F. The resource teacher. Paper presented at the Conference on the Resource Room Teacher. Tucson: University of Arizona, February 28 – 29, 1972.

Sorenson, J. S., Poole, M., and Joyal, L. H. *The unit leader and individually guided education.* Reading, Mass.: Addison-Wesley, 1976.

Spache, G. D., and Spache, E. B. *Reading in the elementary school.* 4th ed. Boston: Allyn and Bacon, 1977.

Speece, D. L., and Mandell, C. J. Resource room support services for regular teachers, *Learning Disabilities Quarterly,* 1980, *3* (1), 49 – 53.

Stahlbrand, K., Pierce, M., and Armstrong, S. Partner learning: A practical guide for teachers and teacher trainers. Unpublished manuscript, 1982.

Stallings, J. A. Teaching basic reading skills in secondary schools. Paper presented at the 1978 Annual Meeting of the American Educational Research Association, Toronto, Canada.

Starlin, C. Evaluating progress toward reading efficiency. In B. Bateman (ed.), *Learning disorders,* Vol. 4: *Reading.* Seattle: Special Child Publications, 1971.

Stauffer, R. G. *The language-experience approach to the teaching of reading.* New York: Harper & Row, 1970.

Stauffer, R. G., and Cramer, R. *Teaching critical reading at the primary level.* Newark, Del.: International Reading Association, 1968.

Stephens, T. M. *Directive teaching of children with learning and behavior handicaps.* Columbus, Ohio: Charles E. Merrill, 1970.

Stephens, T. M. *Social skills in the classroom.* Columbus, Ohio: Cedars Press, 1978.

Stewart, C. J., and Cash, W. B. *Interviewing: Principles and practices.* Dubuque, Iowa: Brown, 1974.

Strauss, A. A., and Lehtinen, L. E. *Psychopathology and education of the brain-injured child.* New York: Grune & Stratton, 1947.

Strickland, R. *The language arts in the elementary school.* 2d ed. Boston: D. C. Heath, 1957.

Stuart, R. (ed.). *Behavioral self-management: Strategies, techniques, and outcomes.* New York: Brunner/Mayel, 1977.

Stufflebeam, D. L. (Committee Chair.). *Standards for evaluations of educational programs, projects, and materials.* Developed by the Joint Committee on Standards for Educational Evaluation. New York: McGraw-Hill, 1981.

Sulzer-Azaroff, B., and Mayer, G. R. *Applying behavior-analysis procedures with children and youth.* New York: Holt, Rinehart, and Winston. 1977.

Summers, E. G. *Literature preferences of elementary age children.* Vancouver, Canada: University of British Columbia, 1979.

Sund, R. B., and Carin, A. *Creative questioning and sensitive listening techniques. A self-concept approach.* Columbus, Ohio: Charles E. Merrill, 1978.

Sundbye, N. W., Dyck, N., and Wyatt, F. R. *Essential sight words program: Level I and Level II.* Hingham, Mass.: Teaching Resources Corp., 1979 (Level I) and 1981 (Level II).

Sunflower, C., and McNutt, G. *URICA. Using reading in creative activities.* Austin, Tex.: PRO-ED, 1981.

Swart, W. L. Evaluation of mathematics instruction in the elementary classroom. *Arithmetic Teacher,* 1974, *21*, 7 – 11.

Taba, H., and Elzey, F. F. Teaching strategies and thought processes. *Teachers College Record,* 1964, *65*, 524 – 34.

Taylor, F. D., Artuso, A. A., and Hewett, F. M. *Individualized arithmetic instruction: arithmetic drill sheets.* Denver: Love, 1970.

Teachers' and Writers' Collaborative (eds.). *The whole word catalog.* New York: PS 3, 1972.

Teaching sight words using the kinesthetic method. Originator: the former Special Education Instructional Materials Center, University of Kansas, 1972. Revised and reissued by the National Center on Educational Media and Materials for the Handicapped, Columbus, Ohio, 1976.

Teale, W. H. *Early reading. An annotated bibliography.* Newark, Del.: International Reading Association, 1980.

Temple, C. A., Nathan, R. G., and Burris, N. A. *The beginnings of writing.* Boston: Allyn and Bacon, 1982.

Templin, M., and Darley, F. *The Templin-Darley Tests of Articulation.* Iowa City: Bureau of Educational Research, State University of Iowa, 1960.

Terman, E. L., and Merrill, M. A. *Revised Stanford Binet Test of Intelligence.* Boston: Houghton Mifflin, 1961.

Tharp, R., and Wetzel, R. J. *Behavior modification in the natural environment.* New York: Academic Press, 1969.

Thiagarajan, S. Designing instructional games for handicapped learners. *Focus on Exceptional Children,* 1976, *7*, 1 – 11.

Thomas, E. L., and Robinson, H. A. *Improving reading in every class. A sourcebook for teachers.* 3d ed. Boston: Allyn and Bacon, 1982.

Thompson, R., and Quinby, S. *Individualized interest area contracts.* Austin, Tex.: PRO-ED, 1981.

Thorndike, E. L. Punctuation. *Teachers College Record,* 1948, *49*, 531 – 37.

Thorndike, R. L., and Hagen, E. P. *Measurement and evaluation in psychology and education.* 4th ed. New York: John Wiley and Sons, 1977.

Thurber, D., and Jordan, D. *D'Nealian handwriting*. Glenview, Ill.: Scott, Foresman, and Co., 1979.

Tiedt, I. M. *Individualizing writing in the elementary classroom*. Urbana, Ill.: National Council of Teachers of English, 1975.

Tilley, B. K. The effects of three educational placement systems on achievement, self-concept, and behavior in elementary mentally retarded children. *Dissertation Abstracts* (1970) 4590-A. Ph.D dissertation, University of Iowa, 1970.

Trantham, C., and Pederson, J. *Normal language development: The key to diagnosis and therapy for language disordered children*. Baltimore, Md.: Williams and Wilkins, 1976.

Tull, D. Assessment in learning disabilities. In R. J. Van Hattum, *Seminars in speech, language, and hearing: Screening in school programs*, Vol. 2, No. 2. New York: Thieme-Stratton, 1981.

Van Riper, C. *Speech correction*. Englewood Cliffs, N.J.: Prentice-Hall, 1972.

Vasa, S. F. Alternative procedures for grading handicapped students in the secondary schools. *Education Unlimited*, 1981, *3* (1), 16 – 23.

Veatch, J. *Individualizing your reading program. Self-selection in action*. New York: G. P. Putman's Sons, 1959.

Veatch, J., Sawicki, F., Elliott, G., Barnette, F., and Blakey, Jr. *Key words to reading: The language experience approach begins*. Columbus, Ohio, Merrill, 1973.

Walker, J. (ed.). *Your reading. A booklist for junior high students*. 5th ed. Urbana, Ill.: National Council of Teachers of English, 1975.

Walker, V. S. Efficacy of the resource room for educating retarded children. *Exceptional Children*, 1974, *40*, 288 – 289.

Wallace, G., and Kauffman, J. M. *Teaching children with learning problems*. Columbus, Ohio: Charles E. Merrill, 1973.

Wallace, G., and Larsen, S. C. *Educational assessment of learning problems: Testing for teaching*. Boston: Allyn and Bacon, 1978.

Weaver, C. *Grammar for teachers. Perspectives and definitions*. Urbana, Ill.: National Council of Teachers of English, 1979.

Weed, L. L. *Medical records, medical education, and patient care. The problem-oriented record as a basic tool*. Cleveland, Ohio: Press of Case Western Reserve University, 1971.

Weigand, J. (ed.). *Developing teacher competencies*. Englewood Cliffs, N.J.: Prentice-Hall, 1971.

Weiner, L. H. An investigation of the effectiveness of resource rooms for children with specific learning disabilities. *Journal of Learning Disabilities*, 1969, *2*, 223 – 29.

Weiss, C. E., and Lillywhite, H. S. *Communication disorders*. St. Louis, Mo.: Mosby, 1981.

Weiss, H. *How to make your own books*. New York: Thomas Y. Crowell Co., 1974.

Wepman, J., and Hass, W. *A spoken word count*. Chicago: Language Research Associates, 1969.

White, M. (ed.). *High interest easy reading for junior and senior high students*. 3d ed. Urbana, Ill.: National Council of Teachers of English, 1979.

Wiederholt, J. L., Cronin, M. E., and Stubbs, V. Measurement of functional competencies and the handicapped. Constructs, assessment, and recommendations. *Exceptional Education Quarterly*, 1980, *3*, 59 – 73.

Wiederholt, J. L., and McNutt, G. Evaluating materials for handicapped adolescents. *Journal of Learning Disabilities*, 1977, *10*, 11 – 19.

Wiener, H. *Any child can write: How to improve your child's writing skills from preschool through high school*. New York: McGraw-Hill, 1978.

Wilde, J., and Newkirk, T. Writing detective stories. *Language Arts*, 1981, *58* (3), 286 – 92.

Wilderman, A. Math skills for survival in the real world. *Teacher Magazine*, 1977, *94*, 68 – 70.

Williams, E., and Shuard, H. *Primary mathematics today*. London: Longman Group Limited, 1970.

Williams, F., Hopper, R., and Natalicio, D. *The sounds of children*. Englewood Cliffs, N.J.: Prentice-Hall, 1977.

Williamson, L. E., and Young, F. The IRI and RMI diagnostic concepts should be synthesized. *Journal of Reading Behavior*, 1974, *6*, 183 – 94

Wilson, J. W., and Sadowski, B. (eds.). *The Maryland diagnostic arithmetic test and interview protocols*. College Park, Md.: Arithmetic Center, College of Education, University of Maryland, 1976.

Wilson, R. M. *Diagnostic and remedial reading for classroom and clinic* 2d ed. Columbus, Ohio: Merrill, 1982.

Winegert, K., and Geissal, M. A. Reading miscue modification. Unpublished manuscript, Northeastern Illinois University, Chicago, Ill., 1975.

Winitz, H. *From syllable to conversation*. Baltimore: University Park Press, 1975.

Wolfgang, C. H., and Glickman, C. D. *Solving discipline problems: Strategies for classroom teachers*. Boston: Allyn and Bacon, 1980.

Wong, B. Activating the inactive learner: Use of questions/prompts to enhance comprehension and retention of implied information in learning disabled children. *Learning Disabilities Quarterly*, 1980, *3*, 29 – 37.

Woodcock, R. W. *Peabody Rebus reading program*. Circle Pines, Minn.: American Guidance Services, 1967.

Workman, E. *Teaching behavioral self-control to students*. Austin, Tex.: PRO-ED, 1982.

Workman, E., and Hector, M. Behavioral self-control in classroom settings: A review of the literature. *Journal of School Psychology*, 1978, *16*, 227 – 36.

Wright, H. F. *Recording and analyzing child behavior with ecological data from an American town*. New York: Harper & Row, 1967.

Zifferblatt, S. *Improving study and homework behaviors*. Champaign, Ill.: Research Press, 1970.

Zutell, J. Children's spelling strategies and their cognitive development. In E. H. Henderson and J. W. Beers (eds.) *Developmental and cognitive aspects of learning to spell. A reflection of word knowledge*. Newark, Del.: International Reading Association, 1980.

Author Index

H

I

J

M

N

O

P

Subject Index

A

B

J. Lee Wiederholt has held the position of coordinator of general special education programs at the University of Texas. Included in his list of professional accomplishments are member of the board of trustees for both the Council for Learning Disabilities and the Society for Learning Disabilities and Remedial Education, past-president of the Council for Learning Disabilities, and member of advisory board for *The Journal of Learning Disabilities, Learning Disabilities Quarterly, Topics in Learning and Learning Disabilities,* and *Journal of Special Education.*.

Donald D. Hammill received his doctorate from the University of Texas and was professor of special education at Temple University. His many professional affiliations and honors include past president of the Council for Learning Disabilities, executive director of the Society for Learning Disabilities and Remedial Education, Certificate of Clinical Competence from the American Speech, Language and Hearing Association, as well as serving as editorial consultant for numerous journals. He is presently the publisher of Exceptional Education Quarterly.

Virginia Brown has been associate professor of psychology at the University of Minnesota-Duluth. She received her Ed.D. from the University of Kansas and has served as both elementary teacher and college professor. She has held the positions of supervisor of remedial reading programs and compensatory education in Kansas City, Missouri, and coordinator of public city school programs in learning disabilities and emotional disturbance.

She is currently president of the Council for Learning Disabilities, consulting editor of several journals, member of the governing boards of professional organizations, and consultant for several school districts.

Influence of Business
Firms on the Government

New Babylon

Studies in the Social Sciences

34

MOUTON PUBLISHERS · THE HAGUE · PARIS · NEW YORK

Influence of Business Firms on the Government

An Investigation of the Distribution of Influence in Society

Geert P. A. Braam

Professor of Sociology
Twente University of Technology
The Netherlands

MOUTON PUBLISHERS · THE HAGUE · PARIS · NEW YORK

Originally published under the title:
Invloed van bedrijven op de overheid by
Boom Meppel, The Netherlands.
© Geert P. A. Braam.

Library of Congress Cataloging in Publication Data

Braam, G   P   A   1930–
  Influence of business firms on the government.

  (New Babylon, studies in the social sciences; 34)
  Translation of Invloed van bedrijven op de overheid.
  Includes bibliographical references and indexes.
    1. Lobbying. 2. Pressure groups.   3. Business and
politics.   I. Title.
JF529.B713   322′.3   80–39906
ISBN 90-279-3457-6

ISBN: 90 279 3457 6
© 1981, Mouton Publishers, The Hague, The Netherlands
Printed in Great Britain

The Dutch version of this book was awarded the Kluwer Prize for 1975 (Kluwer is one of the largest publishing companies in the Netherlands). The book was also selected by the Dutch Society for Science to receive the Shell Prize 1975 (the author, however, refused the Shell Prize because he feared that even the slightest association with a multinational corporation might compromise the acceptance of the results of the investigation).

Preface

For many observers the conviction persists that in sociology very little has 'really' been measured over the years, in spite of the enormous volume of data which has been gathered within the discipline. This conviction is especially strong with respect to complex, yet basic, macro-sociological concepts such as integration, social conflict, collective behavior, socialization, etc.

Influence and power must definitely be included in this list. For this reason, this study aims at making a contribution to the measurement of the concept of influence – or more precisely, the influence exercised by firms, by interest organizations, and by private citizens on the government.

The book begins by sketching the theoretical context surrounding the concept, a knowledge of which is essential for a truly adequate measurement procedure (Chapters 2, 3 and 5 in particular). This supplies an answer to the question 'What has to be measured?' Inspired by numerous insights and discussions in the literature, I tried to do justice to several core elements of the concept of influence as described in the fifties by March, Dahl, and, in particular, by Simon (1953, 1957). The latter placed heavy emphasis on the *process* of *the exercise of influence*, but at the same time highlighted many other aspects (anticipation). Bachrach and Baratz made a powerful case for the importance of these anticipations in their discussions of '*non-decisions*' (1963).

Another aspect of the concept of influence which must be incorporated into any responsible research design is its *relational* character. Two or more actors are always involved in an influence relationship. This involves an *assignment* problem. It has to be stressed that investigators must take into account the *interests* of the actors involved (compare Coleman, 1973). At the beginning of this study, the interests of business firms are made the central issue (Chapters 2 and 5). Further on in the book, the interests of government agencies are also taken into consideration by using a decision-making model with corresponding criteria (Chapters 8, 9 and 10). It proved possible to do justice to core elements – *processes, non-decisions* and *interests* – within the context of a measurement procedure which is inspired by Lazers-feld's 'Empirical Analysis of Action'.

Measurement in the social sciences is usually quite crude. In particular, when only a few measurements are available, a solid interpretation is virtually impossible. In our case, once the influence has been determined for a certain business firm, how can an assessment be made of whether the influence is strong or weak. Interpretation is only feasible when there is a solid basis for comparing measurements. Thus the second primary building block of the book is the development of such a basis for comparison (Chapters 3, 4 and 5).

The third building block – which is certainly not the least in importance – is the actual application of the measurement model. For measurement procedures in particular it is true that 'the proof of the pudding is in the eating'. Application of the method in the field, as described in this book, was shown very clearly to be feasible. Yet in a certain sense, this is only *one* trial of the method, though in fact a fairly comprehensive one. It is therefore interesting to note that tentative tests have been made using the measurement procedure in allied fields, and in at least one other European country. The results were promising. Even more important, measurements in completely different fields – e.g. the influence of schools on the municipal government – proved very successful (Elting and Even, 1977). Thus the possibilities for application of the measurement procedure appear to be sufficient, or even considerable.

A final comment on the practical significance of this study. The preceding discussion emphasized the scientific aspects of the measurement procedure. However, a very important dimension of the concept 'influence exercised on the government' is exactly what the private citizen has managed to obtain from the government. As a result, measurements of influence give a definitive picture of one aspect of government policy-making – or, more specifically, about 'distributive justice'. Looking at it this way, this investigation can be regarded as a special type of evaluation-research.

Acknowledgement

The research for this study was originally financed by the State University of Groningen and by the Netherlands Organization for the Advancement of Pure Research. The latter organization also made possible the translation of the study. At a later stage, the Twente University of Technology made a number of facilities available.

My thanks to Professor Jo E. Ellemers of the University of Groningen for acting as my mentor for the investigation. My wife, Marijke Braam-Voeten, as well as the economist Professor Jan Pen, and Professor Ivo Molenaar (both of the State University of Groningen) gave invaluable advice in the shaping and editing of the manuscript.

Finally, my thanks to Ms. Nancy Boeije-Kelley for doing the translation.

Contents

1. Introduction: Goals and Basic Principles

Goal: the measurement of 'influence in society' – This is a study of the influence which business firms exert upon decisions of the Dutch government. The research question which I have posed is an offshoot of a very general problem whose ramifications are felt in numerous areas of social life. My question is as follows: Do some people, groups or organizations exert more influence upon the government than others? Specifically, this study will report an attempt at determining such distributions of influence as accurately as possible. 'Measurement' is therefore its primary goal.

Let us begin with some general observations about the theme 'distribution of influence'. The subject is, of course, far from new. Influence and power have demanded a great deal of attention over the years, and are still a central topic today. We speak of the influence of business, the banks, the trade unions and the farmers.

'Influence' is a most vital force in society as we observe it from day to day; it sets processes in motion or it brings them to a halt. In addition, its possession can procure prestige and personal gain for the holder. It is not surprising, then, that influence is a valued asset; as a result the question constantly arises whether or not it is 'fairly' distributed in society. Sometimes it is given another name; in the last twenty years such words as 'participation' and 'social action' have become familiar. Different words, but the same phenomena.

In this century the expression 'distribution of influence' cannot in fact be separated intuitively from the ideals of democracy. The actual distribution of influence can tell us something about the extent to which these ideals have been realized, or if they have in fact *not* been realized. Hopefully, this brief discussion has sufficiently demonstrated the importance of our subject matter.

An extremely thorny problem immediately presents itself, however. If we speak of the distribution of incomes or of marbles, then everyone knows what we mean; these are *tangible* objects. Influence is different; it is often elusive and even has something mysterious about it. This is immediately obvious if we ask ourselves exactly what we mean by it. Its elusiveness is also evident from the way we speak of its well-known misuse. 'Power corrupts . . .' – and don't we believe this to be equally true of influence? It seems as though we are dealing with some mysterious forces; we notice regularly that they are there, but they elude our systematic and direct observation.

This emphasis on the elusive character of influence may seem somewhat exaggerated. After all, in our every-day experience we usually produce simple answers to the question of how influence is distributed in society. We have our sacrosanct convictions about whether or not an 'establishment' exists, about the power of the bureaucracy, about the influence of large companies, etc. When the question of how influence is distributed becomes a subject for scientific research, however, things become much less simple. Following the publication of Mills' *The Power Elite* (1956) a tiresome discussion has raged in the United States as to whether or not a closed 'military-industrial complex' exists (Aron, 1960; Kornhauser, 1966; Parsons, 1957; Rose, 1967; Domhoff and Ballard, 1968; Lieberson, 1971). Many years later, a similar discussion began in the Netherlands in the wake of a union leader's contention that 200 persons were the true holders of all the power in that country (the '200 of Mertens', Helmers *et al.*, 1975).

The crucial point is that these scientific discussions often have the characteristics of any ordinary struggle among poorly-grounded opinions. There is a clear lack of research methods which would resolve such differences of opinions with facts.

Significant advances have, however, been made in the development of research methods. The simplest procedure is to determine who fills positions in an official or semi-official hierarchy (positional approach). In a variant of this positional approach, the researcher studies 'overlapping memberships' in particular. He tries to determine, for example, whether or not members of Parliament are concurrently sitting on the Board of Directors of a company, or he investigates interlocking directorates. Conclusions are also reached on the basis of 'switches' of positions at high social levels, such as when government functionaries and highly-placed military personnel become members of Boards of Directors and vice versa.

A somewhat more advanced method works with 'reputations for power or influence'. A selected number of respondents are asked who is 'influential' in their community in order to discover if and where influence is concentrated. Interest for this method was generated by the work of Hunter in 1953. Much research activity in the areas of influence and power has followed in the United States, but primarily at the local level.

Repeated criticism of the reputational approach arose at the end of the 1950s. A new method, the decision or issue method, appeared (for example Dahl, 1961). The researcher determines who has taken part in decision-making on important matters which have arisen in the community. The *participants* are thus ascertained (see Dahl, 1961). This method also generated criticism.

The discussion of methods has raged with a violence that one often meets in such elusive matters. Characteristic of these discussions is the misgivings as to whether or not the methods presently existing are in fact measuring influence at all (among others: Dahl, 1961, p. 330; 1968, p. 414; Walton, 1971; Frey, 1971). Up to the present this problem has not satisfactorily been resolved, notwithstanding the advances in conceptualizing (among others Coleman, 1977) and in the use of sophisticated techniques of analysis (for example Laumann and Pappi, 1973; see also Liebert and Immersheim, 1977). It must be concluded that the simple methods which have been used until now are inadequate.

For this reason the testing of a new method for determining influence is the primary goal of this study.

*The basic framework of this study: problems–influence attempts–success (compliance)–*In designing a new method I proceeded from the principle that the existing methods were too superficial, as I suggested above. Positions, reputations and participants can certainly be useful for certain purposes. They cannot, however, provide any decisive answers; in other words, they cannot deliver the definitive criterium for answering the question whether or not one individual has more influence than another. For this it is necessary to observe *actual processes of influence* (Simon, 1957) including their outcomes. Several studies have been carried out in which this was done (for example Bauer, de Sola Pool and Dexter, 1964). They are, however, limited in number, and usually fall short in one crucial aspect: the mutual comparability of the influence processes. (Gamson, 1966, is perhaps one of the few exceptions.)

We are thus faced with the task of producing hard and clearly comparable data. But this emphasis on better measurement can lead to a slight misunderstanding. Our intention is certainly not to design new and complicated scales, but to measure in such a way that we encompass as full a meaning of the concept influence as possible. This means in part that we must take both the *background* and the *consequences* of influence in society into account (compare Coleman, 1964, p. 62). For this reason, my starting point was the principle stated above: the study should be based as much as possible on the processes of influence – that is, on what *actually happened.* Our goal is, among others, to investigate whether or not one actor has obtained more benefits from the government than another.

In order to reach this goal we have determined the following data for a number of groups:

who has   *problems* (and what are their determinants);

do these lead to   *influence attempts* (requests of or demands upon the government),

and are these attempts   *complied with (government decisions).*

A small *chain* of data must therefore be collected for each group. The observation of one element (one indicator) is insufficient for the determination of influence; all the elements in the chain must be recorded (see also Figure 1.1).

The basic outline shown in Figure 1.1 forms the foundation for the method of measurement which we will use in this study. The method is based upon a synthesis of insights available in the literature, as will be explained in Chapter 2. My impression is that such a sociological method has never been applied in this form.

There is yet a second point of departure. Producing 'hard' data, which this design aims at, is in itself not sufficient. The determination of influence becomes much more meaningful scientifically when the relationship of the influence with *another variable* is investigated (Coleman *et al.*, 1970, p. 11). In this study I have chosen the size of the business firm as one such variable. The groups themselves (the business firms) are of course the research units, but we are primarily concerned

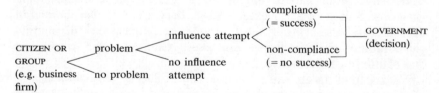

Figure 1.1
Problems, influence attempts and compliance (decisions) in their mutual relationship

here with one of their properties (size). This may seem to be a trivial observation, but those whose are even slightly familiar with studies of influence and power will agree that this statement is anything but superfluous.

We shall use the outline shown above primarily for *influence from below*, that is, for influence *upon* the holders of power. Many types of power holders exist in society; from them, we have chosen to examine *the government* in our study.

Let us denote the different persons or groups whose influence we wish to determine with A_1, A_2, and so forth. We visualize the amount of their influence, which we infer from the chain above, with the length of an arrow. Thus our research problem can be schematically rendered as follows:

A_1 ⟶

A_2.

A_3 ⟶

A_4 ⟶

GOVERNMENT

The *mutual* influence, if any, which A_1, A_2, A_3 and A_4 might exert on one another *is left out of consideration*. Our goal is simply to compare the 'amounts' of the influence of different groups, that is, to describe a *distribution* of influence. The word 'distribution' should be interpreted here as a *frequency distribution* of the amount of influence (in its dependence upon another variable such as the size of the firm).

It goes without saying that I proceeded from the assumption that influence upon the government *does* exist in society; more strongly stated, I presumed that this phenomena would be ubiquitous. *The* relevant question, then, is whether or not comparable individuals, or comparable groups, receive benefits to an equal degree.

The objective sketched above cannot be reached by limiting the scope of our study to a local level. Many important processes of influence simply do not end at the city line. This goes almost without saying; it also proved to be true in some exploratory research. In principle, therefore, this study touches upon the municipal, provincial and national levels. The Netherlands has *three* administrative levels: the municipal, the provincial and the national government (there are approximately 850 municipalities and there are 11 provinces).

The visualization which we have presented here contains many simplifications which may understandably occasion objections. We will of course consider these objections fully in the text which follows. The core of the study and our research has, however, been presented here.

Note that I shall usually speak of *influence* and not of power. The choice of the word is not so important. Terms only have meaning when they are placed within a framework of concepts. We will return to this later. We shall see that for the phenomena with which we are concerned in this study the term influence is slightly preferable.

Social relevance: distributions of influence; the role of government – The primary goal of this study is to measure influence. In fact, the basic research design that I have just described already contains a more applied objective as well. The measurement of influence in this design is aimed at the determination of *distributions* of influence. Additionally, influence is confined to influence on the government. This further specification has been deliberately chosen for reasons which seemed to be practically relevant.

First, influence has consequences for the group or for society. Establishing with precision whether or not one person can be more sure of determining these consequences than another is therefore an important task. Continuing in this line of thought, we see that knowing how influence *is distributed* is of practical interest. Such distributions touch directly upon the functioning of groups and societies and on the problem which we refer to in passing as 'the problem of democracy'.

Secondly, thoughts of influence call to mind the advantages reaped by those who exert influence. Principles of social justice become directly involved here. Investigations of the distribution of influence are therefore likely to have a strong normative accent; is the distribution 'fair'? To be able to answer this question we need to investigate *a special type of influence, namely, the influence by which the persons concerned are pursuing at least in part some advantage for themselves*. Self-interest (problems) must therefore enter the picture. Only then are statements possible about *who gets what and how much* (this is an alternative reading of the well-known theme 'who gets what, when and how?; Lasswell, 1936).

Another practical question follows this one directly; if necessary, how can the distributions be changed? This is of course a problem area in itself. One thing is certain; if there is no clear regulating force, then changes will be very difficult. Much can be said for directing our efforts toward the investigation of situations where a *center* more or less controls such distributions. In most societies, government is both highly visible and accountable to its citizens for public policy. This study will therefore direct its attention to the role of the government in the distributions of influence which have been tracked down.

A further breakdown of the problem is necessary, since a pure measurement of influence is both difficult and time-consuming. Other elements in the research design must be kept as simple as possible. This simplicity is achieved by, among other things, measuring the influence of groups which are highly comparable, namely *business firms*. I have determined besides the influence for *comparable* problems, and primarily for *problems which were related to the material facilities for transport by water* (*harbors, canals, locks, bridges, etc.*). In the Netherlands, virtually all the harbors, canals, locks, etc. are administered and financed by government bodies.

The related question which receives the emphasis in this study is equally simple: Do larger firms have more influence on the government than smaller ones and if so, why?

The question is highly relevant in spite of its simplicity. Don't we all have our established ideas about the influence of big business? Aren't they the ones who pull the strings via the government, while the smaller fry often go unheard? This study will reveal that the answer to this question is somewhat surprising.

The study will offer still other insights. We will, for example, investigate whether or not differences in influence are related to:

- characteristics of the municipality or region in which the business firm is located (for example, central versus peripheral location in the state).
- differences between 'growing' and 'not-growing' business firms
- 'connections' between business firms and the government
- 'social circles' such as the Rotary
- positions in interest organizations.

In addition, we will examine the influence exercised by coalitions of business firms.

Though the question of differences in influence among business firms is an interesting one in itself, it involves only one of the many distributions which are found in society (for examples see page 69). The primary goal of this study is the testing of a method which can be used for the determination of *many* distributions. That is, *we are striving towards a method which is generally applicable*, to groups as well as whole societies, and to both Western and non-Western types of societies.

Again, I would like to stress the practical significance of such a method. We can, of course, talk about how a society can be reconstructed without a precise knowledge of the state of affairs. But what are we actually talking about? What is there exactly wrong, and what must be changed? Many discussions seem to be in full swing long before the actual initial situation has been precisely observed and analyzed. It would be, I think, an illusion to maintain that effective remedies can be prescribed without good diagnoses, that is, without knowing what the shortcomings are. Here, as I see it, is an important task for sociology: to carefully investigate what the state of affairs in society is.

The type of research needed to obtain such information has many of the features of a diagnostic examination; its primary goal is to gather data in order to point out possible defects.

Resistance to this type of research can be expected from two sides:
1. From holders of power, aspirants to power and the influentials if they are bent upon camouflaging reality.
2. From the theoretically-inclined scientists if they subscribe to the 'explanation' as the credo of science.

In the diagnostic investigation facing me here the primary requirement is 'pure measurement', and 'explanation' is of secondary importance. Yet I believe that it is just this type of research which we need to throw a more precise light on problems in complex societies.

2. 'Influence in Society': The Concept, Specifications, and a Procedure for Measurement

The contents of this chapter–Before we begin to measure something, two things must be clear:

(a) *What* is to be measured? We must circumscribe the concept of influence. This is the first task which I have tackled in this chapter. I have striven toward a definition in which the macro-sociological dimension is represented as completely as possible.

Next we must consider within what social area we intend to ascertain influence. The area chosen, I repeat, is that of citizens (here business firms) in their relation to the government. Further we will briefly discuss the division of labor which underlies this field of influence in order to see whether or not the amorphous and complex 'problem of the functioning of democracy' can be separated into unambiguous sub-problems.

(b) *How* must the measurement take place? Influence is a very broad concept; in the terms of De Groot (1968) we would say that it is a concept with a 'surplus' meaning. To measure such a concept it is absolutely necessary that limitations–specifications–be introduced. This is no simple task, since we must 'lose' as little of the concept as possible.

As we have already noted, we shall further specify the concept influence as *influence exercised at least in part for one's own gain.* A still further specification will be *the number of effects brought about in a given period.* These effects can have been produced:

1–as the result of an *influence attempt* by a private citizen

2–as the result of *anticipation by government agencies* (that is, if the government has taken the interests of a private citizen into account in making a decision, without that private citizen having made an attempt to influence that decision).

We will concentrate on the first type of effects–those which have resulted from influence attempts. In sketching the background of these effects, we have distinguished three partial *aspects* of influence. These

aspects, which are easily derived from the scheme in Figure 1.1 (p. 4) are:
1 – *tested influence*, that is, the percentage of influence attempts which have been complied with (of the total number of attempts to influence the government which have been undertaken);
2 – *manifest anticipation*: the percentage of the "problems" for which influence attempts have been made.
3 – *latent anticipation*: the number of problems perceived.

In all probability the reader expects at this point an extensive discussion of various definitions of the concept influence. He will not, however, find much emphasis on such discussions in this book. There are myriad studies in which the many nuances and controversies surrounding the concept have been illuminated. I will name but a few: Van Doorn, 1962; Dahl, 1957; 1968; McFarland 1969; Wagner, 1969; Ellemers, 1969; Riker, 1964; Wrong, 1968. There is an "absence of a standard terminology' (Dahl, 1970, p. 15).

The studies in which justice has been done to as many nuances as possible in a research situation are much less numerous. My view is that there are enough building blocks in the literature which can be accumulated to fashion a manageable measurement procedure. And this is the aim of this study: to attempt to synthesize various nuances – a synthesis which must additionally lead to a workable measurement procedure.

2.1 'Influence in society' as a macro-sociological concept

A broad characterization – Four elements are central in my more-or-less intuitive conception of 'influence':
1. Influence can put something into motion; it has *effects*.
2. These *effects* must have an impact on *society*.
3. Consequently, the influence not only of *persons*, but especially of *groups and organizations* is central to our study.
4. Influence has a more-or-less *permanent* (or lasting) character.
    Let us examine these points more fully.
    The first, that influence can 'put something into motion' requires little explanation. The examples of people attempting to get something done with influence are legion: minority groups petition the government for anti-discrimination laws; political parties press for changes in income distribution and for measures combating traffic accidents; companies ask for improvement of roads or canals; the New Left

propounded changes in thought and action. Attempts are constantly being made to bring about effects.

Influence is not always likewise 'societal influence'. Influence can be exerted by children on their parents and vice versa, by pupils on their teacher, and by one company director on another. We can only speak of 'societal influence' if the effects touch upon the *functioning of the society*. This is then the second element. Societal influence is a special instance of the general phenomenon 'influence'.

It is absolutely necessary to bear this last point clearly in mind, or we arrive all too quickly at a kind of one-sided definition. The crux of many definitions is that the exercise of influence is considered as a process occurring between two persons. This is naturally also an indispensable element in our own definition, but it must be supplemented with a macro-sociological viewpoint. That is, the effects must have consequences for the functioning of society as a whole. This can, of course, mean many things: the effects can refer to social relations as well as to government regulations, social rules, norms and distributions. The direction in which the influence works is not given either. It is possible that something may change, but equally possible that a change will be impeded. But in all these different situations it is still true that the effects relate to *larger social systems.*

The third element is closely connected to this second one. If we want to study influence in large social systems, then we must devote at least as much attention to organizations as to persons. Companies, churches, unions, sport clubs, pressure groups–they are all more important in the ongoing flow of social events than the individual persons that comprise them.

The fourth element, 'the more or less permanent character of influence', can be illustrated as follows: Influence naturally manifests itself in individual effects. A tariff for the textile industry, a deepening of the channel to Rotterdam (the Nieuwe Waterweg), a broadening of the Delaware Canal, could be the results of forceful influence attempts on the part of companies. Yet as such they are nothing more than casual events. Influence includes more; it has a more lasting character. It suggests a possession, a potential, a capacity. Obtaining the tariff and a deeper channel are 'only' events from which we must derive these potentials. (For a closer examination of the term 'potential' see Section 2.3 and further.)

In this sense, therefore, influence refers to a more or less permanent relation between business and government. A more technical denotation is that 'societal influence' is an *institutionalized phenomenon.* It is maintained by the organization of social life itself (naturally with the possibility that the potential can be 'exhausted', but this is a borderline case). Stated in this terminology, influence is an aspect of the social order which has consequences for other aspects of the social order.

We will now combine the four elements which have just been discussed in a definition: *The societal influence of a person, group or organization* (3) *is the potential* (4) *to determine at least partially* (1) *social rules, relations, regulations and so on* (2) (the numbers between the parentheses refer to the elements discussed above).

This definition – 'characterization' is perhaps a better word – is still, however, so broad that as it stands it cannot be incorporated directly into any research design. These difficulties with concepts such as influence are familiar. Weber (1922, p. 28) was conscious of this problem in his definition of the concept power, which is comparable to influence; he called the concept amorphous and turned directly to a special case, 'Herrschaft' (see also Pen, 1971, p. 107).

The various elements of our definition must, then, be narrowed down – particularized – so that we can obtain empirical specifications.[1]

The main line of particularization following from the goal of this study: '*influence by which someone is pursuing, at least in part, advantage for himself*' – One of our research objectives, stated briefly in Chapter 1, was to ascertain 'who gets what and how much' in order to determine the distribution of influence. This implies that we must only consider that kind of influence which has been exercised, at least in part, to obtain advantages for those concerned. In this way we have particularized the 'effects' in the definition (or 'the partial determination of social relations, etc'.). Influence has become influence which is exercised *for one's own gain*. Of course, this does not preclude social relations and rules also being affected by the exercise of influence (which is required by our definition). Even stronger, the distribution of the gains can be an important factor determining social relations.

Later I will sketch in greater detail the exact form which these specifications will take in our investigation.

The concept of influence in this study: *no distinction according to means* – Another customary direction in which specifications have been made is according to the means used in exercising influence. This option has not been taken here because for our purpose – finding out 'who gets what and how much' – the means used are not of primary importance. The overriding objective is to discover whether or not there are differences among citizens in the gains that they have obtained through exercising influence.

Our concept of influence, therefore, remains broad with regard to the means employed–which likewise do not appear in our definition. We also find a similar kind of broad definition in the work of other authors (for example Dahl, 1970). Sometimes the word power is used instead of the word influence, likewise in a broad sense (for example Simon, 1957; Harsanyi, 1962).

Another category of authors, on the contrary, use means as an important characteristic in distinguishing between concepts. The distinction between influence (in the narrower sense) and power is well-known in this respect (Lasswell, see Walton, 1971, p. 192; Parsons, among others 1963a; Ellemers, 1969, p. 10; see also Mulder, 1973, p. 146 and Pen, 1971, p. 110).[2]

Power is generally associated with processes in which something is compelled. Taxpaying, compulsory schooling, conscription, and the building codes are all matters which can be enforced by negative sanctions (Parsons, 1963a, p. 237 and 1969, p. 335; Olsen, 1970, p. 13). Influence in the narrow sense of the word is first and foremost associated with 'persuasion' as far as means are concerned. If Arthur Burns or the Club of Rome speak, it can have effect. The same holds true when the Presbyterians, the Trustees of a university, a pressure group or the International Paper Company express an interest in public issues. Although negative sanctions may also play a part in these cases, they are not the primary means employed.

'Persuasion,' by the way, must be very broadly interpreted in this connection. Burns can get something done because he is a man of authority; he does not even need to be telling the truth. International Paper can convince with the argument of employment opportunities, even if employment has little to do with the issue at hand. Of course, the persuasion can be based on concrete information, but this is not a necessary condition; of primary importance is *who* has said it, and *not what* has been said (Parsons, 1963b, p. 50; for a further elaboration of the dimensions which play a role here, see Chapter 10 of this book). The person or group that wants something is *trusted*. The term 'persuasion,' therefore, has a much broader meaning than only 'rational argumentation'.

At first sight this distinction between power and influence may not seem so problematic. We can attribute power to those who threaten with or impose negative sanctions; if this is not the case, then we can speak of influence. If someone robs a bank, then he knows that the state has negative sanctions at its disposal. But it is not always so simple. In the first place, persuasion and negative sanctions may be used concurrently. Secondly, it is often impossible to distinguish between the two, especially if we consider persuasion in the broad sense given above and if negative sanctions are understood to include the more subtle forms such as 'loss of esteem'. If, for example, I do not let someone's rational argument convince me, then his esteem for me will almost certainly be diminished. It depends, therefore, on the field of research whether or not it is wise to choose differences in means as the basis of a terminological distinction between power and influence.

As I have already pointed out, a distinction according to means does not seem to be of primary importance for this study. If we concentrate on the question 'who gets what', it is not necessary to consider the difficult problem of what means were used. We are therefore using a broad concept of influence, in which the means, in principle, can differ widely–from rational argument to extortion. In the area of social relations which we investigated–briefly outlined in the following section–the actual phenomena, in my opinion, generally seems to be influence as persuasion, but this is perhaps open to debate.

Before presenting further empirical specifications, we must deal with another problem. According to the definition, everyone can have influence on everyone else, at least in principle. Theoretically considered, this is indeed true, but no single investigation can completely cover such a complex field. Some selection and schematization is needed, which we will attempt to do below.

2.2 Influence in the context of the division of labor in society

The choice of a specific field of influence relations – Considered theoretically, the number of influence relationships which can occur in society is nearly infinitely large. I will now explain how I have selected a certain field of relations from the larger universe.

Many writers state with considerable emphasis that influence is a relation between people or parties (for example Dahl, 1970, p. 17). In the jargon of sociological research, we speak in such a case of a 'relational property'. This is a property which characterizes a *relation* between two or more individuals rather than the individuals themselves.

The authors referred to may be right, but they usually overlook some important consequences of their observation. What is in fact the problem? In reasonably large groups, the number of possible combinations of elements greatly outnumbers the number of elements themselves. If we also take into account the fact that every relation has two directions, then the number of possible relations increases still further. This poses considerable problems for the investigator. A selection is needed – preferably a selection which will yield a limited and more-or-less *structured field of relations.*

Reality helps us here to some extent. The number of factual relations is much, much smaller than the number of possible ones, because a large degree of *division of labor* exists among people and organizations in society. This means that well-defined patterns can be distinguished in the tangle of influence relations. Some examples are: consumers versus producers, unions versus organizations of employers, government civil servants versus politicians and patients versus doctors.

The field of relations which *I have chosen as the object of this study* is by now a very familiar one: that of *private citizens versus the government* (under 'private citizens' I also understand organizations, business firms, companies and so on). The connection with the division of labor is obvious.[3] The government is clearly one of the central organizations in society which has the task of regulating issues and relations in society. This is embedded to a certain extent in the Constitution.

The government has a whole scale of jurisdictional powers for the performance of this task. To illustrate which influence relations we are primarily interested in, we will select a clear-cut power – *the power to dispose of finances*[4] *and the control over public-owned facilities.*[5] Now the essential point is that this 'power of the purse' is limited by the other party involved, the 'private citizens'. They also have powers. In the first place, they can periodically change government policy via the ballot box. It is, however, widely supposed that the government still retains considerable freedom of action and discretion. The second 'right' of the citizens is therefore certainly just as important. They can always exert pressure to affect *how* the government spends the money, and what kind of policies it pursues; the citizens can exert this pressure at any time without confining their efforts to election years. Instead of 'pressure' we can use Parsons' more general term *interest-demands* (among others 1963a, p. 260). We have chosen the influence which is involved in these interest-demands as the object of our study – that is, the influence of *private citizens on the government.*

The parties in this field and their connections are schematically presented in Figure 2.1.

The 'private citizens' can be persons, but are usually organizations, as we have noted in the preceding section. (Parsons speaks of 'solidary groupings', 1969, p. 437.) It is exactly these organizations which we

```
                                     control of public-
                       influence     owned facilities
private citizen ─────────────→ government ──────────────────→ social rules,
                                                              relations, etc.
```

Figure 2.1
An influence relationship of a 'private citizen' on the government

may rightfully expect to have influence of a more-or-less permanent character. They form a part of the framework within which the processes take place.

Now that we have selected a concrete field of influence relations, we must reexamine the assumptions underlying the specifications which have been discussed in the preceding section. Clearly, an important argument for the choice of this field is that our specification of influence as 'effects partly for one's own self-interest' would seem to be reasonably feasible.

Once more the question arises whether or not a distinction according to means used in exercising influence is possible within this concrete field. This remains, however, far from simple. If, for example, a business firm requests the city to improve the roads to its plant location, it may first attempt to persuade. In these attempts the firm may advance arguments that appeal to the city government, such as the favorable consequences for employment. It can perhaps increase the strength of its argument by submitting a good cost-benefit analysis (see for example Dasgupta and Pearce, 1972). But if the city government continues to resist, the firm has other means available which come very close to being negative sanctions: it can mobilize the press, go immediately to a higher level of government, or threaten to close the plant or move it to another location. But the city must *perceive* these means as being negative sanctions before they have any meaning. Whether or not this perception actually occurs varies according to time and place. It is even possible that the firm must first conduct a campaign leading to the acceptance of the value 'employment opportunities' before the city in fact considers the sanctions to be sanctions. Moreover, the distinction among means was very difficult to handle empirically, as became clear during some explorative research carried out by Ellemers and Braam in the Dutch Delta area. This difficulty appeared especially with processes of influence which lasted many years. This was for me all the more reason to leave out of consideration a distinction which is not strictly necessary for the goal of this study, and to definitely abandon any specification in the direction of a type of means.

Distinguishing problem areas: (1) *the powers of the government* (2) *distributions of influence (on the government)*–If we ask which private citizens have a great deal of influence and which have little–that is, what the frequency distribution of their influence is–we accept in a certain sense the *existing* division of labor between private citizens and the government as given. This division of labor can, of course, be considered an important problem in itself. What is the number and nature of the powers that the government must have? After all, every power means that the citizens have conceded a part of their autonomy, that they have delegated 'power' (see Coleman, 1973; Braam, 1973). This is, of course, an important problem area. However, as soon as one accepts that a division of labor in society is necessary to a certain degree–that such an institution as government must exist at all–the problem area chosen for this study, in which the influence *on* the government agencies is the central question, becomes just as important. If the government has power, one of the questions which becomes important is *how* these powers are used. In my opinion the position can rightfully be defended that every citizen should have an equal amount of influence in determining the use of government powers.

Even if this principle is *not* accepted, however, there are pressing arguments for devoting more attention than usual to the distribution of societal influence. I noted earlier that voters can only *periodically* call the government to account through the elective process. A great many issues are settled *between* elections, however; it is exactly these issues which are likely to be the object of influence attempts. More important, there are often no formal rules regulating these influence processes.

Thus a number of processes which play an essential part in the functioning of society unfold outside 'official' boundaries–which means, of course, that the distribution of influence in turn is not, on the whole, formally regulated (which of course does not mean that no regularities occur).

This has important practical ramifications. It is namely difficult to imagine how the distribution of influence in a modern society can be 'formally' regulated. No matter what is done to the Constitution, to the system of voting or about the recruitment of politicians, influence processes can always occur outside the formal framework. Influence will not allow itself to be contained within formal structures. Concealment always remains an attractive option in such a vital area.

Regulating influence 'in advance', then, appears to be very difficult.

This is, however, no reason for remaining idle in such an important problem area, especially since, in my opinion, 'unfair' distributions of influence are at the root of many social grievances. Can a remedy be found?

We might begin by considering the popular demand for 'public accountability' or 'openness', which is often proposed as a solution. Presumably it is hoped that this openness will lead toward control of the influence processes. In a certain sense this demand does hit the nail on the head; the 'distribution of influence' and 'power' are cloudy areas, as the present state of research on them can testify. But can openness really change anything? This seems extremely unlikely for two reasons: (1) it is rather naive to think that obligatory openness will actually cause all the information to be brought to light (2) even if a great deal of information is available, determining influence distributions on the basis of simple, unstructured observations is a highly dubious procedure.

'Public accountability' as a remedy, therefore, would require considerable modification, more specifically in the form of *periodic structured investigations of the distribution of influence in the different sectors of society.* Such a solidly-grounded diagnosis would make possible a subsequent appropriate control; the government might then be granted the 'power' to make 'adjustments'.

This exposition has hopefully made a convincing case for the practical relevance of determining the *actual* distribution of influence.

A knowledge of influence distributions is also of outstanding theoretical relevance. The central part which such distributions play in descriptions of social systems is self-evident. Whether it concerns communistic or democratic countries—whether families, clubs or societies are involved, whether the time of measurement is before or after a revolution—data telling how influence upon the government is distributed are indispensable if we are trying to reveal the functioning of the social system. These data, however, are not so easily obtained—which is why we are attempting to develop a new method in this study.

To sum up this section: The number of influence relations in a society can be extremely large. It appears, however, that clear patterns—fields or areas—can be distinguished more or less following the lines of the social division of labor. The field I chose for closer examination was the relationship of private citizens with the government.

To determine influence within this field, we must make some further specifications.

2.3 Particularization of 'influence': a set of concrete effects

Synopsis–In the first part of this chapter we have characterized the concept of influence. We selected one area–the influence of private persons on the government–to be the particular object of our study. Thus *what* we intend to measure has become more or less clear; the question now facing us is *how* the measurement must be carried out. We begin answering that question in this chapter by particularizing the concept, by breaking it down into single, measurable elements.

Several questions follow directly from our definition and shape the lines along which our particularization unfolds. The first question is how can we infer a 'potential' from individual events. The section dealing with this topic immediately follows this synopsis. A second question is how we can conclude that a 'partial determination of social rules, relations, regulations and so on' is present. This will bring us to a discussion of causal relationships, which are an essential element in the concept of power and influence.

At the same time, we must keep in mind that our aim is to obtain a sufficient level of *comparability* of measurements to allow us to reach conclusions about differences between persons or between groups in the amount of influence they exercise.

Particularization of influence as a 'potential': a 'set' of concrete effects – Sociologists face considerable problems with the term 'potential'. 'Potentials' themselves cannot be observed. The presence of magnetism, for example, can only be derived from the *effect* it produces: a piece of iron in the vicinity of a magnet begins to move.

The problem is that we cannot 'test' whether or not a 'potential for influence' is present, or if it is present, what its magnitude is. Magnetism can be ascertained experimentally, while influence cannot, or only with very great difficulty.

To determine influence we must therefore rely upon effects which *spontaneously* occur. This results in considerable extra problems, since such spontaneous occurrences are not comparable, taken as they stand. An 'exact' measurement is therefore extremely difficult.

Is it possible then, to remove the term 'potential' from our definition? The answer is simple: certain dimensions of influence, which we intuitively feel to be important, would disappear completely if our definition were changed in this way. The use of the term potential effectively emphasizes the more or less permanent, lasting character of influence. It is not the individual effects which interest us, but the 'institutionalized relations' which lie at the root of them. The social order is at least partially revealed by exactly these relations. The term 'potential' is therefore in my opinion indispensable in a definition of influence.

But the heavy consequences of its inclusion must then be faced; that is, in some way or another we have to derive these potentials from effects which have spontaneously occurred 'in the field' (see also Coleman, 1970, pp. 9 ff).

We must begin by postulating how this invisible potential is related to the observable phenomena. The specification which I have chosen to represent this relation is a very simple one: *influence as a potential* we will consider to be the *set of concrete effects brought about* by the potential *in a given period of time* (for example five years) (see also Harsanyi, 1962, p. 68 for the term 'effects').

This means that we intend to determine influence from a *number* of events in a given period, and not from one single event (of course, it is possible that only one effect has, in fact, occurred). It is plausible that this specification will allow us to come to grips with the more-or-less permanent character of influence. The representation of influence just outlined is presented in Figure 2.2.

I have already intimated that my specification is less simple than it may at first appear. There are problems inherent in the data on which our investigation must be based: we must constantly come to grips with the question of whether or not 'spontaneously-occurring events' *can be compared with one another*. If two private citizens have brought about a different number of effects, it is not necessarily due to a difference in their 'potentials'. Perhaps the two individuals were faced with entirely different situations. Imagine, for example, that two business firms are located at two different industrial sites. The first firm has persuaded the government to improve the road to its plant–an 'effect'; the second firm has no effects. If further inquiries should reveal that the second

private citizen	number of effects in a 5-year period
A1	× × × ×
A2	×
A3	(none)
A4	× × × ×

Figure 2.2
Influence as potential considered as a set of effects

firm already had good access roads, then the observed difference has not been a proper indicator of a difference in a 'potential' for influence.

It follows that differences in potentials can only be derived from differences in effects if as many factors as possible are 'controlled'. Without such controls, the specification of influence 'as potential' is clearly not valid.

This need for 'controls' is also highlighted by the radical nature of the specification. It means, for example, that if someone has achieved no effects in the 5 years in question, then no 'potential' can be ascribed to him. But how would we classify him if he were not at all *motivated* to obtain effects? (in the terminology which I will use in this book, this would mean that he had no 'problems' in this period). Yet intuitively we do not want to accept the conclusion that the 'potential' is absent in such a case (compare with Dahl, 1970, p. 28).

This problem can be solved in two ways:

1. by not using the concept influence 'as potential' at all. This is most unsatisfactory, as we have shown in the preceding paragraphs.
2. by considering motivation as one of the essential components of a human potential; this means that if two people, *under the same conditions*, are unequally motivated to use their influence, then their 'potential' can also be considered unequal. This formulation is not completely satisfactory, but it is adequate for our purposes (compare with Wrong, 1968, p. 679, who launched the suggestion not to consider 'merely possible' influence as potential influence).

I have opted for the second solution. Yet it retains its validity only if we can compare the motivations for the use of influence as accurately as possible, that is, if we can manage to hold under control as many of the conditions as possible which may determine this motivation. The requirement of *comparable conditions is thus partially inherent in the nature of the concept for which we are carrying out the measurement.* How I have strived toward comparability in this investigation will be explained in Chapter 4.

There is another point which must be considered. An 'effect' is the final result of an influence process which takes place in different phases; these phases constitute what we may call the background of the effect. To be able to make a selection among the conditions which must be controlled, it is necessary to trace this background. For this purpose we will analytically distinguish three aspects: tested influence, manifest anticipation and latent anticipation. This distinction also allows us to illuminate separately the roles of the two parties in the influence process–the governmental decision-maker and the citizens.

We shall see that *the effects form the tip of a pyramid of data* which considerably enhance our insight into the phenomena influence and make possible a better comparison among individuals. This will be considered in the next paragraph.

We will now first discuss *what* exactly we consider an effect to be.

Influence as a cause–effect relationship–Once influence has been further specified as a set of effects, we must describe which kind of phenomena can be considered to be a 'produced effect'. One of the best ways to achieve this is by studying concrete *influence processes.*

The influence process plays such an important role in some definitions of influence that its use can be recognized as a certain 'definitional trend'. Simon (1957), March (1955) and Dahl (1957) devoted considerable attention to influence processes in the 1950s. 'Behavior'–or that which is clearly observable–was always central in these studies. Their definitions actually emphasize the *exercise* of influence (Simon, 1957, p. 65) rather than a potential for influence (see Van Doorn, 1957). In a certain sense this trend was a reaction to earlier definitions in which influence was equated with *sources* of influence. The weakness of this kind of definitions is that they leave no room for data demonstrating whether or not the potential is actually utilized.

Objections can of course also be made to the defining of influence as a concrete process. This easily leads to a 'behavioristic' one-sidedness. However, according to our measurement approach, there is a compelling reason for avoiding this one-sidedness. As we will demonstrate, this follows from the specification which we have chosen above. Such a specification makes it necessary to also consider *the extent* to which influence processes have occurred. This means that we must also take into account the *absence* of influence processes. This problem will be dealt with in the following section when we discuss the 'anticipation' of the private citizen. We will observe that this behavioristic one-sidedness disappears automatically.

Though we must be careful not to treat influence and the exercise or process of influence as being identical, influence processes remain our most important point of orientation: (1) *if* they occur, then we have to incorporate them into our measurements, and (2) we must also consider the *degree* to which they occur, or do not occur.

What exactly is involved in the definition of influence as a process? This can be illustrated with a simple example. Suppose that a businessman (A) asks his city government (B) for a new road to the industrial park in which his company plant is located. The businessman has had influence if his request is granted – with one reservaton: if the city had already planned to construct the road, but for other reasons, then the businessman cannot, of course, be credited with any influence.

Dahl describes this process well in his definition (1970, p. 71): 'Influence is a relation among actors in which one actor induces other actors to act in some way they would not otherwise act' (see Figure 2.3).

Essential to this definition is thus:
1. that the *direction* of B's behavior *is changed*
2. that this happens *as a consequence* of A's action

Both elements must be *inextricably* connected with one another before we can speak of influence of A on B. This amounts to the same

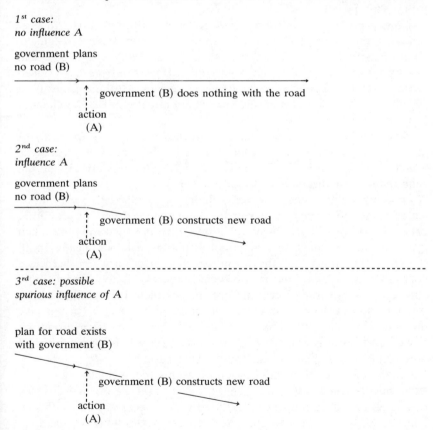

1st *case:*
no influence A

government plans
no road (B)

government (B) does nothing with the road

action
(A)

2nd *case:*
influence A

government plans
no road (B)

government (B) constructs new road

action
(A)

3rd *case: possible*
spurious influence of A

plan for road exists
with government (B)

government (B) constructs new road

action
(A)

Figure 2.3
A schematic representation of the process of influence

thing as the requirement in our specification that effects must have been 'brought about'; the 'partial determination' in our definition is also consistent with the schematization of influence processes just presented.

Various authors have considered influence as a special case of the *cause-effect relation* (Simon, 1957, p. 65–67; March, 1955, p. 434; see also McFarland, 1969). In our example this means that A's action is the cause, and the change in the behavior of B the effect. According to the philosophy of science, this inclusion of cause-effect relations, or causal relations, in our definition can lead to considerable difficulties. This was reason enough for Dahl, 1957 to exclude the term from his definition. But this is a solution in appearance only; the notion of causality is present in his definition as well, if only implicitly (compare Bell, 1969, p. 20).

What problems exactly are involved with causality? First, the essence of the concept cannot be captured by our 'formal language' (Blalock, 1964, p. 9). Causality means 'producing a change', and exactly this process eludes our observation. If we think we have traced a causal relation between variable A and variable B, there is always a possible variable C between the two which might explain the change-producing activity.

This problem can be solved if we re-define causality in terms of *necessary and sufficient conditions* (Riker, 1964) rather than processes. Statements of the type 'If, and only if A, then B' do meet the requirements of the philosophy of science.

Complex reality can, however, seldom be reduced to such simple statements–which means that we are immediately faced with another problem. There will always be additional factors which must be taken into account in an actual research situation. Blalock (1964, p. 9) therefore maintains that the terminology of necessary and sufficient conditions cannot be used in the social sciences. In non-experimental situations, where conditions can never be completely controlled, causal relationships must be formalized in some other way. The specific method which he proposed has deservedly received much attention; however, it is not suitable for the purposes with which I am concerned here (as will be explained in the following pages).

On the surface, Blalock's reasoning seems highly plausible. Yet a basic flaw becomes evident when we realize that we do in fact often conclude that there are causes in the sense of 'necessary and sufficient conditions' in our day-to-day experiences: Mr. Johnson causes an accident; a woman seduces a man; A & P causes problems in the milk industry.

In addition, the situation is not necessarilly as complicated as Blalock suggests. In our case, for example, it is questionable whether A's action must be required to be *both* a necessary and a sufficient condition. This seems unrealistic. Of course there are other conditions besides A's action which are needed to achieve a change in B's behavior. It is only necessary that these other relevant conditions be 'controlled' in comparing *different* groups or persons. *It is, however, an indispensible requirement that A be a necessary condition before we may ascribe influence to him* (compare Wagner, 1969, p. 5). We cannot attribute influence to A if A has not had a part in the behavioral change of B; A must have *achieved* something with B.

This means that we have *not* accepted Blalock's conclusion: we *shall* indeed use the expression 'necessary condition'. The means by which we intend to determine influence will, consequently, differ sharply from methods like those of Blalock (and other somewhat related methods such as those of Lazarsfeld and Hyman).

This difference in method is closely related to a difference in the context in which the concept 'cause' is placed. With influence as 'effect' we think first of an *individual* in one single influence process. Causes must therefore already be determined in an early stage of the study. The usual causal analyses in survey research, however, make statements about causal connections among *variables*. As a consequence the causal analysis is carried out at the end of the investigation, after all the individuals have been classified according to several variables. Statements about causes in such cases concern the sample of individuals as a whole.

In practice, using such a method means that processes which take place *between* individuals no longer play a central role. Since the study of these processes themselves is *the* core of my investigation, I have deliberately departed from the current approaches in this respect. An elaboration of the reasons for making this choice now follows.

That processes are seldom studied in sociology is a more general problem. A process is a much more difficult unit to manipulate than a clear-cut 'statistical' one such as an individual or a group. Much information is lost as a result; research is seldom based on processes such as 'Monique is flirting with Erik'; 'The government is conducting negotiations with the business world'; 'Tensions are increasing in the AFL-CIO'. At most, such processes become the object of case studies. And there are good reasons why social scientists generally abandon any aspirations towards greater generalization. A major one is that a sample of 'processes' is extremely difficult to select because it is almost impossible to determine the universe from which they are being taken.[6]

This is by no means a reason for refraining from studying such processes thoroughly. *Why* they take place, and what their *consequences* are, is of utmost importance for changes in both personal and more general social relations. Clearly, therefore, the search for cause and effect in the cases just mentioned must be made for each *process* or for each *interaction* (compare Lazarsfeld and Rosenberg, 1955, p. 387).

This is immediately evident with a concept such as influence. The concept implies that the behavior of one actor is closely *linked* to that of another, or that a private citizen *obtains* something from the government. Additionally, we would very much like to know whether or not one private citizen has obtained *more* than another. I believe that it would be too great a departure from reality if we did not determine this causality for each process separately. We would otherwise fail completely to characterize real human life with our concept of influence.

Of course the individual process is only the building block for general statements which are based upon a large number of similar cases. This poses no particular problems. The real difficulty is that Blalock's method makes it impossible to arrive at general statements about processes of influence, simply because these processes have not been observed.

If we take the processes themselves as our point of departure, then we must first determine for each process separately whether or not A has been the cause of a behavior change in B before we can conclude that influence can be *ascribed* to A.

The observation of the influence process as a causal relationship–In order to decide whether or not a causal relationship is present between A and B we must first set forth which requirements the relation must meet. Simply presented, these requirements are as follows:

a–the two elements must *covariate*; that is, something must change in A as well as in B;

b–the relation must be *a-symmetrical*; that is, the change in A must not be a result of the change in B. There must usually–but not necessarily–be a time-lapse between the change in A and the change in B. In these cases, the *direction* of the relation is fixed.

c–the relation must not be *spurious*; the changes in A and B must not both be the result of a third factor.

(For these requirements compare Stinchcombe, 1968, p. 19; Dahl, 1968, p. 410 ff; Simon, 1957, pp. 65 ff and 50–61.)

How can we set about determining whether or not these requirements have been met in one single case, that is, in one separate process? According to requirement (a) two observations are needed, one of A and one of B. Both actors must therefore be involved in the observation. This double observation is difficult in practice, which is why so many social scientists seek refuge in indirect methods.

Requirement (b) will be treated more fully when we discuss the final formulation of the hypotheses. We will also return later to requirement (c)–that the relation may not be spurious (as we shall see, a classification of 'problems' can be very helpful in meeting this requirement, see p. 60).

Requirements a, b and c encompass the formal characteristics of a causal relation. As soon as we attempt to investigate the differences in influence in the real world, however, the additional requirement of *comparability* remorselessly presents itself (compare Dahl, 1957, p. 205; 1970, p. 19). This also has its advantages, however. It means, for example, that it is not necessary to require that absolutely no other conditions besides A have been involved in the relation. It is sufficient if we know that these other conditions can be assigned a comparable weight in the various cases.

In the beginning of this section I emphasized the primary importance of comparability. We will return to this topic repeatedly when we formulate our hypotheses and discuss our research design.

Our first concern must be to ensure that requirement a (covariation) is fulfilled. The questions are: *what exactly about A and B must be observed,* and for which elements do we intend to determine the occurrence of changes. In our definition of the exercise of influence we referred to a *change in behavior* in B (in our case the government). It is obvious that we must also investigate what action A undertakes in relation to B, thus the *change in behavior* in A (this alone, by the way, is not sufficient because A can have effects through other means than behavioral changes on its part; I will return to this topic in 'anticipation by government agencies').

In examining these behavior changes more closely, we quickly realize that radical specifications must be introduced.

Specifications: influence attempts and government decisions–Many authors interpret the term 'behavior' in a broad sense, including emotions and attitudes in their definitions (Dahl, 1970, p. 18). Indeed, there are ample investigations of influence processes which focus on attitude changes.

My initial specification here, and one which shaped the course of later specifications, is a limitation to *manifest* behavior, both of (1) the private citizens, and of (2) the government officials. Corrections must be made later, but this is a clear point from which to begin.

(1) Manifest behavior of private citizens, aimed at exercising influence, can be further characterized as *influence attempts*, or in our case '*demands made on the government*'.

(2) Behavior changes in those who have been the object of influence attempts can be specified as '*decisions*' in which the influence attempts proved to be *successful* or *unsuccessful*. Decisions of the government in particular are behavior changes which are clearly observable (see also Figure 1.1, p. 4).

If we have observed that the influence attempt of a private citizen A1 is followed by a decision which is favorable to him, we can only label A1 as a necessary condition if the decision would *not* have been made, or would have been made differently, *without* the influence attempt. We must therefore investigate whether or not the government had already planned to make the decision in question for another reason than that influence had been exerted upon it (for an exception see the following section on 'anticipation by government agencies'). A thorough search must be made to discover other possible reasons why a decision produced that particular outcome (for further discussion of this problem see Chapter 3, p. 55, Chapter 4, p. 79 and Chapter 6, Sect. 6.1). In Chapter 3, for example, the special case in which two or more private citizens exercise influence for the same goal will be extensively discussed.

We have now essentially completed our characterization of influence as a set of concrete effects. The influence of a private citizen within the period specified is simply equal to the number of influence attempts which have been complied with or, stated differently, the number of successes. This influence will be denoted by the symbol S.

Our discussion of causal relations itself, however is not yet complete. A private citizen can also possess influence *without* having made an influence attempt. This eventuality will now be considered.

A complication: influence without an influence attempt (anticipation by government agencies)–The influence of a private citizen can be traced through the two specifications which have been presented–influence attempts and decisions respectively-*if* that citizen has made an influence attempt, that is, if his behavior aimed at affecting the decision was clearly observable. In this case we encounter the least difficulties in ascertaining a causal relation.

Yet more factors must be considered. If the government *takes a private citizen into account* in making a decision, even if that citizen has not requested such consideration, he has just as surely exercised influence as in the previous case. The government's behavior in this situation can have various causes. Possibly the interests of a company are considered in order to promote a more general interest such as employment opportunities. Or the government may be wary of a public outcry if it were to make another decision than it has.

Whatever the reasons may be, in such cases A is the cause of a given behavioral change in B, because B is *anticipating* the interests associated with A. We owe this wording to Friedrich, who spoke of 'the rule of anticipated reactions' (Friedrich, 1941).

The only requirement for a causal relation is, therefore, *that A be present in B's 'life-space' at the moment that B is making his decision, and that B take A into account in this decision-making process* (Nagel, 1968, p. 132).[7]

We can now distinguish two situations in which influence is present:
1. influence attempt by A → compliance by B
2. anticipation by B (government) of A → decision by B to the advantage of A.

We should note that a decision can also be to A's disadvantage. Since we are always concerned in this study with comparisons among different A's, this statement adds no new complication to the measurement problem. The actual question is simply which A has had relatively the least amount of disadvantages.

Our subsequent task is to determine when anticipation by the government has taken place.

The assessment of 'anticipation by the government'–For the *private citizen*, anticipation by government agencies can manifest itself in two ways: first, when he enjoys advantages, secondly, when disadvantages are avoided: In both cases the decisions have not originated with the private citizen. It is possible that the latter is not even aware that he has influenced the outcome of the decision. In these cases the observations must therefore begin with the decision itself, or with the government agencies. We must assess whether or not the decision would have been different if the private citizen *had not* been there. This difficult task can only be accomplished if, first, the research is confined to certain types of decision, and secondly, if the positive and negative consequences of these decisions can be clearly established. If these requirements are fulfilled, then *an inventory must be made of these 'other' decisions, and they must be screened for their relevance for private citizens* (for the practical research procedure see the chapter 'Problems of Business Firms').

In the first case, that is when the private citizen has obtained advantages, this is the only feasible way to discover the governmental anticipation.

In the second case, that is when disadvantages for the private individual have been avoided, the observation can perhaps be carried out more easily. We can also study those situations in which government plans *threaten* to, or do have a *negative* effect for the citizen. The citizen will usually be vividly aware of these negative effects. Thus the differing perceptions of private citizens concerning the negative effects which government decisions threaten to have for them, can serve as an indicator of differences in government anticipation with respect to those private individuals (for the practical implications, see Chapter 5).

Following the guidelines sketched above, we can construct several simple indicators. My intention, however, has been to make *effects resulting from influence attempts* the primary concern of this study. Since determining these effects involves a laborious measurement procedure, and since overburdening of the investigation must be avoided, I intend to confine myself to the broad indicators of government anticipation just described. On the basis of these indicators we can introduce any corrections which might be necessary in the numbers of effects which have resulted from influence attempts (see p. 116 ff.).

Effects and their backgrounds (decision–makers, petitioners and influence aspects) – As we noted previously, the influence of a private citizen within the requisite five-year period can be represented simply by the number of influence attempts which have been successful (S).

Although this simplicity seems too good to be true, considering our specification, this index is accurate. The amount of information which it provides, however, is scanty. The index falls short as a means of *illuminating* differences in influence. For example, the number of influence attempts which have *not* been successful is not included. Likewise, we cannot trace which *actor* is responsible for differences in S; it is possible that one individual has made many more influence attempts than another, but it is also possible that the decision-maker has given one of the two 'preferential treatment'.

We must therefore analyze the influence process more precisely so that we can outline the background of the effects. As I stated earlier, three *aspects of influence* will be distinguished; with these different aspects we are able to describe separately the behavior of the *decision-maker* and that of the private citizen, the *petitioner*.

The three aspects are:

on the side of the decision-maker: *tested influence*
on the side of the petitioner: *manifest anticipation* and
                                    latent anticipation[8]

This does not affect our specification 'influence as a collection of concrete effects', for as we shall see later, the number of effects is equal to the product of the three aspects.

The section which follows will be devoted to the development of these aspects.

Summary – In this section we have taken the following steps:
1 – we have provisionally specified the concept of the 'potential', influence, as a set of produced effects within a given period of time;
2 – the determination of a *produced effect* requires an assessment of a causal relationship; there must be certainty that the action of a *private citizen* has been the cause of *a change in behavior of the government*;
3 – further specifications necessarily follow – of *influence attempts* (by the private citizen) and of *decisions* (by the government):
4 – the government can also take a private citizen into consideration in making a decision when no influence attempt has been made; this *'anticipation' by the government* can likewise clearly be termed influence. The 'private citizen' in this case can also be considered a cause.

Schematically presented, the following elements must therefore be observed in the investigation:

	with private citizens	*with the government*
effects as a result of influence attempts:	influence attempts ⟶	decisions
effects as a result of anticipation by the government	advantages ⟵---------- disadvantages ⟵----------	other decisions

In order not to overburden the investigation, we will only take effects resulting from government anticipation into account when it is strictly necessary.

The emphasis in this book, therefore, will be placed primarily on effects which have resulted from influence attempts. We can safely assume that this procedure will assure a reasonably close approximation of our specification of influence as the number of effects produced in a given period.

The number of effects, though in itself a valuable piece of information, leaves us in doubt as to how these effects have come into being. The backgrounds of these effects will be the subject of the following section.

2.4   Backgrounds: Effects as the product of three aspects of influence

Introduction – In this section we will trace the background of influence; in order to accomplish this task, we shall separate the influence process into three partial aspects. It will be shown that the product of these three aspects is equal to the number of effects – that is, to the index which we suggested in the preceding section.

The first aspect – tested influence – is related primarily to the behavior of the decision-maker. The second and third aspects – manifest anticipation and latent anticipation respectively – largely characterize the behavior and the perceptions of the 'petitioner'; the latter two aspects make their appearance when we ask *why* influence attempts have been undertaken.

The first aspect: tested influence (T); the fraction of influence attempts which are successful – When a private citizen has made a number of influence attempts within the chosen time period, the behavior of the decision-maker in relation to *this* particular individual can be characterized by the fraction of total number of his influence attempts which have been complied with (or, if we multiply by 100, the *percentage* of influence attempts which have been successful). We call this fraction T.

$$T = \frac{\text{number of successful influence attempts}}{\text{total number of influence attempts}}$$

$$\text{or} \quad T = \frac{S}{IA}$$

Where IA is the number of influence attempts.

This aspect of influence has a clearly explicit character; it is concerned with the influence that a private citizen has deliberately and overtly tried to use. I shall therefore speak of the influence which has in reality been tested, or, more succinctly, 'tested influence'. This index is well-known in the literature (see among others Goldhamer and Shils, 1939; Lippit, Polansky, Redl and Rosen, 1960, p. 753; March, 1955, p. 448).

The index clearly has a number of advantages. It reflects not only the number of effects, but also the number of unsuccessful influence attempts. Imagine a situation in which two citizens A_1 and A_2 have achieved an equal amount with the government; for example, both have had two successes. A_1, however, has made three additional influence attempts which have been unsuccessful. The index for A_1 is therefore 2/5, for A_2 1 (viz. 2/2). The difference in governmental behavior towards the two private citizens is clearly reflected in these numbers.

The index T, however, also makes apparent the need for further supplementation, for we have now switched from the set of effects over to another set, namely that of influence attempts. Our original set, effects, is only a part of this new set (a subset, see Figure 2.4). It must be emphasized that the size of the set 'influence attempts' is also a meaningful datum. If the fractions of successful influence attempts (T) are the same for A_1 and A_2, and if A_1 has made many more influence attempts than A_2, then, considered absolutely, A_1 *has actually achieved much more than A_2*. This is not revealed by the index T. It does not reflect the fact that one citizen can be much more active in making influence attempts than another. In other words, *we must also take possible differences in the number of influence attempts into account.*

This is also quite clear when considered arithmetically. If we have accepted the number of effects (S) as being a good index in itself, then T must be multiplied with a certain factor to get S. This factor is the number of influence attempts (S = T × IA, namely S = S/IA × IA). The

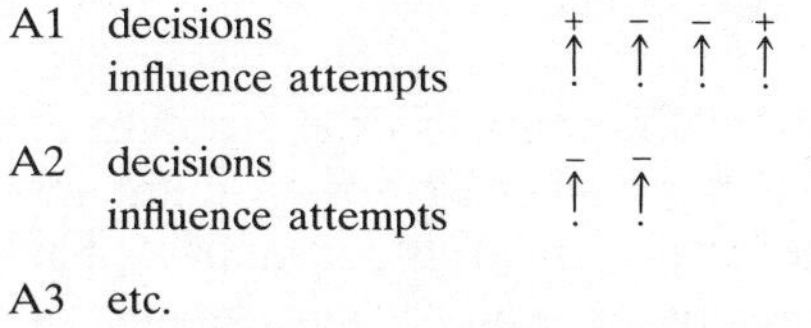

A1   decisions
      influence attempts

A2   decisions
      influence attempts

A3   etc.

1.   + : successful influence attempt (an effect)
    − : unsuccessful influence attempt

Figure 2.4
The set of effects as a sub-set of the set influence attempts[1]

crucial point in this exposition is that 'the number of influence attempts' refers to the *behavior of the petitioner*, thus *to the other actor* in
the influence process. This is the meaning of the statement, in itself
trivial, that the number of effects will depend upon the number of
influence attempts.

It is this second party–the petitioner–whose influence we wish to
determine. It is therefore desirable in every respect that we pay
relatively much attention to 'the number of influence attempts' and
that we thoroughly examine the background of this datum.

*How does an influence attempt come into being? Sets of influence
attempts and sets of interests*–The size of the set of influence attempts
which a private citizen undertakes reflects the extent to which he has
tried to use his potential influence. Without further information, this
number of influence attempts is also a rather vague piece of information. To what extent are these sets a good basis for comparing[9] the
potentials which we are seeking to establish?

On page 21 we stated that the motivations for using influence were
to be considered a real component of 'potential influence' provided
that–and this is the crucial addition–we specify the conditions (and
hold them constant) when we make comparisons.

But which conditions must we select as relevant for the purpose of
controlled comparisons in our study? This question cannot be answered unless we go further into the *reasons* why people make influence
attempts, that is, why they strive for *effects*.

Roughly three factors can be mentioned which will determine
whether or not an influence attempt will be made (see Chapter 5 for a
more detailed discussion). These three factors are:
– interests
– daring
– the extent to which self-interest is perceived as such.

First the 'interests'. It is plausible that differences in the strength of
an interest will determine at least in part whether or not an influence
attempt is made. *We must therefore hold these interests constant* so that
we can validly compare the set of influence attempts. This means, of
course, that these interests must first be operationalized. We will
return to this topic later.

But much more is involved here. The interests may be the same, yet
one citizen may make an influence attempt which another does not.
The cause can be a difference in daring (this is, of course, a very rough

formulation; technically stated, we are concerned here with the level of aspiration and the 'perception of the probability of success'). But don't we instinctively tend to consider this difference to be actually a difference in influence? In other words–when the number of interests and their strengths are equal, then it holds true that the more influence attempts, the greater the probability of influence. This points to a *second index* for influence, that is the size of *the set of influence* attempts. Again, we will return to this point later.

All this still assumes that 'interests' are a good basis for comparison. But this is also doubtful. In our daily experience we often maintain that some people don't 'realize' what their own interests are. Some people are very keen about promoting their interests, others are not. In studies dealing with the subject 'social justice' it has been found, for example, that those who have received less than their share feel themselves less underprivileged than might be expected. They do not see their own 'relative deprivation'; they are 'resigned' (see Runciman, 1966, 1972; Pinker, 1971; Braam, 1972). So not being aware of one's own interest already limits the number of influence attempts and 'effects' *in advance*. Provisionally formulated, *the size of the set of interests constitutes a third index* for the amount of influence.

Our exploration into the background of the set of influence attempts has therefore led us to two other aspects of influence. The last aspect especially has become more visible because we have focused our attention on the mechanisms which have *prevented* effects from occurring. This touches closely on the theme 'non-decisions' which is well-known in the literature; I will now discuss this topic briefly.

A closely related problem area: '*non-decisions*': *anticipation by private citizens of the government*–The 'decision-making approach' has long enjoyed much popularity in investigations of local power. Dahl's study *Who Governs*, 1961, serves as a classical example in this field. My method, which I shall develop further in this section, is similar to Dahl's only in that 'decisions' play a part in it. In other respects the differences between the two methods are very great (see Appendix 2A for an explanation).

Bachrach and Baratz (1962, 1963, 1970) have launched a trenchant attack on the decision-making approach as it has been applied by Dahl and others. Summarized, their objections are as follows: Decisions reveal only a very limited part of power and influence. Exactly those matters about which decisions are never made are extremely relevant for power and influence. Such 'non-decisions' (however curious the term may be) must be accounted an equal importance with 'decisions' in investigations of power and influence.

In their own words: 'But power is also exercised when A devotes his energies to creating or reinforcing social and political values and institutional practices *that limit the scope of the political process to public consideration* of only those issues which are comparatively innocuous to A (1962, p. 948);

and:

'To measure relative influence solely in terms of the ability to *initiate* and *veto* proposals is to ignore the possible exercise of influence or power in *limiting the scope of initiation*' (1962, p. 952).

I will not review here the heated debates on these ideas which have been waged in the literature (see among others Merelman, 1968; Parenti, 1970; Wolfinger, 1971; Frey, 1971). It must be admitted that Bachrach and Baratz have pointed out some important gaps in the research practices which prevailed until their work appeared. The idea of 'non-decisions' is related directly to the question I posed above— how do influence attempts come about, and especially, why do they *fail* to occur?

Bachrach and Baratz suggested that, for example, manipulation of values could be the reason for this non-occurrence. Human beings are politically socialized in a certain way (Frey, 1971, p. 1094)– 'indoctrinated' is the fashionable term. As a result some people feel that influence attempts are 'not respectable'. Questions about motivation are, however, long familiar to sociologists. Max Weber refers to approximately the same phenomenon when he says that some kinds of human behavior can be explained by an orientation towards 'order' in itself (Weber, 1922, p. 16). It is equally well-known that a tendency toward 'acquiescence' can lead to the non-recognition of interests. The demand that people become conscious of their situations, based upon these ideas, is likewise a familiar one.

What is, of course, important to know in determining influence is *whether or not such internalized values are partially responsible for one individual's attempting to exert more influence than another.* We will roughly characterize the effects of the internalization of these 'values' on private citizens with the term *'anticipation by private citizens'*.[10]

To cover this aspect of influence more fully we need yet another supplementary definition. I refer to *negative* anticipation if a person has 'inhibition' about making an influence attempt, and to *positive* anticipation when the opposite is the case–when he is eager to make such an attempt. I consider positive and negative anticipation here to be complementary. If one is strong, the other is weak and vice versa.

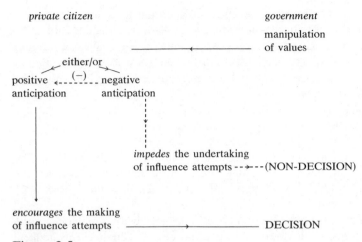

Figure 2.5
Example of a process that encourages or prevents the undertaking of an influence attempt

For convenience sake in this book I will use the term *anticipation* when referring to 'positive anticipation' (this conceals no deeper meaning; it is purely a question of assigning a name). So, *stronger anticipation means that the probability of influence is deemed to be greater.*

Various possibilities can be schematically represented as can be seen, for example, in Figure 2.5. Specialists in this field are pessimistic about the possibilities for investigating processes such as those depicted in Figure 2.5. Fortunately, it is not necessary to know such a process entirely–and its duration can be very long indeed–in order to determine influence. It is sufficient that we establish the differences in anticipation as displayed by the *private citizens themselves*. I already suggested in the previous section that this was feasible, provided that the interests are comparable (compare Frey, 1971, p. 1088 ff.).

While attempting to cope with comparable interests, we are led nearly automatically toward a further elaboration of the specification 'influence by which someone is pursuing, at least in part, advantage for himself' which we already realized to be essential at the beginning of this study. This elaboration now follows.

Elaboration of the specification 'influence by which someone is pursuing, at least in part, advantage for himself'–The concept 'interest' is still extremely broad. Clear self-interest, involvement in the political struggle, ideals focused on a far-removed future–all can be considered to be interests. For example: even if a citizen has no self-interest, or if its presence can only be vaguely hypothesized in the distant future, he can still be the cause of a given government decision. With a number of decisions it is even difficult to establish to whose advantage or disadvantage they are–that is, whose 'self-interest' would be served by them (compare Bauer, 1964, p. 129).

We stumble here upon the two 'facets' that the term influence can have in common usage. On the one hand the term indicates the determination of 'a general state of affairs', on the other hand, the probability that people are obtaining advantages for themselves. The first aspect has been sufficiently represented in our definition; the second, the 'probability of personal advantages' has until now been clearly less present.

As we have just seen, the two aspects do not always coincide; in any case, it is conceivable that an individual could influence the general state of affairs without obtaining advantages for himself, thus without 'serving his own self-interest' (of course, the opposite case is also conceivable). Our previous discussion amounts to the following: the general term 'interest' is a catchall for numerous *dissimilar types of interests. This causes great difficulties in the measurement of anticipation* because few or no examples exist showing how this measurement should be carried out. The heterogeneity of interests can be reduced to some extent by considering only 'self-interest' in the narrow sense of the word. This is additionally in accordance with the specification 'influence aimed at least in part at gaining advantage for one's self' which we already developed at the beginning of this book (see Chapter 1 and Chapter 2 p. 12). Naturally this does not preclude the possibility that 'the general state of affairs' is being partially determined at the same time, but this no longer has first priority. The definition of influence has become 'ego-oriented' (Riker, 1964, p. 344).

On the one hand, this specification introduces a restriction which is somewhat unwelcome. There is less emphasis placed on the explanation of societal rules and relations than is perhaps desirable.

On the other hand, the specification has certain advantages for the social relevance of this study. Influence is now directly related to the distribution of the marbles, to 'gains'. This contributes to the requirement of practical relevance, since we can now clearly determine whether or not certain individuals or groups are privileged or under-privileged as a result of a set of influence processes.

Thus another specification evolves along with this one, namely *that the social consequences of the influence are at least in part personal consequences for those involved,* and also that the point *at which they can be measured* is with those actually involved in the influence process.

Summarizing, the specification has the following consequences for the three basic elements which we have used up to this point:

interests   →   'self'-interests (for brevity: interests)
influence-attempts →   interest-demands
decisions   →   decisions at least partially to the advantage of
                             the private citizen making the interest-demand

Finally, the specification has many *advantages for the feasibility of the investigation.* The actual observation of influence-attempts becomes much easier when these attempts can be characterized as interest-demands. If the investigator knows that 'self-interests' are at stake, then he must be aware of the *possibility* of influence attempts. This in turn promotes the reliability of the procedures used to determine the causal relations discussed earlier in this chapter. In short, the whole procedure for determining influence comes to rest on more solid foundations through this specification.

A provisional statement about the operationalization of 'self-interest': *problems* – How shall we operationalize interests? Earlier investigations are of little help on this point. The idea that interests must be taken into account in the assessment of influence is not in itself new. Harsanyi (1962, p. 73) mentions the 'utility function' in this connection. March (1966, p. 60) cites the idea, agrees with it, but notes that there are as yet practically no procedures for making the concept empirically manipulable.

I have opted for a step-by-step operationalization of 'self-interest' in this study. I will deal with this subject matter more extensively in Chapter 5. At this point suffice it to say that the first step consists of recording *problems which can be relevant for interest.* As soon as there is a problem, we can assume that an interest is involved. The *strength* of that interest must then be separately determined – this is the second step.

To simplify the discussion, I will therefore speak of *problems, rather than interests,* in the remainder of this book.

The second and third aspects of influence: manifest anticipation and latent anticipation by private citizens (with two new indices) – After discussing a rough operationalization of interests we can now return to the two supplementary indices for influence which we have already provisionally described.

We are first looking for an index for *the relative size of the set of* influence attempts. Assuming that we succeed in determining the influence-relevant problems which a private citizen has experienced within a certain period, we can then subsequently investigate those cases where an influence attempt has been made, and those where no attempt has been made.

Now the ratio between all the problems and the problems with an influence attempt reflects the anticipation. If, for example, a private citizen generally estimates that he has little chance of success then he will only undertake influence attempts for a few problems. We can therefore use the following index for the relative size of the set of influence attempts:

the fraction of problems accompanied by influence attempts (out of the total number of all the problems).

Anticipation takes place here in the presence of problems which have already been perceived; this anticipation is therefore clearly observable. In such cases, then, I will speak of *manifest* anticipation (symbol AM). The index for manifest anticipation is therefore:

$$AM = \frac{\text{number of problems with influence attempts}}{\text{total number of problems}}$$

$$\text{or} \quad AM = \frac{IA}{P}$$

in which P represents the total number of problems. The stronger the (positive) anticipation, the greater the value of the index.

The third index which follows here must indicate to what degree some people are more conscious of their self-interest than others. An underlying assumption seems to be that we *can* identify such a phenomenon as an "objective" interest. Theoretically considered, this is impossible; determining an 'objective' interest for one single person is out of the question. But the *comparison* of individuals presents some possibilities. The difference in awareness of self-interest, or the difference in the degree to which individuals are 'conditioned', is indicated by the *difference in the number of perceived problems*. This is only true, of course, if the other conditions which determine the perception of these problems are held as constant as possible.

This form of anticipation is much less directly observable than manifest anticipation. I will therefore refer to it as *latent* anticipation (symbol AL). The index for this aspect of influence is simply:

$$AL = P$$

where $P =$ the number of perceived problems (under certain constant conditions).

As far as I know the two aspects of influence just discussed are new, as are their accompanying indices; the insights on which they are based, however, are far from new. Tendencies are evident in earlier studies which also point in the direction of the criteria presented above. For example, Frey (1971, p. 1093) presents a line of thought which is surprisingly similar to the one I have followed; only the operationalization and the accompanying investigation are lacking in his presentation.

Although I have presented several more or less intuitive reasons for the necessity of introducing the third aspect of influence in setting up my investigation, the following comments may perhaps be helpful.

Our provisional specification of influence was 'the number of effects produced' (S). The first two aspects of influence (tested influence and manifest anticipation) do not cover this specification completely. The *number* of problems has not been taken into consideration (this is clearly evident with manifest anticipation, where the number of problems is the divisor). This has some advantages, since the two indices involved are comparable from citizen to citizen, even when the conditions are not exactly identical. But we have failed to capture something about the influence process as a whole.

The following example serves as an illustration: There are two business firms, A_1 and A_2, which face exactly the same conditions with respect to an access road. Assume that firm A_1 does not perceive a problem; firm A_2 does, and undertakes an influence attempt. For firm A_2 the indices for tested influence and manifest anticipation can be calculated normally, but for firm A_1, which has perceived no problem, the indices are *indeterminate* (that is, 0/0). According to our specification (number of effects), however, we are inclined to state that A_1 has clearly had *no* influence. This difficulty is resolved by introducing my third aspect. Having or not having a problem does, therefore, tell us something about influence – something which has not been reflected in the first two aspects.

The number of effects as the product of the three aspects of influence – It is not surprising, after the discussion above, that the number of effects proves to be equal to the product of the three aspects of influence, namely:

$$S = T \times AM \times AL = \frac{S}{IA} \times \frac{IA}{P} \times P$$

The number of effects and the number of problems can always be determined–they always have a value which can be expressed with a natural number. The tested influence only has a value *if* influence attempts have been exercised, and the manifest anticipation only has a value *if* there have been problems.

In this study we will usually consider the three aspects separately; we will rarely work with the number of effects. Hypotheses will also be tested for the three aspects separately.

The primary point of observation: *citizens instead of decisions* – As we have seen above, the problems of private citizens play a very important role in our specification of the concept of influence. More precisely, the problems can make the citizen's anticipation actually accessible to investigation. This emphasis has consequences for the primary point at which our observations must begin. In principle an investigation of influence can begin either with decisions or with the citizens. It is, however, clear that the two new indices which have just been intro-duced leave us no choice: the citizens are the only point at which we can begin. Otherwise it would be impossible to determine differences in numbers of problems and influence attempts. If we begin with the citizen, we can observe, for example, whether or not an influence attempt has been made in the presence of a problem; in this way a 'non-decision' immediately becomes evident. In other words, it is simply true that before we can ascertain the sub-sets we must first determine what the 'mother set' is.

If, on the contrary, we begin with the decisions themselves, then tracing back to a 'non-decision' is much more difficult, and there is a *good possibility that the results are open to diverse and arbitrary* in-terpretations. This is a significant danger, since the investigator can then arrive at the conclusions which fit in best with his own pre-existing opinions, perhaps without his being aware of it himself. I call the reader's attention to the fact that the *usual* initial point of observation in this type of investigation is not the citizen. Vital questions of public interest often receive the emphasis in the mass media–that is, objects for which the decision-making has already begun. Social-science studies of power and influence often revolve

around 'issues' as well. In policy analysis, which seems to be receiving
increasing attention from social scientists, decisions also play a central
role. It should be realized that for this investigation an emphasis upon
decisions or issues is definitely not suitable. For the achievement of our
goal, the observations must begin '*from the bottom*' (compare Parenti,
1971).

Summary–I proposed the following tentative specification for influence in the preceding section: the set of concrete effects within a
given period. In order to determine these concrete effects we needed
to ascertain a cause-effect relationship. If a private citizen has achieved
an effect, this means that he can clearly be indicated as the cause of a
change of behavior in the government (see the summary of the
preceding section).

The number of effects, considered by itself, and however accurate
the datum may be, gives us virtually no insight into the way in which
these effects have come into being. We have therefore distinguished
three aspects of the influence process in this section in order to be able
to analyse the roles of the decision-maker (government) and the
petitioner (private citizen) separately.

The first aspect has been labeled 'tested influences'. It primarily
describes the behavior of the decision-maker; its index is the fraction
of influence attempts which have been successful.

We have called the second aspect 'manifest anticipation'. It reflects
how 'keen' a citizen is about making influence attempts.

The third aspect also refers to the private citizen and has been
named 'latent anticipation'. This reflects to what extent the citizen is
conscious of his interests, or in other words, to what extent the *initial*
conditions for the exercise of influence are present.

The two anticipatory aspects are complementary to the so-called
non-decisions which Bachrach and Baratz brought to the attention of
the social scientists. In order to construct an index for these anticipatory aspects we must track down the set of influence attempts, and,
even more important, the set of interests from which the influence
attempts arise.

The achieved effects are then the tip of a small 'iceberg' of data:
'interests'–influence attempts–effects.

The basic set, interests, plays a crucial role in this study. There are,
however, various types of interests. I have therefore introduced a
specification in order to promote the comparability of these interests;
that is, interest is to be conceived as 'self-interest' in the narrow sense
of the word. This enables us at the same time to specify 'influence in

Private citizen A1

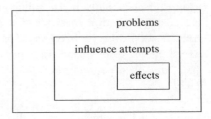

Private citizen A2

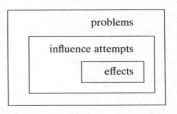

Figure 2.6
The sets of elements required to determine the three aspects of influence

society' as *influence by which someone is pursuing, at least in part, advantage for himself* – a specification which we said would be necessary in Chapter 1.

I will operationalize 'self-interest' in two steps. The first step consists of the determination of 'problems'. These indicate that there is a minimum interest present. The second step is the establishment of the strength of the interests.

The anticipation of the private citizen can now be adequately characterized with the two 'mother' sets, problems and influence attempts respectively (see also Figure 2.6). The manifest anticipation is the fraction of the problems which have been followed by influence attempts, and the latent anticipation is the number of problems under 'controlled' conditions.

Schema of the phenomena to be observed and their meaning – Figure 2.7 is a condensed presentation of the phenomena we must observe and of their relations to the concepts we have discussed.

The three aspects of influence – tested influence, manifest anticipation, and latent anticipation – constitute the framework which can be used to sketch the backgrounds of the effects. Additionally, the number of effects is equal to the product of the three aspects of influence.

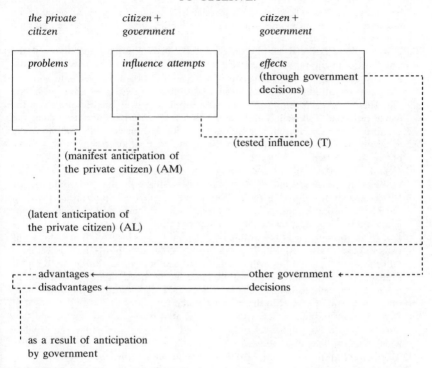

Figure 2.7
Schema for the observations

The preceding elaboration of the concept influence makes it necessary to begin our observations with the problems of the citizens, and *not* with the effects.

Notes

1. This means inevitably that the 'full' meaning of the concept can never be covered by one investigation. In this area especially it is necessary to be conscious of the limited importance of one single research study. More investigations are needed with still other empirical specifications.
2. Still further distinctions within these concepts are often made according to means or 'bases' (see, for example, with regard to power: Pen, 1971, pp. 107 and further, and with regard to influence: Parsons, 1963b, p. 52).
3. What follows can easily be subsumed under 'systems theory' (compare Parsons, 1959; 1969; Easton, 1966; see also Ellemers, 1969). For our purposes an extensive discussion of this link is unnecessary.

4. The use of the term power is probably justified in this case because the government has *scarce* goods and services at its disposal. The negative sanction involved in the use of this power is the withholding of these scarce goods if they are desired by a private citizen (Pen, 1971, p. 111).

5. Perhaps the reader is wondering whether or not there is still a connection with the social rules, relations, etc, which form one of the core elements in our definition. Even in this simple case this connection is clearly evident, for example with the allocation of subsidies for certain regions and through zoning decisions permitting the establishment of retirement centers as well as industry. The appearance of the whole province of Zeeland (until the sixties a land of farmers and fishermen) was changed by the Sloe Harbor. Or *both* air pollution and further industrialization can 'stagnate' as a result of government policy concerning the development of the area of the New Rotterdam Waterway.

6. Considerable attention has been devoted to such questions in theoretical works. Games theory and simulation research also concentrate on the study of processes. But in field-studies either only a few case studies are carried out, or, when a greater number of processes are studied, the methods used are largely of an indirect character (for example, the reputational approach).

7. Even this formulation is too restrictive. It is also possible that B is anticipating without being conscious of it. This can happen if, for example, A has succeeded in influencing B's values or in manipulating information (Nagel, 1968, p. 132). This is similar to the mechanism which will be discussed in the section on anticipation by business firms on page 39 ff. Because it is of little significance for our schematization, I will confine myself to the wording in the text.

8. Both these two aspects of anticipation are related to the private citizen and they must therefore be emphatically distinguished from the *government* anticipation which has just been discussed.

9. This is an old problem, as the following quote testifies: 'Obviously, there can be no direct operational definition of this concept (potentiality), because so many situations and interactions would have to be explored to discover the exact boundaries of "potential power"' (Lippitt, Polansky, Redl and Rosen, 1960, p. 746). My assumption is that the beginning of this sentence (namely, 'obviously') is not necessarily correct.

10. Of course, we have already encountered the concept 'anticipation' in 'anticipation by the government'. Needless to say, the anticipation by *both* actors must be considered in the determination of influence on the government. This section, however, is concerned with anticipation by the private citizen.

3. Formulating Hypotheses

In this chapter, after first considering several general points, we will arrive quickly at the basic hypotheses: the influence of comparable social units is proportional to their size. I have chosen business firms as my comparable social units. The hypothesis, however, cannot as yet be tested. We must first consider the question of exactly to whom influence can be assigned. This makes it necessary to subdivide the basic hypothesis into sub-hypotheses. Further, a selection must be made from the total possible objects of influence attempts. My choice of the material facilities for transport by water as the object in my study contributes considerably to the feasibility of the investigation. Finally, I will try to demonstrate the fruitfullness of testing these basic hypotheses in other sectors of society and for other problems.

3.1 Choosing a hypothesis

Preliminary considerations – The goal of this study is to determine influence, and more specifically, to ascertain the distribution of influence. It may be open to debate whether or not we should construct hypotheses *in advance* for such an investigation. It is possible, after all, to isolate a certain research field and register the distributions which are considered to be relevant within that field, without indicating in advance what we expect to find. This is the method employed in a considerable number of investigations of power and influence. A serious objection to such an approach is that it allows great freedom of interpretation *a posteriori* because the research design is not focused sharply enough upon an exact goal. Arbitrarily-drawn conclusions can easily be the result.

I have tried therefore to avoid arbitrariness by formulating hypotheses *a priori*, and by selecting a research design in which these hypotheses can be tested as exactingly as possible. This last requirement – testability – limits our freedom of choice considerably in formulating hypotheses. This becomes evident when we examine more closely the elements which must be present in any hypothesis about a distribution.

The elements are the following (compare Galtung, 1967, p. 310):

a1   the units (persons, groups) of which a distribution is being described

a2   the attributes of the units

b   the phenomenon whose distribution is being sought (influence)

c   a proposition about the shape of the distribution.

The units (a1) must *have clear boundaries* and must be *comparable*. In principle there is great freedom of choice with respect to the attributes of the units (a2). We must realize, however, that the hypotheses should not become too complicated. This is a well known problem in all investigations of complex phenomena; in one way or another simplifications must be introduced. Up to now, *the necessary simplification which have systematically been introduced in the research have led primarily to a neglect of the measurement of influence* (b). This is precisely what should be avoided. If we are serious about the considerable importance which is usually assigned to power and influence in society, and if we simultaneously realize that these concepts are elusive ones, then we must make as few concessions as possible when it comes to their measurement. This leaves the investigator, however, with a most difficult task. We must, therefore, keep other aspects simple wherever it is at all possible. For this purpose the *attributes* of the units, as well as the units themselves, must be kept as simple as possible. Or in other words, the independent variable for which a distribution of influence is being described must be as uncomplicated as possible.[1] Since our hypotheses must be testable, their formulation will have to meet the requirements which have been mentioned up to this point, namely: simple units and simple attributes, comparability of units, as well as the comparability of the influence itself, already mentioned in Chapter 2.

There is yet another aspect that should be taken into account. Usually there is a hypothesis derived from the theory and the hypothesis which is to be tested. The latter form–the testable one–is usually a particularization of the theoretical hypothesis; this process allows for greater freedom of choice in working out the testable hypothesis than with the 'theoretical' one. It is, however, unwise to introduce specifications which are too drastic: the 'gap' between the theoretical hypothesis and the 'testable hypothesis' can easily become too large. The contribution which testing can make to the confirmation of the more general hypothesis would be minimal in such a case. The requirements which we have set forth must therefore already be kept in mind when formulating a theoretical hypothesis. This means that the theoretical hypothesis must be rather simple. I will discuss this in the next section.

In formulating an hypothesis of a theoretical nature, modest as it may be, yet another requirement must be met. The units to be investigated must be available in *sufficiently large numbers* in the social system. If, for example, we wish to determine the difference in influence between employers' organizations and unions during the year 1979 in the Netherlands alone, then this aspect is no longer at issue. We can compare the three (or two) employers' organizations and the three (or two) unions. If, however, we want to consider the results as an indication of the difference in influence of the categories more generally, thus for other years besides 1979, then it is highly probable that the results are too strongly influenced by random factors, owing to the small number of units. Either we must extend our investigation to a large number of other points in time, or we must formulate another hypothesis relating to units which are available in greater numbers in society. Investigations at different points in time seem difficult because 'influence' must already refer to a longer time span anyway (see Chapter 2, p. 19). Only the second possibility, therefore, remains: to choose an hypothesis in which a considerably large number of units required for testing are present in the society.

A basic hypothesis: the influence on the government of comparable social units is proportional to their size – We are searching for the simplest possible terms with which we can describe persons and groups. As far as individuals are concerned, a 'role' is the attribute which can be useful in this context. Significant hypotheses can then be formulated about differences in influence between persons fulfilling different roles. We have studied, for example, differences in the external channels of influence between members of the council, the burgomaster and aldermen in several communities (Braam and Swinkels, 1969).

The emphasis in the present study, however, will be placed on social *groups* rather than individual persons. Although role-connected aspects are also involved here, a simpler *attribute* stands in the foreground – namely, the *size* of the group, that is, simply the *number of persons* of which it is composed. The number of members is a factor of which unions, churches, armies, etc. are constantly aware. There are 'majority rules' in most institutions and groups. Of course, numbers are not always the deciding factor; organizational strength, cohesiveness, etc. are also important ('union is strength'). But wouldn't it be a valuable contribution to subject the very general factor of size to an investigation, testing at the same time the popular notion that the 'giants' have more influence than the 'pygmies'?

Of course we are concerned with more than pure numbers alone; we are not investigating every arbitrary set of individuals. From a sociological point of view, these individuals exhibit a certain minimum of integration, either in the sense of 'belonging' together, or of being joined together in an organizational bond. This is the meaning which we wish to give to the term *'social groups'*.

Yet as it now stands, the term 'social groups' is still covering too broad an area. A certain group can have relations with all kinds of other groups. I stated in the previous chapter that I would choose to investigate one field, chosen from the myriad fields of influence relations, namely, the influence of *private citizens on the government*. The reason for this choice was that we wished especially to examine that influence which is closely connected to the functioning of the *social system as a whole* – that influence which is related in one way or another to the working of the entire system. I will investigate the influence of the groups which appear as units in our hypotheses only insofar as they are a part of this larger system. I conceive of them not simply as groups, but as *social sub-units or societal units* (compare Blau, 1964, p. 282 ff.).

The choice of a unit is now fixed, as is the choice of the characteristic of that unit (size). Simply stated, we intend to compare the influence of large and small social units.

We must now, however, turn our attention towards the comparability of the units. Though we could conceivably compare the influence of large football teams and small business firms, large problems in interpretation are sure to ensue. A far better course is to confine our comparisons to the units composing one specific type of group – that is, to compare either football teams with one another, or to compare various business firms. That is the reason why we state in the hypothesis that the social units must be *comparable*.

The basic hypothesis for our investigation can now be formulated, namely, *the influence on the government of comparable social units is porportional to their size*. Undoubtedly objections can be raised against 'size'. Isn't 'size' too simple, and influence more probably connected with the bases of influence such as prestige, social relations and 'connections'? We shall, in fact, examine these factors in more detail in a later interpretation as 'explanatory' variables (see Chapters 9 and 10 for several secondary hypotheses).

My tentative assumption underlying the main hypothesis has been that 'size' can be considered as a 'cluster' of a number of factors. It is this cluster as a whole which will be investigated as a condition of influence. In the second place, we will examine whether or not such a cluster does, in fact, exist, and if it can be broken down into components.

The current practice of survey research has placed the analysis of individuals and their backgrounds sharply in the foreground, to the detriment of the analysis of larger social units (this is an opinion that has long been voiced by Lazarsfeld; see also Coleman, 1965 and 1970; Galtung, 1967, p. 150). This objection is removed to some extent by choosing societal units as our research units. We will discuss later the complications this introduces in our research design.

Specification of 'comparable social units': business firms – Which social sub-units can be chosen? We have stated the requirements that the units must be available in sufficiently large numbers, that they must have clear-cut boundaries, and that they must be highly comparable. Provinces, for example, do not come into consideration because there are too few of them in the Netherlands. But groups large enough for our research purposes still abound. Large football organizations can be expected to obtain more support from the government than small ones, as can large hospitals and similar organizations – and even large ad hoc pressure groups.

The requirement of unambiguous boundaries is less easily met. My preference has been for *business firms*, or sub-units of the economic sector. The determination of their boundaries does not present much of a problem. Because business firms have a clearly 'private' character in our western society (with the exception, of course, of nationalized industries), their boundaries with government are fairly clear. Confusion with 'public' functions, which can appear, for example, in such sectors as public health, are avoided in the case of business firms.

Finally, units from the economic sector have the advantage that a number of factors can be expressed in terms of money. This is true not only because influence is often exercised in order to obtain money from the government, but also because financial damages are suffered if no influence is exercised. The numerous examples in the Netherlands of business firms who appeal to the government to save them from bankruptcy are excellent illustrations of this principle.

The next question which must be faced is whether or not we should restrict ourselves to one level of government – only provinces or districts, for example. We have, after all, placed considerable emphasis on the comparability of the influence. Yet I feel that such a restriction would be misplaced. Distinguishing different governmental levels is unimportant and even misleading if we interpret the question of the distribution of influence among business firms as the socially relevant question of the justice of government decision-making as a whole. From the viewpoint of the business firms themselves it is equally unimportant whether they are located in a country with one or ten governmental levels. Of course, the possibility remains that the chances of success at a lower level are different from the chances at a higher level – but that is another problem area.

There is another objection to confining the study to one governmental level from the practical point of view. The level at which a decision is finally made is determined by numerous factors which have nothing to do with the phenomena being studied. For example, issues that a large municipality can decide for itself, must in a small municipality be referred to the provincial government, or even to the national government. A comparison of influence from firm to firm would be seriously hampered if we considered only one level of governmental decision-making. This is only one of many possible complications. Another, for example, is that different levels of government are often involved in one-and-the-same decision.

In our hypothesis the government must therefore be considered as a whole entity. *The only important point is what 'movements' take place over the boundary line between government and 'non-government'.*

Our theoretical hypothesis in the preceding sub-section has now been particularized to the following form, which is central to this study, namely: *the influence of business firms on the government is proportional to their size.*

The hypothesis is not, however, testable in this form, in particular because the comparability of the influence is not guaranteed. I will devote considerable attention to this topic in the present chapter. But first I will present an example of the types of 'cases' which I will use in testing the hypothesis.

An example: the importer of timber and the lock – The business firm, with 70 employees, is located on a canal in the eastern part of Holland. The importer obtained his timber from Scandinavia; the shipments were brought to his sheds by small coasters, and the importer had never experienced any problems with this means of delivery. About 1962 this situation began to change. The costs of transport with these fairly small ships rose steadily and the competitive position of the business firm was endangered. The cost of transport would be considerably diminished if larger ships could be used. But these larger ships could not reach the firm because of a narrow lock in the canal. The dealer approached the administrator of the canal, in this case the Provincial Board of Waterways, and requested that the lock be widened. Such a change, however, would cost about ten million guilders. The Provincial Board of Waterways replied that it was impossible to carry out such an expansive project for the benefit of only one company.

The three elements of the concept of influence, as we have sketched them in Chapter 2, are clearly evident. The dealer has a *problem,* he tries to persuade the government to solve this problem (*influence attempt*), and the government makes a decision about *complying with his request.*

3.2 Some additional remarks

What is and what is not included – By confining ourselves to differences in influence exercised by large and small business firms we have excluded a number of other phenomena from our research design.

We have, for example, not considered the influence which the business firms exert upon each other. We already noted that these relations are not primarily at issue. The central point of this hypothesis is the differences among business firms in their relations with a third and always the same actor, the government. Nevertheless, it may be necessary in several cases to introduce a discussion of the influence that firms exert upon each other; the emphasis, however, remains upon the relation government-business (see the section on assignment of influence).

What we have said up to this point means, more or less, that the influence of the 'the business world' as a whole is not at issue. The central element in the hypothesis is the influence of individual business firms, or, at most, of small groups of business firms. We intend here to investigate the influence of certain *definite* economic units on certain *definite* political or administrative decisions and not the influence of *the* economy on *the* polity (of course the latter influence possibly can be inferred from the former, but this can certainly not be done on the basis of this study alone).

My study is likewise not concerned with the power of business companies over consumers, or over other companies (or, in other words, over the market); nor is it devoted to the power of the government over companies or citizens (or at most indirectly, through the refusal of requests such as that of the timber importer). But it *is* concerned with the 'requests' or, using a more common term, with the pressure of business firms on the government.

Expectations about the 'amount' of influence which really exists – One of the greatest concerns before I began the investigation was whether or not a sufficient number of influence attempts actually do occur. If this were not the case then a very large sample would have to be drawn to allow for the comparison of a sufficient number of cases.

A preliminary investigation in the province of Zeeland provided some basis for the expectation that a sufficient number of influence attempts by business firms would actually occur. I found it necessary, however, to direct the investigation towards a sector having a large probability of the occurrence of influence attempts (see the section 'The choice of the object of influence attempts'). The risk of doing superfluous work is in this way minimized.

Cost-benefit analysis and the hypothesis for this study – The possibility remains that we have not attached sufficient importance to the fact that governments, in their own eyes at least, make their decisions 'rationally'. We are forced to consider this point when we observe that governments in recent years have strived increasingly toward greater rationality in their decision-making – for example, by promoting cost-benefit analysis.[2]

Our hypothesis certainly does not exclude a certain measure of rationality. It implies at the same time, however, that other factors in addition to rationality can determine the outcome of a decision – the prestige of a business firm, for example.

Unfortunately it is not possible to use cost-benefit analysis for our research design.

An ideal research design could be constructed if a completely rational decision-making model existed. Then we could decide, for example, how decisions are supposed to work out on the basis of an ideal cost-benefit analysis, and we could then use these results as a standard. A comparison with the actual outcomes of the decisions may then reveal a number of departures from the standard; these departures would then possibly be a very good measure of influence.

Because the amount of rationality in the decision-making process is always limited to some extent (Simon, 1957[2], p. 76 ff.), such a procedure does not adequately reflect reality. A cost-benefit analysis always begins with 'values' which are chosen by those who are doing the analysis themselves, and which may be consequently subject to disagreement.

Influence will in fact often exist precisely by virtue of a change in these values, or in the strength with which they are held. At first sight, the values of the administrative agencies responsible for the Dutch waterways and harbors, which we have chosen as the object of influence attempts within our research area, do not seem to be very much in doubt. In a number of cases this has proved to be true in appearance only; an example is when the extension of a harbor attracts industries which threaten the environment. During our investigation, we noted that the opinions differed widely as to how heavily the environment should be allowed to weigh compared with employment opportunities. Putting these considerations aside, we would have had to carry out so many cost-benefit analyses in our investigation that it would have proved impracticable with the means at our disposal.

3.3 The problem of accurately assigning influence; types of problems and types of influence

The business firm as a necessary condition for a change in behavior of the government–Suppose that the influence attempt of the timber dealer is in fact followed by the construction of a new lock; yet more information is needed in order to conclude that the business firm has in fact had influence. Influence can only be ascribed to the firm if the behavior of that firm has been a necessary condition for the change in behavior of the government (see Chapter 2 p. 25). This is *not* the case if *other* conditions were already sufficient – for example, if difficulties with drainage presented a pressing reason for the government to widen the lock. The change has been advantageous for the business firm, but it has been 'lucky' rather than influential. The two data, influence attempt and decision are therefore not enough; the other possible conditions ('causes') must also be sought and taken into account. These conditions may be primarily governmental plans and the problems of other firms which may be interested in the same objective.

In order to be able to find out these conditions, we have carried out small case studies, one by one, of the influence attempts that have been tracked down. Lazarsfeld has given this procedure the name 'Empirical Analysis of Action' (Lazarsfeld and Rosenberg, 1955, p. 387 ff.). 'Causes' in this method are determined for each process separately, and it can then be ascertained whether or not a firm has been a necessary condition for a change in behavior of the government. In addition, the study of the process must give an insight into the *strength* of the other conditions. These conditions were in some cases possibly almost 'sufficient' – for example, if the government already had plans but was waiting for an extra 'push'; in other cases these other conditions were perhaps not at all sufficient. In order to be able to compare influence from firm to firm, we must be reasonably sure that the other conditions are in all cases approximately equally strong.

Things remain relatively simple as long as the influence attempt originates from one business firm only. We shall speak in such cases of *individual* influence. But it is not always so simple. People can act individually, but they often act in collaboration with others. This is, of course, also true of business firms. They can form 'coalitions', form pressure groups, or call existing lobbies to their aid. We are, in fact, involved here with the well-known sociological problem of the relation between the individual and his group, or of units within other units. The individual business firms – thus the units which serve as primary 'mover' – will from time to time, but certainly not always, be absorbed by larger units which themselves operate as more or less independent units. Of course we can refer then to the *influence of a coalition.* But shouldn't some measure of influence be assigned to the business firms individually, since they can clearly have achieved individual gains in the process? We will try to answer this question by introducing further distinctions among types of problems and types of influence exercised. We will discuss several examples in the following section in order to develop these distinctions. The first example clearly reflects joint action, but in other respects it is still fully comparable to individual action. The cases which are subsequently introduced become successively more complicated.

Two business firms demand two objectives; the coalition as a unit – Suppose that two business firms located on different branches of a canal both have a similar problem. Each wants a new wharf for the mooring of the ships which transport goods to and from his business locations. Together they approach the city council, which administers the canals and their banks, with their problem. It is clear that the business firms in this case have formed a coalition.

If the two firms' request is granted, to whom exactly must the influence be assigned? According to the basic principle which we stated previously, this must be the person or group which was the necessary condition for a change in behavior of the government (in the future I will simple speak of causes when I mean 'necessary conditions'). We can only conclude from our example that the firms jointly have been the cause. We can therefore speak in this case of the *influence of a coalition,* a case which, as I have previously noted, can be distinguished from *individual* influence (one business firm demands one wharf).

It would, of course, be convenient for our investigation if we could analyse the relationship of the influence of coalitions to their component individual influences – for example, by partitioning the influence of the coalition into parts, and by assigning one part to each of the members as individual influence. Unfortunately it is highly doubtful whether or not this procedure is admissible. This can be easily seen if we compare the example of the two firms which act jointly with a situation in which the first firm requests a wharf individually, and the second does the same immediately afterwards. The chance of success now, when both firms approach the council as individuals, is likely to be different than when the firms acted jointly. The city government can conceivably refuse exactly because the firms have not made their appeal jointly. Doesn't the adage say that in union there is strength?

It is therefore possible that another dimension, another *quality* has entered the picture – that is, the 'weight' of the group as a whole. The possibility of course remains that in the future the individual and group levels can be easily and accurately related to each other. At the moment, however, the relation between the two levels have been poorly explored (see for example Coleman, 1965; Olson, 1965). I therefore feel justified in continuing to distinguish between the two types or levels of influence exercised for the time being.

But the subject is not yet closed, since a certain type of reduction to the individual firms remains possible. In our example, after all, both firms have 'received' a wharf via the coalition. While this cannot be expressed in terms of individual influence, it can still be stated in terms of individual *gains*. Whether or not one firm receives more gains than another in a given period via one or more coalition is, after all, an extremely relevant question. In the situation sketched above we can therefore compare the *gains via coalitions*. The distribution of gains, rather than the distribution of influence is the central theme here.

Two business firms demand one objective; gains of a firm via a coalition – The case in which two business firms request one wharf for common use – or more generally stated, one *indivisible object* which is important for both – is more difficult. Only one wharf is now being considered; we therefore cannot rightfully say that each firm has received a wharf. That this one gain came *via a coalition* does, however, remain a useful piece of information.

As a provisional check of this proposal let us examine an entirely different example. One hundred residents of a street ask the city for a sidewalk. The request is successful. Each resident has exactly the same 'benefit' from the sidewalk (irrespective of differences of location on the street and differences in use). Each resident has therefore received a whole sidewalk via the coalition. Yet intuitively this statement occasions some objections. It is difficult, however, to see how these objections can be maintained if we exclusively consider the gains of the petitioners. Perhaps these intuitive reservations would disappear completely if we used the term successes rather than gains via coalitions. This is, in my opinion, not a fundamental distinction.

But doesn't it make a difference whether a sidewalk is built for ten or for one hundred people? From the standpoint of the decision-maker this is of course true. It implies that a small coalition has had just as much influence as a large one. But this is not the point we are concerned with here. The size of the coalition makes no difference at all for the benefit of the individual resident, for his gain (supposing, of course, that the number of residents does not affect the individual benefit owing to differences in the population density on the sidewalk).

To summarize, the following distributions can be distinguished:
– individual influence (of the individual business firms)
– influence of coalitions (of coalitions of business firms)
– gains via coalitions (of the individual business firms)

Influence within coalitions; exposing spurious coalitions – Various processes, also having something to do with influence, may have taken place before the business firms have jointly approached the government. For example, one business firm may not even have 'wanted' a new wharf; it therefore had no problem but was merely persuaded to join the coalition by another firm. An extensive process of negotiations possibly preceded the collective request. Influence *within* the group of business firms may have played a part *in the process of forming the coalition*. But our hypothesis does not take this influence into consideration. (Analysis of these processes does show clearly that the dynamics of coalition formation vary widely.)

Are such differences in the genesis of coalitions worthy of our attention? Can it make a difference in our determination of influence and to whom it can be assigned? In any case, the coalition in the example just presented would seem to demand closer inspection. The one firm has gotten a wharf, but it had, in fact, no need for it. It would be a mistake here to assign the influence to the coalition as a whole, because the interests of only one of the firms have been served, and because only one firm has set the process in motion. We can call the coalition in this respect a *spurious coalition*, which we must expose as such in our investigation (see Figure 3.1).

I propose the following procedure: Establish for each business firm what problems it has and, consequently, its interest. Then investigate whether or not the problem is an *individual* one, or whether it is a *problem for more than one business firm*, and determine how important the problem is for each firm.

This summarizes the primary data needed to reveal whether or not a real coalition has been involved in the influence process. More data of

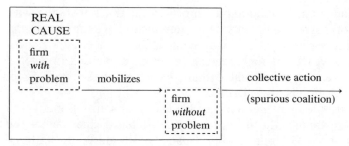

Figure 3.1
Assignment of influence in the case of 'spurious coalitions'

a similar nature will also be needed, but those mentioned above are the most fundamental ones.

It is obvious, of course, that we must be able to determine the *interests* which are at issue in the problems with reasonable reliability. This is no simple task. We cannot, for example, trust to the statements of company officals alone. After a director of a firm has been persuaded to join a coalition, the chances are good that he will begin to identify his partner firm's interest with his own, or at least will appear to. We will see how this source of error can be avoided to some degree when we discuss the choice of the object of influence attempts.

Spokesmen or advocates for the coalition – Coalitions of petitioners do not always have direct contact with decision-makers in the social system. There is often a mediating link in the form of an organization which promotes the interests of its members. It is by now common knowledge that a modern society has an elaborate system of interest organizations. Municipal administrations and provincial agencies also often act as advocates for the interests of their citizens when confronting higher governmental agencies. They function in such cases as *spokesmen* for coaltions. This can, I think, without objection be included under *influence of coalitions*; at the same time, no complications concerning the *gains* of the members arise.

Independent action of agencies at the group level; collective problems – Interest organizations and provincial or municipal administrations do not only make influence attempts *at the request* of one or more of their members. They can also make such attempts *independently*.

After the disastrous flood of 1953, the national Delta-plan to close off the Oosterschelde in the Southwest of the Netherlands threatened the destruction of the oyster and mussel cultures there. The municipal administrations of the communities involved (at times together with fishermen's organizations) made many attempts to have the Delta-plan changed. Another example is: many municipalities have 'approached' the national government for financing for industrial sites without the firms which were already located there having expressed any direct interest in such grants at that time.

In such cases either the almost-identical problems of many are involved (for example the fishermen), or problems which affect the structure of a whole municipality (roads and waterways, harbors, industrial sites). The administrators of a fishing-village 'think' in terms of harbors; in a commuter area the overriding concern is with train and highway connections, in a recreation area with camping grounds, etc. I shall speak in such cases of *collective* problems, and of influence attempts by administrative agencies.

In addition, individual inhabitants sometimes use their influence on a municipal administration to treat a certain issue as a problem for the community as a whole, thus as a collective problem; the reverse, of course, is also known to occur (!). We have to reduce, however, the possible combinations of modes of interaction before we can go to work.

Types of problems and types of influence–I now will summarize the foregoing section. In order to assign influence to a business firm or to a coalition we must first know who has initiated the activity (influence attempts). This is not sufficient, however, as has already been demonstrated. Sometimes coalitions occur in which only one business firm has any real interest involved, and where others merely have been persuaded to join it. In this case, in fact, only the one business firm with a real interest can be considered as a cause. Interests must therefore be determined before situations like those sketched above can be unraveled. In this study, as I have observed previously, I accomplish this by noting the 'problems' (and interests) of the individual firms.

I have introduced several distinctions among these problems for the purpose of accurately assigning influence (compare Coleman, 1976, p. 568). These distinctions correspond to the different units to which the influence must be assigned; they are as follows:

individual problems of business firms	$\longrightarrow$	individual influence
problems for more than one business firm	$\longrightarrow$	influence of coalitions
	$\longrightarrow$	individual gains via coalitions
'collective problems'	$\longrightarrow$	influence of collectivities

3.4 Assigning influence and the further specification of the hypothesis

Of course the hypothesis (size – influence) must be developed further on the basis of the distinctions we have introduced above. First, we must consider the difference for business firms between individual and non-individual problems. This leads to the following hypothesis:

HYPOTHESIS 1: *In solving their individual problems, business firms have the more influence on the government, the larger they are in size.*

This first hypothesis is the simplest one and the most clear in a number of respects, and we will therefore devote the most attention to it in our investigation. The research design, for example, will be attuned primarily to the testing of this hypothesis; a primary goal is to obtain the greatest possible comparability between large and small business firms.

It has become evident that our hypothesis is no longer sufficient in cases where problems occur in more than one business firm and when these problems are interrelated in one way or another. We must study the situation at both the level of the coalition as a whole and at the level of the individual business firms which constitute that coalition. For the coalitions as a whole I propose:

HYPOTHESIS 2A: *The greater the size of a coalition of business firms, the greater the influence it will have on the government in solving the common problems of its members.*

An hypothesis also can be constructed concerning the 'gains' discussed previously for the components of a coalition, thus for the separate business firms which comprise it:

HYPOTHESIS 2B: *The larger a business firm which participates in a coalition attempting to exercise influence on the government, the more 'gains via coalitions' it will obtain.*

I will use the same research design for testing this hypothesis as the one I will develop for Hypothesis 1. We will return to the implications of this decision in Chapter 7.

The third type of problems, the collective problems, concern issues which are primarily important for the collectivity as a whole (for example, industrial sites, recreation areas, roads). The promotion of solutions for these problems is carried out by the formal organizations of the collectivity. In selecting our research units we must now choose between municipalities and provinces. Because in the Netherlands *municipalities* occur in far greater numbers, I chose them for reasons of optimal testability. The following hypothesis results:

HYPOTHESIS 3: *The greater the size of the municipality, the greater the influence it has on 'higher' public authorities in solving 'collective' problems.*

3.5 The choice of the object of the influence attempt: the material facilities for transport by water (harbors, canals, locks, bridges, etc.)

Problems and influence attempts can of course refer to many different things. Business firms can ask for street lights on their access roads, for housing, bus service and sport accommodations for their workers, for subsidies to secure their competitive position internationally, for orders from the government and for the discontinuance of price control mechanisms (all of which are common practices in European countries). The object of influence attempts are thus varied. In order to make reasonable comparisons of problems and influence attempts we must introduce rigorous limitations.

Partly as a result of experience gained in a preliminary study in the province Zeeland, I have chosen problems and influence attempts related to the *material facilities for transport by water.* I will thus deal with desired changes in harbors, canals, bridges, locks and anything which is connected with these objects. As we shall see later, this choice has far-reaching consequences for the selection of business firms which must be included in the sample. The arguments which plead for this choice will now be reviewed.

(a) *The material facilities for transport by water are a 'stage' upon which influence processes are acted out.* To begin with we must realize that in a number of sectors of governmental policy-making few influence attempts by business firms will be observed – few, for example, in the area of social work. A sector must therefore be chosen which will demonstrate pre-eminently the influence of business firms on the government. The material facilities for water transport were in such a sector in the sixties. In the budget year 1967 – that is, several years before our investigation began – the Department of Waterways of the central government alone invested no less than 1.4 billion guilders in these facilities, of which 300 million guilders went to shipping routes and harbors.

There are, of course, other sectors where the exercise of influence is prevalent. The most obvious is perhaps policy-making concerning tariffs. However, we must also take into account the current status of influence research, which is yet in its infancy. For the reasons cited below (b until d), the sector of material facilities for water transport is definitely preferable to other sectors.

(b) *Unambiguousness in identifying 'problems'*. We have seen repeatedly how desirable it is that the *problems* which business firms experience be clearly identifiable. This is necessary in the first place for the classification of problems as individual, not individual (of business firms) and collective. If this distinction should prove impossible to maintain in research practice, then it will be virtually impossible to determine exactly to whom influence can be assigned. In short, the testability of the hypothesis is dependent upon the unambiguousness in identifying the problems.

I have tried to improve the chances of encountering unambiguous problems in two respects by choosing the material facilities for transport by water as the object of influence attempts
1. because it is likely that the problems will be reflected in *physical and geometrical dimensions*, and can therefore be relatively precisely determined;
2. because the *group* involved can be readily overseen.

Let us examine point number 1 more closely. It may seem obvious, at first sight, that many problems of business firms can be unambiguously identified because they lie within the 'hard' economic sphere. At times, however, this may be true in appearance only; consider, for example, occasions in which the internal organization or the competitive position of a firm is at issue. In such instances it is apparently difficult to determine exactly what the problems are and in what direction a solution must be sought. There are good reasons why firms engage efficiency and marketing bureaus to gain more insight into such matters.

If we were to include a consideration of such problems in the present investigation, then it would be equally necessary for us to call upon such experts for advice. Financial and practical considerations force us to discard this possibility.

There is, however, another possibility for circumventing this difficulty – by making sure that ambiguous cases seldom or never occur in the investigation. Now it would be incompatible with the requirements of testing hypotheses if such ambiguity were eliminated *after* the data had already been collected. This would be a means of selection which could make the conclusions of the investigation doubtful. Decisions about which category of problems will be included in the investigation must be explicitly made *in advance*. But we *are* free to choose our categories in such a way that as few ambiguous cases as possible are included.

Problems connected with material facilities for transport by water seemed to form such a category.

There are several reasons why these problems are relatively clear for those concerned. For instance, matters concerning water transport facilities are easily located because of their physical and geometrical nature. It is, for example, sufficient to compare the dimensions of the existing lock with those of the ship which the firm wishes to use for the transport of goods to be able to determine what the shortcomings are and what has to be changed. In addition, in numerous cases the financial *losses* resulting from the inadequacy of the existing facilities can be estimated with reasonable accuracy.

By choosing the material facilities for water transport as the object of our study, we have ensured that the problems unfold in a sphere in which the elements of calculability and observability for those involved are definitely present.

This clarity in the identification of problems is also present for the investigators, and for the same reasons. Even as outsiders we can make a reasonable estimate of what physical aspects are involved, and even of the financial damage suffered by the firm.

Reliability in the determination of problems by the investigator is therefore promoted by the unambiguous observations of those involved, and by the possibility which the investigator has to check such observations. Add to this that in the sixties we could expect a considerable number of problems because of the steady growth in the average size of ships, and we can expect that the choice of material facilities for water transport serve a number of research purposes simultaneously.

Note – Once again emphasis laid upon reliability in the determination of problems is especially necessary when we realize that the possibility of exaggeration by the respondents cannot be excluded. It is conceivable that they may accentuate their problems in the hope that more attention will be paid to them as a result of the investigation. If the problems can be checked to some extent by the investigator independently, then this risk is in any case diminished.

Let us now return to point number 2. Unambiguousness in identifying the problems is also promoted by making sure that the group involved remains well-ordered.

The material facilities for transport by water, like any other physical facility, are by definition attached to a particular location. This is a trivial statement, but it does point out that the category 'interested parties' will be smaller and more manageable than social categories based on problems unconnected with any point in physical space – for example, problems resulting in requests for subsidies for an entire industrial sector, which are not restricted to one location. It is apparently not a coincidence that pressure groups promoting the interests of localities or regions usually have this kind of material issues – roads, bridges, harbors and canals – on their list of requests.

The character of the object being considered, then, determines at least in part what the *spatial configuration* of the category of *interested parties* will be. Now we have been told repeatedly by sociologists that the groups with which individuals associate themselves have in the last one hundred years tended less and less to be directly connected with the place of residence (Parsons, 1960; Coleman, 1976); in other words, there has been an enlargement of scale. Groups or organizations concerned with material facilities are, in my opinion, a clear exception to this trend, though of course in different degrees.

This all means that we can generally expect to obtain a group of interested parties that is relatively small and well-ordered geographically if we choose problems related to the material facilities for water transport. We can, after all, find out easily enough which business firms are situated on a canal, and which ships they use for transport. We would, on the other hand, meet with great difficulties if we tried to determine for the whole of the Netherlands which business firms have an interest in a particular subvention policy. 'Collective problems' in this area are also relatively clear-cut because they are restricted to a locality; harbor approaches can be too small, fishing ports can suffer from lack of space, locks can have insufficient capacity – problems, therefore, in which a large category of business firms may have an interest, or which are important for the prosperity of a region as a whole.

When the group of interested parties can be clearly outlined, the determination of the type of problem – that is, one in which one business firm, more than one business firm or a collectivity has an interest – is simplified. I emphasize once again that in a *behavioral* analysis, which is what we are aiming at, the essential operation is ascertaining which persons are involved.

(c) *Unambiguity of decisions.* The determination of influence requires that the presence of a cause-effect relation be established. Unambiguity in the registration of problems of business firms and municipalities, which we have just discussed in (b), provides an important step in the procedure of indicating a cause. But the effects must also be unambiguously determined. As we have seen previously, the effects in our investigation are the behavioral changes of the government as a result of requests (influence attempts). Decisions serve as an indicator for these behavioral changes; these decisions, therefore, must be clear and unambiguous.

This is not always the case, however. Bauer (1964, p. 426), for example, complained that legislation regulating tariffs seldom involves distinct decisions. Such legislation is often composed of nothing more than general formulas, with many specific aspects left open to debate. Decisions involving material facilities for water transport, however, usually go hand in hand with *costs for the government.* These costs can be estimated fairly easily, because it is exactly in this area that the government has developed considerable technical and economic know-how.

A decision in this area, therefore, means that money is either spent or not spent. This makes vague formulas unlikely since the expenditures must appear explicitly somewhere in the budget. Besides, the consequences of the expenditures are often very concrete; for example, work is begun on visible projects.

Decisions are therefore characterized by a sphere of visibility and calculability, which increases both the clarity with which government administrators perceive the issues, and the probability of reliable observations by the investigators.

Note that for this investigation it is not only important to know whether or not the decision involves compliance with the the request. The *amount of money* which compliance involves is also important. As we shall see, it has often been possible in this investigation to obtain information about costs for the government, or to estimate them reasonably accurately.

(d) *Material facilities for transport by water as a strategic variable in processes of social change.* A final reason for our choice of these facilities as the object of our study is that they can be a *strategic variable* in the process of economic – and consequently also of social – development. The Sloe Harbor in Zeeland was the impulse for a process which has drastically changed the social structure of that province. The number of managers and technicians increased, and new pressure groups were formed to combat air pollution (an example of a similar phenomenon in the United States is the processes of change connected with the development of the Tennessee Valley Authority). Of course these facilities are not a sufficient condition for economic development; some new industrial locations do not attract any firms, or industries are located on waterways which they do not use. But in the Netherlands these facilities *are* an important, if not a necessary condition for new economic and social developments.

The requirement in the definition in the previous chapter, that the effects of influence must have consequences for the functioning of the *society*, has therefore been met with our choice of the material facilities for transport by water. The study does not, however, aim at an explanation of developments within these facilities, though such a misunderstanding is likely to arise. The point is to study the distribution of influence; the objects for which this influence is exercised are matters of secondary importance.

Summarizing – The choice of the material facilities for transport by water as the object of influence attempts is an extremely important one for this study. The cause-effect relations, with which an investigation of influence and power is primarily concerned (or ought to be concerned), are brought within the investigator's grasp in one broad sweep.

The concept of 'influence' in our definition can therefore be further specified as *influence primarily concerning the material facilities for transport by water.*

The specification in retrospect and the 'problem of generalization' – One more step is needed to make the hypothesis testable; we will select 'business firms dependent upon waterways' from the total population of possible business firms (see Chapter 4). The specification of our basic hypothesis is now completed; we have progressed from 'comparable social units' to 'business firms located on waterways' and from 'influence' to 'influence specifically with respect to the material facilities for transport by water'. Our basic hypothesis, 'The influence of comparable social units on the government is proportional to their size' can therefore never be more than partially confirmed. This is also true of the specified version 'The influence of business firms on the government is proportional to their size' (thus without restricting influence to 'influence with respect to waterway-connected facilities').

Such restrictions are almost always found in investigations which aim at testing hypothesis, They form the basis of 'the problem of generalization' (see De Groot, 1969, p. 155). These restrictions are the reason why the generalization problem is present in this investigation; also partially responsible is the absence of other, similarly-oriented research (as far as I know, this investigation is one of the first of its kind).

The possibilities for generalization are therefore uncertain until more research is done using *this* method.

3.6 The government and the citizen: distributions of influence as a dimension of the system of society; other areas on which the basic hypothesis can be applied

The question that we want to answer with our basic hypothesis is, simply stated, whether or not the 'giants' of industry succeed in obtaining more from the government than the 'pygmies'.

Current thinking among some politicians and social scientists, with their emphasis on 'structural changes' in society, would be quick to point out that this theme is too limited. Is the system as a whole being taken into consideration; are we analyzing at the system level?

Such a question invites an automatic 'yes' or, more likely, 'no', depending on the ideological predilictions of whoever is answering. Such a polarization is likely to have been produced unnecessarily, because the question has not been posed properly. When a 'system' is being discussed, it is nearly always only a limited number of aspects of that system which are actually being considered. And a thorough discussion of whether or not one certain aspect is of overriding importance can only be held if the various aspects are well known and if they can be compared with one another.

Therefore I will confine myself here to pointing out why an influence distribution must be considered as a consequence of a system, and, still stronger, why *the distribution of one aspect of influence, the tested influence, is complementary to the criteria of the central parts of the system* (thus of governmental agencies).

We can perhaps clarify this with the following elucidation. Government decisions determine at least in part the influence which a business firm has. The results of these decisions depend on the criteria which the decision-makers – perhaps even unconsciously – use. The size of the business firm can be such a criterium. When we test our hypothesis we are in fact trying to find whether or not such a criterium has actually been used. This could also be investigated by asking the decision-makers whether they did in fact use that criterium.

This latter procedure has, however, its disadvantages. Discovering criteria of whose use decision-makers are totally or partially unaware would be technically extremely difficult. With the hypothesis we have formulated and the specification we have developed, a much better way has been found for tracking down such criteria. We are then namely investigating the working of this criterium (or, more broadly put, of policy) through the *concrete effects* which it has on the citizens.

This basic principle also has important consequences for the research design. It means that we need not determine whether or nor an agency which does or does not comply with a business firm's request was really aware of the size of that firm. The 'perception of the decision-maker' does not appear in the procedure we sketched for assigning influence to a petitioning business firm. If these perceptions concerning the size of the firm investigated are incorrect, then this only means that the condition, size, does not work. We may have to reject the hypothesis as a result, but that is as it should be.

The thoughts of the decision-makers may in the first instance be considered as a 'black box'; yet we *can* trace down one of the criteria from this black box, namely, the size of the business firm (see further Chapter 8, Section 8.4).

The significance of distributions as an aspect of the social system will be more evident when we examine several other possible ways in which the basic hypothesis could be applied.

Other possible applications of the basic hypothesis – It is but a small step further when we consider the variable 'size of social units' as a specification of 'social stratification'. The basic hypothesis can then be formulated at a higher level of generalization as the relation between the status hierarchy and influence.

When this is done, other possible applications become evident. For example:

– the social status of those seeking housing (there is a housing shortage in some areas of the Netherlands) and their influence in obtaining it;
– the social status of the elderly and their influence in obtaining accommodation in a home for the elderly;
– the social status of architects and their influence in obtaining design commissions from the municipal government;
– the social status of social service organizations and their influence in obtaining subsidies.

In other words, the schema 'problems – requests to the government – degree of compliance' can be applied to any area in which the social 'weight' of the petitioner fulfills a role as an independent variable. And also in the background is the same question, 'Do the "giants" succeed in obtaining more from the government than the "pygmies" '?

Notes

1. I note in passing that this can serve another purpose as well. It is very important to test whether or not simple parameters can be utilized for predicting complex phenomena such as influence. This is not, however, a primary goal of this investigation.
2. Roughly stated, with this method decision-makers attempt to arrive at a more responsible choice between policy alternatives by determining the ratio between the expected costs and benefits for each alternative, and by then comparing these ratios (see for example Rossi and Williams, 1972, p. 23).

4. The Research Design, the Sample and Methods of Observation

4.1 The design for testing the main hypothesis concerning business firms and their influence aimed at solving their individual problems

A design for comparable measurements – Several different hypotheses have now been formulated. Each hypothesis in fact requires a separate, and somewhat different, research design. It is already difficult enough to construct a reasonably appropriate design for testing even one hypothesis involving complex phenomena, let alone for a number of such hypotheses. I have decided, therefore, to mainly consider our major hypothesis in shaping the research design. That hypothesis is:

HYPOTHESIS 1: *In solving their individual problems, business firms have more influence on the government, the larger they are in size. (We specified problems further as those problems connected with the material facilities for transport by water).*

What requirements must such a research design fulfill? In the first instance we need an investigation which *tests* a hypothesis – this goes without saying. We are justified in postulating that this is a 'testing investigation' because the hypotheses have been formulated *in advance* (otherwise the investigation would be explorative rather than testing, De Groot, 1969, p. 52).

If the investigation's primary concern is to satisfy methodological requirements, then the only fully satisfactory context in which research can be carried out is undoubtedly the laboratory. Our field of investigation unfortunately precludes a laboratory treatment. One of our primary goals was, after all, to accurately observe influence processes as they took place *concretely* in society. It is difficult to imagine that laboratory experiments could be suitable for this task, at least at the present state of our knowledge.

Field research is therefore best suited to our needs. Yet the choice of a design is likewise limited by the conditions just described. A 'field experiment', for example, is impracticable: we would have to set up artificial situations in which influence attempts were carried out, thus losing just that element of realism which we are trying to preserve. We have therefore finally fixed upon the 'experimental survey' (compare Hyman, 1954, p. 66), with which we determine the influence of a number of business firms during a certain fixed period. What we are attempting is thus definitely broader in scope than what the term survey generally implies: one simple 'round' with a questionnaire.

A further explanation is in order here. Our intention is to compare several categories of business firms with respect to their influence. For simplicity's sake I will restrict the number of categories to two: small business firms and large business firms (we shall see later that the boundary between the two classes has been set at 100 employees. Additionally, besides as a dichotomy, I will consider the number of employees in greater detail as a continuous variable).[1] We must determine the influence of each business firm and subsequently calculate the mean value for each category. This is schematically sketched in Figure 4.1. To simplify the presentation, only one measure for influence has

	S1	I_{S1} (problems, influence attempts, successes)
	S2	I_{S2}
condition 1	.	mean I_S
(small business firms)	.	(AL, AM, T)
	.	
	Sn	I_{Sn}

. . . .

	L1	I_{L1}
	L2	I_{L2}
condition 2	.	mean I_L
(large business firms)	.	(AL, AM, T)
	.	
	Lm	I_{Lm}

Key: S   = small business firm (with numbers 1 to n, inclusive)
       L   = large business firm (with numbers 1 to m, inclusive)
       I_{S1} = influence of business firm S1
       etc.
       AL = latent anticipation
       AM = manifest anticipation
       T   = tested influence

Figure 4.1
The research design

been presented in this schema. As we have seen in Chapter 2, at least three measures are essential in our actual analysis, but are not needed for the present discussion. The following points must be considered here:

(a) First the problems of the business firms, then the influence attempts which result from them, and finally the successes which may have been scored must be observed for computing I_{S1}, I_{S2}, etc.

As we have seen in the previous chapters, this means among other things that a cause-effect relationship must be established. This has to be carried out for *each business firm* and even for *each separate influence process.* The more generally accepted procedure, however, in investigations of cause and effect relationships is to draw conclusions about the causal working of a factor through observations of the categories *as a whole.* Blalock (1964) introduced this method; the so-called path-analysis is also based on it, and it was used earlier still in the 'elaboration' of Lazarsfeld and Hyman (Lazarsfeld & Rosenberg, 1955, p. 115 e.v.; Hyman, *op. cit.*). The investigation of causes for each process separately, on the other hand, is less prevalent, but the method *has* been used – in motivation research, for example. Lazarsfeld and Rosenberg call it 'The Empirical Analysis of Action' (*op. cit.*, pp. 387 ff.). It is important to note, however, that the determination of the cause-effect relationships which we have been discussing has no consequences for our research design, or for our sample (see also Chapter 2).

(b) We have as yet said little or nothing about the design as a whole, which is in essence extremely simple. By determining 'only' the mean influence of both small and large business firms, we have at the same time determined the 'distribution' of influence (of course, *three* means must in fact be computed, one for each aspect of influence).

But several preliminary measures must be taken which will determine, for example, exactly *which* business firms we will compare. As we demonstrated in the previous chapter, we want to investigate not only whether or not the influence varies with the characteristic 'size of the business firm', but also whether or not it varies *with that characteristic alone.*

We therefore need a research design in which additional explanatory factors in the influence process are eliminated as rigorously as possible. It is, of course, likely that many other factors besides the size of the business firms are responsible for the degree to which problems, influence attempts and successes occur. If small and large firms are not affected equally by these conditions, then our conclusions about the effect of the size of the business firm will be highly dubious. The possibility then always remains that conditions other than the size of the business firm are responsible for observed differences in influence. *Our research design must therefore guarantee a comparative measurement between large and small business firms, under measurement conditions which are held as constant as possible* – that is, under conditions which approach the controlled measurement situation of the laboratory as nearly as possible (compare Dahl, 1957, p. 205).

Such a design can be obtained: first, by choosing business firms which are themselves highly comparable, such as those from a single branch of business, and, secondly, by ensuring that as many conditions as possible have the same frequency distribution in the sub-samples of both small and large firms (for example, if they are both located in small communities in the same percentages). That is, we try to secure *controls*, which are the means pre-eminently used in experimental research (controls ex-post factor can, of course, also be applied). We can call our design a quasi-experimental one (compare De Groot, 1969, p. 144 ff.) if we remember that the meaning of this term is here *observations carried out under controlled conditions*.

The several consequences for the research design have been listed below to avoid possible misunderstandings:

1 – The design *as a whole* is not concerned with causes, but with a condition (size).

2 – This 'condition' is the primary experimental variable. We can manipulate this variable in only one way, namely by selecting the business firms; the condition 'size' is, after all, not a variable which can be manipulated by the investigator in a strict sense of the word. (Or, in other words, in this case there is no 'treatment' – a term often used in the literature about experiments; see, for example, Campbell and Stanley, 1966.)

3 – Since we cannot manipulate our experimental variables, we likewise are unable to 'randomize' – that is, randomly assign the 'subjects' (business firms in this case) to an experimental group and to a control group. Size, our 'experimental' variable, is a condition given in advance.

4 – By introducing controls both before and after the actual 'experiment' an attempt can be made to eliminate 'spurious' factors, or to make large and small business firms as comparable as possible.

5 – In a quasi-experimental design, investigators often use measurements at two different points in time (see Campbell and Stanley, 1966 and Ross and Smith, 1968). Influence as defined in this study can only be determined over a time period in which a number of influence

processes actually can be brought to a completion. For this reason, my choice was for a period of five years. This five-year period is in fact the only point in time with which this investigation needs to concern itself. It seems obvious that at only one point in time are observations needed – that is, at the *end* of this five-year period.

Complications can arise, however. There may have been fluctuations in the size of the business firm before this final point in time has been reached. Distortions may arise from the disappearance or appearance of business firms (this is the so-called self-selection of units; see Hyman, 1954, p. 211). The consequences for the conclusions of this investigation are apparently not serious (see Appendix 4A for a justification of this statement).

A measurement at two points in time would also be helpful in the determination of causes for each separate influence process. A vice-president can, for example, forget some problems. The data gathered in our investigation, however, do not suggest that the results may have been distorted by such factors (these data are discussed in Appendix 4A).

One important methodological implication must still be considered before we continue with our exposition of the research design.

The choice of a design and the problem of generalization – The choice of a research design determines in part the meaning of the results. This is especially true of the degree to which the results can be generalized. The choice of a design brings with it a very limited choice of research units, such as business firms in this case. We must therefore try to indicate to what extent our results also apply to other business firms which we have not included in our sample (some authors refer to 'external validity' as a synonym for the extent to which results can be generalized; for example, Campbell and Stanley, 1966, p. 5).

We are, therefore, clearly obliged to reveal the limitation which arises from our particular research design. The first restriction has more to do with our specification of influence than with the design. For reasons of clarity I have selected influence specifically with respect to the material facilities for transport by water from all the possible domains of influence. Business firms which never transport over water are, of course, not at all interested in these material facilities. It is therefore obvious that this *sub-population* (see De Groot, 1969, p. 183) must be limited to *those business firms which are dependent on transport by water.*

For our sample the business firms must be selected from this

sub-population. But before that can be done, we are forced to introduce a limitation which follows clearly from the research design. Our
aim, after all, is to select large and small business firms which are
comparable – and we intend to use 'controls' as a means of achieving
that end. For example, we try to arrange a situation in which large
business firms are located relatively just as often in large communities
as the small firms. In fact we are not selecting our sample from the
entire sub-population cited above, but from a part of it which meets
certain requirements concerning the distribution of control variables.
Following De Groot, we could call this the 'operational population'. Of
course, generally speaking, a so-called 'disproportional' sample is often
necessary when selecting a sample from a set of business firms. After
all, there are in actuality many more small than there are large
business firms. But the requirements of our design go further because
we must also try to 'standardize' other factors.

Our sample will therefore not reflect the set 'business firms dependent on transport by water' as it existed concretely at the time of the
investigation. In other words the sample will not be 'representative'.

Because the word 'representativeness' is more or less sacred in
sociological research, I will explain my position on this matter more
fully (compare Philipsen, 1969). The core of my argument follows from
one of my research goals: comparing measurements obtained under
comparable conditions. Imagine that the size of the community in
which a business firm is located actually is a factor diminishing the
influence of that firm. If large business firms happen to be located
relatively much more often in large communities than the small firms,
then, if the sample were representative, we would measure 'too little'
influence for the large firms. Our hypothesis, after all, is concerned with
establishing a test of the 'pure' relationship between the size of a
business firm and the amount of its influence. (If our aim in the
investigation was to find a procedure for making actual predictions,
rather than to test an hypothesis, then such a concern for 'pure'
relationships would, of course, be misplaced; compare De Groot,
1969, p. 191.) In other words, if the most important variables in the
population were unevenly distributed, then, given the goal of the
investigation, the *requirement of representativeness* would lead to *incorrect results*. We must, for example, ensure that the percentages of small
and of large business firms located in small communities are the same.

Such problems are encountered fairly often in sociological studies. In
this branch of the social sciences it is very difficult to carry out true
experiments. The experiment, however is all but indispensible in any

responsible search for general theoretical regularities. As we have just seen, this gap is not closed with demands for representative samples. A more effective solution is to aim at quasi-experimental approaches.

Yet this is a rather rigid statement of the principle; there are other methods conceivable for securing comparability. For example, a representative sample can be drawn, and then certain controls can be applied after the fact, such as only comparing business firms which are located in small communities. This results, however, in distinct difficulties when the total population is actually small, as is the case in our study (this is due to the social units being business firms rather than persons; see also Galtung, 1967, p. 150). Because of the distinctive composition of the population, the sample may contain too few cases in a given 'cell' – for example, too few large business firms in small communities. Increasing the size of the sample is not always the solution for such a problem. It is always possible that there are also few cases in the total population within the category we are trying to fill out. Further, the practical problems inherent in increasing the size of the sample are immense. The sample had to be kept limited in size (about 130 business firms) largely because we anticipated that considerable follow-up work would be needed to thoroughly investigate the problems and the influence attempts which were discovered (this included the collection of supplementary information from other business firms, as well as from governmental agencies). Therefore, controls in advance, or assembling a set of business firms which were reasonably comparable seemed to be the most suitable method. This method is in fact the most common one in experimental and quasi-experimental research; the requirement of *homogenity* dominates over that of representativeness (Hyman, 1954, p. 81; Ross and Smith, 1968, p. 337).[2]

We are now prepared to estimate the possibilities for generalizing our findings as follows. The results of our investigations will not apply without qualification to those Dutch business firms which are dependent upon waterways for their transport.

The results *are* applicable to a clear-cut, though theoretical population: the *comparable* firms which are dependent on waterways for transport. It is precisely when a relationship between influence and *one distinctive attribute* is being investigated that an attempt to generalize to an actual universe may be misplaced. In these instances it is better to aim at a generalization to a *theoretical universe*. The universe has therefore been manipulated to promote comparability (De Groot, 1969, p. 191).

Unfortunately, this ordering of priorities means that the value of our results for practical predictions is inevitably somewhat diminished (De Groot, 1969, p. 191; Blalock, 1964, p. 43 ff.).

On the other hand, generalizing to a concrete business sector is not as precarious as might be expected from the previous arguments – as a result of various factors which we will discuss later. This is, of course, important, since it means that the results retain at least some of their value for practical predictions.

The selection of business firms and controls. Shipyards as the most unambiguous category – The unit upon which our sample is based is the business firm. However, the term 'business firm' has not yet been defined precisely enough (compare Neth. Centr. Bureau of Statistics, 1968, p. 10). In this study, a business firm will be 'every individually-located factory, workshop, store, office or other business location, or complex of business locations, of one company' (C.B.S., 1968, p. 14). The essential notion here is of a unit which is *geographically* clearly identifiable (compare Philipsen, 1968, p. 109). This separate geographical identity usually also implies that the managers of such units normally have a clear responsibility for the day-to-day business at their own branch. When we speak of the number of workers in a business firm, we therefore mean *the number of workers at a particular business location.*

We should keep in mind that the concept 'company' is much broader than 'business firm' as we have used the terms in our investigation. A company can have one location, but it can also have two or more. Because the sample is being drawn from locations, it is possible that two or more locations are included from one and the same company (for example, a large concern).

As we have demonstrated repeatedly, we are attempting to construct a research design in which comparative measurements are made possible. We must therefore point out which factors must and can be brought under control.

Exactly which factors contribute to making a business firm's influence greater or lesser? There is very little empirically-grounded information available in sociological literature. As a result, common-sense considerations have largely guided my choice of such factors. This is, of course, far from a satisfactory solution, but will have to suffice as a beginning.

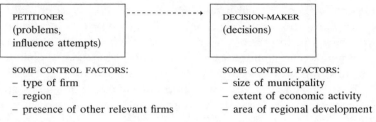

| PETITIONER (problems, influence attempts) | - - - - - - - - - - - - → | DECISION-MAKER (decisions) |

SOME CONTROL FACTORS:
- type of firm
- region
- presence of other relevant firms

SOME CONTROL FACTORS:
- size of municipality
- extent of economic activity
- area of regional development

Figure 4.2
Two categories of control factors

For convenience sake we have taken the two 'parties' in the influence process, potential petitioners and decision-makers, as points of orientation. Factors contributing to the increase or decrease in the amount of influence play a role for both parties. For the petitioners, or business firms, these factors are conditions which are partially conducive to the perception of problems and influence attempts; for the decision-makers, these are the conditions of compliance (see Figure 4.2).

The 'petitioners' – There are numerous conceivable factors which might determine the occurrence of influence attempts on the part of business firms, all of which, of course, can never be subject to controls. *A priori* controls can only be applied to factors which can be selected in advance, prior to the field work. On the other hand, it will be evident from what follows that the a priori controls which *are* possible usually concern important factors. Three general categories can be distinguished: factors connected (a) with the business firm itself (b) with the physical environment, or the material facilities for transport by water (c) with the socio-political environment (for example, other business firms, administrative conditions).

(a) *Factors connected with the business firm. Shipyards as the most important category; inclusion only of shipyards already in existence.* How should we select business firms which are comparable in the sense of their being dependent upon waterways. I have looked first for business firms of the same type, with the following considerations guiding my decisions. First and foremost, transport to and from the firm must be by water as a *necessary* condition. Other forms of transport (by train, car or airplane) must be either impossible in practice, or so much more expensive that it would endanger the very existence of the firm. Secondly, *because of the extent of investment in non-transferable goods, such as buildings, etc., the firm must be tied by force of circumstance to its present location.* If a change to a location on other waterways were possible which did not involve prohibitive costs, then the urgency of demands for improvement of the existing accommodation concerning waterways would be drastically diminished.

An exhaustive search reveals one, and only one, unambiguous and yet useful category of business firms for our investigation – namely, *shipyards* (in the terminology of The Netherlands Central Bureau of Statistics, this is an industrial sub-group). These firms produce or repair *the means itself of transport by water;* besides, this transportation medium is large in size, and to a large extent cannot leave the yard in sections. Moreover, exceptionally large investments are required for the slipways or docks necessary for shipbuilding, which means that a change in location is very difficult. The foregoing, however, does not hold true for shipyards which build yachts exclusively, since yachts can be transported to and from the yard with trucks. Shipyards which build yachts therefore cannot be included in our population. Since most yacht-building shipyards are small, we can be reasonably sure of a considerably more homogenous population if we do not include smaller shipyards. We have therefore 'drawn' our sample from firms with twenty or more employees. The one yacht-building yard with more then twenty employees which appeared in the sample was eliminated.

I subsequently sought diligently for other, equally unambiguous categories. Several categories which seemed promising later had to be abandoned because they failed to meet one or more of the requirements. Ship-owner's firms, for example, are not always inextricably connected to one particular place. Business firms dealing in products which can only be won from aquatic environments (sand from river or ocean, fish) or firms which are dependent upon bulk transport over oceans, or those which make large, unwieldy constructions which can best be transported by water were other possibilities. In these last three cases, however, there is a greater possibility of 'transshipment' to other ships or trucks and/or the investment in immovable goods is less significant. The only categories which remained belonged to the true harbor industries. These were discarded for other reasons: either the categories were too small, or they exhibited too little variation in the size of the firm.

To conclude, I was unable to find a second homogeneous industrial sub-group, after a diligent search. My intention was, however, to also compare a number of these 'business firms other than shipyards'. We will return to this later. At this point we have established that *shipyards* are the most important homogeneous sub-group which meets our requirements. Seventy-three of these business firms were included in our investigation.

Of course, it will have become evident that only business locations *which are already in existence* can be taken into consideration. The necessity of these firms being located on waterways is not open to doubt in such cases. Firms which are in the process of selecting a new location will in all likelihood choose a site with the least possible disadvantages. Additionally, firms seeking new locations are usually in a favorable negotiating position because the administration of municipalities, at least during the period in which we made our observations, competed fiercely for the recruiting of new industries. New and established firms are therefore very likely to be faced with highly dissimilar conditions, both in their relationships with the government, and in their possibilities for mobility.

After narrowing down the field to one industrial sub-group, we can consider which factors connected with the business firms might fruitfully be subjected to controls. Two factors are immediately evident. The first one is whether the firm is primarily concerned with *shipbuilding* or with *ship repairing*. The second factor is the *degree of independence of the business firm*. A number of firms may be parts of larger companies. Whether or not a firm is 'absentee-owned' is frequently a variable in American research on local power (see, among others, Fowler, 1964). These two variables could be measured in advance only with great difficulty, which is why we decided to control them after the fact.

(b) *The existing material facilities for transport by water.* The question of how comparability of these physical environments can be achieved is difficult to answer. The weight that has to be attached to a number of factors, such as sand bars, narrow locks and dimensions of bridges, varies sharply with the type of ship that is being built. For example, we cannot simply state that the size of the waterway, expressed in the maximum admissible tonnage, should be held constant. Smaller business firms, which will usually build smaller ships, would then certainly have fewer problems than large firms. We would have to conduct a separate preliminary investigation in order to gather all the detailed information we must have before our sample could be drawn.

Yet some simple attempts were possible. In any case, it should be clear from what has just been said that *small business firms* located on *smaller* waterways must also be included in the sample.

Further, a number of *regions* were indicated on a map of waterways in the Netherlands; we planned to limit the sample to business firms located within one of these regions (see Appendix 4B for a description of this procedure). The regions were chosen from all over the Netherlands, with the exception of the following areas:

– *Zeeland* (too much information from a preliminary investigation)
– the harbor areas of *Rotterdam and Amsterdam* (there is such an enormous activity in these areas on the waterways, and such a high concentration of yards, that they are almost certainly atypical; it would require a separate investigation).

The *population* obtained *up to this point* consisted, therefore, of *shipyards with more than twenty employees, located mainly within a number of previously indicated regions spread throughout the Netherlands* (see Table 4.1).

Table 4.1 demonstrates that our freedom of choice is limited with regard to the boundary to be drawn between large and small firms. In order to obtain a sample size of sixty to eighty shipyards, in which the number of small and large firms is about the same, then the boundary will have to be set at about 100 employees.

(c) *The socio-political environment of the business firm.* A business firm can be expected to become aware of problems more quickly the more stimuli the environment provides. Another firm in the area can, for example, provide such a stimulus; the presence of such another firm

Table 4.1
The population of shipyards classified according to region and size of firm, and the sample drawn from it

	number of employees							total number of yards with more than 20 employees
	21–49	50–	100–	200–	500–	1000–	>2000	
population size of yards outside Amsterdam, Rotterdam and Zeeland*	57	40	23	10	6	5	1	142
population of yards located in selected regions with the addition of three 'solitary' ones outside these regions†	34	29	22	10	5	4	1	105
sample	24	19	14	9	4	3	—	73

* Based on the Business Census of C.B.S. (Netherlands Central Bureau of Statistics) 1963 with corrections based on data from Economic-Technical Institutes and telephone directories.
† Some limited adjustments in regions and size of the work force had to be made during field work (among other things, because of changes in the number of employees).

can result in the problems becoming collective rather than individual. And the opposite can also be true: problems which involve a number of negative consequences for other firms are likely to be 'repressed' (compare Bauer, 1964, p. 218) – or, stated in our terminology, the latent anticipation diminishes.

The simplest way of dealing with these complications is by attempting to select a number of municipalities where one, and only one, shipyard was located. We will call this a *solitary shipyard*. This solution is, of course, still not quite satisfactory; business firms other than shipyards can also affect the awareness of the firms in our sample. But as we have seen, the interests of shipyards are shaped by very specific conditions connected with their location on waterways, so that we can be confident that our approach will allow us to weigh the importance of potential allies and opponents.

A typology has therefore been constructed in which two variables are combined, namely the number of shipyards in a municipality and the size of the shipyards.

This typology of configuration of shipyards per municipality is essentially a simple one:

A   = small solitary
B   = large solitary
C   = equals, small (more than one small firm in the same municipality)
D   = equals, large (more than one large firm in the same municipality)
CD = mixed large and small

(the construction of this typology is in fact somewhat more complicated; a complete discussion is given in Appendix 4B).

It was decided that the selection of the sample should be carried out in such a way that an accurate *sub-sample of solitary shipyards* (abbreviated SS) could be obtained. In this way one possible disturbing variable has been eliminated. The sub-sample finally obtained consisted of *forty-one shipyards* (located, of course, in forty-one municipalities). Because, understandably, these solitary shipyards were not located exclusively within the previously selected regions, it was necessary to make a small adjustment; that is, some yards outside the regions were included. However, only three cases were actually involved here.

Another fundamentally different factor which can promote the perception of problems and the making of influence attempts is the general industrial 'climate'. Of particular importance, of course, is whether or not the area in which the firm is located has been singled out by the government for special regional development aid. Because this factor can also have significance for the decision-maker, it will be discussed in the subsequent section.

There is a final, fundamental point which is important for comparability, but which could only be sketchily taken into account in advance: namely, possible controls of the 'objective' interests. The choice of a homogeneous branch of industry is, of course, a very important step in the right direction, but it is questionable whether this provides sufficient comparability for the following reasons. As we demonstrated in Chapter 2, the latent anticipation of a firm is determined from the number of problems it perceives. This figure has only a *comparative* value; information about the absolute number of problems has in itself no definite conceptual meaning. But for the sake of comparison it is absolutely necessary to hold constant those conditions which can give rise to the perception of problems, or to assure ourselves that the frequency distribution of these conditions is the same in the category of large and the category of small firms. It is not feasible to do this prior to the investigation. During the field work we gathered a number of relevant data: size of the waterway, size of the ships being built, economic performance. This data made it possible to apply reasonably effective controls after the fact.

The decision-makers – We will now briefly discuss several factors which may influence the decision-making process leading to compliance, and to which we can apply controls.

The variation in possible decision-makers seems the most obvious factor to be controlled. However, it is questionable whether or not much can be gained from such a restriction (see page 51). Because other important controls must also be applied, it is also extremely difficult to carry out in practice. For example, if we want to include a sufficiently large number of 'solitary shipyards', we must realize that this will involve an equal number of decision-makers, since in practice, each 'solitary' will be located in a separate municipality, and most likely a separate province as well. Diminishing the number of decision-makers would result in a reduction in the number of solitary shipyards; most probably the number of individual problems will likewise be diminished. The disadvantages of retaining fewer 'pure' cases weighed more heavily in my judgment than the advantage of a homogeneous population of decision-makers. Controls on decision-makers were therefore only carried out after the fact.

Several other factors could possibly influence government decision-making. The following controls proved practically feasible:
– *the size of the municipality* in which the shipyard is located; this can be roughly considered as an indicator of the *relative social position*

occupied by the firm within the municipality. A large firm in a small community could conceivably weigh more heavily in decision-making than a large firm in a large community.
- *the volume of goods* which are transported to and from the municipality over waterways; this can be considered as an indicator of the amount of *economic activity* connected with water transport.
- the location of the firm in or outside an area of *governmental regional development aid.*

Note that the different factors may also affect the petitioners, but this is only a fortunate circumstance.

The previous control requirements played a decisive role in the *definitive selection* of the business firms, to the extent to which it proved practically feasible. To begin with, freedom of choice was limited by the 'large-solitary' firms. The frequency distributions of the control factors cited above were therefore fixed, so that 'small-solitary' firms had to be chosen in such a way that the frequency distributions of the control factors were the same as with the large-solitaries. This turned out to be successful in the categories 'size of municipality', 'transport by water' and 'area of regional development aid'. (See Appendix 4C.)

The sample of *solitary shipyards* (SS) which resulted was composed of:
- nineteen small firms (fewer than 100 employees)
- twenty-two large firms (100 or more employees); (of these, five firms had 500 or more employees, to be called 'giants').

The previously sketched procedure for arriving at comparable measurements was designed – I repeat – for individual problems. The procedure is admittedly of only limited value for problems shared by more than one business firm; for high comparability, other factors would have to be considered such as the geographical distance between firms. One investigation cannot, however, do justice to all the possible facets of a concept like influence. The comparative measurement is consequently of a more explorative character for the types of problems shared by more than one firm.

4.2 Verification criteria for the sample results

Based on our hypothesis, a prediction can be made about the differences in influence of business firms in a concrete sample, Now exactly what criteria will allow us to conclude that the results are in agreement with the predictions? We are referring, of course, to the verification criteria which are essential to any investigation to avoid arbitrariness in arriving at conclusions (De Groot, 1969, p. 93).

For statistical testing we are, as usual, stating a null-hypothesis: there is no difference in influence on the government between large and small business firms. We will adopt a 5% level of significance (one-sided). This is admittedly a rather steep requirement for a small sample. However, the difference in influence between large and small business firms seems so obvious that a rigorous test seems to be clearly justified.

The use of tests of significance is in many cases somewhat controversial (see Morrison and Henkel, 1971). Since we have considered our universe to be a *theoretical* one, the objections to this procedure should not be too great. This is less obvious in two other small samples which will be discussed in the next section. Yet the use of significance tests can be supported, as long as they are clearly understood to be aides rather than an end in themselves. A test of significance can be an extremely useful supplement to a global inspection if an estimate of the *order of magnitude* of the differences within the results is being sought. That is, it is an aid and nothing more – stripped of the weighty pretensions generally associated with it.

Because the size of the sample is small I felt it necessary to search for other criteria of verification. A *replication* is often recommended for exactly this kind of investigation, where the size of the actual population is small, and the units are business firms rather than individuals (compare Lipset, Coleman and Trow, 1956, pp. 482 ff; De Groot, 1969, p. 157; Galtung, 1967, p. 150). My approach to a kind of a replication has been to *divide the sample* in two parts, and then to see whether the results obtained from the two samples are in agreement. Of course, the samples so obtained are even smaller than the original one. The same argument as above applies here: the trends which are suggested in our hypothesis are supposed to be so strong that we expect them to be clearly manifested in even small samples. Before the data collection began, therefore, the shipyard sample was divided into:
– *shipyard sample* 1 (SS1) and
– *shipyard sample* 2 (SS2)
(in which the assignment of shipyards to SS1 and SS2 was determined by random selection).

4.3 The generalization problem: striving for extension

Strictly speaking, the results which can be obtained from following our research design are only valid for a theoretical universe. We are thus limited in generalizing our conclusions by the conditions which have been imposed upon the sample: for example, the distribution of the size of the municipalities in which shipyards are located. Our criteria of verification apply only to the hypothesis under the conditions as stated; they say nothing about the truth of the hypothesis under other conditions (De Groot very properly emphasizes the difference between the confirmation of a hypothesis and the verification of a prediction derived from it. This derivation almost always involves particularizations and specifications, which are in turn shaped by the general structure of the investigation, 1969, p. 147). It is, of course, of considerable importance that the scope of the validity of our conclusions are as broad as possible. We have therefore sought to increase the extent of our generalization by choosing two new samples (De Groot, *op. cit.*, p. 155).

They consisted of:
(a) Another shipyard sample (that is, the third shipyard sample, SS3). The sample can be seen more or less as a set of *non*-solitary shipyards, located therefore in municipalities with 'equals, small', 'equals, large' and 'mixed large and small' configurations. (C, D and CD, see p. 83). Shipyards located in municipalities within the selected regions were designated as this sub-population before data collection began. The set proved to be so small that no sample was drawn from it, but the selected units accounted for a large part of the entire set. Controls were out of the question.

This sample is admittedly somewhat heterogeneous, but this should not lead to serious objections if we remember, again, that the trends suggested in our hypothesis are so pronounced that they should become clearly evident under uncontrollable conditions.

To summarize: our aim in introducing this third sample was to make the set of selected shipyards more representative of the actual population of Dutch shipyards, thereby increasing somewhat the predictive value of the results.

The sample SS3 was composed of:
– twenty-four small shipyards
– eight large shipyards (of which two were 'giants', namely, 500 employees or more).
(See also Appendix 4B; for the composition of the entire shipyard sample see Table 4.1.)

(b) A sample of business firms from other *industrial sub-groups*. The validity of the hypothesis for other types of firms than shipyards is of course vitally important. As explained previously, it proved impossible to find another industrial sub-group with sufficient homogeneity in problems associated with the material facilities for transport by water (harbors, canals, locks, bridges, etc.), and which additionally was not composed exclusively of solely large or solely small firms. Dealers in sand and gravel are an illustration of this heterogeneity: some are completely dependent on waterways for the transport of sand dredged from rivers, while others are not even located on waterways.)

Yet simply as newspaper readers we were aware that important issues were at stake for other groups than shipyards alone. An example is the channel which was dredged in the New Rotterdam's Waterway to allow for the passage of supertankers.

Thus the task facing us is to achieve some increase in generalization potential, without obtaining a sample containing to many unsuitable units (that is without problems) or which is too extensive.

The procedure was as follows: A number of *municipalities* were first selected in which *considerable transport by water* took place (based on data from the Neth. Central Bureau of Statistics). We approached key informants (port-wardens, municipal officials) in these municipalities with a *preliminary interview*. We thus discovered which business firms were dependent on water for transport, and which were reasonably likely to have problems related to the material facilities for transport by water.

Let me emphasize at this point that the composition of this fourth sample is dependent on the following factors:
1. the perceptions of the key informants
2. the perceptions of the investigators of the probability of problems related to the material facilities of transport by water.

As a result, it is not quite clear whether this sample of remaining business firms (RF) is either somewhat aselect, or on the other hand has real possibilities for comparison. The question is whether or not this sample can still be of value in making generalizations. The answer is either yes or no, depending on which aspect of influence is being considered. The sample seems to me least suitable for the number of problems (latent anticipation). In cases where the number of problems plays no role in itself, as in manifest anticipation and tested influence, there is less reason to seriously question the value of this sample. Because we are only designing a first, tentative attempt to broaden the generalization potential, it would seem permissible here to omit the detailed discussion which would be necessary to clarify the matter completely.

Classified according to size, the sub-sample RF consisted of:
– thirty-four small firms

– twenty-three large firms (eight of which had 500 or more employees).
Included were firms dealing in timber, construction materials, in cereals
and forage; also paper mills, cement factories, machine works, 'sea-
harbor' industries, transshipment firms, ship-owners and chemical industries (see Appendix 4D).

Further, the question arises whether or not giant concerns and/or
multinationals are present in our set. This, indeed, is true – both of
shipyards and non-shipyards. Table 4.1 illustrates the situation with
shipyards.

To summarize: I have attempted to broaden the area of generalization
by adding two samples in which controls were either absent or only
sketchily applied: a third shipyard sample and a fourth sample of 'firms
other than shipyards' (abbreviated to 'remaining firms' or RF).

4.4   A summary of the characteristics of the sample

In striving toward a research design in which comparable measurements would be possible I decided to look for a category of business
firms which was clearly dependent on transport by water. I decided on
shipyards, excluding those yards building only yachts. A sample was
drawn from units having as great a comparability as possible. In order
to achieve this comparability, frequency matching was applied with the
following factors:
– *region* (for example, located on the same waterway);
– *solitary* or not (i.e., located in municipalities without or with other
  shipyards);
– *size of the municipality* in which the shipyard is located;
– the amount of *transport by water* in the municipalities in question;
– whether or not located in an *area of governmental regional development aid.*
The most important sub-sample, *solitary shipyards* (SS) ultimately
contained:
– nineteen small business firms (less than 100 employees)
– twenty-two large business firms (100 or more employees, of which
  five firms had 500 or more employees).

Criteria were than sought for deciding whether or not the prediction
derived from the hypothesis had actually been fulfilled. The criteria
applied included, apart from levels of significance, especially the consistency of results obtained from two separate *sub-samples*. To carry

Table 4.2
*Composition of sub-samples according
to size of firm*

	number of employees	
	0–99	100 or more
SS1	11	11
SS2	8	11
S3	24	8
RF	34	23
Total	77	53

out this comparison of results the solitary shipyard sample was divided
in two parts (see Table 4.2):
– solitary shipyards 1 (SS1)
– solitary shipyards 2 (SS2).

This research design makes it possible to make uncontaminated comparisons of measurements, but at the cost of having the results be valid
only under restricted conditions. In order to increase the breadth of
our generalizations, we selected two more samples. The third shipyard
sample (SS3) consisted of twenty-four small and eight large shipyards
(non-solitary). A fourth sample was obtained by interviewing key
informants in communities where a large volume of transport by water
takes place; these informants were asked to indicate which firms other
than shipyards in their communities were highly dependent on water
transport. This *fourth* sample of remaining business firms (RF) consisted of (Table 4.2):
– thirty-four small and
– twenty-three large firms.
   Finally, the investigation was retrospective in character. It was
primarily directed towards influence which had already been exercised.

4.5 Data collection and processing

The primary source for the necessary data are the 'petitioners'; interviews had to be conducted with spokesmen from the business firms
(vice-presidents or their direct representatives). Supplementary information was obtained in a number of cases from various documents
(newspapers, etc.).

We would, however, be open to charges of bias if all the observations were confined to one side of the interaction process which plays such a central role in this investigation. I therefore investigated a number of influence attempts at the decision-maker's end as well (municipalities and agencies of the provincial and national Departments of Waterways). Interest groups were also approached for information when necessary.

As we have seen in Chapter 3, one of our hypotheses concerned the influence of municipalities on higher government levels in cases where 'collective problems' were present. Interviews with burgomasters from communities where firms from a sample were located therefore served a triple function: first, a check on the information obtained from the business firms; second, a reconnaissance of possible 'anticipation' by the government in decisions where no influence attempts of business firms are made; and third, registration of 'collective problems' within municipalities (see Figure 4.3).

During the first phase of the study, in the summer of 1969, seven undergraduates and myself conducted interviews with the business firms and the municipalities. We used structured questionnaires, largely composed of questions of a closed-answers type. However, the interviewers were instructed to introduce an 'open section', probing for any hint of possible problems of business firms, or of influence processes. In addition, the interviewer had at his disposal structured questionnaires for the problems of the firms and municipalities (of course, he always had available a number of 'sets' of these problem questionnaires for the possibility that the firm had more than one problem).

It was almost immediately evident that it would be impossible to get all this accomplished in one single interview. A follow-up interview

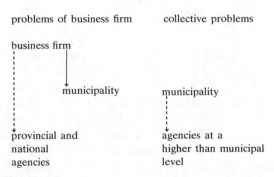

Figure 4.3
Schema of the points at which information is gathered

was therefore planned to allow us to track down problems and influence attempts in greater detail. Intensive work was involved in this
follow-up phase, since we were reconstructing actual processes, or
chains of decisions. To make matters even more complicated, an
unexpectedly large number of business firms' problems ultimately
came to light – 279. Luckily, much of the supplementary information
could be obtained by telephone, although entire new interviews with
vice-presidents or others were sometimes necessary.

The number of research workers in this stage of data collection had
to remain limited to assure the comparability of these case studies – for
that is what these 'problems' and 'influence-attempts' in fact implied.
Four undergraduate assistants and myself – subsidized in part by the
Netherlands Organization for the Advancement of Pure Research –
spent several months analyzing, categorizing and coding these problems and influence processes of business firms, as well as about eighty
collective problems of municipalities.

A final phase of interviews with a number of representatives of
agencies dealing with the material facilities connected with transport
by water completed the data collection. These interviews were mainly a
check on the obtained information concerning problems of business
firms and collective problems of municipalities with which the official
in question was possibly familiar, or which he himself had handled.
The data collection was definitively ended in the autumn of 1970 with
the completion of this final phase.

On the basis of the collected information, a series of punch cards
was obtained per business firm and per municipality. The analysis,
using among others self-developed Algol programs, could then com-
mence.

4.6 The response

Business firms cooperated most satisfactorily with the investigators, as
testified by a refusal percentage of somewhat less than 4%, which is
very small for sociological research (Bauer's in some respects similar
investigation in the U.S.A. had a refusal percentage of 17%; 1964, p.
109). Cooperation was further evident from the fact that interviewers
rated the degree of interest of 60% of the firms (even 67% of the
shipyards) as good to very good (on a five-point scale).

None of the burgomasters refused an interview. However, interviewing them did cause us some problems, since it was often very difficult
to obtain concrete information from them: they were often apt to hide

behind generalities. Other government officials, and especially officials of the Departments of Waterways were comparatively easier to interview.

Notes

1. The operationalization of the 'size of the business firm' will therefore be 'the number of employees'. This seems to me to be a sufficiently 'hard' datum which is also easily obtained. We have, nevertheless been able to test the validity of this indicator somewhat further by computing the correlation coefficients with the annual turnover. This relationship proved to be most satisfactory (see Appendix 6B).
2. Of course, controls after the fact remain necessary as well. We shall, among other methods, compute partial correlations (see Blalock, 1964).

5. Problems of Business Firms: Conceptual Analysis, Operationalization and Results

5.1 Conceptual analysis of 'self-interest'; specification and operationalization

Statement of the problem – We stated briefly in Chapter 2 that in our study 'self-interest' would be operationalized in two successive steps. We would first isolate 'problems which are relevant to influence', and would then attempt to determine the *strength* of the interests coupled with these relevant problems.

In the ensuing pages it has become increasingly evident how essential the 'problems' are in the determination of influence. They constitute the most important observable phenomena which can be used to track down processes of influence; they are additionally indispensible elements in two aspects of influence, namely:

(1) the manifest anticipation, that is, the percentage of the problems for which influence-attempts have been undertaken. Without the variable 'problems' our study would be ill-equipped to answer the crucial question of whether one business firm makes relatively more influence attempts than the other. 'Problems' comprise here a *basis for comparison.*
(2) the latent anticipation. As stated previously, differences in latent anticipation are determined by comparing the number of problems perceived by the firms in the study. 'Problems' are in this case the *dependent* variable.

Our use of problems in the operationalization of self-interest therefore constitutes an essential link in this study. For this reason, in the present section I shall explain in greater detail my reasoning in making this methodological choice. In this connection I again proceed from the question, 'How does an influence-attempt come into being?' We have answered this question briefly and in general terms in Chapter 2. Following the more specific exposition of the hypothesis developed in

Chapter 3, we can now explore this aspect of influence in greater detail.

A note before we begin: The credo of comparability, which I have repeatedly defended, can easily lead to misinterpretation. At times we are referring to comparability of research situations; at other times we are alluding to the comparability of the perceptions of the situation by the firm. One way in which *we* are striving for comparability in the research situation is by setting up controls. This is the measurement situation, for example, in which we compare two importers of timber behind a too-small lock (See also below under 'influence-relevant problems'). Whether or not they actually perceive a problem is, as we have previously stated, an indicator for one aspect of influence, latent anticipation. But this is of course a dependent variable, and naturally no attempt must be made to control it. In the subsequent step, however, we *do* treat the total number of problems of a firm as a basis for comparison; we investigate which firm undertakes relatively more influence-attempts (manifest anticipation). In this case both the particular problems and the sets of problems as a whole must therefore be sufficiently comparable. One of the ways in which this can be achieved is by confining ourselves to certain *types* of problems. Hopefully this brief discussion has lessened the chance of a misunderstanding of our methods.

Determinants of an influence-attempt–We proceed from the assumption that the research situations are as similar as possible. Our research design has been developed in agreement with this assumption; other precautions will be discussed in the section 'problems and influence-relevant problems'.

We can assume with confidence that a vice-president of a firm will only launch an influence-attempt if he has been sufficiently motivated, that is, if he *perceives its utility* (compare with Harsanyi, 1962, p. 73). This is in fact a necessary condition for his making an approach toward the government. A number of other circumstances, however, must precede this necessary condition of perception, that is:
The vice-president must:
A believe that the firm's *performance* can be improved by
B changing some aspect of the *situation* (the environment) of the firm (recall the example of the lock above). It may be possible for the firm itself to effect the needed changes; for the initiation of an influence-attempt therefore it will also be necessary that
C *the means* at a firm's disposal for improving the situation *on its own* (private solutions) are relatively *expensive*, or are *impossible* (this is clearly true of the lock);
D *government action* is seen as *a means* for improving the situation (the importer of timber will almost certainly have this perception, but the situation is not always this clear-cut);

A. perception of a possible improvement in the firm's perfor- $\xrightarrow{\text{no}}$ no activity
    mance by the respondent?

    $\downarrow$ yes

B. perception by the respondent of some element in the $\xrightarrow{\text{no}}$ no activity
    situation which can bring about this improvement?

    $\downarrow$ yes

C. 'private solutions' are relatively expensive or impossible $\xrightarrow{\text{no}}$ firm changes the
                                                                                         situation itself
    $\downarrow$ yes

D. *government action* is seen as a *means* for improving the
    situation? $\xrightarrow{\text{no}}$ no activity

    $\downarrow$ yes

E. positive appraisal of the chance that the government can
    be activated? $\xrightarrow{\text{no}}$ no activity

    $\downarrow$ yes

undertakes an influence-attempt

Figure 5.1
The series of conditions which must be fulfilled before an influence-attempt is made

E   the *chance of success* of the influence-attempt is rated reasonably
    high.
These conditions must all be met (see also Figure 5.1). This could be
called a decision-making model for an influence attempt.

This schematic representation takes sufficient account of several
motivational theories, such as those of Lewin and Atkinson; it incorpo-
rates their basic elements: the values of the actor, the goal, and the
means of achieving the goal (Lewin, 1952, pp. 258, 273; Deutsch,
1954; Atkinson, 1964, pp. 256 ff.; Atkinson and Birch, 1970, pp.
182 ff.).

But let us examine the conditions in greater detail. Our diagram
begins with the firm's 'interest' (A). Several authors have expressed
serious reservations about the use of this term (for example Bauer,
1964, pp. 473 ff.). Common sense, as well as the knowledge that
concepts such as 'interest' or 'values' are basic elements in almost all
motivation theories, provide a defense for this usage. In recent years
the concept of 'interest' has been stressed again by Coleman (1973).

It is, of course, essential that we use the concept as consistently and
concretely as possible. We are on the right track, for example, if we
consider 'interest' not as an abstract concept existing in itself, but as a
condition which is always related to *certain very concrete changes in the
situation* (B). This is nothing new; common usage speaks of someone

being interested *in* something, or someone's interest being damaged *by* some event or action. That is, A and B must always be considered in combination.

It is exactly these '*interests in certain changes in the situation*' which can serve as an excellent basis of comparison for influence-attempts. We can arrive at a score for manifest anticipation by listing these interests, and determining for each of them whether or not an influence-attempt has been made. Moreover, the possibility of 'private solutions' must also be comparable (C).

Care must be taken to avoid contamination of our indicators. The decision to make or not to make an influence-attempt, once we have established the presence of 'interest in certain changes in the situation', will be determined by the next two factors in the model: government action is seen as a means of improving the situation (D), and appraisal of the chance of success is high (E). Whether these latter two perceptions are positive or negative determines the presence or absence of manifest anticipation.[1] It is of the utmost importance that these two factors be excluded from our indicator for latent anticipation–that is, from our basis of comparison. Failure to do so would involve *contamination* of our variables; that is, we would allow the very factors we are trying to determine (the *dependent* variable) to become a part of our independent variable (for a further discussion of contamination see, among others, Hyman, 1954, p. 179 ff.). The operationalization of 'interest' must therefore incorporate *only* aspects of the situation (B) and the firm's performance or the possibility of its improvement (A).

The 'interests in certain changes in the situation' are themselves–but in this case as a *dependent* variable–a good measure of latent anticipation. These interests are in themselves not 'objective' data, but are likewise perceptions, as we have noted in Chapter 2. Some importers of timber do not even *see* that their interests would be served by widening of the lock; others are always on the lookout for an advantageous change. A complicating factor is that this perception (that one's interest might be served by a change in the situation) may itself once again be influenced by the factors (D) and (E), the perception of government as a means of change, and the perception of the chance of success.

In this case, however, these factors have had a far more profound effect on the decision-making process of the petitioner. There is, in fact, a feedback at the level of *perception* of interests. In the case of manifest anticipation, on the other hand, the interests are given; feedback refers only to *behavior*, and particularly, to the initiation of an influence-attempt.

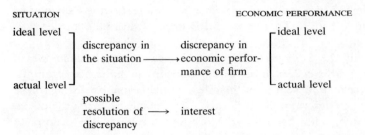

Figure 5.2
Discrepancy in the situation and interest of the business firm

Emperical specification of 'change in the situation': the resolution of a discrepancy; 'problems' – How can 'interest in a chance in the situation' be operationalized? The previous discussion has lightened our task considerably.

The perception within a firm that a certain change in the situation would be in that firm's interest implies a perceived difference between the *actual level* of the situation and the *ideal level.* This difference is in turn seen as the cause of another gap–that between the *actual* and *ideal* performance (see Fig. 5.2).

The difference between the actual and the ideal levels of the situation we will call the perceived '*discrepancy* in the situation'. The disappearance of such a discrepancy leads to a rise in the actual level of the firm's performance. This expected difference between the actual level of the firm's performance before and after the resolution of the discrepancy we will call the 'interest'.[2]

Although discrepancies in the situation are directly linked with interests, the two remain separate concepts. Two firms can, for example, have an equally large situational discrepancy with regard to the width of a lock, while the interests involved may be very different. A given discrepancy is thus a guarantee that a *minimum interest* is present, but the *strength* of the interest must be determined *independently.*

There are various possibilities open in the investigation for obtaining a set of 'interests in changes in firms' situations' which can be compared with one another. I have opted for a technique which will presumably guarantee the most unambiguous comparability: that is, by starting with a list of a number of aspects of business firms' situations (for example, bridges, locks, etc.), and then asking for each aspect whether or not discrepancies existed. The final step was determining the strength of the interests connected with these discrepancies.

A satisfactory operationalization of the concept 'discrepancy' can be made by investigating the possible presence of the (perceived) *problems*. All those discrepancies with a minimum interest at stake are obtained in this way. At a later stage the strength of the interest must be held constant to provide an unbiased basis for comparisons.

Operationalization by using the term 'problems' guarantees to some extent that the interest situations which are to serve as a basis of comparison are not diffuse in character. Benefits are often anticipated in a firm as a result of certain changes in its situation, but their exact extent and the time lapse before they can be expected to materialize remain to a large extent uncertain. Bauer's investigation demonstrated that even in the economic sector, 'interests' are not as hard data as would be expected (1964, pp. 128, 152, 473). It would be a vital blow to the comparability of elements of the investigation if the 'hardness' of the interests differed greatly. The advantages gained in using the term 'problems' is that the interest thus brought to light will almost certainly be *a clear occurrence in the firm's life-space*. The interests come to a head in a problem *concretely*. The term 'problems' should therefore ensure that the more diffuse interests are kept out of the investigation.

What is now the exact nature of the specification of the concept 'interest in a change in the firm's situation' which we have just introduced? If we ask a firm's vice-president what his 'problems' are, what are the chances that some of his 'interest in a change in the situation' will *not* be included?

This is indeed a serious point for discussion. Referring to Figure 5.2, we can distinguish two separate reasons why a firm's vice-president perceives such an interest:

(a) *a lowering of the actual level of the situation,* which is equivalent to a worsening of the existing situation. In this case the firm is afraid that 'normal' operations will be disturbed: there are *difficulties, bottlenecks* which *hamper* operations (or which are expected to hamper operations in the near future). In such cases the firm's emphasis will most probably lie on consolidation of existing assets rather than the search for new ones. It will pursue a 'satisfactory' policy, or, as formulated by Simon, it strives toward 'satisficing' (Simon, 1957^2, p. xxv and 261; also March and Simon, 1958, p. 140). In this case, 'problems' are probably an ideal tool for tracking down an 'interest in a change in the situation'.

(b) *an elevation in the ideal level of the situation* – In this case the existing state of affairs is not necessarily threatened, but the firm's vice-president is especially eager for improvements – or, he has a high level of aspiration (Lewin, 1942, 1952, p. 81). He will perceive a relatively large number of possible changes in the firm's situation as contributing positively to his interests. Contrary to the previous case, an *optimal* behavioral policy is sought (in Simon's terms 'maximizing', *op. cit.* p. xxv). The situation in such cases is a dynamic one: an eagerness for improved benefits dominates. (In such cases, the term 'desires' may perhaps be used instead of 'needs', Krech and Crutchfield, 1968, p. 216 ff.). In this case, however respondents may fail to mention their perceived 'interests' when the interview question is couched in terms of 'problems'. On the one hand, the existing situation is not seen as being 'problematical'; on the other hand, 'problems' will have to be solved if the envisioned goal is to be reached. The term 'problems' is therefore somewhat ambiguous here.

Yet we must make sure that cases of the second type are also consistently tracked down; they are as much an impulse for the undertaking of an influence attempt as the 'problems' in the first type of cases. In fact, it may be *exactly* a strong anticipation which they are reflecting. We tried in the following way to ensure that these interests would on no account be overlooked: Before asking about problems in the interview we posed a number of questions about the general situation in which the firm found itself, its material facilities and its contacts with the administrative agencies (among others with the Boards of Waterways). Thus the interviewer was instructed to be on the lookout throughout the interview for possible interests and for any connections which might exist between business firms and government as a result of a concern for material facilities for transport by water. In this manner, 'interests in a change of the firm's situation' not mentioned along with the respondent's 'problems' could be pinned down; 'interests' obtained in this way were added to the 'normal' problems (see also Appendix 5C for a more detailed discussion).

Therefore the first step toward operationalizing 'interest in a change in the firm's situation' has consisted in tracking down 'problems' *plus* any other interests which might not have come to light as a result of probing into 'problems'.

This form of operationalization can only be justified if there are good reasons for expecting the search for additional interests to have a subsidiary character only, with the supposition that the majority of the interests will be discovered by asking about problems. And, indeed, reasons can be cited to show that this is the case. According to the theory of Simon (*op. cit.*, 1957[2]), firms strive more often toward 'satisficing' than toward 'maximizing'. Even in simple situations, an actor is not likely to follow an optimal line of behavior; he is usually happy enough to find a 'reasonably' satisfactory pattern of behavior. Why this is so can be easily explained. The world in which he lives is so complex that he can only proceed step by step. Bauer's investigation (1964, pp. 152, 474), which showed that the attitudes of firms toward tariffs were more strongly determined by the fear of losses than by the prospects of gain, also supports this theory. The primary concern was, and usually is, with maintaining the situation as it is (satisficing). We can thus be reasonably sure that the great majority of firms' interests will come to light when they are asked about their 'problems'. (This was confirmed by the data; see Appendix 5C.)

Our operationalization using the term 'problems' thus consists more or less of retaining only those 'interests in a change in the firm's situation' which are relatively unambiguous. A consideration of some alternative possibilities for operationalization will make this more clear.

Alternative operationalizations of 'interest of a firm in a change in the situation' – It is of course possible to pose questions about interests more directly, and to investigate at the same time which changes in the situation are needed for them to be realized. There are two reasons why I rejected this form of operationalization. First, I suspected that direct questions about interests would in the Netherlands meet with resistance on the part of the respondents. Secondly, and more importantly, there was too great a danger that the set of interests obtained in this way would be composed of a string of utopian statements, too little tied to reality. After all, endless numbers of improvements are conceivable which are in the 'interest' of a firm. Difficulties of this sort were encountered in interviews designed to discover living preferences.

A question about problems, on the other hand, is more directly concerned with interests which the respondent has *already consciously experienced as such*. A 'problem' has a relatively small 'psychological distance' from concrete behavior; a 'mere interest's' distance and link to behavior can vary widely.

Another possible operationalization of 'interest of the firm in a change in the situation' uses the concept 'satisfaction' (see Berting and De Sitter, 1971; March and Simon, 1958, pp. 47 ff.). Analogous to our question about problems, a list of aspects of the environmental situation could be presented to the respondent, and he could be asked to indicate which aspects he would consider to be satisfactory for his firm, and which not. If we introduced another specification by asking only which aspects were *unsatisfactory* (thus the *dis*satisfaction), then we are coming close to our 'discrepancies'. Nonetheless, this approach is more likely than our 'problem'-oriented one to lead to arbitrary listings of situations whose connections with reality are tenuous.

Perceived problems as an indicator of latent anticipation; the 'objective' situation – In the foregoing section I have attempted to make plausible the argument that 'problems' are a good basis of comparison for manifest anticipation.

The number of problems per business firm is in itself an equally good index for latent anticipation. A good case can be made for this proposition: Stated in terms of the previous section, some firms can be expected to have higher ideal levels of the situation than others (the term 'aspiration level' could also be used. This could be seen as determined by McClelland's 'achievement motivation'. This in turn increases the number of perceived problems).

Comparability is delicate and therefore vitally important in the case of latent anticipation, as I have pointed out previously. The most desirable basis of comparison would be one which is identical for small and large business firms. This can be achieved by measuring all other factors which help to determine the perception of problems, and by introducing controls after the fact (for example, 'size of the waterway'). This is a reasonably trustworthy procedure for taking into account a comparable 'objective' situation and 'objective' interests. (Compare Berting and De Sitter, 1971, p. 135.)

Problems and 'influence-relevant problems' – Not all the problems experienced by business firms are important for our investigation. We must be wary of the following points in our search for a good basis of comparison for influence attempts:

Suppose, as a rather far-fetched example, that one firm is experiencing problems with its internal organization, while another's problem lies with a lock in an important waterway. Internal reorganization is a job which must be accomplished by drawing on the firm's own resources, but the problem of the lock can only be solved by involving the government. Clearly, the disparate nature of these two problems makes it far less likely that an influence attempt will be made in the first case than in the second. Therefore, the criterium 'the discrepancy in the situation experienced by a firm' is not in itself sufficient. For a crucial requirement for comparing the problems of business firms must be their relevance for the exercises of influence.

An additional criterium must therefore be set–that of a comparable *latitude* for influence. The problem must be of such a nature that influence exercised by the firm can, in fact, result in benefits from the government. We can call the category obtained in this way *influence-relevant problems.* This specification is thus introduced to make the *research situations* comparable.

Two dimensions therefore have to be combined to form the concept of an influence-relevant problem: a discrepancy in the situation, and latitude for influence (once more–the latter implies a possible relation with the government).

Our choice in this study of the material facilities for transport by water as the object of influence attempts has already fulfilled this last condition for a large number of problems. These facilities are to a large extent *owned,* or at least administered by the government. One category of influence–relevant problems has now clearly been indicated– those which the firm sees as a sufficient inducement for making a legitimate appeal to the government to make a change in the material facilities for transport by water.

If we based our domain of objects of influence on the points made in the previous discussion, we would be able to confine ourselves to asking the respondents one question about problems related to the material facilities for transport by water. There is, however, another type of problem which satisfies both requirements–those which come into being *as a result of governmental behavior.* These problems do not necessarily need to be connected with material facilities for transport by water. A preliminary investigation showed that it is not uncommon for problems to arise in the wake of government plans. A plan for development, a proposed filling-in of a canal or the closing-off of an estuary, for example, can suddenly face a firm with serious difficulties. The two dimensions discussed previously are automatically present: governmental behavior leads to a discrepancy for the firm, and at the same time the government is creating a relationship with the firm which often has an accompanying effect of giving the firm latitude for exercising influence (that is, in this case, to get some extra benefits).

This category of influence-relevant problems is characterized by their cause: governmental actions which threaten the firm in some way. We have attempted to track down these problems by asking about '*plans of others*' (see Section 5.2 and Appendix 5B).

Concealing the goal of the investigation–In the period covered by the
gathering of data in the field (1969 and 1970) questions about power
and influence were treading on somewhat ticklish ground in the
Netherlands. This was demonstrated repeatedly in both the preliminary investigation and in investigations of local power. It seemed clear
that the goal of the investigation would have to remain hidden, and
that the words power and influence should not be used in the interviews. The exact intentions of the investigators were relatively easy to
hide because the concept of influence had already been broken down
into three elements (problems–demands upon the government–
successes). As a result, conscious concealment was in a certain sense
superfluous, except, of course, in the introduction.

This problem of the introduction was solved in the following way:
the investigation was labeled as a survey of factors which determine
social-economic development. Material facilities for transport by water
can be an important link in the chain of developmental processes. An
example was given when necessary (like: a harbor is deepened to aid
shipping, which in turn opens new developmental opportunities for
other economic sectors). The interviewers were permitted to choose
examples which were more directly connected with the life-space of
the individual firm–for example, how the removal of bottlenecks for
business firms can contribute to a type of development which changes
the character of an entire region (for example, the Sloe-harbor project
in Zeeland, and the Tennessee Valley Authority in the U.S.A.).

Actually, this is a perfectly valid way of looking at the investigation,
only the investigation was really concerned with one special aspect of
such developments (that is, influence of business firms).

The fact remains, however, that I personally find such concealment
unpleasant. Yet I fear there is no other way to obtain 'objective'
information–and by 'objective' I mean information which is not distorted by marked resistance to the object under study, or the reverse,
by excessive interest in it.

5.2 Problems of business firms; results of the investigation

A first inventory of problems relevant for influence–The respondents
were asked:
> 'What were the principal problems related to the material facilities for
> transport by water which your firm has experienced in the last five
> years?'

They were then handed a list of objects (aspects of the situation) which
might possibly be the cause of problems for the firm (see Table 5.1).

Table 5.1

Objects which were possible sources of problems for business firms (with respective frequencies of answers)

objects	number of firms with *at least one* problem connected with the object at the left	
– height of bridges	16	12.3%
– harbor entrances	17	13.0%
– accommodations for maneuverability	8	6.1%
– harbor accommodation: cranes	6	4.6%
– harbor accommodation: quays and wharves	18	13.9%
– harbor accommodation: harbor dues	4	3.1%
– harbor accommodation: dredging operations	17	13.1%
– beam of canals (possibly plus bridges, locks and depth)	30	23.0%
– beam of bridges	21	16.1%
– beam of locks	12	9.2%
– draft of waterways (also dredging operations)	37	28.5%
– water levels (in connection with slipways)	37	28.5%
– space to put out the ships built	5	3.8%
– other objects	31†	23.8%
		(n = 130 business firms)*

* Business firms can have problems relating to more than one object, so that the total of the percentages does not have to be equal to 100.
† The total of business firms with at least one problem, or the sum of the figures in this column, has no actual significance. Besides the point made in the previous note, it should be realized that one and the same firm can have more than one problem relating to the same object. The sum is therefore *not* equal to the total number of problems.

Subsequently, questions were asked about the *nature* of the problem, the *timespan* during which they were experienced, and the *rank-order* of their importance.

The second supplementary question concerned the 'plans of others', where we tried to uncover governmental planning which might be threatening to the firm, and which creates a situation in which influence is likely to be exercised (see the previous section; see Appendix 5B for the precise formulation of the question). The results of this part of the investigation are given in Table 5.2.

It should be added that only 15 of the 130 business firms, or less than 12%, had no problems whatsoever (not visible in Table 5.2). There is therefore a quite broad basis for comparison, which is

Table 5.2
Number of business firms for whom plans of others could be a source of 'problems'

plans relevant for:	number of firms with at least one problem	
– manpower (for example, industrialization)	3	2.3%
– infra-structure and possibilities for expansion (for example, plans for development)	23	17.7%
– other aspects	29	22.3%
		(n = 130 business firms)

especially important for any conclusions to be drawn about manifest anticipation and tested influence.

The term problems-'in-use' – The problems tracked down by the foregoing procedures thus formed the basis for making comparisons of influence attempts.

In the course of the investigation, however, it became clear that the word 'problem' was not interpreted uniformly by all the respondents. In some cases a problem was defined in terms of a refractory government, that, for example, refused to raise a bridge; here, of course, problems were stated in terms of solutions and influence attempts and not in terms of 'problems' along the lines envisaged in our study. This was taken into account in our coding and in subsequent operations.

In other cases, where the problems were more generally well-known, respondents tended to apply these general problems to their own particular firms. We tried in these somewhat doubtful cases to discover whether or not the firm experienced any *concrete inconvenience*. 'Concrete' means that the inconvenience already had to be present, or had to be likely to appear in the near future.

Influence-relevant problems: equal importance for small and large firms? – Influence-relevant problems, as we have previously argued, are a significant help in determining the various aspects of influence. It is important, for the following reasons, to establish whether or not these problems have the same importance for both small and large business firms. People – and therefore also vice-presidents of business firms – cannot do everything at the same time. This is a simple though basic point in Simon's theory of human behavior (March and Simon, 1958, p. 11, among others). Its significance for our investigation is that the presence of a number of other problems, not directly relevant for influence, could mean that the comparability of one firm with another is severely lessened. Suppose that there are two firms, one large and one small, which are both concerned with a lock that is too narrow. If for example, the large firm is involved at the same time in an extensive internal re-organization (not an influence-relevant problem), then its vice-president will obviously be less likely to take immediate steps to have the lock enlarged. The small firm, on the other hand, with fewer things on its mind, will most probably devote itself heart and soul to the problem of the lock. The *perceived* interest in a given problem will therefore depend on the degree to which there are other urgent problems which demand attention.

This difficulty can be conceptualized as the need to know the relative *weight* of influence-relevant problems within the totality of problems of a firm. This knowledge was sought by posing an *open* question about all the main problems which had been experienced in the last five years *before* the question about problems related to the material facilities for transport by water (for a detailed presentation of the frequencies of responses to this question see Appendix 5A). The answers to this open question showed, as was to be expected, that a number of firms had other problems, not related to waterway facilities. Some examples: 57% had personnel shortages, 30% problems with financial results. To compare: 61% cited problems related to material facilities for transport by water (for shipyards 64%). It follows that the danger that the time at a vice-president's disposal *cannot* be devoted to influence attempts because of the presence of problems unrelated to influence – Simon's theory – is far from an illusory one. To safeguard comparability this 'danger' should be equally great for large and for small firms. In other words, the average weight of water-related problems compared to other problems should be about equal for large and for small firms. An indicator of this relative weight is the order in which the problems are ranked according to importance. To save time, an approximate ranking was derived from the sequence in which the problems were spontaneously revealed. The sequential numbers varied in practice between one and four. The averages in the categories of large and small firms differed very little, as can be seen in Table 5.3. This is, by the way, also true of personnel problems which are included in the table for reasons of comparison.

Conclusion: the usefulness of the variable 'influence-relevant problem' – An 'influence-relevant problem' must serve many purposes in this investigation (see the aspects of the concept of influence discussed in

Table 5.3

Problems relating to the material facilities for transport by water compared with other cited problems (the average of the rank-order numbers)

average rank-order number, in which a *problem related to the material facilities for transport by water* was cited by	firms' numbers of employees	
	0–99	100 and more
shipyards	2.19 (16)†	2.41 (17) n.s.* (U = 119)
remaining firms	1.73 (15)	2.17 (6) n.s. (U = 31)
average order-number in which *manpower problems* is named by		
shipyards	1.48 (25)	1.78 (23) n.s. (Z = 1.16)
remaining firms	1.78 (9)	1.66 (12) n.s. (U = 52)

* Mann-Whitney U test (Siegel, 1956, pp. 116 ff). The difference in all cases was not significant, even at the 10% level (two-sided).

† Only those firms which clearly ordered the problems in answer to *this* question were taken into consideration in this comparison. In some cases the problem was spontaneously revealed at an earlier point in the interview so that when the *planned* question was posed the problem could no longer be neatly placed in a sequence. The firms where this had happened were not used for this comparison.

The number of firms which were finally compared are in the table between parentheses.

Chapter 2). It is therefore a variable which in use must meet several simple requirements. In the first place, the value of the variable would be diminished if there were a large number of firms without such problems. It would then be impossible to carry out the comparison of manifest anticipation and tested influence, because too few cases would be left over.

Secondly, the comparison of the influence of large and small firms would be seriously hampered if the relevance of the variable was not the same for the two categories. Results of the investigation have indicated, however, that there should be no difficulties in this respect: the 'weight' of the influence-relevant problems compared to other problems of business firms is about the same for large and small firms.

5.3 **Further selection of problems of business firms for extensive consideration**

The selection procedure – The preliminary inventory of business firms' problems which we have just discussed must now be elaborated. More clarity is needed about whether or not a problem is influence-relevant.

While water-related problems are very often influence-relevant, there are exceptions. On the other hand, there are also problems in other areas which are sometimes influence-relevant. A *definitive* selection of influence-relevant problems was therefore made in a *second phase of the investigation.* Each interviewer reviewed all the material–composed of the actual interview results, documents, observations made during the interview and maps of areas with material facilities for transport by water–one more time together with me to arrive at this selection.

If both of the previously-stated requirements
– 'problems' (or possibly eagerness for improved benefits)
– 'latitude'
were met, further 'consideration' was decided upon (for details about this sort of decisions see Appendix 5C).

The number of business problems relevant for influence which remained following this definitive selection greatly exceeded our expectations. For 130 business firms there were:
– 192 water-related problems[3]
– 87 other problems
  (total 279 problems).
The remaining analysis in this investigation will now be based on this set of 279 problems–or, whenever necessary, a selection from them.

Following this selection, a large amount of additional data needed to be gathered. Since business problems are to serve as a basis for comparisons of influence, all the associated concrete behavior which is relevant for influence must be tracked down: for example, the importance of the problem, whether or not an influence attempt has been made, the way in which the government has been approached, what the financial costs were, and so forth. The *concrete interactions* with the *government* in particular, as empirically observable behavior, must now be investigated.

A *block of information* must therefore be assembled *for each problem.* For convenience sake we will bundle all this information under the term 'problems of business firms'. The number of problems will clearly vary from firm to firm, so that the collected information displays a pattern like that in Figure 5.3. The information was complemented for each problem with follow-up interviews with the business firms involved, and also with news items from newspapers and magazines, etc.

Reliability of the information: controlling with information obtained from burgomasters and administrators of departments of waterways–As I said

number of firm	standard information	variable information

number of firm   *standard information*   *variable information*

number of business problem (with
associated influence attempts etc.)
no. 1   2   3   4   etc.

1   ———————————————   — —
2   ———————————————   — — — — —
3   ———————————————
4   ———————————————   —
5   ———————————————   — — —
etc.

Figure 5.3
The pattern of information for each business firm

previously, the information obtained from the business firms was
controlled as exhaustively as possible. This is not too difficult for larger
projects, because their various aspects are public knowledge, and
written information is usually available concerning them. Problems
which were shared by more than one business firm presented possibilities for controlling information both with the other firms involved,
and often with the various formal interest-groups in addition (information was controlled with such organizations for thirty-six problems).

Control was more difficult when small projects were involved, especially if only one firm was interested. To give some impression of the
reliability of the information obtained: burgomasters and administrators of waterways were asked for 113 problems – a little more than
one third of the total – if they were familiar with them. In 100 cases, or
88%, the answer was positive. Considering that not all problems lead
to influence attempts, and thus may remain unknown, this percentage
is very satisfactory. There was, of course, much more control information available than only for these 113 problems (information received
from other firms, interest organizations, etc.).

And, working from the other side, government agencies were continually asked if influence attempts had taken place which we had not
discovered – for example, because a firm concealed a problem. We
documented only one clear case in which this occurred.

Checking for possible bias in our selection – It remains perfectly possible,
of course, that despite all our precautions our choice of the problems
of business firms to be considered has been biased in one way or
another. It is not, however, very probable. The concept of influence
has, after all, been broken down into different aspects; thus a number
of different measurements are being made. Additionally, the number
of business problems dealt with varied widely from firm to firm.

Table 5.4
The percentages of problems selected for the investigation according to the size category of the business firm

number of employees*	percentage of problems selected by the investigator per category†
0–49	57% (n = 133)
50–99	57% (n = 108)
100–199	62% (n = 68)
200–499	57% (n = 74)
500 and more	70% (n = 73)†

* The number of firms in the five size classes are 42, 34, 18, 19 and 14 respectively. The total number is 127 (some data were missing for the computations of the percentages; this concerns three firms which were omitted).

† There were a total number of 456 problems *designated* by the respondents from the 127 firms. The number of problems selected for consideration is 274 (five problems were cited by respondents in the three firms which were not included in this table).

There is one possible bias which fortunately can be controlled after the fact using results of the investigation. It is conceivable that more influence-relevant problems have been selected for large firms than for small ones or vice versa. To check this out we computed for each size category the percentage of problems that we had considered, thus:

$$\frac{\text{number of influence-relevant problems considered}}{\text{total number of problems cited by respondents}} \times 100$$

The results are shown in Table 5.4. It is shown that our selection from all the problems mentioned (including problems which are not relevant for influence) was about the same in all the different size categories.

5.4 **The set of selected business problems: An impressive source of impulses for change**

What is the significance of the set of selected problems as a whole which are relevant for influence? I will first consider its importance for the firms themselves, and then its importance for government policy.

As far as the business firms are concerned:
– a business firm has on the average *slightly more than two* business problems which are relevant for influence;
– concerning the nature of these problems: no less than 35% are related to *large objects* (bridges, locks, waterways) and another 10%

to expensive adaptations of slipways required, among other reasons, because of changing water levels as a result of the Delta plan (made after the Holland flood disaster in 1953);
– a reasonably accurate estimate could be made for a number of problems (sixty-two cases) of their *costs for the firm;* no estimate can be made of the degree in which these cases are representative for all the problems (see Appendix 5D). They do give a very clear picture, however, of the order of magnitude of the costs involved; these costs were *per problem:*

for fourteen problems   less than *f* 100,000
for twenty-five problems   between *f* 100,000   and   *f* 500,000
for eleven problems   between *f* 500,000   and *f* 1,000,000
for twelve problems   more than *f* 1,000,000

(for a more detailed survey of problems of business firms and the determination of costs for the firm see Appendix 5D).

Considering that these figures concern the period between 1965 and 1970, this has, I think, demonstrated quite graphically the considerable significance of the problems for the business firms themselves. It is also clear that all the problems are far from being equally 'serious'. We will have to take this into account in our further analysis.

The significance of problems of business firms *for governmental policy* is an equally important point. To be sure, the goal of this investigation is *not* to determine this significance, but we would very much like to know whether the totality of business problems is a pin prick or a hefty blow directed toward this governmental policy. We thus arrive at the question: How important is our set of business problems as a motive force for the total of expenditures for changes in the material facilities for transport by water?

As I have pointed out before, there are undoubtedly a number of such expenditures which have only the slightest connection with the problems of our firms: 'traffic flows' and other 'collective' problems are at least as important as sources of change. The new canal from Antwerp to Rotterdam is a good example. In addition we are only working with a sample of business firms in this investigation. Business firms which were not included in the sample can naturally have made influence attempts as well.

In spite of all of these qualifications, 'our' business problems are certainly a source of impulses for change which cannot be neglected. The following discussion should help to illustrate this point.

When the influence attempts arising from problems of business firms are successful, they result in *costs for the government.* We have determined the costs per influence attempt. This could be easily accomplished in some cases because the sums involved could be located in written documents. There were a number of cases, however, for which we ourselves had to make an estimate of the costs. Problems related to the material facilities for transport by water were especially amenable to making such estimates; there were sometimes comparable projects whose costs were known and we were also able to obtain the prices of a number of 'units' making up the larger projects (for example, dredging operations per meter^3, wharfs per meter). Finally, a number of checks could be made in interviews with engineers at the Department of Waterways. In a small number of cases it proved impossible to determine the costs.

There was a total of 195 influence attempts:
in 138 cases (71%) the costs were determined;
in 38 cases (19%) licences and so forth were involved;
in 19 cases (10%) it was impossible to determine costs.

The total costs amounted to 600 million guilders (about 260 million dollars). I of course took account of the fact that different firms sometimes make influence attempts aimed at the same objective; no duplications are included in the figure cited above. If we estimate roughly that the compliance with influence attempts in our investigation stretches out over a period of about six years, the figure amounts to about f 100 million per year.

The logical question at this point is what percentage of the total government budget is covered by this amount. An answer to this question, however, would require a complete investigation for itself: the costs can appear on budgets of the national government, the provinces and municipalities, and at each of these levels in various different departments. The figure presented (f 100 million) cannot therefore be compared validly with one budget item. Nevertheless, to give a rough idea about the order of magnitude of this figure I will do just that.

I will compare it with the item 'shipping lanes and harbors' in the budget of the Ministry of Traffic and Waterways. In 1966, this item was f 300 million (Budget figures 1966, nr. 2, p. 14). Half, at the most, of 'our' influence attempts would fall under this budget item (that is, only those projects related to the material facilities for transport by water which are financed by the national government); on the other hand, roughly half of the projects falling under this budget item are totally unrelated to the influence attempts of the business firms in our samples.

According to this rough estimate, the influence attempts of the business firms in our sample would lay claim to a figure amounting to about *one third* of the item 'shipping lanes and harbors' on the national budget for the period under consideration. Not all the influence attempts are complied with. Half at the most of the f 600 million that were requested by the business firms in our sample was actually 'granted' by the government. Figured per year, the actual amount spent by the government would then be maximally f 50 million. This is *one sixth* of the 'shipping lanes and harbors' item on the national budget. I repeat–the absolute value of this figure (one sixth)–should not be overrated. There is too large a margin of uncertainty. The fact remains, however, that there are sufficient grounds for concluding *that the influence attempts which arise from our set of business firms' problems are not merely a marginal phenomenon, but are a significant source of impulses for government policy.*

5.5 Individual and non-individual problems of business firms

It became clear that during the formation of hypotheses that differences in influence could most easily be investigated in the case of individual problems of business firms. It is for this reason that the research design is attuned to the testing of a hypothesis which applies to this category of problems. Our first task was therefore to classify the problems in one of the two above categories.

The classification – The classification into individual and non-individual categories was accomplished in the following way: The investigator, using all the information available, classified all the problems. The crucial question was which vice-president judged the problem to be important for his own firm. A difficulty which arises when such procedures are used is obvious: the interest in a problem must sometimes also be assessed for business firms which are not in the sample.

In the majority of cases, however, the *object* with which the firm's problem was concerned could serve as a check for the categorization. The familiar borderline cases which must be dealt with in any categorization were of course present here as well.

An impression of the *reliability* of the categorization was obtained by comparing the result with the assessments of the interviewers. It was, however, no more than an impression, since the judgements are *not completely independent*, because a great deal of preliminary deliberation was necessary to 'measure' each problem.

Twenty cases proved to be classified differently (see Table 5.5). They were considered again. No changes in my first judgement seemed necessary.

Another control was applied for individual problems. We compared our judgement with that of the respondents who had been asked whether they considered the problem to be of interest for other firms as well. Answers were available for 104 individual problems. In 70% of these cases the respondent considered the problem to be only of interest for himself, in 30% of the cases for others as well. We did get the impression, however, during our consideration of the problems that respondents tend to answer rather quickly that the problem is also of interest for others (a 'socially desirable' answer).

Table 5.5
The categorization of problems of business firms as individual and non-individual

	judgement of interviewer		
judgement of investigator	solely or mainly in one firm's interest	in the interest of two or more firms	total
individual	136	10	146
non-individual	10	123	133

If we check the problems which I have classified as individual to see whether a firm made an influence attempt *together with other business firms*, we find that this was the case for only seven of the ninety-two problems (this is 8%; see also Table 5.6).

It is also true of Table 5.6 that the two variables are not independent. The judgement about categorization of a problem as 'individual' or 'non-individual' is, after all, made by considering many aspects of the problem. We can only maintain that this judgement is reasonably consistent. Attempts to discover more sophisticated operationalizations of this variable should definitely be encouraged.

Is the proportion of individual problems about the same for large and small firms? – The emphasis in the following section will lie on individual problems. Our first step in the next stage of the analysis is to ask whether or not individual problems have the same 'weight' in large and small business firms. This is computed by comparing the number of individual problems with the total number of business problems considered. The percentage of problems of shipyards having an individual

Table 5.6
Nature of the problem* and type of influence attempt

	influence attempt:			
type of problem	none	alone	together with other firm(s)	total
individual	33	85	7	125*
non-individual	41	39	53	133

* With the exception of 21 'Delta-problems'.

character was exactly the same (65%) for the three size classes (that is, number of employees less than 100, from 100–499, and 500 or more). The percentages for firms other than shipyards were 28%, 55% and 23% respectively. The second category is thus somewhat high.

There is on the whole no reason for supposing that individual problems should be afforded an unequal weight in different size classes of business firms; this will, however, be controlled in another way later on in the study.

5.6 Has some aspect of influence escaped detection by using 'problems' as an indicator? (Anticipation by the government.) Influence as an institutionalized phenomenon?

The set of business problems tracked down during this investigation is by now familiar. It is now high time that we ask what constrictions have been placed on the concept of influence by the *actual* composition of this set. Are there some (important) aspects of influence which have been lost in the shuffle? The most important source of errors is the possibility that problems do *not* come into being. Certain processes may have been operative which prevented the awareness of problems from forming. We pointed out one of such processes, anticipation by government agencies, in Chapter 2. This will be discussed further below. We will subsequently consider another conceivable source of error, which I have called 'inconspicuous influence as a result of permanent relationships with the government'.

Anticipation by government agencies–A business firm can exercise influence on the government without there having been any actual interaction–as I made clear in Chapter 2. It is, after all, perfectly plausible that the government *takes the mere presence of the business firm into account* when making its decisions. The only requirement for influence is then that the business firm is present in the 'life-space' of the governmental administrator (Nagel, 1968, p. 132).

This anticipation can manifest itself in two ways:
a   by the firm's obtaining *advantages*;
b   by the firm's *avoiding disadvantages*.

What is involved in both cases is not decisions which have proceeded from influence attempts with which the firms from our sample were involved. In Chapter 2 we called them '*other*' governmental decisions. All the decisions for a given region relating to the material facilities for transport by water which have been made in the previous five years are to be taken into account.

In order to pinpoint cases of governmental anticipation we tried in particular to obtain information from burgomasters to allow us to make an inventory of these 'other' governmental decisions. This number proved, however, to be so small that it could virtually be ignored. There was almost always some connection with the set of business firms' problems and the influence attempts. This point must be accepted with some reservations, because our procedures are here certainly open for improvement.

Other indicators are possible for point b – the case in which disadvantages for a business firm are avoided by the government. We can in this context examine those situations where government plans (and therefore proposed decisions) *have had or threaten to have* a negative effect. This can be observed *at the business firm itself*. We assume concurrently, of course, that the firm is aware of these negative effects.

I reasoned this way: if the government takes large firms more into account than small ones in its planning, then the former can be expected to experience relatively *less* inconvenience than the latter as a result of governmental planning. As we have pointed out before, the effect of these plans have been inventorized under the heading 'plans of others'. These plans of others were almost always government plans which might have caused inconvenience (negative effects) to a particular business firm – at least in the first instance.

The share of 'plans of others' in the total number of problems per size class of the business firms turn out to be as follows:
for shipyards:
– less than 100 employees: 29%
– from 100 to and including 499 employees: 20%
– 500 or more employees: 35%

Another index which can be used is the *average* number of plans of others per size category. These averages are 0.54, 0.43 and 0.86 respectively. These figures most definitely do not indicate that there is stronger government anticipation for large than for small firms; large firms *do not* experience less negative effects than small ones as a result of government planning.

The same conclusion holds concerning the 'remaining business firms'. The share of 'plans of others' was here 22%, 39% and 14% (with the average numbers 0.35, 0.73 and 0.50) for the three respective size–classes of business firms.

A second possible procedure for determining whether or not large firms experienced relatively less negative effects than small ones was based on a question in the interview: 'Have you sometimes felt that an *industrialization plan* was prejudicial to your interests'? The question was answered in the affirmative by 24% of the small firms and by 34% of the large ones. This failed also to indicate that government anticipation was relatively more advantageous to large firms than to small ones.

Further evidence was obtained in a third way: the respondents were asked questions about their *appraisal* of government activity related to the material facilities for transport by water. For example, one question was: 'Do you find your municipal government very active, reasonably active, or not active enough compared to other municipalities with respect to the material facilities for transport by water?'

Similar questions were asked concerning the activities of provincial and national governments. A *negative* appraisal was made:

- for municipal government: by 28% of the small firms and 37% of the large ones;
- for provincial government: by 17% of the small firms and 18% of the large ones;
- for the national government: also 17% of the small firms and 18% of the large ones.

There are therefore absolutely no indications that government anticipation works to the advantage of large firms more than to that of small firms. The answers received for another question also support this conclusion. The respondents were asked: 'What are your feelings concerning more extensive industrialization in this area?' (there were five possible answers ranging from strongly negative to strongly positive). There were slightly less small firms with a negative attitude than large ones (24% of the small firms had a negative attitude, 39% of the large ones). This is in itself not so significant; however, combined with other data—namely, that 80% of the *burgomasters* in our sample gave positive or very positive answers to the same question, and only 10% negative ones—this piece of information gains added importance. It shows that the burgomasters were willing to create a favorable climate for industrialization. Since the large firms had more negative reactions than small firms toward continuing industrialization, it would be going against the evidence to say that any government anticipation of the needs of especially larger firms could be detected.

The answers given to another question asked of the burgomasters gave a final weak indication of the impartiality of government anticipation. In this question we sough information about their knowledge of problems relating to the material facilities for transport by water experienced by shipyards in their community (of course, shipyards we

Table 5.7
The knowledge possessed by burgomasters about the problems of the shipyard in their municipality (solitary shipyards)

number of employees of shipyard	burgomasters answer		
	no answer	incorrect	correct
0–99	3	4	11
100 or more	4	8	11
total	7	12	22

had investigated). Their answers were classified by the interviewer as being a correct or incorrect assessment of the actual state of affairs. The result for the solitary shipyard sample is shown in Table 5.7. This shows that knowledge about the small shipyards is no less than that about the large ones. Of course, this knowledge as such does not exhaust the question of whether the two size classes of business firms are actually taken equally into account in decision-making processes. But this knowledge is at least a necessary condition for making equal handling possible.

I believe that these indications give us a reasonable basis for concluding that there is no evidence pointing toward governmental anticipation favoring large business firms.

Taken separately, these indications certainly cannot be taken as a definitive proof. It is remarkable, however, that considered together they reveal not one hint of a relatively strong government anticipation favoring the larger firms. As a result, I see no reason for taking this factor into account in any further conclusions which are made. *Government anticipation will therefore no longer be taken into consideration in this study.*[4]

A marginal note: Manipulation of information? – The 'sin' of manipulation of information or of values can be 'committed' by both the government and the business firms. To the extent that this is done by the government, we can leave it out of our consideration here; it should have an effect on the latent and the manifest anticipation of the business firms, and that will be exactingly tested later.

What then of the possible manipulation of information or values by the business firms? A firm can exercise influence not only in the case of concrete problems, followed by concrete decisions, but also in a more general sense, by changing the world of opinions and ideas of the government agencies. This is a neglected point in Dahl's 'decision-method' which is often criticized: 'Power is also exercised when A devotes his energies to creating or reinforcing social and political values' (Bachrach and Baratz, 1962, p. 948).

Exactly what significance does this have for our investigation of influence? The question is once again whether or not the large firms are favored by this mechanism: that is, whether they succeed in reducing the number of problems they experience by continually 'indoctrinating' the government. If this was the case, then its effect would have to be seen in the 'anticipation by governmental agencies' just discussed. There was, however, no evidence for this to be found at all. Therefore our sample of business problems cannot be easily distorted as a result of these processes.

The fact remains, however, that manipulation of information can have effects of a somewhat different nature–namely, on more general government policies. The crucial question is then whether or not some of these policies have something *other* than concrete business problems as their source. My impression is that this is very seldom the case. These problems do sometimes merge into a 'collective' one (or vice versa), but government policy in this field does not originate in a vacuum. This is true of issues relating to the material facilities for transport by water; I am not in a position to make a judgement in any other area.

To summarize, I propose that the mechanism of information manipulation:

- has apparently caused no distortion in the comparability of small and large firms with respect to their number of problems,
- has apparently not been the source of influence 'external' to the business problems for the objects of this investigation,
- nevertheless causes us to retain some reservations, especially because further research is needed in areas other than those related to the material facilities for transport by water.

Inconspicuous influence through permanent relations with the government–Some firms may conceivably have such a good relationship with the government that there is practically nothing that can develop into a problem for them any more. In such cases a casual remark or a telephone call from the firm to their 'good friend' in the government agency is sufficient, and the 'problem' is simply solved before it has time to develop into a real problem. This is in fact a way of asking whether or not the 'set' of decisions which we are using as a basis for determining influence is large enough (see McFarland, 1969, p. 102).

A number of reasons can be given to show that this possible source of error is not a very plausible one.

First, a detailed list of a large number of specific objects (that is, those related to material facilities for water transport) was handed to the firms' vice-presidents. Secondly, the possible solution of problems often has such drastic consequences that it is highly improbable that they would be casually solved by the government. Finally, the governmental apparatus has a considerable number of branches: the municipality must be approached for some aspects of the problems, provincial agencies for others and so on. A very large number of permanent relationships would be necessary to achieve the desired effect.

If a distortion were to occur nevertheless, it would have to find its expression primarily in *smaller* problems, since these are the easiest to settle 'unofficially'. This makes possible the following check.

It seems obvious that we would expect to encounter these permanent influence relations by the large firms more often than by the small ones. Continuing this line of reasoning, we would expect large firms to mention small problems relatively less often than small firms. But what is relatively less often? Maybe large firms have fewer small problems by the very nature of their size. I have chosen a safe standard: the percentage of small problems in the total number of problems should be about the same for large and small firms. If this proves to be true, then it will in any case be impossible to conclude that small problems are underrepresented in large firms.

There are two ways of checking whether this is so. The first possibility is to exclude from consideration *the large objects* of possible influence attempts and to compare the numbers of problems remaining for small and large firms. I have selected bridges and locks as being large objects. What percentage of problems per size class of business firm is there now remaining? For shipyards, the figures are as follows:
- for firms with less than 100 employees: 74%
- for firms with 100 to and including 499 employees: 65%
- for firms with 500 or more employees: 71%.

These percentages certainly do not give any occasion for fearing a serious distortion (this comparison could not be carried out for the 'remaining firms' because the numbers of problems relating to bridges and locks were too small).

A second possible way of testing for a difference in small and large firms' proportions of small problems is to compare the share of problems involving relatively low costs for the government. For shipyards, the share of problems with costs less than f 75,000 were:
- for small firms: 17%
- for large firms: 7%

Virtually no problems occurred under f 75,000 for the *'remaining firms'*. If we look at costs for the government under the f 250,000 level, then we find that the percentage of problems is:
- for small firms: 11%
- for large firms: 14%.

It can therefore be seen that for large shipyards, problems involving 'low' costs for the government are slightly underrepresented. This is not true of the other types of firms.

These data allow us to make the following conclusions:

If large firms have more permanent relations with government agencies than small firms, then the number of problems experienced by large firms may be diminished. For reasons explained above, this would be reflected primarily in a smaller share of relatively small problems on the part of these large firms. One indication based on data from the investigation provides some support for this hypothesis; two other indications give no evidence to justify it. To eliminate any doubt I have applied a correction factor for the results for manifest anticipation and tested influence that we will discuss later. Here is an example of the outcome when a correction is applied to tested influence in connection with the individual problems of the entire sample of shipyards (see also Chapter 6). If we add eight influence attempts of large firms to the twenty attempts already registered – an increase of 40% – and if we assume that all eight attempts have been successful, then the over-all percentage of successful attempts becomes 82% (75% before the correction). The corresponding figure for small shipyards is 74%. Thus, although there is a slight observable difference between large and small firms, it is far from being significant. The correction affects the results hardly at all. I therefore believe that *the possible effects of permanent relations between the firms and the government will not endanger any further conclusions of the investigation.*

'Institutionalized' influence?–We must at this point examine critically whether or not our methods are sufficient for tracking down the effects of the social 'order'. Social relatinships, after all, are 'patterned', that is, relatively rigidly structured; there is a pattern of *norms* which define

what the *correct* modes of behavior or *social relationships* are (Chinoy, 1967, p. 28). Such normative patterns are called *institutions* (the doctor-patient relationship is a good example).

One of the main questions of this investigation is, in fact, whether government agencies use *other* norms in their behavior towards large firms than they do towards small ones—or, in terms of the layman, whether there is evidence in society of a discriminatory behavior, depending on the size of the firm. It is clear that this question can only be conclusively answered if this institutionalized aspect is sufficiently represented in our material. And one prerequisite for this representation is that we work with an accurate set of situations which are considered as a basis for our determination of influence.

In what respects can our set of situations be inadequate?

1 – A distortion can have been introduced in the process of specifying the concept of 'situation' with the term 'problems'. I have devoted considerable attention to this possibility in this chapter. More research is needed, however, with other specifications to gain more complete insight into the matter.

The fact remains, however, that we *have* devoted considerable attention to the question of to what extent the set of problems of business firms is sufficiently representative of the universe of situations in which influence could manifest itself. We have searched for any evidence indicating that large firms are less likely to have some kinds of problems because other mechanisms work so to their advantage that the awareness of problems simply fails to come into being. Results of several tests (possible anticipation by the government, among others) have shown that there is no indication that such a state of affairs exists.

2 – The set of problems of business firms can be of insufficient magnitude. I believe that our inventory of problems of a large number of firms over a five-year period definitely does satisfy at least minimum requirements.

To summarize, I am convinced that the 'institutionalized' aspect of influence can certainly find its proper expression by means of our set of problems of business firms. *That is, I maintain that we are most definitely measuring the effects of the social order in this investigation.* It remains nevertheless true that the measurement in this one investigation cover only a part of this order.

Notes

1. We must again emphasize that perceptions of different firms can only be compared if the *research situations* are as rigidly controlled as possible (see below, 'influence-relevant problems').

2. The interest–or perceived discrepancy–is very similar to what Lewin calls the 'tension' within an individual (which in our case is the firm's management) (Lewin, 1952, p. 11).

3. As a result of the selection, the number of problems is naturally smaller than the number revealed by the respondents in the first inventory.

4. The discussion has only been concerned with the variable 'size of business firms'. As will be shown later, this is crucial for this variable because the relationship between size and influence predicted by the hypothesis will prove to be only very partially present.

Strictly speaking, the effect of government anticipation should also be examined for other variables (growth, for example). Since these are usually variables which appear in subsidiary or new hypotheses, I have not included them in the analysis.

6. Large and Small Firms Compared: Influence Exercised for Solving Individual Problems (Results)

Content of this chapter–The testing of the *first* hypothesis is discussed in this chapter. This hypothesis is (see p. 61),

'*In solving their individual problems, business firms have the more influence on the government, the larger they are in size.*'

Comparable measurements of influence are needed to test this hypothesis. We have seen how the research design was tailored to guarantee the comparability of individual problems in particular (controls in advance).

Our testing consists of two main steps: first, an overall test, then a test in which as many factors as possible are held constant (controls after the fact). These controls are usually used to check whether or not the relationships established in the initial testing are spurious ones.

The overall test is discussed in this chapter; the 'controls' will be handled in a later one.

6.1 The overall test of the hypothesis

Brief survey of the three aspects of the concept of influence and their corresponding indices–We have, I think, by now convinced the reader that the concept of influence is a very complex one. It does therefore seem natural that we test the hypothesis first for the three different *aspects* of influence separately. In Section 2.4 we suggested three such aspects by basing them on three fundamental elements of the concept of influence:

problems – influence attempts – successes (compliance)

These elements have a definite logical connection. After all–before there can be any effects, there must have been an influence attempt; before there can have been an influence attempts, a problem must have been present.[1]

Each element thus is a necessary condition for the succeeding one. This structure was portrayed earlier in Figure 1.1.

A firm can, of course, have no problems, or one problem, but it can also have several problems. The same is true for influence attempts and successes (compliance). The corresponding symbols are:

P   (number of problems),
IA   (number of influence attempts),
S   (number of successes, or IA's complied with).

The three aspects of influence already introduced in Section 2.4 are then:

(1) *tested influence* (symbol T); the index representing this aspect is the fraction of the influence attempts that are successful:

$$T = \frac{S}{IA}$$

(2) *manifest anticipation* (symbol AM); the index is the fraction of the problems for which influence attempts are actually made:

$$AM = \frac{IA}{P}$$

(3) *latent anticipation*; the index of this aspect is the number of problems (P), under constant conditions, for large as well as for small business firms (these conditions will be specified later; see also Chapter 4).

We should keep in mind that these three aspects are intimately connected with the various stages of an influence process.

Testing for each aspect separately – As we have seen in Chapter 2, the three aspects of influence can be very simply combined arithmetically: their product is equal to the number of successes (effects). But the combination of these aspects is much more difficult to interpret than the aspects separately. Therefore, to avoid this difficulty we will *test the hypothesis for each aspect of influence separately*. Naturally, it can also be said that we are now concerned with three sub-hypotheses.

We will consider the three aspects in the order followed above. In this way we are in effect beginning with the surface phenomena and working toward 'deeper levels'. The first aspect clearly lies in the sphere of actual, observable interactions with the government; the other two aspects become progressively less directly observable. I emphasize, however, that I am not maintaining that any of the aspects is the most important. For the time being I am considering them all to be equally significant.

Before presenting the results I will have to discuss several operationalizations.

Operationalization of 'influence attempt' and 'compliance' (successes) – The operationalization of problems was already discussed in the preceding chapter. The operationalization of *influence attempts* presents few difficulties. For each problem of the firm the respondent was asked:

'Have you ever tried to find a solution for this problem

a   by using your own resources

b   by asking the government for help?'

Very tersely formulated, an influence attempt is thus operationalized as a 'request made to the government'. In the actual practice there were, of course some complications, especially if the influence attempt was aimed at an objective that the government was planning to carry out anyway.

Such cases were only coded as influence attempts if something additional was requested by the firm. We also counted only the costs connected with the 'extra' portion as 'costs for the government' (see also below under 'compliance').

Some control of the reliability of our operationalization of problems was obtained by a number of checks carried out with burgomasters and with officials of the provincial and national agencies responsible for the material facilities for transport by water.

If an influence attempt had taken place, the respondents in the business firms were asked a series of follow-up questions about such topics as the frequency and nature of the contacts with the government and the mobilization of the help of interest organizations.

'Compliance' (*successes*) was operationalized by means of the following question:

'Has your objective been reached?'

Taken by itself, this operationalization presents no problems. It is, however, not conclusive; more information is needed to be able to conclude that influence can be assigned to the firm on the basis of this compliance. In assigning influence or failing to do so, it is vitally necessary that we be sure that the government decision in question would *not* have been made had the influence attempt not been undertaken. In other words, the firm's influence must be a *necessary condition* for the decision (see Chapter 2 p. 25 and Chapter 3).

Further information is therefore needed to obtain definite knowledge concerning the following points:
- that there are no other firms which have undertaken influence
  attempts aimed at the same objectives; since in this chapter exclusively individual problems are treated, this point has already been
  resolved by the classification of the problems;
- that the problem does not just 'happen' to fit into plans of the
  government which would have been carried out *in any case*; in such
  a way an individual problem could merge into a collective one. This
  possibility has been provided for to a certain extent by the classification of problems as collective and non-collective. As a further check,
  burgomasters from the same municipalities were interviewed immediately after our visits to the firms so that direct information
  could be obtained about whether or not a particular firm's problem
  could be subsumed under collective problems present in the community. This was the beginning of the small 'case-study' of each
  problem which I spoke of earlier.

Finally, it should be noted that in actuality there are of course
'degrees' to which success is achieved. Initially we therefore distinguished among three categories: successful, partially successful and
unsuccessful. The second category was combined with 'successful' at a
later stage in the analysis, leaving us with a dichotomy (however, only
the costs which could be specifically assigned to a particular influence
attempt were considered as 'relevant government expenditures').

Table 6.1 gives an overall picture of the total number of individual
problems, influence attempts and successes.

6.2   First aspect: tested influence (results)

Tested influence and government behavior – We have seen that this
aspect of influence is reflected in the proportion of influence attempts
which have been successful, or, *the percentage of influence attempts with
success*. This index has long been familiar in the literature (see Chapter
2). It is comparable to what March (1955, p. 448) calls the 'measure of
influence attempts'.

We pointed out earlier that this aspect is clearly connected to actual,
observable interactions between business firms and the government.
The firms are experimenting as it were with their influence with their
'demands upon the government'. They are 'trying out their influence'.

It is important to pause for a moment here and consider the reverse
side of this interaction. The government is confronted with a number

Table 6.1
The number of individual problems (P), influence attempts (IA) and successes (S) in the period from 1965 to and including 1969

SHIPYARDS‡	all problems	portion of problems which were brought to some conclusion†
individual problems	108 (59)*	84 (56)
portion with influence attempt	71 (43)	47 (36)
portion which was successful		35 (27)
REMAINING BUSINESS FIRMS		
individual problems	38 (25)	26 (16)
portion with influence attempt	31 (21)	18 (11)
portion which was successful		16 (11)

* The numbers of firms are given in parentheses. For the problems is given the number of firms having *at least one* problem, and so forth.
† 'Brought to some conclusion' means:
–either the firm has definitely decided against making an influence attempt
– or the government has made a definite decision about the object of the influence attempt.
‡ The figures refer to all the shipyards. We will divide this sample into three sub-samples for testing (see also Chapter 4).

of influence attempts for which it has to make decisions. These influence attempts are originating partly from small firms and partly from large ones. The pattern formed by these decisions thus reveals something about the differences in *behavior of the government towards these two different categories of business firms.* The results can provide a basis for the assessment of the *justice of government decisions.*

Weighted or unweighted averages?–There are still various ways to compare the tested influence $(T = S/IA)$ of large and small firms. Besides the normal average of T, it is also possible to work with a weighted average, using the number of influence attempts per firm as the weighting factor.

This can result in considerable differences, as the following example will show. In this example, two pairs must be compared with one another–for example, a pair of small firms (a) with a pair of large firms (b).

pair a:　firm 1:　two influence attempts, two successes, $T_1 = 1$
　　　　　firm 2:　eight influence attempts, two successes, $T_2 = \frac{1}{4}$
pair b:　firm 3:　five influence attempts, two successes, $T_3 = \frac{2}{3}$
　　　　　firm 4:　five influence attempts, two successes, $T_4 = \frac{2}{5}$
The 'normal' average for pair a is $\frac{5}{8}$.
The 'normal' average for pair b is $\frac{2}{5}$.
There does seem to be a definite difference. If, however, we consider the *total number of successes* and the *total number of influence attempts* of the pairs as a whole, then there is no difference whatsoever; the figure for both pairs is $\frac{4}{10}$. This latter ratio, $\sum S / \sum IA$, is equal to the weighted averages of T, namely:

$$\frac{\sum S}{\sum IA} = \frac{\sum \frac{S}{IA} \times IA}{\sum IA} = \frac{\sum T \times IA}{\sum IA}$$

An extensive treatment of these differences can be found in Kish (1965, p. 564). The following remarks will have to suffice here:

The number of influence attempts varies from firm to firm. These numbers can have a different dispersion within categories of firms. As a result of this alone, there can be dissimilarities in the 'normal' averages of T (= S/IA) (this is very roughly formulated; see Kish for more details, *op. cit.*). We should be on the lookout for this possibility; therefore, we will work with *weighted averages* for the overall testing in this chapter.

The 'normal' averages were also computed, but were not presented in the tables. They did not provide a basis for making any other conclusions. This is a fortunate state of affairs, since working with weighted averages sometimes leads to practical difficulties–for example, when applying some tests of significance. It is then more convenient to have the unweighted scores of T per business firm available for use. These scores can also be used to compute correlation coefficients, which will be used extensively in the following chapters.

The percentage of successful influence attempts –The figures for the tested influence are given in Table 6.2. They are based on all the individual problems, most of which are related in some way to the material facilities for transport by water. Following the line of reasoning used when we were developing our research design, the comparisons were carried out separately for the four sub-samples.

Table 6.2
'*Tested influence*' ($T = S/IA$) *of small and large business firms in four sub-samples* * (*individual problems*)

size of firm (number of employees)	percentage of influence attempts with success (of the total number of influence attempts)† in sub-sample‡			
	SS 1	SS 2	S 3	RF
less than 100	86 (5)	67 (7)	73 (8)	83 (4)
100 or more	71 (5)	75 (10)	100 (1)	92 (7)
total	79 (10)	71 (17)	75 (9)	89 (11)

* The computations are based only on those firms with
1 individual problems, which
2 are followed by influence attempts, which
3 are brought to a conclusion (that is, for which the success or failure is definite).
The numbers of these firms are in parentheses (compare with Table 6.1, the second and fifth line respectively in the last column).
† The percentage of successful influence attempts is the weighted average of T (weightings factor: number of influence attempts per firm) or;

$$\frac{\sum S}{\sum IA} = \frac{\sum T \times IA}{\sum IA} \text{ (see text)}$$

Of course, we must multiply by 100 to obtain percentages.

‡ SS1: sub-sample solitary shipyards 1
SS2: sub-sample solitary shipyards 2
S3: sub-sample shipyards 3 (not-solitary)
RF: sub-sample 'remaining' business firms

Note that the number of business firms here is considerably smaller than the total amount in the sub-samples. Only a limited number of firms has undertaken one or more influence attempts which were based on individual problems, and which additionally were brought to a complete conclusion (that is, 47 of the 130 business firms).

'Tested influence' is in fact only concerned with the 'super-structure' of influence. More firms will automatically be involved when we handle the other two aspects.

The results shown in Table 6.2 are somewhat surprising. *There is no evidence whatsoever to support the hypothesis* that large firms have more tested influence than small ones. If the various shipyard sub-samples are combined this conclusion remains the same (the percentages are then 74% and 75% for small and large shipyards respectively).

Significance tests are of marginal usefulness for the sub-samples because the numbers involved are too small. Nevertheless we did carry out a Fisher exact test (T dichotomized) with not one significant result (see also the correlation coefficients following on p. 133).

Refinement: *government expenditures per employee* – But a more precise index for tested influence can be constructed. Until now the *amount of the expenditure* that the government must make if it complies with the influence attempt has not been taken into account. Meeting the wishes of the larger firms may conceivably involve more government expenditures, even though these firms have not been successful relatively more often. However, it is necessary as a further refinement that we also take into account the *number of employees* who profit from this expenditure.

A simple index can be constructed in this way, namely, *the government expenditure per employee* (from firms with IA)

$$= \frac{\text{total government expenditures}}{\text{total number of employees}}$$

See Chapter 5, for the way in which costs for the government were determined. Note that the costs could be determined for sixty percent of the sixty-five influence attempts resulting from individual problems that were brought to a conclusion.

The government expenditures per employee are presented in Table 6.3. For shipyards, it can be seen in the table that this index also fails to lend the slightest plausibility to the hypothesis that larger firms have a greater tested influence than small ones. The reverse is more likely. The result is different for the 'remaining' firms. The differences there are in the direction predicted by the hypothesis.

Our conclusion must be that *in three sub-samples there are no indications that point to a confirmation of the hypothesis and that in the fourth sub-sample there is only one out of two indications that points to a greater tested influence of large firms.* This fourth sub-sample is additionally the poorest in quality; the criteria on the basis of which the firms have been selected are unambiguous enough in themselves, but the information needed for establishing the existence of these criteria is obtained from key informants, which means that it is secondhand

Table 6.3
'Tested influence' expressed in government expenditure per employee

size of firm (number of employees)	government expenditure per employee* (in Dutch guilders)			
			in sub-sample†	
	SS1	SS2	S3	RF
less than 100	19,664 (4)	1,087 (3)	917 (7)	8,227 (4)
100 or more	304 (3)	862 (6)	— (0)	42,460 (3)
total	5,809 (7)	883 (9)	917 (7)	37,301 (7)

* Basis: number of employees in firms with
1. individual problems,
2. followed by influence attempts,
3. which have been brought to a conclusion and
4. for which the costs to the government could be determined.
† See Table 6.2 for legend.

(see Section 4.3). Further, the sample is heterogeneous in composition, and the share of individual problems in the total number of problems is relatively small (34% for remaining firms compared to 65% for shipyards).

The most important problem remaining is whether or not the conclusion just formulated will stand up to further analysis. We will return to this more fully later.

One of the more obvious suspicions should be dealt with immediately: that is, is the result perhaps caused by the choice of the cutting point of 100 employees in forming size classes. Can a firm with 100 employees already be called 'large'? To test whether this can have distorted the results, we have distinguished a separate class of large firms having 500 or more employees. The percentages of successful influence attempts than become:

for all shipyards:		remaining firms:	
less than 100 employees	74% (20)	83% (4)	
100–499 employees	73% (12)	100% (4)	
500 or more employees	80% (4)	80% (3)	

There is no indication that very large firms occupy a special position.

Even when class limits are ignored and correlation coefficients are computed, no relationship appears. The computation is carried out for all the shipyards: the correlation coefficient between T and number of employees of the firms is 0.055 (n.s. n = 36; one-tailed testing). In the following, unless explicitly stated otherwise, testing is always one-tailed. It makes no sense to compute correlation coefficients for the remaining firms because the dispersion of T is too small (see Appendix 6A for a more completely worked-out justification for using correlation coefficients for the somewhat skewed distributions in this investigation).

Consequently, our conclusion remains that there is almost no evidence pointing to large firms having more tested influence with respect to individual problems than small ones. And a complementary conclusion: our findings give no reason for assuming that the government applies other standards for large firms than for small ones in making its decisions about individual problems. This result is surprising.

6.3 Second aspect: manifest anticipation

The percentage of problems with influence attempts – Until now we have been examining that aspect of influence which can be measured clearly on the basis of influence attempts and the *decisions* of the government. We indicated previously that this is only an aspect of influence that is on the 'surface'. More information is needed – for example, about *which problems are laid before the government, requiring decisions, and especially, for which problems this does not happen.* It is the question about 'non-decisions' as well as decisions, as posed in particular by Bachrach and Baratz (1963, p. 632) (see Chapter 2 for further details).

As stated earlier, I will try to answer this question by using the two 'anticipation' aspects; manifest anticipation will be considered first.

If a firm has an influence-relevant problem, it is faced with the choice of whether or not to undertake an influence attempt. Now our assumption is that this choice will depend in part on whether or not the firm regards government behavior as a means for solving the problem, and on its perception of the probability of success of the influence attempt (see Section 5.1). We have summarized these factors under the term 'anticipation' of one's own influence. This is the concrete manifestation of the influence which a firm believes itself to have: the stronger the influence, the more pronounced the just-mentioned perceptions, and the more influence attempts there are to be expected.

The comparison of the percentages of problems followed by influence attempts (weighted averages) is shown in Table 6.4. Note that all the business firms having individual problems (even when not brought to a conclusion) form the basis of comparison here.

No indications can be found in the table to support the hypothesis with respect to manifest anticipation (AM) (no significant results were

Table 6.4
Manifest anticipation $(AM = IA/P)$: *percentages of problems with influence attempts of large and small firms in four sub-samples**

size of firm	*percentages* of individual business problems with influence attempts†			
		in sub-sample‡		
(number of employees)	SS1	SS2	S3	RF
less than 100	64 (9)	92 (8)	45 (16)	73 (12)
100 or more	71 (10)	91 (10)	33 (6)	87 (13)
total	68 (19)	92 (18)	42 (22)	82 (25)

* Basis of the computation: business firms with individual problems (the number of firms are in parentheses; compare with Table 6.1, first column, the first and third figures).
† The percentage of problems with influence attempts is the weighted average of AM (weighting factor is the number of problems per firm) × 100; compare the weighted average of T.
‡ See Table 6.2 for legend.

obtained for any of the four sub-samples with the Fisher exact test). Neither are the correlation coefficients between the number of employees and AM significant at the 5% level: the coefficient is 0.107 ($n = 59$; non-significant) for shipyards and 0.232 ($n = 25$; non-significant) for remaining firms. The most that can be said is that, for the remaining firms, a very slight tendency can be detected in the direction predicted by the hypothesis, both in the correlation coefficient and in the fractions in the table (primarily responsible for this tendency were the four firms with 500 or more employees, whose separately computed percentage was 100%).

Refinement: the government expenditures requested per employee – The percentage of problems with influence attempts is not the only relevant datum for the manifest anticipation. The *magnitude of the influence attempt* can also differ widely. In constructing an index for this magnitude *we consider primarily the amount of government expenditures which the business firm demands for its problem*. Analogously to the tested influence, we divide by the number of employees, and we get as our index the government expenditure *requested* per employee

$$= \frac{\text{total amount of government expenditure requested}}{\text{total number of employees}}$$

Table 6.5
Influence attempts expressed in terms of 'requested' governmental expenditures per employee

	requested government expenditure per employee in firms with influence attempts that have been brought to a conclusion (in Dutch guilders)*			
size of firm		in sub-sample†		
(number of employees)	SS1	SS2	S3	RF
less than 100	17,600 (4)	19,063 (3)	2,880 (7)	10,614 (4)
100 or more	40,743 (3)	14,393 (6)	— (0)	47,661 (3)
total	36,221 (7)	14,786 (9)	2,880 (7)	42,079 (7)

* A difference from the previous table is that the basis of the computations here is the number of business firms with influence attempt that have been brought to a conclusion. Further, only those influence attempts involving costs, and whose costs could be determined, are included; compare Chapter 5, p. 113.
† For legend see Table 6.2.

Of course, employees are only included from those firms which have undertaken individual influence attempts. The amount of government expenditures requested per employee is shown in Table 6.5 (the requested expenditures per employee can also be computed for *all* the firms instead of only those firms *with* influence attempts: I will not give these results here because they revealed the same tendencies as those seen in Table 6.5).

No conclusion can be reached on the basis of sub-sample S3. The relevant figures for two of the three other sub-samples lend some support to the hypothesis that *influence attempts of large firms involve more costs for the government than the influence attempts of small firms.*

To summarize the findings of the two tables: *Faced with individual problems, the large firms do not undertake influence attempts relatively more often than small firms, but there is evidence to show that 'the weight' of their influence attempt is greater* – or in other words, they ask for more.

The results for tested influence which we saw in the previous section are placed in a clearer perspective by these findings. When Tables 6.5 and 6.3 are compared, it can be seen that the more expensive requests of large shipyards are not honored commensurately by the government. There is, on the other hand, a slight tendency for requests to be commensurately honored for the 'remaining firms' (what is involved here is the discrepancy in the results for tested influence in the remaining firms, which we discussed in the previous section).

Tested influence in retrospect: the amount of money requested as a determining factor? – The differences just discovered in government expenditures requested call for a pause in the argument in order to return once more to an inspection of tested influence.

Did differences in tested influence (T) perhaps fail to appear because the large firms make more expensive requests, and for that very reason are often confronted with negative decisions? In other words, do differences in tested influence come to light if the *size* of the expenditure requested is kept reasonably constant? To test this we computed the fraction of influence attempts meeting with success separately for problems involving limited or extensive government expenditures respectively. The boundary between limited or extensive costs was set at about the median (f 750,000).

The data in Table 6.6 do lead us to believe that the extent of the costs is indeed relevant for the percentage of successes (see the total percentages, for example): the greater the costs, the smaller the probability of success. There may be a 'ceiling effect' for influence attempts – an amount involved above which it becomes far more

Table 6.6
'Tested influence' in relation to the amount of government expenditures requested

	percentage of influence attempts with success* (out of the total number of influence attempts involving costs)			
	SHIPYARDS (all) *costs*		REMAINING FIRMS *costs*	
size of firm (number of employees)	low†	high‡	low	high
less than 100	67 (13)‡	50 (2)	100 (4)	100 (1)
100 or more	100 (4)	20 (5)	100 (2)	67 (1)§
total	76 (17)	29 (7)	100 (6)	89 (2)

* See Table 6.2 for legend.
† 'Low' costs: less than f 750,000 per influence attempt: 'high' costs: f 750,000 or more per influence attempt.
‡ Naturally, one and the same firm can have problems with *both* low and high costs. The same firms can therefore appear in both the first and second columns. The same is true of the third and fourth columns.
§ It should be pointed out once more that the percentage can also lie between zero and 100 for only one business firm – if the firm has more than one problem.

difficult to have influence attempts be complied with (compare Zeisel, 1968, pp. 10 ff).

It is further revealed that for the shipyards with requests involving low costs, the difference in tested influence is, in fact, somewhat to the advantage of the large firms.[2]

Exactly the opposite seems to be true for high costs, and this is true for the remaining firms as well.

Of course these indications are only based on small numbers of cases. They do, however, allow us to make a reasonably coherent interpretation of the results obtained up to now. This interpretation can be summarized as follows:

Summary – The probability of a firm's undertaking an influence attempt to resolve a problem is not dependent on the size of the firm. It should be added that attempts of large firms are relatively expensive for the government. This perhaps explains in part why the percentage of successes (tested influence) is not a function of the size of the firm. If the relatively cheap (for the government) influence attempts are examined separately, then our data support the suggestion that for these cheaper attempts the tested influence of large firms is relatively greater. But for the expensive attempts, the reverse seems to be true.

Taken as a whole, then, it is clear that no convincing evidence has been found to support our hypothesis for tested influence and for manifest anticipation.

6.4   Third aspect: latent anticipation (number of problems)

The number of problems – Even though we have been unable to establish differences between small and large firms for two aspects of influence, we are not finished yet. Both aspects have, after all, been determined by using 'relative' standards: we divided by the number of influence attempts or the number of problems respectively. This, however, leaves room for considerable differences. If, for example, the large firms were to have more problems than the small ones, then the *absolute* number of influence attempts would be accordingly larger (compare two firms with ten and four problems respectively; if the percentage of influence attempts is 50% for both of them, then they have undertaken five and two influence attempts respectively).

The absolute number of problems of business firms is thus an essential aspect of influence. It can also be seen as a partial reflection of the kind of influence relationship a firm has with the government. If a firm is fully aware of what the government can do for it, it will be quicker to perceive problems than a firm which does not include the government in its 'life space'. In the terminology of Lewin–a person's situation is partially dependent on his perception of the environment (Lewin, 1952, p. 239). We discussed this more fully in Section 5.1. The (latent) anticipation of one's own influence, therefore, can be expressed in the number of problems.

The number of individual problems are shown in Table 6.7. In the table can be seen that there are tendencies in the same direction in all the sub-samples, but the result is only significant in one of the four cases. These outcomes of the statistical testing makes the interpretation of the result somewhat difficult. Yet I consider the fact that the tendencies are consistently in the same direction to be most convincing; the hypothesis has, in my opinion, been reasonably confirmed. This interpretation is also supported by the following argument: If the three shipyard samples are combined, there is a significant difference when the Mann Whitney test is applied. Further, when the correlation coefficients are computed between the size of the firm and the number of problems–a similar check to the one applied in the previous sections–we find:

for all the shipyards $r = 0.259$ (sign. 2.5%)

for remaining firms: $r = 0.137$ (n.s.)

Table 6.7

The number of individual problems (latent anticipation)

size of firm	average number of individual problems* in sub-sample†			
(number of employees)	SS1	SS2	S3	RF
less than 100	1.27 (11)*	1.63 (8)	1.21 (24)	0.44 (34)
100 or more	1.55 (11)	2.09 (11)	1.50 (8)	1.00 (23)
total	1.41 (22)	1.90 (19)	1.28 (32)‡	0.67 (57)‡
Mann-Whitney test§	z = 0.7 (p = 0.24)	z = 1.43 (p = 0.08)	z = 0.7 (p = 0.24)	z = 1.88 (p = 0.03)
	all shipyards: z = 2.16 (p = 0.02)			

* Basis for the computation: all the firms in the sample.
† See Table 6.2 for the legend.
‡ The total number of problems is given in Table 6.1 (first column, first and third figures).
§ The computation of z can be considered a reasonable approximation (using this number of cases).

We see that the result is not significant for the remaining firms, in contrast to the difference in 'averages' (see Table 6.7). The correlation coefficient has presumably been lowered because the distribution of the problems over the size classes of firms displays irregularities in the remaining firms.[3]

Surveying the statistical tests, I believe that its results lie on the border between significant and non-significant. Combined with the consistency of the tendencies in the four sub-samples, these results justify the following conclusion:

Our hypothesis that large firms have relatively more influence than small firms is reasonably confirmed for that aspect of influence which we have called latent anticipation. This is in contradistinction to the two aspects of influence examined previously.

A reminder: the neccessity of controls – For the aspect of latent anticipation in particular objections may arise concerning the purity of the comparison. Perhaps there are a number of other factors which contribute to determining the perception of problems, and we can ask whether these factors are effective to the same degree in both categories of business firms. If, for example, all the small firms are located on large waterways, they will naturally have fewer problems than the large firms, which generally build larger ships. These possible disturbing factors must, of course, be more closely examined, and we shall consider them in greater detail in Chapter 8. We have confined ourselves until now to an overall testing of the hypotheses.

6.5 The three aspects combined: the number of effects

The number of effects (successes) with large and small firms – We concluded in Chapter 2 that the number of effects is equal *to the product of the three aspects* (tested influence, manifest and latent anticipation), namely:

$$S = T \times AM \times AL \left(= \frac{S}{IA} \times \frac{IA}{P} \times P \right)$$

This is also true for the averages of categories of firms, provided that we work with the weighted averages of T and AM.[4]

$$\frac{\sum S}{n} = \frac{\sum S}{\sum IA} \times \frac{\sum IA}{\sum P} \times \frac{\sum P}{n}$$

(with n the number of business firms)

The average numbers of successes are shown in Table 6.8. The higher average number of problems—the third aspect—in large firms is only weakly reflected in the average number of successes. In only two of the four sub-samples is the average number of successes higher for large firms than for small ones. (The difference for RF is a significant one, however, if we look at the corresponding correlation coefficient 0.236, n = 55). Now we saw earlier in our data that large firms have a greater number of problems which are not brought to a conclusion than do small firms; this may be a cause of a somewhat weak result (remember: problems and influence attempts are determined for all the problems; successes are only determined for problems which have been brought to a conclusion). With corrected (estimated) figures (based on *all* the problems), the average number of successes are higher for large firms than for small ones in all four subsamples (see the bottom section of Table 6.8).

This leads us to conclude that *the greater number of problems perceived by large firms is reflected in a somewhat greater number of*

Table 6.8
Average number of successes for all the business firms.

(number of employees)	average number of successes			
	in sub-sample*			
size of firm	SS1	SS2	SS3	RF
	SUCCESSES WHICH ACTUALLY OCCURRED:			
less than 100	0.55 (11)	0.75 (8)	0.33 (24)	0.15 (34)
100 or more	0.46 (11)	0.82 (11)	0.13 (8)	0.48 (23)
total	0.50 (22)	0.79 (19)	0.28 (32)	0.28 (57)
	SUCCESSES WHICH WOULD PRESUMABLY HAVE OCCURRED IF ALL THE PROBLEMS WERE BROUGHT TO A CONCLUSION†			
less than 100	0.70 (11)	1.01 (8)	0.39 (24)	0.27 (34)
100 or more	0.78 (11)	1.36 (11)	0.50 (8)	0.80 (23)
total	0.76 (22)	1.24 (19)	0.40 (32)	0.48 (57)

* See Table 6.2 for a legend of the symbols.
† Successes which have actually occurred are, of course, based only on problems which (via influence attempts) have been brought to a conclusion. *All* the problems are used as a basis for estimating the presumable number of successes in the bottom section of the table. The figures seen in the table are obtained by multiplying the number of problems with the *actually*-occurring fractions for tested influence and manifest anticipation— $(S_{estimated} = T \times AM \times AL)$.

successes for the former. This tendency is strong for the remaining firms, and rather weak for the shipyards.

This difference between shipyards and remaining firms becomes even more evident when we use another standard for the total successes: the government expenditures per employee, computed this time with the employees in *all* the firms (not only with those in firms with influence attempts as for tested influence). These expenditures for small and large firms

were f 1633 and f 158 respectively for shipyards,
and f 1271 and f 4861 for remaining firms.

To summarize: the three influence aspects can be combined through multiplication into one index: the number of successes. We have seen that there is only minimal support for our hypothesis using this index. There has most certainly been no definite confirmation.

Retrospect – Again: why aspects of influence? – Why has the concept of influence been separated into three aspects when, as we have just shown, they can so easily be combined into one standard? A reason given in Chapter 2 was that the separate aspects could illuminate the background of the achieved effects. With the results before us, we can now reexamine this argumentation and supplement it with reasons of a more practical and methodological nature. I believe that it is definitely preferable to treat each aspect separately for the following reasons:

(1) *More precise application of 'controls'.* The two anticipation aspects are clearly localized in the 'requesting' actor in the influence relation; the 'tested influence' aspect is associated with the deciding actor. While introducing further refinements to the overall methods of testing used until now, we must hold other variables constant. It is, however, highly possible that these other variables are not the same for the petitioner and the decision-maker. Controls can therefore be more effective when they are applied for the three aspects separately.

(2) The *practical interest* in the separation is actually obvious. Because the different aspects are associated with the different actors in the influence relationship, it can be clearly seen which actor is the cause of possible differences in influence. Or, stated in terms of a strategy for change: if the results are known, then it is also known which actor must be changed to level out the observed differences – if, at least this is the goal. Seen in the light of our results, this means that, considering that virtually no difference in the tested influence was observed, there is no reason to assume that the large firms in our sample are preferentially treated by the government. On the other hand, the number of

perceived problems was different for large and small firms. If the overall outcomes in connection with influences are to be changed, therefore, either the large firms will have to perceive fewer problems, or the small firms will have to perceive more (or the latter group must become conscious of its situation, to use an old, but these days again fashionable, phrase). In short, the division into aspects makes it possible to determine in which category of firm a change must take place, and what kind of change this should be (assuming that a change is desired).

(3) *Localizing the uncertainties in the operationalization.* The tested influence and the manifest anticipation were determined using indices of a 'relative' nature. This has important advantages. Even if through external circumstances the absolute number of influence attempts and problems respectively are highly divergent for the various categories of firms, the possibilities for comparing within the two aspects are not severely endangered. The case is of course different with the third aspect–the absolute number of problems. A relative index *could* also be constructed for this aspect: for example, the number of perceived problems divided by the number of problems that people 'objectively' should have. A panel of experts might be consulted, but their judgement would at the most be intersubjective–and besides, such a panel was not available for our investigation. In Chapter 8 we will nevertheless see that at least one other method exists. Yet the third aspect still remains the weakest link in the chain.

Now the combination of aspects is naturally also formed using this link. The choice is therefore between one total index containing a weak link, lessening the reliability of the index as a whole on the one hand, and three separate aspects, only one of which is relatively weak, on the other. The proper choice seems obvious.

6.6 Summary of the overall testing

The testing of the hypothesis, 'in solving their individual problems, business firms have the more influence on the government, the larger they are in size', produced the following results:

(a) There were no differences exhibited in the 'tested influence' between small and large firms. For shipyards, neither the percentages of influence attempts, nor the government expenditures per employee indicate a confirmation of the hypothesis; for 'remaining firms' only the government expenditures per employee point in the predicted direction. It can justifiably be concluded that government decisions clearly do not give preferential treatment to large firms (nor do they to small firms).

(b) The manifest anticipation of the firm is not dependent on the size of the firm when the percentages of problems with influence attempts are used as an indicator. The probability that a firm with a problem will make an influence attempt is about equal for large and small firms–but the large firms do make more expensive requests. The government expenditures requested per employee are higher for large firms. As we have seen with tested influence, the government does not, however, comply with these more weighty requests.

The findings with regard to tested influence and manifest anticipation differ sharply from those of a study by Salomon and Siegfried (1977). It should be kept in mind, however, that these investigators omitted the *influence process* from their research. They also made no distinction between individual problems and problems of more than one firm (see also Chapter 7).

(c) The hypothesis *is* confirmed for latent anticipation, using the average number of problems as an index: the large firms do have slightly more problems, which is also reflected to some extent in the absolute number of successes.

Summarizing, we find that our hypothesis–which seemed to be so cut and dried–is only reasonably confirmed for one of the three aspects. I reiterate that these conclusions are primarily applicable for influence which is exercised to obtain advantages for oneself, and for decisions which are concerned with the material facilities for transport by water.

Notes

1. This is only true for the specification of influence which I have used in this investigation: influence by which someone is pursuing, at least in part, advantage for himself, and in which no anticipation of the government is involved (see Chapter 2).
2. Without the amount received per employee, not shown here, being any greater.
3. This can be illustrated with the category of problems relating to the material facilities for transport by water, which will receive the most attention in later chapters. The average number of water-transport related problems for the five size-classes of remaining business firms are:
   0–50 employees: 1.31 (n = 19)
   –100 employees: 0.87 (n = 15)
   –200 employees: 2.20 (n = 5)
   –500 employees: 0.60 (n = 10)
   >500 employees: 2.50 (n = 8)
4. See p. 129 for an explanation of the difference between weighted and unweighted averages.

7. Non-individual Problems

Problems involving interests of more than one business firm and coalitions; the role of interest organizations and government agencies at lower levels

7.1 Statement of the problem and operationalization

The level of the individual business firm and the level of the coalitions – Up to now I have investigated the influence of business firms on the government using individual problems. The concept of influence encompassed in this phase of the investigation was fairly unambiguous (see Chapter 3, Section 3.3). Our in certain respects unexpected results provide a strong impulse for also considering non-individual problems. It is certainly conceivable that large firms prefer to use non-individual problems as a vehicle for part of their influence. It is, after all, often assumed that influence tends to be disguised, and non-individual problems could provide a good cover. If large firms were much more likely to disguise their intentions in this way, then we might have a partial explanation of why large firms do not have more influence than small ones for individual problems (at least for two of the three aspects of influence).

We explained earlier that when we enter the realm of non-individual problems it becomes difficult to speak of influence of individual firms; as soon as there is more than one interested party, the assignment of influence becomes very difficult. Yet it does seem vitally important that this category of problems be included in our analysis; we cannot, however, always use the term influence in this new context.

As we explained in Section 3.3, two aspects must be distinguished in the analysis of non-individual problems: one at the level of the individual firm, and one at the level of the coalition as a whole.

(a) The level of the *individual business firm*. Though the term influence cannot validly be used here, it *is* important to find out whether or not differences exist in the *gains* which large and small firms obtain *via coalitions* (or, in other words, successes via coalitions). We therefore formulated the following sub-hypothesis, parallel to our basic hypothesis (2B): *The larger a business firm which participates in a coalition attempting to exercise influence on the government, the more* '*gains via coalitions*' *it will obtain* (see Chapter 3, p. 61). The testing of this hypothesis is discussed in Section 7.2.

(b) The level of the *coalition as a whole*. At this level we can still validly use the term influence. The hypothesis covering this aspect is then simply: *The greater the size of a coalition of business firms, the greater the influence it will have on the government in solving the common problems of its members* (Hypothesis 2A; see Chapter 3).

The data on which our testing of both hypotheses is based is *the set of problems which involve the interests or more than one firm* (abbreviated Pom). This is used as a basis for the existence or non-existence of coalitions; the result is a *set of coalitions*.

A few remarks should be made about the sample. As we have seen, the research design was primarily constructed to test the hypothesis about influence exercised in an effort to solve individual problems. Are our samples suitable for testing an hypothesis based on Pom's and coalitions?

The answer seems to me to be yes for Pom's. The individual business firm still remains as the unit of analysis here.

The answer is much harder to find for coalitions. After all, social units are involved here which are totally new elements in the social world. They arise, exist for a certain period of time, and fade away into nothing. Questions like: 'what is the theoretical universe of coalitions'? and 'what are the conditions for their coming into being'? would certainly need to be closely examined (compare with the origins of collective actions, Braam and Swinkels, 1969). The precise characteristics of a coalition must be enumerated – a far from simple task. Special procedures must be followed in selecting units in the sample to ensure that the majority of firms comprising each coalition is investigated (compare with Coleman, 1959, who cites the familiar 'snowball technique', among others).

This complex of difficult problems, can, I believe, best be approached in the following way:

(1) We will consider only those coalitions in which at least one of the firms already in our sample is involved. A narrow interpretation must therefore be given to our hypothesis about the influence of coalitions. There is no attempt being made to obtain a sample of coalitions as such; we are only concerned with coalitions here to the extent that they acted as a 'super-structure' of individual business firms in the sample.

(2) We have observed only one characteristic of coalitions: their size, indicated in number of employees.

(3) We made only limited use of the snowball technique. We only consulted firms not in our original sample when some piece of

information about the influence process was vitally needed. These firms were then added to the original sample. This occurred several times for the 'remaining firms', and almost never for the shipyards. This was, of course, no problem in the 'remaining firm' sample, since it had been originally drawn anyway using '*a priori*' information.

To summarize, the following points must be considered for an accurate appraisal of the range of generalization of results obtained in this chapter:
- to the extent that the individual business firm is our point of reference, the results are subject to no other restrictions than those which were applicable to influence exercised to solve individual problems;
- conclusions concerning coalitions are subject to one additional restriction; they do not apply to a hypothetical set of coalitions, but only to *a set of coalitions in which at least one firm from our sample was involved.* Therefore we make no claims that coalitions as such have been investigated.

Operationalization of 'coalition'; coalitions and collective actions (or movements) – Pom can be operationalized simply as: all the problems of business firms which are not individual. The distinction between individual and non-individual problems has already been drawn in detail in Section 5.5, making further comment here unnecessary. One particular point should be noted here, however: When more than one firm has an interest in solving a common problem, this only implies that at least one firm is present in our sample. It is perfectly possible that the other interested firms are *not* included. We will embellish upon this presently.

But first, the operationalization of 'coalition'. The presence of a Pom does not always mean that the firms involved will actually perform as a coalition. We circumscribed a coalition as follows (see also Figure 7.1):

A – An influence attempt must have taken place.

B – One of the following states of affairs must exist:

    a The business firms must all be aware of the fact that their problem is shared by *the other firms* involved; in addition, they have undertaken the influence attempt *concurrently*, and the attempt has preferably been directed toward the *same government agency* (thus several questions in the interview had to be included to obtain three different types of data).

    b The firms have undertaken an influence attempt' *together*. A question was posed about such an attempt in the interview. At

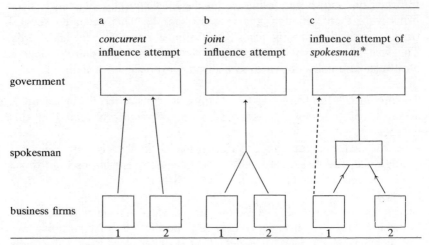

* The dotted line indicates that a firm sometimes makes an influence attempt parallel to, but more or less independent of, the spokesman.

Figure 7.1
The three cases considered to be coalitions

       least one interested firm must have reported this joint influence attempt.

c   The Pom must have been 'adopted' by an organization; this organization then acts as a *spokesman* (see Chapter 3). It then undertakes an influence attempt itself, sometimes with and sometimes without influence attempts of the interested firms. Interest groups or lobbies are not the only organizations which can function as spokesmen. Municipal governments and even provincial agencies also promote the interests of the firms located in the area under their jurisdiction. *Ad hoc* interest groups which are especially formed to further the particular interest of the coalition also fall into this category of spokesmen. These spokesmen were tracked down, interviewed when necessary; and the data thus obtained were coded.[1]

This completes the operationalization of the concept 'coalition'.

In addition to 'coalitions', *collective actions* (or movements) will also be afforded consideration. No sharp distinction can be made between these two types of joint action (compare Coleman, 1973, p. 60 ff). A collective action can best be described as a *special case* of a coalition in which:

1.   the number of firms involved is rather large (at least eight, although this number is rather arbitrary),

2. the element of representation through committees and so forth is very pronounced,
3. the problems of some members are rather diffuse,
4. the emotional character is marked.

The basic data – Once more I emphasize the importance of the following points:
(1) a coalition must include *at least one business firm from the sample;* of course, firms not present in the sample can also be found in the same coalition. There are likewise no Pom's from the latter group present in 'our' set of coded Pom's (there is further only very limited information available concerning the firms not included in our sample);
(2) one and the same Pom can occur in different firms in our sample, and it is coded each time it appears.

We must therefore distinguish between
(a) – the set of Pom's *as a whole* – this consists of the total number of coded Pom's (thus including duplications; see Table 7.1);
(b) – the set of separate Pom's (no duplications).

Table 7.1 reviews the total number of Pom's coded, and the number of separate Pom's which appear in our material.

7.2 The individual business firms and their gains via coalitions

Three aspects again: number of problems, participation in coalitions, gains via coalitions – The hypothesis restated at the beginning of this chapter is our point of departure for the analysis of gains obtained via coalitions. This hypothesis predicted that large firms would obtain more 'gains' via coalitions than small firms. The term 'gains' is preferred to 'influence' because the latter term is difficult to apply to Pom's. Yet when their formal characteristics are considered, they are highly analogous – if, at least, gains are interpreted broadly enough. This can be seen, for example, if we look at the antecedent processes upon which the gains which a firm can obtain via coalitions are dependent. We must then look *beyond* the contributory factor of the number of coalitions which have been successful to the *number* of Pom's that a firm has. The Pom's are as it were the starting points at which gains may be initiated. Next we have to consider the proportions of Pom's which end up in coalitions (abbreviated: *participation in coalitions*). Three aspects can again be distinguished. (The three aspects of influence should be sufficiently familiar by now to consider them here in

Table 7.1
Review of problems which can be of interest for more than one firm (Pom)

		total number of *codings*
the number of *separate* Pom's each involving at least one firm from the sample is:	85	
of these are coded:		in the business firms:*
in 1 firm:	56	56
in 2 firms:	19	38
in 3 firms:	6	18
in 4 firms:	1	4
in 5 firms:	1	5
in 6 firms:	2	12
total *separate* Pom's:	85	total Pom's 133
of these can be classified as coalitions:		
– spokesmen:	32	
– other coalitions:	32	
total coalitions:	64	
Pom's which could not be coded as coalitions:	21†	

*These figures are obtained by simply multiplying the two columns of numbers on the left side of the table.

†The computations carried out in the following section are based on the coalitions. For several computations, *all* the Pom's can also be used. Though we did carry out some of these alternative computations, their results have not been reported here because they did not deviate from what will be presented shortly.

the reverse order of the previous chapter; this means that we must begin with the least well-known aspect of influence, but hopefully also bring with it an improvement in the logical structure of our argument:

a   the *number of Pom's* of a business firm

= Pom

(compare with latent anticipation for individual problems)

b   the *proportion* of a firm's Pom's that winds up *in a coalition* (that is, for which the firms participate in coalitions)

$$= \frac{(\text{Pom}) \text{ in C}}{\text{Pom}}$$

(compare with manifest anticipation for individual problems) c   *gains via coalitions: the proportion of all the coalitions* in which a firm participates which has *success*

$$= \frac{S}{(Pom) \text{ in } C}$$

(compare with tested influence for individual problems)

The total number of successes that a firm achieves via a coalition is once again equal to the product of the three aspects:

$$S = Pom \times \frac{(Pom) \text{ in } C}{Pom} \times \frac{S}{(Pom) \text{ in } C}$$

It is here also perfectly permissible to work with weighted averages of a category of firms. A $\sum$ must then be placed in front of each term in the formula, and two terms must be divided by n, the number of business firms.

$$\frac{\sum S_B}{n} = \frac{\sum Pom}{n} \times \frac{\sum (Pom) \text{ in } C}{Pom} \times \frac{\sum S_B}{\sum (Pom) \text{ in } C}$$

(S_B is the number of successes of business firms, *not* that of coalitions).

It should be kept in mind that there may be duplications contained in any or all of the terms. For example, if the same Pom occurs for two firms in the sample, then it will be present twice in $\sum$ Pom. This follows from the fact that a successful influence attempt via a coalition results in a 'gain' for more than one firm.

We can now proceed to the testing of these three aspects of our investigatory material. Note that no tests of significance are used in this section. This is impossible because, as I just explained, the units involved are not independent. For example, two successes for business firms can be attributable to one success of a coalition. The utmost caution is therefore called for in reaching conclusions on the basis of our data.

Results

(a) *The number of Pom's per firm.* The average number of Pom's for small and large firms is:

small shipyards: 0.70
large shipyards: 0.94
small 'remaining' firms: 1.15
large 'remaining' firms: 1.57

The same trend as with individual problems is evident here. Large firms have slightly more problems (Pom's) than small ones in both samples.

(b) *Participation of large and small firms in coalitions.* The degree to which a firm participates in coalitions is a factor contributing to his likelihood of receiving 'gains'. We must therefore determine whether or not large and small firms display different tendencies in this respect. Stated simply, the question is: 'Given that they both have a Pom, do large firms participate more often in coalitions than small ones'? Before the participation in coalitions can be determined, it must be known which of the Pom's have become involved in coalitions. This has been carried out by the operationalization of coalitions. On the basis of these data, the results are as follows:

small shipyards have 30 Pom's; in coalitions are 25 (83%)
large shipyards have 28 Pom's; in coalitions are 22 (79%)
small 'remaining' firms have 39 Pom's; in coalitions are 32 (82%)
large 'remaining' firms have 36 Pom's; in coalitions are 29 (81%)

We can conclude on the basis of these figures that participation in coalitions is about the same for large and small firms. Here, as well, the same tendency is evident as with the individual problems.

(c) *Gains via coalitions.* This has been defined as the proportion of all the coalitions in which a firm participates that is successful. We begin by determining for each category of business firm the total number of coded Pom's that appear in a coalition. We then determine the number of these Pom's that has been involved in a successful coalition. Thus the percentage of 'gains via coalitions' is:

$$\frac{\text{number of successful Pom's}}{\text{total number of coded Pom's in coalitions}} \times 100$$

I would like to call attention here to the fact that it is practically impossible to convert these successes into government expenditure per employee. To accomplish this, the sample would have to be expanded to include all business firms which appear in coalitions. These new firms, however, will also appear in coalitions. These new firms, however, will also appear in new coalitions, for which the government expenditures would also need to be known. This is feasible, but then another sample would have to be drawn with a much greater density.

The percentage of successes obtained via coalitions is presented in Table 7.2.

Table 7.2
Percentage of successes (gains) via coalitions

size of firm (number of employees)	percentage* of Pom's that appear in a successful coalition†	
	SHIPYARDS	REMAINING FIRMS
less than 100	67 (11)	38 (12)
100 or more	44 (16)	72 (10)
total	55 (27)	56 (22)

*The computations are based on all the firms with at least one Pom that has been brought to a conclusion and which have become involved in a coalition (the numbers of firms are in parentheses); the bases of the percentages are the numbers of Pom's appearing in coalitions which *have been brought to a conclusion.*
† The percentage of successes of *all* the Pom's can also be computed – that is, including the Pom's which have not been made part of a coalition. The results are virtually identical with the figures shown in this table, and have therefore not been presented separately.

For shipyards, as was the case for the tested influence for individual problems, the hypothesis has not been confirmed here (there is even a slight tendency in the opposite direction).

There is, on the other hand, a definite difference between large and small 'remaining' firms in the direction predicted by the hypothesis. The percentage of gains is twice as high here for large firms as it is for small ones. Thus this result is only marginally analogous to the tested influence for individual problems (the hypothesis was only somewhat confirmed for tested influence when the government expenditure per employee was used as a basis for judgement).

Some hard thinking is needed to reconcile these contradictory results. In the first place, I tend to attach the most importance to the shipyard results, because that sample was drawn using the most unbiased procedures. This was less true of the sample of remaining firms, making it possible that a number of firms – and especially small ones – which received benefits via coalitions, have wrongly not been included in our sample.

To probe more deeply into this problem, let us examine once more the basic structure of the relationship between individual business firms and coalitions. Reading from Figure 7.2, we can make the following observations:

1 – the coalitions 'cover' all the firms in our sample, with no exceptions; as soon as one firm from the sample had taken part in a coalition, this coalition was coded as such;

2 – the reverse, however, is far from true – the firms do not completely

*firms in
the sample*

*firms not in
the sample*

coalitions

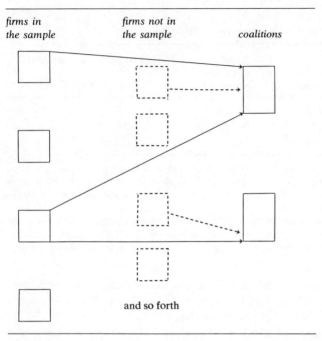

and so forth

Figure 7.2
Coalitions seen with respect to firms within and outside the sample

'fill' the coalitions; many firms outside the sample are also members of a coalition. In other words: the firms from our sample constitute only a subset of all the firms in the coalitions.

The latter point can have repercussions for the distribution of benefits among the firms *within* the sample. The crucial factor, in my opinion, is the way in which the sample has been drawn. If procedures have been followed which were precisely laid down in advance – as was the case with the shipyard sample – then there is very little likelihood of distortion. If, however, we must depend on hearsay evidence, as was the case for the 'remaining' firms (for compelling practical reasons), then the probability of distortion is greatly increased. The key informants that we interviewed might, for example, have had the personal conviction that large firms obtain more gains via coalitions than small firms – that is, identical to my hypothesis. Consciously or unconsciously, this belief may have an effect on their listing of firms that have had problems. More specifically: large firms which benefit from coalitions usually have a higher visibility than small firms whose problems are solved through this mechanism.

Thus conclusions concerning the remaining firms must be accepted with some reservations which I have not been able to remove. This topic does provide one more unequivocal demonstration of the importance of unbiased sampling, especially in investigation of such a complex concept as influence.

In spite of the reservations just revealed, the results obtained for the remaining firms are not entirely compromised. We saw under point b, after all, that large and small firms participate to an equal degree in coalitions (based on Pom's). The question whether or not equal participation in coalitions results in equally distributed gains is then still a meaningful one, in spite of any criticism of our methods just cited. I believe that the results must be accepted for what they are, namely: *that the gains via coalitions do not differ for large and small firms under some conditions, and that they do differ, on the other hand, under other conditions.*

What, exactly, these conditions are would need to be investigated separately. A central theme of such an investigation would be the determination of the extent to which a less satisfactory comparability of the business firms also has repercussions for the resulting distribution of influence (note that in our 'homogeneous' sample influence was equally distributed). Another factor might be the distance between firms; virtually all our 'remaining' firms are located at small geographical distance from one another within a community or region.

Summary – In this section we have discussed the extent to which large firms reach more successes via coalitions than small firms.

Three aspects were investigated:
(1) the average number of problems of more than one firm (Pom); as in the case of individual problems, large firms have a slightly higher average than small ones;
(2) the participation in a coalition when a Pom is present; we found no differences for this aspect;
(3) the gains via coalitions; for the shipyards there was no tendency in the direction predicted by the hypothesis. For the remaining firms, on the contrary, the large firms had a higher percentage of successes than the small firms. When compared with the results for tested influence, based on individual problems, this outcome leads one to suspect *that large firms acting through coalitions are slightly more likely to be favored by government decisions than when they acted individually;* though this is apparently only true under certain conditions. There are, in my opinion, urgent practical reasons for discovering as soon as possible exactly what these conditions are.

7.3 The relationship between influence of coalitions and their size

Influence of coalitions – We move on now to the influence of coalitions, that is, to a discussion at 'group level', leaving the individual business firms behind us.

The hypothesis formulated in Chapter 3 was: 'The greater the size of a coalition of business firms, the greater the influence it will have on the government in solving the common problems of its members'. The delineation of a coalition has been given in Section 7.1. We saw in Table 7.1 that of the eight-five different Pom's,

64 were classified as coalitions;

61 of these could be used for testing (three cases were incomplete or ambiguous); in

37 of these 61 coalitions the influence attempts were brought to a conclusion.

The index of the size of the coalition is the *number of employees of all of the firms participating in the coalition* (therefore also including the employees of the firms outside the sample; this made it necessary for us to collect this information separately).

This relationship between the size of the coalition and its influence is shown in Table 7.3.

There does seem to be a definite tendency for the relative number of successes to increase along with the size of the firm. Although the numbers involved are too small to allow us to draw a definite conclusion, I believe that these results provide a *reasonably good confirmation of the hypothesis*. This result points in the same direction as that of Salomon and Siegfried (1977). This is contrary to what we saw with

Table 7.3
Size of coalitions in relation to compli-ance with their influence attempts

| size of coalition | success | |
(number of employees)	no	yes
less than 100	1	1
100–499	7	6
500–999	2	4
1000–2499	3	7
2500–4999	1	2
5000 and more	0	3
	14	23

individual problems (Chapter 6); it should be stressed that these authors made no distinction between the individual level and the level of coalitions.

The logical question at this point is why size plays a role in obtaining successes here when it did not in the hypotheses which were tested earlier in the investigation. There are two possibilities:

(1) The fact that the firms acted *as a coalition* may have been the crucial factor. In other words, the factor of size only begins to have an effect when it is associated with a coalition (a possibility which we already touched upon in Chapter 3, p. 57).

(2) The absolute number of employees that are involved in coalitions is much greater. Yet if this were a decisive factor, the very large firms in our sample should also have more influence in solving their individual problems (note again that the very large concerns, or multinationals, are represented in our sample by some of their component subsidiaries). We saw in Section 6.2 that this was not the case. The boundary there between large and 'very large' firms was drawn at 500 employees. We see in Table 7.3, however, that *coalitions* do begin to be more effective, beginning at the 500 employee level.

This does seem to be an initial, if still a somewhat weak, indication that the first explanation is the more plausible one: 'size' only begins to play a role in achieving effects when there is a coalition. One reason supporting this explanation is that an essential aspect of a coalition is a certain *degree of organization among* the firms. The results to be analyzed below also support this supposition. Finally, it will be shown in Chapter 10 that interest organizations are important factors in the influence relationship, even for individual problems.

The role of spokesmen for coalitions – The final question to be considered is whether or not the success of the influence attempt is at all affected by the action of spokesmen. Note that there are spokesmen of every hue: *ad hoc* interest groups, advisory committees, chambers of commerce, large-scale interest organizations and lobbies, municipal and sometimes even provincial governmental administrations. The term 'interest organization' as it is commonly understood is too narrow to cover all these gradations. I will therefore use the term 'organizations' (cases in which a few firms have formed such an organization *ad hoc* are also included, if, at least, it has been given a label – for example 'Committee for this or that').

Thus the coalitions can be divided into two categories according to whether they are represented by spokesmen or not. If we compare the successes of the two categories it turns out that:

of the 22 coalitions without spokesmen, 12 were successful (55%);

of the 15 coalitions with spokesmen, 11 were successful (73%).

The spokesmen thus increase the probability of success. When the effect of spokesmen is considered separately for large and small coalitions, it is found to manifest itself solely for the smaller coalitions. The limit between large and small coalitions has been set at 500 employees. Small coalitions with spokesmen are successful three out of four times, without spokesmen, four out of eleven. For large firms, the percentage of successes is identical with and without spokesmen (eight out of eleven times in both cases).

Thus the supposition is born that the effect of organizations is primarily manifested in coalitions which are not too large; the set of data is, however, too small to provide decisive evidence.

7.4　Other results: activities from within coalitions and size of business firm (compared to collective actions)

Given that a coalition has been formed, it can be asked whether or not large and small firms differ in the amount of activity that they undertake *individually* in relation to the decision-makers. This is important, because the way in which the problem is defined by those involved, and the way in which it will be solved, can usually undergo transformations. Therefore a firm can, though working from the basis of a coalition, try to ensure that any transformations will take place to its advantage.

We tried to determine if large firms in the given coalitions take part more often in influence attempts than their smaller partners in coalitions. These influence attempts can have been undertaken individually or jointly; indirect influence attempts were not counted (an influence attempt is qualified as indirect if it takes place through the intercession of an organization). In other words, there must have been *direct contact* with the government.

It can be seen in Table 7.4 that for the shipyards the differences in percentages of influence attempts for small and large firms are very slight. The difference is somewhat greater for the other firms but not large enough to be convincing.

It is interesting to compare these results with those obtained in an earlier study of *collective actions* (Braam and Swinkels, 1969, pp. 82 ff). These collective actions were concerned with problems shared by a rather large number of large and small business firms in

Table 7.4
Percentages of influence attempts originating from coalitions

size of firm (number of employees)	percentage of influence attempts undertaken for problems in coalitions*	
	SHIPYARDS	REMAINING FIRMS
less than 100	64 (16)†	75 (18)
100 or more	68 (18)	93 (12)
total	66 (34)	84 (30)

* Bases for the computation:'
(a) all firms with at least one Pom in a coalition (also those not brought to a conclusion)
(b) all the Pom's in a coalition
† Between parentheses the number of firms

municipalities in the Netherlands. We compared the firms involved according to the channels of influence which were at their disposal – that is, their contacts with agencies of government higher than the municipal level. These channels – or, more concretely, the degrees of participation – are to a certain extent comparable with the above-mentioned influence attempts issuing from coalitions.

The differences in participation in these collective actions of large and small firms were in general fairly pronounced. Replications in other municipalities revealed similar tendencies (see in Braam, Dijkstra *et al.*, 1976). There is thus a marked difference between the outcomes for the collective actions and the coalitions.

How can these contradictory results be explained?
(1) First, it should be noted that the boundary line for the coalitions between large and small firms in the investigation was set at 100 employees; additionally firms with less than twenty employees were almost entirely absent in our sample. In the investigations of collective actions the boundaries were set much lower, often at ten employees or less. It is therefore conceivable that the *differences in contacts* with the government *only manifest themselves when the very small firms are included in the analysis.*
(2) Further, according to our definition (p. 148) the number of firms involved in collective actions is generally much greater than the number of firms participating in a coalition. Conceivably, 'when a greater number of firms becomes involved, it is primarily 'the notables', or the large firms, which act as spokesmen. *The distribution of*

'channels' should therefore be the more skewed, the greater the number
of interested firms involved
(3) A complementary factor is the essentially different characters of
a coalition and a collective action. Our impression is that coalitions
more often involve a purely business like coordination, with a certain
degree of hard-headedness as a primary characteristic. Different firms,
sharing a common problem, appeal to the government *after the problem
has been clearly defined.* The formulation of the problem usually
remains more vague in collective actions.

An example is the fishermen in various communities in Zeeland who
in 1950 already felt threatened by the proposed closing of a number of
estuaries. The definition of the problem went through various stages,
often with an attendant high level of emotionality. Waves of unrest ran
through the various villages. As happens more often in situations of a
threatening character, there may have been a tendency to turn to the
powerful elements[2] in the community to act as leaders in the struggle,
abandoning – perhaps from force of necessity – the principle of proportional representation. In this type of situation, therefore, which are
perceived as critical by all the interested parties involved, the participation of the powerful in the influence process is generally accepted as
being legitimate.

The preceding ideas have hopefully provided a reasonable interpretation of the reasons for the contradictory outcomes for coalitions and
collective actions.[3]

7.5 Summary of this chapter

Summary[4] – In this chapter we have been occupied with problems of
business firms involving the interests of more than one firm (Pom).
These problems often lead to the formation of coalitions, defined as
two or more firms which, in one way or another, *jointly* undertake an
influence attempt aimed at the government.

The analysis can now proceed on the two levels, namely the level of
independent business firms (A) and the level of coalitions (B).

(A) On the level of the individual business firms, we must adapt our
terminology, substituting *'gains via coalitions'* for influence. We can
then investigate the differences between large and small firms with
regard to this less abstract, but still highly significant variable. Three
aspects can also be distinguished here, which are analogous to the
aspects derived for individual problems. The following results for these

aspects were found from testing our central hypothesis:

	relationship with size of firm
number of problems:	yes (shipyards), yes (remaining firms)
participation in coalitions:	no (shipyards), no (remaining firms)
gains via coalitions:	no (shipyards), yes (remaining firms)

These results are virtually identical to those obtained for individual problems (with the one exception of the gains of remaining firms via coalitions).

(B) On the level of coalitions as a whole we can again use the term influence. The results give to a reasonable extent a confirmation of our Hypothesis 2A: *the influence of coalitions increases with their size.* (This result points in the same direction as those of Salomon and Siegfried, 1977. With regard to individual problems we saw in Chapter 6 that the results differed sharply. However, Salomon and Siegfried made no distinction between the level of individual firms and the level of coalitions.)

Another result was that coalitions were found to have greater influence when *spokesmen* were explicitly present (interest-organizations, for example). This is an indication that the 'degree of organization' of the coalition can be an important factor. This conclusion must, however, be regarded as provisional because the number of cases on which it is based is rather small.

We incidentally examined – given that a coalition had been formed – which activities the separate firms undertook *individually* in relation to the government. These activities, or channels of influence, can illuminate possible discrepancies in participation in decision-making. These data have much in common with those yielded by the decision or issue method. In our investigation we found *no differences* in the activities undertaken from the coalitions between small and large firms. This result contradicts findings of other studies – that is, those examining 'collective actions'. In these 'collective actions' – in which a larger number of firms were involved than in the coalitions – the larger firms usually had a much higher participation rate than the small firms.

A number of highly significant questions are raised by these contradictory outcomes for coalitions on the one hand, and collective actions on the other. Only one possible explanation is: considering that *very* small firms were often involved in collective actions (which was not the case in coalitions), it may be exactly this category which is severely underrepresented in participation; the discrepancies between large and small firms may diminish above a certain minimum of size of firm.

Considerations for further testing. Opting for individual problems – In the preceding analysis I have repeatedly maintained that I do not consider the overall testing done thus far to be conclusive. We will have to see whether or not the same results are obtained when possible 'third' factors are held constant.

We will have to look for such factors, among others, in the characteristics of the units (firms, coalitions) whose influence is under study. I have already emphasized the practical difficulties of tracing the distinguishing features of coalitions, which is for me reason enough to refrain from applying controls on that level. A supplementary reason for dropping coalitions as such in our further analysis is our decision to concentrate on influence relating to *individual problems* in the remainder of the investigation. Conceptually and methodologically we then stand on firmer ground. Thus non-individual problems remain outside our scrutiny when controls are applied in the following chapter. This limitation will not, I believe, have any serious consequences.

Notes

1. How the coalition came into being is not examined. The processes involved are very difficult to track down in retrospect, and are, in addition, of no real importance for our research problem.
2. The demands for forceful leadership in times of crisis has been commented upon before (Mulder and Stemerding, 1963 and Ellemers, 1956, pp. 51 ff).
3. It should be noted that there can be other situations besides coalitions and actions in the collective sphere which have not been investigated. Situations in which the interests are limited, or will only become manifest in the future, come first to mind. The degree of participation would in these two cases probably be much lower than in either the coalitions studies here, or in the collective actions which were cited. Further research would be welcome in this area.
4. In Chapter 3 a third hypothesis concerning the collective problems of municipalities was also presented. However, it falls somewhat outside the scope of this study. See Appendix 7A for a very brief discussion of this topic, with testing results.

8. Controls Applied to the Results:
Determinants of Problems and of Influence Attempts; Criteria Employed in Government Decision-Making

8.1 Objective of the controls and procedures used

The necessity of controls – The overall testing of the hypotheses dealt with in the preceding chapters does not yet provide conclusive evidence. The credo which primarily determined the focus of our research design was: 'Our measurements must be carried out under comparable conditions'. We therefore endeavored to obtain the greatest possible comparability of the units in the main part of the sample. Additionally, the small and large firms were 'matched' with respect to a number of factors. For the 'petitioners' we tried to 'match' the branch of industry, the region and the solitary or non-solitary status. We did the same for the decision-makers with respect to the size of the municipality, the amount of transport over waterways and whether or not located in an area of governmental regional development aid. We handled this subject-matter in Chapter 4.

In that chapter it was pointed out that controls in advance of testing almost always prove to be inadequate for covering the area under study. This is sometimes even true of laboratory experiments, and of course even more so in field research, where a number of the factors involved only can be observed during the course of the study. These newly-emerged factors must now be 'controlled' after the fact.

In this chapter it will be our task to determine whether or not the results obtained up to this point must be at least partially ascribed to possible 'third' factors.

Comparative measurement and causal relationships – A point which must be considered before we can begin to carry out controls is whether or not the relationships we are studying are causal ones.

This problem has remained in the background in the overall design of the investigation; we saw in Chapter 4 that the main focus was the achievement of *comparable measurements* of influence for different values of one condition (that is, size of a business firm). In this context, the concept of cause was superfluous.[1] We have reserved the use of the term cause for that phase of the investigation in which it is indispensible—that is, for determining influence 'per event', or, in other words, for each separate influence process.

In applying controls after-the-fact it also becomes clearly necessary to consider the role of causality in the research design as a whole. We can, of course, stick with the general formulation that we must hold all other 'relevant' conditions constant when carrying out our measurements. These conditions are those which we presume to be relevant for the variance of influence.

From a formal standpoint, such a procedure is perfectly permissible. We simply record the strength of a relationship when all other variables are held constant (compare Blalock, 1972, p. 150).

This is unmistakably an important piece of information. However, the insights which such methods can deliver are rather limited. Does, for example, the variable in question have a direct or an indirect effect? If a deeper understanding of the processes at work is the goal, then some other procedure must be used than simply holding all the variables constant.

A more refined analysis must take the following into account: *Even if a condition varies with influence, it is not always permissible to use it as a control variable.* This decision to apply controls has to be based on knowledge of the causal interrelationships of each variable with the base variables (size of firm and influence). Additional outside information—that is, whether the 'third' variable is antecedent or intervening—is therefore needed to discover exactly what these causal interrelationships are.

Extensive literature exists over this topic concerning causal inferences in non-experimental research; I will confine myself in the following section to a short discussion of points directly relevant for this study.

The selection of control variables—The primary question with which we are occupied is whether or not an established relationship is a 'spurious' one. In such a case, a relationship does exist (as evidenced, for example, by a high correlation between variables), but either our 'common sense' or our theoretical insight does not attach any importance to it. Take as a well-known example the relationship between the number of storks (A) in an area, and the birth rate of the human population (B). This relationship exists because both variables have a third, common cause—namely the degree of urbanization.

If we call the two base variables A and B, and the third variable

C–the test variable–the relationship can be schematically represented
as:

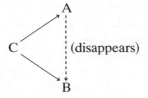

When do we conclude that a relationship is spurious? Two conditions
must be fulfilled:
(1) *When the control variable is held constant, the original relationship*
must disappear; for example, if we consider *only* rural areas, and
investigate whether the number of storks varies with the birth rate,
then no relationship must be revealed.
(2) The *added variable* must *precede in time* both the original variables; if the control variables precedes only one of the two original
ones–that is, if it is intervening–then the relationship can also disappear. The relationship in the latter case is then not spurious, but the
third variable provides an *interpretation* (Hyman, 1954, p. 287).

An equally familiar example: women car drivers are involved in
accidents less often than men. But women drive markedly fewer
kilometres than men. Schematically:

women (compared to men) $\longrightarrow$ fewer kilometres $\longrightarrow$ fewer accidents

The control variable (number of kilometres) is found in between the
two original variables, so that

Therefore the control variable here is an *intervening* variable.

How do we determine whether or not these conditions have been met?
The first–holding a control variable constant–can be carried out by
breaking down the contingency tables into sub-groups, and also by
computing partial correlation coefficients.

The latter procedure–controlling by using partial correlation coefficients has the advantage that it is clear in presentation. This clarity
becomes very marked as the number of variables increases. However,
the use of correlation coefficients can under certain circumstances lead
to faulty conclusions (depending on the nature of the distribution and

the level of measurement; see Appendix 6A). In a number of cases, therefore, we also presented the relevant contingency table. This led very seldom to different conclusions.

Such a check is unfortunately impossible for partials of a higher order because the number of cases in many investigations is too small, as it is in ours. This makes the results obtained when working with partial correlation coefficients of a higher order somewhat dubious. The reason why I have used them anyway, is simply that in a number of cases they were the only possibility open to me. An admittedly imperfect and uncertain aid was in this instance preferable to no aid at all. *However, the higher order particle must always be regarded with the necessary reservations.*

To promote the simplicity of our presentation, we have worked with correlation coefficients[2] in this chapter, only occasionally reproducing a contingency table as a further elucidation. It should be noted that the dichotomy used previously for the number of employees plays no role in the correlation coefficient. In this case, the variable 'size of business firm' is considered in its full range of variation.

One definite *restriction* is inextricably linked to this method of using partial correlation coefficients. A correlation coefficient can give no evidence of whether or not the relationship is only present *under certain conditions.* Even when the partial approaches zero, the possibility remains that there is a relationship at some particular value of the control variable–only for high values, for example (Lazarsfeld, Pasanella and Rosenberg, 1972, p. 122). This is a serious limitation, which can only be dispensed of by working with refined contingency tables. And again, this is impossible in our investigation, considering the small number of cases with which we have to work. We will just have to accept this limitation for what it is and try to make the best of it.

To examine the *second condition,* we must determine whether or not the control variable precedes both original variables in time.[3] In investigations whose design is not longitudinal, this is often difficult to ascertain. This means that we must decide for each control whether or not the temporal sequence has consequences for our conclusions.

Another point to be considered in selecting the control variables is the requirement that the control factor may not be a *dependent* variable. This precaution is especially applicable in the relationship between size of the business firm and tested influence. I will return to this point in Section 8.4.

The preceding discussion may have created the impression that in testing for spuriousness we are only concerned with those cases in which we have concluded that a relationship is *present* between two variables. This is not the case. We are equally interested in finding out if the *absence* of a relationship persists when a control variable is introduced. And cases of both types are, in fact, to be found in our investigation.

The number of control variables. Rule of thumb: economy–The following points were also considered in the selection of control variables:
(1) Control variables closely related to the size of business firms–the independent variables–should not be included, particularly when these variables are all different indicators for the same concept (Gordon, 1968, p. 593). An extreme example: the correlation between size of the business firm and the number of problems would probably disappear if we held the turnover constant. This, however, makes little sense, since turnover and the number of employees are highly correlated with one another, and can both be seen as indicators for 'size of the business firm'. Even if the two correlated variables are clearly indicators for distinctive concepts, then it should be realized that the partials computed for them can be subjected to considerable sampling errors (this is the problem of 'multicollinearity', Blalock, 1964, pp. 87 ff.).
(2) The latter point must also be considered when carrying out more than one control simultaneously–higher order partials (see especially Gordon, *op. cit.*, p. 594). The probability of random fluctuation is very great when highly correlated control variables are used.[4]

The logical consequence is that, particularly when computing partials of the higher order, the number of variables used should be restricted to those which are strictly necessary. This number can, for example, be reduced using factor analysis. This technique allows us to discover how many factors 'actually' are the basis of a greater number of variables. The decision how many variables–or combinations of variables–will be used in this next phase of the analysis can therefore partially be based on the outcomes of this factor analysis. Though we have made use of this technique, it was not the only point considered in choosing the control variables; I also considered conceptual arguments. The reason for this is that, under the special conditions under which our investigation has been set up, factor analysis can be of only limited value. The investigation has not been designed to determine the relationships between control variables. The correlations which are found to exist in our material may have some wider significance, but this is far from certain. Their only positively valid application is within the limits of our particular sample. This is all the more true in our investigation, because our sample has been drawn in a highly specific way. Under such circumstances, no technique is capable of bringing to light 'general theoretical' factors. For this reason, the factor analysis used here is nothing more than an–admittedly very helpful–aid.

Control per aspect of influence–The results of our tests of the hypothesis, presented in Chapter 6, are not the same for all the different aspects of influence. If only for this reason, therefore, controls should be carried out for each aspect *separately*, that is, for each of the three relationships:

size–number of problems
size–fraction of problems with influence attempts
size–fraction of influence attempts with success

The perception of problems and the undertaking of influence attempts are matters involving the 'petitioning' party. Compliance, on the other hand, which determines the third aspect of influence, primarily involves the 'decision-maker'. This is another reason why the controls must be carried out separately for the different aspects since different factors play a role in the processes surrounding these two parties (see Chapter 6).

The choice of a set of problems for further testing–The further testing of two of the three influence aspects will be based on individual problems. The testing of latent anticipation, however, will be carried out using all the problems related to material facilities for transport by water. Thus:

latent anticipation:	problems related to material facilities for transport by water (individual and non-individual)
manifest anticipation:	individual problems
tested influence:	individual problems

A different set of problems has been chosen for latent anticipation for the following reason: Controls must be applied for the relationship between size of the business firm and the number of problems. In such a case, the control variables are related to factors which cause someone to see, or fail to see, a problem. But it only makes sense to hold such factors constant if the possible problem situations are comparable. It would, for example, be pointless to hold the largest ship built (abbreviated LSB) constant for problems totally unrelated to material facilities for transport by water. It thus seems rather obvious that only problems relating to these facilities for water transport should be included (remember that a small fraction of the problems were related to other matters).

This decision also effects the next one, which is to include *both* individual and non-individual problems. When a number of factors combine to cause a problem, it may be a matter of chance whether the problem will be individual or non-individual (specifically: the presence or absence of other firms dependent on waterways, and the pattern of waterways in the wider environment). A failure to include non-individual problems would therefore be likely to lead to distortions of the results.

An entirely separate question is whether or not we can carry out operations on the designated set of problems (that is, problems which are related to the material facilities for transport by water respectively individual problems) while ignoring further distinctions according to strength of the interest, extent of the costs for the government, and so forth. I have usually refrained from making these distinctions in order to avoid reducing the number of cases unnecessarily. For a more complete justification of this decision see Appendix 8A.

8.2 Determinants of problems related to the material facilities for transport by water and controls on the relationship size of the business firm-latent anticipation (number of problems)

Size of the firm and number of problems – We saw in Chapter 6 that there was a correlation between the size of the business firm and the number of individual problems for all the sub-samples (see Section 6.4 for one minor restriction).

We found the same tendencies present for *non-individual problems* (see Chapter 7).

As stated previously, the following analysis will focus primarily on the category 'problems relating to the material facilities for transport by water'. Here as well there is a relationship between size of the firm and number of perceived problems. The averages are:

for small and large shipyards respectively: 1.28 and 2.07 problems
for small and large remaining firms respectively: 1.12 and 1.61 problems.

Is the number of problems really a reflection of latent anticipation? – Our intention is to measure an aspect of influence – in particular, that aspect which is based on expectations about the role of the government, and about the chances of success for any influence attempts which might be undertaken (see Chapter 5, Section 5.1). I have postulated that this anticipation finds its expression in the degree to which an actor (the firm) perceives his own 'self-interest', in which he 'anticipates latently' his own possibilities for influence. For this concept of 'latent anticipation' we are using as *indicator* the number of perceived problems (see Chapter 5).

The question to be answered, then, is actually: '*Are the differences in numbers of problems actually an expression of latent anticipation, or can the differences be explained by other factors?*'[5] In terms of our hypothesis, this means that we must examine whether the correlation between size of the firm and number of problems is in fact based on latent anticipation.

We must therefore search for factors which could explain this relationship. For example: since larger firms build larger ships, they can be expected to have more problems. The 'largest ship built' (LSB; see shortly, p. 177) can therefore explain the number of problems. To make certain that the correlation between the size of the firm and the number of problems is, in fact, due to differences in latent anticipation, we must hold a factor like this one constant (bring under control).

When this example is examined more closely, we see that it involves at least one serious difficulty. It is, after all, possible that the latent anticipation is also reflected in the size of the ships that are built, thus:

latent anticipation ⟶ LSB ⟶ number of problems

In other words, the latent anticipation can already be concealed in the control variable. This would mean that when we control for LSB, of course, the correlation between problems and size disappears *unjustly*; exaggerating somewhat: it is exactly the factor which we want to measure which is being held constant. A rigorous solution of this methodological problem would require knowledge of the order in which the variables occur in time; however, it is impossible to make any reliable estimates of this kind in this investigation.

There is, of course, a method which sacrifices some elegance but which is nevertheless effective: that is, simply by controlling for this type of variable anyway. We may then at times be testing the relationship size-number of problems too rigorously, but we are also assuring ourselves that – if the correlation is not too greatly weakened – our conclusions will only err on the side of caution. It would also seem advisable to choose a significance level of 10%.

In *this* section, we also intend to control for 'intervening' variables (p. 170). It is therefore usually *unimportant* to know exactly in what way one variable relates to the other in time. If the partial correlation between size and the number of problems disappears when a control is applied, we have gained sufficient information. The variable LSB can be used to illustrate this very nicely (provided, of course, that LSB is not itself already an indicator for latent anticipation; see p. 170). When controls are applied, the correlation can disappear for one of the two reasons discussed in the previous section:
(1) If LSB is the common cause of both the size of the firm and the number problems, then the original correlation is spurious:

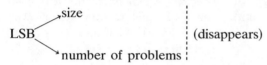

(2) If the size is the cause of LSB, and LSB is in turn the cause of the number of problems, then the correlation is 'explained':

size $\longrightarrow$ LSB $\longrightarrow$ number of problems

The cause of the problems in such a case is then not latent anticipation, but simply a technological condition.

For this aspect of influence, therefore, we will, with a very few exceptions, not concern ourselves with the order of the variables in time.

Determinants of problems: two categories of control variables – Which factors are now likely to stimulate or prevent the occurrence of problems? In other words, what are the determinants of these problems.

These determinants can be divided into two broad categories, namely:[6]

(A) factors in the realm of the *business firm* and the aspects of its *environment relating to the material facilities for transport by water* (or shortly: *water-related environment* of the firm) (see Figure 8.1);
(B) factors connected with the *socio-political environment* (see Figure 8.2 p. 181).

This categorization is comparable along broad lines with that introduced in Chapter 4 for the *a priori* controls. Here we will first consider the factors in the realm of the business firm and the aspects of the environment relating to the material facilities for transport by water.

(A) *Factors in the realm of the business firm and the environmental aspects relating to the material facilities for transport by water* – Perceived discrepancies in the situation were operationalized as problems (Chapter 5). Such a discrepancy is described simply as the *difference* between two levels – the level seen as *ideal* and the *actual* level.

The perception of a discrepancy is thus promoted by both a relatively *high* ideal and a relatively *low* actual level (see Figure 5.2). Problems can therefore be caused either by factors which make the ideal level relatively high, or by factors which make the actual level relatively low. Several more-or-less obvious factors are shown in Figure 8.1. We should, for example, expect a high level of aspiration for the economic performance of the firm (1) to result in a high *ideal* level (compare Chapter 5 p. 98).

On the other hand, the *actual* level will be lower when:
– economic performance is worse (2)
– technology 'makes more stringent demands' on environmental aspects relating to material facilities for transport by water (3); this corresponds to the *type* of business firm (indicator: percentage of new building of the total of building and repairing, abridged 'new building', see p. 176).
– the environmental aspects related to the material facilities for transport by water are already in relatively poor condition (4) (indicator: largest ship built along with the size of the waterway).

These factors, their accompanying indicators and the resulting controls applied for the relationships between size of the firm and number of water-related problems will now be discussed more fully. Our sample consists of *all the shipyards* (a different pattern of determinants would need to be worked out for 'remaining firms'). The shipyards afford the best guarantee of reasonably good comparability.

(1) *The level of aspiration in relation to economic performance* – It would be very difficult to operationalize this concept directly, because it would have to apply to the last five years. We will, however, see presently that the concept has in a way apparently 'operationalized itself'.

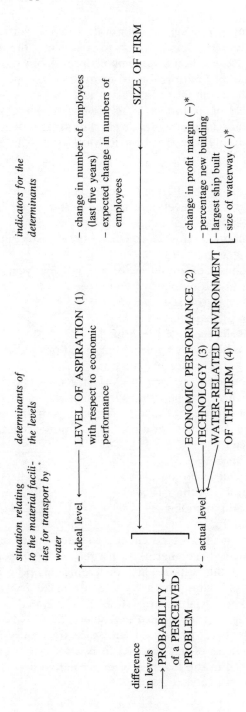

*The sign relates to the connection with the *difference* between levels (the connection with the height of the level itself has the opposite sign).

Figure 8.1
Determinants of problems: factors in the realm of the firm and the water-related environment

Aside from this point, however, it is doubtful whether controls for the factor considered here are desirable. On the one hand, the *aspiration level for influence* is, we should remember, *included* in the problems, and it is of course not permissible to control for this particular factor. On the other hand, the latter aspiration level does not have to be identical to the *level of aspiration in relation to economic performance*. If we can operationalize this latter concept separately, then it would certainly be desirable to control for it. More on this later.

(2) *Economic performance*–The better the economic performance of the firm, the higher the actual level, and the fewer the problems that would be expected to appear.[7]

Exact figures on economic performance could not be easily obtained. I worked instead with five indicators:
– the change in the number of employees in the last five years,
– the expected change in the number of employees,
– the change in turnover in the last five years,
– the change in the profit margin,
– the prospects for development of the firm.
(these indicators are based upon corresponding questions in the interview; see Appendix 8B for further explanation).

The last variables could not be used because the dispersion of the values was too small, which left us with four indicators.

A three-point scale was used for the 'expected change in the number of employees'; the other variables were pre-coded on five point scales with the following classes:
– decrease of 30% or more;
– decrease of 10% to and including 29%;
– decrease or increase of less than 10%;
– increase of 10% to and including 29%;
– increase of 30% or more.
(The variables 'change' and 'expected change' in the number of employees were incorporated, since there was no reason to suspect any resistance on the part of the respondents concerning this point.)

The next question is of course whether we cannot make do with less than four indicators. The variables are, after all, correlated to some extent with one another, as can be seen in Table 8.1.

A factor analysis was therefore carried out. An extraction of factors to the very low eigen-value of 0.2 resulted in two factors; there was virtually no change noted in the loadings after a rotation according to the Varimax criterium was carried out.

Table 8.1
Correlations of four indicators for 'economic performance' of 72 ship-yards

		1	2	3	4
1	Change in number of employees in last 5 years	1.000			
2	Expected change in number of employees	0.307	1.000		
3	Change in turnover in last 5 years	0.530	0.210	1.000	
4	Change in profit margin	−0.036	0.077	−0.017	1.000

Indicators 1 and 3 had a high loading on the first factor, indicator 4 on the second. Indicator 2 loaded high on both factors. This pattern is already visible in the correlation matrix. Factor analysis served therefore as nothing more than a check of the reasonably clear picture provided by the correlation matrix.

It is now possible to reduce the number of variables by computing factor scores. This procedure has not been followed in the present investigation, because I preferred to base any insights gained from data on the original variables. Instead, another, very simple method was used: namely, by discarding 'superfluous' indicators. In the present case, at least one indicator with a high loading on the first factor can be dispensed with. I chose the least 'hard' one, namely, the change in turnover (3).

The three remaining indicators yielded the following correlations with the *number of problems relating to the material facilities for transport by water*:
- change in the number of employees   0.282 (sign. 1%)
  in the last five years
- expected change in number of   0.158 (sign. 10%)
  employees
- change in profit margin in the   −0.141 (not significant)
  last five years

The sign of the first two correlations are the opposite of what our hypothesis would lead us to expect. Only for the third correlation are our expectations in agreement with the observed direction (the better the results, the fewer the problems).

If the *change in number of employees* is considered to be an indicator of the *level of aspiration* rather than of company performance, than a logical final picture results, as follows:

higher level of aspiration → higher ideal level → more problems
(indicator, growth of the
number of employees)

better economic performance → higher actual level → fewer problems.
(indicator, higher profit
margin)

If this proves actually to be the case, then an incidental operationalization of level of aspiration has been achieved. It should be remembered, however, that this is only an interpretation after the fact, based largely on observed correlations.

Now if we control the correlation of size of the firm with number of problems for each of these indicators, the partial correlation coefficients of the first order become for:
– change in number of employees in the last five years: 0.277
– expected change in number of employees: 0.331
– change in profit margin: 0.311.
None of the controls causes the correlation to disappear (the critical value at a 5% level of significance is 0.195 for a first order partial). This provides a satisfactory answer to our question of whether or not our control of the level of aspiration was justified. This question was raised because there might have been a narrow connection between the level of aspiration in relation to economic performance on the one hand and the level of aspiration in relation to influence on the other. But the latter aspect is included in the perception of problems. If this narrow connection does exist, then the control on the first two variables would have caused the correlation to disappear unjustly. However, the correlations remained, and thus our fears were unfounded.

(3) *Technology* – Another factor in the realm of the business firm is the amount of *new building* as compared to *repairing*. The trend since the second world war has been to use increasingly large ships (of course, in recent years this trend has drastically come to a halt). It seems highly plausible that this tendency has caused more problems for shipyards primarily oriented toward building than those primarily concerned with repairing existing ships. Yards oriented toward reparations can, after all, work on the entire scale of ships, including older, smaller ones–

those constructing new ships, however, are obliged per definition to concern themselves with 'the vanguard' of the shipping world.

It is therefore not surprising that we observe a significant correlation (r = 0.271) between the percentage of new building of the yard and the number of problems.

The relationship between the size of the business firm and the number of problems also remains the same here when the percentage of new building is held constant. The first order partial correlation coefficient then becomes 0.260 (significant at level 2.5%).

(4) *Water-related environment of the firm* – The question here is again whether large firms perceive more problems than small firms under the condition of an identical water-related environment. It is, however, virtually impossible to consider this environment entirely *independently* of the situation of the business firm. For example, if we hold the size of the waterway constant, we are sure to find the large firms having more problems than the small ones, because they naturally build larger ships.

This methodological problem can be solved by *concurrently* considering both the situation as it relates to the material facilities for transport by water, and the 'largest ship built'. Moreover, a *separate* control for LSB would, after all, be unwise also; even if it is assumed that all the firms build equally large ships, in actual fact, the larger firms are located more often on larger waterways. The large firms should then have *fewer* problems than the small ones. By holding constant LSB, the correlation size of the firm – number of problems would be subjected in this way to much too stringent controls. Therefore both variables have to be held constant concurrently (we will see later in Table 8.2 when we control for LSB separately that, notwithstanding, the correlation does not disappear).

The size of the waterway is coded according to the *maximum permissible tonnage* of the waterway. A conventional classification into seven classes varying from 150 to more than 2000 tons was used. The *largest ship built or repaired* (abbreviated LSB) was also placed in this scale, with the addition of one class (for very large ships). The actual measures of a ship were sometimes also taken into account – this is primarily for deviant types of ships such as dredgers, heavy lift driving cranes, derricks and so forth.

Now, if we hold both variables constant *simultaneously*, we are examining the correlation between size of the firm and number of problems, under the conditions that all the firms build ships of the same size, and are located on equally large waterways.

The second order partial correlation coefficient then becomes 0.243 (sign. at level 5%). The correlation size of firm–problems thus remains.

Another means of considering both variables simultaneously is to construct a new index which gives a direct indication of the existence of 'bottlenecks' in the systems of waterways. This index 'bottleneck' is constructed in the following way:

0: LSB smaller than the maximum tonnage of waterway
1: LSB equal to the maximum tonnage of waterway
2: LSB larger than the maximum tonnage of waterway

This index is therefore no longer directly dependent on the size of the waterway itself. It is the most direct indicator of the 'objective' situation. Based on this index, it should be possible to determine when a firm 'should' experience a problem. However, the far-from-high correlation (0.268) between 'bottleneck' and number of problems (even though it *is* significant) shows that even this 'objective' measurement is far from perfect.

When this 'objective situation' is held constant, the correlation between size of firm–number of problems still remains. The partial correlation coefficient is 0.271 (sign. at level 5%).

Finally we have to consider a final plausible explanation for the difference between large and small firms in the number of problems. The small shipyards may be confronted much less than the large ones with the phenomenon of the steadily-increasing size of ships ordered– because, for example, ships in the middle class are disappearing entirely from the market. Naturally, the large firms would then have more problems.

We have, however, indirect evidence showing that this explanation is not a correct one. The cause *for each problem* has been coded. The average number of problems that was caused by an *increased size of ships* was 0.86 for small yards and 1.06 for large ones. This can have had only a slight effect on the difference between the averages of the total number of problems relating to the material facilities for transport by water (these averages are 1.28 and 2.07 for small and large firms respectively).

Summarizing, we wanted to test whether the differences in numbers of problems actually are an expression of differences in latent anticipation, or whether they can be explained by other factors. We have found that the relationship between size of the firm and number of problems *does not* disappear when we hold constant six variables,

related to the following four factors:
1. the level of aspiration relating to economic performance
2. economic performance
3. technology
4. the water related environment (or: the environmental aspects relating to the material facilities for transport by water.)

A summary of the controls applied thus far is given schematically in Table 8.2 (for further data concerning the variables see Appendix 8B).

Table 8.2
The correlation between size of firm (Fs) and number of problems relating to the material facilities for transport by water (P) under control of factors relating to the firm (including the water-related environment) (all shipyards = 72)*

concept with corresponding variables (V)	zero order correlation		first order partial correlation** (0° order: 0.315)	
	(Fs) with V	P with V	(Fs) with P with V constant	
LEVEL OF ASPIRATION:				⎫
– change in number of employees in last 5 years	0.193^+	0.282^{++}	0.277^{++}	
– expected change in number of employees	-0.072	0.158^+	0.331^{++}	
ECONOMIC PERFORMANCE:				
– change in profit margin in last 5 years	-0.052	-0.141	0.311^{++}	sixth order 0.222^{++}
TECHNOLOGY:				
– percentage new building	0.276^{++}	0.271^{++}	0.260^{++}	
WATER-RELATED ENVIRONMENT OF FIRM:				
– largest ship built	0.425^{++}	0.372^{++}	0.187^+ ⎱ second	
– size of waterway	0.360^{++}	-0.039	0.353^{++} ⎰ order 0.243^{++}	⎭

* The sample consisted of 73 shipyards. One case was omitted because of large gaps in the information.
** $^+$ significant at the 10% level
   $^{++}$ significant at the 5% level.

I emphasize again that some of the control factors have subjected the relationship to a rather heavy test. For example, the level of aspiration relating to economic performance of the firm may already contain 'latent anticipation' of a firm's own influence. Nevertheless, the original relationship between size of firm and number of problems does not succumb to the pressures of the controls. The uncertainty about whether or not the number of problems is in fact a reflection of the latent anticipation is therefore considerably reduced.

Finally, we can hold the six variables (as indicators of the four factors) constant simultaneously by computing partial correlation coefficients of the sixth order.

While carrying out these computations, however, we must be wary of high correlations among the control factors themselves. However, this point is somewhat less important here because the factors are conceptually clearly distinct. It should therefore be sufficient to report that the highest correlation among the factors themselves is 0.435 (between percentage of new building and LSB).

The *sixth order* partial correlation coefficient is 0.222 (sign. at level 5%).

Thus the correlation size of the firm – number of problems also remains when controls are applied for six variables simultaneously.

Note–to get a broad idea of the total explanatory value of the control variables used–that the multiple correlation coefficient between P and the seven variables (including size) is 0.50. The explained variance is then 25%. So it certainly makes sense to consider still other control variables.

(B) *The second group of control factors: factors connected with the socio-political environment*–We saw in Section 5.1 that the degree to which firms become aware of their problems can depend upon their perceptions about the possibility of influence attempts. More particularly, this perception involves how the role of the government is interpreted, and what the assessment is of the probability of success.

We must now investigate which are the factors in the environment on which these perceptions can depend. We can then control the correlation of the size of the firm with the number of problems for these factors–unless, of course, this has already been done *a priori*.

Firstly, there may be stimuli present in the environment which cause firms to pay attention to certain problems. The most pronounced case is when the firm is located in an area of governmental regional development aid. It is then made explicit public knowledge that possibilities are open for receiving subsidies for projects connected with the infrastructure. There are also other stimuli of this type. We have summarized them all with the term *'climate'* (1).

Next, *the social structure* (2) can be an important factor in determining whether or not these stimuli can reach the firm easily, and conversely, in determining whether or not the firm has 'social channels' available which it can use to communicate its wishes to the government. In constructing our research design, we did try to take these types of factors into account whenever possible. We will now consider 'the environment' in greater detail. For practical reasons, we will concentrate primarily on the municipality, or the most immediate environment. There is, namely, a large body of statistical material concerning the municipalities already made available by the Central Bureau of Statistics (CBS), which can be used to form a number of indicators for climate and structure (compare Gadourek, 1967). Regions and provinces can also be taken into account as factors. For a review of the factors which will be discussed in the following pages, see Figure 8.2.

1. The 'climate' factors can be divided into the following categories:
1a the climate generated by governmental development policy (abbreviated, the governmental stimulation climate); the following variables were chosen as indicators:
   - the percentage unemployed in the municipality;
   - the net migration (municipal); abbreviated, the emigration;
   - population growth (municipal);
   - the growth of the work force in the industrial sector (municipal);
   - centrality of position of the province (broadly, whether or not located in the urban 'core' of the Netherlands, including Amsterdam, Rotterdam, the Hague, and Utrecht, and a number of smaller cities located between them);
   - area or centre of governmental regional development;
1b the general level of economic activity on the waterways; sufficient

---

1. *'Climate'*
   1a. governmental stimulation climate
   1b. level of economic activity on waterways

2. *Social structure*
   2a. relative social position of the firm
   2b. formal economic power structure (municipal)
   2c. integration *of* the environment

Figure 8.2
A review of the environmental factors

data could be obtained for one variable:
- the amount of goods (tonnage) transported over the waterway (note that the size of the waterway itself has already been taken into account in the category of the water-related environment).

2. *The social structure.* A number of different dimensions of this aspect can be distinguished. These dimensions are roughly parallel to three well-known sociological concepts, namely status, social distance and integration.

2a The *social position* of the firm. Of course, this is partly indicated already by the size of the firm. A possible refinement can be achieved by also considering the size of the municipality and the size of the province. The following variables were selected as indicators for these two aspects:
- population size of the municipality (number of inhabitants);
- number of inhabitants in the province;
- relative position in the municipality (percentage of the work force that works in the firm in the sample).

2b *The formal economic power structure of the municipality.* The primary distinction made in the literature is between a *monolithic* and a *pluralistic* power structure (see, for example, Fowler, 1964, p. 63; Aiken and Alford, 1970, pp. 651 and 656). One of the more widely-shared assumptions is: the more power is concentrated, the fewer power centers there are, and the easier it will be to make decisions (Aiken and Alford, *op. cit.,* p. 655). We are primarily concerned here with the following derivation of this thesis: the more the large firms dominate in a municipality, the more the frame of reference of the municipal officials will be likely to be shaped according to the wishes of these large firms. This can be the case, for example, in the area of employment opportunities and housing. It can also encourage compliance with influence attempts undertaken by the large firms. Cases where there is clearly a pattern of dominant large firms can be called monolithic formal power structures.

Finding an index for this 'domination', however, is more difficult. In line with other investigators, we will use the distribution of the size of the firms in a given community. It is, of course, pretentious to maintain that we are accurately measuring the 'formal economic power structure'. Nevertheless, I have maintained this terminology to emphasize that this is the ideal concept at which our approximations are aiming. The dubious validity of the indicator is painfully obvious.

The following variables have been chosen to characterize this dimension:
- the concentration of employment opportunities (the percentage of the work force working in firms of 500 employees or more; Fowler, 1964, p. 63);
- the number of firms with 500–999 employees;
- the number of firms with 1000–1999 employees;
- the number of firms with more than 2000 employees;
- the 'density' of the firms (number of firms per 1000 inhabitants; compare Fowler, 1964, p. 40 and Aiken, 1970, p. 496); roughly speaking, the power structure is more flat when the density is greater.

2c *The degree of integration of the environment.* The concept of integration–long a part of the sociological tradition–has received a very specific interpretation here. The question is whether the structure of the environment is such that a firm has easy *access* to government agencies–in other words, if there are accessible social channels in existence. When such a structure does exist, the environment can be considered to be integrated. This in turn is conducive to the integration of the firm into the wider environment (compare Stinchcombe, *op. cit.*, p. 188; Lipset, Coleman and Trow, 1954, p. 82 ff.). Various authors (Coleman, 1971,[3] pp. 673 ff.; Stinchcombe, *op. cit.*, pp. 188 ff.) have demonstrated that this integration can be enhanced by the *presence of organizations.*

I constructed two indexes to characterize the municipalities in this respect:
- general organization density; this indicator should reflect the existing 'social meeting places' where representatives of the various firms come into contact with one another and exchange ideas; we tried to include primarily those 'social meeting places' which were also open to administrators. An index was formed on the basis of three elements: the presence of industrial clubs, commercial clubs and groups which promoted the interests of more than one branch of trade and industry (compare: shopkeepers' associations); both local and regional groups were included (the data on these organizations were obligingly provided by the Chambers of Commerce);
- the presence of organizations whose primary goal was the promotion of interests in connection with the material facilities for transport by water.

In Appendix 8C can be found more details concerning all eighteen of these variables.

Table 8.3
The relationship between size of firm (Fs) and number of problems relating to the material facilities for transport by water (P) under control of socio-political environmental factors (solitary shipyards n = 40)*

concept with corresponding variable (V)	zero order correlation**		first order partial correlation (0° order: 0.323)		
	Fs with V	P with V	Fs with P under V constant		
1a GOVERNMENTAL STIMULATION CLIMATE:					
– emigration	−0.168	0.179	0.364^{++}		
– area or center of regional development	−0.189	0.167	0.366^{++}		
1b LEVEL OF ECONOMIC ACTIVITY ON WATERWAY:					
– tonnage transported	0.060	−0.165	0.338^{++}		
2a RELATIVE SOCIAL POSITION OF FIRM:					
– population size of municipality (—)	−0.005	−0.066	0.324^{++}	eighth order 0.408^{++}	fourteenth order 0.286^{+}
2b FORMAL ECONOMIC POWER STRUCTURE					
– concentration of employment opportunities (percentage of work force in firms with 500 or more employees)	0.214^{+}	0.189	0.295^{++}		
– density of firms (number of firms per 1000 inhabitants) (−)	$−0.248^{+}$	0.161	0.380^{++}		
2c DEGREE OF INTEGRATION OF ENVIRONMENT:					
– density of organizations	0.097	0.147	0.313^{++}		
– density of interest organizations concerned with material facilities for transport by water	−0.047	0.010	0.323^{++}		
– preceding six variables (Table 8.2)					

* One solitary shipyard was omitted because the municipality in which it was located had a very large population, and might have had a seriously disturbing effect on the correlation coefficients.

** $^{+}$ significant at the 10% level

$^{++}$ significant at the 5% level.

Possible correlations among these eighteen variables makes a reduction desirable here as well in order to avoid 'double' indicators. A factor analysis delivered eight factors. In the same way as previously, a variable was chosen for each factor. This selection of factors and variables proved to be a reasonably good representation of the various conceptual dimensions which were involved in our assumption about socio-political factors. The variables chosen are shown in Table 8.3.

We can now answer the question whether or not the correlation between size of the firm and number of problems remains when these variables are held constant. Here we use *solitary shipyards* only. This has the advantage that they are *all located in different municipalities.* Since most of the environmental variables are based on statistical data related to the municipality, we can ensure that one and the same enviroment cannot effect the results more than once. This is, I think, the most sound procedure, in spite of the fact that it reduces the number of cases at our disposal.[8] The unit of analysis thus remains most explicitly 'the business firm'.

The results are shown in Table 8.3. It turns out that *not one environmental variable* causes the correlation to disappear when used as a control.

The eighth order partial correlation coefficient is also significant at the 5% level.

To give a rough idea of the total 'explanatory' value of the environmental variables, a multiple correlation coefficient was again computed for P, this time for the eight environmental variables. This was equal to 0.44, with which 20% of the variation was explained.

To compare: the multiple correlation coefficient of P with the seven variables related to the business firms is 0.50 (25%) and the coefficient with all fifteen variables is 0.65 (42%). Seen in retrospect, the inclusion of the environmental variables is justified by the increase in explained variance.

Controlling for all the variables simultaneously – Fourteen control variables have been taken into account in all: six variables relating to the business firm, and eight environmental variables. We can finally examine what happens when all fourteen of these are held constant simultaneously. The fourteenth order partial is 0.286. This is not much lower than the coefficient of the zero order, and is amply significant at the 10% level.

As we have just seen, the fifteen variables (including size of the firm) explain 42% of the variance. We can therefore be confident that we have applied controls for a reasonable sufficient number of relevant variables.

A reservation: change of firm's location primarily by small firms – The number of problems of a firm can be decreased by a change of the firm's location in the past. This has occurred far more often with small firms than with large ones: fifteen of the forty-three small yards have changed locations in the past compared to three out of thirty large firms. The latter are apparently much less mobile than the former. Yet it is doubtful whether this can provide an explanation for the difference in problems in the year 1969, since fifteen of the eighteen moves were made before 1960 – some of them, in fact, a great deal earlier.

I believe, however, that the results must be accepted with some reservations: the greater mobility of small shipyards could be a reason for their having perceived fewer problems during the period of the investigation than the large shipyards.

On the other hand, it is conceivable that the number of problems of large firms have been underestimated for another reason. Interviews with firms which had a large number of problems taxed the patience of both investigators and the vice-presidents of the firms; more problems are likely to be left out in these situations.

Conclusion: size of the firm and latent anticipation – In the previous chapters, a significant correlation was found between size of the firm and the number of problems. In this section we have investigated whether or not this correlation remains when other variables are held constant. Or, in other words, we have investigated whether the number of problems is, in fact, a reflection of the latent anticipation. The variables that we held constant were therefore related to factors which could also explain how problems come into being. These factors could be divided into two categories:

(A) the firm's environment, and the environmental aspects relating to the material facilities for transport by water. Selected for consideration were:

 – the level of aspiration with respect to economic performance,
 – the economic performance of the firm,
 – technology,
 – the water-related environment (environmental aspects relating to the material facilities for transport by water): the largest ship built in

relation to the size of the waterway;
(B)   the socio-political environment:
(a1) the governmental stimulation climate,
(a2) the level of economic activity on waterways,
(b1) the relative social position of the firm,
(b2) the formal economic power structure in the municipality,
(b3) the integration of the environment.

Fourteen variables were used as indicators of these factors. The correlation between size of the business firm and number of problems remained in every case when controls were applied with these variables separately and also simultaneously. This means that it is most probably true that the greater number of problems in large firms is due to latent anticipation, and not to other factors.

In other words, the hypothesis: 'The influence aspect "latent anticipation" increases as the size of the firm increases' is more fully confirmed in this section (for shipyards only).

8.3   Determinants of influence attempts and controls on the relationship between size of the firm and manifest anticipation

*The percentage of problems with influence attempts examined more closely–*We used the percentage of problems accompanied by influence attempts as an index of the second aspect of influence, manifest anticipation (AM). The results of the overall testing showed that this percentage did not have any relationship with the size of the firm. For individual problems, the correlations between size of the firm on the one hand and the percentage of problems with influence attempts on the other were for:

all shipyards: 0.107 (n = 59);
solitary shipyards only: 0.005 (n = 37);
remaining firms: 0.232 (n = 25).

It is important to ascertain whether or not more extensive testing leaves these results standing. The basic question to be answered in this regard is whether and to what degree the interference of other factors has caused a spurious non-correlation. We will therefore attempt to discover any such factors.

In a sense, our task here is less complicated than in the previous section. There should be no problem in determining whether or not our index is, in fact, a real measure of the influence aspect under consideration here. It is certainly plausible that the percentage of problems for which influence attempts have been made is a good index of manifest anticipation. Controls can therefore be applied according to the procedures outlined in Section 8.1.

We are thus searching for other factors which contribute to determining whether an influence attempt will be made or not, assuming that a problem is already present. These factors can be divided into three groups:

a   factors related to the *business firm*,
b   factors connected with the *problem itself*,
c   factors related to the *environment*.

ad (a) and (c)–Roughly speaking, we can use the by-now familiar variables (see Section 2.4) to represent factors relating to the *business firm* and the *environment*. It is, after all, also anticipation which is actually involved here.

ad (b)–The different aspects of the problem itself must be taken into account for this aspect of influence; that is:
– the specific *interest* associated with the problem,
– the *priority* accorded the problem,
– the *possibilities for a private solution of the problem*.

The characteristic feature of these factors is that they vary not only from firm to firm, but also from problem to problem within the same firm. Partial correlation coefficients are therefore inappropriate and even impossible here; another method must be found for applying controls. Because of their relative complexity, we will consider these latter factors first.

Factors related to the problem itself: interest, priority, possibilities for a private solution–The decision-making model describing how an influence attempt comes into being (see Section 5.1) can be used as a basis for categorizing those factors which are directly related to the problem itself.

A brief review therefore follows of the conditions which must be met before a business firm undertakes an influence attempt:

A   the vice-president of the business firm must perceive that an improvement of the firm's economic performance can be obtained by
B   changing some aspect of the situation (the environment) of the firm;
C   a *private solution* must be deemed too expensive or impossible;
D   *government action* must be seen as a possible *means* of effecting

the improvement of the situation, and

E   there seems to be a reasonably high *chance of success* in persuading the government to follow the desired line of action.

A + B = perception of the problem
D + E = determination of the manifest anticipation

The point of departure, of course, is a problem that has already been perceived as such (A + B). But with this perception the *intensity* of the firm's *interest* in the problem (A) is not given. Additionally, some problems can be solved relatively easily through *private solutions* (C); for others, this is virtually impossible. It is therefore necessary to investigate whether or not a correlation between size of the firm and percentage of influence attempts also fails to materialize when these factors are held constant.

I emphasize once again that factors D and E are definitely not suited for use as controls. They are a virtually direct reflection of the *dependent* variable: manifest anticipation.

(1) *Controls for the strength of the interest in the problem and the priority given it.* The comparisons of the percentages of problems accompanied by influence attempts can be disturbed because of unequal distributions in:

the *strength of the interest* in the problem,
the *priority* given the problem in relation to other problems.

Although the priority may be closely connected with the strength of the interest, it seems useful to consider the two as separate dimensions. The differences between the two come most sharply into focus when a firm has a large number of problems involving approximately equal strengths of interests; in such a situation, the setting of priorities will often be necessary.

The *intensity of the interest is operationalized* by asking the question: 'If this problem were not solved, what would be the consequences for your firm?' The respondent could choose from five possible response categories: negligible, slight, moderate, serious, disastrous. In the first–overburdened–stage of the investigation, this operationalization was somewhat lost in the shuffle. The omission was rectified later as well as possible, but unfortunately, estimations of the interviewers had to suffice for a small portion of the problems. The measurement of this already elusive concept of 'intensity of interest' therefore leaves something to be desired. However, a reasonably reliable method for independently validating this measurement is by relating it to the *financial disadvantage* which is a consequence of the firm's problem (see Section 5.4). Of course, these financial disadvantages could only be determined for a limited number of problems.

The correlation between strength of interest and financial disadvantage (converted per employee) is:

for shipyards: 0.375 (n = 30, significant at 2.5%)
for remaining firms: 0.296 (n = 32, significant at 10%).

It can be concluded on the basis of these correlations that our scale for measuring strength of interests is a valid one, although the correlations are lower than I had anticipated.

The priority was operationalized by determining the rank order assigned to the problem in relation to all the other problems (including problems which were not relevant for influence). Here it was also necessary to depend in part on estimates.

It is inappropriate in this case to inquire into whether or not 'strength of interest' or 'priority' are intervening variables, for which controls should not be applied; they are namely to be regarded as *conditions* for which we are interested in knowing, come what may, whether a relationship does in fact make its appearance when they are held constant.

Another significant feature of the variables 'strength of interest' and 'priority' is that they cannot be held constant *for each business firm* separately. The reasoning goes as follows: one particular firm can have various problems whose strengths of interest differ. Because the scale we have constructed for strength of interests is ordinal at best, it is impossible to combine these various values into one average value.

The differences between firms in percentages of problems with influence attempts when 'strength of interest' is held constant is presented in Table 8.4. In this table the same comparison is also presented, with 'priority' held constant.

For shipyards, our conclusion that there is no difference between large and small business firms in the percentage of problems with influence attempts holds true. The differences increase somewhat when interests are strong and priority is high, but the values remain far from significant. For remaining firms, the tendency is more pronounced when *the strength of the interest is weak,* and *the priority is low. The supposition therefore arises that when less important problems are involved, the large firms undertake influence attempts more often than do the small ones.* Since this tendency was not observed for the shipyards, this supposition is only weakly supported. On the whole, therefore, the outcomes obtained after application of the controls give no reason for

Table 8.4
Manifest anticipation $(AM = IA/P)$ *controlled for the strength of the interest and the priority of the problem*

size of firm (number of employees)	percentage of problems with influence attempts (out of the total of all the individual problems per category)*			
	SHIPYARDS† strength of interest		REMAINING FIRMS† strength of interest	
	not great	great	not great	great
less than 100	61 (28)	60 (18)§	64 (9)	100 (4)
100 or more	69 (22)	75 (16)§	92 (10)	80 (7)
total	65 (48)	68 (34)	79 (19)	86 (11)
	priority		priority	
	low	high‡	low	high
less than 100	47 (10)	64 (19)	50 (4)§	100 (5)
100 or more	60 (14)	79 (13)	100 (5)§	100 (6)
total	54 (24)	69 (24)	82 (9)	100 (11)

* Computations are based on firms with at least one individual problem.
† It also holds true for this table that one and the same firm can be included in both columns because it can have problems for which their interests is strong, *and* those for which their interest is weak.
‡ A problem having high priority is one which is given a rank of 1, $1\frac{1}{2}$ or 2 ($1\frac{1}{2}$ means: two problems with the highest priority).
§ The significance of this difference is tested with the Fischer exact test with AM dichotomized per firm. The result was in both cases not significant at the 5% level.

questioning our previous conclusions; that is, even when controls are applied for strength of the interest and priority, there are little or no indications that the manifest anticipation is different for large and small business firms.

(2) *The possibilities for applying private solutions.* It is perhaps instructive, before discussing controls using this factor, to make a brief survey of the degree to which 'private solutions' have actually been applied.

When a firm has a problem, it can choose from among various different behavioral alternatives:
a   it can do absolutely nothing

b   it *can* do something
   b1: solve the problem with private resources
   b2: demand the cooperation of the government (alone or in con-
       junction with other firms)
   b3: *both* b1 and b2.

The respondents were asked for each problem which alternative they
had chosen, using roughly the wording of the schema above.

The answers to this question gave an impression of how business
firms react to their problems. To achieve a broad orientation, in the
following table, as many problems as possible (that is, all the problems:
individual *and* non-individual) and all the firms were used:

a	did nothing	29	7.4%
b1	private solution only	45	17.5%
b2	demand of government only	87	33.9%
b3	both b1 and b2	91	35.4%
–	not applicable	15	5.8%
	total	257	(no answer in two cases)

We see from this data that only in a few cases has no action at all been
taken, which seems to be in accordance with the general gravity and
magnitude of the problems involved. The relatively small percentage of
problems for which a purely private solution is sought (17.5%) also
supports this view. The line of action most often followed (35.4%) was
one in which an appeal was made to the government *and* a private
solution was sought concurrently. Considering the large span of time
involved first in reaching governmental decisions about the projects
concerned, and then in making the changes in the material facilities for
transport by water called for in these decisions, it is perfectly understandable that there is an immediate search for a provisional private
solution.

We asked the following question to investigate to what extent
private solution were *possible*:

'If you had to solve this problem solely with private resources, what
would be the consequences for your firm?'

Once again, there were five response categories: negligible, slight,
moderate, serious, disastrous.

The percentages of problems with influence attempts can now be
compared for large and for small firms while holding constant the
(financial) 'consequences of a private solution'. Those comparisons are
shown in Table 8.5.

Table 8.5
Manifest anticipation controlled for the possibilities for a private solution

size of firm (number of employees)	percentages of problems with influence attempts (out of the totality of all individual problems)*			
	SHIPYARDS† consequences of a private solution		REMAINING FIRMS consequences of a private solution	
	negligible, slight or moderate	serious, or disastrous	negligible, slight or moderate	serious, or disastrous
less than 100	47 (28)‡	82 (17)	67 (7)	83 (5)
100 or more	61 (23)‡	86 (15)	85 (9)	90 (9)
total	54 (51)	84 (32)	77 (16)	88 (14)

* Computations based on firms with at least one individual problem.
† For further legend see preceding table.
‡ This difference is not significant at the 5% level (Fischer exact test with a dichotomized AM).

When private solutions are difficult, no difference can be observed between large and small firms. When the consequences of the private solution were less serious, the differences in percentages of problems with influence attempts increased somewhat (although they were not significant). This trend could be an indication that *large firms are slightly less hesitant about undertaking influence attempts;* they are more likely to appeal to the government, even for problems which are relatively well-suited for a private solution. A similar trend was also observed with the remaining firms for problems involving less serious interests (Table 8.4). However, the principal conclusion is that when this control is applied, no definite differences can be observed between large and small firms in their manifest anticipation.

Factors related to the business firm and environmental factors–These factors have already been extensively treated in the section on latent anticipation. Can we in fact carry out controls with these fourteen variables? Some of them may be intervening variables (see Section 8.1); this cannot, however, be established with certainty. In this case, however, knowing whether or not a variable is an intervening one is

not very important for the following reasons:
1. It is improbable that variables which are indicators of the socio-political environment are intervening ones;
2. Since the business-firm-related variables have been shown not to be correlated with manifest anticipation (see Table 8.6), they cannot in any case be real intervening variables; they clearly do not constitute a link in the processual chain. Controls can therefore have no negative effect. (Strictly speaking, it is in fact unnecessary to apply these variables as control factors. This has been done anyway primarily because using the same set of variables contributes to the simplicity of the presentation.)

The results obtained when the controls are carried out are presented in Table 8.6. It can be seen that the relationship between size of the firm and manifest anticipation remains absent under all the controls, even when applied concurrently (higher order partial).

The multiple correlation coefficient of AM with fifteen variables (including size) is 0.67 (explained variance 45%). With some qualifications we can state that we have carried out controls for a reasonably large number of variables.

Conclusion: size of firm and manifest anticipation – In this section, we have investigated what changes if any can be observed in the relationship size – manifest anticipation when a number of other factors are held constant. The absence of that relationship – the conclusion reached in Chapter 6 – may, after all, be spurious.

We first held constant several variables which were related to the problem:
– the strength of the firm's interest in the problem,
– the priority accorded the problem,
– the possibilities for finding a private solution for the problem.

We next held constant for the fourteen firm- and environment-related variables discussed in the preceding section (once again, this was done only for solitary shipyards).

On the whole, the results obtained with the controls give no reason for changing our conclusion: *no relationship appears to exist between size of the firm and manifest anticipation.* We can at most suppose that under some special conditions a weak relation does exist. The most important of these is that large firms tend to undertake influence attempts relatively more often than small firms when less important or less urgent problems are involved. This result is not, however, significant, which means that this supposition requires further testing.

Table 8.6

*The relationship between size of the firm (Fs) and manifest anticipation (AM), controlled for factors relating to the business firm and to its environment (solitary shipyards)**

concept with corresponding variable (V)	zero-order correlation†		first-order partial correlation (zero-order: 0.09)†
	Fs with V	AM with V	Fs with AM, V held constant
Firm and water-related environment			
LEVEL OF ASPIRATION			
– change in number of employees in‡ the last 5 years	0.12	0.06	0.00
– expected change in number of employees	−0.12	0.19	0.03
ECONOMIC PERFORMANCE			
– change in profit margin in the last 5 years (−)	−0.02	0.08	0.01
TECHNOLOGY			
– percentage of new building	0.35++	0.00	0.01
WATER-RELATED ENVIRONMENT			
– largest ship built	0.45++	0.11	−0.04
– size of waterway	0.43++	−0.05	0.03
Socio-political environment			
1a GOVERNMENT STIMULATION CLIMATE			
– emigration	−0.16	0.15	0.03
– area or centre of regional development	−0.20	0.11	0.03
1b LEVEL OF ECONOMIC ACTIVITY ON WATERWAYS			
– tonnage transported	0.06	−0.17	0.02
2a RELATIVE SOCIAL POSITION OF FIRM			
– population size of municipality (−)	0.01	0.03	0.01
2b FORMAL ECONOMIC POWER STRUCTURE			
– concentration of employment opportunities (percentage of work force working in firms with 500 or more employees)	0.20	0.01	0.01
– density of firms (number of firms per 1000 inhabitants) (−)	−0.25+	−0.12	−0.02
2c DEGREE OF INTEGRATION OF ENVIRONMENT			
– density of organizations	0.10	−0.40∞	0.05
– density of interest organizations concerned with material facilities for transport by water	−0.06	0.01	0.01

fourteenth order 0.09

* Computations based on all the solitary shipyards with at least one individual problem (*n* = 36).
† + significant at 10% level; ++ significant at 5% level. When the direction of the correlation is *opposite* to what was expected, a two-tailed test was carried out (°: 10% level; ∞: 5% level).
‡ The third decimal in the correlation coefficient has been omitted in this and the following tables.

8.4 Controls on the relationship size of firm – tested influence; criteria used in governmental decision-making

Tested influence examined more closely – In this section, the controls of the relationship between size of the firm and tested influence (the percentage of successes) will be discussed. We concluded in Chapter 6 that in this case as well, no relationship existed.

For individual problems the correlations between size and tested influence were:

for all the shipyards: 0.055 (n = 36)
for solitary shipyards only: 0.020 (n = 26)

For the remaining firms (n = 11), a Fisher exact test yielded no significant result (computation of correlations was not permissible because of the small standard deviation in the sample).

As in the previous section, we are going to investigate whether or not 'third' factors are responsible for the absence of this relationship between size of firm and tested influence.

Our first task, therefore, is to determine exactly which these possible third factors are – a gargantuan task, considering that we are here being asked to enumerate the determinants of governmental decisions. Finding control factors thus involves ascertaining *which criteria are used by the government in reaching a decision.* For example, a possible criterium might be 'the significance for employment opportunities'.

But such a criterium does not always carry the same weight in different situations. The 'significance for employment opportunities' will, for example, depend on the degree to which unemployment is a problem in the region under consideration. Thus the *conditions* determining their strength, as well as the criteria themselves must be held constant.

This line of reasoning is schematically presented in Figure 8.3.

Before considering the ramifications of this scheme, let us interject two preliminary observations.

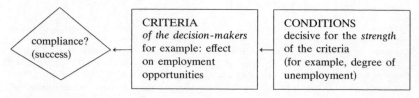

Figure 8.3
Determinants of the decision

(1) The decision-making process is extremely complicated. Although it is possible to construct a model which is a reasonably accurate representation of the essentials, the application and operationalization of that model is far from simple. Approximations must be made, and some aspects will have to be neglected.

In particular, those factors are omitted which represent *aspects of the problem itself*. As I stated earlier, partial correlation coefficients cannot be computed when these factors are incorporated; the level of measurement – ordinal or lower – makes it impossible to assign one value per business firm for the types of factors under consideration.

(2) We shall see that the firm- and environment-related variables encountered in the two previous aspects of influence will once again make their appearance as control factors. I have, in fact, consciously worked in this direction to promote the comparability of the influence aspects (see also Chapter 9). This is not stretching things as far as it may at first seem. A number of variables can be at issue in both the behavior of the petitioners and the behavior of the decision-makers. For example, 'growth' of the firm can be a *condition* for a petitioner's undertaking an influence attempt, but it can at the same time be used as a *criterium* in the behavior of the decision-maker.

Other variables are those related to the linkage of relationships among the various parties involved – the organizational density, for example. These can play a significant role, both in the undertaking of an influence attempt (the behavior of the 'petitioner') and in the granting of the request (the behavior of the 'decision-maker').

It should be noted that in such cases the variables (indicators) are, true enough, the same, but the conceptual meaning assigned to them in relation to the petitioner may be a different one than that assigned to them in relation to the decision-maker.

A theoretical schema of the decision-making process and the criteria employed in it – In seeking to establish which criteria were involved in the governmental decision-making process in the area covered by this investigation, we found that there were very little empirical data available from other studies. The selection of criteria which may be relevant for this decision-making process will therefore have to be based on theoretical knowledge which has been adapted somewhat to fit our needs.

Of course, the criteria obtained in this way are of a purely hypothetical character and together form a kind of theoretical model. Whether they are actually used or not is an empirical question which will be examined in the following chapter. Our primary goal here is to discover criteria which can subsequently be held constant when carrying out controls on the relationship size of firm – tested influence.

Simon (1957[2]) describes a decision as a choice among alternatives. This can be applied to decisions about the compliance with influence attempts, where the alternatives simply are:[9]
– to comply with the demand
– to reject the demand.

How is this decision made? Roughly sketched: the decision-maker will evaluate the *consequences* of each particular choice. In theory, he is able to estimate a list of consequences for each alternative and compare these lists. His preference for one particular combination of consequences is determined by his values, or the criteria which he uses to evaluate the consequences of the decision as he perceives them.

The process of choosing thus consists of comparing the evaluations which have been made of two or more sets of consequences. In reality, however, this weighing of pros and cons is never carried out completely; a decision (or the choice) is thus always characterized by 'bounded' rationality.

Thus the decision-making process is formally described in terms of: behavioral alternatives – consequences – evaluations. This schema can only make clear how the criteria are conceptually 'situated'. The exact number and contents of the criteria have to be based on other considerations.

Which concrete criteria are likely to be involved? In seeking to answer this question, I proceed from the assumption that the 'life-space' of the decision-maker is comprised of four fields (compare Parsons, 1966, pp. 28 and 29):
– the technical field
– the economic field
– the sociological field
– the cultural field.

A decision can have consequences in any or all of the fields. A reasonably responsible decision-maker will make sure that those consequences meet certain criteria.

This is a postulate, or point of departure in the theory which cannot be proved. It is based on the assumption that the prestige, and consequently the position of the decision-maker will be threatened if he seriously neglects these requirements. Stated theoretically, the decision-maker, for reasons of *his own interest*, will take certain criteria into consideration in making his decision. This is not such a bold assumption since, as we will see later, the requirements involved are extremely elementary (nevertheless – it should be stressed once again – the question of whether criteria are actually used or not can only be answered on the basis of data).

Let us first examine the technical field. The decision-maker can certainly be expected to evaluate whether the project for which the influence attempt is made is *feasible* or not (a).

In the economic field, there will be investigated whether the costs of the proposed projects will be covered by the gains in the future. The project must be *profitable* (b).

Various sociological aspects will also need to be considered by the decision-maker. The first question is whether or not there is enough *support* for compliance with the firm's request (c1). Active resistance from other groups, business firms, or agencies higher in the administrative hierarchy, will act as a brake on compliance. This is the first sociological criterium. In the second one, the probability of compliance will depend on the amount of *pressure* which is applied by the firm itself or by its possible partisans. Closely connected with this aspect is the degree to which the petitioning firm has the *trust* of the decision-maker (Coleman, 1963, p. 66). I have combined these two aspects into the sociological criterium 'is there *pressure* and *trust*'? (c2).

These two sociological criteria (c1 and c2) are analogous to what Easton calls 'support' and 'demand' (1966, p. 151, and other works). They are components of the 'input' of the political (and administrative) system. Parsons' concepts are somewhat analogous (1963, p. 260, and other works).

The fourth, cultural, field is in a way prior to, and a basis for, the previous three fields. For example, they can only have any significance if 'economic activity' is a positive value shared by the actors involved in the influence relationship.

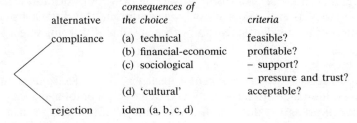

	consequences of	
alternative	*the choice*	*criteria*
compliance	(a) technical	feasible?
	(b) financial-economic	profitable?
	(c) sociological	– support?
		– pressure and trust?
	(d) 'cultural'	acceptable?
rejection	idem (a, b, c, d)	

Figure 8.4
A global model of the criteria determining compliance with an influence attempt

This example is perhaps too simply presented, since even though such a value may be present in a society, it is the degree to which it is held that is decisive. It is probably accurate to say that the value 'economic growth' has diminished in strength in the last ten years, while a 'clean environment' has risen in importance.

These cultural criteria can be summarized under the term '*acceptability*' (d).

The criteria used by the decision-makers in the four categories[10] are shown schematically in Figure 8.4.

The following remarks may serve to prevent several misunderstandings which are likely to arise.

(1) The schema of criteria is designed for obtaining a global organization of the control variables, and has therefore purposely been kept simple. For example, the possible existence of a hierarchy among the criteria has been left out of consideration. This complication can, in any case, be neglected, since as will be seen below, the control factors can be considered side by side. The criteria can also be interwoven with one another. For more complex models it would be necessary to cover this and other nuances, but their application would in my opinion be inappropriate in the present stage of the research in this field.

(2) In reality, the criteria will most probably be flexible. In some cases, the petitioner may manipulate them to his advantage. The model is an approximation in this respect as well.

(3) It might be argued that a criterium such as 'justice' or 'fairness' should be included. Such criteria may, in fact, be applied in actual decision-making, but it would clearly be a mistake to propose them as control variables. It is exactly from the results of our investigation – distributions of influence – that the application of the criteria of 'fairness' can come to light. They should therefore be regarded as dependent variables.

With a global model at our disposal, we can now look for indicators for each of the criteria selected for consideration. But first a brief consideration of an incidental feature with a possible disturbing effect.

Location and level of the governmental agencies? – The decisions with regard to the influence attempts are made by governmental agencies in different locations and at different hierarchical levels. Is it safe for us to neglect this diversity?

First the location. This concept will presently be analytically divided into a number of characteristics which will be familiar from our

Table 8.7
Tested influence at different decision-making levels

	SHIPYARDS			REMAINING FIRMS		
	decision-making level			decision-making level		
size of firm (number of employees)	municipal	provincial*	national*	municipal	provincial	national
less than 100	78 (8)	57 (7)	82 (8)	83 (4)	—	—
100 or more	67 (3)	80 (4)	75 (11)	100 (3)	100 (2)	80 (3)
total	75 (11)†	67 (11)	78 (19)	91 (7)†	100 (2)	80 (3)

percentage of influence attempts with success

* Provincial level inclusive the Provincial Department of Waterways. National level, inclusive the National Department of Waterways.
† One and the same firm can also appear in several different columns in this table as well – namely, if it has made influence attempts which have been directed toward decision-making agencies at different levels.

previous analysis (size of municipality, area of governmental stimulation, etc.). Differences in locality, region and so forth are thus thoroughly taken into account after all.

Apart from that, the level at which the decision is made is also variable. The decisions about influence attempts can be taken by municipal governments, by a provincial, or even the national government.

Therefore, we have investigated whether or not the tested influence is dependent upon these three levels of government. Table 8.7 provides reasonably convincing evidence that the level of decision-making is not a significant factor. The tested influence is virtually constant from one category to the next, as are the differences in tested influence between large and small firms. It appears that we are justified in ignoring this variable.

Characteristics of business firms as indicators for criteria employed by decision-makers – pushing things too far? – Characteristics of the *business firms* will presently be used as indicators for criteria employed by the decision-makers. For example, the economic criterium 'profitability' is indicated by the change in the profit margin, using the data provided by the firm itself.

This is clearly an artificial solution. Is it a responsible one? Supposing that the change in the profit margin does, in fact, tend to increase the tested influence, is it then possible to conclude that the criterium 'profitability' is used by decision-makers?

This question can be answered in the affirmative because a process of interaction can be treated as a unit of analysis, so that our conclusions can be based on the final results of these processes (that is, on the decisions). An example drawn from another area can perhaps make this clearer. Let us assume that we want to investigate whether or not a certain group of boys uses the criterium 'color of hair' in choosing a girl friend: for example, girls are more highly preferred the darker their hair is. We can investigate this in the following way. We first determine the hair color of a sample of girls. We then record which *interactions* can be *empirically demonstrated to have occurred* between (a number of) these girls and the group of boys. Explore whether, following *these* interactions, the group of boys is married to relatively more girls with dark hair than with light hair. If this is the case, we can conclude that the boys have used the criterium 'hair color' in their choice of a partner. The important point is that the conclusion that a certain criterium is being used has been based on the result of a process of interaction: marrying or not marrying (assuming, of course, that all other conditions are equal).

I would even go so far as to say that this is the most correct method for investigating how such criteria are used. In applying another method – for example, asking the decision-makers what criteria they used in their decision – we are supposing that they are conscious of both the criteria and the hierarchy which exists among them. It is tantamount to asking them why they arrived at a particular decision – a question which it is doubtful will yield valid answers.

This is not to deny that a decision-maker's sensitivity for a particular criterium can be inquired into. We will in fact do this in a number of instances using information obtained from burgomasters.

On the whole, I believe that using characteristics of business firms as indicators for criteria used in decision-making is a justifiable procedure. Of course, it may then be asked why we do not simply keep calling them firm-related variables instead of criteria for decision-making. There is a practical reason for using the latter terminology. The decision-makers function, after all, is a distributive mechanism in the society – *a mechanism which is in addition responsible for the distribution of influence, and which is in a position to amend or alter these criteria, and the distributions as well.*

It is within this context that my choice of the term 'criteria' has been determined.

One more consequence of the choice of firm-related variables as indicators for decision-making criteria should be noted: one and the same firm may have undertaken a number of different influence attempts, for which more than one decision must naturally be made. Thus different criteria may be applied in decisions involving different objects requested by one and the same firm. It is impossible to do justice to these nuances if firm-related variables are used as indicators for decision-making criteria. This difficulty can be skirted by looking at the situation on a problem-for-problem basis or – as in the preceding section – by holding constant those variables which can vary along with the problem (for example, 'strength of the interest'). This aspect has been taken into consideration several times in the discussion of criteria which follows.

Choice of control variables within the context of the decision-making model – The ramifications of the model presented in Figure 8.4 will be explored here, and specific control variables will be selected (the list of definitive choices is shown in Figure 8.5). For each criterium I will at the same time report which aspects I have been forced – at times unwillingly – to leave unconsidered.

(a) *The criterium 'practicability'* (technical field). The large majority of our influence attempts were undertaken by people whose primary orientation lay in the technical realm. It is hardly credible that they would propose plans which were technically impossible to carry out. I therefore think that this criteria can safely be omitted.

(b) *The criterium 'profitability'* (economic field). This criterium is relevant for so many consequences that it is practically impossible to provide a sufficient number of indicators which will cover its full meaning. That this criterium does play a role in the decision-making process is testified by the fact that compliance with an influence attempt is to a large degree dependent on the *costs* associated with that attempt. We saw in the previous chapter that the probability of an influence attempt's meeting with success decreases as the costs for the government increase (Table 6.6). This trend is especially pronounced for shipyards.

Another factor determining whether or not the government perceives a project as being profitable is the 'economic health' of the business firm involved. The previously-used variable change in the profit margin' can be used as an indicator of this factor (Figure 8.5, variable number I).

(c) *The criteria 'support'* (c1) *and 'pressure and trust'* (c2) (sociological field).
c1 *Support.* The crucial element here is the support of relevant groups. This support can also be tacit. First and foremost, support means the *absence of conflict.* This is based on the supposition that

compliance will be seriously hampered if the project threatens the interests of other firms or groups. This point proves to be insignificant for the individual problems; there were only three cases in our material where opposition from other firms was clearly involved. This point can therefore be neglected.[11]

Secondly, consensus and support can be promoted by *complementarity of influence attempts and projects already planned by the government.* It is difficult and expensive for the government to heighten a bridge for one business firm. The request is much more easily complied with when there are other reasons for building a new bridge – for example, the capacity of the old one is no longer adequate for increased traffic flows. The extra change necessary for the special needs of the firm will most likely involve extra costs, but this will be perhaps more easily accepted than if the influence attempt had stood alone. A rough survey of our data shows that such cases do occur; the strength of this phenomenon could only be guessed because of the difficulty of making a definitive classification. It should be recalled, however, that in these cases an influence attempt was coded only when there were extra costs (p. 127). Therefore, there is always complementarity only to a limited extent (compare Schuyt, 1974). This aspect will therefore also be omitted – though theoretically less justifiably than in the previous case.

c2   *The experienced pressure and the trust in the firm that undertakes the influence attempt.* Even when there is sufficient support for an influence attempt, success will depend on how the decision-maker *perceives* the strength of that attempt. This strength will be determined by:

– the activity displayed by the firm in trying to reach its goal;
– the degree to which interest groups 'take over' the influence attempt (the allies in some cases may be administrative agencies which are lower in the governmental hierarchy in cases where a decision about compliance must occur at a higher level).

The activities displayed by a firm are problem-connected, and therefore cannot be included in the set of variables. They have, however, been considered separately. Tables constructed for this purpose (not shown here) make clear that the differences in activity – for example, in the number of organizations which have been approached, in the number of different governmental agencies appealed to, the degree to which concrete plans have been submitted, etc. – are seldom highly correlated with the probability of success.

When governmental agencies or interest organizations take over the influence attempt, the relationship is stronger: in these cases the percentage of successes is 88% (n = 8), as opposed to 58% (n = 57) when the firms were acting alone. The difference is, however, not significant; this lack of significance, though, should not be taken all too seriously, considering the small number of cases included in the category with the highest percentage.

The 'pressure' which the decision-makers experience is more or less theoretically interwoven with the *trust* that they have in the actor which is making the influence attempt. If, for example, the influence attempt is taken over by an interest organization, it means more than simply that another party is exerting additional pressure. It means at the same time that the other party is a 'significant other' who is an *acknowledged* factor in negotiations with the government. Because they are familiar and accepted as being legitimate negotiating partners, they enjoy governmental trust.

Trust can also be based upon characteristics of the business firm itself – this will be treated more fully in Chapter 10. We will see that this trust can have different foundations which will be called bases of influence. Only one of these influence bases will be dealt with now: the *prestige* enjoyed by the petitioner in the eyes of the decision-maker. The theory is that the higher a firm's prestige, the greater the capacity to convince it will have. Our basic hypothesis has as one of its underlying suppositions that the size of the firm confers prestige.

This supposition is of course supported by the results of other investigations, for example in Van Heek's *et al* study of stratification (1958, p. 39) and Hodge, Siegel and Rossi, 1963 (see also investigations of local power structures, for example Schulze, 1958; Braam and Swinkels, 1969).

The *size of the firm* (II) (number of employees) can therefore be used as an indicator of prestige (and therefore also of the criterium trust) – not such a surprising step in this investigation. The *largest ship built* (III) and the *percentage of new building* (IV) will also be incorporated as indicators for prestige.

As stated earlier, my aim is to form a series of variables identical to the one used for the first two aspects of influence. I do not think that this is pushing things too far; after all, clearly visible characteristics of the firm are involved.

Two obvious indicators remain to be considered. Prestige may also depend on the 'legal status' of the firm (in The Netherlands whether an 'open' or 'closed' corporation: in the former stocks can, and in the lattter cannot, be bought and sold on the open market), whether or not it is a part of a larger concern outside the community ('absentee-owned', see Fowler, 1964, p. 168 ff, among others). Neither variable was used in later analysis. The overwhelming majority of the shipyards

(85%) had the same legal status, that is, they were closed corporations. Thus this distribution was so skewed as to make this variable unsuitable for incorporation in the further analysis. The same holds true for the variable 'absentee-owned'. In addition, both variables were relatively highly correlated with business firm size (coefficients of 0.58 and 0.31 respectively). Controls using partial correlations are therefore undesirable (see the first section of this chapter). Finally, the zero order correlations with tested influence was not significant for either variable (−0.172 for legal status and −0.242 for absentee-owned). Therefore, it is unlikely that this ommission will have any serious effects (see also Appendix 8D).

Let us turn for a moment to the indicators which have already been selected (size of firm, and so forth). The degree to which pressure is experienced by the decision-maker can depend in turn on other conditions within the *social structure*. Familiar factors appear in this sector as well. According to the most prevalent supposition, a *pyramidal power structure* should serve to increase the influence of business firms. Indicators for this type of structure used earlier in this study are: percentage of the work force working *in business firms with* 500 *or more employees* (1), which gives some idea of the *concentration* of power in the structure and *density of the business firms* (2). This latter is in turn an indication of the flatness of the structure, which should mean that influence is relatively low.

The *organizational density*, which may be functionally related to the integration between the administrative and business worlds, should promote the tested influence. The respective indicators are: *organizational density* (3) *and density of the interest organizations which are concerned with the material facilities for transport by water* (4). A survey of the criteria and conditions treated can be seen in Figure 8.5.

(d) *The criterium 'acceptability'* (cultural field). This criterium is a product of the basic cultural principles which prevail during a given historical period. In the timespan covered by the investigation (±1964–1970) and in the selected field (material facilities) two principles seem to be the most important: *economic growth* (V) and the *share of employment opportunities* of the firm (VI)[12] (compare Andriessen, Miedema and Oort, 1968, pp. 164 and 181). Of course, these principles are not conceptually independent. But we shall see later that it is nevertheless highly desirable that they be considered separately.

Characteristics of business firms will also be used as indicators of these criteria. Their effects will be determined by observing the interactions which actually occurred between business firms and government.

This would seem, for the reasons discussed on p. 202, to be the only correct method for pinning down how, if at all, these criteria play a part in the decision–making process.

They are, however, some data available which enable us to determine how dominant a role these criteria play in the life space of one category of decision-makers – the burgomasters. Of course, they represent only in part 'the decision-makers' – in the first place, because the City Council (composed of aldermen and city councillors) also takes part in decision-making, and secondly, because there are also other levels of decision-making. Apart from that, in the latter case burgomasters and city councils often act as intermediaries between firms and higher levels. These qualifications should be kept in mind in considering the following analysis.

The burgomasters were asked which sector of the municipality deserved the most attention. They were then handed a list from which they were asked to make a choice. The percentages of those citing a given sector in the first place, or in the second place, is shown below for sixty-seven municipalities:
- culture (arts)   7.5%
- recreation   16.5%
- industrialization   38.9%
- sport   4.0%
- social services   7.5%
- agrarian sector   6.0%
- municipal planning   53.7%
- other sectors   9.0%

The accent seems unmistakably to have been laid on 'growth', both in terms of living accommodations and of employment opportunities.

This can also be concluded from the answers given to the question 'what is your position with regard to ongoing industrialization?' (there were five response categories varying from highly in favour to completely opposed). Approximately 80% of the burgomasters was highly favorable; it should be noted that the percentage of those in favor was lower among the firms' directors (63%). In addition, fifty percent of the burgomasters answered an open question about their reasons for this choice by citing increased employment opportunities (yet signs of an imminent turning point in prevailing criteria was also apparent: air or water pollution was cited in eighteen percent of the cases).

Thus, in my opinion, 'growth' was demonstrably a definite decision-making criterium in the period under consideration.

How, then, can this criterium be operationalized for firms making concrete influence attempts?

We can safely assume that governmental agencies are aware of the significance of a given firm for 'growth'. This growth factor can be indicated by two already-familiar variables:

– *change in the number of employees of the firm in the last five years* (V_A)

– *the expected change in the number of employees* (V_B)

To check the assumption whether these very concrete indicators play an important role in the life space of the burgomasters, they were asked how shipyards' production had changed in their municipality in the last five years. In a municipality with a *solitary* shipyard, the answer of the burgomaster can only refer to this specific firm from our sample. We could then check whether or not the burgomasters' judgements were *correct*, that is, whether they were in agreement with the data supplied by the firms themselves. If the criterium of growth is an important factor in decision-making, then the burgomasters should be especially likely to give correct answers for the firms whose number of employees has increased.

The percentages of correct answers by burgomasters are the following for firms whose number of employees has

diminished	17% correct judgements	($n = 12$),
remained unchanged	31% correct judgements	($n = 13$),
increased	70% correct judgements	($n = 10$).

(no answer in five cases).

The same answer can be set off against the change in turnover. The analogous percentages are then 0%, 18% and 56%.

These data are a reasonably good confirmation of the heightened sensitivity of burgomasters for those solitary firms in their communities which are growing.

Because the accent has been laid so heavily on the criterium growth, the second criterium, 'share of employment opportunities of the firm' threatens to be overshadowed. Yet is likely that this criterium does fulfill an independent – and important – function in the decision-making process. Even if a large firm is not growing, it can nevertheless have a considerable significance for employment opportunities in a particular area. The sensitivity of the decision-makers for this criterium was measured indirectly by asking, 'How do you rank the shipbuilding industry in importance within the economic sector of your municipality'? (five response categories).

Table 8.8

Share of the solitary shipyard in the community's total employment opportunities, and the importance attached to this relative position by the burgomaster

shipyard: number of employees per thousand of work force in municipality (in 0/00)	burgomaster: significance (solitary) shipyard			
	not coded, etc.	minimal, slight*	moderate– very great*	total
0–19.9	5	9	6	20
20 or more	1	5	15	21

* When the column 'not coded' is omitted, the result is significant (Fisher exact test, at 5% significance level).

These answers were compared with data obtained from independent computations, providing an objective measure of each solitary shipyard's portion of the community's total employment opportunities' we could then determine whether the burgomasters' answers were reasonably correct or not (see Table 8.8).

There is a significant relationship. This is an indication that burgomasters are definitely aware of the magnitude of the employment opportunities afforded by each individual firm. Again, this cannot, of course, be regarded as definite evidence that this factor is also used as a criterium in decision-making. Once more, we have to rely on the outcomes of the decisions. Which indicators do we have to use? We have just seen that the share in employment opportunities of a firm can be operationalized simply using the *percentage of the employment opportunities* in the community which the firm provides. Earlier I called this the 'relative position' of the firm. However, in our material this correlates highly with the size of the firm ($r = 0.829$ for the forty *solitary* shipyards). This is a serious obstacle for the computation of a partial correlation (see the beginning of this chapter). It would therefore be preferable to use the *population size* (VI) as an indicator instead, as we did in the preceding sections. Of course, the assumed relationship with influence will then be a negative one: the larger the size of the municipality, the smaller the share of employment opportunities of the firm.

Finally, we should consider the *strength* in which the criteria are operational, and the conditions which can determine this strength. We could expect the 'governmental stimulation climate' to play an important role in this respect. The variables involved here are: *emigration* (5) and *area or center of regional development* (6), The 'level of economic

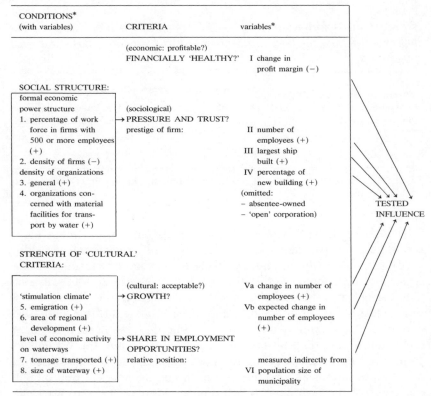

* A (+) or a (−) behind a variable means that a positive or negative relationship is expected.

Figure 8.5
Decision-making criteria, with associated conditions, and their indicators

activity on waterways' also seems relevant here: as variables can be used the *tonnage transported* (7) and the *size of the waterway* (8).

This concludes the selection of control variables on the basis of decision-making criteria and the conditions determining their strength. A summarizing schema of these variables is given in Figure 8.5.

Controls of the relationship between size of the firm and tested influence – The control variables relevant for the relationship between size of firm and tested influence have been discussed extensively. Let us now turn to the results of the controls.

In controlling, the variables were handled without taking into account whether they applied to criteria or to conditions. The variables have been placed alongside one another, as it were. This should have no serious consequences for the controls (it would never be justified, however, for testing the model as such).

It is, of course, important to know whether or not any of the variables are intervening ones. This does not seem to be the case. The various characteristics of the firm impinge upon the 'life-space' of the decision-maker at exactly the same point in time. The possiblity does, of course, remain that they take on a certain chronological order in the decision-maker's head, but this does seem to be pushing things a little too far. It therefore seems safe to state that the variables act simultaneously. Controls are thus unquestionably permissible.

Another important question is whether any of the variables are *dependent* upon the tested influence. Take 'growth' as an example. A firm could undergo a growth spurt *because* a number of its influence attempts had been successful. This is not too probable, because a considerable amount of time usually elapses between the point when the firm's request is granted and when the project is finally brought to completion. And it seems more likely that growth is primarily caused by other factors (for example, market conditions).

Examined from another, more empirical, perspective, our data yields an indication which is an even more convincing argument for the supposition that growth is not caused by the tested influence. This argument goes as follows: the same amount of government money is spent on the successful influence attempts of small firms as on those of large firms (see Chapter 6, Table 6.3). If growth were dependent on the tested influence (T), then when T was the same for both groups, the smaller firms would grow at the same rate as the large ones (as measured by the *absolute* increase in number of employees). But the *relative* increment should then be greater for small firms than for large ones. Using our set of gathered data, we can look to see if this is the case. Table 8.9 shows that almost the reverse situation actually exists. In the bottom section we see that the percentage of growth for large firms is at least as high as that for small firms (for a high value of T). This seems to me to be sufficient reason for rejecting the hypothesis that, according to our data, the growth of a firm is a dependent variable.

The variable 'expected growth', which is measured at the end of the five-year period, presents a somewhat more complex case. I believe that the risks involved in also treating this variable as non-dependent are not too great. When the variables 'change in profit margin', 'the

Table 8.9

Percentual change in the number of employees in large and small firms when the tested influence (T) is held constant (all shipyards)

		percentual change in number of employees		
	size of firm (number of employees)	less than 10.5%	greater than 10.5%	total
T = 0.5 or less	less than 100	6	1	7
	100 or more	5	0	5
T greater than 0.5	less than 100	10	3	13
	100 or more	4	7	11
			total	36

largest ship built' and 'the percentage of new building' are considered, they can be shown not to be significantly correlated with T. It is therefore virtually impossible for them to be true dependent variables.

The 'variables related to the environment' have been left out of the preceding discussion. The probability of their being intervening or dependent variables is very small.

A presentation of all the partial correlations between size of the firm and tested influence is given in Table 8.10. The fifteen variables (including size of the firm) explain 63% of the variation in the tested influence (the multiple correlation coefficient is 0.79). This indicates that our selection of variables satisfies fairly stringent requirements.

We see that when each of the variables is held constant separately (first order), no relationship emerges. When all of the fourteen variables are held constant simultaneously, there is no significant relationship, although the correlation coefficient has increased somewhat.

Thus the relationship between size of the firm and tested influence remains absent when controlled for decision-making criteria and their underlying conditions.[13]

Conclusion: size of firm and tested influence – In the overall testing, no relationship could be demonstrated between size of the firm and tested influence. In this section we have investigated whether or not this relationship remains absent when other relevant 'third' variables are held constant. In selecting these factors, we have been guided by a model of the criteria used in decision-making. These criteria relate to

Table 8.10

*The relationship between size of firm (Fs) and tested influence (T), controlling for decision-making criteria and conditions determining their strength (solitary shipyards)**

criteria (I to/incl. VII) and conditions (1 to/incl. 8) with associated variable	correlation zero-order†		1st order partial correlation (zero-order: 0.02)	
	Fs with V	T with V	Fs with T V held constant	fourteenth order
(economic) HEALTHY?				
I. change in profit margin in last 5 years	−0.05	0.23	0.03	
(sociological) PRESSURE and TRUST				
II. Number of employees	—	0.02	—	0.20
III. largest ship built	0.51⁺⁺	−0.18	0.13	
IV. percentage new building	0.31⁺	−0.26	0.11	
Conditions (SOCIAL STRUCTURE):				
– Formal economic power structure:				
1 percentage of work force in firms employing 500 or more	0.24	−0.03	0.03	
2 density of firms (—)	−0.24	0.29	0.10	
– density of organizations:				
3 general	0.07	0.07	0.02	
4 Interest organizations concerned with material facilities for transport by water	−0.12	0.22	0.05	
(cultural) GROWTH?				
Va. change in number of employees	0.23	0.30⁺	−0.05	
Vb. expected change in number of employees	−0.25	0.42⁺⁺	0.14	
(cultural) SHARE IN EMPLOYMENT OPPORTUNITIES?				
VI population size of municipality (approximation) (—)	−0.11	0.13	0.04	
Conditions for STRENGTH OF CULTURAL CRITERIA:				
– stimulation climate				
5 emigration	−0.41°°	0.23	0.13	
6 area of regional development	−0.27	0.16	0.07	
– level of economic activity				
7 tonnage transported	−0.11	0.08	0.03	
8 size of waterway	0.44⁺⁺	−0.04	0.04	

* Computation based on: solitary shipyards with at least *one* influence attempt which was brought to a conclusion (n = 26).

† ⁺ significant at 10% level; ⁺⁺ significant at 5% level. In two-tailed testing, indicated by ° (10%) and °°(5%).

four fields:
- the technical
- the economic
- the sociological
- the 'cultural' (growth, for example).

'Size of a business firm' is classified under the sociological criteria. The procedure used is to examine the effects of this single criterion, while eliminating the effect of all the others. A number of criteria had to be omitted, for example, because they varied from problem to problem and were difficult to combine into one index per firm. In a number of other cases, information gained from our data indicated that these omissions caused no serious difficulties (for example, the criterium 'absentee-owned'). The plausibility of some of the variables could be increased using an indirect method: that is, by asking (potential) decision-makers several questions. In this way some powerful evidence was obtained pointing to the empirical existence of a criterium 'economic growth'.

Our final selection was composed of fourteen variables: six criteria and eight conditions determining the strength of the criteria (see Figure 8.5).

Here once more, the results obtained after application of the controls did not bring the original conclusion into doubt: no clear relationship can be demonstrated between size of the firm and tested influence.

Controls of the results: concluding remarks of this chapter – The hypothesis which was subjected to more refined testing in this chapter was: *In solving their individual problems, business firms have the more influence on the government, the larger they are in size.*

The testing was carried out for the three aspects of the concept of influence which we had distinguished. The results were as follows:

size of firm – *latent anticipation*
          (= the number of problems)   hypothesis *confirmed*
size of firm – *manifest anticipation*
          (percentage of the problems   hypothesis *not*
          for which an influence attempt *confirmed*
          has been undertaken)
size of firm – *tested influence*
          (percentage of the influence   hypothesis *not*
          attempts that has been   *confirmed*
          successful)

The summary of Chapter 6 can be consulted for a deeper insight into these conclusions.

Here I only want to stress the most remarkable finding: tested influence, which consists of the effect of governmental decisions, displays *no* relationship with size of the business firm.

The actual testing of the hypothesis has been brought to a conclusion. However, a number of intriguing questions remain. For example, if tested influence is not related to size of the firm, is it perhaps related to other factors? The tables in this chapter have provided several suggestions. In the next chapter we will subject these suggestions to a more systematic examination.

Notes

1. The design with respect to the main hypothesis is in my opinion comparable in form with the investigation of Barendregt, as discussed by De Groot (1967). There as well as here, the primary concern was not with a cause-effect relationship, but with a co-variation: in Barendregt's case, between the nature of a disease and characteristics of the personality structure.
2. An exception is made in those cases where a factor must be held constant which is correlated with *the problem itself* (see Sections 8.3 and 8.4).
3. It should be noted that even if the control variables precede the two original variables in time, they cannot always be used to test for a spurious correlation. They could, for example, represent a developmental sequence (Blalock, 1964, p. 86, see also Hyman, *op. cit.*).
4. Later, we examine the relationships of influence with other conditions, and likewise compute partial correlation coefficients, it will also be important to take care that the *number* of variables used as indicators for these conditions do not vary widely from condition to condition. When the number of variables varies widely, there is a risk that the value of the partial is dependent on the mere number of other indicators. (See Gordon, 1968, pp. 595 ff).
5. Strictly speaking, then, the 'latent anticipation' is measured more or less indirectly. A more direct measurement was made using three questions:
   'In your opinion, does the municipality have a responsibility for the maintenance of the material facilities for transport by water in this area such as harbors, canals and so forth?' (this question was repeated with regard to the provincial and national administrations).
   In coding the answers to the question, respondents who perceived government agancies as having a *specific responsibility toward the business firms* were assigned to a separate category. The three questions were combined into an index which reflects the *firms' expectations* concerning the government's promotion of their interests.
   This index has reasonably high correlations with the number of problems (shipyards: $r = 0.344$, significance level 0.5%; contingency table significant 10%; remaining firms: $r = 0.164$, not significant; contingency table significant 10%). This is an empirical indication that the number of problems is, in fact, an index for latent anticipation.
   However, I consider an index constructed on the basis of the first type of question a much less hard datum than the number of problems.
   A different point is whether the *number* of problems is the right indicator to choose. For example, a large firm may mention more problems, but a relatively large

percentage of them may be considered rather unimportant. It can be seen in Appendix 8A that the percentages of 'important' problems is virtually the same for large and small firms. I believe, therefore, that the distribution of 'interest' does not pose any problems for the choice of 'number of problems' as an indicator for latent anticipation.

6. One of the reasons why this categorization has been used is a practical one: the first category of factors was gathered per firm; the second category – the factors related to the socio-political environment – consists primarily of variables which were constructed on the basis of statistical material from the Central Bureau of Statistics in the Netherlands.

7. This is a simplified way of looking at the matter. After all, a better economic performance can result in a rise in the aspiration level; this in turn may cause the probability of perceived problems to remain the same (March and Simon, 1958, p. 162; this process is also known as the mechanism of 'rising expectations'). If, however, the aspiration level is operationalized independently, the statement in the text should meet with no objections. We shall see shortly that such an operationalization is apparently available to us.

8. One environmental variable is left out of consideration by limiting ourselves to solitary shipyards – of course, that of being or not being a solitary shipyard. As we saw in Chapter 6, when non-solitary shipyards are being considered, large firms also have relatively more problems than small ones. Thus the same basic relationship between size of firm and number of problems is present. This is also true of the category of problems relating to the material facilities for transport by water, which are analyzed in this section (average number for small and large firms 1.42 and 1.62 respectively). I am convinced, therefore, that the sacrifice of this variable has no serious consequences. An additional fact: the *average* number of the individual problems for non-solitary shipyards was lower than for solitary ones (1.46 and 1.71 respectively; compare Table 6.7).

9. This dichotomy is, of course, an extremely simplified diagrammatic representation of reality. In actuality, negotiations can produce a modification of the original influence attempt, with a compromise resulting. Or, the decision-maker can propose an alternative solution (see also Appendix 5C).

10. These categories are roughly comparable to those of Parsons (1966, p. 29, among others). If we consider the decision-makers to be representative of the political system – Parson's 'polity' – then we know it to be surrounded by three other 'systems': the economic (b), the integrative (c), and the 'pattern maintenance' (the cultural (d)). I have added yet another, the 'physical environment' (a). At the risk of being redundant – 'administration' must also be considered to fall under 'polity'.

11. There was very rarely any opposition to the problems studied in this investigation. This is true of opposition not only from other firms, but also from interest organizations and political parties, including their branches. This may be due to the nature of the objects of the influence attempts. Additionally, firms may be hesitant to unleash any action which threatens the interests of their colleagues. Bauer (1964, p. 218) believes that there are definite *norms* guiding behavior in this area. And, of course, a firm is fairly likely to invite counter-actions if it violates these norms.

12. The question may arise why these criteria were placed in the cultural, rather than the economic field. Of course, neither can be completely separated from the other, but nevertheless, they can be distinguished. This can be seen when we ask how the criteria change in the course of time. For example: the principle of economic growth has received a great deal of emphasis since the second world war, but some doubts

are arising about it now. 'Profitability', on the other hand, has existed for a much longer time as a criterium, and is much less likely to be discarded. Thus, the latter criterium is less subject to short-term fluctuation in the 'culture'.

13. An obvious factor which may contribute to a decrease in tested influence is, simply, the number of influence attempts: the probability of success may diminish as the number of influence attempts increases. If large firms undertake more influence attempts than small ones, then this factor could tend to minimize the relationship between Fs and T. This effect, however, was not observed in our data: the first-order partial of Fs with T, holding the number of influence attempts constant, is 0.06 (zero-order: 0.05 for all 72 shipyards).

9. Alternative Hypothesis: Growth of the Business Firm Instead of Size of the Business Firm

Statement of the problem – The result obtained by testing our hypothesis was most certainly an unexpected one: two of the three aspects of influence, manifest anticipation and tested influence, did not have a relationship with the size of the business firm.

The question thus arises whether or not there are other factors which exhibit a relationship with these influence aspects. The data needed for supplying an answer to this question are already at our disposal. In the preceding chapter we worked with fourteen variables which were chosen because they might possibly disturb the relationship between size and influence; in other words, there might be a relationship between these variables and influence. These possible relationships will now be investigated.

More specifically, with regard to tested influence, the following question will be considered: Since the size of the firm does not appear to be used as a criterium in decision-making, what other characteristics of the firm do play a role in governmental compliance with an influence attempt?

This section of the investigation is most definitely exploratory in nature. Since the research design was specifically shaped around the factor 'size of business firm', it is not quite certain whether it is likewise suitable for testing other hypotheses. In addition, the number of cases to work with is small, especially for tested influence. The investigation can nevertheless provide us with a richness of data which can be used to *form* new hypotheses. It may even be possible in some cases to test these hypotheses as well.

The explanatory value of variables relating to the business firm compared to variables relating to the environment – What is the significance of the variables for the different aspects of influence? A first inspection can be carried out on the basis of the variance, which is explained by two groups of variables:
- variables relating to the business firm itself
- variables relating to its environment.

Table 9.1
Explained variance by groups of variables (firm-related and environment-related)

| By | solitary shipyards: percentage explained variance* in: | | |
	AL: latent anticipation (PETITIONER)	AM: manifest anticipation (PETITIONER)	T: tested influence (DECISION-MAKER)
7 firm-related variables (including size)	25% (0.50)	6% (0.24)	38% (0.62)
8 environment-related variables (socio-political)†	20% (0.44)	37% (0.61)	16% (0.40)
all 15 variables (including size)	42% (0.65) n = 40	45% (0.67) n = 36	63% (0.79) n = 26
size only‡	10% (0.32)	0% (0.01)	0% (0.02)

* In parentheses the multiple correlation coefficients.
† The eight environment-related variables are those variables which were identified as such during consideration of the two influence aspects reflecting anticipation. The factors for tested influence were arranged somewhat differently in the first instance. In Table 9.2 which follows later, the two arrangements can be found side by side.
‡ In this row the previously-computed correlations with size of the firm alone.

The absolute value of these variances must be regarded with some reservations. The multiple correlations upon which these explained variances are based are 'inflated values' (the multiple R represents the *maximum* possible correlation between the dependent variable and a weighted combination of independent variables. Guilford, 1965, p. 401). This is especially likely to have an effect in small samples. We will therefore take only their ratio's into consideration.

The following trends within the two parties can be observed in the table:
(1) *The 'petitioners'* – The latent anticipation (the perception of problems) is determined almost as strongly by variables relating to the socio-political environment as by firm-related variables. The effect of firm-related variables on manifest anticipation is virtually nil; the environment-related variables are clearly dominant here.

These results lead us to believe that the *anticipation of the firms does depend to a real extent upon variables relating to the socio-political environment of a firm.*

The figures for manifest anticipation show this the most clearly, but I consider the results for latent anticipation to be even more significant.

We would, after all, expect the perception of problems to depend primarily upon the situation of the firm in combination with the water-related environment. These two categories do, of course, leave their traces, but *the simple fact of where a firm is located is also an important source of differences in anticipation.*

This also has its practical implications. Distributions of influence can be 'skewed' as a result of differences in environment. Exactly which environmental factors these are is an important topic for further research (some suggestions are given in the following sub-section).

(2) *The decision-makers* – Almost the reverse conclusion can be drawn for tested influence: environment-related variables here explain relatively less variance in two respects. First, when compared to the variance which these variables explain in latent and manifest anticipation. This result points to the conclusion that *the behavior of the decision-makers is less dependent on environmental factors than is the behavior and the perception of the firms.*

Secondly, we see that the environmental factors explain less of the variance in tested influence (16%) than do the firm-related factors (38%). It appears that the decision-maker thus is guided primarily by *the situation of the firm itself* (including the water-related environment). And this holds true in spite of the fact that the size of the firm is not a factor of any significance in the decision-making process of the government, as concluded in a previous chapter. We will shortly begin the search for the firm-related factors which are significant in this process.

Finally, Table 9.1 shows that firm-related variables explain considerably more variance in tested influence than they do in anticipation of the business firms.

Two conspicuous points emerge from the preceding analysis. First, the importance of the socio-political environmental factors is manifested primarily in the anticipation of the business firms. Secondly, firm-related factors (including the water-related environment), while being reasonably significant for latent anticipation, are even more important for tested influence (thus for the behavior of the decision-maker). As for the government, we may advance a conclusion that the decision-making criteria are 'universalistic' rather than 'particularistic' (they do not show variation with the region, for example).

The effect of the variables considered one by one – We will now begin to test the relationship of each individual variable with the various aspects of influence. Fourteen independent variables, in addition to the size of the business firm, were discussed in the previous chapter. In Table 9.2

are presented the computed correlations of these variables with the three aspects of influence, both without controls (zero order) and under the control of the fourteen remaining independent variables.

As I stated earlier, it is undoubtedly a weakness of the control procedure that it cannot reveal possible conditional relationships. In addition, as a result of this procedure, the importance of each of the individual variables can only be estimated (Blalock, 1972, pp. 150 and 156). Thus the only thing actually being determined is what correlation coefficient if any remains when other variables are held constant. We do not get more information about the 'real' causal working of the variable – until we manage to learn more about the configuration of the variables, especially their *temporal sequence.*

However, the following points were observed in the previous chapter:

a – with latent anticipation, we must also control for intervening variables, because the variable 'number of problems' was a somewhat indirect indicator for this concept; as a result, some controls are perhaps too stringent (see Section 8.2), and the disappearance of some correlations may be unwarranted;

b – with manifest anticipation, controls can emphatically only deliver an estimate of the importance of the individual variables;

c – with tested influence, the control variables can be considered to *stand alongside* one another; in this case, cautious conclusions can be drawn about causal relationships.

We are following a safe strategy when we regard the partial correlations as only a *tentative* indication of the effect of the variables. This strategy has its advantages for other reasons as well. The number of cases at our disposal is small, especially for partial correlation coefficients of a higher order. To be sure, this is taken into account by the increased critical value of the correlation coefficient with a given level of significance (Guilford, 1965, p. 341: the number of degrees of freedom diminishes by one each time a new control variable is added). However, it would, in my opinion, be unwise to base our conclusions on a significant partial alone. More evidence is needed. I will try in such cases to find additional supportive indication in *other sub-samples.*

We will now delve deeper into the results (Table 9.2), considering them first *per variable,* and then *per aspect of influence.*

Factors relating to the business firm
– No relationships are evident for the *change in profit margin* as an operationalization of 'economic performance of the firm'. Improved economic performance does not result in a decrease in the number of

Table 9.2

Correlations of the fourteen variables with the three aspects of influence

	latent anticipation (n = 40)		manifest anticipation (n = 36)	
	zero order	14th order	zero order	14th order
ECONOMIC PERFORMANCE:				
– change in profit margin (—)	−0.20	−0.14	0.08	0.19
SIZE OF FIRM:				
– number of employees	0.32††	0.29†	0.01	0.09
FIRM AND WATER-RELATED ENVIRONMENT (I):				
– largest ship built	0.38††	0.27†	0.11	0.20
TECHNOLOGY:				
– percentage new building	0.35††	0.07	0.00	0.03
FORMAL ECONOMIC POWER STRUCTURE:				
– percentage of work force working in firms with 500 or more employees	0.19	0.14	0.01	−0.15
– density of firms (—)	0.16	0.33°	−0.12	−0.25
DEGREE OF INTEGRATION OF ENVIRONMENT:				
– density of organizations	0.15	0.09	−0.40°°	−0.56°°
– density of interest organizations concerned with material facilities for transport by water	0.01	−0.23	0.01	0.03
LEVEL OF ASPIRATION:				
– change in number of employees	0.23†	−0.08	0.06	−0.17
– expected change in number of employees	0.11	0.08	0.19	0.16
RELATIVE SOCIAL POSITION:				
– population size of municipality (—)	−0.07	0.01	0.03	0.02
GOVERNMENTAL STIMULATION CLIMATE:				
– emigration	0.18	0.10	0.15	0.21
– area or centre of regional development	0.17	0.16	0.11	0.24
LEVEL OF ECONOMIC ACTIVITY ON WATERWAYS:				
– tonnage transported	−0.17	−0.08	−0.17	−0.15
FIRM AND WATER-RELATED ENVIRONMENT (II):				
– size of waterway	0.02	−0.02	−0.05	−0.07

* †: significant at 10% level; ††: significant at 5% level.
When the direction of the relationship is *opposite to* that expected, then a two-tailed test was used:
°: 10% level; °°: 5% level.

and with the number of successes (40 *solitary shipyards*)*

criteria (I to/incl. VI) and conditions (1 to/incl. 8) with associated variables	tested influence (n = 26)		number of successes (n = 40)	
	zero order	14th order	zero order	14th order
(Economic) HEALTHY?				
I. change in profit margin (+)	0.23	−0.03	−0.05	0.01
(Sociological) PRESSURE AND TRUST				
II. number of employees	0.02	0.20	0.14	0.24
III. largest ship built	−0.18	−0.49	0.04	−0.01
IV. percentage new building	−0.26	−0.17	0.11	0.03
Conditions (SOCIAL STRUCTURE)				
– formal economic power structure				
1. percentage of work force in firms with 500 or more employees	−0.03	0.21	−0.05	−0.07
2. density of firms (−)	0.29	0.54°	0.15	0.09
– density of organizations:				
3. general	0.07	0.19	−0.11	−0.17
4. interest organizations concerned with the material facilities for transport by water	0.22	−0.10	−0.03	−0.17
(Cultural) GROWTH?				
Va. change in number of employees	0.30†	0.34	0.34††	0.05
Vb. expected change in number of employees	0.42††	0.42†	0.35††	0.29†
SHARE IN EMPLOYMENT OPPORTUNITIES?				
VI. population size of municipality (approximation)	0.13	−0.04	−0.10	−0.06
Conditions for STRENGTH OF CULTURAL CRITERIA				
– stimulation climate				
5. emigration	0.23	−0.35	0.30††	0.12
6. area or centre of regional development	0.16	0.17	0.12	0.18
– level of economic activity				
7. tonnage transported	0.08	0.31	−0.16	−0.02
8. size of waterway	−0.04	0.34	−0.12	0.06

problems (latent anticipation) or the manifest anticipation; in the opposite direction, improved economic performance does not foster compliance (tested influence). We should, however, be cautious in accepting these results, considering the weaknesses of our operationalization of economic performance.

– *The largest ship built, LSB, is* correlated with the number of perceived problems – a plausible result. It should, however, be noted that LSB is a direct, purely technical, causal variable for the number of problems. Consequently, it cannot be inferred as a matter of course that the latent anticipation is also caused by LSB (after all, the number of problems is only an *indicator* for latent anticipation). A spurious correlation may be involved here, inasmuch as latent anticipation can cause an increase in both the LSB and the number of problems:

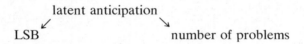

latent anticipation

LSB   number of problems

LSB displayed no significant relationships with any of the other influence aspects.

– *The percentage of new building* (indicator for technology) did not correlate with any of the aspects of influence after computation of the partials.

– Finally, we look at the two variables *change in number of employees* and *the expected change in the number of employees* (see under 'level of aspiration' and 'growth'). We have considered these variables as indicators for the *level of aspiration* of the business firm. When we look at the partials, they no longer display any relationship with the latent anticipation and the manifest anticipation. (A more refined analysis would probably show that the relationship between change in last five years and latent anticipation would remain; compare p. 230). For the decision-makers, these variables have been regarded as indicators for the criteria *growth* and *expected growth. Both show a significant zero order correlation with the compliance (tested influence); after computation of the partials, the relationship with one of the two variables is still statistically significant.*

Variables relating to the environment
(a) *The social structure.* The *formal economic power structure* is indicated using two variables: *percentage of the work force in large firms* (500 employees or more) and the *density of the firms.* No significant relationships with the first variable could be discovered. The concentration of power, indicated by this variable, and which would seem to

be an important datum, does not, in fact, have much of an effect. In the meantime, the results of other investigations have indicated that the supposed relationship between this variable and the 'concentration of power' is far from evident (Aiken, 1970, p. 497; Aiken and Alford, 1970, p. 657). Better indicators are needed for future studies.

The second variable – *the density of business firms* – can be an indicator for the levelness of the structure (this is complementary to 'concentration'). There is a correlation with the perception of problems (latent anticipation) and compliance (tested influence), but in an *opposite* direction than was expected (partials of 0.33 and 0.54). This suggests that the number of firms per 1000 inhabitants is fostering two aspects of influence – one aspect on the petitioner's side, and the other on the decision-maker's side. In other words, the more level the structure, the more influence a firm can exercise.

It would nevertheless be premature to treat these findings as a new hypothesis without digging deeper into the exact meaning of this variable. From the correlation matrix and the factor analysis (which are not represented here) can be seen that social density of firms loads high on a separate factor on the one hand, but it also appears at the same time on another factor – which can be called 'region' (for example, the greater the density the less centrally the municipality is located in the Netherlands). The variable can thus concurrently represent another concept, which gives a possible explanation of the correlations: the less centrally located the region, the greater are the latent anticipation and the tested influence.

A definitive interpretation can only be made in the wake of continued study.

Two variables were used for *the integration of the social structure.* An index was constructed of 'social meeting places' where governmental administrators and directors of firms could come into contact with one another, by discovering what industrial, commercial clubs and the like were present. The indicator thus obtained we called the 'density of organizations'. A separate indicator was chosen for the presence of interest organizations concerned with the material facilities for transport by water (see also Chapter 8).

Only the density of the organizations showed a correlation – with the percentage of influence attempts (AM). The direction of this correlation, however, is opposite to what I expected; this is a remarkable result. *The presence of 'social meeting places' appears to curb the undertaking of influence attempts* (the tentative nature of this result should again be emphasized: the variables in question have a somewhat skewed distribution). In later discussions with vice-presidents a possible explanation was suggested: the organizations are often internally dominated by large firms. They may use these occasions to prevent growth of other firms – for example, with regard to the recruitment of workers, a competitive situation in this period.

(b) *The relative position of the firm*, indicated by size of the municipality, remarkably enough exhibits not a single relationship. I consider it especially surprising that no relationship with tested influence was found. This means that the criterium *share of the employment opportunities* played no role in the decision-making. In any case, it is in accordance with the finding that the size of the firm is unrelated to the tested influence.[1] It is likely that this situation has changed markedly since the period of the investigation, when employment opportunities have radically diminished.

(c) *The stimulus situation* (or, conditions determining criteria in the cultural field) is indicated with the variables *emigration* and *area or centre selected by the government for regional development aid*. No effect was found of these variables on either the anticipation of the petitioner or the behavior of the decision-maker (in the latter case we conceived these variables as conditions determining the strength of the criteria). To illuminate these results, some aspects of the economic planning situation in the Netherlands in the sixties may be considered. Until about 1970, the government's stimulation policy was primarily directed toward encouraging the establishment of *new* industrial sites. Our investigation, however, is concerned with business locations already in existence – that is, locations which are less likely to experience the full effects of this policy package. A number of our respondents were definitely aware of the content of this policy, as evidenced by the frequent complaints which were expressed concerning it. Yet the already-existing locations were not totally removed from the realm of this policy; for example, extra subsidies for material facilities for transport by water were often available in areas of governmental economic development aid.

The second dimension of the stimulus situation – the level of activity on the waterway – is indicated by the *tonnage transported* and the *size of the waterway*. Neither of the two variables furthered the perception of the problems (P) or the percentage of influence attempts (AM). As *conditions* affecting the criteria used by decision-makers they have likewise shown no significant relationships.

The influence aspects in combination: the number of effects (successes)– In several lines of Table 9.2 can be seen that a given factor is positively correlated with one aspect of influence, but negatively correlated with another; on other lines, there is a weak correlation in the same direction with several aspects. This leads to the question of what the resultant is when we combine the influence aspects.

The answer can be seen in the last column of Table 9.2, where the correlations of the variables with number of successes have been presented; the number of successes, after all, is equal to the product of the three influence aspects. Only one significant partial of the four-teenth order results – for the expected change in the number of em-ployees. One environmental factor, the emigration, does have a sig-nificant zero-order correlation, but it disappears after partializing.

Characteristics of firms, decision-making criteria and the distribution of influence – The principal question in this study is how influence is actually distributed in society. The hypothesis that the size of the firm is correlated with the amount of influence was only confirmed for one aspect – for latent anticipation. We have just examined which factors if any are related in any degree to the other aspects of influence. A summary of the information obtained is shown in Figure 9.1.

If we now restate our question about the distribution of influence among business firms, we can at this point omit the environmental variables; it is sufficient to merely hold them constant. After all, our primary interest in the influence distribution is in finding out whether or not there are characteristics of the business firms themselves with which the influence varies.

The *latent anticipation* has already been discussed sufficiently: it varies in the direction predicted by the hypothesis. There is with other characteristics of the firm either no relationship at all, or a relationship which is possibly spurious (largest ship built).

The *manifest anticipation* – the percentage of problems for which influence attempts have been undertaken – did not display a relation-ship with any of the firms' characteristics. This is in line with the slight percentage of the variance of this aspect (6%) which is explained by variables relating to the business firm.

The *tested influence*, as we have seen, does not correlate with size of the firm. It is striking that a relationship still fails to appear when we interpret the number of employees more strictly as 'share of employ-ment opportunities'. Neither size of the firm, holding size of the municipality constant, nor size of the municipality, holding size of the firm constant, showed any relationship. It does appear as though this criterium is not effective in steering governmental decision-making.

	the latent anticipation is greater when	manifest anticipation (AM) is greater when	tested influence (T) is greater when
firm-related factors	the firm – is larger (– builds larger ships)†	----------	– the firm expects the number of employees to increase
environment-related factors	– the number of firms per 1000 municipal inhabitants is greater (?)*	– there are *fewer* organizations such as industrial clubs etc., in the municipality or region (?)*	– the number of firms per 1000 inhabitants is *greater* (?)*

* A (?) behind a result means that the relationship cannot yet be readily interpreted.
Italicized items mean that there is a relationship, but in the opposite direction to the one expected.
† It is possible that a spurious correlation is involved here (see text).

Figure 9.1
Review of the variables with demonstrated correlations with an aspect of influence when fourteen variables are held constant (level of significance at least 10%)

Nor is there any relationship with the change in profit margin. Strangely enough, this implies that there is likewise no indication that the criterium 'economically healthy firm' had any effect on decision-making (with, of course, the reservation that the operationalization is possibly not as adequate as would be desirable).

There is a clear, positive relationship with the change in the number of employees in the *previous* period, and with *expected change* in the number of employees. This latter relationship also remains after partialization (at a 10% level of significance). In addition, the expected change in the number of employees also shows a relationship with the combined influence aspects – that is, the number of successes.

Further exploration of the effect of the decision-making criterium 'growth' – An important new hypothesis has now emerged, namely, that the tested influence of a firm is greater, the more the number of employees has increased and/or when an increase in employees is expected. As set forth in the preceding chapter, these variables can be considered as indicators of the decision-making criterium 'growth'.

Of the many diverse criteria reviewed in this study which can be involved in the decision-making process, the only one which we have observed as having any effect is 'growth'.

This is true no matter what the 'region' – that is, no matter whether or not the firm is located in an area of governmental regional development aid (this is, after all, a variable which has been held constant; in addition, this latter factor is not in itself of any significance for decision-making).

The question, of course, is whether or not there is any other evidence supporting this hypothesis.

In the first place, I have checked to see if the relationship remains when 'growth' is inferred from the answers of the burgomasters rather than the data supplied by the firms. The burgomasters, it should be remembered, were asked their evaluations of the increase or decline in production[2] in the shipyards in their municipalities. In municipalities with only one shipyard, this answer must apply as a matter of course to this one shipyard. If we compute the correlation coefficient between this change in production as seen by the burgomasters and the tested influence, *then we are subjecting the relationship 'growth' – tested influence to a very stringent test.* The perceptions of the burgomaster may, after all, be distorted in some way, and equally important, some influence attempts may escape the attention of a given burgomaster entirely (that is, it is unlikely that he knows the 'objective reality' of

Table 9.3

The relationship between tested influence and growth (for all the shipyards and all the remaining firms)

firm-related variables (criteria for decision-making)	tested influence* of SHIPYARDS (n = 35)		REMAINING FIRMS (n = 18)
	zero-order	6th order partial†	zero order
(GROWTH) change in the number of employees in the last five years	0.27+	0.14	0.62++
(EXPECTED GROWTH) expected change in the number of employees	0.39++	0.41++	0.29

* The tested influence of shipyards applies to individual problems. The number of individual problems of the remaining firms was too limited, so that another set – problems relating to the material facilities for transport by water – was chosen.

† If the 'expected change' is omitted as a variable, then the coefficient for the 'change in the last five years' jumps to a significant value (fifth order: 0.37).

tested influence; besides burgomasters are scattered all over the country). Nevertheless, we obtain here a correlation coefficient with T of 0.48 (significant at a 5% level, for n = 17). The relationship is also significant when we construct a contingency table (that is, when we transform the data to a nominal level). This result is, I believe, very *strong evidence that the criterium 'growth' does function as a criterium in decision-making.*

As a further test, we next looked to see if the relationship still holds when all the shipyards – thus including non-solitary ones – are used in the computations (see Table 9.3; data for 'remaining firms' are also included).

The relationship is, in fact, again present. When controls are applied for the other firm-related variables, the correlation between the expected growth and tested influence remains significant (sixth order). The partial correlation with the growth in the past, on the other hand, disappears (this was also the case for the solitary shipyards). This is not so surprising, since the two variables are rather highly correlated with one another (0.46 for n = 35).

To eliminate this effect, the fifth-order partial correlation of the growth in the past with T was computed, omitting the expected growth. This partial is 0.37 (significant at the 5% level).

Further, the zero-order correlation of growth in the past with tested influence was checked once more with a computation at the nominal level. We found that when a firm:

has grown: then 94% of the influence attempts are successful;

has not grown: then 65% of the influence attempts are successful.

Further evidence was sought in the sub-sample of 'remaining firms'.

No computation of correlations could be made here for tested influence involving individual problems; the T showed too little dispersion. I therefore substituted another set of problems – those related to material facilities for transport by water – for a computation of the correlation between the growth indicators and the percentage of successes (T) for influence attempts. Non-individual problems are thus also included in this set. This is not so serious a disadvantage as it may seem. For it should be recalled that for non-individual problems, T can be validly interpreted as 'gains via coalitions, and so forth' (see Chapter 3). The result of this computation shows that one of the two growth variables was again significantly correlated with T (Table 9.3).

A final possible difficulty should be discussed. That is, the scale used to categorize the change in the number of employees in the preceding time period can be called into question. We are, after all, working with a proportional change (and on a five-point scale besides; see p. 174). The following check was applied: the change in the number of employees in the past was given in absolute numbers in the interviews for a large number of the business firms. The correlations of these values with T were computed; the result for shipyards was 0.33 (28 cases; sign. 5%), and for other firms 0.30 (15 cases; not significant, apparently due to the elimination of extreme values). The outcomes in this final stage of testing can, in my opinion, be interpreted as a reasonably good confirmation of the new hypothesis that tested influence depends on the decision-making criterium 'growth'.

Growing business firms and government agencies – harmony of interests? – All in all, we are driven to the conclusion that *decision-makers' behavior is determined rather one-sidedly by the criterium growth.* This is understandable from several points of view: burgomasters attach considerable significance to industrial growth, as we have seen in the preceding chapter. And it is all the more plausible when we consider that their own 'interests' are also involved: the growth of the municipality can be a crucial factor determining their prestige. Besides, the fact that salaries of burgomasters and municipal officials depend on the number of inhabitants under their jurisdiction can, of course, also play a role in these 'interests'.

It is true that municipal governments make definitive decisions only in a fraction of the cases being studied. Yet they clearly have an important role in other decision-making processes as well: for the 130 influence attempts where a final decision was made at a higher level than the municipal, the petitioners involved *also* appealed to the municipality in at least 80 instances (62%). *Thus local administrators function as a kind of 'first line' for the demands, and in some cases completely 'take over' the influence attempt.*

Leaving this out of consideration, it is highly probable that at higher administrative levels as well, a high value is attached to growth; and that is used as a criterium in decision-making.

The evidence points to a kind of harmony of interests: growing firms have more tested influence than non-growers, apparently because growth is also in the interest of the administrators. And, once made, the affirmative decision is likely in its turn to increase employment opportunities.

In all probability this conception of a harmony of interest based on 'growth' is now outdated to a certain degree (no further material was gathered for this investigation after 1970). At the present, it is more likely that a greater number of criteria are in conflict with one another (for example, growth vs. pollution), or that the criterium 'share of employment opportunities' has become a more dominating one.

Notes

1. Of course, the two data can also be combined expressing the number of employees in a firm as a percentage of the work force. This percentage likewise had no relationship with T (zero-order: -0.12).
2. Of course, change in production is something different than change in the number of employees. I do not believe that it would be too risky, however, to use them both as indicators of growth. Looking back, the best procedure would naturally have been to ask the burgomasters in their interviews about the change in the number of employees.

10. A Further Look at the Bases of Influence

Interest organizations, 'social relations', unified elites and the deficiencies of indirect indicators for influence

Statement of the problem – The hypothesis that a firm's influence in solving its individual problems is related to its size has only been shown to be true for one out of three aspects of influence. This is a serious blow to a very widely held opinion which is generally defended using numerous arguments. One argument has already been mentioned in this book: size is supposed to be associated with prestige, and prestige is likely to contribute to an increase in influence. This theory is a plausible one, but it is not supported by the results of this investigation – and this calls for some further probing for an explanation.

Some clarification of the problem was achieved in the preceding chapter when other characteristics of business firms were taken into account. Our principal finding was support for an alternative hypothesis with regard to the aspect tested influence: the higher the growth rate of a firm, the greater its tested influence.

However, a further consideration of the criterium 'trust' and 'confidence', introduced in Chapter 8, may be an equally fruitful basis for further explorations. This criterium can be based on a number of different factors which we will call influence bases. Prestige, mentioned above, may be one of these bases, but there are also several others conceivable. There are a number of popular assumptions about their exact nature. Often cited as influence bases are such factors as level of education, 'connections', and social circles, like the Rotary, where influence could be exercised 'behind closed doors'.

I have tailored this phase of my research design to a number of these popular assumptions; a number of subsidiary hypothesis have been formulated, which, stated briefly, maintain that:

A firm's influence will be greater when
- the technical expertise is greater (*education*);
- the socio-organizational expertise is greater (that is, when the firm has more positions in *interest organizations* and/or *governmental committees*);

- the firm belongs more often to a '*social circle*' such as the Rotary;
- the firm has more extensive '*connections*' (contacts) with government agencies;
- the firm's directors have a more *cosmopolitan* orientation.

In this chapter we will investigate whether these more-or-less stereotyped ideas are supported by evidence gleaned from our investigation. These particular assumptions often lend support to a general conception of a society dominated by a three-pronged 'power elite' composed of the top figures in business, government, and the military (Mills, 1956). We will discuss what light our data can throw on some elements of this controversial social theory.

Finally, from the standpoint of research techniques, the results can be used to examine whether or not the various influence bases are, in fact, good indirect indicators for influence.

These questions will be considered with respect to two aspects of influence only–tested influence and latent anticipation; the reason is that at first inspection, no significant correlations with manifest anticipation could be detected for any of the influence bases. I have therefore omitted this aspect, which will enable us to concentrate more intensively on the two other aspects of influence.

10.1 **Tested influence in relation to prestige, expertise and particularism**

Possible bases for tested influence: prestige, expertise and particularism ('*social circles*' *and* '*connections*')–I stated in Chapter 2 that, although our concept of influence was broadly defined with regard to the means employed in the influence process, I expected that our investigation would reveal that the primary means used in exercising influence was persuasion (*persuasion* in direct contrast to *negative sanctions*). I did add to this statement that persuasion had to be considered in a much broader sense than only 'rational argumentation'. Thus, it is important for influence not only *what* is said, but also *who* is saying it. Or, in other words, the private individual undertaking the influence attempt must enjoy the *trust* of the decision-maker. In this way we arrive once more at the *sociological criteria* from the preceding chapters, to which we must now add some depth and refinements.

The question is thus: *in which social characteristics of the petitioner does the decision-maker repose his confidence?*

I have distinguished three dimensions in these characteristics which can partially be traced back to Parsons (1963b, p. 49 ff.) and Coleman

(1963, p. 70). If we imagine ourselves in the decision-maker's position, it becomes clear that he needs to 'locate' the firm in some way. He can then orient himself by attaching a number of 'labels' to the firms in question. I suggest that the decision-maker asks the following three questions:

A – Is the firm *respected*? In sociological terminology, this is a question about 'prestige' or 'social status'. This aspect has been treated earlier, so I will not repeat myself here. We indicated 'prestige', for example, with *size of the firm* (among other indicators).

B – Does the firm undertaking the influence attempt provide an impression of *expertise*? The decision-maker may feel safer about the firm if he sees that it is making 'responsible' requests.

For example, he must be able to trust the firm's judgement that the facilities requested are indeed necessary in the context of developments in the shipbuilding industry. The decision-maker, it is true, can find this out for himself, but the necessity of his doing so decreases when he knows that the petitioner is competent in his field. This is an example of what we would call *technical expertise; the 'level of education'* in the firm was chosen as its indicator.

The index set up to measure this dimension could assume values from zero to–and–including four. It was constructed in the following way. It was established for four categories–for the respondent (usually vice-president), for the other members of the Board of Directors, for the technical personnel, and for the personnel in other sectors of the firm–whether or not there was one person who had graduated from a College of Advanced Technology or a (Technical) University. One point was awarded for each category for which this was the case. These points were totalled. The index is thus a representation of the *minimum* level of education.

However, a completely different kind of expertise is also of importance here–that is, insight into the complex world of relationships between the business world and the government. We could call this *expertise in the area of social organizations* (abbreviated to *organizational expertise*).

The index for this dimension is constructed on the basis of membership in interest organizations from the industrial sector at the local, regional and national level, plus eventual membership in 'broader' interest organizations at a national level (for example, employers' organizations; in Holland, employers as well as employees are organized at a national level, and take part as a group in negotiations over wages, working conditions, etc.). The factor labeled 'organizational expertise' is thus indexed with 'membership in interest organizations' (see Appendix 10A).

We base our estimation of the importance of this dimension on the following assumptions: If the petitioner is active in organizations, he will know exactly through which channels he can best make his demand known in order to reach his goal. On the other hand, the decision-maker may be conscious of the petitioner's knowledge in this area, perhaps taking into account that the petitioner will immediately appeal at a 'higher level' if his demands are not met. A petitioner may also, by making use of the facilities of organizations of which he is a member, apply negative sanctions–for example, by creating an unfavorable opinion in a broader public about the functioning of some government officials (we see in this connection that it is difficult in this investigation to maintain a strict separation between 'persuasion' and 'applying negative sanctions'; I already pointed this out in Chapter 2, p. 13).

As a second indicator for organizational expertise was chosen the *membership in government committees* (0 = no memberships, 1 = membership in local committees only, 2 = in regional committees, possibly also in local ones, 3 = in national committees, possibly also in regional and local ones). This leaves us with three indicators for 'expertise'.

C–*Particularism* ('*social circles*' *and* '*relations*'). Does the decision-maker base his basic 'trust' in the petitioner on his 'familiarity' with the latter? That is, it is assumed that compliance will occur more readily when the petitioner moves in the same social circles as the decision-maker–that he can be considered 'one of us'. The petitioner may as a result have a kind of continuous credit, ensuring him a willing listener whenever a problem crops up.

I tried to indicate this possible source of influence by asking questions about memberships in (a) Rotary, Lions, etc., (b) the Association for Industry and Commerce (a Dutch association with a 'social' rather than 'interest' character) and (c) regional commercial or industrial clubs. An index was obtained which represented the number of memberships (maximum of three). This is the indicator for '*social circles*'.

Since governmental officials also belong to these circles, this index is an indicator of the *probability* of business directors and government officials coming into contact outside of (semi-)official channels.

In addition, we tried to indicate '*connections*' with government officials more directly by establishing exactly what *contact* there is with *governmental* agencies. One word of warning–influence attempts, of course, *always* imply contacts. Our aim, however, is to measure the

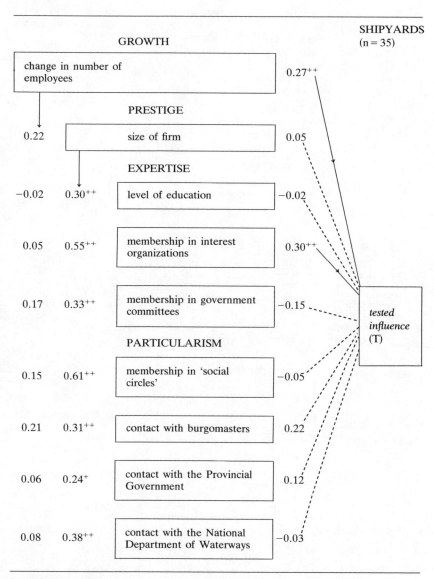

⁺ significant at 10% level
⁺⁺ significant at 5% level
Only those correlations represented by a *solid* line remained significant when controls
were applied.

Figure 10.1
*Prestige, expertise and particularism in relation to tested influence for
individual problems (shipyards)*

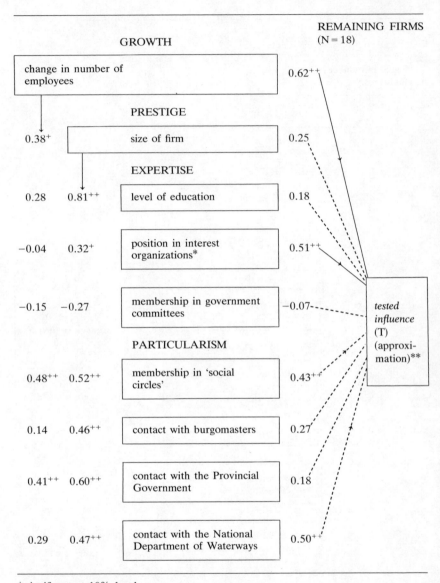

REMAINING FIRMS
(N = 18)

GROWTH

change in number of
employees   0.62⁺⁺

PRESTIGE

0.38⁺   size of firm   0.25

EXPERTISE

0.28   0.81⁺⁺   level of education   0.18

−0.04   0.32⁺   position in interest   0.51⁺⁺
                  organizations*

−0.15   −0.27   membership in government −0.07
                  committees

                                            tested
                                            influence
                                            (T)
PARTICULARISM   (approxi-
                                            mation)**

0.48⁺⁺ 0.52⁺⁺   membership in 'social   0.43⁺⁺
                  circles'

0.14   0.46⁺⁺   contact with burgomasters 0.27

0.41⁺⁺ 0.60⁺⁺   contact with the Provincial 0.18
                  Government

0.29   0.47⁺⁺   contact with the National   0.50⁺⁺
                  Department of Waterways

⁺ significant at 10% level
⁺⁺ significant at 5% level
Only those correlations represented by a *solid* line remained significant when controls
were applied. Other notes see next page.

Figure 10.2
*Prestige, expertise and particularism in relation to tested influence for
water-related problems (remaining firms)*

concept of particularism, which covers much broader ground than merely a few specific contacts. In the interview, the questions regarding 'contacts' were therefore posed before the questions about the firms' problems.[1]

To track down possible contacts, the respondents were given a list of eleven different government agencies and political organs (beginning with harbor masters and councilmen, and ending with Cabinet Ministers). It was asked per agency whether the firm had been consulted by it or vice versa. The contacts determined in this way were coded as: none, sometimes, frequently. The answers to these eleven contact questions were, understandably, rather highly correlated with one another. A reduction was called for.

Depending on the sample, a factor analysis resulted in two to four factors. I therefore chose to retain the three primary levels:
– contact with the burgomaster
– contact with the Provincial Government
– contact with the National Department of Waterways
which corresponded to a reasonable degree with the factors yielded by the factor analysis.

Together with the preceding indicator for 'social circles' this yielded *four variables for particularism.*

(See Appendix 10A for further information about the variables just discussed).

Results: the relationships between tested influence and the influence bases – The correlations of the preceding indicators with tested influence (T) were computed. Following the same lines as in Chapter 6, computations of these correlations were made solely for firms with influence attempts which had been brought to some conclusion. The correlations are presented in two figures. Figure 10.1 includes all the shipyards, Figure 10.2 the remaining firms.

In the shipyard sample, the correlations of the various influence bases with tested influence, located on the right side of Figure 10.1, are extremely low. Only the variable 'membership in interest organizations' shows a correlation (that correlation was also present in the corresponding contingency table which has not been presented here).

---

* The variable 'positions in interest organizations' applies in this sample only to national organizations of a general character (for example, National Assocation of Employers). Since firms from a number of different industrial sectors are included in this sample, interest organizations specific to a particular sector cannot be included. There are three classes: non-member, member, officer.
** See text for clarification.

In the sample of remaining firms (Figure 10.2) we worked once more
with a substitute for tested influence (that is: the T was computed on
the basis of *all* problems relating to the material facilities for transport
by water rather than only individual problems. It should be remembered, however, with respect to the non-individual problems, that T
can be validly interpreted as gains via coalitions).

The overall picture is somewhat different here (Figure 10.2) than it
was for shipyards. In addition to 'positions in interest organizations',
two indicators for particularism ('connections') are correlated with the
tested influence.

Way in which the results should be interpreted – What is the correct
interpretation of the significant correlations which have just come to
light? While it is in itself interesting to know that 'social circles' is
correlated with tested influence, this result only attains any real value
when the relationship can be shown to have an *independent significance*. If there are a number of 'growers' in the 'circles', it may actually
be the factor 'growth' which has been the origin of the correlation
between 'circles' and 'tested influence'.

We can determine the independent significance of a factor to a
certain extent by computing partial correlations. When the original
correlation remains, we can conclude that the variable has an independent significance. When, however, the partial correlation coefficient
approaches zero, it is more difficult to arrive at a conclusion. The
independent significance of the correlation is, of course, called into
question, but there is not enough information available to make a
definitive decision possible.

In this particular case, the reason for our uncertainty is that we are
unable to discover whether or not the correlation, despite its apparent
disappearance, does, in fact, remain in existence under certain *conditions.* For example: we shall see that the partial correlation between
social circles and tested influence approaches zero when growth is held
constant. However, the possibility always remains that under a certain
condition – rapid growth, for example – the correlation will remain in
existence. A definitive answer can only be obtained by splitting up the
contingency table; unfortunately, the number of cases for tested influence is too small to make this possible.

The chronological order of the variables is less problematic. The sole
question is which factor makes an impression on the decision-maker at
the moment that the influence attempt is undertaken (see also Chapter

8). We can thus be reasonably certain that the factors make their appearance *simultaneously* in the decision-making process. It is then less important to know whether or not the membership in social circles was a cause of the firm's growth in the past or whether it was the other way around.

There is one further difficulty resulting from the relatively strong correlations of the variables with one another. I made it clear earlier that in such cases a reduction of the number of variables is desirable. Again, a factor analysis was carried out for the seven variables, but interpreting the two or three factors (depending on the sample) which resulted proved to be very difficult. It was particularly difficult to place them in a clear relationship with the dimensions in the conceptual schema. Factor analysis was in this case an unsuitable method for reducing the number of variables.

A simple solution to the reduction problem is to follow the rule: do not choose a control variable from the same conceptual group, and control, when necessary, for only one variable at a time. In addition, only those correlations which already show a significant zero-order coefficient are to be subjected to further testing. This procedure will suffice for testing the independent significance of the few most important factors (for example, 'social circles' and 'membership in interest organizations').

Growth, integration in interest organizations and particularism further considered – As announced above, the significant zero-order correlations from Figures 10.1 and 10.2 will be examined for their independent significance.

Membership or position in interest organizations, with 'growth' held constant. For the shipyards, the partial correlation coefficient of the first order turns out to be 0.31 (significant at level 5%). (These were the only variables for the shipyards which displayed significant correlations with tested influence.) For the remaining firms, the correlation between 'position in interest organizations' and tested influence was controlled for three other variables; the results were:

controlled for 'growth' (first-order):	0.68 (significance level 5%)
controlled for 'social circles' (first-order):	0.41 (sign. at 5% level)
controlled for 'contacts with the Department of Waterways' (first-order):	0.35 (sign. at 10% level)

There is no longer any doubt that the correlation between tested influence and membership or positions in interest organizations has an independent significance. The correlation remains in existence in both samples under the application of each of the controls.

The obvious next question is, in turn, whether or not the independent significance of the factor *'growth'* can be demonstrated when controls for the variables just used are applied (variables which had not yet been introduced in the preceding chapter). Growth turns out to be significant once more. For shipyards: a control for 'membership in interest organizations' gives a first order partial between 'growth' and T of 0.32 (sign. at 5% level). For the remaining firms we find that the correlation of 'growth' with T,

controlled for 'position in interest organization' is (first order):	0.74 (sign. at 5% level);
controlled for 'social circles' is (first order):	0.52 (sign. at 5% level);
controlled for 'contacts with Department of Waterways' is (first order):	0.57 (sign. at 5% level).

'Social circles' and 'contacts with the Department of Waterways' show significant zero-order correlations with tested influence only for the remaining firms. However, the independent significance of 'social circles' is highly doubtful. The first order partials for 'social circles' with T are namely:

controlled for 'growth':	0.19 (not significant)
controlled for 'positions in interest organizations':	0.29 (not significant)

(No controls were carried out for 'contacts with Department of Waterways' because this variable was an indicator of the same conceptual dimension.)

Attaching an independent significance to 'contacts with the Department of Waterways' does seem a bit more justified. Control for 'growth' gives a first-order partial of 0.42 (significant at 5% level); the control for 'positions in interest organizations', however, results in a diminished first-order partial (0.33), which is not significant at a 10% level.

On the whole, the correlations between tested influence on the one hand and the indicators for particularism on the other are only present for the remaining firms; and the independent significance of the variables is additionally not too convincing. We conclude that there are only weak indications pointing to 'connections' having any effect on tested influence. The findings of this investigation *provide very little reason for believing that governmental decision-making is determined by particularistic relations.* The possibility does remain, however, that these variables are significant under certain conditions–see the preceding sub-section for a discussion of this point. In spite of this negative evidence, it can, of course, be maintained that even the weakest of indications gives cause for concern. Additionally, all the evidence is not yet in for the other two influence aspects (see latent anticipation, Section 10.2).

The following conclusion now appears justified: The variables *growth* and *membership or positions in interest organizations* are a better basis for a description–or, what amounts to the same thing, are better indirect indicators–of the distribution of tested influence among business firms than are the indicators for particularism.

For example, while the correlation between growth also remains in existence when there is, for one reason or another, no variation in 'social circles', a variation in 'social circles' is not accompanied by a difference in tested influence when the growth is held constant.

Interest organizations and governmental agencies: complementary interests?–We just saw that the degree to which a firm is a member of or has positions in interest organizations is related to tested influence. The assumption that the 'label' interest organization increases the chance of a favorable decision does seem to be firmly grounded in fact. Just as was the case with the 'growers' the idea begins to form that there is to a certain extent a harmony of interests between interest organizations and government agencies.[2] The interest organizations are, after all, usually the designated partners of the government in any negotiations over important decisions–and this occurs steadily, over a number of years rather than at any one fixed point in time. It is reasonable to suppose that the governmental agencies will do all they can to maintain good relations with social units which are to a certain extent relevant for their reputation. Thus, the government's interest may well lie in the area of 'political support'.

The idea of a unified power elite in the field of this investigation–The idea of a unified power elite 'at the top' was vigorously defended by C. Wright Mills (1956). Mills based his postulates of the existence of a 'power elite' on an analysis of 'big decisions' at 'high levels' of government and industry. Although the parallels of my investigation with his are far from complete – our 'objects', while large, are not likely to be categorized as 'big decisions', and our concern is with government at *all* levels – we can usefully employ the data presented in this and preceding chapters to test certain aspects of the power elite theory.

The particular aspects I would like to consider here are some of the basic ideas on which Mills' theory rests: that is, that 'a shared body of interests' and 'social connections' provide the bases for the unified elite (Mills, 1956, pp. 19 and 292).[3] The social connections form in a certain sense the structural dimension, consisting of patterns of contact and so forth. Exactly what happens in the course of these contacts is another question. Therefore, following Mills, a second, cultural, dimension is needed representing the *substance* of these contacts (the interests).

Mills' conception of the exact nature of the cohesion of the elite remains rather vague. Must both social connections and a harmony of interests be present, or is one or the other sufficient in itself?

This is not intended as a denial of the importance of the elements with which Mills has built up his theory. I will appropriate them here, however, with my own adjustments, describing the elite in terms of the picture emerging from the results of my investigation. Of course, *tested influence* is here again considered as the *decisive* variable.

The results obtained for tested influence gave reasons for supposing that *shared interests* existed between
1.   growing firms and the government
2.   firms well-integrated in interest organizations and the government.
However, we noticed that the variables 'growth' and 'membership or positions in interest organizations' were *not* related to one another, and that they both had an *independent* effect on tested influence. There seemed clearly to be two distinct spheres of interest involved.

We can consider *social connections* as being identical to our concept of 'particularism'. Only for the remaining firms – the weakest sample – do our indicators show any correlations with tested influence. On the whole, therefore, in our set of data social connections have at most a very limited independent significance.

Finally, if we bring the size of the firm into the picture, we see that it is primarily related to 'membership or positions in interest organizations' and to 'particularism', but it shows much lower correlations with growth.

The following conclusions can be drawn:
1 – If Mills' assertion is taken to mean that an elite exists which is based on both shared interests and social connections, then it is not supported for the field of our investigation. One of the two bases is actually not even effective: 'social connections' shows little or no relationship with tested influence.

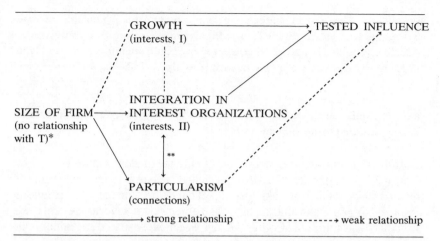

* Size of firm shows no relationship with tested influence. When the integration in interest organizations and the growth is held constant for this relationship, the correlation coefficient even becomes negative (second order: −0.22: non-significant at 10% level, two-tailed testing).
** The coefficients relevant for this relationship have not been presented in any of the preceding tables. An example may therefore be illuminatory: the correlation coefficient between 'membership or positions in interest organizations' and 'social circles' was 0.49 (significant 5%) for shipyards and was 0.39 (significant 10%) for remaining firms.

Figure 10.3
Schematic representation of the separate influence elites

2–There are signs pointing to the existence of elites based on complementarity of interests; however our data do not point in the direction of one and only one elite, but rather toward two sharply distinct spheres:

growing firms–government:
interest organizations–government.

Based on these considerations, and assuming for a moment that we can appropriately use the concept 'elite', our conclusion must be that *there are two elites which are at least to some degree independent of one another.*

This is, of course, a surprising result, but it should be remembered that it applies only for tested influence, involving individual problems which are mainly concerned with the material facilities for transport by water. Thus it would certainly be a mistake to base any generalizations on results from a fairly limited field. The situation may be entirely different for collective problems, or in other domains of influence. In some cases there may indeed be one power elite. Yet the reverse extreme is just as surely false: it is highly unlikely that one power elite, based on the two factors above, reigns in all societal sectors. Even Mills clearly did not want to carry matters this far (Mills, 1956, p. 268).

10.2 Latent anticipation in relation to expertise, particularism and cosmopolitanism

Possible bases for latent anticipation (= *the perception of problems*)–For shipyards, the size of the firm is clearly related to the number of perceived problems–a conclusion reached in one of the previous chapters. When this relationship was subjected to several controls, we came across a number of other factors which were also determinants of perceived problems, such as the largest ship built.

The question at this point–analogous to the one in the preceding section–is whether or not there are still other factors which have a relationship with latent anticipation. In other words, which as yet undiscussed factors can possibly promote the perception of problems? More specifically, we can try to discover which conditions contribute to the firm's seeing *social channels* leading to the decision-makers, and which contribute to its *perception of a reasonably high probability of success* (*see Sections 2.4 and 5.1*, conditions D and E). The assumptions being tested in the process of finding answers to these questions are the following:
A firm perceives problems earlier to the extent that:
– its own *expertise* is greater,
– its relationships are more *particularistic* (the more extensive and intensive the contacts with administrative agencies, the more it will know about the proper 'channels' to use),
– its orientation is more *cosmopolitan* (that is: the focus is on a broader environment; the opposite of a cosmopolitan orientation is a 'local' one. Compare, among others, Merton, 1957, p. 393).

We can use the same indicators for expertise and particularism as in the preceding section. Cosmopolitanism is indicated by the following variables:

(1) *Perception of government policy*–An index for this variable was constructed based on the answers to four questions: knowledge of the report of a governmental committee on the shipbuilding industry, which had appeared a short time before the investigation; knowledge of governmental papers on industrial and regional policy; knowledge

of whether or not one's own region was selected for industrial stimulation, or had been designated as a special 'centre' in this respect; knowledge of local or regional reports on economic questions, or topics regarding town and country planning (resulting scale: 0 to/including 4).

(2) *Cosmopolitanism, general*–In American studies, respondents are often asked whether or not they read local or regional newspapers. In our investigation we could not obtain a satisfactory frequency distribution for this question–too few people in our sample read only local or regional papers. We therefore chose the number of business trips in the last year as our variable for this factor. Unfortunately, this indicator is not entirely satisfactory.

(3) For shipyards, an additional variable was included, consisting of the *number of technical magazines subscribed to, which were primarily oriented to research*. This variable can, by the way, equally justifiably be considered as indicator for expertise (see also Appendix 10A).

Once more we have now at our disposal a series of variables which may determine an aspect of influence. These variables will also be called influence bases. Latent anticipation should, after all, be considered as an equally valuable aspect of influence in spite of the fact that it is 'only' composed of perceptions.

Results: latent anticipation and influence bases–The correlations between the indicators discussed above and the number of problems relating to the material facilities for transport by water are shown in Figure 10.4 (for shipyards) and Figure 10.5 (for remaining firms).

The factor 'growth' has not been included in this series, since as we saw in the preceding chapter, the correlation between growth and the number of problems tends to disappear after partializing.

The results in Figure 10.4 reveal that in the shipyard sample only three variables show a significant correlation with the number of problems (size of firm is not included in the computations). These variables are:
– level of education: 0.21,
– social circles: 0.19,
– cosmopolitanism (technical magazines): 0.18.

The question once more arises whether or not these variables have an independent significance. We are handling this problem in the same way as we did for tested influence.

(a) The size of the firm has been shown earlier to be clearly related to

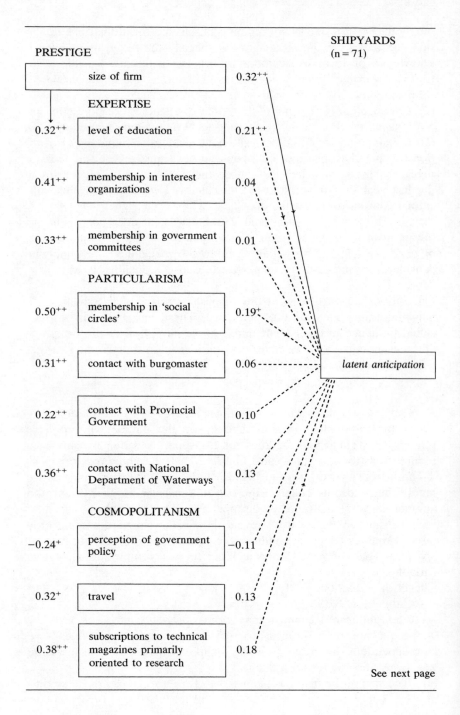

See next page

the number of perceived problems. Does this relationship remain when there is no variation in the level of education, etc.? And indeed, this is the case, even when we control for all three variables at the same time (third-order partial between size of firm and number of problems: 0.22; significant at 5% level). The first-order partials also remained significant: 0.28, 0.28 and 0.27, respectively.

(b)   When the size of the firm is held constant, do the other influence bases demonstrate any effects? Computation of the first-order partials holding the size of firm constant gives:
- level of education   – P: first order: 0.11;
- social circles   – P: first order: 0.04;
- cosmopolitanism (technical magazines) – P: first-order: 0.07.
None of these partials is still significant at the 10% level.

We should be aware, however, that for this aspect of influence it is uncertain whether size is actually the intervening variable. If that were the case, the disappearing correlation would say very little about the independent significance of the variables. 'Intervening' would mean here that size of the firm is a result of 'level of education' etc. Unfortunately, it is virtually impossible to unravel the exact time sequence; in fact, there is probably a causal effect in two directions.

Thus we can only conclude that we are somewhat dubious about the independent significance of the three variables. Once again, the possibility remains that the variables would indeed have importance under certain (unknown) *conditions*. It is impossible to reach any conclusions on these matters on the basis of partial correlations.

For the remaining firms (Figure 10.5) all the indicators for particularism and one indicator for cosmopolitanism are clearly correlated with the number of problems. Social circles, connections with governmental agencies and the perception of government policy are all correlated with the number of problems. Here as well, we would like to know whether or not the correlations disappear when the size of the firm is held constant. The formal operations involved are simple enough.

[+] significant at 10% level
[++] significant at 5% level
Only those correlations represented by a *solid* line remained significant when controls were applied.

Figure 10.4
Prestige, expertise, particularism and cosmopolitanism in relation to latent anticipation (shipyards)

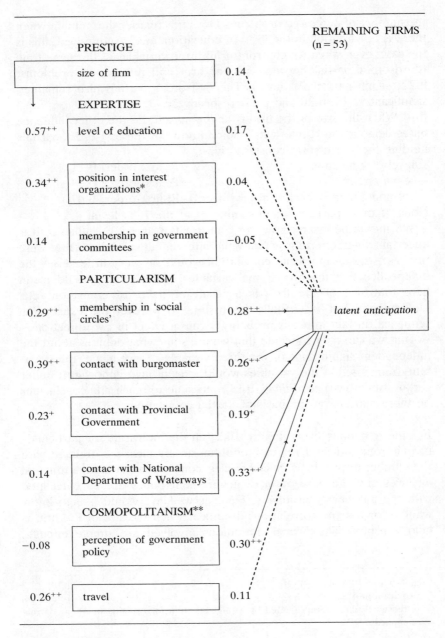

Figure 10.5
Prestige, expertise, particularism and cosmopolitanism in relation to latent anticipation (remaining firms)

Understandably, the correlations do not disappear–because there was no correlation between the size of the firm and the number of problems to begin with. However, the latter coefficient has probably been reduced due to the fact that the number of problems is unevenly distributed among the various sizes of business firms (see Chapter 6, p. 144). No hard conclusions can be drawn under these conditions.

Another problem is experienced with the indicators for 'connections' (contacts). The possibility of contamination is fairly evident for latent anticipation in particular: the more problems, the more contacts. Whatever the reasons, the *indications that 'particularism' partially determines the perception of problems are stronger for the remaining firms than for the shipyards*. Thus there is a possibility here that 'social circles' and 'connections' do have an effect.

What is the explanation of the difference between these two samples? The answer cannot easily be given using the results of this investigation alone. As I pointed out while introducing my research design, the shipyard sample is considerably more homogeneous than the sample of remaining firms; the remaining firms all come from very divergent branches of industry. On the one hand it is possible that the differences in this latter sample are actually representative of the differences in particularism as it occurs in reality. On the other hand, the fact remains that the method used to construct this sample (information obtained from key informants) was not entirely satisfactory. Latent anticipation, as I noted in Chapter 4, is the influence aspect most likely to suffer the deleterious effects of this methodological weakness. All in all, the results obtained for remaining firms cannot provide entirely definite conclusions.

To summarize: The results of our investigation suggest that the perception of problems is partially determined by particularistic relationships and a cosmopolitan orientation, but only under certain conditions. The indications were very weak for shipyards, but somewhat stronger for the remaining firms.

+ significant at 10% level
++ significant at 5% level
* The variable 'position in interest organizations' applies in this sample only to national organizations of a general character (for example, National Association of Employers). There are three categories: non-member, member, officer.
** The variable 'technical journals' as an indicator of cosmopolitanism has not been included here (the industrial sectors are not comparable).

Conclusions of a similar character can be drawn about the effects of another influence basis, namely the expertise within the firm as indicated by the level of education. There were some signs pointing to an effect of this factor for the shipyards, but not for the remaining firms.

In comparison to the findings for tested influence (and as is to be expected), a completely different set of influence bases is apparently involved in perception of problems than those which played a role in governmental compliance:

(1)　The results of the investigation give rise to the supposition that particularistic relationships are of importance in the perception of problems – at least for the remaining firms. The significance of this kind of particularistic relation is, on the other hand, much more limited for tested influence.

(2)　The influence basis 'memberships or positions in interest organizations' played a role primarily for tested influence; no effect was revealed for latent anticipation.

Stated more boldly, the perception of problem is, under certain conditions, fostered by connections and social circles. These two factors stimulate the firm's becoming aware of influence-relevant problems. But, in order to 'push things through', that is, to achieve successes with the government, the firm must be well integrated into interest organizations, or occupy positions in them.

It should be added that this is in all probability an exaggerated picture: the relevant correlation coefficients usually are not very high, and a number of other indicators do not display any relationships at all.

Secondary result: differences in the 'life-space' of large and small firms – When we look again at Figures 10.4 and 10.5 we see a fairly distinct difference between large and small firms in a whole complex of factors. We find that *the larger the firm:*

– the higher the level of education;
– the better the integration into interest organizations;
– the more often it is a member of government committees;
– the more often it is a member of social circles like the Rotary;
– the more often it has contacts with government agencies (at all levels);
– the greater the degree of cosmopolitanism.

These results, which run along the same lines as those of Bauer (1964), are not very surprising. Yet they are important as background factors for distributions of influence. A difference in these factors can, after all, lead to a difference in influence. It should, however, be kept in mind that our findings only point in this direction to a limited extent. The popular conception of an elite in which big business and government continually play into each other's hands is–in the field which we investigated–highly exaggerated.

10.3 The dubious value of indirect indicators

In most of the investigations carried out thus far, the methods employed for measuring influence usually made use of indirect indicators. Some of these indicators were very similar to the variables which I used in this chapter to indicate influence bases:
– membership or positions in influence organizations are very similar to the 'positions' in the positional method;
– 'social circles' and 'connections' are variables with a marked resemblance to the data obtained using the sociometric method touted by some authors as a worthwhile method for uncovering configurations of power (compare Kadushin, 1968, and Felling, 1974).

If it did prove possible to determine influence with this kind of indicator then it would save investigators a good deal of time and effort. The critical question, of course, is whether, and under what conditions, such indicators can safely be accepted as valid ones. This is closely connected with the definition of influence which serves as the investigator's point of departure. Simon suggests that the '*exercise* of influence' must absolutely be regarded as the key element in the definition (1957, p. 65). This suggestion has to a large degree guided us in our choice of the method of measurement described and applied in this book.

Only *after* an empirical relationship between this 'real' measurement of influence and an influence base is established can the latter be regarded as an indicator for influence (again, Simon, 1957, p. 78). Even then, the validity may very well be tied to certain conditions.

Following this line of reasoning, influence as measured with our method can be considered as the criterium. Then we have a solid procedure for evaluating the bases of influence as indicators. As a rule of thumb, an indicator can be assigned a certain validity if the zero-order correlation with our measurements is significant, and if in addition these correlations occur in both samples.[4] We considered the validity of the indicators for tested influence and latent anticipation separately.

(a) *Tested influence*–As can be seen in Figures 10.1 and 10.2, only the variables 'membership or positions in interest organizations' is of any value as an indicator. There is little or no evidence attesting to the value of the other indicators (six variables).

The following example demonstrates once more that it is extremely important to proceed with caution when using indirect indicators. Almost all the indicators are highly correlated with the size of the firm (see the left side of Figures 10.1 and 10.2, second column), but size of the firm shows no correlation with tested influence. On the other hand, only a very few of the indicators are at all correlated with 'growth', but it is exactly growth which is an important factor in determining tested influence (see once more Figures 10.1 and 10.2).

(b) *Latent anticipation* – To begin with, the size of the firm itself can be used as an indicator (although for the remaining firms the correlation coefficient does not show that there is a relationship; see p. 140). The only other indicator having any value whatsoever, as can be seen in Figures 10.4 and 10.5 is 'membership in social circles'. The value of 'connections' is questionable, because the corresponding variables only display significant correlations in one of the two samples. This means that sociometric data alone cannot be regarded as an adequate indicator of latent anticipation. Only a specifically-tailored application of the sociometric method – that is, by tracking down the memberships in social circles – provides a possible reliable indicator.

Our conclusion is that the 'rough' indirect methods of measurement cannot entirely be dismissed:
– 'membership or positions in interest organizations' is a reasonably good indicator of tested influence (positional method);
– 'memberships in social circles' points under some conditions to latent anticipation (sociometric method).

But, it must be immediately admitted that interpreting the data obtained by applying these indirect methods involves almost insurmountable difficulties. After all, each separate indicator applies to only one aspect of influence. It is also doubtful whether the indicators used in this study are also valid to the same degree for other areas of social life.

Of course, our conclusions are only valid for *influence* exercised with regard to *individual problems* and perhaps to a certain degree for *gains* via coalitions as well. The situation may be entirely different for collective problems such as 'issues' which have been the object of most of the previous studies of influence. Since these investigators usually maintain, wrongly, that they are studying influence or power – in fact they are at the most measuring 'participation' – I believe that the time has not yet come for discussing this point any further.

Notes

1. We have tried to minimize in this way the danger of contamination between contacts and influence. This danger is in any case the most pronounced for the influence aspect 'latent anticipation': the more problems a business firm has, the greater the number of contacts which can be expected. Nevertheless, it will be seen later (p. 247 ff.) that our results do not point strongly in this direction. In my opinion, therefore, the probability of contamination in this case is so minimal that it can be neglected.
2. Has this interpretation been made too hastily? It could be countered that the greater tested influence of firms with strong and extensive ties to interest organizations can be traced back to their social-organizational expertise. These firms in particular may perhaps *only* undertake influence attempts when they are virtually certain of success. Our data pointed–be it weakly–in this direction: the correlation coefficients between manifest anticipation and 'membership and positions in interest organizations' are slightly negative (though far from significant). On the other hand, firms which are comfortably familiar with a scale of interest organizations will also be more likely to possess the skills needed to ensure that their own problems are seen and treated as non-individual ones, as common problems. It thus appears unlikely that our interpretation that a 'harmony of interests' exists between interest organizations and government agencies is seriously threatened by suggestions that social-organizational expertise is the actual key factor.
3. Mills in fact uses a somewhat stronger term, 'social intermingling'.
4. The customary methods make no distinction among the 'parties' in the influence process. In such cases, measurements are carried out both of private citizens and government agencies. This section considers the possible value of indirect indicators *exclusively* for private citizen.

11. Summary and Concluding Discussion

11.1 Summary of the main results of the investigation

In this investigation, the influence of business firms on the government has been investigated by inquiring into the degree to which the problems of firms are solved by the government. Simply stated, influence on the government is thus considered as persuading the government to 'get something done'. The number of effects which the firms have achieved in a given period is thus the ultimate criterion for establishing the existence of influence.

It should be kept in mind, however, that 'getting something done' implies investigating *the influence process*. In other words, there is a difference between benefits and influence. Benefits may result from many causes, and only one of these is influence. Therefore the influence process has to be at the core of the measurement method (Simon, 1957). This investigation has adhered to this principle (in contrast to Salomon and Siegfried, 1977, who omitted the processes).

Additionally, the number of effects (benefits) reveals little or nothing about the source – which party in the influence relationship – of possible differences in influence. Influence can result from efforts of the business firms, but can also be a consequence of their being a 'willing' government in power.

In an effort to gain an insight into this process of influence as well, we have divided influence into three influence aspects.

Two of the aspects characterize the business firms (the 'petitioners'):
a. *latent anticipation*, which is the degree to which the firms are aware of their problems, and the possibilities available to them for exercising influence.
b. *manifest anticipation*, the degree to which the firms turn to the government for a solution of their problems – that is, the degree to which they undertake influence attempts.

The third aspect primarily characterizes the behavior of the government (the decision-makers):

c. *tested influence* – the degree to which the government complies with the influence attempts of the business firms. (It should be recalled that there is also influence without influence attempts – that is, by anticipation *by the government*. In this investigation, this kind of influence was empirically negligible).

For this investigation I selected as objects of influence mainly the material facilities for transport by water; the sample was composed of 130 firms, all of which were dependent upon transport by water (there were two sub-samples: 73 shipyards and 57 'remaining' firms – paper mills, for example). The research design could be characterized as quasi-experimental (Chapter 4).

A number of popular assumptions were put to a test in this investigation. The most important results are:

– The *main hypothesis* that *large* firms have more influence on the government than small ones was *not* confirmed for two of the three aspects of influence (Chapters 6 and 7). This is a surprising result. In particular the tested influence was not correlated with size of the firm; thus government decisions did not tend to favor the large firms. We also investigated separately whether or not there was any indication that subsidiaries of multinational concerns (present in the 'remaining firms' sample) had relatively more influence than other firms. Contrary to what is a currently widely-accepted opinion, this did *not* prove to be the case.

The manifest anticipation likewise displayed no correlation with the size of the firm. These findings differ sharply from those of Salomon and Siegfried (1977), although it should be noted that these authors disregarded the *influence process* in the investigations.

Only the latent anticipation – the number of problems which the firm perceives – increased along with the size of the firm.

Let us return for a moment to the surprising results for tested influence. I have of course examined the data in great detail in an effort to find an *ad hoc* explanation of these findings. In the first place, there appeared to be absolutely no reason to doubt the validity of the results. Once the results were accepted, only one adequate explanation – the following one – could be found: Large firms have more influence attempts that are relatively expensive for the government. This perhaps explains in part why the percentage of successes (tested influence) is not a function of the size of the firm. If the relatively cheap (for the government) influence attempts are examined separately, then our data support the suggestion that for these cheaper attempts the tested influence of large firms is relatively greater. For the expensive attempts, however, the reverse seems to be true.

– A second hypothesis was, that when business firms have formed coalitions, the greater the size of the coalition, the greater the influence it will have on the government in solving the common problems of its members.[1] This assumption was supported to some extent by our findings (Chapter 7). In this respect, the results are similar to those of Salomon and Siegfried, 1977.

We can, of course, only offer an *ad hoc* explanation for the intriguing puzzle of why 'size' has no effect when individual firms are at issue, but does have an effect when coalitions are being considered. The most probable explanation is that size only begins to play a role when it appears in *combination* with another factor – that is, the '*degree of organization*'. We can be reasonably certain that 'coalitions' imply a relatively high 'degree of organization' (in any case *between* firms).

This latter factor has a significance of its own as well. That is, the data indicated that the influence of coalitions was relatively greater when they were represented by 'spokesmen' (for example, interest organizations, municipal administrations). The representational role played by spokesmen in such cases can validly be considered as an element of the 'degree of organization'.

A secondary outcome was that the *degree of participation* in the activities of the coalition was more or less equal for the large and the small firms. This is a radically different finding from one obtained in studies for collective actions (Braam, Dijkstra and others, 1976). The larger firms clearly had higher rates of participation in these collective actions. However, the makeup of coalitions and collective actions exhibits considerable differences. Many more firms, as well as many more *small* firms, are involved in collective actions; in addition, the emotional overtones are much stronger in collective actions than in coalitions.

– A *third* assumption applies only for tested influence, and was formulated after the fact. It states that the tested influence – the degree to which the government complies with influence attempts – depends upon the *rate of growth* of the business firm. There is much evidence in support of this hypothesis. 'Growers' were found to extract more favorable decisions from the government than 'non-growers' (see Chapter 9). This is in agreement with the values of the decision-makers, which could to a certain extent be pinpointed by analyzing the interviews with the burgomasters.

– We tested a number of subsidiary assumptions relating to the *bases of influence* to see whether or not they are related to the three influence aspects, and whether or not an *independent significance* could be attributed to the statistically significant zero-order correlations which were found (see Chapter 10).

A. Contrary to our expectations, the *tested influence* does *not* show a relationship with
– *expertise* within the firm,
– membership in '*social circles*' such as the Rotary,
– the '*connections*' maintained with government agencies.

The tested influence *does* correlate with:
– the degree to which memberships or positions are occupied in *interest organizations*.

B. Virtually no relationships are found to exist between the various influence bases and *manifest anticipation*.

C. The latent anticipation is *not* correlated with:
– the degree to which memberships or positions are held in *interest* organizations.

The latent anticipation is presumably correlated *under certain conditions* with
– *expertise*,
– membership in '*social circles*' such as the Rotary.
– '*connections*' with government agencies,
– *cosmopolitan* orientation.

(All these factors also showed high correlations with size of firm. It is impossible, and probably not even desirable, to make a statement about the independent significance of the correlations. That is why I have qualified my statement affirming the existence of these correlations with 'presumably'.)

Roughly speaking, tested influence only appears to be related to 'growth' and to 'memberships or positions in interest organizations'. The latent anticipation, which is more or less the source from which the influence springs, has a demonstrated relationship with size of firm and – apparently closely associated with this factor – sometimes with expertise, 'social circles', 'connections' and cosmopolitan orientations.

The results with regard to tested influence can be used to highlight several aspects which lie at the heart of the theory of C. W. Mills in the *Power Elite*. It is obvious that the present investigation is only to a limited extent concerned with the 'top elite'. We are not testing Mills' theory as such. Nevertheless, it is useful to review some of the dimensions of Mills' theory which are significant in the present investigation, using 'tested influence' as a criterion (in my view a very plausible and important one).

1.　According to Mills, a power elite is based on two factors, shared interests as well as social connections. In the field covered by this investigation this assumption turns out to be invalid. The 'social connections' show only weak correlations, and in some cases no correlations at all, with tested influence;

2.　There are indeed indications attesting to the existence of an elite based on a harmony of interests; however, our data, rather than pointing toward only one exclusive elite, seem to indicate that there are two fairly distinct spheres in which a harmony of interests exists, namely:

growing firms – government

interest organizations – government.

We must therefore conclude that there are two *elites which are at least to some degree independent of one another.*

One investigation, using the method employed here, does not provide us with sufficient evidence for answering the question of whether or not these results can be generalized to other domains of influence, and to other types of business firms. Perhaps we have to abandon the goal of generalizing in this subject matter. It is, after all, one of the essentials of the meaning of 'measurements' that they reveal different patterns at different times, places, domains or whatever.

11.2　The significance of this study from a methodological point of view

The measurement of influence – The primary goal of this study was to test a method for measuring influence which could do justice to the full measuring of the concept, with the influence process as the "core" – whether present or absent (non-decisions). There are perspectives for application of this method of testing for much-needed research in other spheres of social life. The obvious rejoinder is that the sphere which I chose to study had influence objects which were of unusual clarity and simplicity. However, in the course of the investigation we came into contact often with influence in other spheres than in the water-related infrastructure, and I am convinced that these areas are in no instance so complex as to make an investigation along the same lines as this one impracticable. In the mean time, some attempts in a quite different fields – namely influence of schools on the local government (Elting and Even, 1977) and of football-clubs on the government (Bos and Braam, to be published 1980), have succeeded very well.

One word of caution should be added: The method described will perhaps be applicable mainly to areas where the government has a *monopoly* for distribution. Nevertheless, the number of such areas is large (see also Schuyt, 1974).

The value of indirect indicators – The measurement of influence using our method is, of course, time-consuming. Thus it is understandable that in the past, *indirect* indicators – positions, reputations, participation and sociometric patterns – have been favored most often by researchers. When we use the data derived from the *influence process* as the criterium-variables in our investigation, we are able to establish the validity of these indicators (compare Simon, 1957, pp. 65 and 78), and especially of 'positions' and 'sociometric patterns'. In Chapter 10 I came to the conclusion that the value of this type of indicators is at this stage highly problematical. The most that can be said is that they are valid under some conditions and for some aspects of influence only. In all probability, it is the uncertainty concerning the value of the indicators which has been responsible for the heated and highly partisan discussions which have surrounded the controversy over the reputational and the decision-making methods, the study of Mills (1956), and, in the Netherlands, the study of Helmers and others (1975). The data produced by most of these investigations are real enough, but interpretations of this data in terms of influence and power are precarious. Much can be said in such situations for an all-out drive toward terminological purity and consistency. If it is actually 'participations', 'reputations' and so forth which are being measured, then the original terms should be used *consistently* rather than substituting power or influence at some point in the discussion. This is a persistent instance of slovenliness which crops up again and again in sociological praxis.

I hope that this investigation has demonstrated convincingly that influence is a concept which is clearly susceptible to operationalization and measurement using the influence process as a 'core'. If it proves possible, as I think it will, to apply our method to other fields of influence (the feasibility of such studies has, after all, been proven to a certain extent), then we should abandon the use of surrogates once and for all, even though a better measurement will undoubtedly cost more in time and money. We are, I fear, as sociologists too often satisfied with irresponsible short cuts and half solutions when studying and observing these kinds of sensitive topics involving fundamental sociological concepts in complex settings. Comparing our level of aspiration with that in the sciences – take astronomy as an example – would provide us with some serious warnings.

Statements of famous sociologists and empirical investigations – The results of this investigation highlight once more the problem that statements of renowned sociologists which are not derived from exhaustive research must be regarded skeptically. Mills, for example, maintains that although the business world and the government used to occupy independent spheres in what he called a 'balancing society', the present state of affairs is one of 'governmentalization of the lobby'. 'The old lobby, visible or invisible, is now the visible government', (1956, p. 267). Anyone who has ever worked in a government agency will probably agree that there is certainly some truth in this statement. And our results do not entirely contradict this. If we assume that the 'membership or positions in interest organizations' is a reasonably good indicator for a lobby – the former is, after all, consulted regularly prerequisite to governmental decision-making – then lobbies are certainly working to the advantage of individual problems. But Mills' statement can also be interpreted as meaning that the government has been 'annexed' as it were by interest organizations. Yet this is at most only partially true, since we have seen that the criterium 'growth' also plays a significant role in decision-making – a factor whose effect is independent of the integration in interest organizations. In the area covered by our study, the government clearly has a considerable measure of autonomy. The situation is thus more complex than Mills realizes – or at least seems to realize.

Other statements insufficiently grounded in empirical data are not hard to find. Parsons (1970, p. 274) says: 'The participation of big businessmen in governmental processes is by no means to be interpreted as a simple index of their power to dominate government in their own interest, as Mills often seems to maintain'. This statement cannot, of course, be entirely disproved – it is itself too complex and vague, and our investigation covers too limited a range. But the impression which Parsons is trying to create here is clearly false, according to our data. 'Membership or positions in interest organizations' does indubitably contribute to an increase in influence exercised in the interest of individual problems.

Thus there is reason enough to be suspicious of any statements purporting to relate to empirical reality unless they are clearly and directly linked to exhaustive investigation.

11.3 Influence and inequality in the area under investigation (interpretation)

In this study, the concept of influence was further specified as 'influence exercised, at least in part, to pursue some advantage for one's self'. The more influence a firm has, the more 'gains' it has booked through the intercession of the government. Differences in influence can therefore be an important cause of *social inequality*.

Differences in influence can in their turn be traced back to differences in the *three* aspects into which we have divided this concept. To illuminate the causes of social inequality – concentrating on differences in influence as their source – we will review separately the principal results for two of the three aspects (since very few correlations were observed with manifest anticipation, I will omit discussion of it here, as I did in Chapter 10).

The consciousness of problems (latent anticipation) – Small firms appeared to perceive fewer problems than large firms (or, the latent anticipation of small firms was weaker than that of large firms).

Thus because they are less conscious of the number and extent of their problems, they have fewer starting points from which influence can be initiated. The same is sometimes true in cases where the firm possesses relatively less technical 'expertise', or when it is not a member of 'social circles', or when it has a weaker network of 'connections' with the government, or when it has a less cosmopolitan orientation. In many cases, these factors in turn are closely connected with the size of the firm.

In all these cases, there is a relatively high probability that the firm will remain unaware of a number of problems which the government could have acted upon. *Such firms are thus likely to be underprivileged as a result of their own perceptions (or lack of them) of the number of problems.* This is an important piece of information which can be used in the search for strategies for changing influence distributions. We will return to this topic in Section 11.5.

The differences in influence just mentioned are primarily related to the private citizens (business firms) themselves. Possibly even more important are the differences in influence which come into being as a result of the behavior of governmental agencies.

Government policy and tested influence (the government as 'distributive actor') – 'Tested influence' is the degree to which the government complies with the influence attempts made by business firms. Thus the magnitude of the tested influence is a reflection of the government's behavior toward a given business firm. Comparison of different firms can reveal which firms receive relatively many or relatively few benefits as a result of government policy. We discover how the government has fulfilled its role as the *'distributive actor'* in the relationship. This 'distribution' takes on a very concrete meaning in our investigation, because compliance involves expenditures for infra-structural objects. It is no exaggeration to say that this study is examining how our tax dollars are distributed by the government in one particular budget area.

The interpretation of our main findings will now take place in the light of these considerations.

(a) *Government decision-making does not favor large firms over small ones.*
We saw that one possible partial explanation of this result was that large firms make requests relatively more often for more expensive objects, and are successful relatively less often as a result. We can only speculate as to the complete interpretation of this finding. Perhaps the decision-makers are extremely anxious to avoid any suggestion that they favor large firms over small ones; they are, of course, painfully aware that rival politicians and the mass media are always ready to pounce upon even the slightest hint of an instance of favoritism. Whatever the reason, our results with respect to size of firm give us no grounds for doubting the impartiality or the 'justice' of government decision-making.

The exact content of the concept 'impartiality' or 'justice' can, of course, be a topic of endless 'learned' discussion. In my opinion, the matter is quite easily settled within the context of our research design. We can conclude that decision-making is impartial when firms in *comparable* situations obtain an equal amount of gains from the government (in this study we call it – from the point of view of the business firms – equal tested influence). I emphasize strongly that a sound judgement about impartiality can only be made when the situations are highly comparable. We took great pains to incorporate this element in our research design (Chapter 4), and extensive controls were also carried out after-the-fact (Chapters 8 and 9). Since the 'gains' must also be comparable, we have expressed them wherever possible as government expenditure *per employee*.

(b) *The employment opportunities already in existence: 'stepchild' of the government in the late sixties?*
In Chapter 9 we observed that growing firms receive relatively more benefits from the government than 'non-growers'. There appeared to

be a harmony of interests between growing business firms and government agencies, because the principle of 'growth' was highly valued by the decision-makers (at least during the period covered by this investigation).

A harmony of interests, benefiting a number of parties, is, of course, in a certain sense a positive state of affairs. But the non-growing firms, as well as their employees, are then left in a relatively unfavorable position. A disproportionate amount of attention is given to the *increase* in employment opportunities. Concern with the enhancement of employment opportunities is, however, only a very small part of the concern with *employment opportunities as a whole*. It can justifiably be maintained that *consolidation of existing employment opportunities* is at least equally important. In many industries – textiles, metals – employment actually decreased to a considerable extent – due perhaps in part to governmental neglect of these 'non-growth' industries.

Our results indicate that this latter aspect was more or less ignored during the period of the investigation. I do not base this conclusion on the finding that neither the size of the firm itself, nor the 'share in employment opportunities' correlate with tested influence. After all, this does seem to be a proper state of affairs from the point of view of justice. However, the assumption that there is only limited governmental interest in 'preservation of existing employment opportunities' is derived from the fact that the condition 'governmental stimulation climate' does not appear to have any effect on the tested influence – at least not for firms which are already located in the areas selected for this policy (see Chapter 9). Thus, this condition, which is in large part of the government's own creation, fails to bestow any extra advantages on firms which are already located in economically backward areas; they thus receive in fact no more advantages than firms located in economically 'healthy' areas. Of course, objections can be made to looking at the problem this way (competitive relationships and so forth). The fact does remain, that there is no special attention paid to firms which are located in areas with limited employment opportunities. This, in combination with our finding that non-growing firms receive less benefits than growing firms, supports the assumption that the government was relatively unconcerned with the *preservation* of existing employment as opposed to its considerable concern for *growth* of employment opportunities (business closures 'appearing out of the blue' fits perfectly into this picture).

This picture may have changed drastically since 1970, or even been completely reversed. Yet the same general advice applies: the government should think through, and possibly modify the precise criteria which play a role in its decision-making.[2] If government is seen as having some responsibility for overseeing employment opportunities, then it should at least be required that it be impartial in its treatment of growers and non-growers with respect to their influence attempts.

(c) *Interest organizations: Influence elites with individual advantages?* Interest groups, in the sense of lobbies or pressure groups, can be conceived as communication links between private citizens and government. A number of observers and social scientists believe that they fulfill a useful, even necessary function in this respect (see for example Key, 1942, Truman, 1958). This standpoint, though true enough in itself, does not tell the whole story; *interest organizations can also constitute a cause of social inequality.* This problem does not, in my opinion, receive the attention it deserves; I will therefore discuss it more deeply here, using the results of this investigation as my point of departure.

As we saw in Chapter 7, interest organizations certainly are an important factor within the area covered by our investigation. They sometimes fulfill a function as 'spokesmen' for coalitions of business firms, and there is evidence showing that they contributed to the success of those coalitions. In another investigation we discovered intensive participation by the leaders of interest organizations when problems which were more collective in nature were involved (Braam and Swinkels, 1969, and Braam, Dijkstra and Others, 1976). However, these data do not provide decisive evidence for reaching any conclusions about social inequality. We can only suppose that those who are closest to the sources of power will benefit the most from it. But the possibility always remains, that the leaders of interest organizations act in the interests of the group as a whole, because they see it as being their *responsibility.*

We found in Chapter 10, however, that a connection with interest organizations also resulted in *individual* advantages. The better a firm was integrated into the interest organizations, the higher was the tested influence for individual problems (that is, the problems in which only one firm was involved).

Thus those firms which were highly integrated into interest organizations seemed to form an *influence elite* which reaped a relatively large amount of individual benefits.[3]

We therefore conclude that, while *interest organizations* are on the one hand an effective means of promoting the interests of their members in their relations with government, *they are on the other hand also very likely the cause of new social inequalities.* The source of these inequalities are the differences in the *members' involvement in the organizations* – a phenomenon whose occurrence seems inevitable.

This brings us to the end of our analysis of governmental policy. The government certainly does seem liable to serious criticism on the basis of the relationships which we have observed. *Its policy, subject as it is to influence issuing from the society, causes inequality in some respects; however, there are also apparently areas of relative independence, with, as a consequence, a number of 'fair' distributions* (look at 'size of firm', for example).

Another possible source of inequality is a difference in participation for problems in which a number of firms are interested. Although this theme is a bit out of place in this chapter, it is important enough to devote a short section to a discussion of it.

The problem of equal representation in large groups – In Section 7.4 we reported some results recording the *participation* of firms when problems of interest to more than one firm were involved, and when the firms formed *coalitions* on the basis of these shared interests. It is unclear to what degree these participations are related to benefiting relatively too much or too little. At most, they provide a hint about differences in influence *possibilities*. However, in this investigation, no differences were observed between large and small firms in their levels of participation in coalitions.

In another investigation, carried out with other researchers, we looked into the rate of participation in collective actions (these actions have been numerous in the Netherlands during the last ten years). Considerable differences *were* observed in these cases: among all the firms interested in a problem, the large firms showed relatively more participation. This was the case not only because the firms were operating via the interest organizations, but also because they were using communication channels 'outside' these organizations.

There are several possible reasons for this difference between coalitions and collective actions. In the first place, a number of very small firms – with less than twenty employees – participated in the collective actions. It could be posited that the category 'very small firms' has very little influence possibilities, and that there is a sharp jump in influence possibilities above a particular size class; however, these possibilities level off when the firms pass a certain size. A second reason could be that the level of the threat is higher and the accompanying strength of the emotions is greater for collective actions (compare Mulder and Stemerding, 1963). So far, the difference between (small) coalitions and collective actions is more or less in line with the theory of Olson (1965).

Another explanation is possible. The difference may originate from the greater possibility for domination by the 'big ones' in larger groups. In that case, from a practical point of view, the difference between the (small) coalitions and the (larger) collective actions is extremely important. It could mean that the ideal of 'equal representation' is in greater danger as the group involved becomes larger and/or the emotions become stronger. It does seem to be a point to keep in mind with the numerous efforts that are being made in the Netherlands to increase participation in a number of areas: when large groups are involved, the basic principles of equal representation are all too easily ignored. This problem can be dismissed quickly enough by maintaining that 'representation' does not mean much in itself until the exact dimension which is involved is specified. There is, however, one dimension which is a hard and ubiquitous reality no matter what the social system: the social stratification. Whether it is operationalized as the size of the business firm, education, income, property, or party positions, the distributions are in every case so skewed that they *must* be considered in any attempts to construct a system of equal representation. At this particular moment in history, when new horizons seem to be opening up in the realm of participation (at least in this country), this principle can be all too easily forgotten.

11.4 Influence and inequality in general

Influence distributions as a fundamental problem of society – The significance of influence for inequality is by no means restricted to the area covered by this investigation. Yet I am convinced that this is accorded far too little attention in discussions of inequality. It is generally realized that social inequality is created and maintained in part by social institutions themselves. We assume, for example, that our educational system does not provide equal opportunities for the different strata in our society (for example Peschar, 1978). The point of view that this educational system is itself a product of influence processes which are steered by certain social groups is less widely shared. The 'background' of influence relationships is perhaps less imediately obvious in education than in some other areas, but myriad examples can be cited in support of their importance.

Whether or not foreign workers have inferior housing to native Dutchmen, whether accommodations for the elderly are on an equal level with other age groups, whether some categories of the population are forced to live in high-rise apartments, while others are not, whether or not people with a low IQ earn less than people with a high IQ, whether or not there are more facilities available for the married than the unmarried – all these differences and many others will always be partly determined by the differences in the influence at the disposal of the categories involved. The central question is simply whether different citizens or groups can get the government to do things for them in equal measure: that is, whether or not influence is equally distributed. Differences in influence – as we have defined them – involve discrepancies in the *benefits* which are received from the government. Since in our Western societies the government has enormous financial resources and legal power at its disposal, any discrepancies in the benefits which it grants (and thus also in influence) have far-reaching consequences for inequality. *In effect, the influence processes constitute one of the mechanisms through which inequality is produced.*

In the area covered by our investigation, this inequality was caused by three different factors: The awareness (of citizens) of problems, the 'growth' criterium (used by the government), and the degree of integration in interest organizations (or its complement: the decision-making criteria 'pressure and trust').

When we take a closer look at governmental policy, we see that the primary significance of influence is likely to be the role it plays in setting priorities. Decisions about which problems need to be solved first, and for which problems the most resources will be used, are more likely to be affected by influence issuing from a society than by 'hard' calculations. I believe that it is no exaggeration to state that the distribution of influence is the most fundamental problem in our – and, in fact, in every – society (compare Chapter 2). One important dimension of this problem which I have chosen to highlight once more in the next section is the operation of interest organizations.

Interest organizations in our society: a pattern resembling 'early liberalism' – It should be recalled that the interest organizations in the area we were studying were partly responsible for the pattern of influence distributions which we observed. They were thus a partial cause of inequality.

It would be going too far to generalize this finding to other areas of influence and other social sectors. However, there is an urgent need for further research along the lines of this study in these other areas and sectors. After all, the sector of shipyards can be surveyed rather easily. The total number of shipyards in the Netherlands is only two hundred or so (not counting firms with less than twenty employees). If distributions are already markedly unequal in a category as small as this one, what must the situtation be in very large sectors?

There is yet another impetus for further research. The interest organizations which made an appearance in this investigation were all paid for by the members themselves. In some other social sectors, interest organizations are subsidized by the government – in the Netherlands, for example, on a large scale in the areas of health care and social work. The pressing question here is whether or not the interests of private citizens in such cases are much more likely to be subordinated to the interests of the interest organizations – the service organizations included – than when interest organizations maintain their independence and pay their own way.

It is a small step from our tentative findings to the widely-shared supposition that *groups* in society which are *relatively poorly represented* by interest organizations receive fewer 'benefits' than groups which are well-represented. In the Netherlands groups and categories that immediately come to mind are foreign labourers and the elderly, though there are, of course, many more (see, for example, Braam, 1972; 1973).

How interest organizations actually operate, the roles which they fulfill, is from this standpoint perhaps the most fundamental problem facing our democratic way of life. In this part of the social structure, to an even greater extent than in the economic sector in a narrower sense, 'laisser faire' is the guiding principle in both thought and action. However, although government spending has increased enormously, and the government has placed its administrative stamp on ever-widening sectors of social life, there has not been a concomitant broadening of democratic controls on these expanded governmental powers and the influence exercised on it. It is especially true here that 'the law of the jungle' is a *reality*. Seen in this perspective, our society still finds itself in a stage of early liberalism, yet this fact usually remains unacknowledged because discussions of other 'issues' channel attention into other areas. Certain topics – capitalism versus socialism, for example, or change 'from the bottom up', or workers' self-management – though in themselves important enough, threaten to crowd out even the possibility of looking at things from a completely different theoretical framework (in recent years, the necessity of coping with increasingly serious economic problems has been a factor strengthening this trend), and thus causing us to forget the role played by interest groups and the inequality issuing from them in and by the area of social influence.

Interest organizations: a paradox – From time to time, some awareness of this problem crops up in society. *New* interest groups or 'collective actions' make their appearance, undertaking influence attempts aimed at eliminating a particular set of inequalities. At times they are successful in these attempts, but exactly as a result of these successes, new inequalities can be brought into being. These inequalities thus can be directly linked to the activities of those new interest groups (see the results of the present investigation). We are therefore faced with a paradox: the social processes which are working to do away with inequalities, are themselves the immediate cause of making further corrective measures necessary.

11.5 Influence and the diminishment of inequality: 'learning' and 'regulation'

How can the mechanism discussed above, which produces inequality in a society, be brought under control? Influence exercised on the government is a phenomenon which is here to stay. If we want to diminish the inequality which can result from this influence, the only really effective solution is to regulate the distribution of influence. In this closing section, I intend to propose several lines of action which could be followed to achieve this end. The main prerequisite to all these possibilities for action is that the influence distributions which are to be regulated be known *empirically* to those doing the regulating. After all, our results in this investigation have made it clear enough that the actual situation does not always jibe with what 'common sense' tells us to expect. Empirical investigations must therefore stand in the forefront.

In order to achieve a diminishment of discrepancies in influence, changes will virtually always need to be made with respect to *both parties* in the influence relationship, the *private citizens* and *the government*.

The private citizens: learning, participation and mobilization – The 'awareness' of individual problems has a relationship in our investigation with the size of the firm, and at times with expertise, membership in 'social circles', the availability of connections and a cosmopolitan orientation. Which of these factors can be eliminated or altered? It would be impracticable to do anything about 'social circles' and 'connections' – besides the fact that we would probably create a new 'circle' with every measure that we took.

It is, on the other hand, possible to increase expertise – and in particular, a person's or group's capability to recognize its own problems and its possibilities for exercising influence to solve them. Mulder (1973, pp. 148 ff) has made several valuable suggestions concerning how this process can be fostered; beginning with the seventh grade, these matters should be considered an integral part of the learning process, and as such handled *in the schools*.

Our results point to some other possible lines of action which the private citizen has at his disposal:

1 – *participation in interest organizations* was shown to be significant for tested influence;

2 – *mobilization* of others may be a prerequisite for forming the interest organizations *and* for supporting and intensifying individual influence attempts (the significance of 'spokesmen' in our field of investigation, as well as that of coalitions).

Skills are involved here which can also be 'learned' to a certain extent.

As important as these skills may be, it would be quite unrealistic to maintain that when they are acquired, inequalities will be totally eliminated. Differences in predisposing factors, be it 'nature' and/or 'nurture' (environment), might conceivably even be accentuated as a result of an improvement in skills. As I see it, these measures must therefore be supplemented by adjustments in the behavior of the second party in the relationship – the government.

Evaluation, inspection, correction (*government policy and the parliament*)–In this study, we have considered the government as being the *distributive party* with respect to influence. We have seen how that government policy – consciously or unconsciously – can be the cause of inequalities. No doubt can exist as to who is responsible for this state of affairs. All the decisions which were explored in this investigation were governmental decisions. Thus the responsibility simply lies with the government – and with the parliament. In the Netherlands, it is sometimes assumed, the parliament in particular has steadily increased the strength of its 'watchdog' function as compared to its function as a *legislative* body. Yet, while we observe on the one hand that some members of parliament frequently express their concern about parliament's total inability to exert any control over far-reaching decisions made by powerful business firms, on the other hand we see them fail repeatedly to act decisively in areas which do clearly fall under their jurisdiction. They are in fact responsible – in part at least – for the inequalities which resulted from the influence distributions we tracked down since they failed to fulfill their 'watchdog' function by making adjustments in these distributions, which were caused, in part at least, by the government.[4]

It is quite clear, however, that it is virtually impossible for the parliament to carry out those controls for which it is in a formal sense responsible – at least not at the present time. Parliament, facing a huge governmental bureaucracy, simply does not possess the instruments which it needs to assess the enormous area covered by influence distributions and related government decision-making, as well as the inequalities which can result from them. I said in Chapter 1 that 'influence' was an elusive phenomenon. Especially in complex societies like ours, its distribution can become easily and even unconsciously unequal. Parliament would need extensive and precise knowledge of particular influence distributions in order to be able to *evaluate* their effects and what can be done about them.

Evaluation can therefore only take place if the social sciences, on the basis of *evaluation research* can provide the knowledge which is needed. I believe that this study is an example of such an investigation – an example which I hope will give others confidence in their ability to develop research projects along these same lines. Furthermore, whereas we were forced to feel our way carefully, step by step, new investigators should be able to obtain results much more quickly.

There are two necessary preconditions for this type of investigation – information and autonomy.

Information – Providing the necessary information to the scientists carrying out these investigations would need to be made compulsory. This is certainly the case for government information. Such a requirement does, in fact, make perfect sense: since citizens are obliged to provide information for the *collection* of government funds (taxes), it would seem normal to require that government be held publicly responsible for how it *spends* its money, and the reasons behind the fiscal decisions which it makes. The information which can be gleaned from present-day budgets is insufficient. They are not detailed enough, and are too difficult to interpret accurately for an outsider who is trying to set up an investigation of influence (of course, the investigator will still have to proceed carefully to ensure the reliability of the information; see Section 5.1).

Autonomy – The autonomy of the scientists who seek to evaluate government policy is a factor whose importance cannot be emphasized enough. The achievement of this autonomy is a serious practical problem, but a solution can certainly be found if the political will is present to strive toward it. Some examples of institutions with a certain amount of autonomy already exist – the university and the General Accounting Office, for example. More is needed, however. Research produces information. Information and information flows are vitally important elements in our societies. Such an important social factor should not be left to the mercy of chance factors and political machinations. I believe that the solution must be sought in information and research agencies which are backed up by a status anchored in the Constitution.

Inspection and evaluation should naturally be followed by *correction* of the undesirable situation. This may appear to be a somewhat naive suggestion at a time when 'fundamental reforms' are called for in quite other fields. But one thing is certain: the correction or adjustment of influence distributions is perhaps one of the most fundamental reforms which a society can set about to make. What is involved here is nothing less than the functioning of the government – of the whole complex of central 'regulatory organs' of society – as an institution capable of creating and removing inequalities. In addition, we gain much-needed clarity when the corrections are directed towards influence distributions whose existence has been empirically established by concrete investigations. And clarity in politics, still a very 'scarce good', is certainly a goal worth striving towards.

Of course this view will only be endorsed by those who would like to clear politics from the fog which is persistent and which often seems to be deliberately maintained. It may be true, as Simmel pointed out (1908, p. 257 ff), that the lie is an element in nearly all social relationships, as it is in politics. It is also true, however, that social scientists should continuously insist upon governmental decision-making being based on truth and facts rather than phantoms and fallacies.

Notes

1. The first and second hypotheses both rest on one basic hypothesis – namely, that the influence of comparable social units is proportional to their size. This – very general – hypothesis was not confirmed in this investigation for some social units (business firms), but was confirmed for other social units (coalitions of business firms).

2. The results may point to another consideration. Only one of the six characteristics of business firms discussed in Chapter 9, p. 228 turned out to be a criterium in decision-making. This is to a certain extent a satisfactory result as far as justice is concerned.

   It is also conceivable, however, that the government – consciously or unconsciously – actually works with very rough rules of thumb, and perhaps even with only one rule of thumb. It is, for example, difficult to conceive that no effect at all was revealed for the criterium 'firm economically healthy? (Chapter 9, p. 221). I believe that a cautious proposition can be put forward that the decision-making process is marred by a *certain one-sidedness* in the use of criteria.

3. Of course, this is not to deny that a greate deal is achieved for 'others' at the same time. The theme *here*, however, is inequality.

4. I am ignoring for the moment a rather serious complication: the 'inspection apparatus' and the 'influence apparatus' are *intertwined* with one another. Members of parliament often have close ties with the interest organizations. This could also be observed in the area covered by our investigation.

References

Aiken, Michael, 'The distribution of Community Power: Structural Bases and Social Consequences', in: Michael Aiken and Paul E. Mott (eds.), *The Structure of Community Power:* An Anthology, N. York, 1970.

Aiken, Michael and Robert R. Alford, 'Community Structure and Innovation: The Case of Urban Renewal', *Am. Sociological Review*, 35, 4, 1970, pp. 650–665.

Andriessen, J. E., S. Miedema en C. J. Oort, *De sociaal-economische besturing van Nederland (The Social-economic Governing of The Netherlands)*, Groningen, 1968.

Aron, R., 'Social Class, Political Class, Ruling Class', in: Bendix and Lipset, 1966², see pp. 210–218.

Atkinson, John W., *An Introduction to Motivation*, Princeton, 1964.

Atkinson, John W. and David Birch, *The Dynamics of Action*, N. York, 1970.

Bachrach, Peter and Morton S. Baratz, 'Two Faces of Power', *American Political Science Review*, 56, 1962, pp. 947–952.

Bachrach, Peter and Morton S. Baratz, 'Decisions and Nondecisions: An Analytical Framework', *American Political Science Review*, 57, 1963, pp. 632–642.

Bachrach, Peter and Morton S. Baratz, *Power and Poverty*, N. York, 1970.

Bauer, Raymond A., Ithiel de Sola Pool and Lewis Anthony Dexter, *American Business and Public Policy*, N. York, 1964.

Bell, Roderick, 'Political Power: The Problem of Measurement', in: Bell, Edwards and Wagner, 1969, see pp. 13–27.

Bell, Roderick, David V. Edwards and R. Harrison Wagner (eds.), *Political Power*, N. York, 1969.

Bendix, Reinhard and Seymour M. Lipset (eds.) *Class, Status and Power*, N. York, 1966².

Berting, J. and L. U. de Sitter, *Arbeidssatisfactie (Satisfaction of Workers)*, Assen, 1971.

Blalock, Hubert M., *Causal Inferences in Nonexperimental Research*, Chapel Hill, 1964.

Blalock, Hubert M. and Ann B. Blalock (eds.), *Methodology in Social Research*, N. York, 1968.

Blalock, Hubert M., 'Evaluating the Relative Importance of Variables', in: Paul F. Lazarsfeld, Ann K. Pasanella, Morris Rosenberg, *Continuities in the Language of Social Research*, N. York, 1972, see pp. 148–157 (Earlier in *Am. Soc. Rev.*, 26, 1961, pp. 866–874).

Blau, Peter M., *Exchange and Power in Social Life*, N. York, 1964.

Bonjean, Charles M., Terry N. Clark and Robert L. Lineberry (eds.), *Community Politics*, N. York, 1971.

Braam G. P. A. and J. Swinkels, 'De verdeling van invloedskanalen bij collectieve acties vanuit plaatselijk niveau' (The Distribution of Channels of Influence within Collective Actions from the Local Level), *Sociologische Gids*, 16, 2, 1969, pp. 82–102.

Braam G. P. A., 'Het bejaardenbeleid' (Aging Policy in the Netherlands), in: Hoogerwerf, 1972, part 2, pp. 85–108.

Braam G. P. A., 'Van individuele mensen naar politieke macht en terug' (From Individuals to Political Power and Backwards), *Acta Politica*, 8, 2, 1973, pp. 113–133.

Braam G. P. A., A. Dijkstra, a.o., *'Collectieve acties' (Collective Actions)*, Meppel (Neth.), 1976.

Campbell, Donald T. and Julian C. Stanley, *Experimental and Quasi-experimental Designs for Research*, Chicago, 1966. (Earlier published in: N. L. Gage (ed.), *Handbook of Research on Teaching*, 1963).

C. B. S. (Netherlands Central Bureau of Statistics), *Derde algemene bedrijfstelling; deel I (Third Census of Business Firms; part I)*, The Hague, 1968.

Cninoy, Ely, *Society*, N. York, 1967[2].

Clark, Terry N. (ed.), *Community Structure and Decision Making: Comparative Analysis*, San Francisco, 1968.

Coleman, James S., 'Relational Analysis: The Study of Social Organizations with Survey Methods', *Human Organization*, 17, 1958–59, pp. 28–36.

Coleman, James S., 'Comments on "On the Concept of Influence",' *Public Opinion Quarterly*, 17, 1963, pp. 63–82.

Coleman, James S., *Introduction to Mathematical Sociology*, Glencoe, 1964.

Coleman, James S., 'The Use of Electronic Computers in the Study of Social Organization', *Archiv. Européennes de Sociologie*, 6, 1, 1965, pp. 89–107.

Coleman, James S., Amitai Etzioni, John Porter, *Macrosociology: Research and Theory*, Boston, 1970.

Coleman, James S., 'Community Disorganization and Conflict', in: R. K. Merton and R. A. Nisbet (eds.), *Contemporary Social Problems*, N. York, 1976, see p. 568.

Coleman, James S., 'Loss of Power', *Am. Sociological Review*, 38, 1, 1973, pp. 1–18.

Coleman, James S., *The Mathematics of Collective Action*, London, 1973.

Coleman, James S., 'Notes on the Study of Power', in: Liebert and Immersheim, 1977, see pp. 183–199.

Dahl, Robert A., 'The Concept of Power', *Behavioral Science*, 2, 1957, pp. 201–215.

Dahl, Robert A., *Who governs (Democracy and Power in an American City)*, N. Haven, 1961.

Dahl, Robert A., 'Power', in: David L. Sills (ed.), *International Encyclopedia of the Social Sciences*, vol. 12, N. York, 1968, pp. 405–415.

Dahl, Robert A., *Modern Political Analysis*, Englewood Cliffs (N.J.), 1970.

Dasgupta, A. K. and D. W. Pearce, *Cost-Benefit Analysis: Theory and Practice*, London, 1972

Deutsch, M., Field Theory in Social Psychology, in: G. Lindzey (ed.), *Handbook of Social Psychology*, Cambridge, Mass., 1954.

Domhoff, G. William and Hoyt B. Ballard (eds.), *C. Wright Mills and the Power Elite*, Boston, 1968.

Doorn, J. A. A. van, 'Sociologische begrippen en problemen rond het verschijnsel macht' (Sociological Concepts and Problems on the Phenomenon of Power), *Sociologisch Jaarboek*, XI, 1957, pp. 73–135.

Doorn, J. A. A. van, 'Sociology and the Problem of Power', *Sociologia Neerlandica*, I, 1962–63, pp. 1–18.

Easton, David, 'Categories for the System Analysis of Politics', in: David Easton (ed.), 1966, pp. 143–153.

Easton, David (ed.), *Varieties of Political Theory*, Englewood Cliffs (N.J.), 1966.

Ellemers, J. E., *De Februari-ramp, (The Holland Flood Disaster of 1953)*, Assen, 1956.

Ellemers, J. E., *Macht en Invloed, (On the Concepts of Power and Influence)*, Meppel, 1969.

Elting, L. and M. Even, *Onderwijis, invloed en sociale ongelijkheid. Een empirisch onderzoek naar de invloed van scholen op het overheidsbeleid, (An Empirical Study on the Influence of Schools on Government Policy)*, Groningen, 1977.

Felling, A. J. A., *Lokale macht en netwerken*, (*Local Power and Networks*), Alphen a.d. Rijn (Holland), 1974.

Fowler, Irving A., *Local Industrial Structures, Economic Power and Community Welfare*, Totawa N.J., 1964.

Frey, Frederick W., 'Comment: On Issues and Nonissues in the Study of Power', *American Political Science Review*, 65, 1971, pp. 1081–1101.

Friedrich, J., *Constitutional Government and Democracy*, Boston, 1941.

Gadourek, I., 'Political Radicalism and Social Change', *Mens en Maatschappij*, 42, 2, 1967, pp. 117–133.

Galtung, J., *Theory and Methods of Social Research*, Oslo, 1967.

Gamson, W. A., 'Reputation and Resources in Community Politics', *Am. Journal of Sociology*, 72, 2, 1966, pp. 121–131.

Goldhamer, H. and E. Shills, 'Types of Power and Status', *The Am. Journal of Sociology*, 45, 1939, pp. 171–182.

Gordon, R. A., 'Issues in Multiple Regression', *The Am. Journal of Sociology*, 75, 5, 1968, pp. 593–616.

Groot, A. D. de, *Methodology: Foundation of Inference and Research in the Behavioral Sciences*, The Hague (Holland), 1968.

Guilford, J. P., *Fundamental Statistics in Psychology and Education*, N. York, 1965.

Harsanyi, J., 'Measurement of Social Power, Opportunity Costs and the Theory of Two-person Bargaining Games', *Behavioral Science*, 7, 1, 1962, pp. 67–75.

Heek, F. van, a.o., *Sociale stijging en daling in Nederland* (*deel I*), (*Social Mobility in the Netherlands*, part I), Leiden, 1958.

Helmers, H. M., R. J. Mokken, R. C. Plijter and F. N. Stokman, *Graven naar macht*, (*A Search for Power Positions*), Amsterdam, 1975.

Hodge, Robert W., Donald J. Treiman and Peter H. Rossi, 'A Comparative Study of Occupational Prestige' in: Reinhard Bendix and Seymour Martin Lipset, *Class, Status and Power*, N. York, 1966, pp. 309–321.

Hoogerwerf, A. (ed.), *Beleid belicht*, (*Government Policy*), part 2, Alphen a.d. Rijn, 1972.

Hunter, Floyd, *Community Power Structure*, Chapel Hill, 1953.

Hyman, Herbert, *Survey Design and Analysis*, N. York, 1954.

Kadushin, C., 'Power, Influence and Social Circles: A New Methodology for Studying Opinion Makers', *Am. Sociological Review*, 33, 5, 1968, pp. 685–699.

Key, V. O., *Politics, Parties and Pressure Groups*, N. York, 1942.

Kish, Leslie, 'Sampling Organizations and Groups of Unequal Sizes', *Am. Sociological Review*, 30, 1, 1965, pp. 565–578.

Kornhauser, William, 'Power Elite or Veto Groups', in: Seymour M. Lipset and Leo Lowenthal (eds.), *Culture and Social Character*, N. York, 1961 (also in Bendix and Lipset, 1966 and Domhoff and Ballard, 1968).

Krech, David and Richard S. Crutchfield, *Elements of Psychology*, N. York, 1968.

Labovitz, S., 'The Assignments of Numbers to Rank Order Categories', *Am. Sociological Review*, 35, 3, 1970, pp. 515–524.

Lasswell, Harold D., *Politics: Who gets What, When, How*, N. York, 1936.

Laumann, Edward O. and Franz Urban Pappi, 'New Directions in the Study of Community Elites', *Am. Sociological Review*, 38, 2, 1973, pp. 212–230.

Lazarsfeld, P. F. and M. Rosenberg, *The Language of Social Research*, N. York, 1955.

Lazarsfeld, Paul F., Ann K. Pasanella and Morris Rosenberg, *Continuities in the Language of Social Research*, N. York, 1972.

Lewin, Kurt (ed. Dorwin Cartwright), *Field Theory in Social Science*, London, 1952.

Lieberson, Stanley, 'An Empirical Study of Military Industrial Linkages', *The Am. Journal of Sociology*, 76, 4, 1971, pp. 562–84.

Liebert, Roland J. and Allen W. Immersheim, *Power, Paradigms and Community Research*, London, 1977.

Lippitt, Ronald, Norman Polansky, Fritz Redl and Sidney Rosen, 'The Dynamics of Power', in: Dorwin Cartwright and Alvin Zander, *Group Dynamics*, London, 1960[2], see pp. 745–766. (Earlier published in: *Human Relations*, 5, 1952, pp. 37–64).

Lipset, Seymour M., Martin Trow and James Coleman, *Union Democracy*, N. York, 1962 (Earlier published in 1956).

March, J. G., 'An Introduction to the Theory and Measurement of Influence', *American Political Science Review*, 49, 1955, pp. 431–451.

March, J. G., 'The Power of Power', in: Easton, 1966, pp. 39–71.

March, J. G. and H. A. Simon, *Organizations*, New York, 1958.

McFarland, Andrew S., *Power and Leadership in Pluralist Systems*, Stanford, 1969.

Merelman, Richard M., 'On the Neo-elitist Critique of Community Power', *Am. Political Science Review*, 62, 2, 1968, pp. 451–460.

Merton, Robert K., *Social Theory and Social Structure*, Glencoe, 1957.

Mills, C. Wright, *The Power Elite*, N. York, 1956.

Mokken, R. J. and F. N. Stokman, *Traces of Power II*. Interlocking Directorates between Large Corporations, Banks and Other Financial Companies and Institutions in the Netherlands in 1969, (Paper Joint Session Eur. Cons. for Pol. Research, Strasbourg, March 1974), Amsterdam, 1974.

Morrison, Denton E. and Ramon E. Henkel, *The Significance Test Controversy*, Chicago, 1970.

Mulder, M. and A. Stemerding, 'Threat, Attraction to the Group and Need for Strong Leadership', *Human Relations*, 16, 4, 1963, pp. 317–334.

Mulder, M., 'De grijpbare macht' (The Seizable Power), *Acta Politica*, 8, 2, 1973, pp. 133–153.

Nagel, Jack H., 'Some Questions about the Concept of Power', *Behavioral Science*, 13, 1968, pp. 129–137.

Olson (jr.), Mancur, *The Logic of Collective Action*, (Public Goods and the Theory of Groups), Cambridge, 1965.

Olsen, Marvin E. (ed.), *Power in Societies*, London, 1971.

Parenti, Michael, 'Power and Pluralism: A View from the Bottom', *The Journal of Politics*, 32, 3, 1970, pp. 501–532.

Parsons, Talcott, 'The Distribution of Power in American Society', in: Olsen (ed.), 1970. (Earlier published in *World Politics*, 10, 1957, pp. 123–143).

Parsons, T., 'General Theory in Sociology', in: R. K. Merton, L. Broom, L. S. Cottrell jr. (eds.), *Sociology Today*, N. York, 1959 (1965), part I.

Parsons, T., *Structure and Process in Modern Societies*, Glencoe, 1960.

Parsons, T., 'On the Concept of Political Power', *Proc. of the Am. Philosophical Society*, 103, 3, 1963 (a), pp. 232–262 (Later a.o. in Parsons, 1969).

Parsons, T., 'On the Concept of Influence', *Public Opinion Quarterly*, 27, 1963 (b), pp. 37–62. (Later a.o. in Parsons, 1969).

Parsons, T., *Societies* (Evolutionary and Comparative Perspectives), Englewood Cliffs, N.J., 1966.

Parsons, T., *Politics and Social Structure*, N. York, 1969.

Pen, J., 'Bilateral Monopoly, Bargaining and the Concept of Economic Power', in: Rothschild (ed.), *Power in Economics*, (Penguin Books), 1971. (Earlier published a.o. in J. Pen, *The Wage Rate under Collective Bargaining*, Harvard, 1959).

Peschar, J. L., 'Educational Opportunity within and between Holland and Sweden; the Semi-experimental Approach', *Sociologische Gids*, XXV, 4, 1978, pp. 273–97.

Philipsen, H., *Afwezigheid wegens ziekte* (*Sickness Absenteeism*), Leiden, 1968.

Philipsen, H., *Steekproeven* (*Samples*), Leiden, 1969.

Pinker, R., *Social Theory and Social Policy*, London, 1971.

Riker, William H., 'Some Ambiguities in the Notion of Power', *Am. Political Science Review*, 58, 2, 1964, pp. 341–349.

Rose, Arnold M., *The Power Structure*, N. York, 1967.

Ross, John and Perry Smith, 'Orthodox Experimental Designs', in: Blalock and Blalock (eds.), 1968, see pp. 333–390.

Rossi, P. H., and W. Williams (eds.), *Evaluating Social Programs*, N. York, 1972.

Runciman, W. G., *Relative Deprivation and Social Justice*, London, 1966, 1972.

Salamon, Lester M. and John J. Siegfried, 'Economic Power and Political Influence: The Impact of Industry Structure on Public Policy', *The American Political Science Review*, LXXI, 3, 1977, pp. 1026–43.

Schulze, R. O., 'The Role of Economic Dominants in Community Power Structure', *Am. Sociological Review*, 23, 1, 1958, pp. 3–9.

Schuyt, C. J. M., (Discussion), *Beleid en Maatschappij*, I, 4, 1974, p. 138.

Siegel, Sidney, *Nonparametric Statistics*, N. York, 1956.

Simmel, Georg, *Soziologie: Untersuchungen über die Formen der Vergellschaftung*, Berlijn: Duncker, 1908, 1958.

Simon, H. A., *Administrative Behavior*, N. York, 1957[2].

Simon, H. A., 'Notes on the Observation and Measurement of Political Power', in: *Models of Man*, 1957, pp. 62–78 (Earlier published in *Journal of Politics*, 15, 1953).

Stinchcombe, Arthur L., 'Social Structure and Organizations', in: J. G. March, *Handbook of Organizations*, Chicago, 1965.

Stinchcombe, Arthur L., *Constructing Social Theories*, N. York, 1968.

Truman, D. B., *The Governmental Process*, N. York, 1968[5].

Wagner, R. Harrison, 'The Concept of Power and the Study of Politics', in: Bell, Edwards and Wagner, 1969, pp. 1–13.

Walton, John, 'The Vertical Axis of Community Organization and the Structure of Power', in: Bonjean, Clark, Lineberry, 1971, pp. 188–197. (Earlier published a.o. in Clark, 1968).

Walton, John, 'A Methodology for the Comparative Study of Power: Some Conceptual and Procedural Applications', *Social Science Quarterly*, 52, 1, 1971, pp. 39–60.

Weber, Max, *Wirtschaft und Gesellschaft*, Tübingen, 1922.

Wolfinger, Raymond E., 'Nondecisions and the Study of Local Politics', *Am. Political Science Review*, 65, 1971, pp. 1063–1087 and 1102–1104.

Wrong, D., 'Some Problems in Defining Social Power', *The American Journal of Sociology*, 73, 6, 1968, pp. 673–81.

Zeisel, Hans, *Say it with Figures*, N. York, 1968[5].

Zetterberg, H. L., *On Theory and Verification in Sociology*, Totowa N.J., 1965[3].

Appendices

For Use with Chapter 2

Appendix 2A
The difference between the decision-making method and the method used in this investigation

In investigations of local power the decision-method–sometimes also called the issue method–is well-known. 'Decision-making' is also a central element in the method used in this investigation, but that is virtually the only point that the two methods have in common.

Some differences between the two methods:

(1) *The decision method begins with the selection of decisions.* My initial point of departure is private citizens and their interests. It is an entirely open question whether or not decisions will flow from these interests.

(2) The decision method aims primarily at pinning down the *degree of concentration* of influence and power in a municipality. It has always been a mystery to me how it can be maintained that this concentration has been 'discovered' when *only the participation* in decision-making of citizens or their organizations has actually been observed. This is, after all, a far cry from determining influence. My method is based on the supposition that the influence must first be determined *for each private citizen or organization separately* before we can begin to talk about concentrations. The first step is thus simply to describe the *distribution* of influence among the citizens.

(3) The decision-method ignores those phenomena which are not involved in decision-making, giving rise to '*non-decisions*'. In the method used in this study, they receive full treatment.

Bauer's *et al* (1964) working procedure shows the most points of similarity with my own. Although they do begin by selecting an 'issue' (legislation involving tariff barriers), they at least take the trouble to gather data for all firms which *might conceivably* be interested parties.

For Use with Chapter 4

Appendix 4A
The absence of a longitudinal design: consideration of the possible consequences for the results

In Chapter 4, while setting up and discussing our research design, I briefly remarked that–strictly speaking–measurements should be made at two different points in time. This was not done, however, thus we must try to determine what consequences this has for the results. I will organize the discussion of consequences along the same lines followed in setting up the design, distinguishing between (a) *the research design as a whole*, and (b) *the determination of influence for each process.*

Let us consider first several practical aspects. The solution of a problem usually takes a very long time–five years or more is not unusual. This implies that the measurements for an investigation would have to be stretched out over at least five years. At the same time, the whole approach toward the measurement of influence which I was introducing was new and untried, and I was in fact putting it to its first test. Balancing all these aspects, I was unfortunately forced to abandon the requirement that measurements be made at two separate points in time. So this investigation has, in fact, turned out to be a *retrospective* one (Zetterberg, 1965, p. 136). The material *is* suitable for use in a new investigation; the results of this present study could serve as a first measurement in a prospective design.

Whatever the practical reasons, it remains a necessity that we thoroughly analyze the implications of the retrospective design I have used.
(a) This concerns in the first place the implications for the research design as a whole; we will confine ourselves to a discussion of the principal variable, size of business firm. The sample was drawn on the basis of one point in time, about one year before the field work began. Because I wanted to consider the problems over a period of five years,

this should strictly speaking have been 1964. This was not done because the reconstruction of the population of shipyards was already difficult enough for 1968. There is no publicly-available registration of business firms like there is for private citizens, complete with names, addresses and number of employees. And in fact, during the field work, a number of corrections had to be made. A reconstruction of this population for 1964 would in itself have been a topic for an entire investigation.

The first possible source of errors is that the size of the firms *in* the sample changed during this time period. The danger of this change taking place is in all probability negligible, since very broad categories were chosen for 'number of employees'. It is almost impossible for any significant number of shifts over category boundaries to have taken place.

A second possibility has to do with the composition of the sample. New firms can have appeared since 1964, old ones may have gone bankrupt. This is comparable to the 'experimental mortality' (see Campbell and Stanley, 1966, p. 5). Thus a number of young firms may have been unjustifiably included in the sample, and a number of firms who disappeared between 1964 and 1968 may have been omitted unjustifiably. We encountered in fact very few of these 'new' firms in our sample, in all probability because the shipbuilding industry as a whole was going through difficult times in this period. The only possible distortions, then, are those resulting from firms which are unjustifiably absent from the sample because they went bankrupt between 1964 and 1968. Since, as I said before, a reconstruction of the 1964 population would have been very time-consuming, I will confine myself to several conjectures about the seriousness of this distortion.

In the sample which we drew on the basis of data from 1968, we found one business firm that had just gone bankrupt (we were, by the way, unable to come into contact with the former owner despite considerable effort on our part). To give some impression of what significance this has for our results: figured over five years, this would be five bankrupcies in a sample containing seventy-three shipyards. This is not enough to entirely eliminate our uneasiness on this point.

We will therefore discuss to what degree our results would change in several hypothetical cases (I confine myself here to the shipyard sample and to the hypothesis about influence with respect to individual problems; see Chapters 3 and 4).

1–*Latent anticipation.* Our results in Chapter 6 indicate that there is a relationship between size of the firm and latent anticipation (or the number of problems). Let us consider two extreme possibilities. The first possibility is that the five shipyards which went bankrupt had relatively few individual problems–say one per firm–and they all fell under the category 'large firms'. If these firms were added to the sample, the average number of problems for large shipyards would drop from 1.73 to 1.63. The comparable average for small firms was 1.28. Thus a considerable discrepancy does remain between the two categories of firms.

Another extreme possibility is that all the firms that 'disappeared' were small ones, and they had a great many problems. A modification of the results using hypothetical data from this example would yield about the same outcome as in the previous case. Neither–rather extreme–possibility has much effect on the results: the relationship between size of firm and latent anticipation remains.

2–*Manifest anticipation.* Possible modifications of the results would at the most have the same order of magnitude as those we will find for tested influence. The latter aspect is, after all, determined on the basis of a smaller number of business firms and is therefore more 'vulnerable'. I will therefore proceed immediately to a consideration of the tested influence.

3–*Tested influence.* The results in Chapter 6 *do not* indicate the existence of a relationship between the size of the firm and tested influence (= percentage of influence attempts which are successful). Suppose that all five of the shipyards that went bankrupt each undertook one influence attempt which was not successful. Suppose further that all of these shipyards were small. If we add them to the sample, the percentage of successful influence attempts within the class of small shipyards as a whole will drop from 74% to 63%. The percentage for large shipyards is 75%. In other words, a difference would appear between the two groups in the direction predicted by the hypothesis; the difference is, however, far from being significant (Fisher exact test).

Likewise, if a reverse situation were true–all the 'disappearing' firms were large and had a relatively large number of influence attempts which were successful–a similar, equally insignificant change in the outcome would result.

In short, I do not believe that the sample's having been drawn in 1968 rather than in 1964 can have had any serious consequences for the results of the investigation.

(b) The absence of a measurement in 1964 may also affect *the determination of influence for each separate process.* The most important difficulty may occur with the problems of business firms: four- or five-year-old problems can obviously be forgotten.

There are several rough indications that no serious distortions need be expected on this score. Consider the following indirect test, for example. It is most likely that problems which lasted only a short time will be the first to be forgotten after a passage of time. So the farther we go into the past, the fewer short-term problems we should expect to be reported. We checked the figures for forty-eight firms in the shipyard sample, with the following results:

time period ending	in 1969:	41% short-term problems (one year or less)
time period between	1964 and 1969:	32% short-term problems (one year or less)
time period ending	1964 or earlier:	45% short-term problems (one year or less)

(See Chapter 5 for the relevant interview questions.)

The percentages indicate that fears of distortions in the results caused by selective perceptions are unfounded.

The distribution of the *data of origin* of business firms' problems is another indication that 'forgotten problems' are not a disturbing factor in the investigation. The distribution is as follows:

date of origin	1969	7%
date of origin	1967 or 1968	20%
date of origin	1965 or 1966	21%
date of origin	1960 to/including 1964	19%
	before 1960	33%
	total	100% (n = 258 problems; 21 problems which were highly a-typical were not included)

Going back as far as 1965, the number of problems *per year* is roughly the same. There is a slight decrease in problems per year prior to that date, but this can very well be ascribed to the fact that respondents were specifically questioned about problems experienced in the last *five* years.

Both indications support the supposition that 'forgetting' of business problems is not a significant source of error. This may, of course, be due in part to the unambiguousness in identifying the problems (and their objects)–the respondents were even presented with a list of possible problem-related objects (aspects of the situation).

To conclude: the absence of a measurement at the beginning of the time period for which the firms' influence was being determined, has not apparently had any adverse effect upon the results of the investigation.

Appendix 4B
Discussion of several units used in drawing the sample

Business firm will be taken to mean *business location* as used in the 1963 Netherlands Central Bureau of Statistics report (see p. 78).

Municipality. Only municipalities which are located on waterways are relevant for this investigation.

Region. This was defined as an area containing a number of municipalities varying from one to seven, which are reasonably comparable with respect to their 'economic climate' and location of a waterway. A number of weaknesses in the preliminary regional categorization were revealed during the field-work. This should have no serious consequences, since the sample was large enough relative to the size of the total population.
The regions chosen were:

Groningen	– Eemskanaal/Damsterdiep
	– Winschoterdiep (including the city of Groningen)
Friesland	– Prinses Margrietkanaal
	– Van Harinxmakanaal
Drente	– Meppelerdiep
Overijssel	– Zwarte Water
Gelderland	– Rijn
	– Waal
Gelderland/N. Brabant	– Bergse Maas
Utrecht	– Amsterdam-Rijnkanaal
Noord-Holland	– Zaan
	– Spaarne/Zijkanaal C
Zuid-Holland	– Oude Rijn
	– Lek
	– Noord
	– Dordtse Kil
	– Beneden Merwede
N. Brabant/Limburg	– Maas

The typology of shipyards according to their 'spatial' relationships with one another. As was explained in Chapter 4, to meet the requirements of the research design it was necessary to choose those large and small shipyards whose position relative to other shipyards in the municipality were comparable. We concentrated primarily on shipyards located in municipalities where no other shipyards were present: we called them the 'solitary' shipyards (SS). Our aim was to compare a category of 'small-solitaries' with a category of 'large-solitaries' (the boundary between large and small firms was placed at 100 employees).

The categories 'solitary' and 'non-solitary' are of course rather straightforward–as long as 'solitary' is narrowly interpreted. In some cases, however, a strict application of the term leads to unrealistic classifications in practice. If, for example, there are two shipyards in one municipality, one with 600 employees and one with 60, we are faced with a hybrid category which is basically the same as the category 'large-solitary'. I have called this hybrid category 'dominant'. This category was combined with the 'real' large-solitaries in the sample, partly because of the practical necessity of obtaining a category with a sufficient numbers of cases. To ensure the unambiguity of our typology we adopted the classes used in the C.B.S. census, based on the number of employees:

1. 21–49 employees
2. 50–99 employees
3. 100–199 employees
4. 200–499 employees
5. 500–999 employees
6. 1000–1999 employees
7. ≧2000 employees

We use the letter W to stand for a shipyard; WW indicates that there are *two shipyards* in one municipality. We used i to indicate one of the seven classes of number of employees. A class i-2 means that a firm falling into this class is *two* classes lower than a firm located in class i. This is especially important for the 'dominant' type. The definitive typology is shown in Figure 4B.1. (It should be noted that municipalities with three or more shipyards can be classified according to an analogous procedure.) This typology was used to categorize the municipalities, using data from the C.B.S. business census of 1963. Addresses were looked up in the telephone directory. Adjustments were then made when necessary, using more recent data generously supplied by the Economic and Technological branches of the Provincial Governments. In spite of all these precautions, corrections also needed to be made during the field work. Table 4B.1 shows the distribution which was obtained for all the harbor areas *except* those of Rotterdam, Amsterdam and Zeeland.

					number of municipalities in sample
A	W_i	$i < 3$	(less than 100 employees): small solitary		19
B	W_i	$3 \leqq i < 5$	(100 to 500 employees): large solitary		11
	or W_iW_{i-2}	$3 \leqq i < 5$	(100 to 500 employees): large dominant	all grouped under 'large solitary'	6 } 22
	or W_i	$i \geqq 5$	(500 or more employees): giant solitary		2
	or W_iW_{i-2}	$i \geqq 5$	(500 or more employees): giant dominant		3
C	W_iW_i	$i < 3$	(less than 100 employees): 'equals' small		} 6
	or W_iW_{i-1}	$i < 3$	(less than 100 employees): 'equals' small		
D	W_iW_i	$i \geqq 3$	(more than 100 employees): 'equals' large		} 3
	or W_iW_{i+1}	$i \geqq 3$	(more than 100 employees): 'equals' large		
CD	W_iW_{i+1}	$i < 3$ and $i+1 \geqq 3$	(less than 100 employees): mixed large/small		5

Figure 4B.1
Typology of shipyards according to their 'spatial' relationships with one another

Table 4B.1

The municipalities, classified according to the configuration of the ship-yards located within their borders

type of municipality, classified according to configuration of shipyards	total number of municipalities with shipyards (within regions)*	*munici-palities* in the sample	firms in the sample			
			number of ship-yards in SS†		number of ship-yards in S3†	
			S	L	S	L
A = small solitary	45	19	19			
B = large solitary	27	22		22	6	1
C = equals, small	15	6			8	
D = equals, large	6	3				3
CD = mixed large/small	6	5			10	4
municipalities without a shipyard (but with 'remaining firms')		11				
Total	99	66	19	22‡	24	8§

* excepting the Rotterdam and Amsterdam harbor areas and Zeeland
† SS = solitary shipyards; S3 = third supplementary shipyard sample; S = small shipyard; L = large shipyard
‡ of which five were 'giants' (500 or more employees)
§ of which two were 'giants' (500 or more employees)

Appendix 4C
Composition of the sample solitary shipyards (SS), with regard to a number of variables used in matching (Table 4C.1)

solitary shipyard (cutting point 100 employees)		size of municipality*		transport by water†		area of regional development‡	
				Lt	5	D	2
						nD	3
		Lm	7	St	2	D	2
						nD	0
small	19			Lt	9	D	2
						nD	7
		Sm	12	St	3	D	1
						nD	2
				Lt	9	D	2
						nD	7
		Lm	12	St	3	D	2
						nD	1
large	22			Lt	3	D	0
						nD	3
		Sm	10	St	7	D	0
						nD	7

THE SAME AS ABOVE, BUT WITH
THE TOTAL FREQUENCIES

small	19	Lm	7	Lt	14	D	7
		Sm	12	St	15	nD	12
large	22	Lm	12	Lt	12	D	4
		Sm	10	St	10	nD	18

* Lm = large municipality; Sm = small municipality; cutting point between the two categories 9500 inhabitants. Size of municipality determined by number of inhabitants as of January 1, 1968.
† Lt = large amount of tonnage transported; St = small amount of tonnage transported; cutting point between the categories set at 175,000 tons. The tonnage is the total amount of goods delivered and received in 1966 (sea traffic, international and national inland navigation).
‡ Area of regional economic development aid, or an area singled out for significant economic reorganization in one or more four-year periods after 1959: D. Not one of these regions: nD.

Note: because the sample 'solitary shipyards' was the purest in its composition, the variable 'absentee owned (or not)' could seriously distort the results. During the field work it was found that only one of the small firms and eight of the large firms were absentee-owned. This had to be taken into consideration after-the-fact (see p. 206).

Appendix 4D
The composition of the sample 'remaining firms' (that is, not ship-yards) with regard to number of employees and type of firm (Table 4D.1)

| type of firm | number of employees | | | |
	1–99	100–499	500 and more	total
– timber dealers and paper mills	6	4	4	14
– cement factory or dealers in construction materials	8	3	—	11
– machine works	1	1	—	2
– dealers in cereals and forage	8	3	—	11
– 'sea-harbor' industries	—	—	2	2
– trans-shipment firms	4	—	—	4
– ship-owners	5	1	1	7
– chemical industries	1	2	1	4
– other	1	1	—	2
total	34	15	8	57

For Use with Chapter 5

Appendix 5A
Infra-structural problems compared with other problems (Table 5A.1)*

nature of problem	TOTAL NUMBER OF FIRMS (130) number of firms having at least one problem in the last 5 years		1969		(SUB-TOTAL) NUMBER OF SHIPYARDS (73) number of shipyards having at least one problem in the last 5 years		1969	
– personnel shortages, etc.	75	57.6%	71	54.4%	54	74.0%	53	72.7%
– credits	40	30.7%	29	22.3%	20	27.4%	15	20.6%
– orders	35	26.9%	29	22.3%	27	37.0%	19	26.0%
– internal organization	35	26.9%	26	20.0%	15	20.6%	11	15.1%
– *material facilities for transport by water*	79	60.8%	48	36.9%	47	64.3%	28	38.4%
– other infra-structure (roads, etc.)	7	5.4%	7	5.4%	2	2.7%	1	1.4%
– expansion, change of location	21	16.1%	10	7.7%	12	16.4%	6	8.2%
– cooperative agreements, mergers	5	3.8%	4	3.1%	2	2.7%	—	0.0%

* Presented in the table are the response frequencies to an open question about (1) the principal problem which the firm had experienced in the last five years and (2) the principal problems which were present at the time the question was being asked. It should once again be noted that the summation of the frequencies per column does not yield a total whose meaning can be easily interpreted.

A suggestion: the difference between the number of problems in the last five years and the number at the time of the interview may be an indication of the degree to which something has been achieved through the exercise of influence. The discrepancy is especially pronounced for the material facilities for transport by water.

Appendix 5B
Questions concerning plans of others

The relevant questions in the interview were the following ones:
'I would like to conclude with several questions about the plans of others.
a–Have other agencies or firms in your area had plans in the last five years which have affected you in any way?' (Instructions for the interviewer: what we are looking for here is (1) plans involving the material facilities for transport by water, such as filling up a canal, removal of a bridge, etc. (2) but also those involving more general topics such as industrialization. Be especially on the lookout for plans of firms in the neighborhood and municipal governments, as well as the national and provincial departments of Waterways.)
b–'What is the rank-order of these plans as far as their importance *for your firm* is concerned'?
c–'During what time-period did these plans play a role'?

Appendix 5C
Selection of those problems of business firms which are relevant for comparison of influence

The first criterium which an influence-relevant problem always had to meet was that there be sufficient *latitude* present in the situation for the exercise of influence.

The second criterium, *discrepancy in the situation*, which was also a necessary condition of influence-relevance, determined the choice of two categories:
1–problems relating to the material facilities for transport by water in which the *objects* involved were owned by the government. The majority of problems in my final selection belonged to this category (that is, 180 problems, or 65%).
2–problems of business firms directly related to governmental planning (town planning, filling up of canals, etc.) which we have grouped under the term 'plans of others' (66 problems, or 25%).

As we explained earlier, the term 'problems' was conceived in a broad sense to prevent the exclusion of the type of cases in which 'eagerness for benefits' dominates (*maximizing* rather than satisficing). In such cases we were more strongly dependent on information about *whether or not an influence attempt had been made.* 'Problems' are in this respect a somewhat less reliable basis of comparison. Two categories were involved here:

(1) objects relating to the material facilities for transport by water which are owned by the firms themselves; although these objects are clearly *not* government property, the firm makes an appeal to the government to make changes in them (for example, subsidies for a large dock). There are only twelve such cases in our research data; additionally, these cases are equally distributed among large and small firms (seven to five respectively);

(2) other objects such as: making available of sufficient industrial building grounds to allow for expansion, subsidies for re-location of a part of a firm, lowering of energy prices–even airport accommodation (total, 21 cases).

The objects in these two categories were generally cited by the respondents as 'problems' because of the difficulties encountered in persuading the government to come to the firm's assistance. This is not, however, completely in accordance with our basic concept 'perceived discrepancies' in which the government played no role in a direct sense. However, there are so few of this type of 'problem' (33 in all) that I believe that this inaccurateness can be disregarded. It would, after all, be highly undesirable to discard a category of influence attempts such as this one, since it is also central in the tracking down of 'influence'.

A great deal of time was spent in the selection of the problems, the gathering of information about these problems, and their categorization. Yet this time was certainly not wasted, as testified by a number of complexities which had to be unraveled with the information so obtained.

– There was sometimes a very large number of problems. Some important ones in the first instance escaped the attention of both interviewer and respondent. However, check-questions were incorporated into the interview at other points, bringing omissions to light which could be rectified with follow-up interviews.
– Some respondents only began to formulate their problems in detail after intensive 'probing' by the interviewer. A tongue-in-cheek example: one respondent maintained originally that a problem was of no consequence for his firm, but later declared that he might as well close down if the problem were left unsolved.
– There were a number of highly complex problems which had to be

unraveled and broken down into separate problems. This was necessary when:

1. There were clearly different *objects* involved, and influence attempts had to be made through different channels;
2. *Phases* could clearly be distinguished, especially when the problem was present over a long period of time. Problems were divided when an influence attempt had failed (for example, a request for the raising of a bridge) and a new attempt was made, but with another formulation of the request (for example, making a part of the bridge a drawbridge).

– Individual problems usually were easy to identify. The assignment was often difficult for problems which were shared by a number of firms, and which were common knowledge within a certain area: was a change in the situation in the interest of this firm *and* that firm, or was the latter's interest really nothing more than an expression of sympathy. However, the 'visible' situation with respect to the material facilities for transport by water usually provided a 'hard' basis for making a decision in such cases.

Appendix 5D
Types of problems of business firms

Table 5D.1 presents the problems of business firms classified according to type. Note that here the unit under consideration is the *problem* rather than the firm. For example, *one* firm can have two problems relating to locks. And just the reverse, one problem can be shared by more than one firm.

Losses suffered by the firm as a result of the problem. In many cases it simply proved impossible to make any accurate estimate of the costs which a problem implied for a firm. A case in point would be when a firm is prevented from obtaining a share of the market for larger ships because of a lock which is too small. Therefore, we only included cases where a reasonably accurate estimate could be made: for example, if a firm experiences costs in order to get a ship under a bridge which is too low (dredging the channel or river under the bridge, loading and unloading extra ballast on the ship, completing construction at another location).

Table 5D.1

Problems of business firms* classified as influence-relevant according to type of problem

| type problem | number experienced by | | | |
	shipyards	remaining firms	total	
1. height of bridges	15	2	17	6.1%
2. harbor entrances	5	11	16	5.8%
3. accommodations for maneuvarability	2	2	4	1.4%
4. harbor accommodations: cranes	—	4	4	1.4%
5. harbor accommodations: quays and wharves	5	11	16	5.8%
6. harbor accommodations: harbor dues	3	4	7	2.5%
7. harbor accommodations: dredging operations	14	1	15	5.4%
8. beams of canals	1	3	4	1.4%
9. beam of bridges	11	9	20	7.2%
10. beam of locks	6	1	7	2.5%
11. draft of waterways	16	19	35	12.6%
12. combinations of 8 to/including 11	11	4	15	5.4%
13. water levels (in connection with slipways)	24	4	28	10.0%
14. space to put out the ships built	4	—	4	1.4%
15. negative aspects of plans of others (industrialization)	3	1	4	1.4%
16. negative aspects of plans of others (zoning, development plans)	23	18	41	14.7%
17. negative aspects of plans of others (other)	13	8	21	7.5%
18. other problems	10	11	21	7.5%
total	166	113	279	100.0%

* This table presents the number of *problems*. Note that in Tables 5.1 and 5.2 are presented the *firms*.

For Use with Chapter 6

Appendix 6A
The use of correlation coefficients in this investigation

According to the requirements of the research design, the primary variable in this investigation, the size of the business firm, was dichotomized. The most important results, then, have also been presented using this dichotomy: small and large business firms. This results, however, in some loss of information, since there is also a wide variation within these two classes which cannot be done justice in this way. The obvious solution is to compute correlation coefficients between the number of employees and the aspects of influence. This has the additional advantage of allowing for the utilization of a higher level of measurement of the size of the firm (ratio scale).

However, a number of other variables do not satisfy the requirements of this high measurement level. Neither can another classical requirement for testing with correlation coefficients–that the frequencies of the variables follow a 'normal distribution'–be met in these cases.

Finally, we have no reason for supposing that eventual relationships will always be linear; the correlation coefficient can only measure the linearity of a relationship.

However, if quite a large number of variables must be considered simultaneously, the use of correlation coefficients has a number of solid advantages: the surveyability of the data is enhanced, a maximum of information is retained, and the option of multivariate analysis is kept open (for example, see Blalock, 1964).

Besides, an inability to meet all the requirements for testing with correlation coefficients does not always have serious consequences (Labovitz, 1970, p. 515). These positive aspects not withstanding, caution is called for.

Therefore, the following procedure has generally been followed: in most cases where correlation coefficients are used, a simple contingency table has also been constructed. Although complete agreement is too much to expect, it was, in fact, often encountered. In cases where agreement was lacking, the relationship in question was often afforded special attention. Such procedures are not, of course, very sophisticated, but they are effective. Much more complex would be a decision as to how far we may deviate from the requirements stated earlier without making computation of correlation coefficients inadmissible (such theoretical derivations, by the way, will undoubtedly prove to be of great value in the future).

Taking this all into consideration, we will present correlation coefficients in the more exploratory phases of this investigation. However, when we clearly enter the stages where we *test* formally-stated hypotheses, then it is the contingency tables with the size of the firm dichotomized, rather than the correlation coefficients, which must provide the decisive evidence. In these cases the correlation coefficients are merely a source of additional information.

Appendix 6B
The number of employees as an indicator for 'size of firm'
and 'annual turnover'

'Size' in this study is meant to be size of social units. The number of employees seems to be the obvious choice as an indicator of the size of the business firm.

As a check on the value of this indicator, respondents were also asked the amount of annual turnover of the firm. Thirteen percent of the respondents refused to answer this question – a lower percentage than we had expected.

After elimination of fifteen extreme values, *the correlation coefficients* between number of employees and turnover were:
for shipyards: 0.95 (n = 51)
for remaining firms: 0.82 (n = 44)
These coefficients are so high that we may safely assume that the number of employees also reflects the economic-financial situation of the firm.

For Use with Chapter 7

Appendix 7A
Collective problems of municipalities

In Chapter 3, a third hypothesis was formulated: The greater the size of the municipality, the greater the influence it has on 'higher' public authorities in solving 'collective' problems.

A collective problem in this respect is defined as a problem which is important for a *large number* of people and/or firms in the community. Two types can be distinguished: the first, a summation of a large number of individual problems (unemployment, for example); the second, a problem at a group level (for example, deficiencies in road and water connections). In this second type, the point at issue is the functioning of the municipal 'economy' – or the social welfare system – as a whole. Of course, this latter type can in turn affect the first type, employment opportunities. Thus in some cases the two types will correspond to different *phases* in the definition of the problem. It is, however, not uncommon for administrators to think in terms of the second type, so that the connection with individual problems is not directly evident.

Here, as with the problems of more than one firm (Pom's; see p. 145), two levels can be distinguished: (A) the level of the individual private citizen (or firm) and (B) the level of the municipality.

(A) Our primary point of orientation in the first level is the interest of the individual private citizen. The term 'gains' could again be used as it was with coalitions (p. 57), but now via influence attempts made by the municipal government while seeking solutions for collective problems. This subject-matter is, in my opinion of enormous practical significance. Questions such as the following are at issue here:

How does the municipal government define collective problems, and what are the possible implications for the interests (and needs) of the private citizens?

What kind of activity does the government undertake concerning these interests (directly or indirectly), and under what conditions does this activity meet with success?

Obviously, we would need to enlarge our investigation considerably to be able to answer questions such as these. As it is, they have only been answered for the firms in our sample–several of the coalitions which were analyzed under the Pom's had municipal administrations as spokesmen. However, the share of such cases within the totality of 'collective problems' in the municipalities studied is negligible. This level will not, therefore, be considered further.

(B) The second level, that of 'the municipality' can be handled on the basis of 'collective problems' as defined by the municipal administrations themselves. This level was explored to some degree in our investigation in the following way. All the problems which were cited in the 'open' part of the interview were counted as collective problems. (We had planned to pose relevant questions more systematically, but the length of the interviews made this impossible). Thus we are by no means truly testing the hypothesis. Besides, we have limited ourselves to the following aspects:

(1) *Only* these problems *for which an influence attempt was undertaken* with a 'higher' government (provincial or national) were considered.

The necessary information was available for sixty municipalities. No such influence attempt was observed for ten of the municipalities. In the remaining fifty there was cited at least one collective problem with associated influence attempt (there was a total of eighty-one such cases).

The eighty-one influence attempts were related to the following topics (whose classification is somewhat arbitrary)

– trying to become a center of development aid	7
– home building	7
– recreation	7
– town and country planning	4
– zoning and development planning	17
– adaptations to changing water levels (Delta-plan)	3
– 'water-related' material facilities	13
– 'road-related' material facilities	11
– water- and road-related material facilities (bridges, for example)	9
– various other	3
(total)	81

Although this is a respectably large number of influence attempts, I suspect that a more systematic investigation would reveal the existence of a great deal more.

(2) It was determined whether or not the undertaken influence attempts had been successful. This could, of course, only be carried out for influence attempts which had been brought to some conclusion – forty in all. These data can be used to test the hypothesis that large municipalities have more influence on higher governments than small municipalities (since our data are rather limited, we cannot attach all too much value to the results of this test). We can determine for large and small municipalities separately what percentage of influence attempts have been successful. This can be seen as the 'tested influence' of municipalities. Setting the cutting point between large and small municipalities at 10,000 inhabitants – roughly the median – we observe the following percentages:

small municipalities   55% successful (n = 14)
large municipalities   83% successful (n = 10)

To promote somewhat greater comparability, we can consider only infra-structural problems. The percentages are then respectively 67% and 89% successful (in both cases n = 6).

Formulating cautiously, we can say that these results provide some preliminary support for the hypothesis. A new investigation would be needed to test this hypothesis more rigorously.

For Use with Chapter 8

Appendix 8A
Differences in problems and the controls

Problems can differ in the strength of the interest at stake, the priority, and so forth. Influence attempts can also differ along various dimensions, such as the costs of such attempts for the government, for example. The question is whether or not these differences can safely be ignored when applying controls. A positive answer to the question would be very welcome, since a reduction of the number of cases available for analysis could thus be avoided. In my decisions over these matters, I have been guided by the following considerations:

If we want to treat the basic set–the problems–as a single unit for both large and small firms, then the *distribution of the interests* must be roughly the same in each sub-set (see p. 189 for the operationalization of 'interest'). The distribution of the interests are given in Table 8A.1.

I believe that these differences are small enough for us to assume a reasonably good comparability of the interests of large and small firms.

This is also true when water-related problems are considered (which is the specific set of problems on which the analysis of latent anticipation was based in this study). A rough indication should suffice–that is,

Table 8A.1
Problems and the corresponding distributions of interest

| size of firm (number of employees) | percentages individual problems with *interest:* | | | |
	negligible or slight	moderate	serious or disastrous	total
	SHIPYARDS			
less than 100	28	36	36	100 (n = 56)
100 or more	40	21	39	100 (n = 52)
	REMAINING FIRMS			
less than 100	34	39	27	100 (n = 15)
100 or more	17	40	43	100 (n = 23)

the percentages of the problems with moderate, great or very great interest:

small shipyards: 72% (total absolute number: 55)
large shipyards: 68% (total absolute number: 62)
small remaining firms: 73% (total absolute number: 38)
large remaining firms: 60% (total absolute number: 37)

Appendix 8B
Indicators for economic performance, technology and the water-related environment (72 shipyards) (Table 8B.1)

variable	scale	midpoint of scale	mean	standard deviation
ECONOMIC PERFORMANCE				
– change in number of employees in last 5 years	five-point*	3	2.86	1.15
– expected change in number of employees	three-point	2	2.36	0.68
– change in turnover in last 5 years	five-point*	3	3.48	1.18
– change in profit margin in last 5 years	five-point*	3	2.30	0.90
TECHNOLOGY				
– percentage new building	ten-point	4.5 (50%)	5.03	3.31
WATER-RELATED ENVIRONMENT OF THE FIRM				
– largest ship built in tons†	eight-point	4.5 (= about 1200 tons)	6.17	1.89
– maximum possible tonnage on waterway‡	seven-point	4 (= about 1000 tons)	5.80	1.54

* Consisting of the following classes:
– decrease of 30% or more;
– decrease of 10% to/including 29%;
– decrease or increase of less than 10%;
– increase of 10% to/including 29%;
– increase of 30% or more.
† When 'abnormal' ships (for example, dredgers, coasters, heavy-lift floating cranes) were being considered, the classification sometimes had to be based on direct measurements of the ship itself.
‡ This scale is based on a classification of waterways which is already in existence and in fairly general use.

Appendix 8C
Means and standard deviations of the dependent variables* (Table 8C.1)

variable	mean	standard deviation	number of firms
	SOLITARY SHIPYARDS		
P (related to material facilities for transport by water)	1.67	1.19	40
AM (= IA/P)	0.77	0.36	36
T (= S/IA)	0.73	0.42	26
S	0.65	0.73	40
	ALL SHIPYARDS		
P	1.61	1.13	71
AM	0.61	0.43	59
T	0.73	0.42	35
S	0.45	0.62	71
	REMAINING FIRMS		
P	1.32	1.61	53
AM	0.71	0.39	33
T	0.55	0.46	18
S	0.34	0.80	53

* For the shipyards, all the variables are with reference to influence attempts and successes related to *individual* problems, with the exception of P, which represents the total number of problems related to the material facilities for transport by water. For the remaining firms, all the variables are with reference to problems relating to the material facilities for transport by water.

Socio-political environmental factors (40 municipalities with solitary shipyards) (Table 8C.2)

	mean	standard deviation	coefficient of skewness
1. number of inhabitants per January 1, 1969	22795	36396	2.28
2. growth of population size in percentages in comparison to 1959	20.7%	20.1%	1.62
3. migration per 1000 inhabitants in 1965	−64.1	192.5	−1.85

Table 8C.2   (contd.)

	mean	standard deviation	coefficient of skewness
4. growth of work force in the industrial sector 1947–1960 in percentages	6.0%	7.39%	0.12
5. number of firms with 500–999 employees (1963)	1.03	2.28	2.99
6. number of firms with 1000–1999 employees (1963)	0.25	0.71	3.14
7. number of firms with 2000 or more employees (1963)	0.03	0.16	6.08
8. percentage of work force in municipality employed in firms with 500 or more employees (1963)	9.47%	14.75%	1.36
9. tonnage of goods transported over waterways in 1966 (in multiples of thousand)	559	972	3.05
10. maximum possible tonnage of waterways (seven classes)	4.58	1.75	−1.13
11. area or center of regional development (three classes)	0.40	0.71	1.45
12. density of organizations (three classes)	0.63	0.74	0.71
13. density of organizations concerned with material facilities for transport by water (three classes)	0.25	0.54	2.07
14. relative position of firm in municipality (percentage of employees of total working population)	8.74%	14.63%	2.92
15. density of business firms (number of firms per 1000 inhabitants)	34.3	11.95	1.38
16. average percentage of unemployed in the work force 1965	0.63%	0.65%	2.11
17. number of inhabitants* in the province in multiple of 1000 on January 1, 1969	(1605)	(903)	(0.14)
18. centrality of province*,†	(1.17)	(0.77)	(−0.35)

* The figures for the variables 17 and 18 have no real meaning, and are only presented as an added piece of information.
† core area (Amsterdam, Rotterdam, Den Haag, Utrecht)–middle area–peripheral area ('the sticks').

Appendix 8D
Tested influence controlled for 'absentee owned' or not (Table 8D.1)

	percentage of successful influence attempts in sample			
	SHIPYARDS		REMAINING FIRMS	
size of firm	absentee-owned		absentee-owned	
(number of employees)	no	yes	no	yes
less than 100	73 (19)	100 (1)	50 (1)	100 (3)
100 or more	78 (11)	67 (5)	100 (3)	85 (3)
total	75 (30)	71 (6)	85 (4)	91 (6)

For Use with Chapter 10

Appendix 10A
Indicators for expertise, particularism and cosmopolitanism (Table 10A.1)

variable	scale (number of points)	midpoint of scale	SHIPYARDS (N = 71)		REMAINING FIRMS (N = 53)	
			mean	standard deviation	mean	standard deviation
EXPERTISE						
level of education	five	2.5	1.56	1.02	1.51	1.36
membership in interest organizations	five	2	2.06	0.68	—	—
position in interest organizations	three	1	—	—	0.56	0.64
membership in government committees	four	1.5	0.79	1.21	0.88	1.10
PARTICULARISM						
membership in 'social circles'	four	1.5	0.94	0.87	1.42	1.11
contact with burgomaster	three	1	1.96	0.80	1.02	0.79
contact with Provincial Government	three	1	0.33	0.61	0.42	0.63
contact with National Department of Waterways	three	1	0.83	0.81	0.74	0.80
COSMOPOLITANISM						
perception of government policy	five	2	2.04	0.82	0.69	0.98
travel	three	2	2.16	1.22	2.18	1.15
subscription to technical magazines primarily oriented to research	three	2	1.51	1.71	—	—

Author Index

Subject Index